Great Lives from History

Latinos

Latinos

Volume II
Mimi Fariña – Miguel Antonio Otero

Editors

Carmen Tafolla
University of Texas - San Antonio

and

Martha P. Cotera
University of Texas - San Antonio

SALEM PRESS

Ipswich, Massachusetts   Hackensack, New Jersey

Library of Congress Cataloging-in-Publication Data

Great lives from history. Latinos / Carmen Tafolla, Martha P. Cotera, editors.
    p. cm.
  ISBN 978-1-58765-810-5 (set) — ISBN 978-1-58765-811-2 (vol. 1) — ISBN 978-1-58765-812-9 (vol. 2) — ISBN 978-1-58765-813-6 (vol. 3)
  1. Hispanic Americans—Biography—Encyclopedias.   I. Tafolla, Carmen, 1951-   II. Cotera, Martha.
III. Title: Latinos.
E184.S75G75 2012
920.009268—dc23
[B]

2011043168

Contents

KEY TO PRONUNCIATION

Many of the names of personages covered in *Great Lives from History: Latinos* may be unfamiliar to students and general readers. For difficult-to-pronounce names, guidelines to pronounciation have been provided upon first mention of the name in each essay. These guidelines do not purport to achieve the subleties of all languages but will offer readers a rough equivalent of how English speakers may approximate the proper pronunciation.

Vowel Sounds

Symbol	Spelled (Pronounced)
a	answer (AN-suhr), laugh (laf), sample (SAM-puhl), that (that)
ah	father (FAH-thur), hospital (HAHS-pih-tuhl)
aw	awful (AW-fuhl), caught (kawt)
ay	blaze (blayz), fade (fayd), waiter (WAYT-ur), weigh (way)
eh	bed (behd), head (hehd), said (sehd)
ee	believe (bee-LEEV), cedar (SEE-dur), leader (LEED-ur), liter (LEE-tur)
ew	boot (bewt), lose (lewz)
i	buy (bi), height (hit), lie (li), surprise (sur-PRIZ)
ih	bitter (BIH-tur), pill (pihl)
o	cotton (KO-tuhn), hot (hot)
oh	below (bee-LOH), coat (koht), note (noht), wholesome (HOHL-suhm)
oo	good (good), look (look)
ow	couch (kowch), how (how)
oy	boy (boy), coin (koyn)
uh	about (uh-BOWT), butter (BUH-tuhr), enough (ee-NUHF), other (UH-thur).

Consonant Sounds

Symbol	Spelled (Pronounced)
ch	beach (beech), chimp (chihmp)
g	beg (behg), disguise (dihs-GIZ), get (geht)
j	digit (DIH-juht), edge (ehj), jet (jeht)
k	cat (kat), kitten (KIH-tuhn), hex (hehks)
s	cellar (SEHL-ur), save (sayv), scent (sehnt)
sh	champagne (sham-PAYN), issue (IH-shew), shop (shop)
ur	birth (burth), disturb (dihs-TURB), earth (urth), letter (LEH-tur)
y	useful (YEWS-fuhl), young (yuhng)
z	business (BIHZ-nehs), zest (zehst)
zh	vision (VIH-zhuhn)

COMPLETE LIST OF CONTENTS

VOLUME 1

VOLUME 2

Volume 3

Contents v
Key to Pronunciation vii
Complete List of Contents ix

Appendixes

Indexes

Mimi Fariña

American folk musician and activist

A key figure in the 1960's folk revival, Fariña also was active in the social protests of the time. Her activism led her to found Bread and Roses, a nonprofit organization that offers free entertainment to people confined to institutions.

Latino heritage: Mexican

Born: April 30, 1945; Stanford, California

Died: July 18, 2001; Mill Valley, California

Also known as: Margarita Mimi Baez Fariña;
    Margarita Mimi Baez

Areas of achievement: Music; activism

Early Life

Margarita Mimi Baez Fariña (BI-ehz fah-REEN-yah) was born in Stanford, California, to physicist Albert V. Baez, a native of Puebla, Mexico, and Joan Bridge, from Edinburgh, Scotland. Fariña was the youngest of three sisters; the oldest was Pauline, and folk singer Joan was the middle child. A product of a Society of Friends school, the elder Joan introduced her husband and children to the Quaker religion. Quaker teachings shaped the family's political and social views and led the daughters to embrace a commitment to nonviolence and pacifism.

Because Albert worked as a researcher and university professor, the family moved frequently and lived in various places around the United States and the world, including Redlands, California; Baghdad, Iraq; and Belmont, Massachusetts. Their sojourn in Baghdad in 1951 was particularly difficult for six-year-old Fariña, who attended a convent school. The nuns' sternness dampened her enjoyment of academics, so she turned to the arts, particularly music and dance, which gave her a sense of accomplishment and self-worth.

In 1958, Albert accepted a position at Massachusetts Institute of Technology in the Boston area, and the family moved to nearby Belmont, where Fariña began high school. The folk era was starting to gain momentum, and the coffee houses in Cambridge were frequented by many rising stars, including Eric Von Schmidt, Jim Kweskin, and Bob Dylan. Fariña and her sister Joan were accomplished singers and guitarists and often performed duets in the clubs around Harvard Square. Joan dedicated herself to building her career, but Fariña did not have the freedom to participate in the folk scene because she was still in high school.

Life's Work

Fariña and her parents moved in 1961 to Paris, where Albert was on assignment with Unesco. There she met Richard Fariña, a charismatic young writer and musician who was eight years her senior. Although he was married to Carolyn Hester, another star of the folk era, Richard was smitten by the fifteen-year-old. Eventually Richard and Carolyn divorced, and Fariña and Richard were married in a secret civil ceremony in Paris in 1963. They later were married in California with family and

Mimi Fariña. (AP Photo)

friends in attendance. Richard and Fariña's wedding marked the beginning of a brief but creatively rich musical collaboration.

After their wedding, the Fariñas moved into a cabin in Carmel, California, next door to Joan, who was living with Bob Dylan at the time. In 1964, Fariña and Richard debuted together at the Big Sur Folk Festival and were warmly received by the audience. By the time they rejoined the burgeoning folk scene in Cambridge that same year, they had built a solid reputation among folk aficionados as an up-and-coming duo known for their fresh, original sound. While Richard wrote most of the songs they performed and was praised for his poetic lyrics, Fariña was known for her expertise on the guitar. They released two albums in 1965, *Celebrations for a Grey Day*, and *Reflections of a Crystal Wind*. During the summer of 1965, they performed at the Newport Folk Festival, where they received a standing ovation. Their personal and professional relationship was cut short on April 30, 1966, Fariña's twenty-first birthday, when Richard was killed in a motorcycle accident.

After Richard's death, Fariña continued to work as an entertainer and musician. In 1967, she joined the Committee, a comedy troupe based in San Francisco. She formed a musical partnership with singer-songwriter Tom Jans and recorded an album with him titled *Take Heart*. The collaboration did not last long, and they split up in 1972.

Fariña, Joan, and B. B. King performed a concert at Sing Sing Prison in New York in 1972. The event was a turning point for Fariña when she noticed that the music had a positive effect on the inmates. Performances in similar venues convinced her that both the audiences and the artists would benefit from the interaction that the concerts provided. In 1974, Fariña founded Bread and Roses, a nonprofit group that organizes free live concerts in institutional settings such as prisons, nursing homes, homeless shelters, special-needs schools, and drug rehabilitation centers. Her connections in the music industry enabled Fariña to recruit well-known musicians to donate performances, including her sister Joan, Pete Seeger, Bonnie Raitt, Judy Collins, Odetta, Carlos Santana, Joni Mitchell, and Neil Young. Fariña headed the organization until her death from neuroendocrine cancer in 2001.

SIGNIFICANCE

Fariña was an accomplished singer and master musician whose artistry shaped the folk revival of the 1960's and who inspired a generation to participate in social action. Her most enduring legacy, however, is the founding of Bread and Roses. Reflective of its humanitarian mission, the title of the organization is derived from a poem by James Oppenheim about a 1912 garment workers' strike in Lawrence, Massachusetts. Bread and Roses is active in the San Francisco Bay area, where it produces 600 shows annually in more than 110 facilities with the help of 1,400 volunteers. It has been the recipient of numerous honors, including the award for Achievement in Nonprofit Excellence bestowed by Marin County in 2008.

Pegge Bochynski

FURTHER READING

Baez, Joan. *A Voice to Sing With: A Memoir*. New York: Summit Books, 1987. A memoir by Fariña's sister that includes details about their upbringing, relationship, and musical collaboration.

Hajdu, David. *Positively Fourth Street: The Lives and Times of Joan Baez, Bob Dylan, Mimi Baez Fariña, and Richard Fariña*. New York: Farrar, Straus and Giroux, 2001. A well-rounded portrait how four young people transformed the 1960's folk scene.

Von Schmidt, Eric, and Jim Rooney. *Baby, Let Me Follow You Down*. Garden City, N.Y.: Anchor Press Doubleday, 1979. A fascinating account of the folk revival in Cambridge, Massachusetts, written by one of the key figures of the movement.

See also: Joan Baez; Jerry Garcia; Trini López; Linda Ronstadt; Carlos Santana.

DAVID G. FARRAGUT

American military leader

Farragut was an aggressive naval officer who by turns became America's first rear admiral, vice admiral, and admiral. His career reflected the growth of the U.S. Navy from a small commerce-raiding force during the War of 1812 to a large international fleet that deployed the newest technologies during the American Civil War. Farragut's seizures of New Orleans and Mobile Bay contributed significantly to the fall of the Confederacy. His leadership style influenced generations of American sailors, while his famous quip, "Damn the torpedoes! Full speed ahead," established an American naval tradition.

Latino heritage: Spanish
Born: July 5, 1801; Campbell's Station, Tennessee
Died: August 14, 1870; Portsmouth, New Hampshire
Also known as: David Glasgow Farragut; James Glasgow Farragut
Area of achievement: Military

EARLY LIFE

David Glasgow Farragut (FA-rah-guht) was born James Glasgow Farragut on July 5, 1801. His father was Jorge Anthony Magin Farragut, a petty noble born in Spain's Balearic Islands. By 1773, Jorge was the captain of a merchant ship that traded between the Mediterranean and the Caribbean. During the American Revolution, Jorge embraced the patriots' cause after delivering a cargo of weapons and munitions to Charleston, South Carolina. He anglicized his name to George, joined the revolutionary forces as a privateer, and served in South Carolina's navy until he was wounded. Discharged, he joined the Continental Army and fought in the guerrilla campaign that resulted in Britain's defeat at the battle of Yorktown. By war's end, George was a major in the cavalry, and in the postwar years he received lands in Tennessee in lieu of pension and wages. He married and began a family.

Patronage played a role in George's ties to the South. The governor of the new Louisiana Territory invited him to relocate to New Orleans to serve as a sailing master and gunboat captain. The newly purchased Louisiana Territory had previously been a Spanish then French colony, so George's Spanish heritage, language skills, and strong pro-government attitude proved an asset to the governor. In New Orleans, George became friends with a U.S. naval officer, David Porter, Sr. In 1808, the Farragut and Porter families suffered intertwined disasters: Porter suffered sunstroke, and while being nursed in the Farragut home, both he and Mrs. Farragut died (of different causes) on the same day. Porter's son, Captain David Porter, Jr., was a rising star in the fledgling U.S. Navy. In gratitude for the Farragut family's efforts on behalf of his father, Porter offered to serve as a guardian for one of George's children. In 1809, James Farragut joined the U.S. Navy as a midshipman under Porter's tutelage. While Farragut would serve and mature under Porter's care, he was not officially adopted.

David Glasgow Farragut. (Library of Congress)

LIFE'S WORK

Farragut's naval career spanned the War of 1812, the Mexican-American War, and the Civil War. Farragut advanced consistently in rank as a result of his attention to detail, strong nationalism, exemplary courage under fire, technical skills, and Porter's patronage. As a midshipman on the USS *Essex*, Porter's ship, Farragut participated in some of the most famous actions of the War of 1812, including the capture of the HMS *Alert*, the first British warship captured during the war. During the *Essex*'s cruise in 1812-1813, Farragut was given his first brief independent command—a captured prize ship. In recognition of Porter's leadership and role as his surrogate father, Farragut legally changed his first name from James to David.

After the war, Farragut served in a variety of posts and progressed through the ranks because of his professionalism and dedication. His first command of a warship, for example, was at age twenty-three. After his first wife died of a wasting disease that afflicted her for sixteen years, he married his second wife, Virginia Dorcas Loyall. She was from Norfolk, Virginia, where Farragut established a home. During these years, Farragut's assignments varied from ship commands to administrative posts ashore. In the 1850's, he worked with John A. Dahlgren, whose ordnance designs included some of the powerful naval guns used during the Civil War. Farragut also oversaw the creation of the Navy's first major base in California, Mare Island Naval Yard. The creation of Mare Island reflected the Navy's transition into a two-ocean force. In 1857, Farragut was given command of the USS *Brooklyn*, the nation's first warship propelled by a steam-powered screw instead of the older-style side paddlewheel.

Although Southern-born, married to a Southerner, and a Virginia resident, Farragut was a devoted nationalist, so when Virginia seceded, he remained loyal to the U.S. Navy and moved to New York. The Union's naval strategy was to stop Southern commerce through a blockade of Southern ports and the capture of the Mississippi River. Based on his proven administrative skills and loyalty, Farragut was appointed commander of the West Gulf Blockading Squadron in January, 1862, and tasked with capturing New Orleans. Farragut's plan was to use the cover of night to run past the coastal defense artillery located in two forts outside the city. Once beyond the forts, soldiers on ships would land and capture the city. In theory, bypassing the forts avoided the defenders and cut off supplies to the forts, thus starving the garrisons into surrender. On April 24, 1862, the

Farragut's Firsts in U.S. Navy History

During the American Revolution and after, the U.S. Navy's highest official rank was captain. The term commodore denoted the overall captain of a squadron or detachment on temporary assignment, but a commodore's official rank still was captain. The founders viewed the rank of admiral as too reminiscent of the customs and titles common in European navies and, hence, undemocratic. During the U.S. Navy's early years, this seemed a reasonable tradition, as most detachments were small and had limited objectives. In 1857, the title of flag officer was formalized as a rank to reflect the expanding responsibilities of squadron command. During the Civil War, the Navy grew so large that individual squadrons in effect became permanent. Consequently, the U.S. Congress authorized first commodore as a rank, then rear admiral and then vice admiral to reflect the officers' increasing responsibilities. David G. Farragut, who was promoted to commodore on July 16, 1862, was among the first officers to achieve this rank. He then became the first commodore promoted to rear admiral on August 12, 1862, and the first vice admiral on Dec. 21, 1864. In the aftermath of the Union victory in the Civil War, Congress voted to create the highest ranks ever given to American military men, general and admiral, on July 25, 1866. On this day, both Admiral Farragut and General Ulysses S. Grant established traditions and ranks that would not be changed until World War II.

squadron attacked. Aided by lax Confederate security and darkness, the forts were bypassed, and the city fell at minimal cost—less than two hundred Union casualties. This removed the Confederacy's most important port and demonstrated to European powers that the Confederacy would not win the war.

After this victory, Farragut moved up the Mississippi to aid Major General Ulysses S. Grant's campaign against Vicksburg and then attacked Confederate defenses of Port Hudson. In 1864, Farragut attacked the Confederacy's last major seaport, Mobile Bay, Alabama. It was here that one of his ships was damaged by a naval mine—what was at that time called a "torpedo." Rather than withdraw, he issued his famous order, "Damn the torpedoes! Full speed ahead." Farragut was promoted after his victories at New Orleans and Mobile Bay; like Grant, Farragut became a favorite of President Abraham Lincoln based on his battlefield success. After Lincoln was assassinated, Farragut served as a pallbearer at his funeral.

Although Hispanic origins had aided his father, they exerted little impact on Farragut's rise. Well-known captains such as Porter favored Farragut for his determination and bravery. When given command, Farragut showed diligent attention to detail and willingness to use new technologies such as steam power and improved naval guns. As America's first admiral, Farragut created a tradition of professionalism that helped the Navy grow from a small, scattered fleet into a global force. Along the way, he taught junior officers such as Winfield Scott Schley and George Dewey, who went on to become important commanders in their own right during the Spanish-American War.

Kevin B. Reid

FURTHER READING

Duffy, James P. *Lincoln's Admiral: The Civil War Campaigns of David Farragut*. Edison, N.J.: Castle Books, 2006. Readable and detailed, this work is an excellent biography and describes the changing technologies and administrative structures that shaped Farragut's career.

Lewis, Charles Lee. *David Glasgow Farragut: Admiral in the Making*. Annapolis, Md.: United States Naval Institute, 1941. This book is replete with anecdotes taken from Farragut's own journals and the biography written by his son. The result is an intimate look at Farragut's personality and accomplishments.

Martin, Christopher. *Damn the Torpedoes! The Story of America's First Admiral*. London: Abelard-Schuman, 1970. Readable and informative, this is one of the best biographies of Farragut available.

Schneller, Robert J., Jr. *Farragut: America's First Admiral*. Washington, D.C.: Brassey's, 2002. The Brassey's Military Profiles series provides short, readable biographies of military men, like Farragut, whose actions shaped their eras.

See also: Santos Benavides; Luis R. Esteves; Pedro del Valle; Loreta Janeta Velázquez.

JOSÉ FELICIANO

Puerto Rican-born singer and musician

Known for his guitar artistry and vocal stylings blending Latin, rock, and jazz elements, Feliciano is one of the best-known Hispanic entertainers in the United States. His long career included early hits such as "Light My Fire" and "Feliz Navidad," and a controversial rendition of "The Star-Spangled Banner" at the 1968 World Series.

Latino heritage: Puerto Rican

Born: September 10, 1945; Lares, Puerto Rico

Also known as: José Montserrate Feliciano García

Area of achievement: Music

EARLY LIFE

José Montserrate Feliciano García (feh-LEE-see-ah-noh) was born in Lares, Puerto Rico, in 1945. The son of a poor farmer with a large family (eleven sons), the infant was afflicted with congenital glaucoma, resulting in permanent blindness.

When Feliciano was five years old, his family moved to New York City, where his father was employed as a longshoreman. The family lived in a Latino neighborhood in Harlem. By age six, the self-taught Feliciano was playing the concertina. He performed at the Teatro Puerto Rico at age nine. Eventually, his grandfather gave him his first guitar—an instrument that would determine the trajectory of his life. Again, the blind Feliciano taught himself to play.

At age sixteen, Feliciano began to contribute income to his family through performing at coffeehouses in Greenwich Village, playing flamenco, folk, and pop guitar. At seventeen, he turned to music full time. His first professional performance came in 1963 in Detroit, at the Retort Coffee House. Then came a performance at Gerde's Folk City in New York, which earned him rave reviews. RCA Records offered Feliciano a recording contract, and his first single, "Do the Click," came out in 1964. That year, he also released an album, *The Voice and Guitar of José Feliciano*, but neither the song nor the album registered on the pop charts.

Feliciano's big break in the music industry came in 1966. In Buenos Aires, Argentina, he had performed at the Mar del Plata Festival before an audience of 100,000, and record executives asked him to record an album. Feliciano chose to record several Spanish boleros. Singles featuring his arrangements of "Poquita fe"

José Feliciano. (AP Photo)

and "Usted" became best-selling records. This success was followed by two additional albums in Spanish, and Feliciano gained fame throughout Latin America and the Caribbean.

LIFE'S WORK

Next, Feliciano relocated to Los Angeles, California, and recorded a distinctive version of the Doors' "Light My Fire." It rose to number one on pop music charts in the United States. Feliciano received his first two Grammy Awards for this recording. He released an album of English-language cover songs titled *Feliciano!* (1968) that became a hit. Although he did not write the songs on *Feliciano!*, his unique blend of Latin and jazz rhythms on acoustic guitar made them uniquely his own.

The year 1968 also brought controversy. Legendary Detroit Tigers broadcaster Ernie Harwell had asked the twenty-three-year-old Feliciano to sing "The Star-Spangled Banner" at the start of the fifth game of the World Series, held in Tiger Stadium. Instead of playing a traditional rendition of the tune, Feliciano performed a slow, soulful version in keeping with his style. Coming at a time when the country was polarized by the increasingly unpopular Vietnam War, many felt his performance to

be unpatriotic and inappropriate. Feliciano meant well and was surprised by the backlash. Although stylizing the song is now common practice, the controversy put a damper on his career in the United States. Disc jockeys refused to play his music, newspapers published scathing editorials, and negative feelings persisted for years.

In 1970, Feliciano released another album, *Feliz Navidad*. The single "Feliz Navidad" eventually became a huge success and remains a staple of the Christmas season. During the 1970's, Feliciano also wrote and recorded the theme song for the television show *Chico and the Man* and was involved with several other television shows and films.

Feliciano's first marriage, to club owner Hilda Perez in the 1960's, ended in divorce. In 1982, he married Susan Omillion, to whom he had been introduced years earlier by Harwell. Feliciano and Susan have three children, Melissa Anne, Jonathan José, and Michael Julian. In the 1980's, Feliciano recorded several albums in Spanish. In 1987, he was honored with stars on the Hollywood Walk of Fame and the Puerto Rico Walk of Fame.

In the early 1990's, Feliciano and Mark Graham hosted a yearlong radio program called *Speaking of Music*. In 1995, he made a brief appearance in the film *Fargo*, performing his song "Let's Find Each Other Tonight." That decadae, Feliciano released several significant albums, including *Señor Bolero* (1998), a return to his Latin roots. In 1998, Feliciano was honored when his East Harlem school, P.S. 155, was renamed the José Feliciano Performing Arts School. A year later, he was featured in two PBS television concert specials.

In 2003, *Guitarra Mia: A Tribute to José Feliciano*, a television special celebrating his life and music, aired in Puerto Rico and in many cities in the United States. In 2006, he was presented with a Lifetime Achievement Award by the Hispanic Heritage Foundation. Recordings of this period included *Señor Bachata* (2007), which earned him his eighth Grammy.

Coming full circle, in May, 2010, Feliciano returned to Detroit to perform his once-controversial rendition of "The Star-Spangled Banner." This time, he performed as part of a memorial ceremony to honor his good friend Harwell, who had recently passed away. Feliciano's slow, soulful vocal rendition accompanied on acoustic guitar was a fitting tribute.

SIGNIFICANCE

Feliciano rose from playing guitar and singing in Greenwich Village coffeehouses to acclaim throughout the

Latin, Rock, and Pop in Feliciano's Sound

José Feliciano grew up poor in East Harlem, New York. His musical precocity appeared early on, and the gift of a guitar from his grandfather led to his life's work. Feliciano taught himself to play the guitar by listening to popular rock albums of the 1950's, as well as classical and jazz guitarists such as Andrés Segovia and Wes Montgomery, respectively. These influences shaped his musical style, which combined Latin sounds with rock and roll and pop. He became a master of the acoustic guitar and developed a soulful singing style to match. Recording in both English and Spanish, with mega hits such as "Light My Fire" and "Feliz Navidad," his music crossed national boundaries and made him a much-loved international star.

world. Performing in both English and Spanish, he often is viewed as the first Hispanic musician to cross over successfully into the U.S. music market. He has won several Grammys and and sold scores of records and albums. He was voted best pop guitarist five years in a row by *Guitar Player* magazine. Further, in 2004, the American Federation of the Blind gave him the Helen Keller

Personal Achievement Award to honor his musical achievements. By 2011, Feliciano had recorded nearly seventy albums in English and Spanish and won acclaim throughout the world for his musical talent, integrity, and charitable work. In the United States, Feliciano remains one the best-known Hispanic entertainers.

Russell N. Carney

FURTHER READING

Feliciano, José. "José Feliciano." In *My America: What My Country Means to Me By 150 Americans from All Walks of Life*, edited by Hugh Downs. New York: Scribner, 2002. Feliciano's short essay reflects on his controversial rendition of "The Star-Spangled Banner" in 1968.

Myers, Alice. "José Feliciano." In *Popular Musicians*, edited by Steve Hochman. Pasadena, Calif.: Salem Press, 1999. Comprehensive summary of Feliciano's career through the 1990's.

Otfinoski, Steven. "José Feliciano." In *Latinos in the Arts*. New York: Facts On File, 2007. Career overview and brief biography of Feliciano. Bibliography.

See also: Rubén Blades; Gloria Estefan; Julio Iglesias; Ricky Martin; Jon Secada.

GIGI FERNÁNDEZ

Puerto Rican-born tennis player

A champion tennis player Fernández was Puerto Rico's first professional female athlete. She won two Olympic gold medals, captured seventeen Grand Slam doubles titles, and reached top ranking in women's doubles four times.

Latino heritage: Puerto Rican
Born: February 22, 1964; San Juan, Puerto Rico
Also known as: Beatriz Fernández
Areas of achievement: Sports; social issues

EARLY LIFE

Beatrix Fernández, better known as Gigi Fernández (JEE-jee fehr-NAHN-dehz), was born in San Juan, Puerto Rico, on February 22, 1964, the daughter of a wealthy physician, Tuto Fernández, and his wife Beatriz. On her eighth birthday, her parents gave her a gift of tennis lessons. Though she enjoyed playing

tennis, she never considered it as a possible vocation because it was unacceptable at this time for a woman to embark upon a career in sports. Fernández did compete in tournaments and by age nine was a celebrity in Puerto Rico because of newspaper coverage of her tennis games. In her teens she was known for her tennis skills and her extravagant lifestyle, which included frequent shopping trips to the mainland and travel for tournaments.

Her junior-league rankings afforded her numerous college scholarships, from which she chose to attend Clemson University. At Clemson she began to play tennis daily, and her skill as a player improved. She competed in the finals of the National Collegiate Athletic Association's singles tennis tournament during her freshman year, but she lost in a very close match. Before the start of her sophomore year, she decided to leave school. She joined the Women's Tennis Association

(WTA) tour in 1983, and this decision made her Puerto Rico's first female professional athlete.

LIFE'S WORK

In 1984, a year after becoming a professional athlete, Fernández represented Puerto Rico in the Olympic Games. At this time, tennis was still an exhibition sport, which meant that no medals were awarded. However, when Fernández competed in the 1992 Olympics in Barcelona, the classification of tennis had changed. Fernández had to decide whether to represent the United States or Puerto Rico. If she represented Puerto Rico, she would have had no chance at a medal because her strength was in doubles tennis, and there was no Puerto Rican player with which to team. She decided to partner with Mary Joe Fernández and represent the United States. It was a good decision, since the pair returned from Barcelona with a gold medal. She also competed in the 1996 Olympics, capturing another gold medal.

From 1991 to 1997, she partnered with Natasha Zvereva, who mirrored Fernández in both skill and passion for the game. Fernández, who had already earned three Grand Slam doubles titles, garnered another fourteen titles with Zvereva. However, Fernández's legendary

Gigi Fernández. (AP Photo)

bad temper kept her from rising higher than number seventeen as a singles player, and it caused her problems with doubles partners, though Zvereva seemed to be able to rein in Fernández. Still, Fernández once mailed a $250 check, equivalent to five warnings from a chair umpire, to the WTA before the start of the season to cover forthcoming fines. She and Zvereva were named the WTA Doubles Team of the Year for three consecutive years, 1993 through 1995, and again in 1997. As of 2010, they held the second-longest Grand Slam title doubles streak, with six wins between the 1992 French Open and the 1993 Australian Open.

In 1996, Fernández made her acting debut in the television series *New York Undercover*, portraying a flirtatious professional tennis player. Although she enjoyed the experience, she did not intend to pursue an acting career after retiring from tennis in 1997 at the age of thirty-three. After retiring, she completed her undergraduate degree in psychology from the University of South Florida, received her real estate license, and earned her master's degree in business administration from Crummer Rollins School of Business in Winter Park, Florida. In 2009, she became the mother of twins, Madison and Karson. She and Zvereva were inducted into the International Tennis Hall of Fame in 2010.

Throughout her career, in addition to playing on the WTA tour for ten months each year, Fernández endorsed sports equipment and other merchandise. She also worked fiercely to raise funds for various causes, including the National Hispanic Scholarship Fund, Yo Si Puedo (Say No To Drugs), and the Puerto Rican Tennis Association. In 2010, with the birth of her twins, Fernández became involved in a campaign to prevent childhood obesity by getting children and their parents to become physically active. She founded a company, Baby Goes Pro, which provided children and their parents with instructional products that taught sports fundamentals and encouraged them to take part in physical activity.

SIGNIFICANCE

Gigi Fernández remains a Puerto Rican woman of firsts. She was the first female to choose to be a professional athlete, paving the way for other Puerto Rican women and generating interest in the sport of tennis. As a professional tennis player, she was also the first Puerto Rican woman to win an Olympic gold medal. During the fifteen years she played professional tennis, she earned sixty-eight career titles and repeatedly held number-one rankings. She used her position as an athlete to raise awareness for health issues, including childhood obesity, and to tirelessly raise funds for charities and Latino causes. In addition, she was recognized as an American Model of Excellence by the U.S. House of Representatives.

Lisa A. Wroble

FURTHER READING

Crouse, Karen. "A Dream Deferred, Almost Too Long." *The New York Times,* August 30, 2010, p. 1 Describes how women athletes risk deferring motherhood, focusing on the problems Fernández faced in putting off motherhood until after retiring from tennis at the age of thirty-three. Includes details of her personal life and professional career.

Jenkins, Sally. "Terrible Two." *Sports Illustrated,* February 20, 1995, 156. Recounts how Fernández and Zvereva came to be doubles partners, and describes their similarities, differences, and strengths as a pair. Offers brief biographical information about Fernández.

Thomas, I. "Olympic Dreams." *Hispanic* 7, no. 7 (August, 1994): 14. Provides brief biographical information and discusses Fernández's career as she considered the 1996 Olympic Games.

See also: Rosie Casals; Pancho Gonzales.

JOSEPH A. FERNÁNDEZ

American school superintendent

One of the first Latino superintendents of a major public school district in the United States, Fernández started his unlikely journey as a high school dropout.

Latino heritage: Puerto Rican

Born: December 13, 1935; Harlem, New York

Also known as: Joseph Anthony Fernández, Jr.

Areas of achievement: Education; social issues

EARLY LIFE

Joseph Anthony Fernández, Jr. (fehr-NAHN-dez) was born in Harlem, New York, on December 13, 1935. His mother, Angela, had met his father, Joseph Fernández, Sr., on a boat carrying immigrants from Puerto Rico to New York City. Joseph, Sr., worked as a construction laborer. Fernández attended parochial Catholic schools in his elementary and junior high years. He started high school at Bishop Dubois High School but was expelled in the tenth grade for misbehavior. By that time, Fernández was associating with a street gang known as the Riffs in East Harlem and abusing drugs. He dropped out of school at age seventeen and joined the Air Force.

Fernández trained as a radio technician and earned his high school equivalency diploma while stationed in South Korea and Japan. He returned to the United States for his final six months of duty and married his high school girlfriend, Lily Pons, in May, 1956. The G.I. Bill supported his enrollment at Columbia University, where he became interested in mathematics. A year later, Fernández moved his family to Miami, Florida, on the advice of physicians because of the ill health of his newborn son, Keith. Fernández graduated from the University of Miami with a B.S. in mathematics in 1963. He was hired as a math teacher at Coral Park High School in Miami's Dade County public school system.

The next year, Fernández was made department chair and a union steward. Earning his master's degree at night at Florida Atlantic University in educational administration opened the door to an assistant principalship at Coral Park in 1971. In 1975, he was named principal of Miami Central High School. He managed to keep teaching one mathematics class per semester while serving in these administrative roles. Two daughters (Kami and Kristin) and another son (Kevin) joined the tightknit family during this time period. By 1977, Fernández had been named director of community services for the Miami-Dade County School District.

LIFE'S WORK

Fernández became an assistant superintendent of the district in 1985, and one year later, he was named deputy superintendent. He was placed in charge of a district task force on school-based management and earned the respect and cooperation of Patrick Tornillo, head of the local teachers' union. Their task force recommended the implementation of school-based management in which individual schools would be given greater autonomy from the dictates of the central administration.

Fernández completed his doctorate in educational administration at Nova University (now Nova Southeastern University) on nights and weekends. In May, 1987, Miami-Dade County's school superintendent announced to the school board that he planned to leave. A discussion ensued about launching a national search, but after brief deliberation, the board named Fernández superintendent. At this time, Miami-Dade County was the nation's fourth largest school district and Fernández wasted no time implementing the school-based management initiative recommended by the task force. He also removed or transferred forty-eight principals in his first year and started several new programs, including Saturday computer and music classes, magnet schools, and preschools. He became a nationally known education reformer.

When the chancellor of New York City public schools died in office, Fernández was a top prospect for the position. His loyalty to Miami and reluctance to leave his influential position eventually were overcome and he was named chancellor on September 21, 1989. He warned the board and mayor that he would implement rapid reform efforts. Within the first two years he substantially reduced central office administrative staff, increased school choice for students, backed the creation of small high schools, chipped away at the autonomy of the thirty-two highly decentralized local school boards that his predecessors had created, decreased school violence, and raised high school graduation standards. The city also underwent a severe financial crisis that led to the school district downsizing teachers and support staff. Most controversially, Fernández pushed for condom availability in the city's high schools and implemented a new multicultural curriculum for the elementary grades ("Children of the Rainbow") to reflect the city's diversity. The need for education about tolerance was underscored during this period by a racially motivated slaying and divisive trial. The implementation of the program's first-grade curriculum prompted an uproar over its inclusion of gay families. Heated debates erupted across the city and among school board members. A 4-3 termination vote ended Fernández's tenure as chancellor on February 11, 1993. He returned to Miami and served in subsequent years as a consultant,

board member for various organizations, and advocate for change in public education.

SIGNIFICANCE

Fernández was a leader in K-12 education who advanced many different strategies as part of a comprehensive school-reform agenda in two of the largest urban school districts in the United States. His example prompted national discussion about key matters related to educational reform and raised substantial questions about the ability of strong leaders to successfully implement such reforms within the sociopolitical context of American public schooling.

Dennis W. Cheek

FURTHER READING

Fernández, Joseph, and John Underwood. *Tales Out of School: Joseph Fernández's Crusade to Rescue American Education*. New York: Little, Brown, 1993. A passionate, detailed look at the factors that shaped Fernández's life, philosophy of education, and actions as a school superintendent.

Kurtz, Howard. "The Report Card on Joe Fernández." *New York Magazine* 23, no. 3 (January 22, 1990): 40-46. A mostly positive profile of Fernández reflecting on his leadership of the Miami-Dade County schools and his early tenure in New York.

Litow, Stanley S. "Restructuring New York City's Schools." *Yale Law & Policy Review* 10, no. 1 (1992): 30-57. The lawyer/education policy specialist chiefly responsible for bringing Fernández to New York City describes his reform agenda. Litow also served as deputy superintendent.

Nelson, Murray R. "No Pot of Gold at the End of the Rainbow." *Journal of Curriculum and Supervision* 16, no. 3 (2001): 206-227. A detailed look at the content and response to the diversity curriculum in the New York City public schools.

See also: Lauro Cavazos; Jaime Escalante.

MANNY FERNÁNDEZ

American football player

Fernández, an American football player of Spanish descent, played eight seasons for the Miami Dolphins, and this nose tackle dominated defensively in three Super Bowls.

Latino heritage: Spanish
Born: July 3, 1946; Oakland, California
Also known as: Manuel José Fernández
Area of achievement: Football

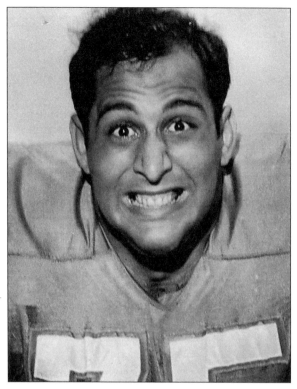

Manny Fernández. (AP Photo)

EARLY LIFE

Manuel José Fernández, better known as Manny Fernández (fehr-NAHN-dehz), was born in Oakland, California, in 1946. He attended San Lorenzo High School and was an excellent athlete, outstanding as a wrestler, discus thrower, and football player. It was perhaps his wrestling skills that best served him on the football field as he had to use "body Braille" in order to take on offensive lineman. His 20/200 vision, which required thick glasses while off the football field, left him able to see no more than flashes of color in front of him while on the field. Night games and dark jerseys effectively blinded him, and he could not see the hand-offs.

LIFE'S WORK

Fernández, who was 6-feet, 2-inches tall and weighed 250 pounds, played defensive tackle at Chabot Junior College and then at the University of Utah. He played well but was not drafted by the National Football League (NFL); Utah's head coach refused to recommend any of his players to NFL scouts because a losing season had gotten him fired. Joe Thomas, the personnel chief of the Miami Dolphins, decided to

sign Fernández almost as an afterthought, with the hope that Fernández would make the squad, and the team would have one player with whom Miami's large Latino community could identify, relate to, and call its own. The only problem with this strategy, which Fernández readily admitted, was that Fernández could not speak Spanish. Fernández debuted with the Dolphins in 1968.

In 1972, Fernández recorded six tackles and one sack and recovered a fumble when the Dolphins lost to the Dallas Cowboys in Super Bowl VI. In 1973, Fernández was a strong contender for Most Valuable Player (MVP) in Super Bowl VII, but the award was given to Jake Scott instead. During the game, Fernández made seventeen tackles and one sack, contributing to the Dolphins win over the Washington Redskins. Nick Buoniconti, another Dolphins player, described Fernández's performance as "the game of his life—in fact, it was the most dominant game by a defensive lineman in the history of the game, and he would never be given much credit for it. They should have given out two game balls and made Manny Fernández the co-MVP with Jake Scott." The MVP was selected by Dick Schaap, editor of *Sport* magazine, who later admitted he had been out late the previous night, had struggled to watch the Super Bowl, and was unaware that Fernández had scored seventeen tackles.

The following year, Fernández scored five tackles and one sack in Super Bowl VIII against the Minnesota Vikings, another victory for the Dolphins. In his three Super Bowls, Fernández racked up twenty-eight tackles and three sacks.

Fernández also garnered postseason honors for four consecutive seasons. He was the second team All-Pro in 1970 and 1973, an All-AFC (American Football Conference) selection in 1971, and a second-team All-AFC choice in 1972 and 1973. In addition, Fernández was voted the Dolphins Outstanding Defensive Lineman from 1968 through 1973.

Fernández's last season with the Dolphins was in 1975. During his football career, he recorded thirty-five sacks, an unusually high number for a nose tackle, and he had a career high of eight sacks in 1971, the most sacks of any player on his team that year. In Dolphins history, only one nose tackle, Bob Baumhower, recorded more sacks. Fernández recorded 5.5 sacks in postseason play, which in 2010 was the third-highest number in Dophins history, behind defensive ends Kim Bokamper (eight sacks) and Trace Armstrong (six sacks).

In 1990, Fernández was voted to the Dolphins Silver Anniversary Team during the celebration of the team's twenty-five years in the NFL. In January, 2001, he was named to *Pro Football Weekly'*s All-Time Super Bowl team; in 2006, *USA Today* similarly included Fernández in its All-Time Super Bowl team. In 2007, Fernández was voted to the Dolphins All-Time team.

Since retiring from football, Fernandez has worked as an executive at First American Title Insurance. On December 2, 2010, he was honored with the Meyerhoff Community Award in recognition of his forty years of charity work in south Florida.

SIGNIFICANCE

Manny Fernández was part of the Miami Dolphins' 1972 "No Name Defense," one of the fiercest defenses in the history of the NFL. The defensive unit was given this nickname because the Dolphins' impressive offense received more publicity that year. Fernández was also one of the first nose tackles in the NFL, and he dominated defensively in his three Super Bowls.

Michael J. Bennett

FURTHER READING

Harvey, Walter. *The Super Bowl's Most Wanted: The Top Ten Book of Big-Game Heroes, Pigskin Zeroes, and Championship Oddities.* Washington, D.C.: Brassey's, 2004. Describes Fernández's spectacular defense in Super Bowl VII.
Longoria, Mario. *Athletes Remembered: Mexicano/ Latino Professional Football Players, 1929-1970.* Tempe, Ariz.: Bilingual Press, 1997. Includes information about Fernández and the Dolphins' 1972 "No Name Defense."

See also: Tedy Bruschi; Jeff Garcia; Tony Gonzalez; Joe Kapp; Anthony Muñoz; Jim Plunkett; Rich Rodriguez; Tony Romo; Eddie Saenz; Danny Villanueva.

ROYES FERNÁNDEZ

American ballet dancer

Fernández was one of the principal male dancers with New York City's American Ballet Theatre. He partnered with some of the world's premier ballerinas for more than thirty years, creating memorable moments in dance history.

Latino heritage: Spanish
Born: July 15, 1929; New Orleans, Louisiana
Died: March 3, 1980; New York, New York
Also known as: Royes Emanuel Fernández
Area of achievement: Dance

EARLY LIFE

Royes Emanuel Fernández (royz eh-MAHN-oo-ehl fehr-NAHN-dehz) was born in New Orleans, Louisiana, on July 15, 1929. His father, Manuel P. Fernández, of Spanish descent, was was a professional dancer, as well as a jeweler, who gave Royes his first dance lesson. Royes's mother, Francoise Blanchine Fernández, was of French descent. Royes's older sister Jeanne also studied dance. Royes began his formal ballet training at age eight with teacher Lelia Haller in New Orleans. Haller once described Royes as a brilliant dancer whose moves were perfectly executed.

Fernández first performed with the New Orleans Opera Ballet in 1944. In 1945, he traveled to New York City to intern at the American Ballet School, and his dancing was so impressive that at age sixteen he was offered a dance scholarship. However, his parents insisted that he return to New Orleans to complete high school. When ballet dancers Alicia Markova and Anton Dolin performed in New Orleans, Fernández auditioned for them following an arranged meeting that was orchestrated by Haller.

After graduating from Fortier High School in June, 1946, Fernández moved to New York and studied with popular dance teacher Vincenzo Celli. Soon thereafter, Fernández joined the Original Ballet Russe (de Basil) company in September, 1946. The following year, Fernández successfully negotiated a solo spot with the Markova-Dolin Ballet.

LIFE'S WORK

Although Fernández's primary affiliation from 1950 to 1973 was with the American Ballet Theatre, he toured with other companies. He journeyed to Australia and appeared as a principal dancer for the Borovansky Ballet Company in 1954, and he made a return appearance with that company in 1964. He also danced with the Eliot Feld Ballet, the San Francisco Ballet, and the Royal Swedish Ballet.

Fernández mentored a number of students who later became principal dancers with major ballet companies. Several of his students also became dance school directors.

Throughout his career, Fernández frequently appeared as a guest artist with various companies, including the Alicia Alonso Ballet Company, the Borovansky Ballet, the Original Ballet Russe, the London Festival Ballet, the San Francisco Ballet, and the New York City Ballet. He was prima ballerina Margot Fonteyn's partner during her 1963 world tour. Fernández often toured as a guest performer, and his frequent guest performances with both major and minor companies throughout the United States received widespread press coverage.

In 1973, Fernández retired from performing and joined the dance faculty at the University of South Florida. He taught there for one year before moving to New York, where he accepted a position as dance instructor at the State University of New York at Purchase. He remained in this position until he died of cancer on March 3, 1980.

Significance

At the height of his career, Royes Fernández was hailed as America's premier male dancer. His principal roles in choreographer David Lichine's *Nutcracker*, *Aurora's Wedding*, *Giselle*, *Swan Lake,* and *La Sylphide* were undoubtedly Fernández's most eloquent episodes on stage. He partnered with the prima ballerinas of his time, including Fonteyn, Kathleen Gorham, Toni Lander, Peggy Sager, Lupe Serrano, Joycelyn Vollmar, and Maria Tallchief. One of Fernández's most memorable performances was the pas de deux from choreographer Marius Petipa's *Don Quixote*, which he danced with Serrano.

Sandra W. Leconte

Further Reading

Dunning, Jennifer. "Royes Fernandez , 50, Ex-Principal Dancer with Ballet Theater." *The New York Times*, March 5, 1980. Obituary details Fernández's life and career.

"Fonteyn and Nureyev." *Australian Women's Weekly*, March 18, 1964, p. 3. Highlights the principal dancers featured in one-act ballets and divertissements with Fernández and Lupe Serrano.

New York Public Library for the Performing Arts. Guide to the Fernandez, Royes (1929-1980) Papers, c. 1942-1982. http://danceheritage.org/xtf/view?docId=ead/danfernaID.xml;query=;brand=default. Provides information about a collection of Fernández's papers, which includes more than 1,100 items of correspondence and contracts dating from 1942 to 1982.

"Royes Fernandez." *Variety*, March 12, 1980. Reviews Fernández's life and career, including his performances with the American Ballet Theatre.

Scott, Harold George. *Lelia: The Compleat Ballerina.* Gretna, La.: Pelican, 1975. Chronicles the career of Fernández's teacher Lelia Haller, who viewed her pupil's dancing as "perfection in motion."

See also: Fernando Bujones; Willie Champion; Evelyn Cisneros; José Arcadio Limón; Rita Moreno; Chita Rivera.

Tony Fernandez

Dominican-born baseball player

Fernandez, a Dominican-born professional baseball player, is considered one of the best shortstops to have ever played Major League Baseball. Fernandez played in the major leagues for seventeen seasons, twelve of which were with the Toronto Blue Jays.

Latino heritage: Dominican
Born: June 30, 1962; San Pedro de Macoris, Dominican Republic
Also known as: Octavio Antonio Fernandez Castro; Professor Gadget; El Cabeza
Area of achievement: Baseball

Early Life

Octavio Antonio Fernandez Castro, better known as Tony Fernandez (TOH-nee fehr-NAHN-dehz), was born in San Pedro de Macoris, Dominican Republic, on June 30, 1962. When he was a teenager he attracted the attention of scouts from American Major League Baseball, who signed him to play for the Syracuse, New York, AAA baseball team when he was nineteen years old. He made his major league debut playing for the Toronto Blue Jays on September 2, 1983, at the age of twenty-one. During his first three seasons with the Blue Jays, from 1983 to 1985, Fernandez played better each year and proved to be a solid hitter and an outstanding defensive specialist. By the 1985 season, he was the starting shortstop for the Blue Jays, playing in 161 games. Much of the Blue Jays' success in the mid-1980's was attributed to the achievements of Fernandez and other Latin American players. Fernandez was known as a fitness fanatic, and his teammates gave him the nickname "Professor Gadget" because of his attempts to turn objects near the baseball clubhouse into fitness training gear.

LIFE'S WORK

Fernandez quickly became one of baseball's most exciting players. During his fourth season, at the age of twenty-four, he was voted a major league All-Star and won a Gold Glove Award for defensive excellence in the infield. He followed this in the 1987 season by setting a Blue Jays' record with 200 hits in a season, and, at .322, he had the highest batting average in the team's history. Fernandez developed a reputation for being an outstanding switch hitter, who could hit equally well from the left or right side. He won three more Gold Glove Awards in 1987, 1988, and 1989. He was part of a trade

Tony Fernandez. (AP Photo)

in 1991 that sent him to the San Diego Padres, and he remained on this team for two seasons and played in the All-Star game in 1992.

In 1993, Fernandez began the season playing for the New York Mets, but he had a slow start and was traded back to the Toronto Blue Jays after forty-eight games. Playing the remainder of the season for the Blue Jays, Fernandez was instrumental in helping the team capture the American League pennant and win the 1993 World Series, in which he set a record for a shortstop by driving in nine runs. In 1994, he played for the Cincinnati Reds and then the New York Yankees and Cleveland Indians in 1995 before returning to the Blue Jays in 1998. In the 1997, season while playing for the Cleveland Indians in the World Series, Fernandez committed a rare fielding error that allowed the series-winning runner to get on base. This error was one haunting memory in an otherwise remarkable baseball career. His return to the Blue Jays in 1998 and 1999 saw him have two good seasons, batting more than .300 in both. In 2000, he played in Japan. He began the 2001 season by playing for the Milwaukee Brewers and ended it by returning to the Blue Jays, retiring from this team at the conclusion of the season. At the time of his retirement, he was the Blue Jays' all-time leader in games played, at-bats, hits, and triples. He ranks second in Blue Jays' history for doubles and is third in batting average and total bases.

Fernandez is a dedicated Christian, and his religion created some challenges for him while playing baseball. In 1988, he outspokenly criticized his team manager for suspending road-trip chapel sessions, which his manager believed distracted the team from focusing on baseball. Since retiring in 2001, Fernandez has spent his time working for the Tony Fernandez Foundation, which provides aid to unprivileged children who want to play baseball. The foundation began helping children in the Dominican Republic and has expanded its work to Canada and the United States. In 2003, he created a baseball camp for children in the Dominican Republic who want to pursue their dreams of playing Major League Baseball.

Fernandez has received the Toronto Blue Jays' Level of Excellence, an award that recognizes his accomplishments as one of the greatest players in the team's history. In addition, his name is proudly displayed on the outfield of the Blue Jays' stadium.

SIGNIFICANCE

Tony Fernandez played the game of baseball with passion. He demonstrated exceptional defensive skills and achieved All-Star status, especially while playing for the Toronto Blue Jays. In retirement he gave back to the Dominican Republic, the country of his birth, by providing financial aid for children who want to play baseball. A four-time Gold Glove winner and five-time All-Star, Fernandez is frequently listed as one of the top five Toronto Blue Jays players of all time.

Timothy M. Sawicki

FURTHER READING

Billheimer, John. *Baseball and the Blame Game: Scapegoating in the Major Leagues.* Jefferson, N.C.: McFarland, 2007. Documents players' major mishaps, including Fernandez's error during a World Series game.

Bjarkman, Peter. *The Toronto Blue Jays.* Toronto: B Mitchell, 1990. Chronicles the history of the team which first began playing Major League Baseball in the 1970's.

Neyer, Bob. *Big Book of Baseball Lineups.* New York: Fireside Books, 2003. A complete guide to the most memorable players in Major League Baseball, including Fernandez's achievements with the Blue Jays.

Stewart, Mark, with Mike Kennedy. *Latino Baseball's Finest Infielders.* Brookfield, Conn.: Millbrook Press. 2002. Fernandez is one of the baseball players included in this account of Latinos' contributions to the game.

See also: Joaquín Andújar; César Cedeño; Roberto Clemente; Pedro Guerrero; Albert Pujols.

J<small>OSE</small> A<small>LBERTO</small> F<small>ERNANDEZ</small>-P<small>OL</small>

Argentine-born physician, scientist, and inventor

Fernandez-Pol is a leader in the field of molecular cancer research. He was the first to decode a novel deoxyribonucleic acid (DNA) sequence associated with cancer known as metallopanstimulin (MPS), which has been shown to play a pivotal role in cancer detection and treatment.

Latino heritage: Argentinean

Born: March 17, 1943; Buenos Aires, Argentina

Also known as: Jose Fernandez-Pol; J. Alberto Fernandez-Pol

Areas of achievement: Medicine; science and technology

EARLY LIFE

Jose Alberto Fernandez-Pol (hoh-ZAY ahl-BEHR-toh fehr-NAHN-dehz-pohl) was born in Buenos Aires, Argentina, in 1943. He earned his B.A. degree from the Colegio Nacional de Vicente López in 1963, and he subsequently pursued a medical degree at the University of Buenos Aires, from which he graduated in 1969.

Fernandez-Pol completed his internship at the University of Buenos Aires's Hospital Escuela José de San Martín from 1969 to 1970 and his residency at the endocrine research laboratory of the university's Center for Nuclear Medicine from 1970 to 1971.

LIFE'S WORK

Fernandez-Pol moved from Argentina to the United States in 1971 in order to accept a one-year residency at the State University of New York in Buffalo. After completing the residency in 1972, he obtained an internal medicine fellowship at Canada's Institute of Medical Sciences and completed two additional research fellowships at the National Cancer Institute (NCI), a division of the National Institutes of Health (NIH). The first fellowship was in the nuclear research laboratory from 1972 to1975, and the second was in the laboratory of molecular biology from 1975 to 1971.

After working at the NCI, Fernandez-Pol moved to St. Louis, where in 1977 he accepted a faculty position as an assistant professor at Saint Louis University School of Medicine. He was quickly promoted to associate professor, a position he held from 1980 to 1985, when he became a full professor. He also had a dual appointment as a professor in the medical school's Department of Radiology, and in 1987 he was appointed chief of the school's laboratory of molecular oncology. In addition to his work at Saint Louis University, Fernandez-Pol in 1977 became the director of the immunoassay laboratory at the Veterans Administration Medical Center.

Fernandez-Pol's research has focused on the genetic causes of cancer and possible treatments of the disease. In 1993, he became the first scientist to describe and patent metallopanstimulin (MPS), a protein that plays an important role in oncogenesis, the process whereby cells become cancerous. MPS was a groundbreaking discovery because it not only can act as a tumor marker for the diagnosis of cancer but also has the ability to assist in the development of new chemotherapy drugs. For example, Fernandez-Pol and colleagues published data on the detection of MPS in patients with breast cancer. This study concluded that increased blood levels of MPS can be used for the early detection of breast cancer and that changes in MPS levels are useful to diagnose disease progression or regression after chemotherapy. In addition, Fernandez-Pol has demonstrated the presence of MPS in colon, liver, prostate, head, and neck cancers.

Fernandez-Pol also studies the effects of chemotherapy treatments. He holds a patent for a method for prevention and treatment of chemotoxicity. In 1995, he patented an antiviral agent that, when applied either on the skin or used intravaginally, may be used to treat findings associated with such conditions as genital warts, psoriasis, skin cancer, and herpes.

In January, 2000, Fernandez-Pol raised more than $3.7 million to form Novactyl, Inc., a pharmaceutical company designed to manufacture and distribute the anticancer agents he spent more than twenty years researching and developing. In 2002, he became president, chairman, and chief scientific officer of Metalloproteomics, LLC, a private laboratory based in Chesterfield, Missouri. He also has served on the editorial boards of *In Vivo: International Journal of Experimental and Clinical Pathophysiology and Drug Research* and *Cancer Genomics and Proteomics,* published by the International Institute of Anticancer Research.

SIGNIFICANCE

Fernandez-Pol's clinical and laboratory research has significantly added to the understanding of the protein composition of cancer. His discovery of MPS is of paramount importance for the field of cancer genetics; this protein has now been found in more than thirty types of cancers. New chemotherapies that were created to target MPS have shown promising results in animal studies and clinical trials, which if translated into human treatment will potentially have a profound impact on patient treatment, prognosis, and outcome.

Janet Ober Berman

FURTHER READING

Daly, James L, et al. "Interactive Data Analysis, Modeling, and Simulation: Available Now on a Desktop Near You." *Proceedings of the Annual Symposium on Computer Application in Medical Care* (1994): 1055. Outlines two new mathematical and statistical tools for medical research that Fernandez-Pol helped create.

Fernandez-Pol, Jose Alberto, Paul D. Hamilton, and Dennis J. Klos. "Genomics, Proteomics, and Cancer: Specific Ribosomal, Mitochondrial, and Tumor Reactive Proteins Can Be Used as Biomarkers for Early Detection of Breast Cancer in Serum." *Cancer Genomics and Proteomics* 2 (January, 2005): 1-24. Describes the important role MPS can play in the detection of breast cancer and how it is comparable or superior to other currently available methods.

Fernandez-Pol, Jose Alberto, et al. "Essential Viral and Cellular Zinc and Iron Containing Metalloproteins as Targets for Novel Antiviral and Anticancer Agents: Implications for Prevention and Therapy of Viral Diseases and Cancer." *Anticancer Research* 21, no 2A (March-April, 2001): 931-957. Reviews the current understanding of MPS proteins and their potential uses in the treatment of cancer.

Ganger, D.R., et al. "Differential Expression of Metallopanstimulin/S27 Ribosomal Protein in Hepatic Regeneration and Neoplasia." *Cancer Detection and Prevention* 25, no. 3 (2001): 231-236. Describes research comparing the presence of MPS in liver diseases, such as hepatitis and cirrhosis, to liver cancer.

See also: Daniel Acosta; Antonia Novello; Marian Lucy Rivas.

LUIS A. FERRÉ

Puerto Rican politician and philanthropist

Ferré founded the New Progressive Party (PNP), the main political party advocating Puerto Rican statehood. From 1969 to 1973, he served as the third democratically elected governor of Puerto Rico. His election marked the first transition of the island's governorship from one political party to another.

Latino heritage: Puerto Rican
Born: February 17, 1904; Ponce, Puerto Rico
Died: October 21, 2003; San Juan, Puerto Rico
Also known as: Luis Alberto Ferré Aguayo
Areas of achievement: Government and politics; business; philanthropy

EARLY LIFE

Luis Alberto Ferré Aguayo (feh-RAY) was born in Ponce, Puerto Rico, to Maria Aguayo Casals, a cousin of cellist Pablo Casals, and Antonio Ferré, a wealthy industrialist and the owner of the Puerto Rico Iron Works. Ferré's paternal grandfather, a French engineer who participated in the ill-fated French attempt to build a canal in Panama, settled in Cuba after the French company building the canal went bankrupt.

Ferré studied civil engineering at the Massachusetts Institute of Technology, earning a bachelor's degree in 1924 and a graduate degree in 1925. While in Massachusetts, he also studied piano at the New England Conservatory of Music. After returning to Puerto Rico, he helped his father expand the family's business holdings, thus making the Ferré family one of the wealthiest on the island. Ferré acquired a small newspaper during the 1940's and turned it into *El Nuevo Día*, one of the most widely circulated newspapers in Puerto Rico. During the 1950's, in an attempt to capitalize on a construction boom, Ferré purchased two cement companies.

LIFE'S WORK

In 1940, Ferré ran unsuccessfully for mayor of Ponce, his hometown. Partially in response to his positive educational experience in Massachusetts during the 1920's, Ferré, who saw the benefits of a closer political and economic relationship with the United States, was an early advocate of Puerto Rican statehood. He was an active member of the Republican Statehood Party (PER); however, in 1951, against the wishes of his party, Ferré boycotted a referendum initiated by the U.S. Congress to determine the possibility of drafting Puerto Rico's

first constitution. He believed that the process would merely reaffirm Puerto Rico's colonial status. Regardless, once the referendum was approved, Ferré, who eventually saw that commonwealth status could be a stepping-stone toward statehood, participated in the constitutional assembly. In 1952, Ferré won election to the Puerto Rican House of Representatives. He consistently argued that commonwealth status, as advocated by Governor Luis Muñoz Marín, made Puerto Ricans second-class citizens.

In 1967, in anticipation of a referendum on the island's future political status, the leadership of the Republican Statehood Party chose not to participate because the results of the referendum would not be binding. Ferré, angered by this decision, left the party to establish the New Progressive Party (PNP). In the 1968 gubernatorial elections, a split in the ruling Popular Democratic Party (PPD), which favored commonwealth status, facilitated Ferré's election. Since the 1968 elections, the governorship in Puerto Rico has been dominated alternatively by the pro-statehood and pro-commonwealth factions.

Luis Ferré. (AP Photo)

Ferré defended the federal minimum-wage laws and the Latino custom of granting Christmas bonus checks to workers. He also visited Puerto Rican troops fighting in Vietnam, created the Puerto Rican Environmental Quality Board to protect the environment, and greatly expanded Puerto Rico's highway system. He lowered the voting age to eighteen and actively sought the participation of young Puerto Ricans in the political system. In 1972, however, he lost his reelection bid to PPD candidate Rafael Hernández Colón. Ferré, who had a close working relationship with the U.S. Republican Party, remained active in politics and was elected to the Puerto Rican Senate in 1976, serving two terms. From 1977 to 1980, he served as president of the senate. Ferré died of respiratory failure in San Juan on October 21, 2003.

SIGNIFICANCE

On November 18, 1991, President George H. W. Bush awarded the Presidential Medal of Freedom to Ferré, one of only a few Puerto Ricans to have received such an honor. Although he is best known as the preeminent champion on the Puerto Rican statehood movement, Ferré also was a philanthropist. In 1959, he established the Ponce Museum of Art with seventy-one paintings from his family's private collection. The museum, whose collection has grown to more than three thousand pieces, is one of the largest and most important art museums in the Caribbean. In recognition of his dedication to building the island's infrastructure, the main highway between Caguas and Ponce, one of Puerto Rico's main transportation arteries, was named in his honor. His daughter, Rosario Ferré, is one of Puerto Rico's most famous writers.

Michael R. Hall

FURTHER READING

Ayala, César J., and Rafael Bernabe. *Puerto Rico in the American Century: A History Since 1898.* Chapel Hill: University of North Carolina Press, 2007. An excellent guide to the history of Puerto Rico during the twentieth century, this source also is of value to students seeking new topics to research on Puerto Rican history.

Dietz, James L. *Economic History of Puerto Rico: Institutional Change and Capitalist Development.* Princeton, N.J.: Princeton University Press, 1987. Dietz contends that Puerto Rico's industrialization campaign has failed to solve the island's economic and social problems.

Morales Carrion, Arturo. *Puerto Rico: A Political and Cultural History.* New York: W. W. Norton, 1984. Although the author's pro-commonwealth stance is obvious, his discussion of Puerto Rican politics is well-researched.

Thornburgh, Dick. *Puerto Rico's Future: A Time to Decide.* Washington, D.C.: Center for Strategic and International Studies, 2007. Former U.S. Attorney General Thornburgh contends that Puerto Rico's current political status denies its citizens the basic right of self-determination.

Trias Monge, José. *Puerto Rico: The Trials of the Oldest Colony in the World.* New Haven, Conn.: Yale University Press, 1999. The author highlights the debates surrounding the nature and future of Puerto Rico's political relationship with the United States, the most contentious issue in Puerto Rican politics.

See also: Pedro Albizu Campos; Rubén Berríos; José de Diego; Rosario Ferré; Lolita Lebrón; Luis Muñoz Marín; Luis Muñoz Rivera.

ROSARIO FERRÉ

Puerto Rican-born writer

One of the most important and prolific contemporary female writers in the Carribean, Ferré is the author of novels, short stories, essays, children's books, poems, and literary criticism. Her writings examine the impact of race, gender, and socioeconomic status on the lives of women living in patriarchal societies, especially that of Puerto Rico.

Latino heritage: Puerto Rican

Born: September 28, 1938; Ponce, Puerto Rico

Also known as: Rosario Ferré Ramírez de Arellano

Areas of achievement: Literature; women's rights; education

EARLY LIFE

Rosario Ferré (roh-SAH-ree-oh feh-RAY) was born to Lorenza Ramírez de Arellano and Luis A. Ferré in Ponce, Puerto Rico. Her father, a wealthy industrialist who founded the New Progressive Party (PNP), the main political party advocating Puerto Rican statehood,

Rosario Ferré. (AP Photo)

served as the third democratically elected governor of Puerto Rico (1969-1973). Ferré's childhood was enlivened by her nanny, Gilda Ventura, who told the young child fascinating stories based on myths and fairytales. Consequently, many of Ferré's literary works, which are steeped in Magical Realism, use myths and fairytales as literary devices.

After completing her primary education in Ponce, Ferré attended the Dana Hall School, a private secondary school for girls in Wellesley, Massachusetts. She began her writing career in high school, publishing several articles in *El Nuevo Día*, a widely read Puerto Rican newspaper owned by her family.

After graduating from the Dana Hall School in 1956, Ferré pursued a B.A. in English at Manhattanville College, earning her degree in 1960. Notwithstanding her father's leadership of the pro-statehood movement, Ferré was a vocal advocate of Puerto Rican independence during the 1960's and 1970's. During the 1990's, however, she changed her political outlook and became a supporter of the pro-statehood movement. When her mother died in 1970, Ferré assumed the role of First Lady for the remainder of her father's term in office.

As a graduate student at the University of Puerto Rico, Ferré helped establish the student-led literary journal *Zona de Carga y Descarga* (*Loading and Unloading Zone*) in 1972. The journal was dedicated to publishing new writers, especially Puerto Ricans. Ferré subsequently earned a Ph.D. in Latin American literature from University of Maryland in 1986. Her dissertation was an analysis of the works of Argentine writer Julio Cortázar.

LIFE'S WORK

While studying at the University of Puerto Rico as a master's degree candidate in Spanish literature, Ferré took courses from Peruvian novelist Mario Vargas Llosa, who encouraged her to pursue a literary career. Many of the stories published by Ferré in *Zona de Carga de Descarga* were reprinted in her first book, *Papeles de Pandora*, in 1976 (published in English in 1991 as *The Youngest Doll*). The recurring motif in the stories is the figure of a doll, a critique of the concept of idealized femininity. Several of the stories debunk the patriarchal view that values women for their social prestige as wives. Drawing upon her early childhood memories of fairytales, one of Ferré's stories recounts how a young woman's hopes of a career as a ballerina were dashed by her father's plan to arrange a socially advantageous marriage for her. Ferré's aggressive and politically astute female characters challenge the stereotypical image of passive and subordinate women in Puerto Rican culture. As such, Ferré is credited by many critics with launching the feminist movement in Puerto Rican literature. In addition, her stories incorporate techniques such as multiple narrators and fragmented time sequences common to Magical Realism.

A frequent theme in Ferré's writings is Puerto Rico's controversial historical and political relationship with the United States. In 1986, Ferré published her first novel, *Maldito amor* (*Sweet Diamond Dust*, 1988). In the novel, the author rewrites Puerto Rican history during the first half of the twentieth century from a woman's perspective. The story, set in the Guamaní Mountains, relates the multigenerational escapades of the sugar plantation-owning De La Valle family and their attempts to resist the encroachment of U.S. corporations. Infused with elements of Magical Realism, the story is told from multiple points of view.

Published in 1995, *The House on the Lagoon* is Ferré's first English-language novel. Nominated for the National Book Award in 1996, the semiautobiographical novel, with multiple narrators and mythical themes, examines the history of the Mendizabal family. The

Ferré's Literary Magazine
Zona de Carga y Descarga

While attending graduate school at the University of Puerto Rico, Rosario Ferré took a course with Uruguayan literary critic Ángel Rama. Encouraged by Rama, Ferré, her cousin Olga Nolla, Eduardo Forastieri, Luis César Rivera, and Waldo César Lloreda established the student-led literary journal *Zona de Carga y Descarga (Loading and Unloading Zone)*. Created as a forum for young Puerto Rican writers, the magazine published nine issues from September, 1972, to June, 1975. Frequent themes included the status of women in a patriarchal society, gay rights, and anticolonialism, especially as it pertained to Puerto Rico. The journal sought a balance between the form and content of literature. As such, it was in the vanguard of the birth of postmodernism in Puerto Rico. Serving as editor of the journal, Ferré also was a frequent contributor, and the journal launched her literary career. Her papers are housed at the Princeton University Library in a collection that primarily consists of her personal and literary correspondence relating to *Zona de Carga y Descarga*. Also included in the collection is a comprehensive index of the magazine.

main character of the novel, Isabel Montfort, a member of the elite social class, embodies the tensions among the various races, genders, and social classes in Puerto Rico. The novel depicts debates about Puerto Rico's political status, with Isabel preferring independence while her husband opts for statehood. Significantly, the book begins on the day that U.S. President Woodrow Wilson signs the Jones Act of 1917, which granted citizenship to Puerto Ricans.

Ferré's second novel originally written in English is *Eccentric Neighborhoods* (1998). Like *The House on the Lagoon*, the novel is a family saga that explores modern Puerto Rican political and social history. The main character, Elvira Vernet, is descended from two prominent families that have contrary views of Puerto Rico's political future. In *Flight of the Swan* (2001), her third English-language novel, the protagonist is Anna Pavlova, a Russian ballerina trapped in Puerto Rico as a result of the Russian Revolution. Rendered stateless by the revolution, Anna experiences a limbo akin to that of the Puerto Ricans before they were granted U.S. citizenship in 1917. *Lazos de sangre (Blood Ties, 2010)* explores the life of Rose Monroig, a member of Puerto Rico's social elite. In addition to her literary pursuits,

Ferré continued to teach at the University of Puerto Rico in the Department of Literature.

SIGNIFICANCE

Running counter to the island's dominant linguistic mode, Ferré set a literary precedent in 1995 when she wrote and published *The House on the Lagoon* in English. Her novels reflect and reinterpret Puerto Rican history, while often engaging in the most controversial debate in Puerto Rico, the future of the island's political status with the United States. Ferré's fiction— suffused with references to Puerto Rico's twentieth century historical experience, Magical Realism, and feminist thought—has made her one of the leading female authors in contemporary Latin American literature.

Michael R. Hall

FURTHER READING

Ferré, Rosario. *The House on the Lagoon*. New York: Farrar, Straus and Giroux, 1995. Ferré's first novel written originally in English, this book is an excellent example of historical fiction.

Henao, Eda B. *The Colonial Subject's Search for Nation, Culture, and Identity in the Works of Julia Alvarez, Rosario Ferré, and Ana Lydia Vega*. Lewiston, N.Y.: Edwin Mellen Press, 2003. Examines the meanings and messages in the novels and short stories of these three Latin American authors.

Lindsay, Claire. *Locating Latin American Women Writers: Cristina Peri Rossi, Rosario Ferré, Albalucia Angel, and Isabel Allende*. New York: Peter Lang, 2003. Part of the Currents in Comparative Romance Languages and Literatures series, this study evaluates the technique and impact of four significant authors.

Ortega, Julio. "Postmodernism in Latin America." In *Postmodernist Fiction in Europe and Latin America*, edited by Theo D'haen and Hans Bertens. Amsterdam: Rodopi, 1988. A well-written chapter that outlines the development of postmodernism in Latin America.

Rivera, Carmen S. *Kissing the Mango Tree: Puerto Rican Women Rewriting American Literature*. Houston, Tex.: Arte Público Press, 2002. Written within the framework of feminist theory, this study examines the work of popular Puerto Rican women writers, including Ferré.

See also: Isabel Allende; Julia Alvarez; Luis A. Ferré; Nicholasa Mohr; Judith Ortiz Cofer; Esmeralda Santiago.

JOSÉ FERRER

Puerto Rican-born actor, director, and producer

In a long and varied career as an actor, director, and producer in the theater, films, and television, Ferrer won an Academy Award and three Tonys and distinguished himself as a versatile performer with a distinctive voice.

Latino heritage: Spanish

Born: January 8, 1912; Santurce, Puerto Rico

Died: January 26, 1992; Coral Gables, Florida

Also known as: José Vicente Ferrer de Otero y Cintrón

Areas of achievement: Theater; acting; filmmaking; radio and television

EARLY LIFE

José Vicente Ferrer de Otero y Cintrón (fur-REHR) was born on January 8, 1912, in Santurce, Puerto Rico, to Rafael Ferrer, an attorney and writer, and Maria Providencia Cintrón. Both parents were originally from Spain. Ferrer first visited the mainland United States as a young boy to have an operation on his palate, and the family moved to New York City permanently when he was six.

Ferrer attended private and public schools in New York and was accepted to Princeton University when he was fourteen, but the university persuaded him to spend a year of preparation at a school in Switzerland. At the time he was a promising pianist and was expected to become a concert performer. Instead, he studied architecture.

Ferrer's goals changed when the president of the Triangle Club, a fellow architecture student, suggested he try out for one of the dramatic club's productions. He did and was rejected but won the leading role on his second audition. Ferrer participated in several campus productions along with fellow students such as future film star James Stewart and Josh Logan, who became a prominent stage and film director. He also organized a band, the Pied Pipers, which performed at Princeton parties.

After graduating from Princeton, Ferrer intended to work on a Ph.D. in Romance languages at Columbia University but could not resist the call of show business. He worked briefly on a showboat on Long Island Sound in 1935 and then joined Logan for a season of summer stock as a stage manager. He made his Broadway debut later that year as second policeman in *A Slight Case of Murder* (1935). Ferrer found steady Broadway work as an assistant stage manager and had supporting roles in eight more plays before landing the lead in *Charley's Aunt* (1892) in 1940. As a young actor, he was greatly influenced by John Barrymore, Alfred Lunt, Osgood

Perkins, Laurence Olivier, Paul Muni (with whom he appeared in 1939's *Key Largo*), and especially Louis Jouvet, for whom Ferrer acted as interpreter on one of the French star's visits to New York.

LIFE'S WORK

Ferrer made his debut as a Broadway director in 1942 with the farce *Vickie*, in which he also starred along with his first wife, Uta Hagen, whom he married in 1938. Ferrer replaced Danny Kaye in *Let's Face It* (1941) in 1943 and costarred later that year with Hagen and Paul Robeson in a legendary production of William Shakespeare's *Othello, the Moor of Venice* (pr. 1604, rev. 1623). After directing Mel Ferrer (no relation) in *Strange Fruit* in 1945, Ferrer landed the role with which he is most associated in 1946, starring in *Cyrano de Bergerac* (1897) under the direction of Mel Ferrer. After divorcing Hagen in 1948, he married Phyllis Hill, one of his *Cyrano de Bergerac* costars later that year.

Ferrer made his film debut as the dauphin in Victor Fleming's *Joan of Arc* (1948) opposite Ingrid Bergman.

José Ferrer. (AP Photo)

Ferrer as Cyrano de Bergerac on Stage and Screen

José Ferrer achieved his greatest success in the stage and film versions of Edmond Rostand's 1897 play *Cyrano de Bergerac*. He won a Tony as the Best Actor in a Play during the 1946-1947 Broadway season for his portrayal of the French nobleman whose skills as a poet, musician, and soldier are overshadowed by his large nose. This defect keeps him from proclaiming his love for his beautiful cousin, Roxane. Ferrer's definitive interpretation of the role attracted the attention of Hollywood and helped launch his film career. His Academy Award for the 1950 film made him permanently identified with the character of Cyrano. Ferrer repeated the role on Broadway in 1953, on television in 1955, and again in Abel Gance's *Cyrano et d'Artagnan* (1964), a merging of Rostand's story with Alexandre Dumas's *The Three Musketeers* (1844). Ferrer said in interviews that he regretted that his film career peaked early with *Cyrano de Bergerac* and *Moulin Rouge*. In both films he captures without sentimentality the sensitivity of souls tormented by their deformities.

In Otto Preminger's stylish psychological thriller *Whirlpool* (1949), Ferrer's murderous con man is distinctive because of the way the actor suggested the character's pleasure in his villainy. In 1950, he played a South American dictator opposite Cary Grant's idealistic doctor in *Crisis* and then repeated his signature role in the film of *Cyrano de Bergerac*. On Broadway, he directed and costarred with Gloria Swanson in a 1950 revival of the Ben Hecht-Charles MacArthur comedy *Twentieth Century* (1934) and followed it by directing the hit World War II comedy *Stalag 17* (1951).

In 1952, Ferrer had another of his best-known film roles as Henri de Toulouse Lautrec in John Huston's *Moulin Rouge*, playing the diminutive artist on his knees. The following year he costarred with Rita Hayworth in *Miss Sadie Thompson*; back on Broadway, he starred in a production of Shakespeare's *Richard III* (pr. c. 1592-1593, rev. 1623) and a revival of *Charley's Aunt* that he also directed and won two Tonys for directing and starring as a victimized husband in *The Shrike*. Continuing to perform in big Hollywood productions, Ferrer played the defense attorney in *The Caine Mutiny* (1954) and starred as composer Sigmund Romberg in Stanley Donen's *Deep in My Heart* (1954).

In 1953, Ferrer achieved another level of celebrity by marrying popular singer-actor Rosemary Clooney. The couple had five children, including future character actor Miguel Ferrer, before divorcing in 1961. They remarried in 1964 and divorced again in 1967. The Ferrers were one the most prominent show business couples of their time, appearing on countless magazine covers and making several recordings and television appearances together.

The Shrike (1955), based on his stage success, was the first film directed by Ferrer, and he began concentrating on this side of his career, directing five films from 1955 to 1958. He had one final Broadway success, directing the Civil War drama *The Andersonville Trial* (1959).

For the rest of his career Ferrer alternated between film and television work, with occasional forays in the theater. He made one of his most indelible film impressions in David Lean's epic *Lawrence of Arabia* (1962), as a sadistic Turkish officer during World War I who has T. E. Lawrence, disguised as an Arab, tortured. The brutality of the scene resulted in the banning of the film in Turkey.

His other notable film roles include *Ship of Fools* (1965), *Enter Laughing* (1967), Billy Wilder's *Fedora* (1978), Woody Allen's *A Midsummer Night's Sex Comedy* (1982), and David Lynch's *Dune* (1984). His final Broadway performances came as a temporary replacement in the musical *Man of La Mancha* (1965) in 1966, and his final directorial effort was another musical, *Carmelina* (1979). Ferrer also acted and directed in London, his native Puerto Rico, and regional theaters, sang opera with the Brooklyn Academy of Music and the Beverly Hills Opera, and served as artistic adviser for Miami's Coconut Grove Playhouse. He was planning a return to Broadway when he died of colon cancer on January 26, 1992.

SIGNIFICANCE

Ferrer's trademark was his deep, resonant voice. He also articulated his lines more distinctly than most actors, especially the method actors of the second half of the twentieth century, without seeming artificial or stagey. Late in his career, Ferrer's unique voice helped him launch a new career as a voiceover actor. Ferrer acted in twenty-seven Broadway plays and directed twenty-one. He acted in forty-nine films and directed seven. In addition to winning three Tonys and one Academy Award, he was nominated for Oscars for *Joan of Arc* and *Moulin Rouge*. He was inducted into the Theater Hall of Fame in 1981 and received the National Medal of Arts in 1985, becoming the first actor to receive the award. Ferrer was the first Latino actor to win a Tony, the first to win an Academy Award, and the first to direct a Hollywood film.

Michael Adams

FURTHER READING

Buckley, Michael. "José Ferrer." *Films in Review* 38 (1987): 66-75, 130-145. Detailed description of Ferrer's film career.

Clooney, Rosemary, and Joan Barthel. *Girl Singer: An Autobiography*. New York: Broadway Books, 2001. Clooney discusses her often turbulent two marriages to Ferrer.

Ferrer, José. "José Ferrer." Interview by Lewis Funke and John E. Booth In *Actors Talk about Acting*, edited by Lewis Funke and John E. Booth. New York: Avon, 1961. Lengthy interview with Ferrer in which he discusses his domestic life and his films but primarily talks about his stage experience and his theories of the theater.

See also: Desi Arnaz; Leo Carrillo; Mel Ferrer; Fernando Lamas; Ramón Novarro; Anthony Quinn; Gilbert Roland; César Romero.

MEL FERRER

American actor, director, and producer

Ferrer had a varied career in the United States and Europe as actor, director, and producer in the theater, films, and television but is best known as the first husband of Audrey Hepburn.

Latino heritage: Cuban
Born: August 25, 1917; Elberon, New Jersey
Died: June 2, 2008; Santa Barbara, California
Also known as: Melchior Gaston Ferrer; Melchior Ferrer
Areas of achievement: Acting; filmmaking; theater

EARLY LIFE

Melchior Gaston Ferrer (MEHL-kee-or fur-REHR) was born in Elberon, New Jersey, to Dr. José Maria Ferrer and Irene O'Donohue Ferrer. His Cuban-born father was chief of staff at New York St. Vincent's Hospital, and his mother was the daughter of a coffee broker who became New York City commissioner of parks.

Ferrer attended private schools in New York and Connecticut before going to Princeton University, dropping out when he won an award for writing a play. He then worked for a newspaper in Vermont and went to Mexico to write. Ferrer collaborated on a children's book, *Tito's Hats* (1940), with artist Jean Charlot.

As a teenager, Ferrer had acted in summer stock theater at the Cape Cod Playhouse, and he appeared on Broadway in 1938 as a dancer in two unsuccessful musicals. He returned to New York from Mexico to act on radio and play small roles on Broadway in *Kind Lady* (1940) and *Cue for Passion* (1940). While recovering from polio, he was a disc jockey in Arkansas and Texas until he found television work with NBC in New York.

He was hired by Columbia Pictures as a dialogue coach before directing the low-budget *The Girl of the Limberlost* (1945).

LIFE'S WORK

Ferrer returned to Broadway to appear in *Strange Fruit* (1945), about an interracial love affair, directed and produced by José Ferrer (no relation). He then directed an acclaimed 1946 revival of Edmond Rostand's *Cyrano de Bergerac* (1897), which made a star of José Ferrer. Determined to establish himself as a film director, Ferrer returned to Hollywood as an assistant on John Ford's Mexican-set *The Fugitive* (1947), in which he played a small role. In 1947, with Dorothy McGuire and Gregory Peck, he cofounded the La Jolla Playhouse in San Diego and remained one of its artistic directors until 1959.

Ferrer was established as a film actor by *Lost Boundaries* (1949), in which he played a light-skinned African American doctor who must pretend to be white to find work. After this success, Ferrer costarred with Joan Fontaine and Robert Ryan in Nicholas Ray's *Born to Be Bad* (1950) and directed the stylish melodrama *The Secret Fury* (1950), with Ryan and Claudette Colbert. Ferrer tried to salvage producer Howard Hughes's *Vendetta* (1950), a troubled production with four earlier directors, including Max Ophüls and Preston Sturges.

Ferrer worked steadily as an actor in Hollywood and Europe throughout the 1950's. Robert Rossen's *The Brave Bulls* (1951) gave Ferrer one of his most notable roles as Mexico's leading bullfighter. Ferrer followed *The Brave Bulls* with Fritz Lang's offbeat

Western *Rancho Notorious* (1952); the swashbuckler *Scaramouche* (1952); the romantic *Lili* (1953), one of Ferrer's most popular films, in which he plays a crippled puppeteer opposite Leslie Caron; and *Knights of the Round Table* (1953), in which he portrays King Arthur opposite Ava Gardner's Guinevere and Robert Taylor's Lancelot.

Before moving to Hollywood, Ferrer had been divorced three times, marrying his first wife twice, and was father of four children. He gained his greatest fame through his relationship with the young actor Audrey Hepburn. The two met in 1953 and starred on Broadway the next year in Jean Giraudoux's *Ondine*. They were married a few weeks after the play closed. Ferrer and Hepburn costarred in King Vidor's *War and Peace* (1956), and he directed her in *Green Mansions* (1959). Neither film was a critical or commercial success, but *Wait Until Dark* (1967), which Ferrer produced, was a hit for Hepburn.

Ferrer starred with Ingrid Bergman in Jean Renoir's *Paris Does Strange Things* (1956), played Robert Cohn in *The Sun Also Rises* (1957), and costarred with Harry Belafonte in *The World, the Flesh, and the Devil* (1959), which explores racial prejudice. While Hepburn remained one of Hollywood's biggest stars, Ferrer's acting and directing careers declined after the 1950's. The disparity in their fame created tensions in the marriage, but the couple remained married until 1968. Their son, Sean, was born in 1960.

Ferrer continued to work regularly as an actor in films and television through 1998. His best-known films were *The Longest Day* (1962), *The Fall of the Roman Empire* (1964), *Sex and the Single Girl* (1964), and Rainer Werner Fassbinder's *Lili Marleen* (1981), but he toiled mostly in obscure low-budget films, especially in Italy. He was best known to the American public for his role in the television soap opera *Falcon Crest* from 1981 to 1984. Ferrer's final marriage, to Elizabeth Soukhotine in 1971, lasted until his death in 2008.

SIGNIFICANCE

Although he was never a major star, Ferrer worked steadily in theater, film, and television for almost six decades. He was essentially a reliable character actor who could adapt his skills to any period or nationality and flourished particularly when Hollywood was still obsessed with costume dramas. Ironically, although Ferrer regularly played French, German, and Italian characters, *The Brave Bulls* was the only film in which

Mel Ferrer. (AP Photo)

he played a Latino. That film, *Lost Boundaries*, and *Lili* constitute his best work as an actor. His most lasting fame results from his association with Hepburn, one of Hollywood's most enduring stars.

Michael Adams

FURTHER READING

Berkvist, Robert. "Mel Ferrer, Reluctant Star, Dies at Ninety." *The New York Times*, June 4, 2008, p. A23. Concise summary of Ferrer's life and career.

Ferrer, Mel. "Audrey Hepburn and Mel Ferrer: Their Homes in Malibu and Beverly Hills." *Architectural Digest* 63 (March, 2006): 160-165. Ferrer recalls the two homes he shared with Hepburn.

Spoto, Donald. *Enchantment: The Life of Audrey Hepburn*. New York: Harmony Books, 2006. Ferrer is presented as domineering husband in this biography of Hepburn.

See also: Desi Arnaz; Leo Carrillo; José Ferrer; Fernando Lamas; Ramón Novarro; Anthony Quinn; Gilbert Roland; César Romero.

AMERICA FERRERA

American actor

Ferrera is best known for her performance in the television series Ugly Betty. *She has received numerous accolades for her acting, including a Golden Globe Award, a Screen Actor's Guild Award, and an Emmy Award.*

Latino heritage: Honduran
Born: April 18, 1984; Los Angeles, California
Also known as: America Georgine Ferrera; Georgina
Areas of achievement: Radio and television; acting

EARLY LIFE

America Georgine Ferrera (ah-MEHR-ee-kah jor-JEEN-eh feh-REHR-ah) was the youngest of six children born to Gregoria and America Ferrera, Hondurans who immigrated to the United States in the 1970's. Her parents divorced shortly after Ferrera was born. Her mother worked as a manager of a hotel housekeeping staff in order to support her children. Ferrera grew up with a strong work ethic and the belief that education was important to lifelong success. She knew that inside beauty was more important than the outside beauty defined by the popular culture.

Ferrera began acting at age seven in a school production of *Hamlet*. She attended Calabash Elementary School in the San Fernando Valley, where she played the Artful Dodger in *Oliver* at age ten. She continued to act in school and community plays while she attended George Ellery Hale Middle School in Woodland Hills, California. Ferrera was valedictorian of her graduating class at El Camino Real High School and studied theater and international relations at the University of Southern California.

Ferrera's mother did not initially support her acting career, so Ferrera waited tables to pay for her acting lessons and the head shots she needed for auditions. Later, her mother came to appreciate her daughter's career choice. Ferrera credits her mother with instilling values that helped her attain success.

LIFE'S WORK

Ferrera was eighteen in 2002, when she got her first opportunity in film with a role in *Gotta Kick It Up!* Ferrera played a Latina teen who loved to dance. That same year, Ferrera attended summer theater camp at Northwestern University in Illinois, where she auditioned for the film *Real Women Have Curves* (2002). She was cast as the Mexican American character Ana Garcia, a first-generation female born in the United States, like Ferrera herself. Ferrera won the Sundance Jury Award for Best Actress in this film. The year 2002 ended with Ferrera playing Charlee in the television series *Touched by an Angel*.

In 2004, Ferrera appeared in the television films *$5.15/Hr.* and *Plainsong*, the television series *CSI: Crime Scene Investigation*, and the feature film *Darkness Minus Twelve*. The following year, she had roles in the films *How the Garcia Girls Spent Their Summer*, *Lords of Dogtown*, *3:52*, and *The Sisterhood of the Traveling Pants*. Ferrera also appeared in the films *Steel City* (2006), *Muertas* (2007), *Under the Same Moon* (2007), and *Hacia la oscuridad* (2007). In 2008, she reprised her original role in *The Sisterhood of the Traveling Pants 2*, hosted the television documentary program *Independent Lens,* and was the voice of Fawn in *Tinkerbell*. Ferrera's 2010 films included *The Dry Land, Our Family Wedding*, and *How to Train Your Dragon*, for which she was the voice of Astrid.

America Ferrera. (AP Photo)

In 2006, Ferrera won the title role on *Ugly Betty* on ABC. This dramedy, with themes of economic disparity and cultural concerns, was based on Fernando Gaitan's Colombian telenovela *Yo soy Betty: La fea* (*I Am Betty: The Ugly One*). Ferrera played Betty Suarez, an intelligent, kindhearted but naïve young woman, who landed her perfect job with *Mode*, a high-fashion magazine. Betty dressed in frumpy outfits and had blue braces on her teeth. Her coworkers made fun of her, but Betty won them over with her genuine nature. A few days before Ferrera's twenty-sixth birthday, the popular television series aired its last show after four seasons on April 14, 2010.

In the fall of 2010, Ferrera performed in a London production of playwright Neil LaBute's *Reasons to Be Pretty*. This production mirrored themes in *Ugly Betty,* addressing superficiality and surface beauty. In July, 2010, she became engaged to longtime boyfriend Ryan Piers Williams, a writer, actor, and director who met Ferrera at the University of Southern California when he cast her in his student film.

SIGNIFICANCE

With her ample, curvaceous body and beautiful smile, America Ferrera has attained her dream of becoming a successful actor. Between 2006 and 2010, she received about thirty award nominations for her role in *Ugly Betty*, winning the Golden Globe, Screen Actor's Guild, and Emmy Awards. In 2007, she was included in *Time* magazine's list of the "100 Most Influential People in the World" and *People* magazine's list of the "100 Most Beautiful." In 2007, Congress recognized Ferrera as a positive role model for young Latinos. Ferrera has proved that Latinos and Latinas can find success in the performing arts and that being yourself is beautiful.

Marylane Wade Koch

FURTHER READING
Anderson, Sheila. *America Ferrera: Latina Superstar.* Berkeley Heights, N.J.: Enslow, 2009. A biography of Ferrera aimed at high school students.
Ferrera, America. Introduction to *Declare Yourself: Speak, Connect, Act, Vote—More Than Fifty Celebrated Americans Tell You Why.* New York: HarperCollins Publishers, 2008. In this book aimed at high school students, Declare Yourself, a nonpartisan group, encourages young people to use their votes to make their voices heard. Ferrera's introduction describes her values and beliefs.
Gauntlett, David. *Media, Gender, and Identity: An Introduction.* New York: Routledge, 2008. Discusses gender identity and its relationship with the media, including Ferrera's role in the television series *Ugly Betty.*
Sandell, Laurie. "Surprise! She's a Bombshell (And You Can Be One Too)." *Glamour*, Sept. 3, 2007. Details how Ferrera defied the traditional image of female actors by not being blond and thin.
Williams, Zella. *America Ferrera: Award-Winning Actress.* New York: Powerkids Press, 2010. Part of the Hispanic Headliner series for students in the second to sixth grades. Highlights Ferrera's acting career, as well as the causes she supports.

See also: Jessica Alba; Eva Longoria; Zoë Saldana.

RICARDO FLORES MAGÓN

Mexican-born activist, journalist, and politician

Flores Magón was a rabble-rousing journalist and dramatist with strong anarchist leanings. Despite constant persecution and frequent imprisonment, he founded the Mexican Liberal Party and a newspaper highly critical of Mexican president-dictator Porfirio Díaz. His eloquence, principles, and courage helped inspire the Mexican Revolution.

Latino heritage: Mexican
Born: September 16, 1874; San Antonio Eloxochitlán, Oaxaca, Mexico
Died: November 21, 1922; Fort Leavenworth, Kansas

Also known as: Cipriano Ricardo Flores Magón
Areas of achievement: Journalism; government and politics; activism

EARLY LIFE
Cipriano Ricardo Flores Magón (SIHP-ree-AH-noh rih-CAR-doh FLOH-rehs mah-GOHN) was born into a poor family in a village in the southern Mexican state of Oaxaca. He was the son of an Indian, Teodoro Flores, and a mestiza (a woman of mixed European and Indian ancestry), Margarita Magón. Seeking better opportunities for their children, Teodoro and Margarita moved

their family to Mexico City in the late 1870's. In the capital, Flores Magón enrolled in the national high school system and graduated from a national preparatory school. In 1893, he entered the National School of Jurisprudence to study law but dropped out after three years without obtaining a degree in order to campaign against the Mexican government.

Flores Magón and his brothers, Enrique and Jesús, had grown up during the rule of Porfirio Díaz, who served as president of Mexico from 1877 to 1880 and from 1884 to 1911. A military hero of the War of Reform, Díaz had been a popular leader early in his tenure who made sweeping social and political reforms as Mexico enjoyed a period of stability, economic growth, and modernization. However, late in his presidency, he became an increasingly repressive dictator, ruthlessly stifling dissent and imprisoning political rivals. Flores Magón, who was well-read in revolutionary and anarchist literature and philosophy, was first arrested as a teenager for speaking out politically. He grew determined to help improve the lot of his fellow citizens, particularly the poor, which he felt could be best accomplished by deposing Díaz.

LIFE'S WORK

After leaving law school, Flores Magón, now living with common-law wife Maria Talavera, worked as a journalist at *El demócrata*, a newspaper opposed to the Díaz regime. The government periodically shut down the paper and had the publisher and writers arrested. In 1900, Flores Magón and Jesús began publishing *Regeneración*, an antigovernment publication of the Mexican Liberal Party (Partido Liberal Mexicano or PLM), which the brothers helped found. Authorities soon closed down the operation, seized the printing equipment, and arrested Flores Magón and Jesús for defamation. The brothers were imprisoned until 1902, when they were released without trial. Flores Magón and Enrique attached themselves to another newspaper, *El hijo del ahuizóte*, to continue the fight against Díaz. This paper was likewise forcibly discontinued, and Flores Magón and Enrique were imprisoned again. Flores Magón became further radicalized and driven towards revolution. Fearing reprisals for their activities, the brothers fled to Texas, where they continued publishing *Regeneración*.

After several assassination and kidnapping attempts, Flores Magón and Enrique moved newspaper operations to St. Louis, Missouri. Local police, in league with Mexican officials, arrested them for defamation.

After their release, the brothers moved to Canada but could not escape persecution. Flores Magón in 1906 secretly moved to El Paso, Texas, where he instigated labor strikes. In 1907, with a price on his head, he relocated to California, where he began a new publication, *Revolución*, which overtly called for the overthrow of Díaz. He was arrested for violating United States neutrality laws. He was tried, convicted, and sentenced to a federal penitentiary in Arizona.

Released in 1910, Flores Magón returned to Los Angeles and resurrected *Regeneración*. After Díaz was toppled in 1911, Flores Magón and Enrique were arrested and again charged with violating neutrality laws. Convicted in 1912, the brothers were sentenced to two years in federal prison. Upon release, they returned to California and resumed publishing their newspaper. In 1916, they were arrested for violating mail laws and once again landed in jail. In 1918, Flores Magón was arrested for sedition and received a twenty-year sentence. He died under mysterious circumstances in the federal penitentiary at Leavenworth, Kansas, in 1922.

SIGNIFICANCE

Flores Magón's contribution to the Mexican Revolution is incalculable. The Mexican Liberal Party, plagued by organizational problems, did not achieve its goal of agrarian reform. As an exile, Flores Magón did not participate directly in the revolution, and the anarchist message printed in his newspapers did not reach the intended audience of Mexican peasants, many of whom could not read. However, Flores Magón and his party constantly expressed dissatisfaction with the Díaz government that eventually resulted in its downfall, and some of his suggestions for reform later were adopted. His consistent, impassioned voice in calling for improvements in the lives of the Mexican poor—in articles, letters and two plays—was acknowledged after his death. In 1945, his remains were placed in Mexico City's Rotunda of Illustrious Men. Revolutionary leader Emiliano Zapata and the contemporary Zapatista movement in Mexico adopted many of Flores Magón's ideas and principles.

Jack Ewing

FURTHER READING

Albro, Ward S. *Always a Rebel: Ricardo Flores Magón and the Mexican Revolution*. Fort Worth: Texas Christian University Press, 2003. A biography of Flores Magón, focusing on his progress from activist to radical to anarchist, set against the backdrop of events leading up to the revolution and afterward.

Bufe, Chaz, and Mitchell Cowen Verter, eds. *Dreams of Freedom: A Ricardo Flores Magón Reader*. Oakland, Calif.: AK Press, 2005. This work provides a biographical overview of Flores Magón's life and a selection of his most important writings: articles, analyses of famous anarchists, letters, and excerpts from his plays. Contains a time line of events, maps, photographs, and bibliography.

Romo, David Dorado. *Ringside Seat to a Revolution: An Underground Cultural History of El Paso and Juarez, 1893-1923*. El Paso, Tex.: Cinco Puntos Press, 2005. An interesting, detailed look—complete with photographs—at the border towns that were hotbeds of radical activity before, during, and after the Mexican Revolution.

See also: José Celso Barbosa; Gregorio Cortez; Juan Cortina; José de Diego; José Antonio Navarro.

Patrick Flores

American religious leader

Flores was appointed the archbishop of San Antonio, Texas, in 1979, becoming not only the titular head of the largest Catholic diocese in the United States but also the first Mexican American cleric to rise to this powerful position in the American Roman Catholic Church.

Latino heritage: Mexican

Born: July 26, 1929; Ganado, Texas

Also known as: Patrick Fernández Flores; Patricio Fernández Flores; The Mariachi Bishop

Area of achievement: Religion and theology

Early Life

The seventh of nine children of Mexican American migrant farmworkers, Patrick Fernández Flores (PAH-trihk fehr-NAHN-dehz FLOH-rehs) grew up during the Depression in the remote southeastern Texas ranching town of Ganado. His father's poor health nearly compelled Flores to abandon his education in the tenth grade; only the financial intervention of a local bishop allowed Flores to complete his schooling at a Catholic school in nearby Galveston. Flores proved a most able student. He dreamed only of being a priest.

When he was ordained in 1956, he was assigned pastoral duties, serving in parishes in the Houston-Galveston area. Charismatic yet humble, Flores enjoyed the love of his parishioners. However, he never forgot the difficult conditions under which migrant workers, who constituted most of his state's large Latino population, lived. He understood the deep reverence the Mexican American people had for their Catholic faith and how the Church provided an important community of support for immigrants adjusting to conditions in their adopted country. During the 1960's, as part of the sweeping changes following Vatican II, Flores spearheaded efforts to establish bilingual parishes in the Galveston area in order to help welcome immigrants, and he championed educational opportunities for promising Hispanic students.

Life's Work

His public efforts to help the Latino population earned him an appointment in 1970 as auxiliary to the arch

Patrick Flores. (AP Photo)

bishop of San Antonio, at this time, with more than a million Catholics, the largest diocese in the American Roman Catholic Church. Even after being named interim bishop later that year, Flores never abandoned the pastoral imperative of his calling, continuing his humanitarian efforts to improve the economic conditions of immigrant Hispanics in parishes throughout the San Antonio area. He gained a national reputation for his compassionate activism, and *Time* magazine named him among the nation's most promising leaders in 1974. He was elevated to bishop for the El Paso diocese in 1978. When the following year the opportunity came for Pope John Paul II to appoint an archbishop for the San Antonio diocese, there was a historic outpouring of parishioner support for Flores's candidacy. Although not bound by such an endorsement, the pope appointed Flores archbishop, the first Mexican American to hold this powerful rank.

As archbishop, Flores continued to work tirelessly for the poor and for the forgotten, most notably mobilizing support groups for parents of death row inmates at nearby Huntsville State Penitentiary and financing shelters for battered women and the homeless. In 1981, he spearheaded efforts to launch a bilingual Catholic television network for his diocese, the first such network in the country. He directed high-profile ecumenical outreach programs to the Protestant and Jewish communities in the San Antonio area. He took the lead when, in the late 1990's, evidence surfaced that the diocese had been less than forthright in handling child molestation charges filed against two of its priests. In the wake of the diocese's multimillion dollar settlement, Flores was not only among the first Church leaders to apologize for the scandal but also challenged the Church to defrock such priests, a far harsher penalty than the Church had endorsed.

Such bold stands only enhanced Flores's appeal in his archdiocese. Flores emerged at the center of a high-profile U.S. Supreme Court decision in 1997 that ultimately redefined the Religious Freedom Restoration Act of 1993, which was designed to protect religious practices guaranteed by the Fourteenth Amendment. When a diocesan church in the small town of Boerne, Texas, filed for the city's permission to enlarge its 1923 structure, the city council stopped construction, citing the church as a protected historic building. Flores was outraged and legally challenged this action, arguing that the ability of the religious community to practice its religion had been usurped by the council's decision. In ultimately finding for the town, the U.S. Supreme Court significantly

limited the power of Congress to extend federal protection of religious practices. Despite this loss, Flores's heroic efforts on behalf of the small Catholic parish made him a folk hero in the Hispanic community.

His stature was enhanced in June, 2000, when an unemployed El Salvadoran immigrant, fearing deportation and armed with a grenade, held the seventy-year-old Flores and his secretary hostage for more than nine hours in the diocesan offices. The long stand-off gained national media coverage. Flores ultimately negotiated the man's surrender, and only then was it determined that the grenade was a fake. Flores later publicly forgave the man and used the opportunity to encourage compassionate treatment of immigrants.

As Flores neared the mandatory retirement age of seventy-five, there was talk that he should be elevated to cardinal, but his health began to fail. He retired in December, 2004.

SIGNIFICANCE

Emerging during a most dramatic era of contemporary Catholicism, Archbishop Patrick Flores perfectly embodied the vision and sensibility of the historic pontificate of John Paul II. Conservative in matters of theology (late in his tenure, he gently compelled religion teachers in the San Antonio diocese to affirm a loyalty oath to the foundational tenets of the Church), but liberal in matters of political and social activism, particularly his efforts on behalf of the indigent, Flores, although he rose through the ranks of the Catholic hierarchy to become the most prominent and powerful Hispanic in the American Catholic Church, was supremely a pastoral priest. Despite an international reputation for voicing the complex problems facing Hispanic immigrants in America, Flores never lost sight of his responsibility to guide, inspire, and, above all, encourage all the people of the Church under his care.

Joseph Dewey

FURTHER READING

Davidson, John. "A Simple Man." *Texas Monthly*, July 1981, 127. A profile of Flores shortly after his ascendancy to the archbishop's position in San Antonio, with particular emphasis on his immigrant roots and his pastoral profile.
McMurtry, Larry. *The Mariachi Bishop: The Life Story of Patrick Flores*. San Antonio, Tex.: Corona, 1987. Still considered the definitive account of Flores's life and theological vision. Written by a Pulitzer Prize-winning Texas author.

Reese, Thomas J. *Archbishop: Inside the Power Structure of the American Catholic Church.* San Francisco: HarperCollins, 1989. Helpful definition of the hierarchy of the Roman Catholic Church and the responsibility of the archbishop. Features revealing interviews with thirty-one American archbishops, including Flores.

See also: Fray Angélico Chávez; Virgilio Elizondo; Oscar I. Romo; Yolanda Tarango.

TOM FLORES

American football player and coach

Born of Mexican American heritage, Flores grew up in poverty in central California. A good athlete in high school and college, he became a star quarterback for the Oakland Raiders in the fledgling American Football League and later coached the Raiders to two Super Bowl victories.

Latino heritage: Mexican
Born: March 21, 1937; Fresno, California
Also known as: Thomas Raymond Flores
Area of achievement: Football

EARLY LIFE

The son of migrant farmworkers, Thomas Raymond Flores (TOM-uhs RAY-mund FLOH-rehs) grew up in the small town of Sanger, California. He enrolled in first grade at the age of five. His family was so poor that they could not afford to buy shoes for their children, so Flores attended school barefoot for several years.

At Sanger High School, Flores excelled in both academic subjects and sports, and despite his slender build he became the starting quarterback for the Sanger Apaches. His athletic abilities enabled Flores to attend Fresno City College from 1954 to 1956, where he played baseball and during two seasons quarterbacked the Rams to an 11-7-1 record. Flores served on the student council and was president of the Associated Men Students, earned an associate degree, and won an academic scholarship to the College of the Pacific (now the University of the Pacific) in Stockton. Here, he again played baseball and was the starting quarterback for the Tigers before graduating in 1958 with a bachelor's degree in education. Despite his college heroics and though he had filled out to weigh around 200 pounds, Flores initially had difficulty landing a job with a professional team. He had a 1958 tryout with the Calgary Stampeders of the Canadian Football League, but he was eventually cut before playing a game for the team. The following year, he had an unsuccessful tryout with the Washington Redskins of the National Football League (NFL).

LIFE'S WORK

In 1960, the American Football League (AFL) started up, and Flores was signed to play with one of the league's charter teams, the Oakland Raiders. He beat out other candidates to become the team's starting quarterback, and he led the league statistically during the AFL's inaugural season, tossing twelve touchdowns while compiling more than seventeen hundred yards and completing over half his passes. He earned his nickname "The Iceman" for his coolness facing

Tom Flores. (AP Photo)

a pass rush. Flores sat out the 1962 season while recovering from a serious lung infection, but he returned strong the following season. During seven years with Oakland, from 1960 through 1966, he completed 810 passes out of 1,639 attempts (49.4 percent) for 11,835 yards, with 92 touchdowns and 83 interceptions. He also totaled 307 yards in 82 attempts while scoring 5 rushing touchdowns. However, he could not lead the Raiders to a championship, so in 1967 he was traded to the Buffalo Bills.

A seldom-used backup in Buffalo, Flores in three seasons completed only twenty-seven passes in seventy-four attempts, with no touchdowns and nine interceptions. However, he did win a ring as a member of the Bills' team in its 1969 AFL-NFL World Championship, the precursor of the Super Bowl. In 1970, Flores was traded to the Kansas City Chiefs, where he threw one pass—a thirty-three-yard touchdown—before retiring as a player.

After finishing his playing career, Flores became an assistant coach in Buffalo. In 1972, he moved back to the Raiders as assistant coach of wide receivers, tight ends, and quarterbacks. Under coach John Madden, he won a ring for the Raiders' victory in Super Bowl XI in 1977. Two years later, Flores took over as head coach. In 1981, Flores guided the Raiders into Super Bowl XV, in which his team defeated the Philadelphia Eagles 27-10 to become the first wild-card team to win the professional football championship.

In 1982, Flores and the Raiders moved south to Los Angeles, where the team would stay for twelve years before returning to Oakland in the mid-1990's. Flores led the Raiders into Super Bowl XVIII in 1983, in which the team thrashed the favored Washington Redskins 38-9, bringing Los Angeles its first NFL championship since the Rams triumphed in 1951. During nine seasons at the helm of the Raiders, Flores posted a record of 83-53. However, after two back-to-back mediocre years in 1986 and 1987, he relinquished the head coaching reins to become a team administrator. In 1989, the Seattle Seahawks hired him as president and general manager. For three years, Flores witnessed the Seahawks' futility on the field (a combined 23-25 record) under head coach Chuck Knox before stepping down from the team presidency to appoint himself head coach in 1992. Flores did not fare any better with a weak offensive club, which went 2-14, 6-10, and 6-10 in three consecutive last-place finishes in the American Football Conference's western division. After the end of the 1994 season, Flores resigned as team general manager and head coach. His final record as a coach, including play-offs, was 105-90-0.

Mexican Americans in American Football

Latinos—Mexican Americans in particular—have made significant contributions to the pantheon of sports in the United States for more than a century. The first Hispanic to play professional baseball, for example, signed with Troy in 1871. Since the turn of the twentieth century Latinos have been prominent in baseball, boxing, horse racing, track and field, and other athletic endeavors. However, they did not appear in American football until the late 1920's and did not participate regularly in the sport for several decades afterward, due largely to a National Football League (NFL) policy of the time that discouraged minority players.

The first Hispanic to play professional football in the United States was a Cuban, Ignacio Molinet, who was briefly a running back with the Frankford Yellow Jackets in 1927. Spanish-born Jesse Rodriguez also served as a running back, playing for the Buffalo Bisons in 1929. The first Mexican American player was Waldo Don Carlos, a center for the Green Bay Packers in 1931. The first true Mexican American star was wide receiver, later coach, and Hall of Fame inductee Tom Fears, who played from 1948 to 1956, and others like Jim Plunkett, Anthony Muñoz, Tony Casillas, and Max Montoya became standouts in illustrious careers. In the twenty-first century, many Latinos—including Louis Vasquez, Greg Camarillo, Roberto Garza, Manny Ramirez, Tony Romo, and Mark Sanchez—are integral to NFL teams featuring Hispanic coaches like Jack Del Rio and Ron Rivera.

Flores afterward returned to the scene of his greatest glory. In 1995, he signed on as a color commentator with the Oakland Raiders Radio Network, and as of 2011, he continued to call the team's play-by-plays alongside two-time California Sportscaster of the Year Greg Papa. Flores, married to wife Barbara and the father of a daughter (Kim) and twin sons (Mark and Scott), also became an author. In 1992, he published a cowritten autobiography, *Fire in the Iceman*, which details his life from birth through his playing and coaching careers. He has since authored or coauthored several other works, including the instructional books *Coaching Football* (1993) and *Football for the Utterly Confused* (2009) and the nostalgic *Tom Flores' Tales from the Oakland Raiders* (2007).

SIGNIFICANCE

Tom Flores is one of just a handful of athletes who played in the American Football League throughout its entire decade-long existence, and he is ranked fifth among the league's all-time passers. The first-ever Raiders starting quarterback, he was also the first quarterback of Hispanic ancestry in the NFL. Flores was the second Hispanic NFL head coach (after Tom Fears, the first Latino to be inducted in the Hall of Fame), the first Hispanic coach to win a Super Bowl, and the first of only three individuals (the others are Mike Ditka and Tony Dungy) to earn Super Bowl rings as both a player and a head coach. Flores has been nominated for induction into the Pro Football Hall of Fame each year since 2001.

He was a charter member of the Pacific Athletics Hall of Fame in 1982, and he has been inducted into the African American/Ethnic Sports Hall of Fame (2003), the California Sports Hall of Fame (2007), and the California Community College Athletic Association Hall of Fame (2011). The Sanger High School football stadium was renamed in his honor.

Flores is also known for his charitable efforts, particularly for the establishment of the Tom Flores Youth Foundation, which benefits Sanger-area schools with funding for science, art, and sports. He received an honorary doctorate from Pepperdine University for humanitarian service. University of the Pacific honored him with the Distinguished Professional Service Award in 1984, and Fresno City College honored him in 2010.

Jack Ewing

FURTHER READING

Flores, Tom, and Frank Cooney. *Fire in the Iceman: Autobiography of Tom Flores, Tales of the Tooz, the Snake, and the Boz.* Los Angeles: Bonus Books, 1992. Flores's autobiography includes many photographs that illustrate his personal and professional life.

Rappoport, Ken. *The Little League That Could: A History of the American Football League.* Lanham, Md.: Taylor Trade, 2010. A detailed account of the new professional league that arose to successfully challenge the domination of the National Football League.

Travers, Steven. *The Good, the Bad, and the Ugly: Heart-Pounding, Jaw-Dropping, and Gut-Wrenching Moments from Oakland Raiders History.* Chicago: Triumph Books, 2008. The complete story of one of the charter AFL football franchises—including its inception and formation, its greatest players and games—and the team with which Flores is primarily associated.

See also: Tedy Bruschi; Manny Fernández; Jeff Garcia; Tony Gonzalez; Anthony Muñoz; Jim Plunkett; Rich Rodriguez; Tony Romo.

MARIA IRENE FORNES

Cuban-born playwright

One of the most important voices in both Off-Off-Broadway theater and Cuban American literature, Fornes has chronicled politics, personal and ethnic identity, feminism, and other social currents since the 1960's. She also is a major influence on a generation of playwrights.

Latino heritage: Cuban
Born: May 14, 1930; Havana, Cuba
Area of achievement: Theater

EARLY LIFE

On May 14, 1930, Maria Irene Fornes (FOHR-nehs) was born in Havana, Cuba. Upon the death of her father, the family was left without financial support, so they emigrated to the United States in 1945, leaving behind one of Fornes's brothers.

Fornes worked for several years in New York City, where she learned English. In 1951, she became a naturalized American citizen. From 1954 to 1957, she lived in Europe, where she studied painting and became interested in the theater after seeing actor-director Roger Blin's original production of Samuel Beckett's *En attendant Godot* (1952; *Waiting for Godot*, 1954). Although she did not speak French, she was deeply influenced by Beckett's style.

Upon returning to New York, Fornes found work as a costume designer for several local theaters. By 1960, she was living with critic and philosopher Susan Sontag, who inspired Fornes to write. Fornes's first play, *The Widow*, was produced in 1961 by the New York Actors' Studio and led to several fellowships. These enabled her to launch her dramatic career in the 1960's.

LIFE'S WORK

Fornes's first major stage production and critical notice came with 1963's *Tango Palace* (also known as

There, You Died!). In the ensuing years, she built a reputation as an Off-Off-Broadway playwright. *The Successful Life of Three* (1965) and the musical *Promenade* (1965) won the writer her first two Obie Awards. She received several fellowships in 1967 and 1968, which she used to work on *A Vietnamese Wedding* (1967), about the war in Vietnam. Her first London production came in 1968 with her one-woman show *Dr. Kheal*, and one of her best-known plays, *Molly's Dream*, debuted that same year. With these successes to her name, in 1972 Fornes co-founded and served as the managing director (until 1979) of New York Theatre Strategy, a company that nurtured new experimental playwrights.

New York Theatre Strategy first produced Fornes's *Fefu and Her Friends* (1977), which won another Obie and quickly became a feminist classic. Other important plays followed, including *The Danube* (1982), *Mud* (1983), and Obie winner *The Conduct of Life* (1985). In addition to New York Theatre Strategy, many of Fornes's plays during this period were staged at International Arts Relations (INTAR)—a New York-based theater group for which Fornes served as the director of the Hispanic Playwrights in Residence Lab—and at the Padua Hills Festival in California.

Through the years, Fornes continued to write prolifically and gain critical acclaim, and also directed both her own works and plays by Henrik Ibsen, Anton Chekhov, and Spanish Golden Age playwright Pedro Calderón de la Barca. Her oeuvre moved from strength to strength, including acclaimed works such as the Obie-winning *Abingdon Square* (1984), *And What of the Night?* (1989), and *Summer in Gossensass* (1998).

Despite this recognition, much of Fornes's work remains all but unknown outside of the New York avant-garde theater scene. However, New York's Signature Theater Company dedicated its 1999-2000 season to her work, including a revival of *Mud* and the premiere of *Letters from Cuba* (2000), a play based on Fornes's correspondence with her brother. In 2010, New York University's English department and INTAR presented the New York Fornes Festival, which mounted a production of *Fefu and Her Friends*; staged dramatic readings of five other plays; and screened the documentary *"The Rest I Make Up": Documenting Irene* (2010).

By 2011, Fornes had written more than forty plays, several musicals, and an opera, in addition to translating and adapting the work of various other writers. She also has served as a teacher of drama both nationally and internationally. Her awards include grants from the Rockefeller Foundation, the National Endowment for the Arts, and the New York State Council on the Arts; the American Academy of Arts and Letters Award in Literature; a Playwrights U.S.A. Award; the PEN/Laura Pels Foundation Award; a New York State Governor's Arts Award; nine Obie Awards for writing, directing, and sustained achievement in theater; a Guggenheim Fellowship; and an honorary doctor of letters degree from Bates College.

SIGNIFICANCE

Fornes has had far-reaching influence in American experimental theater in her various roles as playwright, director, and teacher. This is reflected in her reception by other writers, including three Pulitzer Prize winners: Paula Vogel and Tony Kushner both praised her work, while fellow Off-Off-Broadway dramatist Lanford Wilson called Fornes "the most original of us all." Fornes also is a tireless supporter of new artists, particularly Latinos such as the Cuban American playwright Nilo Cruz, and has helped many to find audiences through New York Theatre Strategy and INTAR.

Leigh Barkley

FURTHER READING

Delgado, Maria M., and Caridad Svich, eds. *Conducting a Life: Reflections on the Theatre of Maria Irene Fornes*. Lyme, N.H.: Smith and Kraus, 1999. Contains contributions from many of Fornes's collaborators and other prominent playwrights, including Tony Kushner and Terrence McNally.

Fornes, Maria Irene. *Letters from Cuba, and Other Plays*. New York: PAJ, 2001. A collection of works including *Letters from Cuba*.

Robinson, Marc, ed. *The Theater of Maria Irene Fornes*. New York: PAJ, 2005. A collection of essays on Fornes's oeuvre, edited by major American theater scholar Robinson.

See also: Mercedes de Acosta; Reinaldo Arenas; Denise Chávez; Eduardo Machado; Piri Thomas; Luis Miguel Valdez; Jose Yglesias.

JULIO FRANCO

Dominican-born baseball player

After a rough start to his career, Franco became a stalwart of Major League Baseball, playing well into his late forties.

Latino heritage: Dominican
Born: August 23, 1958; San Pedro de Macoris,
    Dominican Republic
Also known as: Julio César Robles Franco
Area of achievement: Baseball

EARLY LIFE

Julio César Robles Franco (HEW-lee-oh FRAN-koh) was born August 23, 1958, in San Pedro de Macoris, Dominican Republic. He grew up playing street ball with future major leaguers Tony Fernández, Rafael Ramírez, and Juan Samuel. As a teenager, Franco played for the team sponsored by the sugarcane-processing plant where he and his father worked in nearby Consuelo. Seeing baseball as his only chance to escape a life of poverty, Franco obtained a false birth certificate to cut four years from his age and signed with the Philadelphia Phillies in 1978.

LIFE'S WORK

Franco had a .300 batting average in each of his five seasons as a shortstop in the minor leagues before making his Major League Baseball (MLB) debut early in the 1982 season. Despite the considerable skills he exhibited in the minor leagues and during his brief stint in the majors, the Phillies traded him, along with four other players, to the Cleveland Indians for outfielder Von Hayes in 1982. Franco spent the next five seasons as the Indians' starting shortstop before switching to second base in 1988. He finished second in the 1983 voting for American League rookie of the year. Although Franco had a strong arm, his fielding was erratic, a quality manager Pat Corrales attributed to his lack of concentration. Franco's hitting steadily improved, and he batted over .300 each season from 1986 through 1989.

Franco's tenure with the Indians was an uneasy one because of what was perceived as his immaturity. He was frequently late for team meetings, missed an afternoon game after staying out late the night before, surrounded himself with a growing entourage, was married and divorced twice, and sometimes carried a gun. For these reasons, Franco was traded to the Texas Rangers for three players after the 1988 season.

In Texas, Franco made the American League All-Star team in 1989, 1990, and 1991 and continued to blossom as a hitter, winning the American League batting championship in 1991 with a .341 average and career highs of 201 hits, 108 runs, and 36 stolen bases. He showed new maturity by improving defensively and becoming a clubhouse leader, helping young Latin American players make the adjustment to the big leagues. He also developed a strenuous exercise routine, remarried, and became a born-again Christian.

Franco had knee surgery in 1992 and was able to play in only 35 games. To reduce the wear and tear on his aging body, he became the Rangers' designated hitter in 1993. As a free agent, he signed with the Chicago White Sox for 1994 and, despite playing in only 112 games because of the players' strike, had one of his best seasons, batting .319 with career highs of 20 home runs and 98 runs batted in. Concerned that 1995 might also be lost because of the labor dispute, Franco signed

Julio Franco. (AP Photo)

with Japan's Chiba Lotte Marines and was reunited with Bobby Valentine, his former Texas manager. Playing first base for the first time, Franco was named the best fielder at his position and adapted easily to Japanese culture.

When Valentine was fired, Franco returned to the United States and signed with the Indians, with whom he batted .321. When he was slowed by injuries in 1997, the Indians released him, and he finished the season with the Milwaukee Brewers. Because of his age and history of injury, Franco could find no major league team willing to give him a chance and returned to Chiba Lotte. He played one game for the Tampa Bay Devil Rays in 1999 before spending the rest of the year in the Mexican League. In 2000, Franco became the biggest name ever to play in South Korea. He returned to the Mexican League in 2001 and, after hitting an impressive .437 for the Mexico City Tigers, was signed by the Atlanta Braves.

After batting .300 in twenty-five games at the end of 2001 and hitting two home runs in the postseason, Franco became a Braves fixture as a part-time first baseman and pinch hitter through 2005, hitting .284, .294, .309, and .275. Encouraged by his unprecedented comeback, Franco announced his intention to become the first major league position player to play regularly at age fifty. He became a free agent after the 2005 season and signed with the New York Mets, hitting .273 and making his final postseason appearance. The Mets released him the following July, and the Braves re-signed him to allow him to finish his career in Atlanta. Still hoping to realize his dream, Franco joined Quintana Roo in the Mexican League in 2008 but did not perform well enough to attract offers from the big leagues.

SIGNIFICANCE

With a lifetime average of .298, Franco accumulated 2,586 hits and played in 2,527 games in the major leagues, both records by a player from the Dominican Republic. Equally important was Franco's remarkable second career in the major leagues and his ability to continue to play at a high level until the age of forty-nine. Jerry Browne, Franco's replacement as the Indians' second baseman, played his last game in 1995, twelve years before the retirement of a man eight years his elder. Franco demonstrated what an aging athlete could achieve through diet, exercise, discipline, and determination, and also showed how a rebellious young athlete can mature into a leader.

Michael Adams

FURTHER READING

Eligon, John. "Franco Celebrates His Forty-eighth Birthday but Takes a Pass on the Cake." *The New York Times*, August 24, 2006, p. D3. Describes Franco's role as the Mets' elder statesman.

Pearlman, Jeff. "Oldest Living Major Leaguer Tells All." *Best Life* 3, no. 4 (May, 2006): 54-55. Looks at Franco's diet and exercise routine.

Reilly, Rick. "Old-Timer's Game." *Sports Illustrated* 102, no. 8 (February 21, 2005): 82. Describes the oddity of Franco's playing deep into his forties.

See also: Roberto Alomar; Sandy Alomar, Jr.; Tony Fernandez; Andrés Galarraga; Ozzie Guillén; Rafael Palmeiro; Sammy Sosa.

COCO FUSCO

American artist, actor, and writer

In a career defined by both provocative performance pieces and probing nonfiction about herself and her postcolonial generation of Latino women, Fusco emerged as one of the most insightful commentators on contemporary Latino identity, political and cultural integrity, and sexual and gender issues.

Latino heritage: Cuban
Born: June 18, 1960; New York, New York
Areas of achievement: Art; acting; theater

EARLY LIFE

The childhood of Coco Fusco (FEWS-koh) reflected the pressures of biculturalism. While her mother was pregnant, her father was deported from Cuba shortly after the political upheavals of late 1959 brought Fidel Castro to power. The Fusco family immigrated to New York City, where Coco was born. During Fusco's childhood, her status as an American citizen gave her family security, and dozens of her relatives, fleeing the communist Castro regime, entered the United States legally through her family. Their presence shaped her perception of both Cuban and American traditions and the inevitable collisions of biculturalism, specifically language, religion, and cultural differences.

A voracious reader, Fusco excelled in school. She attended Brown University and, in 1982, completed a dual major, magna cum laude, in literature and society and semiotics, a discipline that investigates the meaning and structures of language. She went on to earn a master's degree in modern thought and literature at Stanford University. Nearly twenty years later, she completed a doctorate in visual culture from London's Middlesex University.

LIFE'S WORK

From 1985, when Fusco graduated from Stanford, to 1995, when she accepted her first teaching position (in the Visual Arts Department at Philadelphia's Temple University), Fusco executed performance pieces, installation art projects, and video productions largely in the New York City area that established her as a cutting-edge theorist in the implications of Latino identity. In 1991, she first worked with Mexican performance artist Guillermo Gómez-Peña—the two collaborated on what would become Fusco's breakthrough piece. In 1992, disturbed by the implications of the international celebration of the quincentenary of Christopher Columbus's "discovery" of the Americas, Fusco and Gómez-Peña mounted a controversial performance piece, *Two Undiscovered Amerindians Visit Spain*, initially for the Columbus Plaza in Madrid. In the piece, the two artists spent three days in a single 10-foot by 12-foot elaborate gold cage portraying indigenous natives from a fictitious Caribbean island supposedly just discovered by European explorers. Without breaking character, the two artists, dressed in primitive costuming, danced and posed for pictures (for money from the audience), interacted with "guards," all the while speaking in a made-up language. The piece exposed the hypocrisy of colonialism, the pernicious stereotypes of native cultures, and European assumption of superiority to native civilizations that, centuries earlier, they had encountered and routinely destroyed. Fusco's piece toured Europe and America for two years.

Over the next decade, Fusco mounted other performance pieces, most notably for the Whitney Museum of American Art; biennials in Sydney, Australia, and Shanghai, China; and the London International Theatre Festival. In 1998, she accepted a faculty position at

Columbia University. At that time, Fusco was involved in one of her more provocative pieces, titled *Stuff*, commissioned by the Institute of Contemporary Art in London. In it, Fusco used the metaphor of cannibalism and the stereotypes that link Latino women to cooking to critique how Latin indigenous cultures had been consumed by whites, in the process making ethnic identity at best difficult, at worst ironic. In 2006, Fusco staged *A Room of One's Own: Women and Power in the New America*. Framed against the American involvement in multiple wars in the Middle East, the piece draws on military imagery (Fusco played a military interrogator, dressed in fatigues) and the writings of Virginia Woolf to suggest empowering women involved not only their interrogating cultural assumptions but also in their serving in the military to protect the democracy that makes such interrogations possible.

Increasingly, Fusco turned toward the possibilities of video production, her commissioned work premiered in venues such as the Rotterdam (2001) and Berlin (2003) international film festivals. Although her multimedia performance pieces, installation productions, street performances, and video works secured her reputation in the international art culture, their appeal was limited—but through more than a decade of publications, Fusco engaged a much wider audience. Her essays have appeared in *The Village Voice*, *Art in America*, and *Ms*. She has published several collections of nonfiction, most notably *The Bodies That Were Not Ours and Other Writings* (2001) and the Critics Choice Award-winning *English Is Broken Here: Notes on Cultural Fusion in the Americas* (1995).

In 2003, Fusco was awarded a $75,000 Herb Alpert Award in the Arts, presented by the California School of the Arts, which annually recognizes creative artists who transform a medium. In 2008, Fusco accepted an appointment to the School of Art, Media, and Technology at the prestigious Parsons, the New School for Design, in New York City.

SIGNIFICANCE

Emerging in the era of popular multiculturalism, Fusco reimagined the potential of theater and the visual arts to provoke difficult questions about the integrity of cultural and ethnic identities against the pressure to homogenize such identities within the larger (Anglo) community. Her work, passionate and prickly, reminded her generation of Latinos that the concept of Latino identity itself was hardly hegemonic (she describes herself as a Yoruba-Taino-Catalan-Sephardic-Neapolitan-Cuban-American) and that artists of color, particularly women, needed to define border identity as part of the celebration of the diversity of postcolonial American culture.

Joseph Dewey

FURTHER READING

Allatson, Paul. "Coco Fusco, Guillermo Gómez-Peña, and 'American' Cannibal Reveries." In *Latino Dreams: Transcultural Traffic and the U.S. National Imaginary*. New York: Rodopi Press, 2002. Sets Fusco's groundbreaking visual narratives within her generation of Latino writers and the particular pressures of minority artists asserting ethnic and gender identity within a larger, dominant culture.

Fusco, Coco. *English Is Broken Here: Notes on Cultural Fusion in the Americas*. New York: New Press, 1995. This collection of seminal essays not only provides meditations on gender and ethnic identity but also offers probing commentary on the influence of other performance artists and on Fusco's own pieces.

Mirzoeff, Nicholas, ed. *The Visual Culture Reader*. New York: Routledge, 1998. Essays by visual artists (among them Fusco) that provide a helpful introduction to the interdisciplinary field of the visual arts, particularly the redefinition of museum, the responsibility of the interactive audience, and the reach of cutting-edge technologies in this art form. Illustrated.

See also: Oscar Zeta Acosta; Denise Chávez; Maria Irene Fornes; Tony Labat; Ana Mendieta.

Guy Gabaldon

American World War II hero

A Chicano who had been adopted by a Japanese American family as a teenager, Gabaldon used his knowledge of the Japanese language to singlehandedly capture more than one thousand enemy soldiers in the battle for Saipan.

Latino heritage: Mexican

Born: March 22, 1926; Los Angeles, California

Died: August 31, 2006; Old Town, Florida

Also known as: Guy Louis Gabaldon; Gabby; the Pied Piper of Saipan

Area of achievement: Military

EARLY LIFE

Guy Louis Gabaldon (gah-bahl-DOHN) was born in Los Angeles, California, on March 22, 1926. One of seven children, he worked as a shoeshine boy in Skid Row at the age of ten. Gabaldon became a member of a multiethnic gang known as the Moe Gang and soon left home. At the age of twelve, he was taken in and adopted by a Japanese American family, the Nakanos. Because he attended language school daily with the Nakano children, he eventually learned to speak Japanese and became versed in their culture and customs.

When World War II broke out, Gabaldon's adoptive family was sent to a relocation camp in Arizona, but the Nakano sons joined the U.S. armed forces. Gabaldon went to Alaska, where he worked in a fish cannery and as a laborer. When he turned seventeen,

Gabaldon joined the Marine Corps. At Camp Pendleton, he received basic training and was assigned duty at the Headquarters and Service Company.

Gabaldon was a mortar crewman and scout observer. Because of his fluency in Japanese, he qualified to be a translator. He also received amphibious training and eventually was sent to the Japanese-controlled island of Saipan in June, 1944. It was there that his heroic acts would occur.

LIFE'S WORK

During World War II, the United States considered the capture of Saipan as critical. The island was needed for airfields to accommodate various aircraft and bombers. In June, 1944, more than five hundred ships carrying more than 125,000 U.S. military personnel began the invasion of Saipan. The troops had been informed that the surrender of Japanese was unlikely; Japanese troops had been instructed by their superiors to commit suicide if captured and to kill as many Americans as possible.

On his first day on Saipan, Gabaldon ventured out alone and used his knowledge of Japanes to capture prisoners. Because of his unorthodox tactics, Gabaldon's superiors reprimanded him and threatened a court-martial. Undeterred, Gabaldon went back out, this time capturing fifty prisoners. His supervisors were persuaded to allow him to continue.

On July 7, 1944, Gabaldon heard the unmistakable drone of hundreds of soldiers and civilians preparing to

Guy Gabaldon. (AP Photo)

attack American troops. After an unsuccessful attempt, they returned to their positions to regroup. The next day, Gabaldon captured two guards. He discussed with them the conditions of surrender and they agreed, bringing with them more than eight hundred Japanese soldiers and civilians, who were given over to United States military authorities. For these exploits, Gabaldon became known as the "Pied Piper of Saipan." He set a military record for most captures.

Gabaldon continued to capture Japanese soldiers until he was wounded in a machine-gun ambush. By that time, he had been credited with the capture of approximately fifteen hundred Japanese soldiers and civilians. He retired from the military as a result of his war wounds.

Gabaldon was recommended for the Medal of Honor by his commanding officer, Captain John Schwabe, the very man who initially reprimanded him for going out to patrol on his own. For unknown reasons, the Marine Corps downgraded the award to a Silver Star.

Gabaldon returned to civilian life and moved to Mexico, where he set up various businesses. His war experiences became public when he was the subject of an episode of *This Is Your Life*, a popular television program in the 1950's. Hollywood producers likewise became interested in his life and exploits and released the film *Hell to Eternity* (1960), which immortalized his heroic feats. Because of this new exposure, Gabaldon's award from the military was upgraded from a Silver Star to a Navy Cross, but the Medal of Honor eluded him. Gabaldon died on August 31, 2006, of heart disease and was buried with full military honors at Arlington National Cemetery.

SIGNIFICANCE

Gabaldon was a hero in various ways. During World War II, he took a practical approach in subduing the enemy: He had only to talk to them, to communicate in their language, mindful of their pride and cultural beliefs. After the war, he worked with troubled youths in Saipan and became an advocate for veterans of foreign wars. Although he received the Silver Star and then the Navy Cross, Gabaldon believed that his race played a part in the military's decision not to award him the Medal of Honor; various groups have campaigned for the award on his behalf.

Yvette D. Benavides

FURTHER READING

Fernandez, Virgil. *Hispanic Military Heroes*. Austin, Tex.: VFJ, 2006. Presents a clear explanation of Gabaldon's military exploits and makes the case that he deserves the Congressional Medal of Honor.

Gabaldon, Guy. *Saipan: Suicide Island.* Saipan: Author, 1990. Gabaldon's self-published memoir details the tactics he used to capture scores of Japanese prisoners on Saipan.

Goldstein, Richard. "Guy Gabaldon, 80, Hero of Battle of Saipan, Dies." *The New York Times*, September 4, 2006. Obituary that summarizes Gabaldon's achievements and includes statements he made in interviews.

See also: Roy Benavidez; Richard E. Cavazos; Horacio Rivero, Jr.

ANDRÉS GALARRAGA

Venezuelan-born baseball player

Galarraga, one of the biggest baseball stars ever from Venezuela, returned triumphantly after missing a season with cancer.

Latino heritage: Venezuelan
Born: June 18, 1961; Caracas, Venezuela
Also known as: Andrés José Padovani Galarraga; Big Cat
Area of achievement: Baseball

EARLY LIFE

Andrés José Padovani Galarraga (ahn-DREHS GAH-lah-RAH-gah) was born in Caracas, Venezuela, on June 18, 1961. He began his professional baseball career at age sixteen in the Venezuelan Winter League, playing for Leones del Caracas along with such future major leaguers as Tony Armas, Bo Diaz, and Manny Trillo. On the recommendation of manager Felipe Alou, the Montreal Expos signed the young first baseman in 1979, even though some scouts felt he was too heavy to be a prospect.

LIFE'S WORK

Galarraga's talents were slow to develop, and he played seven seasons in the minor leagues, being named the most valuable player in the Class-AA Southern League in 1984 and rookie of the year in the Class- AAA International League the following season. He was called up by the Expos at the end of the 1985 season but hit only .187 in twenty-four games. Galarraga was named the Expos' starting first baseman in 1986, but knee and rib injuries forced him to miss fifty-seven games.

Galarraga fulfilled his potential in 1987 by batting .305 and driving in ninety runs. He also improved defensively, prompting Whitey Herzog, manager of the St. Louis Cardinals, to call him the best-fielding righthanded first baseman Herzog had seen since Gil Hodges of the Brooklyn Dodgers in the 1950's. Galarraga's graceful movements, unusual for someone 6-feet, 3-inches tall, weighing 235 pounds, earned him the nickname "the Big Cat." He emerged as Montreal's main offensive threat in 1988 with 29 home runs, 92 runs batted in, 99 runs, and a .302 batting average. He led the National League with 42 doubles and 184 hits.

Galarraga's batting average dropped to .257 and .256 the following two seasons, and he led the league in strikeouts each season from 1988 through 1990. He remained steady as a fielder, winning Gold Gloves as the best at his position in 1989 and 1990. Hobbled by knee and hamstring injuries, he missed fifty-five games in 1991 and batted only .219, resulting in his trade to the Cardinals.

Galarraga continued to struggle with the Cardinals because of a broken wrist but impressed hitting coach Don Baylor. When Baylor became manager of the expansion Colorado Rockies in 1993, he suggested the team sign Galarraga as a free agent. Galarraga responded by putting up impressive offensive statistics during his five seasons with the Rockies, leading the National League in batting with a .370 average in 1993; in home runs with 47 in 1996; and in runs batted in with 150 in 1996 and 140 in 1997. His .370 average was the highest ever by a player from Venezuela and the highest by a righthanded hitter in the major leagues since Joe DiMaggio batted .381 in 1939. His improvement as a hitter was attributed to Baylor's adjusting his stance so that he could react more quickly to inside pitches. *The Sporting News* named Galarraga comeback player of the year for 1993.

Andres Galarraga. (AP Photo)

The thin air in mile-high Denver was said to have contributed to inflated statistics for Rockies players, especially during the team's first seasons. However, Galarraga proved he could produce elsewhere when he was signed by the Atlanta Braves in 1998. He hit 44 home runs, drove in 121 runs, and batted .305, becoming the first major leaguer to accumulate 40 or more home runs in consecutive seasons with different teams.

Galarraga was bothered by a lower back pain toward the end of the 1998 season, and the problem intensified during the 1999 spring training. He was diagnosed with lymphatic cancer and missed the entire season to receive chemotherapy treatment. Galarraga was especially shaken by this diagnosis because his father had died seven years earlier from pancreatic cancer. After his medications caused his weight to balloon to 265 pounds, Galarraga hired a personal trainer to prepare for his return to baseball. He rejoined the Braves in 2000 and delivered another outstanding season, with 28 home runs, 100 runs batted in, and a .302 average, becoming the first person to be named comeback player of the year twice.

Galarraga signed with the Texas Rangers for 2001 and experienced a decline in his productivity. He was traded to the San Francisco Giants that July, returned to Montreal in 2002, and went back to San Francisco in 2003, compiling a .301 average as a part-time first baseman and pinch hitter. His cancer returned in 2004, and he was hospitalized for twenty-three days. He recovered again, signed with the Anaheim Angels, and finished his career with seven games at the end of the season. He went to spring training with the New York Mets in 2005 but discovered his defensive skills had diminished and retired before the season began.

SIGNIFICANCE

Galarraga was one of the most outgoing players of his era, with a constant, charismatic smile. His personality combined with his baseball achievements made him Venezuela's biggest sports hero since the heyday of Luis Aparicio in the 1950's and 1960's. He was the subject of a 2000 documentary, *Galarraga: puro béisbol* (*Galarraga: Nothing but Baseball*). Galarraga hit 399 home runs in the major leagues, drove in 1,425 runs, and had a career batting average of .288. He played in eighteen postseason games with the Rockies, Braves, and Giants, became the first member of the Rockies to be elected to the Colorado Sports Hall of Fame in 2007, and coached the Venezuelan national team in the 2009 World Baseball Classic.

Michael Adams

FURTHER READING

Kindred, Dave. "The Passion Behind the Smile." *Sporting News* 224, no. 18 (May 1, 2000): 62. Describes how Galarraga's positive personality helped him during his illness.

Starr, Mark, and Vern E. Smith. "The Big C Beats the Big C." *Newsweek* 135, no. 20 (May 15, 2000): 56. Account of Galarraga's recovery from cancer.

Vecsey, George. "The Princely Smile Says Galarraga, the Big Cat, Is Back." *The New York Times*, February 16, 2005, p. D1. Details Galarraga's second bout with cancer.

See also: Roberto Alomar; Sandy Alomar, Jr.; Bobby Bonilla; José Canseco; Julio Franco; Ozzie Guillén.

ERNESTO GALARZA

Mexican-born union leader, educator, and writer

Galarza's contribution was to highlight the Chicano identity and describe it; to work politically on behalf of agricultural workers, to better their pay and conditions; and to further the cause of bilingual education. His work was focused on California but had national repercussions.

Latino heritage: Mexican
Born: August 15, 1905; Jalcocotán, Nayarit, Mexico
Died: June 22, 1984; San Jose, California
Also known as: Ernesto Galarza, Jr.

Areas of achievement: Activism; social issues; education; literature

EARLY LIFE

Ernesto Galarza, Jr. (gah-LAHR-zah) was born in a remote Mexican village to Ernesto and Henriqueta Galarza. When he was five years old, his mother and two of her brothers decided to move north to escape political unrest. Galarza began formal schooling the next year in Mexico, but his family soon moved to the United States, eventually settling in Sacramento, California.

His mother died soon after, in 1917 during an influenza epidemic.

Galarza graduated from Sacramento High School in 1923. He won a scholarship to Occidental College in Los Angeles, where he majored in Latin American history, the only student of Mexican origin in his class. Galarza was an outstanding student. For his final thesis, he did research work in Mexico on the role of the Roman Catholic Church there. This thesis was published in 1928 in Sacramento as *The Roman Catholic Church as a Factor in the Political and Social History of Mexico.*

From Occidental College Galaza moved on to Stanford University for his M.A., which he earned in 1929. While there, he met Mae Taylor, a schoolteacher in Sacramento, and the couple soon married. They had two daughters. Galarza planned to do doctoral research in economics and enrolled at Columbia University, where he came under the influence of John Dewey, the famous American educator. At Columbia, Galarza and his wife served as coprincipals of a progressive school on New York's Long Island. Among their innovations, they had the students spend their summers working on a farm, in line with Dewey's learning-by-doing theories. Galarza's second publication, a collection of poems, came out in 1935. He wrote his doctoral thesis on the electrical power industry of Mexico. Even before his dissertation was submitted, his work was so highly regarded that a leading Mexican publisher brought out his research as *La industria eléctrica en México* in 1941. Galarza gained his doctorate in 1944.

From 1936 to 1947, Galarza also served as a research associate of the Pan-American Union, now the Organization of American States, publishing scholarly articles. He traveled throughout Latin America, becoming particularly involved in the Bolivian tin miners' strike in 1942, and the bracero program developed by the United States and Mexican governments. Braceros were migrant workers who came to the United States from Mexico but often were exploited and subjected to low wages and poor working conditions. Galarza's documentation of these activities won him high praise. and he was awarded the Order of the Condor by the Bolivian government.

LIFE'S WORK

Galarza's exposure to the plight of the braceros influenced his decision to take up a post with the National Farm Labor Union. This involved moving to San Jose, California, as the union was trying to organize farmworkers on the large fruit and vegetable farms in the

state. Between 1948 and 1959, the union was involved in some twenty strikes, all of which Galarza helped organize and document. The largest action was against the Di Giorgio Corporation, which had fifty square miles of holdings in the state. The company used Public Law 78, the 1951 formulation of the bracero program, to bring in strike-breaking laborers. It also sued the union, launching legal disputes that lasted fifteen years. Starting practically from scratch, with little money and little support from the large industrial trade unions, Galarza and the union nonetheless managed to win at least temporary concessions and ultimately the withdrawal of the bracero legislation.

Galarza refused to adopt communist tactics—although many activists did at the time—which would have cost him sympathy and support for his movement. He also was careful to document workers' grievances and

Galarza and Bilingual Education

Ernesto Galarza's interest in education can be traced to his graduate-student days, when he wrote an article titled "Problems of Education in the Western Hemisphere" (1939). When his two daughters were children, he wrote for them *Rimas tontas* (1971; *Silly Rhymes*) to help them learn Spanish enjoyably. His interest in bilingual education was renewed in 1971 when he and his wife, Mae, set up the Studio Laboratory for Bilingual Education in San Jose, California. It was meant as a resource center for teachers of the local school district and concentrated on the creative arts for first and second graders. Galarza's philosophy was that children learn by doing, especially in a creative environment. He felt traditional schools' emphasis on reading, writing, and arithmetic did not help Hispanic children and instead created a divide between them and the Anglo culture.

As part of his focus on the arts, Galarza built on his book of poetry for children. Very little literature existed at the time for Chicano children, so Galarza began writing a series of "mini-libros." Five of these works were verse and six prose, the latter being aimed at older children. The series includes *Zoo-Risa* (1968; *Zoo-Fun*, 1971) and *Poemas párvulos* (1971; *Tiny Poems*). The poems are written in both Spanish and English, although the Spanish often tries to mimic English rhythms. One of Galarza's better-known prose books is *La historia verdadera de una botella de leche* (1972; *True Story of a Milk Bottle*). Although the San Jose School Board withdrew funding from the Studio Lab, forcing its closure, the books earned Galarza a Nobel Prize nomination in 1979.

employers' illegal tactics. He described the DiGiorgio struggle in a number of influential books, starting with a report on an accident that killed thirty-two farmworkers, published in 1963, then released in Spanish in 1977 as *Tragedy at Chualar: El crucero de las treinta y dos cruces*. Other accounts of this period come in *Merchants of Labor: The Mexican Bracero Story* (1964), probably the most acclaimed of all his works; *Spiders in the House and Workers in the Field* (1970); and *Farm Workers and Agri-Business in California 1947-1960* (1977).

In the 1960's, Galarza held a number of academic posts at the universities of Notre Dame, Harvard, and San Diego. He also was a consultant with the Ford Foundation, out of which came his coauthored *Mexican-Americans in the Southwest* (1969). He remained politically active in Chicano affairs and served as chair or director for several Hispanic organizations, notably the La Raza Unida Unity Conference and the Mexican American Legal Defense and Educational Fund.

Galarza's best-known book is *Barrio Boy* (1971), an autobiographical account of his journey from Mexico to Sacramento and how he became acculturated into American life. Extracts from this book appear in numerous anthologies, especially those covering Chicano literature.

At that time, Galarza also began to take a renewed interest in education, specifically bicultural education, and he spent much time setting up a learning center in San Jose. From 1968 to 1973, he published eleven bilingual books for young children. His last book of poems, *Kodachromes in Rhyme* (1982), was published two years before his death.

SIGNIFICANCE

Galarza often is referred to as a Renaissance man, in that he accomplished much in many different fields of knowledge and activity. He empathized with Latinos who were unwilling or unable to adapt to life and culture in the United States and sought to ease their transitions. His political and educational impulses were to better the conditions of others who had started from nothing but nevertheless wished to achieve the American dream and all that it represented.

David Barratt

FURTHER READING

Bustamante, Jorge A. *Ernesto Galarza's Legacy to the History of Labor Migration.* Stanford, Calif.: Stanford Center for Chicano Research, 1996. Attempts to establish Galarza's significance in his main field of research.

Cohen, Deborah. *Braceros: Migrant Citizens and Transnational Subjects in the Postwar U.S.A. and Mexico.* Chapel Hill: University of North Carolina Press, 2010. Deals in parts with attempts to unionize the braceros, both in Galarza's time and later, under César Chávez.

Gutiérrez, David G. *Walls and Mirrors: Mexican Americans, Mexican Immigrants, and the Politics of Ethnicity.* Berkeley: University of California Press, 1995. Places Galarza's concerns in the wider context of the economics and politics of the period.

Occidental College. *The Life and Legacy of Ernesto Galarza 1905-1984.* Los Angeles: Author, 1987. Biography published by Galarza's alma mater as part of its centennial celebrations, in conjunction with the Museum of Latino History.

See also: Alma Flor Ada; Monica Brown; César Chávez; Dolores Huerta; Antonio Orendain.

RUDY GALINDO

American figure skater

Galindo overcame poverty and personal misfortune in his childhood to become the United States' first major Latino and openly gay figure skater. He was a two-time pairs national champion with Kristi Yamaguchi and a singles medalist at the national and international level. After he was diagnosed with human immunodeficiency virus (HIV), he became a proponent for HIV/AIDS awareness and gay rights.

Latino heritage: Mexican

Born: September 7, 1969; San Jose, California

Also known as: Val Joe Galindo

Areas of achievement: Sports; gay and lesbian issues

EARLY LIFE

Val Joe Galindo (gah-LEEN-doh) was born on September 7, 1969, in San Jose, California, to Mexican Ameri

Rudy Galindo. (AP Photo)

can parents Jess and Margaret Galindo. Childhood was full of adversities for Galindo as his truck-driver father worked frequently out of town and his mother's undiagnosed bipolar disorder rendered her unable to care for her children consistently. Galindo's elder brother, George, had legal troubles and was expelled from the household when he revealed his homosexuality to his parents.

It was his older sister, Laura, who introduced Galindo to ice skating when he was only six years old. Soon thereafter, the first-grader was taking lessons at the nearby Eastridge Ice Arena and supplementing them with ballet classes. This was especially uncommon in the local Latino community, where many young men were involved with gangs and drugs. Galindo's family made considerable sacrifices to support his skating. Laura began part-time work at a local fast food restaurant to help pay for her brother's lessons. When his long hours of training started to interfere with his education, his parents enrolled him in a more accommodating school. Because competitive figure skating is an expensive endeavor, supporting Galindo's ambitions meant the family was unable to move from their trailer park to a safer, more affluent neighborhood.

LIFE'S WORK

Galindo's labors began to bear fruit in 1982 when he won gold in the novice division of the U.S. championships, followed by a string of national and world medals in the junior division. At age fourteen, Galindo met future figure skating superstar Kristi Yamaguchi, and the two flourished as a pairs team. They placed fifth in their first junior national competition in 1985 and won gold the following year. Although each continued to skate competitively in singles competition, they were the reigning world champions at the junior level by 1988. Their dominance continued at the senior level as the young skaters won gold at the national championships in 1989 and 1990, also placing fifth at the senior world championships those years. Sports pundits projected them as favorites at the 1992 Winter Olympic Games. Over the next six years, Galindo and Yamaguchi won eight medals at major competitions. However, their partnership ended on April 26, 1990, when Yamaguchi decided to focus on singles skating.

The dissolution of the partnership with Yamaguchi was both a personal and professional setback for Galindo. His return to singles competition yielded disappointing results. Between 1991 and 1995, Galindo never placed above fifth at a U.S. national championship competition. Turmoil also marked his personal life. His mother's mental illness intensified, his father suffered a fatal heart attack in 1994, and he lost his brother to complications of acquired immune deficiency syndrome (AIDS) in 1995. Overwhelmed, Galindo turned to alcohol, drugs, and unsafe sexual behaviors to cope. Shortly thereafter, he publicly disclosed his homosexuality for the first time in Christine Brennan's book *Inside Edge: A Revealing Journey into the Secret World of Figure Skating* (1996).

Galindo contemplated retirement for a period before his sister, Laura, became his coach. He trained intensely for the 1996 U.S. championships. Entering the final stretch of the competition behind previous gold medalists Todd Eldredge and Scott Hamilton, Galindo executed eight triple jumps and two triple-jump combinations with flawless precision. Seven of the nine judges awarded him first-place scores. On January 20, 1996, Galindo became the first Latino and the first openly gay man to win a national skating title. His strong performances continued at the world championships, where he won a bronze medal.

Galindo retired from competitive skating in 1996 and began a professional career skating in exhibitions, including the Champions on Ice tour and the Tom

Collins Campbell's Soup Tour of World Figure Skating Champions, before signing deals for his autobiography and a television film. After being diagnosed as HIV-positive in 2000, he went public with the information and became a vocal advocate of AIDS awareness and prevention.

SIGNIFICANCE

With his 1996 gold medal, Galindo became the first American of Mexican descent and first openly gay person to win a U.S. national figure skating championship. Along with fellow openly gay athletes Greg Louganis, Esera Tuaolo, and Billy Bean, Galindo is an advocate for mainstream acceptance of homosexual and transgender people.

Leon James Bynum

FURTHER READING

Anderson, Eric, and Mark McCormack. "Comparing the Black and Gay Male Athlete: Patterns in American Oppression." *The Journal of Men's Studies* 18, no. 2 (Spring, 2010): 145-158. Anderson and McCormack collate patterns of discrimination faced by gay and African American male athletes. Additionally, they argue for Galindo's presence in a unique moment in history, when openly gay athletes were beginning to demand mainstream acceptance.

Brennan, Christine. *Inside Edge: A Revealing Journey into the Secret World of Figure Skating.* New York: Simon & Schuster, 1996. Published just prior to Galindo's victory at the U.S. championships in 1996, Brennan's book contains the first public acknowledgment of Galindo's homosexuality and the effects that it had on his career.

Galindo, Rudy, and Eric Marcus. *Icebreaker: The Autobiography of Rudy Galindo.* New York: Pocket Books, 1997. Galindo offers intimate details of the ways in which personal tragedies inspired him to succeed professionally.

See also: Donna de Varona; Scott Gomez; Pancho Gonzales.

ANDY GARCIA

Cuban-born actor and filmmaker

Garcia is an accomplished actor and filmmaker who rose to fame with his Oscar-nominated role in The Godfather: Part III. *Over two decades in Hollywood, Garcia has produced an extensive body of work in a wide range of roles.*

Latino heritage: Cuban
Born: April 12, 1956; Bejucal, Cuba
Also known as: Andrés Arturo García-Menéndez
Areas of achievement: Acting; filmmaking; radio and television

EARLY LIFE

Andres Arturo Garcia-Menendez was born in the small town of Bejucal, Cuba, the youngest of three children. His mother, Amelie, taught English, and his father, René, was a lawyer and a successful produce grower. Garcia's family was affluent before the Cuban Revolution, after which René was forced to turn over his land to the new communist regime under Fidel Castro. As political exiles, Garcia and his family fled Cuba in 1961 and relocated to Miami. Garcia was five years old when they arrived in America and, for a time, he struggled to learn English.

While attending Miami Beach Senior High School, Garcia was an avid basketball player who had high hopes for a future career in sports; however, he was stricken with mononucleosis and hepatitis during his senior year, crushing any possibility of winning an athletic scholarship. During that time of inactivity, Garcia realized his growing passion for acting. He enrolled at Florida International University and majored in acting, but before long, he decided that more opportunities awaited him, moving to Los Angeles in 1978. Upon arriving, Garcia juggled auditions and earned a living as a waiter, all the while honing his skills as a student of the craft, learning different acting techniques whenever and wherever he could.

LIFE'S WORK

While performing with an improvisational act at the Comedy Store in Los Angeles in 1980, Garcia was spotted by a casting agent, a stroke of luck that led to his first role as a gang member in the pilot episode of the television series *Hill Street Blues* in 1981. Soon after, Garcia made his film debut with *Blue Skies Again* (1983), but it was his magnetic performance in *Eight Million Ways*

Andy García. (AP Photo)

to Die (1986) that caught the attention of director Brian De Palma. Garcia was then cast in De Palma's *The Untouchables* (1987) as George Stone, a tough Italian cop fighting crime alongside Eliot Ness.

Garcia quickly booked more roles as his career gained momentum. He played the second lead in *Black Rain* (1989) and *Internal Affairs* (1990), then won the role of a lifetime in *The Godfather: Part III* (1990). For his performance as Vincent, Michael Corleone's successor as don of the Corleone crime family, Garcia earned critical acclaim and was nominated for an Oscar for Best Supporting Actor.

Following his newfound success, Garcia took on a wide range of diverse roles. He appeared in the comedy *Hero* (1992), as a police officer in *Jennifer Eight* (1992), and as a controlling husband opposite Meg Ryan in *When a Man Loves a Woman* (1994). Garcia's personal passion for Latin music inspired his directorial debut, the stylized documentary *Cachao . . . como su ritmo no hay dos* (1993), based on the life of Israel "Cachao"

López. He also played the lead in *The Disappearance of Garcia Lorca* (1997), a film about a Spanish poet killed at the onset of the Spanish Civil War. Garcia then returned to the commercial arena to play gangster Lucky Luciano in *Hoodlum* (1997); the male lead in the romantic comedy *Just the Ticket* (1999); and the made-for-television films *Swing Vote* (1999) and *For Love or Country: The Arturo Sandoval Story* (2000).

In the 2000's, Garcia joined a number of elite Hollywood actors in the ensemble casts of *Ocean's Eleven* (2001), *Ocean's Twelve* (2004), *Smokin' Aces* (2006), and *Ocean's Thirteen* (2007).

In the midst of such high-profile films, Garcia also directed and starred in his passion project, *The Lost City* (2005). A film that took sixteen years to make, *The Lost City* is a music-filled family drama set amid the Cuban Revolution. He went on to turn in comedic performances in *The Pink Panther 2* (2009) and *City Island* (2009).

SIGNIFICANCE

Garcia found mainstream appeal while showing the willingness to take on independent films that appeal to his passions, regardless of the risks involved. He has avoided typecasting and Latino stereotypes by choosing a wide range of diverse roles. He also has shown an attraction to projects that highlight his Cuban roots. The socially conscious nature of his work has made Garcia a strong voice, not only for his own culture but also for Latin Americans in general.

Kyle Bluth

FURTHER READING

Diamond, Jaime. "Andy Garcia: An Enigma Wrapped Inside Charisma." *The New York Times*, November 22, 1992, p. H12. Profile written as Garcia transitioned from supporting to lead roles after his Oscar nomination.

Ojito, Mirta. "His Homeland, His Obsession." *The New York Times*, February 12, 2005, p. B7. Describes the making of Garcia's *The Lost City*.

Otfinoski, Steven. "Andy Garcia." In *Latinos in the Arts.* New York: Facts On File, 2007. Career overview and brief biography of Garcia. Bibliography.

See also: Benjamin Bratt; Esai Morales; Edward James Olmos; Freddie Prinze; Charlie Sheen; Martin Sheen; Jimmy Smits.

CRISTINA GARCÍA

Cuban-born writer

García is best known for her lyrical novels about Cuban American families, particularly Dreaming in Cuban *(1992). Her writing tends to focus on the implications of international migrations and historical events for individuals and families.*

Latino heritage: Cuban, Guatemalan, and Spanish
Born: July 4, 1958; Havana, Cuba
Areas of achievement: Literature; journalism

EARLY LIFE

Cristina García (gahr-SEE-ah) was born in Havana, Cuba, on July 4, 1958, to a Guatemalan-Spanish father and a Cuban mother. She moved with her parents to New York at the age of two and attended Catholic schools in white neighborhoods in Queens, Brooklyn Heights, and Manhattan. While García has no early memories of Cuba, she was raised speaking English and Spanish and with a strong sense of Cuban identity.

García has studied French, German, Italian, Russian, and Portuguese and originally wanted to work in the Foreign Service. She graduated from Barnard College in 1979 with a major in political science with a concentration in international politics. In 1981, she obtained a master's degree in international relations with a concentration in European and Latin American politics and economics from the School of Advanced International Studies at Johns Hopkins University.

After completing her master's degree, García worked briefly in the marketing division of Proctor & Gamble in West Germany before leaving to become a journalist. She worked at several newspapers before finding a job at *Time* magazine in 1983. García worked as a reporter and researcher until 1985, then as a national correspondent in New York, San Francisco, Miami, and Los Angeles until 1990. From 1987 to 1988, she served as the magazine's Miami bureau chief. In 1990, she left the magazine to write fiction full time. In the same year, García married Scott Brown, a journalist and writer of Russian-Jewish and Japanese descent, with whom she has a daughter named Pilar. The two later divorced.

LIFE'S WORK

García has published in a variety of genres. Her work has been translated into at least twelve languages and won numerous awards, including the Princeton University Hodder Fellowship (1992-1993), the Guggenheim Foundation Fellowship (1995), the Whiting Writers' Award (1996), and the National Endowment for the Arts Literature Fellowship (2004). She tends to focus on themes such as Cuban history and culture, memory, diaspora, intercultural individuals, family, and gender. Many of these issues became important to García after a 1984 trip to Cuba to visit her maternal family awakened her to complexities of Cuban politics and culture generally not discussed in the United States. Much of her writing attempts to provide a more inclusive vision of Cuban and Cuban American society.

García is probably best known for the novels *Dreaming in Cuban* (1992)—which was nominated for a National Book Award—and *The Agüero Sisters* (1997). Along with *Monkey Hunting* (2003), these books examine the diversity of Cuban and Cuban American experience through the stories of transnational, multiethnic families. García's fourth novel, *A Handbook to Luck* (2007), deals with migration and cultural change on a more global scale. Her young-adult novel *I Wanna Be*

Cristina García. (AP Photo)

Your Shoebox (2008), meanwhile, addresses questions of multilayered cultural hybridity.

Additionally, García has published the nonfiction *Cars of Cuba* (1995); a children's picture book, *The Dog Who Loved the Moon* (2008); and a volume of poetry, *The Lesser Tragedy of Death* (2010). She also has edited the anthologies *Cubanísimo!: The Vintage Book of Contemporary Cuban Literature* (2003) and *Bordering Fires: The Vintage Book of Contemporary Mexican and Chicano/a Literature* (2006). García ended the 2000's by releasing *The Lady Matador's Hotel* (2010), a novel, and began the next decade with *Dreams of Significant Girls* (2011), a work of young-adult fiction.

García also has had an active teaching career. Beginning in 1994, she worked at various colleges and universities, notably as a visiting professor of creative writing and Black Mountain Institute teaching fellow at the University of Nevada, Las Vegas (2009-2010). In 2008, she became the artistic director of the Centrum Writers' Exchange.

SIGNIFICANCE

Widely considered the first Cuban American woman to have published a novel in English, García produces work that is innovative in style and content. Her novels are known for their poetic language and for pushing the boundaries of reality. Meanwhile, through her broad range of characters, she breaks with monolithic views of Cuban American society and conservative interpretations of Cuban history and represents a world shaped by transnational historical events and diversity in political, ethnic, and gender identities.

Tom Genova

FURTHER READING

Caminero-Santangelo, Marta. "Contesting the Boundaries of 'Exile' Latino/a Literature." *World Literature Today* 74, no. 3 (Summer, 2000): 507-517. Caminero-Santangelo argues that certain contemporary Latino writers, among them García, are challenging expectations for U.S. Latino literature by writing about both their heritage countries and the experience of being a minority in the United States.

García, Cristina. "A Conversation with Cristina García." Interview by Scott Shibuya Brown. In *Monkey Hunting*. New York: Ballantine Books. 2003. In this interview appended to her novel *Monkey Hunting*, García discusses gender and cultural hybridity.

_____."An Interview with Cristina García." Interview by Ylce Irizarry. In *Contemporary Literature* 48, no. 2 (Summer, 2007): 175-194. García talks about her novels in terms of politics, history, and memory. Influences on her writing are also discussed.

_____. "'. . . And There Is Only My Imagination Where Our History Should Be': An Interview with Cristina García." Interview by Iraida H. Lopez. In *Bridges to Cuba/Puentes a Cuba*, edited by Ruth Behar. Ann Arbor: University of Michigan Press, 1995. García talks about her life, particularly in relation to her Cuban American heritage. The interview also contains a discussion of *Dreaming in Cuban* and U.S. Latino literature and culture.

Mitchell, David. "National Families and Familial Nations: Comunista Americans in Cristina García's *Dreaming in Cuban*." *Tulsa Studies in Women's Literature* 15, no. 1 (Spring, 1996): 51-60. Mitchell discusses the ways in which *Dreaming in Cuban* subverts monolithic views of the nation.

See also: Reinaldo Arenas; Ron Arias; Ruth Behar; Monica Brown; Lydia Cabrera; Norma Elia Cantú; Lourdes Casal; Esmeralda Santiago.

GUS C. GARCIA

American lawyer

A brilliant legal mind who worked tirelessly to establish civil rights for Mexican Americans in Texas, Garcia is best known as part of the legal team that argued in the landmark Supreme Court case of Hernandez v. Texas *(1954) that Hispanics in that state could not be excluded from jury service.*

Latino heritage: Mexican
Born: July 27, 1915; Laredo, Texas
Died: June 3, 1964; San Antonio, Texas
Also known as: Gustavo Charles Garcia
Areas of achievement: Law; activism

EARLY LIFE

Gustavo Charles Garcia (gew-STAH-voh gahr-SEE-ah) was born on July 27, 1915, in Laredo, Texas, along the Rio Grande. His parents were first-generation Mexican immigrants. Although the family struggled with economic hardships typical of the immigrant class, Garcia enjoyed a relatively happy childhood. Before he was ten years old, his parents relocated to San Antonio in search of more promising job opportunities.

Garcia excelled in school, graduating in 1932 from Thomas Jefferson High School as the school's first valedictorian. With the country in the grip of an economic catastrophe that centered on the devastated farmlands of the Midwest and Southwest, Garcia understood that his best hope rested in education. He accepted a full scholarship to the University of Texas (UT) at Austin, where he completed his B.A. in 1936. During his undergraduate study, Garcia came to see the vitality of the judicial system and was determined to become a lawyer. He was accepted at UT's School of Law and earned his law degree two years later in 1938. While at UT, Garcia captained the law school's nationally recognized debate team and relished the dynamic of such a forum (in one memorable debate against the team from Harvard, Garcia got into a heated exchange with future president John F. Kennedy).

After graduation, Garcia remained in San Antonio and accepted a position in the county district attorney's office and then worked for a time with the city attorney's office. In 1941, he was drafted into the United States Army. He served in the judge advocate corps in Far Eastern theater of operations, headquartered in Japan. He served with distinction—indeed, after the war, he was given the chance to serve as part of the American legal contingent that helped establish the operating protocols for the United Nations. In 1947, Garcia returned to San Antonio.

LIFE'S WORK

Garcia joined the law offices of the Mexican Consulate General, which worked to ensure the rights of Mexican American citizens as well as the considerable Mexican immigrant population. Almost immediately, he became involved in an effort to reform San Antonio's public education system, in which Mexican Americans—who were not regarded as a separate racial minority but rather as part of the Caucasian majority—had been for decades segregated into their own schools, facilities that received minimal funding and were viewed largely as vocational schools. At the time that Garcia filed an inquiry with the state attorney general to challenge that system, Mexican Americans in Texas received on average four years of education, compared with nearly eleven years for whites.

Using as precedent a 1947 California ruling that had found such segregation illegal, Garcia, as lead counsel on behalf of the League of United Latin American Citizens (LULAC), filed suit in 1948 against the Bastrop Independent School District (along with three other schools), charging that the system denied equal opportunity for quality education to Mexican American children. The United States District Court agreed. Although it would be ten years before the Texas public school system was entirely desegregated, Garcia's passionate representation of the Mexican American parents is cited as a landmark achievement.

Over the next several years, Garcia worked to promote fair treatment of Hispanics, most notably students, ex-soldiers, and migrant workers. In 1952, Garcia was contacted concerning an appeal of a murder conviction involving a Hispanic defendant, a twenty-one-year-old migrant cotton field worker named Pete Hernandez, who had been found guilty of murder in Edna, a small town in Jackson County, south of San Antonio. The case was considered open and shut: Hernandez had been beaten in a bar and had returned home (a two-mile walk) to get his rifle, walked back to the bar, and killed one of his assailants in front of more than thirty witnesses. And he had confessed. Because the town had no significant Hispanic citizenry, the jury had been all white. Garcia agreed to represent Hernandez for free, recognizing an opportunity to challenge Texas's de facto exclusion of Hispanics from jury duty. When the Texas Supreme Court denied his appeal, Garcia and his legal team filed an appeal to the United States Supreme Court. Garcia, in turn, became the first Mexican American attorney to appear before the Court. The justices, under Chief Justice Earl Warren, unanimously ruled in favor of Garcia's appeal, citing the Texas system as inherently unreasonable, a clear separate-but-equal system, and hence a violation of the constitutional provision guaranteeing equal protection. Hernandez was ordered to be retried, this time with a jury in which no ethnic group was excluded. The ruling was hailed as a triumph in the long struggle of Mexican Americans to be recognized as an ethnic group with its own integrity.

The long and very public case took its toll on Garcia. Between 1955 and 1957, he was in and out of hospitals, and rumors circulated in the San Antonio legal community that Garcia was struggling with alcoholism. He worked briefly at a small law office in Kingsville

Hernandez v. Texas

Long before Gus Garcia had heard of the murder trial of Pete Hernandez, the inequities of the Texas jury system were clear to him. By classifying Hispanics as Caucasian, Texas law could exclude Hispanics from juries without violating the Fourteenth Amendment. Garcia's appeal, filed in 1954, was based on a brilliant interpretation of the Fourteenth Amendment. Because the amendment dealt specifically with issues of black and white races and because Texas considered Hispanics part of the white population, the state of Texas argued the exclusion of Hispanics was not discrimination but simply a matter of coincidence or expediency. Garcia argued that the Fourteenth Amendment could be interpreted to include class as well as race—and because the Hispanic population was among the poorest in the state, the routine exclusion of them from jury service was unconstitutional. Garcia presented powerful evidence: no Mexican American had served on any jury in Texas for more than a generation. In Jackson County itself, where the Hernandez trial had been held, close to 15 percent of the county was Hispanic—yet a Mexican American had never, in the county's history, served on a jury. Although the case and the decision have been largely forgotten in the wake of the historic *Brown v. Board of Education* ruling just weeks later, the Supreme Court's unanimous endorsement of Garcia's position established that the civil rights of Hispanics (and indeed all ethnic groups) were constitutionally protected.

but seldom represented clients in the courtroom. Even as his heroic efforts on behalf of Hispanics were being extended by the Warren Court, Garcia languished in increasing obscurity. After being cited for check fraud in 1960, an action was filed to have Garcia—once the most prominent voice in the Hispanic legal community—disbarred. Given Garcia's reputation, however, the review board recommended a two-year suspension in the hopes that he could return to the law. Shortly after his law license was reinstated, however, Garcia died of a brain seizure in June, 1964. He was buried with full military honors at the Fort Sam Houston National Cemetery outside San Antonio.

SIGNIFICANCE

Although Garcia died largely forgotten, his contribution to the American civil rights movement is secure. By extending the protection of the Fourteenth Amendment to Hispanics, Garcia's brilliant legal argument in

Hernandez v. Texas paved the way for people of all ethnic groups to be explicitly granted the protection of the Constitution. In a career dedicated to challenging the entrenched system of exclusion directed against Hispanics in Texas amid the considerable pressures of such high profile legal work in a white-dominated cultural environment, Garcia persevered and, at enormous cost to his personal life, secured the basic rights of Hispanics in the classroom and in the courtroom.

Joseph Dewey

FURTHER READING

Garcia, Ignacio M. *White But Not Equal: Mexican Americans, Jury Discrimination, and the Supreme Court.* Tempe: University of Arizona Press, 2008. Seminal study of the defining legal battle of Garcia's career. Details the Texas system of exclusion and the legal underpinnings of Garcia's landmark appeal.

Olivas, Michael A. *Colored Men and Hombres Aquí: Hernandez v. Texas and the Emergence of Mexican American Lawyering.* Houston, Tex.: Arte Público Press, 2006. A collection of essays commemorating the fiftieth anniversary of the case that centered Garcia's career. Centers on the role of juries in American jurisprudence.

San Miguel, Guadalupe, Jr. *Brown, Not White: School Integration and the Chicano Movement in Houston.* College Station: Texas A&M University Press, 2005. Scholarly treatment of the public school system similar to the one that Garcia challenged in San Antonio. Includes a helpful discussion of Garcia's role.

Strum, Phillippa. *Mendez v. Westminster: School Desegregation and Mexican-American Rights.* Manhattan: Univ. of Kansas Press, 2010. A case study of the California ruling that Garcia used as precedence to challenge the separate-but-equal status of Hispanic children in San Antonio's school system.

Valencia, Richard. *Chicano Students and the Courts: The Mexican American Legal Struggle for Educational Equality.* New York: New York University Press, 2010. A wide-ranging history of more than six decades of legal proceedings centered on securing Hispanic students access to quality public education across the Southwest. Includes Garcia's challenge to the San Antonio schools.

See also: Joaquín G. Avila; Norma V. Cantú; José Ángel Gutiérrez; Antonia Hernández; Vilma Socorro Martínez; Alonso Perales.

HÉCTOR GARCÍA

Mexican-born physician, activist, and humanitarian

García was a World War II veteran and doctor who became a powerful advocate and activist for Mexican American rights and humanitarian causes. He worked to desegregate schools, restaurants, and other establishments, to secure services for Mexican American veterans, and to improve the conditions of migrant workers.

Latino heritage: Mexican
Born: January 17, 1914; Llera, Tamaulipas, Mexico
Died: July 26, 1996; Corpus Christi, Texas
Also known as: Héctor Pérez García
Areas of achievement: Activism; medicine; military

EARLY LIFE

Héctor Pérez García (PEH-rehz gahr-SEE-ah) was born in Llera, Tamaulipas, Mexico, to José and Faustina Pérez García. Fleeing the Mexican Revolution in 1917, the Garcías and their children moved to Mercedes, Texas, in the Rio Grande Valley. There they found limited professional opportunities, segregated schools, and violence directed against Mexicans and Mexican Americans.

The Garcías had been teachers, but since their credentials were not recognized in the United States, they opened a dry goods store. José expected all of his children to become doctors. Despite the University of Texas medical school system's quota of one Mexican American student per class year, García and five of his siblings became physicians.

García attended a segregated high school, and graduated in 1932, at the same time earning a commission from the Citizens Military Training Corps equivalent to a second lieutenant in the U.S. Army infantry. Although he began at Edinburg Junior College, a daily thirty-mile hitchhike, García received a bachelor's degree in zoology from the University of Texas at Austin (1936). He received a medical doctorate in 1940. In 1942, he completed a surgical internship at St. Joseph's Hospital at Creighton University in Omaha, Nebraska, after being rejected by Texas hospitals because of his Mexican heritage.

After finishing his medical training, García joined the U.S. Army, where he commanded an infantry company and then a company of combat engineers before being transferred to the Medical Corps, where he earned the rank of major and was awarded a Bronze Star with six battle stars for service in Italy and North Africa.

García met his future wife, Wanda Fusillio, a student at the University of Naples, Italy, in 1944. After Fusillio finished her doctoral studies in liberal arts, the couple married on June 23, 1945. They had three daughters—Daisy Wanda, Cecilia, and Susana—and a son, Hector, who died in an accident at age thirteen.

After the war, the Garcías moved to Corpus Christi, Texas, and García and his brother José Antonio opened a private medical practice. García also joined the local chapter of League of United Latin American Citizens (LULAC), an organization formed to defend the rights of Hispanic Americans.

LIFE'S WORK

García quickly found that social gains made during the war by Mexican Americans, who had enlisted enthusiastically, had not lasted. In their medical practice, the García brothers treated many people who could not pay, including poor migrant workers, and García quickly found that many Mexican American veterans were having trouble getting the Department of Veterans Affairs

Hector Garcia. (AP Photo)

(VA) to respond to their claims. Many of his patients were Mexican American veterans who had been turned away by the VA.

García helped other veterans file their claims with the VA. At the same time, he also investigated the conditions of migrant workers in Mathis, Texas, and became determined to end school segregation for Mexican Americans. In 1947, García was elected president of the local LULAC chapter.

In 1948, García called a meeting to discuss discrimination facing Mexican American veterans. The meeting was attended by hundreds of veterans and spawned the American G.I. Forum (AGIF), a Hispanic veterans' and civil rights group. García choose the name to emphasis that Mexican American veterans were patriotic Americans.

Over the following months, AGIF chapters were established throughout Texas. García and the AGIF advocated on many issues, including voting rights (Hispanics had to pay to vote at the time), school segregation, and fair trials. They tackled issues such as restaurants and other establishments with "No Dogs or Mexicans" signs and Mexican American children being whipped for speaking Spanish in school. They also coordinated protests and supported presidential candidates. Some notable early AGIF efforts including obtaining burial for Mexican American private Felix Longoria in Arlington National Cemetery and work on a case that led to a court ruling that the Fourteenth Amendment to the U.S. Constitution applied to Mexican Americans.

In the 1950's and 1960's, García testified as an expert on migrant laborers. AGIF helped to dismantle the Mexican Farm Labor Program (also know as the bracero program), which had been established in 1942. Under the bracero program, the United States could import temporary contract laborers from Mexico. Field workers in particular often lived in substandard conditions, and their mandatory savings accounts were often not paid out to them upon their return to Mexico.

By the 1950's, the efforts of García, the AGIF, and other Hispanic organizations had achieved desegregation for movie theaters, restaurants, and hotels in Texas; barbershops and beauty parlors were opened to Mexican Americans in the 1960's, but swimming pools and cemeteries were not desegregated until the 1970's.

García was instrumental in helping gain the Hispanic vote for numerous local and national politicians, including presidents Lyndon B. Johnson and John F. Kennedy. He also fought against poverty and encouraged education. In 1967, President Johnson appointed

American G.I. Forum

The American G.I. Forum (AGIF) is a congressionally chartered organization focusing on civil rights, veterans' issues, and education for Hispanics. After World War II, Mexican American veterans found that their claims were often delayed or rejected. Héctor García, a Mexican American medical doctor, civil rights activist, and veteran of World War II, founded the AGIF in 1948 to advocate for Mexican American veterans.

The scope of AGIF activities soon expanded to include issues relevant to all Mexican Americans, such as jury selection, voting rights, and desegregation of education. AGIF was organized into local chapters, primarily composed of veterans; in some areas womens' auxiliary and junior chapters also developed. These local chapters were further organized into district, state, and (after 1958) national groups.

AGIF played a key role in the 1954 court ruling in *Hernández v. Texas,* in which the court determined that Mexican Americans, although technically classified as Caucasian, had equal protection as an ethnic group under the Fourteenth Amendment to the Constitution. It also helped achieve desegregation of Texas schools.

García an alternate ambassador to the United Nations. In 1968, García became the first Mexican American on the United States Commission on Civil Rights.

García's dedication to civil rights advocacy continued throughout his life. Even as his own health declined, he also kept practicing medicine. At age sixty-four, he was arrested during a school segregation protest related to *Cisneros v. Corpus Christi Independent School District* (1970), which extended the *Brown v. Board of Education of Topeka, Kansas* (1954) ruling to Mexican Americans.

President Ronald Reagan awarded García the Presidential Medal of Freedom in 1984, one of many awards and honors García received during his lifetime. In 1988, García began his last major project, an effort to improve conditions in poor "colonias" of the Rio Grande Valley.

García's ceaseless work as a civil rights activist, humanitarian, and doctor inspired many, from activists to novelist Edna Ferber, who based the main character of her novel *Giant* on García. However, he also could be hot-tempered and sometimes autocratic, and his daughter Cecilia observed that his work left him relatively little time to spend with his family.

Late in life, García's health declined rapidly. He survived open-heart surgery, but developed stomach cancer. He died of pneumonia complications and congestive heart failure on July 26, 1996.

SIGNIFICANCE

García was a tireless civil rights advocate for both Hispanic Americans and the poor. He believed all Americans deserved the same rights, opportunities, and laws. In addition to his role in numerous legal decisions and political elections benefiting the Mexican American community, García also founded a Hispanic advocacy and assistance group, AGIF, which retained a strong and active membership as of 2011. The work of García and the AGIF paved the way for the Chicano movement of the 1960's. García also provided free medical care to the poor and worked to improve conditions for migrant workers.

Melissa A. Barton

FURTHER READING

Kells, Michelle Hall. *Héctor P. García: Everyday Rhetoric and Mexican American Civil Rights.* Carbon-

dale: Southern Illinois University Press, 2006. An examination of the transition from social marginalization to civic inclusion for Mexican Americans after World War II, and how the work of García and others influenced this change.

Ramos, Henry. *The American G.I. Forum: In Pursuit of the Dream, 1948-1983.* Houston, Tex.: Arte Público Press, 1998. A thoroughly illustrated history of the founding and development of the American G.I. Forum.

San Miguel, Guadalupe. *"Let All of Them Take Heed": Mexican Americans and the Campaign for Education Equality in Texas, 1910-1981.* College Station: Texas A&M University Press, 1987. Describes the Mexican American fight for school desegregation in Texas, with personal stories of school experiences and analysis of the strategies used by organized Mexican American groups such as AGIF.

See also: David Cardús; César Chávez; Gus C. Garcia; Reies López Tijerina.

JEFF GARCIA

American football player

Garcia is a professional football player who has played with different teams and leagues over a long and illustrious career. With his quick feet and accurate passing, he set franchise records and led several teams to winning records and to the play-offs. He is a role model for his perseverance and determination.

Latino heritage: Mexican
Born: February 24, 1970; Gilroy, California
Also known as: Jeffrey Jason Garcia
Area of achievement: Football

EARLY LIFE

Jeffrey Jason Garcia (gahr-SEE-ah) was born in Gilroy, California, on February 24, 1970, to Bob and Linda Garcia. His father worked at Gavilan College in Gilroy as the athletic director and football coach. Garcia's maternal grandfather, Maurice "Red" Elder, played football at Kansas State University and also was head football coach at Gilroy High School. When Garcia was seven years old, his six-year-old brother, Jason, accidentally drowned during a family camping trip. When he was eight years old,

Kimberly, his five-year-old sister, died from internal injuries after falling from a family pickup truck.

When Garcia was a student at Gilroy High School, he played football and basketball. He drew little attention from college recruiters, so he enrolled at Gavilan College in 1989 to play for his father's football team. He threw for 2,038 yards and 18 touchdowns, and rushed for almost 600 yards. After one year at Gavilan, Garcia transferred to San Jose State University. From 1990 to 1993, he started as quarterback for the Spartans football team and became the school's all-time leader in total offensive yards with 7,274.

The National Football League (NFL) did not draft Garcia after he earned a bachelor's degree from San Jose State in 1993. Instead, he signed with the Calgary Stampeders of the Canadian Football League. During five seasons with the Stampeders, Garcia led them to a Grey Cup championship in 1998 while being named most valuable player.

LIFE'S WORK

In 1999, the NFL's San Francisco 49ers signed him as a backup quarterback to Steve Young. In 2000, Garcia replaced Young, who retired. Garcia set a franchise record with 4,278 passing yards and finished second in the league with 31 touchdown passes. He became the fourth quarterback in 49ers history to have 30 or more touchdowns in a single season. He was voted to his first Pro Bowl.

During the 2001-2002 season, Garcia led the 49ers to a 10-6 record and a National Football Conference (NFC) West division title. He recorded his first postseason touchdown during his team's 39-38 win over the New York Giants in the NFC wild card play-off game. The 49ers lost to the Tampa Bay Buccaneers by a score of 31-6 in the divisional play-offs.

Garcia made his second consecutive appearance at the Pro Bowl after the 2001-2002 season. He set a team record by becoming the first quarterback in franchise history to throw for 30 or more touchdowns in consecutive seasons (2000-2001 and 2001-2002). The following season, Garcia had 3,344 passing yards. This was the third consecutive season that he recorded over 3,000 passing yards. Additionally, he completed 328 passes, making him the first quarterback in 49ers history to complete 300 or more passes in three consecutive seasons. He was also voted to his third Pro Bowl.

The San Francisco 49ers released Garcia in 2003 because of injuries, salary cap issues, and declining performance. He spent the 2004 season with the Cleveland Browns, then went to the Detroit Lions for one year in 2005. He replaced Joey Harrington as the team's starting quarterback after leading the team to a 13-10 win over the Cleveland Browns. However, Harrington got the starting position back after Garcia struggled later in the season.

In 2006, Garcia signed with the Philadelphia Eagles as a backup quarterback to Donovan McNabb, then became the starter when McNabb experienced a knee injury that ended his season. Garcia helped the Eagles advance to the NFC wild card play-offs, where they beat the New York Giants 23-20. The Eagles lost to the New Orleans Saints 24-27 in the NFC divisional play-offs. After the 2006 season, the Eagles did not renew Garcia's contract. He signed with the Tampa Bay Buccaneers as the starting quarterback. In 2007, he led the Buccaneers to the NFC wild card play-offs, where they lost to the New York Giants. Garcia made his fourth Pro Bowl appearance in 2008. In April, 2009, Garcia signed a one-year contract with the Oakland Raiders but was released in September, 2009, during final cuts. He signed with the Philadelphia Eagles in September, 2009, when McNabb was injured again. The Eagles

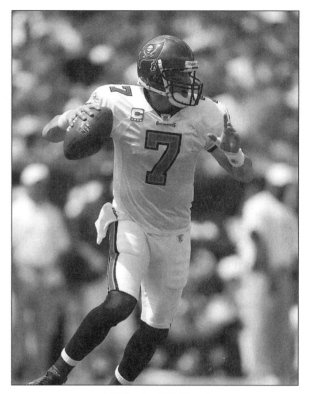

Jeff Garcia. (AP Photo)

released Garcia later that season. In 2010, he signed with the Omaha Nighthawks of the United Football League. Garcia married Carmella DeCesare on April 21, 2007. By 2011, they had three children.

SIGNIFICANCE

Garcia experienced his siblings' deaths early in life but used these tragedies as motivation to succeed. He took a circuitous route to the NFL, starring at a small college and in the CFL before finally achieving his goal of starting for an NFL team. He has had a journeyman career but has found success with many different teams in different football leagues. His passion for and determination to play football are testaments to his love for the game.

Tina Chan

FURTHER READING

Evers, John L., and David L. Porter. "Jeff Garcia." In *Latino and African American Athletes Today: A Biographical Dictionary*, edited by David L. Porter. Westport, Conn.: Greenwood Press, 2004. Biographical sketch that includes statistics from Garcia's college years and early professional career.

Gargano, Anthony. *NFL Unplugged: The Brutal, Brilliant World of Professional Football*. Hoboken, N.J.: John Wiley & Sons, 2010. Offers firsthand stories from professional football players that takes readers inside the game. Includes several anecdotes from Garcia about his experiences.

Layden, Tim. "Rare Birds." *Sports Illustrated* 106, no. 2 (January 15, 2007). Long profile of Garcia written at the time the quarterback resurrected his career with the Eagles.

MacCambridge, Michael. *America's Game: The Epic Story of How Pro Football Captured a Nation.* New York: Random House, 2004. This book chronicles professional football's history in the United States.

Michener, James. *Sports in America*. New York: Random House, 1976. This book examines various factors of American sports from the media's roles to sports financing.

See also: Tedy Bruschi; Tony Gonzalez; Joe Kapp; Anthony Muñoz; Jim Plunkett; Rich Rodriguez; Tony Romo.

JERRY GARCIA

American Grateful Dead guitarist and lead singer

Garcia was the frontman for the legendary psychedelic rock band the Grateful Dead, which inspired and reflected the counterculture movement for decades. The band's music spreads a "hippie" ethos based in freedom, spontaneity, improvisation, and communal spiritual transcendence.

Latino heritage: Spanish
Born: August 1, 1942; San Francisco, California
Died: August 9, 1995; Forest Knolls, California
Also known as: Jerome John Garcia
Area of achievement: Music

EARLY LIFE

Jerome John Garcia was named for the great American songwriter Jerome Kern. Garcia was the second child of Jose Ramon "Joe" Garcia and Ruth Marie (née Clifford) Garcia. A clarinetist, saxophonist, and Dixieland bandleader, Joe had to give up playing professionally after inadvertently violating a union rule, so he made his living owning a bar in San Francisco. Ruth played the piano, and the extended family loved to sing and play music together.

When Garcia was four, he lost most of his right middle finger in a wood-chopping accident. The next year, Joe drowned in a fly-fishing accident. Garcia was unfazed by his own injury, but the the loss of his father left him "emotionally crippled" for five years, he later said.

For the next five years, while Ruth ran the bar, Garcia and his older brother, Clifford, lived across the street with their maternal grandparents. There, they had almost unlimited freedom. In 1953, Ruth married Wally Matusiewicz, and the family moved from San Francisco's tough Excelsior District to Menlo Park. Garcia began to learn rock and roll, singing the harmonies for songs led by Clifford.

Smart, artistic, and troublesome, Garcia started smoking cigarettes and marijuana at age fifteen. For his birthday that year, he received an accordion, which he traded for a Danelectro electric guitar. He often got

Jerry Garcia. (AP Photo)

Garcia's Retaining His Hispanic Surname

In 1918, Jerry Garcia's father's family immigrated to the United States from the fishing village of Sada, in Galicia, Spain. Garcia's father Jose was eager to become Americanized, insisting that his family speak in English at home and calling himself "Joe" or "Joseph." Garcia's mother's roots were Irish and Swedish. Garcia playfully called himself "Atlantean," since the inhabitants of the mythical lost city Atlantis supposedly had come from Iberia and Ireland. Ethnic identity was of no apparent importance to Garcia. He played the Veracruz, Mexico, folk dance "La Bamba," and several Grateful Dead songs bore a Latin influence. However, Garcia's musical roots were deeply and broadly American, especially Southern, and he was influenced by diverse international musical styles, from Indian *raga* to Irish ballads.

Raised Catholic, young Garcia found the Latin Mass spooky and entrancing. Although he eventually became a Buddhist, his Catholic roots were apparent in his mysticism and humility, his insistence that business decisions be righteous, and his decision to pursue communal music rather than solo painting, at which he also was talented.

Garcia explicitly rejected the notion of a stage persona or celebrity. He was among the first American rock stars who was not conventionally attractive and who made no effort to cultivate a public image. Accordingly, Garcia never showed any interest in changing his Hispanic surname, even though it might have hindered him in his early attempts to break into the national bluegrass scene. Changing any part of himself to accommodate the music industry or be more popular would have been antithetical to everything he believed in.

into trouble in school and later was discharged from the Army for being what he called "pathologically anti-authoritarian."

On February 20, 1961, Garcia was involved in a high-speed, drunken-driving accident that killed one of his friends and sent Garcia through the windshield. The incident convinced Garcia to stop idling and to get serious about music. In bands and on his own, he played bluegrass, blues, folk, and old-time music on guitar and banjo around the Bay Area.

LIFE'S WORK
In 1965, Garcia was playing in a band called the Warlocks. After discovering another group had the same name, he

opened the dictionary to a random spot and found "Grateful Dead"—a folktale motif in which the protagonist spends his last penny for a stranger's burial and is later helped by the deceased. This phrase became his band's name.

In 1965 and 1966, author Ken Kesey and his friends—who called themselves the Merry Pranksters—began holding "Acid Tests" up and down the West Coast. The Acid Tests were large public parties at which lysergic acid diethylamide (LSD) was served, multimedia performances were presented, and chaos ensued. The Grateful Dead were the house band for the Acid Tests, with everyone (except keyboardist Ron "Pigpen" McKernan) consuming LSD liberally. During the Acid Tests, Garcia and the Grateful Dead delved deeply into extended improvisation and experimentation.

The rest of the Grateful Dead's thirty-year career bore the influence of the Acid Tests. No two of their 2,318 live performances were identical. The Dead pushed improvisation further than any other rock band, with Garcia leading the way. Unlike most other bands, the Dead did not pause after each song; instead, they wove disparate songs together, and the transitions were energetic creative peaks.

Whether quietly contemplating or ecstatically dancing, the audience was a part of the concert experience—musicians and audience uniting in a greater spiritual whole. As one Grateful Dead lyric puts it, "The music plays the band." Some nights, the Grateful Dead found the magic as Garcia's lead guitar built to wild, electric frenzies. On other nights. his emotional commitment was absent, and the guitar work was lazy noodling. Garcia sung slightly less than half the band's songs. His self-trained, nasal voice was never technically brilliant, but it was soulful, and he thrived as a balladeer.

From 1971 to 1995, Garcia played 1,136 shows with his solo bands, among them the Jerry Garcia Band and the Legion of Mary. However, he was at his best with the Grateful Dead; energetic rhythm guitarist Bob Weir complemented Garcia well, while bassist Phil Lesh, a musical genius with jazz and classical training, kept standards high.

Around the band grew a devoted audience of "Deadheads" who followed the band from show to show. Some attended several shows in a row; others would follow a tour for several weeks at a time. Deadheads also traded tapes of the live shows, with band's approval, and developed a large subculture. When the Grateful Dead and Deadheads toured from city to city, they became a sort of traveling circus, temporarily creating a small town with an alternate reality. The Grateful Dead supported the scene by selling concert tickets through a mail-order operation, thereby ensuring that committed Deadheads had the best chance to attend the concerts. The band also tolerated trademark infringements for what became a vast corpus of fan-created paraphernalia.

Two studio albums—the sweet, country-tinged *American Beauty* (1970) and *Workingman's Dead* (1970)—found appeal beyond the subculture. The live recordings of *Live Dead* (1969 shows), *Europe '72*, and *Without a Net* (1990) captured the band well.

Garcia began to use cocaine heavily in the 1970's, and the addiction drained much of his money. Later, he abused heroin, which eventually took his life. During the early 1980's, he grew morbidly obese. He collapsed into a near-fatal diabetic coma in 1986 and afterward had to relearn how to play the guitar. Garcia came back stronger than ever, however, and the rest of band reached new heights of virtuosity. The 1987 album *In the Dark* garnered a radio hit with "Touch of Grey," a celebration of survival.

Commercial success made the Deadhead scene ever more unmanageable. The band filled bigger venues, but new fans were ignorant of or indifferent to the social norms that had previously governed Deadhead gatherings. Eventually, Garcia relapsed into frequent heroin use; that, combined with obesity and smoking unfiltered cigarettes, led to his death from total coronary occlusion at a rehabilitation facility in 1995. The father of four children, he was married three times and divorced twice.

SIGNIFICANCE

The most successful touring band ever, the Grateful Dead were the founding fathers of the jam band genre that produced rock groups such as Phish. Applying their hippie philosophy of sharing the music, they created a model of social networking that is now studied in business schools. Most of all, Garcia set the standard for live music as more than entertainment, as a communal quest for higher consciousness.

David B. Kopel

FURTHER READING

Garcia, Jerry. *Garcia: A Signpost to New Space.* Interviews by Charles Reich and Jann Wenner. Cambridge, Mass.: Da Capo Press, 2003. Reprints extensive *Rolling Stone* interviews in which Garcia shares his thoughts on music and expanded consciousness.

Greenfield, Robert. *Dark Star: An Oral Biography of Jerry Garcia.* New York: It Books, 2009. Biography based on sixty interviews with almost everyone who knew Garcia well. Captures Garcia's complexities and contradictions.

Jackson, Blair. *Garcia: An American Life.* New York: Penguin, 2000. Definitive biography by a journalist who specialized in the Grateful Dead. Well-written, well-researched, and based on insightful understanding of the scene.

Tuedio, James A., and Stan Spector, eds. *The Grateful Dead in Concert: Essays on Live Improvisation.* Jefferson, N.C.: McFarland, 2010. Twenty scholarly essays examine the music, lyrics, and continuing influence of the Grateful Dead.

See also: Joan Baez; Mimi Fariña; José Feliciano; Carlos Santana; Ritchie Valens.

JOSÉ D. GARCÍA

American physicist and educator

García has had a long career as a physicist and science educator and has made significant contributions to the field of particle physics as well as to improving science education and outreach. He also has encouraged the careers of women and minorities in science, including Latinos.

Latino heritage: Mexican
Born: January 3, 1936; Santa Fe, New Mexico
Also known as: José Dolores García, Jr.; J. D. García
Areas of achievement: Science and technology; education

EARLY LIFE

José Dolores García (gahr-SEE-ah) was born in Santa Fe, New Mexico, in 1936, but grew up in Alcalde, a small, somewhat isolated village in northern New Mexico. García's parents valued education and wanted him to go to St. Michael's High School, a private boarding school in Santa Fe. Although initially reluctant, García enjoyed his time at St. Michael's and credited his math and science teachers there for helping set him on a scientific career path. Attending St. Michael's also helped García earn a cooperative student scholarship to New

Mexico State University. The terms of the scholarship required García to attend classes for half of the year and spend the other half working in a technical job. After receiving a bachelor of science degree in physics in 1957, García studied at the University of Göttingen in Germany on a Fulbright scholarship with some of the world's greatest theoretical physicists.

García continued to the University of California at Berkeley, where he earned a master of science degree in physics in 1959, after which he joined the U.S. Air Force, where he became a captain. After his discharge in 1963, García attended the University of Wisconsin at Madison, where he studied under Julian E. Mack, an internationally known atomic spectroscopist. In 1980, García remembered the scientific atmosphere in Mack's research group as "stimulating and humanely warm." García received his doctorate from Wisconsin in 1966. He soon was offered a professorship in the Physics Department at the University of Arizona (UA).

LIFE'S WORK

García remained at UA, becoming a full professor in 1975. There, he developed a strong research program focusing on theoretical physics. Theoretical physicists use mathematics to describe and model natural phenomena and test these models both physically and by logical "thought experiments." Specializing in atomic physics, García studied time-dependent collisions of atomic particles, such as the interactions among ions, atoms, and surfaces. His research sought to quantify these interactions using quantum models. García also worked on experimental design, research into effective physics education, and improving science teacher training. As a professor, García taught almost every physics course offered by his department, from introductory courses and courses for non-majors to upper-division quantum mechanics.

García's work has demonstrated interest in improving science education at all levels, particularly for underrepresented minorities. He helped high school teachers organize an annual physics competition and hosted a physics night for the public with other members of his department. García was a member of the National Task Force for Undergraduate Physics (2000-2004), which sought to evaluate characteristics of successful physics programs. He also spent twenty years as a coordinator for the local Tucson Area Physics Teachers alliance.

As a program director for the National Science Foundation's Division of Undergraduate Education, García encouraged the publication of physics education articles, leading to an education supplement to the *American Journal of Physics*. Some of García's efforts focused on advancement of women and minorities in physics. He served as charter president of the National Physical Sciences Consortium, a scholarship-granting organization, and as president of the Society for the Advancement of Chicanos and Native Americans in Science (SACNAS), an organization encouraging Hispanics, Chicanos, and Native Americans to pursue scientific careers and leadership positions.

After the passage of SB1070 in 2010, an Arizona law allowing law-enforcement officials to question people suspected of being in the United States illegally, two Mexican universities canceled their academic exchange programs with the University of Arizona. As president of SACNAS, García wrote a letter to Arizona's governor informing her that SACNAS had removed Arizona from consideration for its 2012 meeting because of the inhospitable conditions created by the passage of SB1070. He also chaired the committee that established a Mexican American studies program at UA.

SIGNIFICANCE

García's publications included more than one hundred refereed and peer-reviewed papers, as well as an English translation (with L. Alvarez-Guame) of *Quantum Mechanics I* by Alberto Galindo and Pedro Pascual. García has made major contributions to the field of theoretical physics. In addition to his work as a scientist, García played an active role in UA's Physics Department as a teacher and adviser and served on many university-wide committees. His commitment to improving science education and outreach affected many projects, including the American Association of Physics Teachers' new guidelines for evaluating undergraduate physics programs in 2005.

Melissa A. Barton

FURTHER READING

American Association of Physics Teachers. *75: Celebrating 75 Years of Excellence in Enhancing the Understanding and Appreciation of Physics Through Teaching.* College Park, Md.: Author, 2006. Includes a section examining minorities in physics education and an interview with García.

García, J. D. "Dr. J. D. García: Physicist." SACNAS Biography Project. http://bio.sacnas.org/biography/ Biography.asp?mem=46&type=2. Autobiographical essay aimed at a high school audience.

Newton, David E. "José Dolores García, Jr." In *Latinos in Science, Math, and Professions.* New York: Facts On File, 2007. Profile of García describing his professional achievements and contributions to physics education.

See also: Luis W. Alvarez; Ralph Amado; Albert V. Baez; Manuel Cardona; Vicente José Llamas.

CARMEN LOMAS GARZA

American artist

Garza has enjoyed widespread success as an artist and social activist for her whimsical but realistic portrayals of everyday Mexican American life based on her experiences in South Texas. Through her positive depictions of the Chicano community, she has challenged traditional Eurocentric notions of art while honoring her dual heritage and combating both negative stereotypes and racism.

Latino heritage: Mexican
Born: September 12, 1948; Kingsville, Texas
Areas of achievement: Art; activism

EARLY LIFE

Carmen Lomas Garza (LOH-mahs GAHR-zah) was born in 1948 in Kingsville, Texas, the second of five children. Her father was born in Mexico but moved as an infant to the United States with this family amid the Mexican Revolution. Her mother traced her heritage to grandparents who worked on the well-known King Ranch in Texas. As a self-taught artist who made watercolor paintings and traditional Mexican *lotería* (bingo) cards, Garza's mother greatly influenced her daughter's future career. Citing her family's influence and support, she decided at age thirteen to be an artist.

Although many of Garza's works are fond but realistic portrayals of Mexican American culture, she was a victim of discrimination, which affected her work as both a teacher and artist. She studied art education and studio art at Texas Agricultural and Industrial University (now Texas Agricultural and Mechanical Univeristy) at Kingsville, and after a short break to work as a professional artist, she graduated with a B.S. degree and teacher certification in 1972. It was during this time that she became involved in the Chicano movement, which focused on acknowledging Mexican heritage and recognizing the inequities suffered by Chicanos. She graduated with a M.Ed. from Juarez-Lincoln/Antioch Graduate School in 1973 and received an M.A. from San Francisco State University in 1981. She has won national renown for her unique style of artwork, which encompasses printmaking, sculptures, paintings in oil and gouache, lithography, and writing children's books.

LIFE'S WORK

Garza was raised with a dual heritage but grew up in an English-speaking world dominated by Anglos. Dressed in his naval uniform and on the way home from completing a voluntary tour in World War II, her father was denied service in a restaurant outside Kingsville. As a young girl, she was chastised and ridiculed for speaking her native Spanish at school. Such racism influenced her artwork and her desire to portray the culture of Mexican Americans positively.

While Garza's work is not overtly political or subversive, the bright, detailed images depicting her experiences in South Texas challenge traditional Western notions of art and the place of Chicanos in the United States; in 1992, board members of the El Paso Museum of Art called her *A Piece of My Heart/Pedacito de mi corazón* exhibition an embarrassment. Despite this harsh appraisal, Garza's works have garnered numerous accolades. As a testament to her widespread appeal, Anheuser-Busch and Budweiser used her depictions of Latino life in national ads and her artwork was featured in the film *Selena* (1997).

In 1981, Garza was awarded a National Endowment for the Arts fellowship in printmaking. She was also the recipient of California Arts Council Artist-in-Residence grants in 1979, 1982, 1984, and 1986. In addition to her numerous paper and metal cutouts, paintings, and sculptures, Garza had written and illustrated several bilingual children's books that feature her artwork with related explanations in English and Spanish. Her efforts to honor the customs and celebrations of Mexican Americans earned her a special honor in 2007 when a school in Los Angeles was named the Carmen Lomas Garza Primary Center.

Garza's works have been exhibited across the United States, including places such as the Mexican Fine Arts Center Museum in Chicago and the National Museum of American Art at the Smithsonian Institution. Her art has been part of national shows as well as solo exhibitions.

SIGNIFICANCE

Garza is considered one of the most important modern Chicano artists; her use of printmaking, lithography, and gouache make her one of the most versatile as well. Her folkloric portrayals of colorful scenes from Mexican American life, such as making tamales and breaking a piñata at a birthday party, serve to represent the subjects in a positive manner and combat racism against Chicanos. The flatness of the figures is similar to *retablo* paintings, a style that challenges Western ideals of art while adding a unique facet to the Chicano art movement.

Alyson F. Lerma

FURTHER READING

Congdon, Kristin G., and Kara Kelley Hallmark. "Carmen Lomas Garza." In *Artists from Latin American Cultures: A Biographical Dictionary.* Westport, Conn.: Greenwood Press, 2002. Offers critical information about Garza's artwork and Chicana identity.

Cortez, Constance. *Carmen Lomas Garza.* Los Angeles: University of California at Los Angeles Chicano Studies Research Center Press, 2010. Biography offers critical insight into Garza's artwork, influences, and style. Also addresses racism and the artist's activism.

Easton, Jennifer. "Carmen Lomas Garza." In *Interventions and Provocations: Conversations on Art, Culture, and Resistance*, edited by Glenn Harper. Albany: State University of New York Press, 1998. Provides critical insight into the artist's community activism, development as a Chicana artist, and opinions of art.

Garza, Carmen Lomas. "Oral History Interview with Carmen Lomas Garza, 1997 Apr. 10-May 27." Interview by Paul J. Kalstrom. Archives of American Art, Smithsonian Institution. http://www.aaa.si.edu/collections/interviews/oral-history-interview-carmen-lomas-garza-13540 Lengthy but essential transcript detailing Garza's early life, personal experiences, and development as a Chicana artist.

Vargas, George. *Contemporary Chicano Art: Color and Culture for a New America.* Austin: University of Texas Press, 2010. Book chronicles the history and uniqueness of Chicano art and Garza's contributions.

See also: Judith F. Baca; José Antonio Burciaga; Barbara Carrasco; Gaspar Enríquez; Yolanda M. López; Amalia Mesa-Bains; Yuyi Morales.

ORALIA GARZA DE CORTÉS

American librarian, educator, and activist

Garza de Cortés has dedicated her career to seeking out quality Latino stories and introducing them to children, their parents, and other librarians. A prolific writer and presenter at library conferences around the world, she continues her advocacy work on the importance of early literacy and of multicultural stories for children that stimulate the imagination.

Latino heritage: Mexican
Born: May 1, 1950; Brownsville, Texas
Also known as: Oralia Delfina Garza
Areas of achievement: Scholarship; literature; activism

EARLY LIFE

Oralia Garza de Cortés (oh-RAH-lee-ah GAHR-zah deh cohr-TEHS) was born Oralia Delfina Garza in Brownsville, Texas. Her paternal grandfather, Alfredo E. Garza, was a state senator from the Mexican state of San Luis Potosi, where, in 1923, he signed legislation establish-

ing the Universidad de San Luis Potosi and the archives for the state of San Luis Potosi.

There were no elementary school libraries in Brownsville when she was growing up, so Garza de Cortés's first exposure to libraries for children was through the books her sixth-grade teacher, Ms. Garcia, kept in the classroom. Garza de Cortés was a member of the library club in junior high and high school and worked at the Texas Southmost College's library under the junior college's work-study program, but it wasn't until she became a parent that she fell in love with children's literature.

Garza de Cortés came across many enjoyable stories, but she also came across many stereotypes and token characters and did not see herself or anyone she knew depicted in the books she read to her young children in any meaningful way. When she asked where to find good books for Latino children, her neighborhood librarian directed her to the newly renovated Carnegie

Branch library in Houston, Texas, where she met her mentor and friend Louise Yarian Zwick.

Zwick introduced Garza de Cortés to Spanish-language books, books for children, and multicultural literature. In 1982, Garza de Cortés accepted a position as an assistant children's librarian at the Houston Public Library. She and Zwick collaborated on family literacy programs and on the book *Rimas y cancioncitas para niños* in 1984. Garza de Cortés received her master's degree in library and information science from the University of Texas at Austin in 1988.

LIFE'S WORK

Garza de Cortés has been active professionally in the American Library Association, primarily through the affiliate organization REFORMA, the National Association to Promote Library and Information Services to Latinos and the Spanish Speaking. She became a member of REFORMA in 1986, the same year she met Sandra Ríos Balderrama of the Berkeley Public Library. Together they worked on establishing the children's section of REFORMA, called the Children's and Young Adult Services Committee (CAYASC). Garza de Cortés was a founding member of REFORMA chapters in San Antonio and Austin, Texas, and served as national president from 2000-2001. She won REFORMA's Arnulfo Trejo Librarian of the Year award in 2010.

During their tenure in CAYASC, Garza de Cortés and Balderrama cofounded the Pura Belpré Award. Named after the first Latina librarian at the New York Public Library, the Pura Belpré Award honors excellence in Latino children's literature. The award premiered in 1996, with Garza de Cortés serving as the first chair of the award committee. She served on the book selection committee from 1995 to 1998, and again in 2009.

Garza de Cortés has served on numerous children's book committees including the Américas Children's Literature Award, the Tomás Rivera Mexican American Children's Book Award, the Hans Christian Andersen Award, and the Jane Addams Children's Book Award for Social Justice. In 1995, Garza de Cortés was the first Latina elected to the board of the Association for Library Services to Children (ALSC), a division of the American Library Association, and in 2000 was the first Latina children's librarian elected to serve on the Caldecott Committee.

Recognizing how important it is for children to have books to call their own, she was instrumental in establishing a community book fair called the Feria de Libros: A Family Affair, in East Los Angeles. For this accomplishment, Garza de Cortés received a certificate of recognition from Mayor Antonio Villaraigosa.

Garza de Cortés has played an instrumental role in promoting El día de los niños/El día de los libros (commonly known as Día) in the United States. First celebrated in Mexico every April 30, Día is a community event celebrating families, books, and literacy. Garza de Cortés served as project manager of Día California from 2008 to 2010. In 2010, Garza de Cortés focused on developing a culture of literacy at an international level through Día workshops in Spain and Mexico. She works as a Latino children's literacy consultant and writer in Austin, Texas, where she lives with her husband Ernesto J. Cortes, Jr., a community organizer and 1984 MacArthur Fellow.

SIGNIFICANCE

Today, Latino children throughout the United States can walk into their local public libraries and recognize themselves in the books they read, thanks to the efforts of Garza de Cortés. Many libraries now have books and storytimes in both English and Spanish, which was not the case when she was a child. Librarians looking to expand their collections can readily access award-winning, culturally significant books that recognize the distinctive work of Latino authors and illustrators who write and illustrate for children. Parents can take their children to Latino book fairs and libraries, where they can celebrate as a family the joy of reading together.

Mary Schons

FURTHER READING

Garza de Cortés, Oralia"Getting It Right in the Twenty-first Century." In *Pathways to Progress: Issues and Advances in Latino Librarianship*, edited by John Ayala and Sal Guereña. Santa Barbara, Calif.: Libraries Unlimited, 2011. Garza de Cortés writes an overview of Latino librarianship in the United States.

_____. "Give Them What They Need: Library Services for Latino Children." In *Library Services for Hispanic Youth*, edited by Kathleen De la Peña McCook and Barbara Immroth. Jefferson, N.C.: McFarland, 2000. A critique of the Baltimore County Public Library Blue Ribbon Committee's 1992 publication, *Give 'Em What They Want! Managing the Public's Library*.

Garza de Cortés, Oralia, Jennifer Battle, and Jamie Naidoo. "Celebrating Cultures and Cuentos: Highlighting

Three Awards for Latino Children's Literature." In *Celebrating Cuentos: Promoting Latino Children's Literature and Literacy in Classrooms and Libraries*. Santa Barbara, Calif.: Libraries Unlimited, 2010. This chapter discusses children's book awards as a means to introduce quality Latino literature to children and their families.

See also: Alma Flor Ada; Pura Belpré; Monica Brown; Ana Castillo; Nicholasa Mohr.

JOHN GAVIN

American actor, entrepreneur, and diplomat

Gavin is best known as a Hollywood actor who starred in two of the most celebrated films of the late twentieth century: Psycho *(1960) and* Spartacus *(1960). Although he fell short of attaining the highest ranks of the acting profession, his parallel careers in diplomacy and business also earned him recognition.*

Latino heritage: Mexican
Born: April 8, 1931; Los Angeles, California
Also known as: John Anthony Gavin; John Anthony Golenor Pablos
Areas of achievement: Acting; diplomacy; business

EARLY LIFE

John Anthony Gavin was born John Anthony Golenor Pablos, the son of Herald Golenor and Delia Diana Pablos; both parents were wealthy and came from long-established Hispanic families. This was especially true of his mother, who was born in Sonora, Mexico. His father's family, on the other hand, had lived in the Los Angeles, California, area for more than a century, and, by the early 1900's, had become more fully assimilated. Although the family name was anglicized from Golenor to Gavin, John was reared by his mother to be fluent in both Spanish and Portuguese. At Stanford University, he specialized in Latin American economic history and graduated with a bachelor of arts degree. He was commissioned as a naval officer after going through the Reserve Officers' Training Corps program at Stanford and served from 1952 to 1955, first off Korea on the USS *Princeton* and later as a naval air intelligence office with the Fifteenth Naval District Command. He intended to use his knowledge and expertise in Latin American affairs as a springboard to a career in the Foreign Service. However, Bryan Foy, a friend of Gavin's who worked in the film industry, talked him into taking a screen test, and he thus entered into the acting career that had unexpectedly opened to him.

LIFE'S WORK

Gavin was at first managed by the notorious theatrical agent Henry Willson and touted as a younger version of Rock Hudson, the current Hollywood romantic idol. Willson saw to it that Gavin was hired by Universal Studios; however, Gavin never was comfortable with the controversial Willson or the association with Hudson, and he shook off Willson's tutelage after a year. In 1956, Gavin landed minor parts in the Western *Raw Edge* and *Four Girls in Town* and a more substantial role in *Behind the High Wall*. After appearing in the Western *Quantez* (1957), he came into his own as a lead actor in 1958, portraying a troubled German soldier in the

John Gavin. (AP Photo)

cinematic version of Erich Maria Remarque's tragic war romance, *A Time to Love and A Time to Die* (1958). He had a major breakthrough as Lana Turner's love interest in the drama *Imitation of Life* (1959). In 1957, Gavin married Cecily Evans, with whom he had two daughters, Cristina and Maria. The marriage ended in divorce. He received a Golden Globe Award as Most Promising Newcomer in 1959.

In 1960, Gavin secured important roles in two of the twentieth century's most significant motion pictures: as Janet Leigh's boyfriend and ultimate avenger, Sam Loomis, in Alfred Hitchcock's *Psycho*; and as Julius Caesar in Stanley Kubrick's *Spartacus*. Although the roles brought him fame, Gavin drew criticism over perceived deficiencies in his style of acting. This was especially true from Hitchcock, who was openly displeased with Gavin's performance and never again employed him in such a high-profile manner. Although Gavin continued to regularly appear in films during the 1960's, they were not of the quality of *Psycho* or *Spartacus*. His appearances in major roles included *Midnight Lace* (1960), *Thoroughly Modern Millie* (1967), *Pedro Paramo* (1967), *OSS 117: Double Agent* (1968), *Pussycat, Pussycat, I Love You* (1970), *Murder for Sale* (1970), *Jennifer* (1978), and *The New Adventures of Heidi* (1978). Aside from occasional appearances in *Alfred Hitchcock Presents* and guest appearances on other television shows, Gavin starred as lead actor in two

Gavin's Business Ties with Latin America

John Gavin's family had long-standing business dealings in Mexico; his father held interests in the mining industry, his mother's family in ranching. Gavin founded and operated Gamma Holdings, which is headquartered in Houston, Texas. The company specializes in business consultation, market research, insurance, online education, and entertainment and primarily caters to the Hispanic market.

Gavin served as managing director for the Dallas, Texas-based equity corporation Hicks, Muse, Tate and Furst's Latin America Fund and on the firm's Latin American Strategy Board, investing in cable networks and news and sports media outlets in Mexico, Venezuela, Chile, and Argentina. Starting in 2001, Gavin was a member of the board of directors of Claxson Interactive Group, which provides multimedia entertainment and cable services throughout South America. He was elected as a director of Dresser Industries and was appointed to Chair the Dresser Industries de Mexico advisory board.

television series, *Destry* (1964) and *Convoy* (1965). Both were canceled after one season.

From 1971 to 1973, Gavin served as president of the Screen Actors Guild. In 1974, he married actor Constance Mary Towers, who had a son, Michael, and a daughter, Maureen, from her first marriage to business executive Michael McGrath. Gavin gradually gravitated away from the film industry toward business and international diplomacy. In both fields, his focus was directed toward Latin America. From 1961 to 1968 he held a position with the Organization of American States as a consulting adviser to the secretary-general, Jose Mora of Uruguay, in which position he continued under Mora's successor, Galo Plaza of Ecuador, from 1968 to 1973. He became active in Republican Party circles, identifying with the growing conservative wing.

On May 7, 1981, Gavin was appointed U.S. ambassador to Mexico by his political ally and longtime friend, President Ronald Reagan, who himself once headed the Screen Actors Guild. The nomination was confirmed without controversy by the U.S. Senate but ignited a firestorm in the Mexican news media. Notwithstanding his substantial knowledge of pan-American affairs and his Latino heritage, Gavin was widely viewed as Reagan's crony, and the appointment of a (presumably unqualified) actor to a diplomatic post was considered an insult. Gavin served at the American embassy for five years, resigning on June 10, 1986, and had a mixed legacy as ambassador. He criticized the Mexican government for allowing the Soviet Union to maintain an exceptionally large staff of intelligence agents. On one occasion, he pushed aside a television cameraman who was blocking his way. Gavin also was roundly berated in the media for frequent and lengthy absences from Mexico during his first year in office. After the Mexico City earthquake of September 19, 1985, however, Gavin and his wife were active in offering assistance to victims of the disaster, and by the time he resigned from the ambassadorship in 1986, the Gavins' glamorous style and charm had won them some admirers.

Afterward, Gavin retired to private life, focusing on business ventures, community activities, and occasionally assisting Republican Party candidates in their election campaigns in election. From 1986 to 1987, he was vice president for federal and international relations for ARCO (Atlantic Richfield), and from 1987 to 1989, he served as president of Univisa Satellite. Gavin subsequently sat on the boards of directors of a variety of corporations and educational institutions.

SIGNIFICANCE

As an actor, Gavin never quite shed his early image as a macho romantic figure and consequently was probably underrated and certainly underutilized. His diplomatic career was equally controversial. He was both admired and scorned in Mexico. His blunt, often tactless style of making impromptu statements created frequent controversies. Although he gradually gained the confidence of and favor from a significant portion of the big business community there, he also made enemies. Gavin did, however, retain the confidence of his president. He probably had the most success in business; he was much sought-after as a consultant and board member long after his film and political careers had waned.

Raymond Pierre Hylton

FURTHER READING

Hofler, Robert. *The Man Who Invented The Rock: The Pretty Boys and Dirty Deals of Henry Willson.* New York: Carroll & Graf, 2005. Although Gavin himself is mentioned only briefly, this book provides

a fine background to the Hollywood scene during the 1950's.

McGilligan, Patrick. *Alfred Hitchcock: A Life in Darkness and Light.* New York: Regan Books, 2003. Offers a decent description of the frenetic atmosphere in which Gavin and Hitchcock worked and provides an account of the challenges Gavin endured after incurring the director's displeasure during the filming of *Psycho*.

Staggs, Sam. *Born to Be Hurt: The Untold Story of "Imitation of Life."* New York: St. Martin's Press, 2009. Includes not only a critique of Gavin's role in the film but also an excellent biography.

Wise, James E., and Anne Collier Rehill. *Stars in Blue: Movie Actors in America's Sea Services.* Annapolis, Md.: U.S. Naval Institute Press, 1997. Sheds light on Gavin's career as a naval officer during the early 1950's

See also: Hector Elizondo; Fernando Lamas; Ricardo Montalbán; Carlos Morton; Anthony Quinn; César Romero; Martin Sheen.

FABIOLA CABEZA DE BACA GILBERT

American educator, home economist, and writer

Born into prosperity, Gilbert dedicated her life to helping the poor people of rural New Mexico. Working primarily among Hispanics and Native Americans, she taught the children of farmers and improved the lives of women by instructing them to apply modern methods of home economics to traditional domestic chores.

Latino heritage: Spanish
Born: May 16, 1894; La Liendre, near Las Vegas, New Mexico Territory (now New Mexico)
Died: October 14, 1991; Albuquerque, New Mexico
Also known as: Fabiola Cabeza de Baca; First Lady of New Mexico Cuisine
Areas of achievement: Education; literature; social issues

EARLY LIFE

Fabiola Cabeza de Baca Gilbert (FAH-bee-OH-lah kah-BEH-zah deh BAH-kah GIHL-bahr) was a descendant of sixteenth-century Spanish explorer Álvar Núñez Cabeza de Vaca and a niece of Ezequial Cabeza de Baca, New Mexico's second governor. She was one of four children born to Graciano Cabeza de Baca y Delgado

and his wife, Indalecia Delgado. Fabiola and her siblings—Luis, Guadalupe, and Virginia—grew up in San Miguel County on a large, prosperous land-grant cattle ranch, Llano Estacado (Staked Plain) that had been in the family since the 1820's. Her mother Indalecia died when Fabiola was four years old, and the Cabeza de Baca children were then cared for by their grandparents, Tomas and Estefana, who lived in a large, elegant stone mansion in Las Vegas, New Mexico.

Fabiola attended school at Loretto Academy, a Catholic school in Las Vegas, and spent summers at the ranch, riding her own pony and working alongside her father, especially during branding season. She soon left Loretto (allegedly after a confrontation with a nun) and transferred to a public school. In 1906, she traveled to Spain for a year of Spanish language study before returning home. Fabiola graduated in 1913 from a high school run under the aegis of New Mexico Normal School (now New Mexico Highlands University), having earned a teaching certificate. In 1916, she began teaching the Spanish-speaking children of Hispanic and Indian homesteaders at a rural school in Guadalupe County. During a ten-year teaching career, she also was an instructor at schools in Santa Rosa and El Rita. In 1921, she earned a bachelor's degree in education at New Mexico Normal School, and afterward she returned to Spain to conduct genealogical research. Back in New Mexico, she resumed teaching and was assigned to instruct her students in the relatively new subject of home economics. Intrigued by the possibilities of bringing the modern methodology of family and consumer sciences to traditional domestic chores, in 1929 Gilbert returned to her studies and earned a bachelor's degree in home economics from New Mexico State University in Las Cruces.

LIFE'S WORK

Gilbert immediately put her new degree to good use, landing a position as a home demonstration field agent with the New Mexico Agricultural Extension Service in 1929. For the next thirty years, Gilbert, who at the time of her hiring was the only agent who spoke Spanish, as well as two Pueblo Indian dialects, drove throughout the mostly rural and heavily Hispanic Rio Arriba and Santa

---

Historic Cookery

Fabioloa Cabeza de Baca Gilbert's first book, *Historic Cookery* (1939), originated in 1931, when Gilbert created a brief New Mexico Agricultural Extension pamphlet in which she compiled traditional and modern recipes from Spanish, Mexican, Indian, and Anglo cuisines. Gilbert had closely observed native cooks at work, and she carefully tested each of their recipes in her own kitchen, recording exact measurements of ingredients—customarily a pinch of this or a dash of that—for easy duplication. A popular publication, the pamphlet was reprinted several times before it was released as a book in 1939. *Historic Cookery* sold more than 100,000 copies before the copyright was bought in the 1970's for reprinting. New Mexico governor Thomas J. Mabry, who was in office from 1947 through 1951, helped boost distribution of the book by sending copies to officials of other states as a promotion for New Mexico.

Historic Cookery is the first cookbook detailing the cuisine of the upper Rio Grande region and contains recipes for a variety of chili-based sauces, corn and meat dishes, cheese and egg preparations, salads, soups, breads, desserts, and more. The book, which emphasizes the concept of *guisar*—putting the finishing touch to prepared foods—is widely credited for popularizing New Mexican cuisine in general, and chili in particular.

Fe Counties, bringing the benefits of modern home economics to the wives of isolated, often poverty-stricken farmers. She instructed the women in nutritional values and in techniques of food preparation and preservation, such as how to dry and can fruits or vegetables, and she showed them how to apply new advances in gardening and livestock care to their advantage. She translated useful government bulletins into Spanish for distribution. She also taught wives how to use sewing machines to make traditional craft items, such as quilts and *colcha* (embroidered coverlets), and helped market the finished products to enable impoverished families to earn extra income during the depths of the Great Depression.

In 1931, Fabiola married insurance agent Carlos Gilbert, who was a member of the League of United Latin American Citizens (LULAC), an organization formed to oppose discrimination against Hispanics, especially in the American Southwest. The couple eloped to Mexico; since Carlos had been married before, Fabiola knew her traditionally oriented father would not approve of the union. Though Fabiola would remain active with LULAC for many years—later serving as a national trustee and as president of a local chapter—the marriage did not last. The Gilberts, who had no children, divorced in the early 1940's.

Tragedy struck Fabiola in 1932. A train smashed into her car in Las Vegas, scarring her face and mangling her leg so severely that it had to be amputated. It took two years for her to recover, during which time she wrote extensively on home economics, food preparation, folklore, traditions, and other subjects. After recuperation, she returned to her job as an extension agent with renewed vigor, wearing a wooden leg.

Gilbert not only continued doling out valuable domestic advice to her housewife clients, but also she began gathering information from them. She collected prized family recipes, tidbits of folklore, natural home remedies passed down over the generations, details of religious celebrations, incidents from oral history, and other items of interest from Hispanic and Native American heritages. She used the data she collected to publish many articles in local newspapers and magazines. She also hosted a bilingual radio program about home economics. In 1939, she published the first of three books, *Historic Cookery*, which provided recipes for traditional dishes. In 1949, she released *The Good Life: New Mexican Food*, a fictional account of a typical Hispanic family that explained traditions and rituals and contained recipes for dishes associated with particular festive events. A third book, *We Fed Them*

Cactus (1954), was a history of her family during four generations.

In 1951, through the auspices of the United Nations Educational, Scientific, and Cultural Organization (UNESCO), Gilbert was sent to Mexico to teach home economics to Tarascan Indians. She also trained more than fifty students from Bolivia, Costa Rica, Ecuador, El Salvador, Guatemala, Haiti, Honduras, Mexico, and Peru in modern home-economics techniques. Gilbert retired from the Agricultural Extension Service in 1959, but she kept busy. Always interested in learning about and preserving native customs and traditions, she became an active participant in the Folklore Society of Santa Fe. She lectured widely, wrote copiously, and during the 1960's served as a consultant in home economics to Peace Corps volunteers in training. Still alert and active late in life, Gilbert died in a retirement home in Albuquerque at the age of ninety-seven.

SIGNIFICANCE

Linked by her ancestors to the land for more than four hundred years, Fabiola Cabeza de Baca Gilbert is an important figure in New Mexico's history. She played a pivotal role in the survival of poor Hispanic and Indian residents by giving their children the rudiments of education and by teaching adults efficient methods of home economics designed to improve life during the Great Depression and afterward. Working in both domestic and foreign venues, Gilbert brought the advantages of good nutrition and effective food preparation to the Western Hemisphere, and, through her Peace Corps instruction, to the world. Her writings have preserved traditions and customs that would otherwise have been lost.

Jack Ewing

FURTHER READING

Gilbert, Fabiola Cabeza de Baca. *The Good Life: New Mexican Food.* Drawings by Gerri Chandler. Santa Fe, N.Mex.: San Vincente Foundation, 1949. A fictional account of a typical Hispanic family, including recipes for foods associated with particular holidays.

_____. *Historic Cookery.* 1939. Reprint. Santa Fe, N.Mex: Ancient City Press, 1970. Gilbert's first published book, containing recipes for traditional New Mexican dishes.

_____. *We Fed Them Cactus.* Drawings by Dorothy L. Peters. Albuquerque: University of New Mexico Press, 1954. A four-generation history of Gilbert's family.

Locke, Liz, Theresa A. Vaughan, and Pauline Greenhill, eds. *Encyclopedia of Women's Folklore and Folklife.* Westport, Conn.: Greenwood, 2008. This well-researched, painstakingly documented, two-volume work discusses Gilbert's written works in conjunction with women's traditional occupations, such as cooking, and the relationship of her writings to the preservation of folklore and culture.

Melzer, Richard. *Buried Treasures.* Santa Fe, N.Mex.: Sunstone Press, 2007. Honors notable people in New Mexico's history. Includes a biography of Gilbert that recognizes her work as a cultural preservationist.

Schenone, Laura. *A Thousand Years over a Hot Stove: A History of American Women Told Through Food, Recipes, and Remembrances.* New York: W. W. Norton, 2004. An interesting compendium of cooking history that encompasses a variety of cuisines, including Native American and Hispanic, complete with recipes.

See also: Edna Acosta-Belén; Rodolfo F. Acuña; Jaime Escalante; Arturo Alfonso Schomburg.

MANU GINÓBILI

Argentinean-born basketball player

A dynamic basketball player, Ginóbili has excelled in his sport at all levels of competition, both amateur and professional. He starred in South America and Europe before joining the San Antonio Spurs, and he has won numerous honors for the quality of his individual and team play.

Latino heritage: Argentinean

Born: July 28, 1977; Bahía Blanca, Argentina

Also known as: Emanuel David Ginóbili; The One; Neo; Big Nose; Gino; Narigon; El Contusione

Area of achievement: Basketball

EARLY LIFE

Emanuel David Ginóbili, better known as Manu Ginóbili (MAH-noo jihn-OH-bihl-lee), is the descendant of Italian immigrants. He was born into an athletic tradition, the son of former basketball player and coach

Jorge Ginóbili and his wife Raquel. The youngest of three boys, Manu grew up in the shadow of older brothers Leandro and Sebastián, both of whom played international basketball professionally.

Ginóbili was raised in the basketball hotbed of Bahía Blanca, Argentina, a resort community on the Atlantic Ocean coast, several hundred miles south of Buenos Aires, the nation's capital. He played soccer and basketball as a youth, and from childhood he was an admirer of American National Basketball Association (NBA) star Michael Jordan, whose aggressive playing style he would later emulate. A small, scrawny child, Ginóbili practiced constantly. He shot up in height as a teenager, eventually reaching the height of six feet and six inches. Though still skinny—he would fill out to around two hundred pounds as an adult—he was fearless on both offense and defense. Ginóbili had no qualms about driving to the basket against shot-blockers, or withstanding charges from taller, heavier players.

As an eighteen-year-old, Ginóbili debuted professionally in Argentina with the Andino Sport Club La Roja team. In the 1996-1997 season, he moved to the Estudiantes Bahía Blanca basketball team of the Argentine League, and the following season he led the league in scoring. In 1998, he signed to play in Italy for Viola Reggio Calabria, and in his second season was awarded Player of the Year in the Italian League.

LIFE'S WORK

Ginóbili's heroics did not go unnoticed. In 1999, the NBA's San Antonio Spurs drafted him in the second round. In the meantime, Ginóbili signed with Bologna's Virtus Kinder team in the Italian League, with whom he won the most valuable player award in two consecutive seasons (2000-2002) while leading the team to the Italian Championship (2001), the Italian Cup (2001 and 2002), and the Euroleague Championship (2001). In 2002, he finally signed a one-year, $2.9 million contract with the Spurs. That same year, he played for Argentina at the FIBA World Basketball Championships, leading the team to victory against the highly favored U.S. squad before settling for second place after a hotly contested loss to Yugoslavia.

Injured at the world championships, Ginóbili did not play for the Spurs for a month. However, his physical condition had improved enough that by March, 2003, he won a Rookie of the Month Award, and he became a valuable contributor as a scrappy point guard/forward in his team's drive to the NBA championship—the first Argentinian to play for a title-winning team.

Manu Ginóbili. (AP Photo)

Ginóbili returned to Argentina a national hero. Though he improved statistically during 2003-2004 in points per game, rebounds, assists, and steals, San Antonio fell in the play-offs. Ginóbili's solid performance was good enough to earn him a new six-year, $52 million contract with the Spurs. In 2004, he played for Argentina at the Summer Olympic Games, scoring twenty-nine points to defeat the U.S. "Dream Team." He scored sixteen points and handed out six assists as Argentina triumphed over Italy to win the gold medal. That same year, Ginóbili got married to Marianela Oroño, and his wife gave birth to twin boys, Dante and Nicola, in 2010.

Ginóbili again made an impact in the NBA during the 2004-2005 season, helping the Spurs to another championship in a tense, seven-game final against the Detroit Pistons. Sidelined with lower leg injuries for part of 2005-2006, Ginóbili returned the following year to provide a spark off the bench as the Spurs won their third NBA championship during his tenure.

In 2008, he reached career highs in points per game, rebounds, assists, and three-point field goal percentage, earning him a spot on the All-NBA All-Star team. In the summer of 2008, he again played for Argentina at the Beijing Olympics as the national team captured the bronze medal in basketball.

Through eight seasons (2002-2010) in the NBA, all with San Antonio, Ginóbili racked up respectable credentials, averaging 15 points, 4 rebounds, 3.8 assists, and 1.5 steals per game. His exciting, competitive style of play—featuring long jump shots, slashing drives, no-look passes, and clutch performance—earned him a three-year, $39 million contract extension in 2010.

SIGNIFICANCE

Considered the best basketball player to come from South America, and one of the best international players to perform in the NBA, Manu Ginóbili has led teams to victory at every stage of his career. After Bill Bradley, he is only the second player in history—and the first not born in the United States—to be a member of teams that won a Euroleague title, an Olympic gold medal, and an NBA championship; he has helped win three NBA championships since entering the league in 2002. A three-time NBA All-Star in 2005, 2008, and 2011, he was only the second Latin American to play in the annual game featuring the league's best athletes. In 2008, he also won the NBA's coveted Sixth Man

Award as the reserve player who has contributed the most to his team.

Jack Ewing

FURTHER READING

Hareas, John. *One Team, One Goal, Mission Accomplished: 2005 NBA Champion San Antonio Spurs.* Overland Park, Kans.: Anthem, 2005. A retrospective of the Spurs' drive toward the 2005 NBA championship, complete with player profiles and team highlights.

Hetrick, Hans. *The NBA, a History of Hoops: The Story of the San Antonio Spurs.* Mankato, Minn.: Creative Paperbacks, 2011. A brief history of the franchise for young adults, incorporating the contributions of Ginóbili.

Hofstetter, Adam B. *Olympic Basketball.* New York: Rosen Group, 2007. Aimed at young adults, this book covers highlights of Olympic basketball, including the Ginóbili-led Argentine upset of the U.S. team to win the gold medal in 2004.

See also: Carlos Arroyo; Rolando Blackman; Rebecca Lobo; Eduardo Nájera; Diana Taurasi.

ISAAC GOLDEMBERG

Peruvian-born writer and editor

The author of The Fragmented Life of Don Jacobo Lerner *(1977) and* El gran libro de América Judia *(1998), Goldemberg founded the Latin American Writers Center and has worked as editor of its journals and publishing house the Latino Press.*

Latino heritage: Peruvian

Born: November 15, 1945; Chepén, Peru

Areas of achievement: Literature; poetry; art

EARLY LIFE

Isaac Goldemberg (GOHL-dehm-burg) was born in Chepén, Perú, in 1945. He was brought up Catholic for the first eight years of his life until he moved in with his father in Lima. His father, an Ashkenazi Jew, made sure to reacquaint the boy with his Jewish heritage. During his stay in Lima, Goldemberg developed deep ties with the Jewish community and eventually traveled to Israel, where he lived on a kibbutz for more than a year.

Goldemberg moved back to Peru and soon after he traveled to New York, where he established his permanent residence in 1964. He did not begin to publish his poetry, novels, and essays until he arrived to New York. As he confessed to critic Illan Stavans, he chose to live in New York without mastering the English language so that his Spanish would not become corrupted. He chose to remain an outsider to North American culture in order to reflect on his identity as a Jewish Latin-American. The seemingly conflicted nature of his hybrid identity became Goldemberg's main area of concern in his literary work. Jewish identity traditionally had been perceived as foreign to Latin American cultural identity, especially in the Andean region. While indigenous communities and Catholic Spanish colonizers were perceived as the main components of Peruvian identity, the Eastern European origins and divergent religious practices of the Andean Jewish community were perceived as distinctly foreign.

LIFE'S WORK

Goldemberg is best known for his 1978 novel *The Fragmented Life of Don Jacobo Lerner*, a semiauto-biographic chronicle of his childhood in 1950's Peru. The novel, originally published in English translation, tells the story of Don Jacobo Lerner, a Russian Jew, from the perspective of his son, Efrain, conceived out of wedlock with a Catholic woman. Rather than chronicling the coming of age of the character, the novel portrays his gradual disintegration as an individual. Effrain becomes a symbol of the futile attempts of the Jewish community to become accepted into Peruvian society (Goldberg).

Throughout his literary career, Goldemberg continued reflecting on the challenges of reconciling his Jewish and Latin American heritages in a variety of genres. He has published numerous collections of poetry, including *Tiempo de silencio* (1970), *Hombre de paso* (1981), *La vida al contado* (1991), *Cuerpo del amor* (2000), and *Las cuentas y los inventarios* (2000). He also has written the plays *Hotel AmériKKa* (2000) and *Golpe de gracia: farsa en un acto* (2003). He was also the editor of the anthology of Jewish Latin American writers *El gran libro de América Judía* (1998).

This last work exemplifies Goldemberg's lifelong effort to articulate a coherent identity out of the overwhelmingly diverse experiences of Latin American Jews. The anthology is written as a series of books composed of unidentified fragments from the work of other Jewish writers alternatively suggesting authorial unity and highlighting the polyphonic nature of Jewish tradition in Latin America. Goldemberg's work as an editor is as important as his literary production. In 1987, he founded the Latin American Writers Institute at the City University of New York with the objective of promoting Latin American cultural production in the United States. The institute hosts the Latino Press, the *Brújula/Compass* (a bilingual journal devoted to Latin American literature), and the *Hostos Review* (a journal of international culture). Goldemberg's work as an editor is valued for his ability to raise awareness of the importance of Jewish literature within the Latin American literary tradition.

SIGNIFICANCE

Goldemberg's literary production has greatly contributed to awareness of the contributions of the Latin American Jewish community. As notions of national and cultural identity continue to evolve in a world increasingly defined by transnational economic activity, Goldemberg's exploration of the fragmentary nature of being warn us against essentialist readings of cultural tradition. Individuals become members of a tradition inasmuch as they actively engage with it. In his own professional life, Goldemberg has not only reflected on the significance of his own cultural heritage, but also worked tirelessly as an editor to promote Jewish and Latin American culture.

Adolfo Campoy-Cubillo.

FURTHER READING

Goldberg, Paul L. "Immigration and Childhood Experience in Two Contemporary Andean Jewish Novels." *Shofar: An Interdisciplinary Journal of Jewish Studies* 19, no. 3 (2001): 56-64. This article explores the biographical elements that inform the literary and essayistic production of Isaac Goldemberg and Ecuadorian Jewish writer Diego Viga.

Goldemberg, Isaac. *The Fragmented Life of Don Jacobo Lerner.* London: Sidgwick & Jackson, 1978. Goldemberg's first and most famous novel.

_____. *El gran libro de América Judía.* San Juan: Editorial de la Universidad de Puerto Rico, 1999. An anthology of Jewish Latin American writing, an excellent source to understand the diverse cultural traditions that inform his writing.

Stavans, Ilan. *The One-Handed Pianist and Other Stories.* Evanston, Ill: Northwestern University Press, 2007. A collection of autobiographical short stories that include Stavans's recollections about his first encounter with Goldemberg and his significance in the Latin American literary field.

_____. *The Scroll and the Cross: One Thousand Years of Jewish-Hispanic Literature.* New York: Routledge, 2003. An anthology of Jewish American writing with brief but extremely insightful introductions.

See also: Fernando Alegría; Ruth Behar; Lourdes Casal; Luis Leal; Felipe de Ortego y Gasca.

SCOTT GOMEZ

American hockey player

When he was drafted by the New Jersey Devils in 1998, Gomez became the first Latino to play professional hockey.

Latino heritage: Mexican and Colombian
Born: December 23, 1979; Anchorage, Alaska
Also known as: Scott Carlos Gomez; Scotty
Area of achievement: Sports

EARLY LIFE

Scott Carlos Gomez (GOH-mehz) was born on December 23, 1979, in Anchorage, Alaska. His father was born in Mexico and his mother in Colombia. After watching a University of Alaska hockey game at age five with his father, Gomez wanted to try the sport. Although he struggled to learn to skate and was tempted to quit the sport, Gomez stuck with it. By the age of ten, he was playing on the elite Anchorage North Stars, a team featuring the best players in the city. Gomez often would wake up early and go to the local rink before anyone else was there, and use the free open ice to practice his skills. As he developed into a fast-skating, skilled player, his Alaska All-Stars team won the United States Midget Championship.

By age sixteen, Gomez was one of the top junior players in the United States, and he decided to join the more competitive Canadian junior league to play for a team in Surrey, British Columbia. In his first year in British Columbia, Gomez ended up in second place in league scoring. He was named the team's most valuable player, won the league rookie of the year award, and was named to the All-Star Team. Hockey experts predicted that he would become the first Hispanic player in the National Hockey League (NHL). At first, Gomez was frustrated by the attention he received as a Hispanic hockey player. While growing up in Alaska, he was accepted as a hockey player without regard to his ethnicity.

Gomez moved up a level in play to the Western Hockey League (WHL), a major junior hockey league. In 1998, his second year in the WHL, Gomez was selected twenty-seventh in the NHL draft by the New Jersey Devils. That year, Gomez also was selected for the first All-Star team in the WHL and recorded 108 points in fifty-eight games.

LIFE'S WORK

Gomez was the first Latino ever drafted in the NHL, and he accepted that this distinction made him a role model for Latino children. At 5 feet, 11 inches, he heard speculation that he might be too small to be a force in professional hockey; however, Gomez did not disappoint. In the 1999-2000 season, he won the Calder Trophy as the NHL's rookie of the year. He led all rookies in scoring and was named to the All-Star team. Gomez became the only New Jersey player in history to play all eighty-two regular-season games in his rookie year. To add to his exceptional rookie season, the New Jersey Devils won the NHL championship, the Stanley Cup. The last time an NHL player had won both the Calder Trophy and Stanley Cup in the same year was in 1963.

Gomez had respectable seasons over the next four years. In the 2002-2003 season, the Devils won the Stanley Cup again, giving Gomez two championships in his short career. Gomez was selected by Team U.S.A. to play in the 2004 World Championships and helped the team to a bronze medal. Shortly thereafter, he represented the United States in the 2006 Olympic Games. In 2005-2006, Gomez produced his career highs in goals

Scott Gomez. (AP Photo)

and points. He had achieved superstar status, and as a free agent, he attracted much attention from teams eager to sign him. Gomez signed a seven-year deal with the New York Rangers for $51.5 million in 2007. He also was selected as an NHL All-Star in 2007-2008. At the end of the 2008-2009 season, Gomez was traded to the Montreal Canadiens, where he became the highest paid player in the history of the franchise.

In 2007, Gomez started the Scott Gomez Foundation to help develop the hockey talent and the level of competition in Alaska. His foundation provides hockey equipment to underprivileged children. Because of his generosity, Gomez had his childhood rink in Anchorage named after him.

Significance

Gomez has embraced his heritage of being the first Hispanic to play in the NHL. Gomez enjoys being a role model for Latino children growing up who may aspire to be hockey players. Gomez's success is shown by more and more Hispanic children signing up to play ice hockey. He was named one of the top 50 Latino athletes by *Hispanic Magazine* in 2008. Gomez is truly an inspiration to Latino children, a philanthropist and an international superstar.

Timothy M. Sawicki

Further Reading

Fischler, Stan, and Shirley Fischler. *Who's Who in Hockey*. Kansas City, Mo.: Andrews McMeel, 2003. Profiles Gomez and other hockey stars. Provides career statistics, a list of accomplishments, and other information.

O'Shei, Tim, and Amy Moritz. *Scott Gomez*. Philadelphia: Chelsea House, 2001. A bibliography of the first Hispanic American to play in the National Hockey League. In-depth life details and full color photos make up the book.

Stewart, Mark. *Scott Gomez: Open Up the Ice*. Brookfield, Conn.: Millbrook Press, 2001. Chronicles Gomez's life from his early years playing hockey up to his National Hockey League career.

See also: Donna de Varona; Rudy Galindo; Pancho Gonzales.

Arturo Gómez-Pompa

Mexican-born scientist and environmentalist

Gómez-Pompa was one of the first scientists to powerfully communicate the need to conserve the rainforests. However, some of his greatest achievements have been as a tireless advocate for the rights of the indigenous people who inhabit the Mexican rainforest and for the preservation of their home. Through articles, speeches, and diplomacy, he has worked as a researcher, educator, organizer, and consensus-builder to construct a more environmentally sustainable policy for the Mexican rainforest.

Latino heritage: Mexican

Born: October 21, 1934; Mexico City, Mexico

Areas of achievement: Science and technology; social issues

Early Life

Arturo Gómez-Pompa (ahr-TUH-roh GOH-mehs-POHM-pah) was born in Mexico City, Mexico. He attended the Instituto México and Centro Universitario México in Mexico City, earning his B.S. in biology in 1951. He received his professional degree in botany in 1965 and his doctor of science in botany in 1966 from the National Autonomous University of Mexico. At the age of twenty-four, the Mexican government appointed him to a commission that partnered with pharmaceutical companies to survey medicinal plants. He worked for the commission until 1965, and this work set him on the path of studying the Mexican rainforest. In 1965, Gómez-Pompa was appointed professor of botany at the National Autonomous University of Mexico, a position he held until 1980.

Life's Work

In the late 1960's, Gómez-Pompa made detailed observations of forest ecology at a biological station at Los Tuxlas, Mexico. This work culminated in a database of native plants in the Mexican state of Veracruz. In 1975, he founded the National Research Institute of Biotic Resources in Xalapa, Veracruz, serving as its director until 1984. He examined the agricultural techniques of the indigenous Mayan people who live in the rainforests, discovering that their low-technology cropping methods allowed them to thrive in the rainforest for approximately three thousand years without destroying it. With funds from the John D. and Catherine T. MacArthur

Arturo Gómez-Pompa. (© Keith Dannemiller/Corbis)

Foundation, he organized the Maya Sustainability Project to aid Mayan forest dwellers in southern Mexico. Since the Mayan people were wholly dependent on the rainforest for their sustenance, Gómez-Pompa viewed rainforest conservation as not only an environmental issue but also a human-rights issue. He became a passionate advocate for the Mayan people. In 1978, he was awarded the Al Mérito Botánico Medal of the Botanical Society of Mexico for this work.

From 1984 through 1985, Gómez-Pompa worked as consulting director in the division of ecological sciences at the United Nations Educational, Scientific, and Cultural Organization (UNESCO). In 1984, he received the Alfonso L. Herra Medal of the Mexican government and the Golden Arch medal of the Netherlands government for contributions to the conservation of natural resources. In 1985, he was a Charles Bullard Research Fellow at Harvard University in Cambridge, Massachusetts.

In 1986, the University of California, Riverside, appointed Gómez-Pompa a professor of botany. In 1988, he advised the newly elected Mexican president Carlos Salinas de Gortari on environmental matters. In 1989, his intervention prevented the damming of the Usumacinta River, which preserved the Lacandón Rainforest.

In 1990, Gómez-Pompa helped established the El Eden Ecological Reserve in the state of Quintana Roo, Mexico. El Eden was the first privately owned area dedicated to biological conservation research. In 1992, Gómez-Pompa and his colleagues helped the Mexican government launch a pilot program to stop deforestation in the Mexican rainforests, and four years later, a newly elected Mexican administration initiated long-term forest protection and poverty relief for the indigenous peoples. Gómez-Pompa founded and chaired the Programa de Acción Forestal Tropical (PROAFT) from 1993 to 1999. PROAFT coordinates national and global funding sources for conservation. He was awarded the Tyler Prize for Environmental Achievement in 1994, and in 1996, he was the keynote speaker at the First Sustainable Coffee Congress.

In 1998, the University of California, Riverside, named him a distinguished professor of botany, and one year later, the university promoted him to a full professorship. Under his influence, in 2000 Mitsubishi halted plans to build the San Ignacio Lagoon Saltworks, which would have threatened the El Vizcaino Biosphere Reserve, a breeding site for gray whales. In 2002, the Institute of Ecology in Veracruz awarded him its Honorary Researcher Award, and the University of Veracruz awarded him the Gold Medal Merit Award.

SIGNIFICANCE

One of the pioneers of rainforest ecology, Gómez-Pompa convincingly argued for the conservation of the rainforest and effectively linked ecological concerns with human rights. He also brought a tactful, diplomatic approach to his pursuit of sound environmental policy. Because he never demonized businesses, he was often able to forge consensuses with them and with politicians in order to initiate conservation programs that were mutually beneficial. He is a role model for the constructive use of science in policy making and the creation of respectful relationships between organizations with competing interests in order to establish conservation goals. Gómez-Pompa also challenged many of the assumptions of the environmental movement and helped establish a new paradigm in conservation that included indigenous societies as key factors in ecosystem preservation.

Michael A. Buratovich

FURTHER READING

Gómez-Pompa, Arturo. "Biodiversity and Agriculture: Friends or Foes?" In *Proceedings of First Sustain-*

able *Coffee Congress*, edited by Robert A Rice, Ashley M. Harris, and Jennifer McLean. Washington D.C.: Smithsonian Institution, 1997. A description of the highly sustainable Mayan agricultural methods of coffee cultivation and what modern coffee farmers can learn from them.

_____. "On Maya Silviculture." *Mexican Studies* 3, no. 1 (Winter, 1987): 1-17. A detailed study of the agricultural methods of contemporary Mayan inhabitants of the Mexican rainforests that attempts to reconstruct ancient Mayan silvicultural methods.

_____. "The Role of Biodiversity Scientists in a Troubled World." *Bioscience* 54, no. 3 (2004): 217-225. Addresses the arguments for conservation of biodiversity and concludes that human rights and

justice are better arguments than the overused "new resources" concept.

Gómez-Pompa, Arturo, et al. *The Lowland Maya Area: Three Millennia at the Human-Wildland Interface.* New York: Haworth Press, 2003. An invaluable compendium of research on lowland Mayan forests that covers the geologic history, climate, and biodiversity of the forests, as well as the agricultural techniques of the Mayan people who live there.

See also: Anne Maino Alvarez; Walter Alvarez; Margarita Colmenares; Francisco Dallmeier; Elma González; Eugenia Kalnay; Mario Molina; Severo Ochoa.

PAUL GONSALVES

American jazz musician

Initially playing guitar, Gonsalves switched to tenor saxophone, playing professionally with jazz musicians Count Basie and Dizzy Gillespie before finding a lasting place as one of Duke Ellington's principal soloists from 1950 until 1974.

Latino heritage: Cape Verdean

Born: July 12, 1920; Brockton, Massachusetts

Died: May 15, 1974; London, England

Also known as: Mex

Area of achievement: Music

EARLY LIFE

Paul Gonsalves (pawl gahn-SAHL-vehz) was born in Brockton, Massachusetts, in 1920. Although later nicknamed "Mex," Gonsalves was the son of Cape Verdean immigrants, who instilled in him a love of many kinds of music, including their native folk songs, and he was taught traditional Portuguese folk music from an early age. He was surrounded by music during his adolescence in Providence, Rhode Island, and learned guitar as a boy, playing a variety of music in a string band made up of family and friends. By his early teens he had given up music entirely in favor of sports, although exposure to his older brother's record collection and hearing Jimmie Lunceford inspired him to take up tenor saxophone.

By the late 1930's, Gonsalves was playing in dance bands and jazz groups in the Providence area, and he

had acquired a thorough grounding in technique and tone production from his studies with a classical saxophone teacher. His musical career was interrupted when he served in the Army during World War II, during which he was stationed in India, where he played and recorded with Teddy Weatherford's band. On his return to the United States he joined the popular Boston-based Sabby Lewis Orchestra, with which he played alto and tenor saxophone. While on tour with this band, Gonsalves was heard and hired by Count Basie, who needed a replacement for tenor saxophonist Illinois Jacquet. Gonsalves was an immediate success and remained until Basie broke up his big band in the fall of 1949. For the next year, Gonsalves worked around New York City until he was hired by Dizzy Gillespie for his big band. While working with Gillespie, Gonsalves was exposed to some of the more modern-styled players, although the band did not last long.

After leaving Gillespie's band, Gonsalves was largely unemployed and down to his last few dollars when a chance meeting with Duke Ellington led to an audition with his band in December, 1950. His familiarity with Ellington's style and repertoire, which Gonsalves acquired from his teenage record collection, served him in good stead, as did his appreciation for the saxophone styles of Coleman Hawkins and Ben Webster. Gonsalves's ability to fit into the Ellington band's classic arrangements, as well as his own style, led to his employment in the band until shortly before his death in 1974.

Paul Gonsalves. (Time & Life Pictures/Getty Images)

LIFE'S WORK

While Gonsalves recorded frequently during his tenure with Basie, his legacy was as an Ellingtonian. For the last twenty years of his life, he made numerous recordings with Ellington and participated in many more recording sessions without Ellington's presence. However, virtually all of these sessions were with his fellow bandmates, and the flavor of the music was similar to what was played by the big band.

Gonsalves's greatest recognition in jazz history came from his appearance at the 1956 Newport Jazz Festival. The Ellington band, which at the time was at a low point in its popularity, was to close the festival with a performance of "Diminuendo and Crescendo in Blue." Although this piece was not in the band's regular book at the time, its performance electrified the crowd, especially during the twenty-seven-chorus blues solo by Gonsalves that bridged its two sections. While not extroverted in the style of Jacquet or Lockjaw Davis, Gonsalves's solo brought the audience to a fever pitch and proved to be a rejuvenation of Ellington's band and career. For his part, Gonsalves was elevated to become one of the best-known saxophonists of the day, although most musicians feel that his real strength was in his ballad artistry.

Gonsalves was forced to recreate his marathon solo on almost a nightly basis for the rest of his career, although Ellington thought highly enough of his abilities to feature him extensively on all his performances and recordings. From this standpoint the most notable of their collaborations was on *Duke Ellington and His Orchestra Featuring Paul Gonsalves*, released by Fantasy Records in 1962, on which Ellington had his band record eight of their standard arrangements with Gonsalves playing all the solos. In later years, Ellington was somewhat less willing to assign as much responsibility to Gonsalves, who had become unreliable because of a drug habit.

SIGNIFICANCE

Paul Gonsalves had a long career as a jazz tenor saxophonist. Unlike most of his contemporaries, he did not gravitate to bebop or more modern forms of jazz, preferring instead to work in the swing idiom. His initial influence was Coleman Hawkins, and throughout his career Gonsalves maintained a devotion to tone and melodic construction that he learned from Hawkins and his disciples. That style fit Duke Ellington's palette and Gonsalves is today remembered as one of Ellington's principal voices.

John L. Clark, Jr.

FURTHER READING

Dance, Stanley. *The World of Duke Elllington.* New York: Charles Scribner's Sons, 1970. Includes a chapter on Gonsalves, focusing on his introduction into the Ellington band.

Morton, John Fass. "A Leading Voice Supported by Many Parts: Paul Gonsalves." In *Backstory in Blue: Ellington at Newport '56.* New Brunswick, N.J.: Rutgers University Press, 2008. Describes the Ellington band's performance at the Newport Jazz Festival, devoting a chapter to Gonsalves's now legendary solo on "Diminuendo in Blue and Crescendo in Blue."

Tucker, Mark. *The Duke Ellington Reader.* New York: Oxford University Press, 1993. A collection of pieces of Ellingtonia, including several appreciations of Gonsalves and his role in the band.

Welding, Pete. "Portrait Of Paul." *Downbeat,* February 28, 1963, 18-19. A thorough interview with Gonsalves, detailing many early influences and associations.

See also: Ray Barretto; Paquito D'Rivera; Charlie Palmieri; Tito Puente; Poncho Sánchez; Juan Tizol.

ALBERTO GONZALES

American lawyer and politician

Born into poverty, Gonzales became a partner in a successful law firm. A political appointee under Texas governor George W. Bush, Gonzales followed Bush to the White House as legal counsel and then as U.S. attorney general, the first Latino to hold this office, before being forced to resign.

Latino heritage: Mexican

Born: August 4, 1955; San Antonio, Texas

Also known as: Alberto R. Gonzales; Al Gonzales; Gonzo; Fredo

Areas of achievement: Government and politics; law

EARLY LIFE

Alberto R. Gonzales (ahl-BEHR-toh gohn-ZAH-lehz) was the grandson of undocumented Mexican immigrants; three of his grandparents may have entered the United States illegally. He was one of eight children born to construction worker Pablo Gonzales and his wife, Maria, and was raised near Houston, Texas. Though neither parent was educated past sixth grade, Gonzales became an honors student at Douglas MacArthur High School in Houston. After graduating in 1973, Gonzales joined the U.S. Air Force, intending to become a fighter pilot, and served two years in Alaska. Poor eyesight precluded a flying career, so he enrolled at the Air Force Academy in 1975. Because he did not enjoy the heavily scientific course work and did not want to commit to further military obligation, a requirement if he stayed at the academy more than two years, Gonzales transferred in 1977 to Rice University. He graduated in 1979, majoring in political science. He married for the first time, to Diane Clemens; they divorced in 1982, the year Gonzales earned a law degree from Harvard Law School.

Gonzales subsequently became an associate at a Houston law firm, where over the next dozen years, specializing in corporate law, he rose to become a partner. He married again in 1985, to Rebecca Turner, and the couple had three sons. Gonzales became prominent in the local community, serving as a United Way director, the president of Leadership Houston, and a member of the admissions committee for Rice University.

LIFE'S WORK

In the early 1990's, Gonzales met future Texas governor and U.S. president George W. Bush. Upon assuming the governorship, Bush named Gonzales general legal counsel, and in this position Gonzales gained national recognition and became embroiled in controversy. Gonzales angered civil libertarians for his handling of clemency requests in death penalty cases. He routinely ignored exculpatory information, such as ineffective counsel, conflicts of interest, evidence of innocence, witness recantations, legal improprieties, discrimination, and other factors that might have affected convictions. During Gonzales's two years as legal counsel, only one of the fifty-seven death-penalty rulings was overturned, and Texas executed more individuals than any other state.

In 1997, Bush appointed Gonzales Texas's secretary of state and in 1999 named him to the Texas Supreme Court. When Bush took office as president in 2001, Gonzales was named general counsel. Controversy continued to dog Gonzales. Following the terrorist attacks on September 11, 2001, he argued that physical and psychological torture of suspected terrorists did not violate the Geneva Convention. This stance caused an

Alberto Gonzales. (AP Photo)

international outcry and raised concerns among American military personnel about their own welfare should they be captured. Gonzales also worked to limit the Freedom of Information Act and was a staunch advocate of the constitutionally questionable Patriot Act.

In late 2004, Bush nominated Gonzales to be the U.S. attorney general. Despite widespread doubts about his qualifications for this position, the U.S. Senate confirmed his appointment along party lines in early 2005. Gonzales ran into immediate opposition for his support of illegal wiretapping and warrantless searches of American citizens in the zealous pursuit of terrorists. He maintained that the U.S. Constitution does not guarantee the right of habeas corpus. What ultimately unraveled his career, however, was his firing—and replacing with handpicked Republican Party loyalists—of eight U.S. attorneys, not because of performance (virtually all those dismissed had received outstanding reviews) but for purely political reasons: They were not conservative enough and did not adhere to the presidential agenda. In the process, Gonzales was accused of illegally circumventing the senatorial confirmation process, of incompetence, and of perjury when testifying before legislative oversight committees about his actions. Under mounting pressure from a growing chorus of U.S. senators and representatives of both political parties, who called for his removal or impeachment, Gonzales resigned as attorney general in September, 2007. Other officials, including White House Chief of Staff Karl Rove, also resigned.

SIGNIFICANCE

Though no Latino had ever risen as high in the American government, and none had ever served as both presidential counsel and U.S. attorney general, Alberto Gonzales could not find work at a law firm after leaving office. He began a fee-based lecture tour, speaking before business groups and at educational institutions. In 2009, he was hired as a recruiter of minorities at Texas Tech and Angelo State Universities and as a teacher at Texas Tech, where other professors petitioned to oppose his hiring.

In 2011, Gonzales remained a controversial figure. Supporters maintained he was a victim of circumstance, an ambitious political appointee who cooperated with his superiors, who was elevated beyond his capacities, and who became a convenient scapegoat when the policies he supported became untenable. Detractors have been less kind, calling him a sycophant who served a crony rather than the cause of justice, an enabler, and a willing accomplice in an illegal, unconstitutional, and amoral political agenda that undermined the very fabric of democracy. History, as always, will be the final arbiter of his guilt or innocence.

Jack Ewing

FURTHER READING

Berlow, Alan. "The Texas Clemency Memos." *The Atlantic Monthly*, July/August, 2003, 91-96. An examination of the Texas clemency process during Gonzales's tenure as legal counsel to Governor George W. Bush. The process resulted in an unprecedented number of executions, some of which are highlighted in this article.

Rosen, Jeffrey. "A Unified Theory of Scandal: The Real Roots of the U.S. Attorney Firings." *New Republic* 236, no. 4811 (April 23, 2007): 37-39. An in-depth probe into the U.S. attorney firings, covering Gonzales's testing of the limits of executive power and his illegal use of prosecution for partisan advantage.

Schwartz, Emma. "The Mess He Left Behind." *U.S. News & World Report,* September 10, 2007, 27-28. The story behind Gonzales's resignation: the causes leading up to it and a discussion about what the next attorney general must do to repair damage and restore morale to the U.S. Justice Department.

See also: Joaquín G. Avila; Norma V. Cantú; Henry G. Cisneros; José Ángel Gutiérrez; Antonia Hernández; Manuel Luján, Jr.; Vilma Socorro Martínez; Bill Richardson; Ken Salazar; Hilda L. Solis.

CORKY GONZÁLES

American activist, poet, and boxer

A prominent leader and activist in the Chicano movement of the 1960's, Gonzáles founded the Chicano organization Crusade for Justice. His 1965 poem "I Am Joaquín/Yo soy Joaquín" became the anthem of the *movement. Gonzáles also is responsible for the Chicano Youth Liberation Conference in 1969, at which El Plan Espiritual de Aztlán was conceptualized and produced.*

Latino heritage: Mexican

Born: June 18, 1928; Denver, Colorado

Died: April 12, 2005; Denver, Colorado

Also known as: Rodolfo Gonzáles

Areas of achievement: Activism; social issues; poetry; boxing

EARLY LIFE

Corky Gonzáles (gohn-ZAH-lehs) was born Rodolfo Gonzáles on June 18, 1928, in Denver, Colorado, to Federico and Indalesia Gonzáles. Gonzáles was two years old when his mother died, leaving his father to care for him and his seven siblings. Federico was influential in his son's early understanding of cultural identity, often speaking to him about the history of Mexico and the Mexican Revolution. As the child of a migrant farmworker, Gonzáles had to work in the fields with his father to help support the family. He missed large amounts of school and had to change schools several times because of the nature of agricultural work. Despite these hardships, Gonzáles graduated from Manual High School in 1944 at the age of sixteen. Subsequently, he attended the University of Denver but quickly discontinued his college education because of the high cost of attendance.

Gonzáles's interest in boxing began when he was a teenager. After leaving college, he began to pursue the sport as a career. As a featherweight, he won two amateur national championships. In his professional boxing career, between 1947 and 1955, he was ranked third in his weight class by the National Boxing Association. Despite his high ranking, Gonzáles never was given the opportunity to compete for the world featherweight title.

After ending his boxing career, Gonzáles worked at several different jobs before he finally became part of the local Denver political scene. Between 1957 and 1960, Gonzáles served as district captain in the Denver Democratic Party and worked as the Colorado coordinator of the Viva Kennedy campaign for presidential candidate John F. Kennedy.

LIFE'S WORK

Gonzáles was devoted to advocating social change for the Mexican and Mexican American population in the southwestern United States. Concerned with the economic, educational, and cultural challenges facing the Mexican American community, Gonzáles formed Los Voluntarios, an organization that would later become the Crusade for Justice. He understood that Spanish-speaking youths would be the driving force in the Chi-

cano movement and often spoke publicly about Chicano nationalism and liberation from the oppressive attitudes of Anglo politics.

In 1965, the Crusade for Justice published a poem by Gonzáles titled "I Am Joaquín/Yo soy Joaquín." The poem depicts the struggles of the mestizo community, both in society and with cultural identity, and helped unite Chicanos and the Chicano cause. As the leader of the Crusade for Justice, Gonzáles organized Chicano youths in several protests, including school walkouts and demonstrations against the Vietnam War. In May, 1968, Gonzáles and the Crusade for Justice participated in the Chicano Poor People's March on Washington, D.C. In Washington, he formally introduced his Plan of the Barrio to the American government, calling for better housing, education, and business development for the Denver Chicano community.

A protest against the absence of poverty programs for Chicanos was staged in the basement of the Hawthorne School by members of the Crusade for Justice on May 29, 1968. During the protest, Gonzáles, Reies López Tijerina, and the Reverend Ralph David Abernathy of the Southern Christian Leadership Conference staged a demonstration at the Supreme Court Building

Corky Gonzáles. (© Bettmann/Corbis)

El Plan Espiritual de Aztlán: The Plan of the People

At the Chicano Youth Liberation Conference in March, 1969, El Plan Espiritual de Aztlán was first presented to the Chicano community. The conference was organized by the Crusade for Justice leader, Corky Gonzáles, and intended to raise awareness regarding the societal struggles of the Mexican American and Mexican community. El Plan Espiritual de Aztlán emerged from a poem written by Chicano poet and activist Alurista, which was read at the conference. The ideas presented in the poem represented the concepts and goals of the Chicano movement.

El Plan de Aztlán was accepted by the organizations participating in the conference and declared a symbol of Chicano nationalism. The plan calls for Chicano self-government in educational, economic, and political structures. Liberation from Anglo-determined systems in society was the aim of the plan, and autonomy in the Chicano community was the main goal stated in the document.

to show support for American Indian rights. Gonzáles organized and participated in several other demonstrations during 1968, including a march on the Denver police station to draw attention to the killing of a fifteen-year-old Mexican American youth by a local police officer. These demonstrations and many others added to tensions between the police and the Chicano community. However, Gonzáles worked to unite the Mexican American community through his ethnic nationalist speeches.

Gonzáles continued to stage protests in 1969, including many demonstrations against the unequal treatment of Mexican American students. Focused on creating an educational system that accounted for the cultural conventions and issues facing the Chicano community, Gonzáles sent a list of demands to the Denver Board of Education. These demands included bilingual educationand a requirement that educators live in the communities in which they taught so that they would better understand the needs of their students. These demands were not met, and after the school board's refusal to fire a teacher who had made racist remarks to a student, Gonzáles led a walkout lasting three days. Riots followed the walkout, and Gonzáles was arrested and later released.

These efforts led to the first national Chicano Youth Liberation Conference in March, 1969. Held in Denver, the conference hosted discussions on societal

revolution and Chicano identity. Gonzáles's goals were to unite and involve Chicano youths in the movement. Many student organizations with similar philosophies were involved in the conference. The most significant product of this conference was El Plan Espiritual de Aztlán. This document lucidly stated the ideology of the movement and Chicano nationalism. It represented the needs and demands of the Mexican American community, including a desire for autonomy in its schools, economic systems, and communities. Chicano liberation was the foundation of the movement, and throughout Gonzáles's leadership, he stressed this theme in speeches at events, such as the Chicano Unity Conference in August, 1969.

By 1970, Gonzáles's principles of Chicano unity and liberation had spread through the Southwest, and soon he was influential in the development of La Raza Unida Party in Colorado. Originating in Texas with José Angel Gutiérrez as leader, La Raza Unida Party was developed to proclaim the creation of a national Chicano political party.

Gonzáles's civil rights activism, however, took an unexpected turn as the result of an incident occurring in 1973. In this year, a man was arrested for jaywalking in front of the offices of Crusade for Justice. Demonstrators protested against the man's persecution, and their protest led to a confrontation with police, a gun battle, and a bomb explosion in an apartment house owned by the Crusade. A man was killed and seventeen others, including twelve police officers, were injured in this explosion. While Gonzáles blamed the police for "grenading" the building, a detective concluded that the site of the explosion was a "veritable arsenal."

This incident reduced Gonzáles's national influence, and he maintained a lower profile while remaining active in Denver's Latino community. His health began deteriorating, and he suffered from heart arrhythmia and acute liver disease. In 1995, he was diagnosed with kidney and heart problems, but he refused to obtain hospital treatment. He died at home on April 12, 2005, surrounded by his family and friends.

SIGNIFICANCE

The work of Gonzáles has led to many societal revolutions in the Chicano community. The politics of Chicano nationalism are indebted to the speeches and writings of Gonzáles as his concepts united "La Raza" to fight for justice throughout the southwestern United States. His poem "I Am Joaquín/Yo soy Joaquín" is studied in numerous classrooms, colleges, and universities as influential literature of the Chicano civil rights movement. Gonzáles's contributions to Aztlán, the proposed Chicano community during the movement, are primarily focused on Chicano youth and students. His attention to education eventually led to the development of Escuela Tlatelolco in 1970. Named after the Aztec site for education and art, Escuela Tlatelolco is a school dedicated to motivating Chicano and Mexican children. Gonzáles's dedication to reforming conventional education standards has burgeoned cultural awareness in the Chicano community.

Monica E. Montelongo

FURTHER READING

Gonzáles, Rodolfo "Corky." *Message to Aztlán: Selected Writings of Rodolfo "Corky" Gonzáles*. Edited by Antonio Esquibel. Houston, Tex.: Arte Público Press, 2001. Collection of Gonzáles's writings from the period of the Chicano movement, includ-

ing two plays and the poem "I Am Joaquín/Yo soy Joaquín."

Marin, Christine. *A Spokesman of the Mexican American Movement: Rodolfo "Corky" Gonzáles and the Fight for Chicano Liberation, 1966-1972*. San Francisco: R&E Research Associates, 1977. Mostly concerned with Gonzáles's political career, this is a detailed biography of Gonzáles's early life and part in the Chicano movement.

Rosales, F. Arturo. *Chicano! The History of the Mexican American Civil Rights Movement*. 2d ed. Houston, Tex.: Arte Publico Press, 1997. Gives a history of the Chicano movement and places Gonzáles's activism in context with the politics of his fellow Chicano revolutionary leaders.

See also: César Chávez; Helen Fabela Chávez; José Ángel Gutiérrez; Dolores Huerta; Antonio Orendain; Reies López Tijerina.

PANCHO GONZALES

American tennis player

Gonzales rose from a working-class background to become a champion tennis player over the course of four decades. A fiery competitor and fan favorite, he spent the majority of his career in professional tournaments and tours before the advent of the sport's Open Era.

Latino heritage: Mexican
Born: May 9, 1928; Los Angeles, California
Died: July 3, 1995; Las Vegas, Nevada
Also known as: Richard Alonzo Gonzales; Gorgo; Pancho Gonzalez; Ricardo Alonzo González
Area of achievement: Sports

EARLY LIFE

Richard Alonzo Gonzales (gohn-ZAH-lehz) was the oldest of seven children born to parents who had immigrated from Chihuahua, Mexico, in the early 1900's. His father was a house painter and his mother a seamstress; the family lived in a working-class area of Los Angeles. Gonzales once reflected that, while he was not from the same privileged background as the majority of tennis players of his day, he and his siblings always had plenty of food and clean clothes. At age seven, Gonzales was injured when he struck a car while riding on a scooter,

leaving him with a permanent scar on his left cheek. As he gained prominence in tennis, that scar would come to symbolize prejudice against Mexican Americans, as it was implied that he had been involved in knife fights as a youth.

Drawn to sports, Gonzales began playing tennis at the age of twelve on public courts in his hometown. Tennis consumed all of his time and energy and Gonzales soon became disillusioned with school. His truancy and brief run-ins with the police, coupled with his Mexican heritage, hampered his full acceptance by the established tennis community. Nevertheless, at age fourteen and without the benefit of subsidized training and support, Gonzales became the top-ranked male tennis player in Southern California in his age group, winning several major tournaments. However, in an era when players were selected to advance to elite competition based on factors beyond on-court success, Gonzales was not chosen to represent his region and compete with the best on a national level. Gonzales was shattered and left the game for a while. He soon found trouble and served a year at a boys' prison for burglary. He eventually enlisted in the Navy as World War II ended, serving two years before being discharged, less than honorably, in 1947.

LIFE'S WORK

Gonzales returned to tennis as a nineteen-year-old and quickly picked up where he left off. Although he still was seen as an "outsider," detractors could not ignore the skill and success Gonzales displayed as he resumed his winning ways. He defeated the top players of the day and soon emerged as a rising tennis star through long-overdue national exposure in tournament play. Given the chance to return to Mexico in 1948 and compete as a Mexican, Gonzales was determined to make it in the United States and earned his first U.S. National Lawn Tennis Championship as a twenty-year-old. Although ranked only seventeenth nationally, Gonzales rode his trademark serve and volley to the straight-set championship win at Forest Hills, New York.

Gonzales would repeat that win the following year and remain an amateur through 1949, when he won doubles titles (with Frank Parker) at Wimbledon and the French Championships and helped the United States defeat Australia to win the Davis Cup.

Gonzales was recognized as the top U.S. player by this time and decided to turn professional. He signed a contract to join the professional tennis tour, on which he would play a series of matches against fellow Californian Jack Kramer. As professionals were barred from the "Grand Slam" events at that time, the choice was a logical one for the young Gonzales as it offered him the opportunity to earn a living while playing the game he loved and had begun to dominate. However, the leap to professional play, coupled with the travel and demands of the tour, resulted in another setback. Gonzales only won 27 of the 123 matches he played with Kramer and was dropped from future tours.

Gonzales returned to Los Angeles and played sporadically over the next two years in professional tours in Australia, New Zealand, England, and the United States. He signed an endorsement contract with Spalding that would endure for thirty years. By 1952, he had become a dominant force again in professional tennis and held the top spot in the men's game from 1952 to 1961, with the exception of 1953 and 1960. This included winning the U.S. Championships and Wembley Professional Championships twelve times as well as dominating various touring competitions against all of the leading players of the day. The serve-and-volley game was his signature, but he also became confident in his groundstrokes and in his defensive play, which he performed with speed and agility.

Gonzales often felt that he was not appropriately compensated for his participation in the tour and his success. This led to bitterness on his part and a reputation for aloofness. Tour players were paid a salary regardless of their success, and Gonzales resented his contractual obligations. One year, he earned as little as one-fifth as much as an opponent he regularly defeated. As a member of the tour sponsored by his longtime rival, Kramer, Gonzales often sought equitable pay but to little avail. Nevertheless, Gonzales recognized that he was the featured tennis player and had the record and fan support to prove it. This attitude made him unpopular with his peers, but it fueled his desire to be the best.

Gonzales's longevity was an inspiration to many; he was ranked in the U.S. Top 10 for twenty-four years and secured World Top 10 rankings from 1948 to 1969. When tennis opened its major tournaments to professionals, Gonzales reached the semifinals of the French Open and the quarterfinals of the U.S. Open. However, his performance at the 1969 Wimbledon was one for the ages. Gonzales was forty-one, a grandfather, and matched against twenty-five-year-old Charlie Pasarell in the first round. Gonzales lost the first set 24-22 and, as darkness fell, was dispatched by his younger opponent 6-1 in the second set before the match was suspended. The next day, Gonzales rebounded, winning 16-14, 6-3,

Pancho Gonzales. (AP Photo)

Mexican Americans in Tennis

Although it long has been a popular sport among the wealthy throughout Central and Latin America, tennis had limited appeal to Mexican Americans for many years. Pancho Gonzales overcame discrimination and other struggles to become one of the top players in the world. Following in his footsteps, Raul Ramirez gained fame in the 1970's, primarily for his doubles expertise. Angelica Gavaldon, a former Top 40 player, established a tennis academy in San Diego, California, to promote the development of young players. While Hispanic and Latino players have become prominent in tennis circles since World War II, Mexican Americans have not been as successful or as prevalent as South Americans on the world stage. Various efforts by the United State Tennis Association and local affiliates have been marginally successful in introducing the game to children of color, and diversity is slowly growing.

zales died of cancer in the summer of 1995. He was survived by his wife and eight children.

SIGNIFICANCE

Gonzales competed at a time when many forms of institutionalized racism and segregation were being challenged. His fiery nature may have not always endeared him to the tennis establishment, but he was a leading force in popularizing the game while playing in parts of five decades. Gonzales set the standard for the powerful serve-and-volley style of play that characterized the game for many years and served as a role model for a generation of Americans of color.

P. Graham Hatcher

FURTHER READING

Alamillo, Jose. "Richard 'Pancho' Gonzalez, Race, and the Print Media in Postwar Tennis America." *International Journal of the History of Sport* 26, no. 7 (June, 2009): 947-965. Examines the different perceptions of Gonzales in Mexican and American print media; includes documentation of attempts to shape his image and legacy both positively and negatively.

Gonzales, Doreen. *Richard "Pancho" Gonzales: Tennis Champion.* Berkeley Heights, N.J.: Enslow, 1998. Details Gonzales's playing career, achievements, and drive to excel.

Gonzales, Pancho, and Cy Rice. *Man with a Racket: The Autobiography of Pancho Gonzales.* New York: A. S. Barnes, 1959. Provides insights into the challenges and obstacles Gonzales encountered as a youth and as a tennis champion.

See also: Rosie Casals; Gigi Fernández.

11-9 to take the match. The five-plus hour match stood as a modern-day record for number of games played (112) for forty-one years and was largely responsible for tennis introducing a tie-break procedure for major tournament play. Remarkably, while still an active player, Gonzales was inducted into the International Tennis Hall of Fame in 1968.

Gonzales continued to play competitively throughout the 1970's, finishing his career as a popular member of the Seniors Tour. He eventually moved to Las Vegas, where he directed the tennis facilities at Caesars Palace. He was married six times, the final time to Rita Agassi, one of his protégés and the sister of Andre Agassi. Gon-

ELMA GONZÁLEZ

Mexican-born scientist and educator

The first female Mexican American scientist employed by the Univeristy of California system, González inspired women and Latinos to aspire for careers in scientific fields. As a mentor, she established programs and secured funds to encourage students from ethnic minorities to pursue advanced scientific studies and research careers.

Latino heritage: Mexican
Born: June 6, 1942; Ciudad Guerrero, Tamaulipas, Mexico
Also known as: Elma L. González

Areas of achievement: Science and technology; education; scholarship

EARLY LIFE

Elma L. González (gohn-ZAH-lehz) was born on June 6, 1942, to Nestor González and Efigenia González, both agricultural workers, at Ciudad Guerrero, Tamaulipas, Mexico. When she was six years old, González immigrated with her family to Hebbronville, Texas. She started school three years later and became bilingual. Her father read a geography book aloud to González and her younger siblings, Ovidio, Emma, and Elda. She listened to broadcasts from Mexico City on the family's radio, including a quiz show for children. González credits her early interest in science to her father's urging his children to be inquisitive about local animals and their environment, gathering eggs, nests, and specimens to show them.

During summers and early fall, González traveled with her family to farms in Texas and throughout the Midwest as migrant laborers, weeding and harvesting fruits, vegetables, cotton, and other agricultural products. She labored all day in fields and endured physically grueling tasks, staying in often-crowded migrant camps. In some places, González saw signs forbidding Mexicans to enter stores, restaurants, and other buildings. Knowing she would not begin classes when school opened, González read textbooks while traveling to keep up with her coursework. González's parents wanted her to quit school after eighth grade so she could work full time, but she successfully resisted; her goal was to graduate from college. In high school, González excelled scholastically and belonged to her school's science club. Her teachers encouraged González to request student loans to fund advanced education after her 1961 high school graduation.

LIFE'S WORK

González was the first person in her family to attend college, enrolling at Texas Woman's University, where she concentrated on biology and chemistry classes, intending to become a high school teacher. She worked in a greenhouse on campus. As a summer laboratory intern in the pharmacology department at Baylor University's College of Medicine, González realized that she wanted to pursue a scientific research career instead of teaching. She received a bachelor of science degree in 1965.

The rheumatology department laboratory at the University of Texas's Southwestern Medical School hired González as a technician. She next enrolled in the cell biology doctoral program at Rutgers University, researching the roles of organelles in cell functions. In 1969, her adviser, Dr. Charlotte Avers, took González to a New York Academy of Sciences meeting where she heard Dr. Harry Beevers's presentation. In 1972, González completed her Ph.D. Avers encouraged González to apply for a National Institutes of Health (NIH) postdoctoral position.

In December, 1972, González began a plant physiology fellowship supervised by Beevers at the University of California at Santa Cruz. In 1974, she accepted an assistant professor position in cell biology at the University of California at Los Angeles (UCLA), making her the first female Mexican American scientist to work at any University of California campus. González acquired research grants from the National Science Foundation (NSF) and the National Chicano Council on Higher Education. Her scientific publications were printed in periodicals including *Journal of Phycology* and *Plant Physiology*.

In 1977, González assisted peers to create the Society for the Advancement of Chicanos and Native Americans in Science (SACNAS), serving on that group's board of directors. She established the Center for Academic and Research Excellence at UCLA in 1990, distributing financial support from benefactors to programs including Minority Access to Research Careers (MARC), which González directed. González consulted with the American Association of Hispanics in Higher Education to increase Latino involvement in sciences. Active in UCLA's Chicano Studies Research Center, González belonged to its advisory committee and was on the editorial board of *Aztlán: A Journal of Chicano Studies*.

During a 1998 sabbatical, González was a visiting expert at Leiden University's Institute of Chemistry in the Netherlands. She presented a workshop for the NSF at Woods Hole Oceanographic Institution the next year. After her 2007 retirement, González moved to Newalla, Oklahoma.

SIGNIFICANCE

González empowered Latino Americans to consider and pursue careers in scientific fields because of her example, encouragement, and ability to provide financial and academic sponsors. Her work enabled more minority scientists to supervise laboratories and mentor students. González received honors recognizing her commitment to diversifying science. In 1998, the UCLA College of Letters and Science created the Elma González Award for Distinguished Undergraduate Research. SACNAS presented her with its 2004 Outstanding Scientist Award. The Los Angeles Commission on the Status of Women gave González its 2005 Pioneer Women Award. That year, she also received the Distinguished Teaching Award from UCLA's Academic Senate. In 2009, Texas Woman's University honored González with its Distinguished Alumni Award.

Elizabeth D. Schafer

FURTHER READING

Adam, Michelle. "Science Faculty: Shaping a Different Reality; Thirty-Year Struggle of Elma González,

UCLA." *Hispanic Outlook in Higher Education* 14, no. 25 (September 20, 2004): 36. Incorporates quotations from González and students, emphasizing her efforts to assist Latinos pursuing scientific research.

González, Elma. "What I Did on My Summer Vacation." In *Paths to Discovery: Autobiographies from Chicanas with Careers in Science, Mathematics, and Engineering*, edited by Norma E. Cantú. Introduction by Aída Hurtado. Los Angeles: University of California at Los Angeles Chicano Studies Research Center, 2008. Autobiographical account describes González's migrant worker experiences and development of her scientific career.

Horwedel, Dina M. "How They Beat the Odds: Chicana Scientists Share Stories of Overcoming Obstacles to Achieve Professional Success." *Diverse Issues in Higher Education* 22, no. 19 (November 3, 2005): 8-9. Discusses González's participation at a SACNAS conference, noting mentors, scientists, and family members who supported her scientific aspirations.

Singh, Ajay. "The Importance of Being Elma." *UCLA Magazine* 16, no. 4 (Spring, 2005): 40-43. Profile explores aspects of González's childhood and college years that influenced her scholarly interests and reinforced her work ethic, examining how her background influenced her developing MARC.

See also: Anne Maino Alvarez; Margarita Colmenares; France Anne Córdova; Francisco Dallmeier; Arturo Gómez-Pompa; Adriana C. Ocampo.

HENRY BARBOSA GONZÁLEZ

American politician

In a public career that spanned fifty years, including nearly forty years in the U.S. House of Representatives, González embodied the idealistic fighting spirit of New Society liberalism, confronting with uncompromising vigor institutionalized discrimination against minorities. He also served on a number of critical House committees, most notably as the longtime chair of the powerful House Committee on Banking, Finance, and Urban Affairs.

Latino heritage: Mexican
Born: May 3, 1916; San Antonio, Texas
Died: November 28, 2000; San Antonio, Texas
Also known as: Enrique Barbosa González
Area of achievement: Government and politics

EARLY LIFE
Henry Barbosa González (HEHN-ree bahr-bahr-BOH-sah gohn-ZAH-lez) was born in San Antonio, Texas, in 1916. González's father had been the mayor of Mapimí, a small town in the Mexican state of Durango. His parents had fled Durango in 1911 in the wake of the political oppression and economic uncertainties of the Mexican Revolution. Once safely across the border, González's father joined San Antonio's only Spanish-language daily newspaper, *La Prensa*, eventually becoming its managing editor. Although he faced routine schoolyard brutalities because of his Hispanic

roots, young Henry understood that the key to success rested with education; he mastered his adopted language and excelled in school. He attended San Antonio Junior College before graduating from the University of Texas at Austin and going on to complete a law degree from St. Mary's University in San Antonio, the oldest Catholic university in the Southwest. During World War II, González served in military intelligence as a radio and cable censor.

In 1943, he returned to San Antonio and joined the county's probation office, and within three years he was the city's chief juvenile probation officer. He resigned that same year, however, when he was told he could not hire an African American for his staff. Angered over conditions under which the city's Latino population lived, he served as executive secretary of the Pan-American Progressive Association, a community action organization. Over the next several years, González expanded his citywide grassroots activism on behalf of Latinos.

LIFE'S WORK
González understood that political power was the only way to combat bigotry and racism. In 1950, he ran unsuccessfully for the state legislature. Three years later, however, he won a seat on the San Antonio City Council, the first Mexican American to do so. His aggressive campaign agenda, targeting the city's segregated

Henry Barbosa González.
(AP Photo/Houston Chronicle, Sam C. Pierson, Jr.)

public facilities, attracted a broad coalition of Mexican Americans, blacks, and liberal whites. In 1956, he was elected state senator, again the first Latino ever to serve in that body. He would remain in the senate for the next five years, making a name for himself with his vigorous defense of minority rights, while being dismissed by his political opponents as "that Mexican." Despite González's unsuccessful run for Texas governor in 1958, Democratic presidential nominee John F. Kennedy tabbed him as a national campaign cochair. González helped organize the Viva Kennedy Clubs, a groundbreaking initiative designed to mobilize the Latino vote. Kennedy's strategy worked, and he received nearly 85 percent of the Latino vote nationwide.

In 1961, when President Kennedy named longtime U.S. Representative Paul J. Kilday from San Antonio's heavily Democratic twentieth district to serve as a judge on the federal Court of Military Appeals, González ran for the vacancy in a special election. His victory in November, 1961, marked the beginning of what would become his thirty-seven years of service—the longest tenure of any Hispanic to serve in the House of Representatives. González routinely won reelection by large

margins, often running unopposed, until his retirement in 1999.

Early on, González distinguished himself as a liberal firebrand. In only his second year in the House, at the height of Cold War paranoia, he voted against increased appropriations for the House Committee on Un-American Activities, citing its continuing violation of free speech and privacy, while weathering accusations of being a "pinko." Although he served with distinction on the powerful House Committee on Banking, serving as its chair from 1971 to 1981, it was his uncompromising and passionate support of President's Lyndon B. Johnson's 1964 civil rights initiatives—the Civil Rights Act, Housing Act, and Equal Opportunities Act—that first gained González a national name.

His undaunted, outspoken spirit of a passionate crusader defined González. For example, in the late 1960's, as House liaison on Latin American affairs, he exposed the woeful working conditions on Latin American farms. In 1978, amid growing public skepticism about government findings concerning the lone assassin theories in the shootings of both John Kennedy and Martin Luther King, Jr., González briefly chaired the twelve-member House Select Committee on Assassinations before resigning over a disagreement about the scope of power for the committee's controversial chief counsel.

Even as the American electorate turned to the conservative right with the rise of Ronald Reagan, González continued his unapologetic advocacy of the liberal agenda. He would play key roles in shepherding controversial legislation protecting small businesses, minority rights, the environment, and low-income housing, often battling formidable opposition from right-wing politicians. He emerged as a vigorous critic of the Federal Reserve and the savings and loan industry during the protracted banking crisis in the 1980's. Outraged over the Reagan administration's Iran-Contra dealings, he introduced a bill of impeachment in March, 1987. In January, 1991, he introduced a similar bill against Reagan's successor, George H. W. Bush, over his administration's campaign to wage what González, in an eloquent address to the House, termed an unconstitutional and undeclared Persian Gulf war against Iraq after its invasion of Kuwait.

An early supporter of Bill Clinton, González opposed Republican efforts to investigate Clinton's financial involvement in the Whitewater real estate project just months after Clinton had been sworn in as president. Although nearing eighty, González was a presence throughout the protracted House investigations into

Historical Exclusion of Latinos in Texas Politics

What is most remarkable about Henry Barbosa González is that coming in the late 1950's, nearly a century after Texas independence, he was among the first generation of Latino politicians in a state that is more than one-third Latino. Indeed, González's presence alone represented the breakthrough into the political system that the Latino population had long anticipated. Early in his political career, while serving on the San Antonio City Council, González tackled head-on the inequities of the city's entrenched racism and institutionalized segregation. In the Texas senate, he spoke passionately on the conditions that faced the state's Hispanic population: record unemployment levels, substandard public housing, underfunded public education, inadequate medical care, and voting rights irregularities. For the first time in Texas politics, Hispanics had a voice. Indeed, González first established a national reputation when he, along with a colleague, staged a twenty-two-hour filibuster in order to prevent passage of bills designed to subvert *Brown v. Board of Education*, the U.S. Supreme Court's landmark 1954 ruling mandating desegregation in public school systems.

Following González's election to the U.S. House of Representatives, the first legislation he introduced was designed to outlaw the poll tax, a political maneuver that had long disenfranchised Latinos, as well as other minorities struggling at the poverty line. González had his critics. During the late 1960's and early 1970's, Chicano activist groups advocating violent agitation and street protest dismissed González's strategy of working within the system as ineffective and slow. For a generation of Latinos, however, González himself came to represent their right to participate in the political process of their adopted country.

González, a respected collegiate boxer, remained a fighter for old-school liberal ideology. His most deeply held causes were born of his own upbringing in the working-class neighborhoods of West Side San Antonio, where his immigrant status often marginalized him. González fought to protect the rights of the underclass—the undereducated and the underprivileged—and demanded that the rich and powerful conduct their business with complete transparency and accountability. González was a maverick, who often opposed the House Hispanic Caucus, which he founded in 1976, because of the caucus's lukewarm endorsements for minority rights protection. He distinguished himself by his uncompromising honesty, and he was particularly lauded for his nearly decadelong investigation into the murky dealings that led to the collapse of the savings and loan industry in the 1980's.

Joseph Dewey

FURTHER READING

Auerbach, Robert D. *Deception and Abuse at the Fed: Henry B. González Battles Alan Greenspan's Bank.* Austin: University of Texas Press, 2008. Probing and accessible look at González's historic, and by this account heroic, challenge to the secretive workings of the powerful Federal Reserve and the subsequent revelations of mismanagement.

Bennett, W. Lance, and David L. Paletz, eds. *Taken by Storm: The Media, Public Opinion, and U.S. Foreign Policy in the Gulf War.* Chicago: University of Chicago Press, 1994. Wide-ranging collection of essays that examines the lead-up to the Kuwait invasion, with particular emphasis on the first Bush administration's careful manipulation of public opinion. Includes information on González's quixotic opposition stand.

Haugen, Brenda. *Henry B. González: Congressman of the People.* Minneapolis, Minn.: Compass Point Books, 2005. Careful review of González's public career, with particular emphasis on his liberal populism and his crusading spirit. Designed for young adults.

Rodriguez, Eugene, Jr. *Henry B. González: A Political Profile.* Manchester, N.H.: Ayer, 1976. Still considered the definitive account of González's political rise and his passionate defense of Chicano rights.

See also: Joe J. Bernal; Joaquín Castro; Julián Castro; Eligio de la Garza II; Irma Rangel; Leticia Van de Putte.

Clinton's finances, staunchly defending the administration against what he dismissed as partisan politics at its most vindictive. In failing health by late 1997, González declined to run for a nineteenth full term. His son, Charles A. González, long seen as his protégé, won the seat by a comfortable margin in 1998. González died of a heart attack two years later.

SIGNIFICANCE

Through close to fifty years of public service, even as his fervently held political ideology became the easy hobgoblin of the rising conservative political establishment,

RIGOBERTO GONZÁLEZ

American writer, educator, and literary critic

Known for his straightforward, raw depictions of migrant workers, immigrants, and gay Latinos, González is an award-winning poet, novelist, and writer. His writing transcends boundaries to address issues relevant to children, adolescents, and adults from all cultural and socioeconomic backgrounds.

Latino heritage: Mexican

Born: July 18, 1970; Bakersfield, California

Areas of achievement: Literature; poetry; education; gay and lesbian issues

EARLY LIFE

Rigoberto González (ree-goh-BEHR-toh gohn-ZAH-lehz) was born in Bakersfield, California to a poor family of migrant farmworkers and was raised in Michoacán, Mexico. The extended family often moved across the U.S.-Mexico border following the demand for farm labor in the United States. Accordingly González and his grandfather were born in the United States, but his own father and great-grandfather were born in Mexico.

As a child of the borderlands whose livelihood depended on a successful harvest, González was no stranger to poverty and hardship. Around 1980, his extended family moved to the city of Thermal in the Coachella Valley of Southern California. Three generations including his parents, brother, paternal grandparents, aunts, uncles, and eight cousins lived together under one roof and tried to save enough money to cover basic necessities. After a while, his parents decided to move from the shared house into their own modest apartment. With both of his parents working, the family enjoyed luxuries such as private indoor plumbing and occasional trips for fast food.

González's family life was improving, and he began keeping a journal to document this happy period. However, his mother soon suffered an aneurysm, underwent open-heart surgery, and died a few months later in 1982 at the age of thirty-one. González and his brother went back to live with his paternal grandparents. He attended school and worked in the fields picking grapes. He also spent considerable time reading as a way to escape his difficult circumstances, understand his budding homosexuality, and avoid his abusive grandfather.

After high school graduation, González enrolled at the University of California at Riverside, from which he graduated in 1992 with a bachelor of arts degree, becoming the first person in his family to earn a college degree. Later he attended the University of California at Davis, from which he graduated in 1994 with a master of arts degree. He then enrolled at Arizona State University, where he received a master of fine arts degree in writing in 1997. That same year, he moved with his partner to New York to pursue his writing career.

LIFE'S WORK

In 1999, González published his first book, the poetry collection *So Often the Pitcher Goes to Water Until It Breaks,* which included poems about his family as well as poems addressing social concerns such as immigration, racism, poverty, and exploitation. Drawing on his own cultural roots, the weighty collection eloquently illuminated issues related to the Mexican diaspora that were unfamiliar to many American readers. González's prose was well-received by the literary community, garnering many positive reviews, and his collection was named a selection of the 1999 National Poetry Series. That same year he received *The Crab Orchard Review*'s John Guyon Prize for Literary Nonfiction for his essay "Our Secret Other Worlds," which described his struggles with his sexuality.

González published his first novel, *Crossing Vines*, and his first children's picture book, *Soledad Sigh-Sighs/Soledad suspiros* in 2003. The novel, a winner of *Foreword* magazine's Fiction Book of the Year award, is a gritty, detailed account of the daily experiences of contemporary migrant farmworkers that covers topics such as the threat of immigration officials, abuse, poor living conditions, machismo, violence, and promiscuity that affect this population. *Soledad Sigh-Sighs*, the story of a young Puerto Rican girl who spends most of her time at home alone because her parents work during the evenings, received mixed reviews but exemplified the author's passion to address realistic problems faced by many Latino children every day.

González went on to publish another picture book, *Antonio's Card/La tarjeta de Antonio* (2005), which was a finalist for the Lambda Literary Award for gay literature and describes a young Latino boy's struggle to connect his home life with two mothers to his heteronormative classroom experiences. The next year he published another award-winning poetry collection, *Other Fugitives and Other Strangers*, followed by his groundbreaking *Butterfly Boy: Memories of a Chicano Mariposa* (2006). Winner of the American Book Award from the Before Columbus Foundation, this evocative memoir describes González's coming-of-age experiences as a gay, Chicano adolescent struggling with the societal, cultural, and familial problems common to many gay Latinos. The novel received positive literary praise, securing the author's writing career which has included a collection of short stories, *Men Without Bliss* (2008); a gay-themed Latino young-adult novel, *The Mariposa Club* (2009); and an edited volume of Latino literature, *Camino del Sol: Fifteen Years of Latina and Latino Writing* (2010).

As a result of his writing success, González received numerous invitations to serve as a visiting professor in universities around the world. From 2001 to 2007, he held academic positions as writer in residence in Spain, Brazil, Costa Rica, Scotland, Switzerland, and various cities across the United States. During this time period, he began writing literary criticism of Latino literature for various publications such *The El Paso Times* and serving on editorial boards for publications such as the *Poets and Writers Magazine*. In 2007, he became an associate professor of English at Rutgers University at Newark.

González has received several honors and awards for his writing abilities. Some of these include a John Simon Guggenheim Memorial Fellowship in creative writing (2000), a National Endowment for the Arts grant, and one of *Out* magazine's "One Hundred Men and Women Who Made 2008 a Year to Remember." His collected papers from 1993 to 2008 are available at the University of California at Los Angeles's Chicano Studies Research Center Library.

SIGNIFICANCE

Capturing the emotional experiences and daily lives of both migrant workers and queer Latinos, González's broad body of work transcends cultures, races, and ages, highlighting the universality of the human condition. A fresh voice in the literary field, he significantly contributes not only to the growing body of Chicano and queer literature but also to the careers of budding writers through his numerous appointments on advisory boards and mentoring opportunities as a college professor. At the same time, his literary criticisms of more than two hundred contemporary works of Latin American literature mark him as one of the few mentor-critic-writers in the profession.

Jamie Campbell Naidoo

FURTHER READING

González, Rigoberto. *Butterfly Boy: Memories of a Chicano Mariposa.* Madison: University of Wisconsin Press, 2006. Emotional memoir describing González's coming-of-age experiences as a poor, gay, Chicano teen struggling for acceptance and a sense of self.

_____. "A Home That Won't Refuse Me." *Literary Review* 45, no. 4 (Summer, 2002): 691-700. González describes his experiences as the child of migrant farmworkers, detailing the various hardships of the family and his decision to escape the poverty cycle.

López, Tiffany Ana. "Reading Trauma and Violence in U.S. Latina/o Children's Literature." In *Ethnic Literary Traditions in American Children's Literature,* edited by Michelle Pagni Stewart and Yvonne Atkinson. New York: Palgrave Macmillan, 2009. Critically examines how González addresses the emotionally traumatic experiences of Latino children in his children's picture books *Antonio's Card* and *Soledad Sigh-Sighs.*

See also: Julia Alvarez; Gloria Anzaldúa; Ana Castillo; Junot Díaz; Cherríe Moraga; John Rechy.

TONY GONZALEZ

American football player

Gonzalez is a professional football player who has set franchise and league records as a tight end. He led his teams to winning records and to the play-offs. He is also a role model for his work ethic and determination to succeed.

Latino heritage: Cape Verdean

Born: February 27, 1976; Torrance, California

Also known as: Anthony David Gonzalez

Areas of achievement: Football; basketball

Tony Gonzalez. (AP Photo)

EARLY LIFE

Tony Gonzalez (gohn-ZAH-lehz) was born in Torrance, California, on February 27, 1976. His mother, Judy, divorced his father, Joseph, when Gonzalez was a child. She married Michael Saltzman, a hospital administrator. Gonzalez's paternal grandfather immigrated to the United States from Cape Verde (an island nation off the coast of West Africa that was previously a Portuguese colony); his paternal grandmother was Jamaican, while his maternal grandparents were American Indian (Apache and Sioux), African, Irish, and Polish. Gonzalez's original family name was Goncals, which immigration officials changed to Gonzalez when his paternal grandfather arrived in the United States.

Growing up in Southern California, Gonzalez surfed and skateboarded. His brother introduced him to football, which Gonzalez played in the Pop Warner youth league. He also played basketball in middle school. Gonzalez attended Huntington Beach High School, where he played basketball and football. As a junior, he received an honorable mention on *USA Today*'s All-USA basketball team after averaging 17.1 points and 9.1 rebounds per game. He also developed as a football player. Gonzalez had 68 tackles and 6 sacks

as middle linebacker on his high school team. He also caught 38 passes for 800 yards and 7 touchdowns as a tight end his junior year. As a senior, he recorded 13 touchdowns and caught 62 passes for 945 yards. As a result, he was named a first-team All-American as a linebacker and tight end. In basketball, Gonzalez averaged 22 points per game as a senior. In 1994, he was named Orange County's high school athlete of the year. Although many colleges recruited him for basketball and football, he enrolled at the University of California at Berkeley (Cal).

LIFE'S WORK

After Gonzalez's junior year at Cal, he declared himself eligible for the 1997 National Football League (NFL) draft. The Kansas City Chiefs selected him with the thirteenth pick of the first round. During his first year with the Chiefs, Gonzalez played in sixteen games, accumulating 368 yards, 33 receptions, and 2 touchdowns. He also played on special teams, where he blocked a punt against the San Francisco 49ers. The Chiefs finished the regular season with a 13-3 record, best in the American Football Conference (AFC), but lost in the AFC divisional play-off round to the Denver Broncos.

In 1998, Gonzalez had 59 receptions for 621 yards and 2 touchdowns. The next season, he recorded a team-high of 76 receptions for 849 yards and 11 touchdowns. His touchdown total was the second highest in team history and was second among all AFC pass-catchers. At the end of the season, Gonzalez was named to the Pro Bowl. In 2000, Gonzalez led all NFL tight ends in receptions, touchdowns, and yards. He also was the first tight end in NFL history to have four consecutive 100-yard receiving games. Gonzalez was awarded his second trip to the Pro Bowl and a first-team All-Pro selection.

In the 2001 season, Gonzalez started all sixteen games and caught 73 passes for 917 yards and 6 touchdowns. He earned Pro Bowl and first-team All-Pro selections again, but the Chiefs finished the season with a 6-10 record. During the summer of 2001, Gonzalez tried his hand at professional basketball, playing on the rookie team of the National Basketball Association's Miami Heat. Although he missed the 2002 NFL preseason, he signed a seven-year contract worth $31 million with the Chiefs.

During the 2002 season, Gonzalez started all sixteen games and made 63 catches for 773 yards and 7 touchdowns, earning his fourth Pro Bowl appearance. The Chiefs made the play-offs in 2003, when Gonzalez led all NFL tight ends in receiving yards (916),

Gonzalez's College Basketball Career

In addition to playing football, Tony Gonzalez also was a standout basketball player who played both sports at the University of California at Berkeley (Cal). His basketball position was as a forward. During his freshman year, Gonzalez played twenty-six basketball games, starting three of them. He averaged 7.1 points and 3.9 rebounds per game. He also scored a career-high 29 points versus Washington State University. During his junior year, he played in twenty-eight games, starting six. He averaged 6.8 points and 5.4 rebounds per game. That also was the year the Cal Bears advanced to the Sweet Sixteen round of the National Collegiate Athletic Association basketball tournament, in which he started all three of the team's games. He posted a season high of 23 points in the team's second-round win versus Villanova.

receptions (71), and touchdowns (10). The team won the AFC West division but lost to the Indianapolis Colts in the AFC divisional round. At the end of the season, Gonzalez returned to the Pro Bowl and was selected to his fourth All-Pro team.

The 2004 season saw Gonzalez record 102 receptions (an NFL-high) for 1,258 yards and 7 touchdowns. His total of 102 receptions was the most for a tight end in NFL history. That season also marked the first time since 1986 that a tight end won the league's receiving title. During the 2005 season, Gonzalez became the first tight end in NFL history to record eight consecutive seasons with 50 or more catches. The Chiefs missed the play-offs despite a 10-6 record. They finished the 2006 season at 9-7 record, which earned them a spot in the wild-card round of the play-offs. The Chiefs lost to the Indianapolis Colts, 23-8.

In 2007, Gonzalez led all NFL tight ends in receptions (99) and receiving yards (1,172) and was selected to his ninth consecutive Pro Bowl. In October, 2007, he broke Shannon Sharpe's tight end record for receiving touchdowns. That December, against the New York Jets, he broke Sharpe's record for most catches by a tight end in NFL history and recorded his third season with 1,000 receiving yards. He also earned his tenth consecutive Pro Bowl selection that season, the most for a tight end.

During the 2008 offseason, Gonzalez was traded to the Atlanta Falcons for a 2010 second-round draft pick. In his first season with the Falcons, Gonzalez finished second on the team in receptions (83) and receiving yards (867). His receptions set a Falcons record for most by a tight end in a season. His numbers declined slightly in the 2010 season, but he recorded 6 touchdowns and remained a vital part of the team's offense.

Gonzalez and his girlfriend, October, held a commitment ceremony on July 20, 2007, in Huntington Beach. They have a daughter named Malia. Gonzalez also has a son named Nikko from a previous relationship. In 1998, he established the Tony Gonzalez Foundation, which supports the Boys and Girls Clubs of America and Shadow Buddies. Shadow Buddies provides racially diverse male and female dolls to ill children.

SIGNIFICANCE

Gonzalez is considered one of the best tight ends in football history. Despite playing on teams with mediocre records, he set franchise and league records and earned widespread respect for his durability, dedication, and talent.

Tina Chan

FURTHER READING

Gonzalez, Tony, and Mitzi Dulan. *The All-Pro Diet: Lose Fat, Build Muscle, and Live Like a Champion.* New York: Rodale Books, 2009. Gonzalez discusses the diet and exercise program that changed his life on and off the field.

Sandler, Michael. *Tony Gonzalez.* New York: Bearport, 2010. Aimed at younger readers, this biography offers a concise overview of Gonzalez's life and career.

Stallard, Mark. "Tony Gonzalez." In *The Kansas City Chiefs Encyclopedia.* Champaign, Ill.: Sports Publishing, 2002. Written relatively early in Gonzalez's career, this entry nonetheless describes his importance to the Chiefs and his significance in their history.

See also: Tedy Bruschi; Jeff Garcia; Anthony Muñoz; Tony Romo.

MARTÍN GRAMÁTICA

Argentine-born football player, entrepreneur, and philanthropist

Gramática became a star placekicker for several National Football League teams and was the first Argentine American to win a Super Bowl ring. After ending his playing career, he became a businessman and contributed to a variety of charitable causes.

Latino heritage: Argentinean
Born: November 27, 1975; Buenos Aires, Argentina
Also known as: Automática
Areas of achievement: Football; business; philanthropy

EARLY LIFE

Born of Argentine and Italian heritage, Martín Gramática (mahr-TEEN grah-MA-tih-cah) was the eldest of three sons of soccer professional William Gramática and wife Laura. In the early 1980's the family immigrated to the United States, settling in LaBelle, Florida, a small town with a significant Latino population. William and Laura Gramática opened up a family-style restaurant in town, featuring Argentine and Italian cuisine, where Martín and his brothers often worked after school.

Gramática attended LaBelle High School. In his senior year, the football coach asked him to become the kicker for the team, and he agreed, though he had never played football before. Using the skills acquired from playing soccer with brothers Guillermo ("Bill") and Santiago—both of whom also became professional football kickers—he was successful on 8 of 10 field goal attempts, including one from 52 yards, and he hit 22 extra points. In addition, 77 percent of his kickoffs went into the end zone for touchbacks. Because of his kicking prowess, the 5-foot, 8-inch, 170-pound Gramática was recruited to play at Kansas State University. He played all four years, with a year off as a redshirt because of a knee injury. During his junior year in 1997, he was the top placekicker in the nation, drilling 19 of 20 attempts, setting a school record with 14 points on 3 field goals and 5 extra points in a single game, and tying the Big Twelve record with a 55-yard field goal. He did even better during his senior year, setting a kicking record by tallying 135 points. In a game against Northern Illinois University, he hit the longest field goal in National Collegiate Athletic Association (NCAA) history without a tee: 65 yards. By the time he graduated from Kansas State in 1999 with a degree in social science, Gramática was the school's career scoring leader with 349 points.

LIFE'S WORK

In 1999, the Tampa Bay Buccaneers selected Gramática in the National Football League (NFL) draft. He played for Tampa for five seasons, making the Pro Bowl in 2000 and 2001, and he started for the National Football Conference side in the 2001 game. In 2002, he played for the Buccaneer team that won Super Bowl XXXVII. The following season, he suffered a leg injury that affected his accuracy, particularly on field goal attempts of more than 40 yards. In 2004, the team released him.

Gramática caught on with the Indianapolis Colts at the end of 2004, and he spent the rest of the season solely as a kickoff specialist. During the remainder of 2005, he recuperated from lower abdominal surgery. In early 2006, Gramática signed with the New England Patriots to compete for a vacant placekicking job, but he was released after several months. The Dallas Cowboys signed him in late November, and in his first game with his new team he hit a 46-yard field goal to win the game. In 2007, Gramática signed a two-year deal with the Cowboys. However, he reinjured his leg, and the

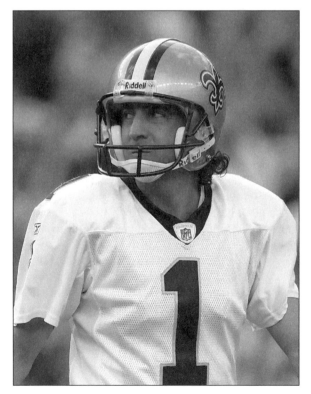

Martín Gramática. (AP Photo)

team released him. The New Orleans Saints signed him at the end of 2007 to replace the injured regular kicker, and two weeks later he matched his personal best as a professional with a 55-yard field goal. He started the 2008 season well for the Saints, but nagging injuries led to crucial misses and the team eventually released him. Gramática ultimately announced his retirement. During his professional career, he made 155 field goals out of 203 attempts, or more than 76 percent. His 13-of-14 field goal conversion rate (92.9 percent) in championship play-offs set an NFL record.

Married to Ashlee Blake Gramática and the father of two sons, Gramática and his family settled in the Tampa area. Thanks to shrewd investments during his professional football playing days, he has become a prosperous businessman. He and his two brothers operate Gramática Kicking Camps locally, instructing athletes in punting and placekicking. Martín is also involved in real estate: In 2010, he sold for $2 million a 560-acre parcel of farmland purchased eight years earlier to an international polo organization, Martín also co-owns Gramática Group, an architectural design and engineering firm.

Another related enterprise is Gramática SIPS (Structurally Insulated Panels) International, of which Martín serves as president and chief executive officer. The company makes layered polystyrene and cement composite panels that make possible the construction of storm-resistant, energy-efficient homes in three to five days. In early 2011, Gramática SIPS donated enough panels to build housing for sixty or more people displaced by the 2010 Haitian earthquake. The company has likewise donated materials to Rebuilding Together, Habitat for Humanity, Wounded Veterans of America, and other charitable organizations.

Martín Gramática has made an especially concentrated effort to assist New Orleans, where he last played football, by working with a local coalition to supply housing materials for low-income families that lost dwellings in Hurricane Katrina. Gramática ultimately intends to open a facility for manufacturing SIPS in New Orleans in order to create jobs while constructing a multitude of sturdy, green-energy prefabricated homes to help rebuild the shattered city.

SIGNIFICANCE

An average-sized man with a powerful leg, Martín Gramática parlayed the soccer skills learned in South America into a successful career as a placekicker in high school, college, and professional football. Nicknamed

---

Evolution of the NFL Kicking Game

American professional football has long been more about players using their hands—to carry, throw, and catch the ball—than their feet. When the American Professional Football Association began in 1920 (the name was changed to the National Football League, or NFL, in 1922), the ball was squat, modeled on a rugby ball. Early professional games were rugbylike in play, too, featuring runs, handoffs, and laterals, with rare forward passes: The shape of the ball made gripping difficult and discouraged overhand tosses. Kicking was an afterthought, used more as a defensive than an offensive weapon. Dropkicks were often used as a surprise tactic to gain position on the field. There were no kicking specialists. In the NFL's first years, position players—quarterbacks, linemen, or running backs—handled kickoffs, punts, and extra points and occasionally attempted dropkicked field goals. A 50 percent success rate was considered acceptable. In the 1920's, all-around athletes like Jim Thorpe, Paddy Driscoll, Al Bloodgood, and Pete Henry were known as effective dropkickers.

The situation began to change in the mid-1930's. The ball became slimmer and more pointed, which made it easier to pass but more difficult to drop-kick because it bounced erratically. Field goals required an accurate long snapper and a sure-handed holder and were reserved as a desperation measure when an offensive drive stalled.

Kicking began to become a more potent offensive weapon in the 1940's with the advent of semispecialists, like Hall of Fame inductees Lou "The Toe" Groza (an all-star lineman) and George Blanda (a quarterback), who each employed a conventional style: a straight-on approach to strike the ball with the toes. Kicking took a quantum leap in the mid-1960's, when Hungarian-born Pete Gogolak pioneered the soccer style, hitting the ball with the arch of the foot, which proved superior for distance and accuracy. Since then, kicking has become an integral part of the NFL game, with specialists, all using the soccer style, routinely hitting 75 percent or more of attempts from long distances and seldom missing extra points. In 2011, the top twenty-five scorers in NFL history were all kickers, led by a Dane, Morten Andersen (2,544 career points), and a South African, Gary Anderson (2,434 points).

"Automática" in college for his uncanny accuracy, he was twice selected for the All-Big Twelve team, won the Lou Groza Award as America's best collegiate kicker, and was later inducted into Kansas State University's Ring of Honor. The first Argentinean to win a Super Bowl ring, with Tampa Bay in 2002, Gramática played with five NFL teams in a ten-year career curtailed by injuries. He has become an ambassador for American football as a sponsor and coach in American Football Argentina (Football Americano Argentina, or FAA), an association that helps local youth through competition in the sport.

Jack Ewing

FURTHER READING

Gay, Timothy. *Football Physics: The Science of the Game.* Emmaus, Pa.: Rodale Books, 2004. A close-up look at the laws of motion at work on the playing field and the aerodynamics affecting the ovate spheroid called a football, particularly when it is passed, fumbled, or kicked.

McGinn, Bob. *The Ultimate Super Bowl Book: A Complete Reference to the Stats, Stars, and Stories Behind Football's Biggest Game—and Why the Best Team Won.* Beverly, Mass.: MVP Books, 2009. A useful resource for detailed information about all aspects of the Super Bowl, from inception through the 2009 game, including Gramática's contributions to Tampa Bay's victory in 2002.

The New York Times. *The Greatest Moments in Tampa Bay Buccaneers History.* Bergenfield, N.J.: Retrographics, 2009. A collection of newspaper clippings illustrating highlights from each of the franchise's seasons, including Tampa Bay's triumph in Super Bowl XXXVII.

See also: Tedy Bruschi; Jeff Garcia; Tony Gonzalez; Tony Romo; Danny Villanueva.

PEDRO GUERRERO

Dominican-born baseball player

One of the most feared sluggers in the National League, Guerrero also was well known for his ability to play multiple positions, including outfield and first and third bases. As a member of the Los Angeles Dodgers, he played a pivotal role during the 1978 World Series against the New York Yankees, shared the most valuable player award in 1981, and was a key figure in the success of the Dodgers throughout the 1980's.

Latino heritage: Dominican

Born: June 29, 1956; San Pedro de Macorís, Dominican Republic

Also known as: Pete Guerrero

Area of achievement: Baseball

EARLY LIFE

Some of the best baseball players to come from the Dominican Republic are born in the city of San Pedro de Macorís. Pedro Guerrero (PEH-droh gah-RAR-oh), the son of Francisco Sanchez and M. Guerrero, was born in this city on June 29, 1956, before the first wave of Latino stars had begun to enter into Major League Baseball. Pedro's older brother Luis would later play minor-league baseball.

Pedro Guerrero. (AP Photo)

In January 1973, at the age of sixteen, Guerrero was signed by the Cleveland Indians for $2,500 after leading the entire roster of Dominican players with a .438 batting average. Relocating in Sarasota, Florida, where he joined an entry-level operation for teenage players, high school graduates, or other newcomers signed from Latin America, Guerrero played third base and shortstop with the Florida Rookie League for a brief period of time. Regie Otero, the Cleveland Indian scout who had previously recruited him, had secured a place in the Los Angeles Dodgers' organization and convinced that team to acquire the young and talented Guerrero, trading him for pitcher Bruce Ellingsen. Guerrero worked his way through the Dodger's system by playing for the team's Triple-A farm club, the Albuquerque Isotopes. On Friday, September 22, 1978, Guerrero made his Major League debut with the Los Angeles Dodgers during a game against the San Diego Padres.

LIFE'S WORK

Displaying his prowess for playing multiple positions, Guerrero played shortstop and was an outfielder in order to stay in the team's batting lineup. Other Dodgers, like Steve Garvey, Davey Lopes, and Ron Cey, played the first-, second-, and third-base positions that Guerrero coveted. Shortly after his debut, Guerrero damaged his ligaments while sliding into second base. He also married the daughter of Denise Chavez, a New Mexico state senator.

In the 1981 World Series against the New York Yankees, Guerrero received the Most Valuable Player award, along with fellow Dodgers Ron Cey and Steve Yeager. Guerrero again covered several positions, switching between center field and right field, and was an unstoppable force during game six, hitting a two-run triple, a two-run single, and a solo home run to enable the Dodgers to win the World Series. Guerrero had an equally good year in 1982, becoming the first Dodger to hit thirty home runs and steal twenty bases in one season. By the 1983 season, he had started playing at third base and was selected for the National League All-Star team. Guerrero scored thirty-two home runs in both 1982 and 1983, although he had defensive troubles in his new position. He was later chosen to play in the All-Star Games in 1985, 1987, and 1989.

Guerrero, who throughout his fifteen-year major-league career suffered from pains associated with knee surgery, pulled hamstrings, a pinched nerve in the neck, strained wrists, a fractured leg, and back spasms, was traded to the St. Louis Cardinals on August 16, 1988, for pitcher John Tudor, the National League leader in earned

---

Guerrero's Post-Major-League Career

Pedro Guerrero's life after professional baseball has been as tumultuous as it has been private. Throughout his career, Guerrero had problems with alcohol and drugs, though his substance abuse did not fully affect his playing In 1993, he played for the Jalisco, Mexico, Charros, a Mexican League team that has appeared, disappeared, and then reappeared more than three times since its debut in 1949. While there is little information about this team, it is known that Guerrero was dropped from its roster in June, 1993. The following month, Guerrero signed a one-year contract with the Sioux Falls Canaries of the Northern League.

Guerrero ran into trouble in 2000, when he was charged with conspiracy to purchase thirty-three pounds of cocaine from undercover Drug Enforcement Administration agents, but he was acquitted of these charges. Several years later, at the age of fifty-three, Guerrero told reporters that he wanted to return to baseball. The man who had been accused of disruptive behavior and conflicts with team members when he was a baseball player now claimed he was a changed person who attended church, read the Bible, and was a lot kinder to his body and to other people.

---

run averages. At the time, it was rumored that Guerrero was being traded because of conflicts with Dodger teammate Kirk Gibson. Believing that the Dodger organization had given up on him, Guerrero made angry statements to the press about the team's management and decision to let him go, which he later apologized for with the help of Dodger manager Tommy Lasorda.

Guerrero's greatest season was in 1989, yet because of his history of injuries, his playing suffered throughout the years and he remained on the disabled list for the majority of 1992. His final game with the St. Louis Cardinals was on October 4, 1992, ending his baseball career after he had played 1,536 games, scored 215 home runs, and garnered a lifetime batting average of .300. Guerrero then played postprofessional baseball with the Sioux Falls Canaries and the Charros of Jalisco, Mexico. In 2000, he was charged with conspiracy to purchase thirty-three pounds of cocaine from undercover Drug Enforcement Administration agents, but he was acquitted after his attorney argued that his low IQ prevented him from understanding that he had agreed to a drug deal. In 2011, Guerrero, his wife, and his daughter Ashley Maria were living quietly in Rio Rancho, New Mexico.

SIGNIFICANCE

Baseball writer Bill James considered Pedro Guerrero to be "the best hitter God has made in a long time." At the time of his greatest successes with the Los Angeles Dodgers, Guerrero's athletic abilities were so respected by team manager Tommy Lasorda and the organization that he was constantly shifted from position to position. A multifaceted, powerful player, Guerrero was a five time All-Star throughout his professional major-league career. Heralded as King of Dodgertown, Guerrero's batting, home runs, and base-stealing skills broke records for the team, and he was crucial to the success that led to their World Series win in 1988, though he had already been traded to the St. Louis Cardinals by the time the team celebrated its victory.

Gustavo Adolfo Aybar

FURTHER READING

Bjarkman, Peter C. *Baseball with a Latin Beat*. Jefferson, N.C: McFarland, 1994. Describes the tremendous influence of Latin baseball players in the United States and discusses baseball's evolution in countries like Cuba, Puerto Rico, and the Dominican Republic.

Klein, Alan M. *Sugarball: The American Game, the Dominican Dream*. New Haven, Conn.: Yale University Press, 1991. Covers the history of baseball in the Dominican Republic and the support of sugar refineries for the nation's teams. Offers a critique of the scouting practices employed by Americans recruiting talented players from the island.

Oleksak, Michael M., and Mary Adams Oleksak. *Béisbol: Latin Americans and the Grand Old Game*. Grand Rapids, Mich.: Masters Press, 1991. A great resource for information on Latin American baseball players and their contributions to the game, containing an interesting section on Pedro Guerrero and other Dominican players of influence.

See also: Joaquín Andújar; César Cedeño; Tony Fernandez; Julio Franco; Andrés Galarraga; Dennis Martínez; Rafael Palmeiro; Fernando Valenzuela.

NICOLÁS GUILLÉN

Cuban-born writer and poet

Guillén is considered the pioneer of Afro-Cuban literature. His literary and journalistic work was associated with the Cuban Revolution from very early in his career. He advocated for a mestiza Latin American identity—an interethnic form of working-class solidarity.

Latino heritage: Cuban
Born: July, 10 1902; Camagüey, Cuba
Died: July 16, 1989; Havana, Cuba
Also known as: Cristobal Guillén y Batista
Areas of achievement: Literature; journalism

EARLY LIFE

Nicolás Guillén (nihk-oh-LAHS je-YEHN) was born Cristobal Guillén y Batista in 1902, only four years after Spain handed Cuba over to the United States and the same year that the island became formally independent. However, the Platt Agreement granted the United States de facto control over Cuba. Guillén's early life was marked by the political and economic instability created by these developments.

The modernization of the sugarcane industry and the massive infusion of American capital between 1890 and 1920 resulted in the displacement of black farmers. Although Guillén grew up in a mulatto, middle-class family, the political unrest that resulted from the reconfiguration of Cuba's economy affected him all the same.

After its independence, Cuba underwent a series of revolts in which farmers struggled to gain recognition and rights in the new republic. In the revolt of 1917, Guillén's father, a journalist and liberal senator, was assassinated by the repressive government of Cuban president Mario García Menocal with the aid of American troops. While the old Spanish colonial government had kept most blacks in slavery and forced servitude, the new Cuban republic continued to marginalize blacks and to favor the interests of the international sugarcane trade.

After the death of his father, Guillén worked as a typographer for the daily newspaper *El nacional* while publishing some of his early poems in local magazines. He began working as a journalist for the daily *Las dos repúblicas* at the age of eighteen. In 1937, Guillén, already a well-known journalist, joined the Cuban Communist Party.

Nicolás Guillén. (AP Photo)

LIFE'S WORK

The publication of Guillén's first poetry book *Motivos de son* (1930), in which he portrays Afro-Cuban culture, coincided with the consolidation of the negritude movement launched by Aimé Césaire, Léopld Senghor, and León-Gontran Damas. While Guillén was certainly influenced by the negritude movement, his exploration of the African contribution to Cuban culture must be understood in the wider context of the efforts of African, African American, and Latin American communities to reinterpret their histories and cultural legacies.

Besides the negritude movement, the end of the nineteenth century and early decades of the twentieth century were also marked by the development of an African American conscience as expressed in such movements as the Harlem Renaissance in the United States and indigenism in Haiti. In fact, Guillén's work is deeply informed by the long Latin American intellectual tradition that explores *mestizaje* (the mixing of races), not just African heritage, as the source of cultural identity. Guillén's did not seek to develop an alternative to Latin American tradition but wanted to expand this tradition to incorporate African heritage. As he explained, "We won't have a well-developed Creole poetry if we

forget the black" who provide "essential ingredients in our cocktail."

Guillén's poetry covered a wide range of topics and styles: European-based modernism, folklorist interest in Afro-Cubanism, overtly political poetry, and the more ironic critique of social issues that characterizes his later work. Some of his most celebrated poetry books are: *Sóngoro Cosongo* (1931), *West Indies, Ltd.* (1934), *Cantos para soldados y sones para turistas* (1937), *La paloma de vuelo popular: Elegías* (1958), and *El gran zoo* (1967). *Prosa de prisa* (1962) and *El diario que a diario* (1972) contain a selection of his best journalistic prose. Guillén's celebration of the Cuban revolution comes across as somewhat complacent, particularly in books like *Tengo* (1964), where he seems to argue that all revolutionary objectives have already been fulfilled.

It is important, however, to remember that Guillén's notion of ethnic and national identity is inextricable from his commitment to class solidarity. Once he overcame his initial folklorist stage, Guillén understood negritude as a transnational, interethnic movement of working-class solidarity. While his commitment to the Cuban Revolution may seem to be uncritical of its shortcomings, Guillén's revolutionary fervor must be understood in the larger context of transatlantic unity.

SIGNIFICANCE

Nicolás Guillén's place in the history of Latin American literature has always been and continues to be controversial. The notion of negritude has been harshly criticized for its essentialist representation of African, African American, and Latin American identity. Although Guillén's *mestizaje* supposedly overcomes essentialist definitions of ethnic identity by celebrating the fusion of races and cultural traditions, his poetry has been criticized for reiterating a traditional patriarchal discourse. Guillén, however, continues to be acknowledged as one of the pioneers who raised awareness of the importance of African cultural traditions in Latin America and as a first-rate poet whose command of the Spanish language combined an excellent knowledge of Spanish literary traditions and Caribbean oral literature

Adolfo Campoy-Cubillo.

FURTHER READING

Adotevi, Stanislas S. K. "Negritude Is Dead: The Burial." *New African Literature and the Arts* 3 (1973): 89-104. One of the first critiques of the notion of negritude, Adotevi criticizes the essentialist representation of African identity.

Andrews, George R. *Afro-Latin America, 1800-2000.* Oxford, England: Oxford University Press, 2004. A thorough analysis of the socioeconomic developments that shaped the experience of Afro-Hispanics during the last two centuries.

Guillén, Nicolás. *The Daily Daily.* Translated by Vera M. Kutzinski. Berkeley: University of California Press, 1989. Collection of journalistic essays and poems in which Guillén critiques prerevolutionary Cuban society.

Kutzinski, Vera M. *Sugar's Secrets: Race and the Erotics of Cuban Nationalism.* Charlottesville: University Press of Virginia, 1993. An in-depth study of Cuban nationalist discourse that pays special attention to issues of gender.

See also: Reinaldo Arenas; Lydia Cabrera; Lourdes Casal; Cristina García.

OZZIE GUILLÉN

Venezuelan-born baseball player

Guillén played shortstop for sixteen years as a member of several Major League baseball teams, most notably the Chicago White Sox, and then shifted his focus toward coaching and managing. As manager of the White Sox, he led the team to a World Series victory in 2005.

Latino heritage: Venezuelan

Born: January 20, 1964; Ocumare del Tuy, Miranda, Venezuela

Also known as: Oswaldo José Guillén Barrio; Paio

Area of achievement: Baseball

EARLY LIFE

Oswaldo José Guillén Barrio, better known as Ozzie Guillén (AH-zee gee-YEHN), was born on January 20, 1964, in Ocumare del Tuy, Miranda, Venezuela. By the age of nineteen, Guillén had married Ibis Cardenas, with whom he had three sons: "Ozzie, Jr.," Oney, and Ozney. His professional career as a ballplayer began in the San Diego Padres organization, where he spent four seasons (1980-1984). Prior to the 1985 season, he was traded with pitchers Tim Lollar and Bill Long and infielder Luis Salazar to the Chicago White Sox in exchange for pitchers LaMarr Hoyt, Todd Simmons, and Kevin Kristan. Guillén played his first game in the majors with the White Sox on April 9, 1985, at the age of twenty-one. As the team's shortstop, the 5-foot, 11-inch Guillén garnered a batting average of .273 and earned both the American League and *The Sporting News* rookie of the year awards in 1985, his first full season.

LIFE'S WORK

Guillén played in three All-Star Games in 1988, 1990, and 1991. In 1990, he earned the Gold Glove Award for his defensive play with a .977 fielding percentage (a measurement of defensive proficiency). In his last three years in the major leagues, Guillén played with the Baltimore Orioles (1998), Atlanta Braves (1998-1999), and Tampa Bay Devil Rays (2000). During his 1999 season with the Atlanta Braves, the team won the National League pennant but lost the World Series to the New York Yankees in four games. He played his last game

Ozzie Guillén. (AP Photo)

in the majors with the Tampa Bay Devil Rays on October 1, 2000. After sixteen years in the major leagues, he amassed a .264 batting average, 1,764 hits, 28 home runs, and 619 runs-batted-in in 1,993 games. He also holds a .974 fielding percentage mark, which as of 2010 was the top spot for infielders in the White Sox organization.

Upon retiring as a player in 2000, Guillén coached third base for the former Montreal Expos in 2001 and the Florida Marlins in 2002-2003. While coaching with the Marlins in 2003, the team made the play-offs as a "wild card" team and defeated the New York Yankees in the World Series. At the end of the 2003 season, Guillén was hired to manage the Chicago White Sox, becoming the thirty-seventh manager in team history. Guillén managed the White Sox to a World Series championship in 2005, when the team swept the Houston Astros. This was the first championship for the White Sox since 1917, and Guillén was awarded manager of the year honors.

As manager of the White Sox, Guillén has been outspoken both on and off the diamond. He has become known for his colorful use of language and candid talk and as someone who is not afraid to share his opinions with the public. In the process, Guillén has made controversial statements to the media about Major League Baseball (MLB) officials and the press. In June, 2006, Guillén, according to one reporter, made comments about *Chicago Sun-Times* columnist Jay Mariotti, launching "into a profanity laced tirade . . . including a derogatory term that is often used to describe someone's sexual orientation." As a result, the MLB commissioner ordered Guillén to pay an undisclosed fine and undergo sensitivity training. Guillén apologized for the use of the term and agreed with the MLB ruling, yet he refused to apologize to Mariotti, stating, "The commissioner did what he had to do. They don't agree with what I say. Me either. I agree with what I say about Jay . . . I'm not going to change. One thing I'm going to make clear is I apologize to the community, but to Jay, no chance. This thing is on and on for good."

In August, 2008, Guillén was suspended for comments he made to the media after being ejected during a bench-clearing brawl in which he had instructed his pitcher D. J. Carrasco to throw at Kansas City's Billy Butler, who was to lead off the inning. In May, 2010, Guillén was fined $7,000 by MLB for arguing balk calls made by umpire Joe West against White Sox pitcher Mark Buehrle.

In addition, Guillén has been outspoken in condemning the use of performance-enhancing drugs, a controversial practice that has plagued baseball since the 1980's. He argues that players knew whether or not they used these drugs, stating "I don't believe players come out and say, 'Well I don't know what I was doing.' Wow, you're not five years old, you should know what you were doing." He has strongly advocated that "We should apologize to the fans, truly. I think everybody involved in this game, you have to do something. I think everybody should feel guilty about it. I think everybody should know about it." Guillén has argued that players who violate MLB's performance drug policy should be banned from playing for one year.

Guillén has also become an active member of the Chicago community, using his postgame interviews as an opportunity to promote particular initiatives, such as wearing apparel with messages supporting Easter Seals of Chicago, autism awareness, and the Roberto Clemente Foundation.

SIGNIFICANCE

Ozzie Guillén, the ballplayer, amazed fans with his glove-work at the shortstop position and was part of the rich tradition of light-hitting Venezuelan middle-infielders who have redefined how their positions are played defensively. He was considered one of the best defensive shortstops of his era. As of 2010, Guillén ranked among White Sox all-time leaders in games played (1,726), hits (1,608), and at-bats (6,633). In the words of one writer, Guillén will be remembered as being "unmatched among Latin middle-infielders of the 1970's and 1980's."

As a manager, Guillén has been notable for being the first Venezuelan manager to win a World Series championship. He is recognized as one of baseball's most outspoken personalities, and he has won admiration, as well as criticism, from many sports fans and the media in the process. Guillén's active, aggressive leadership style and plain-spokenness have contributed to his success, while also forcing many to question traditional notions of what it means to be a Major League Baseball manager.

Kevin-Khristián Cosgriff-Hernández

FURTHER READING

Bjarkman, Peter C. *Baseball with a Latin Beat: A History of the Latin American Game.* Jefferson, N.C.: McFarland, 1994. Provides a focused review of the experience of Latin American ballplayers and traces their contributions to the game up to the early 1990's.

Conner, Floyd. *Baseball's Most Wanted II: The Top 10 of More Bad Hops, Screwball Players, and Other Oddities.* Dulles, Va.: Brassey's, 2003. Documents some of the more humorous and odd stories about ballplayers, including Ozzie Guillén, illustrating why he is considered such a colorful character.

Gano, Rick. "Guillen: Baseball Needs to Put Steroids in Past." *USA Today*, February 15, 2009. Features an interview with Guillén, in which he candidly discusses what he thinks MLB should do about the issue of steroids.

Telander, Rick. "Exit Interview: Ozzie Guillen, the Animated Chicago White Sox Manager on Fidel Castro, Battle Scars, and Marrying Young." *Men's Journal,* October 1, 2008. This interview with Guillén, in which he expresses his opinions on various social issues, is a great example of his candor.

See also: Roberto Alomar; Sandy Alomar, Jr.; Bobby Bonilla; José Canseco; Tony Fernandez; Julio Franco; Andrés Galarraga; Rafael Palmeiro; Sammy Sosa; Fernando Valenzuela.

JOSÉ ÁNGEL GUTIÉRREZ

American activist, educator, and writer

Best known as a founder of La Raza Unida Party, Gutiérrez has maintained a busy life as a civil rights activist, an educator, a political scientist, a judge, and a prolific writer.

Latino heritage: Mexican

Born: October 25, 1944; Crystal City, Texas

Areas of achievement: Activism; government and politics; education

EARLY LIFE

José Ángel Gutiérrez (hoh-ZAY AHN-hehl goo-tee-AHR-ehz) was born in Crystal City, Texas, on October 25, 1944, to Angel Gutiérrez Crespo and Concepcion Gutiérrez. His father, a trained physician from Mexico, and his mother raised him in the Mexican section of Crystal City, where his parents tended to the medical needs of the impoverished residents. At his father's behest, Gutiérrez spent the summers of 1954 and 1955 working as a dishwasher and tortilla maker at a local labor camp. His father believed this manual labor would prepare him to be a man.

In 1957, at age twelve, the age at which his father had said a boy becomes a man, Gutiérrez's life changed dramatically when his father died. The Anglo residents of Crystal City, who had been cordial to his father, began treating Gutiérrez and his mother much as they did other Mexicans, like inferiors to be exploited. This ill treatment informed Gutiérrez's politicization and his understanding of the inequities that Mexicans suffered under Texas's segregation. Even though she had managed her husband's medical office and helped him as a midwife and X-ray

technician for more than a decade, Concepcion could not find employment.

At Crystal City High School, from which he graduated in 1962, Gutiérrez showed great promise as a debater, honing oratory skills that would serve him well. As a teenager, he became politically involved and gave impassioned speeches in the community in support of

José Ángel Gutiérrez. (AP Photo)

Mexican American candidates who were seeking to break the Anglo political monopoly in Crystal City. His speeches drew the attention of the local Anglos who did not take kindly to him stirring up other Mexican people. One day, Gutiérrez and some friends were harassed by a Texas Ranger until his mother interceded with a loaded shotgun. On another occasion, he was held against his will and threatened for hours by the same Texas Ranger and a justice of the peace, both of whom insisted that he disavow his speeches and confess to being a paid agitator connected to the Teamsters Union and the Political Association of Spanish Speaking Organizations (PASO). Gutiérrez refused to comply and was released. The latter incident, which Gutiérrez claims made him both a man and a militant Chicano, convinced him that the Anglo political establishment was willing to go to extremes to maintain its dominance.

LIFE'S WORK

After graduating from high school, Gutiérrez attended Southwest Texas Junior College and then transferred to Texas Arts and Industries University at Kingsville (now Texas A&M at Kingsville), from which he graduated in 1966 with a B.A in government. In 1968, he received a master's degree in government from St. Mary's University in San Antonio. While at St. Mary's University, Gutiérrez cofounded the Mexican American Youth Organization (MAYO) in 1967. Gutiérrez honed his community activist skills by participating in the civil rights work of MAYO, particularly voter registration drives and helping organize numerous school walkouts.

On January 17, 1970, Gutiérrez and other Mexican Americans who felt that the Democrats and Republicans were unresponsive to the needs of Mexican Americans met in Crystal City and founded an independent political party, La Raza Unida Party (The United People's Party). That same year, at the age of twenty-six, Gutiérrez and two other members of La Raza Unida Party were elected trustees of the Crystal City Independent School District. Gutiérrez served as both trustee and president of the district's school board from 1970 to 1973, during which time the district hired Spanish-speaking teachers and school administrators, established bilingual education programs, and introduced courses about the contributions of Mexican Americans. He also served two terms as a judge in Zavala County, from 1974 through 1978 and from 1978 through 1981.

While serving as an elected official, Gutiérrez made time to both write two works that would prove seminal to understanding the sociopolitical condition of Mexican

Americans and to further his education. In 1972, he published *El Político: The Mexican American Elected Official*; two years later, after being rejected by numerous publishers, Gutiérrez published *A Gringo Manual on How to Handle Mexicans*. When he sought to cross the border with copies of his book, customs agents requested that he pay an import tax, even though the tax does not apply to books. Unwilling to pay, Gutiérrez smuggled the books into the United States. Before long, he had personally sold thousands of copies of his satirical examination of how Anglos kept Mexicans politically and economically subjugated. He went on to receive a Ph.D. in government from the University of Texas at Austin in 1976.

Gutiérrez spent the first half of the 1980's residing in Oregon, moving there from Texas in part because of the hostility being directed at him by Texas law enforcement and political adversaries. While in Oregon he held various teaching posts, including stints at Colegio Cesar Chavez (1980) and Western Oregon University (1981-1985).

Gutiérrez returned to Texas in 1986 to pursue a law degree, which he earned from the Bates College of Law at the University of Houston in 1988. The following year, having passed the bar exam, he began practicing law part-time. In April, 1990, Gutiérrez established his own law firm, José Angel Gutiérrez, P.C., in Dallas, Texas.

While serving as president of his law firm, Gutiérrez continued to expand his political thought, write, and document the contributions of Chicano civil rights leaders. In 1994, Gutiérrez founded the Center for Mexican American Studies at the University of Texas at Arlington, for which he was the director until the end of 1996. In 2002, the university made available The Tejano Voice Project, an archive of seventy-five oral history interviews that Gutiérrez conducted with Mexican American leaders in Texas. Gutiérrez joined the faculty of the University of Texas at Arlington as an associate professor of political science in January, 2005. As of 2007, he had published twelve books, including a translation of Reies López Tijerina's autobiography, *They Called Me King Tiger* (2000), and a second, revised edition of *A Gringo Manual on How to Handle Mexicans* (2001), in which he redefines the term "gringo" to include all racist people.

SIGNIFICANCE

As a leader in the Chicano movement, José Ángel Gutiérrez was a steadfast organizer who helped bring Latinos and Latinas into the political realm as both voters and politicians. With his civil rights activism, his founding of La Raza Unida Party, and his many written works, he has demonstrated that progressive social change is

La Raza Unida Party

La Raza Unida Party was founded in 1970 and in its earliest years organized local elections in Crystal City and other cities in South Texas. Soon the party had chapters in various states. However, the party's success was limited to victories in city and county elections in Texas. Conservatives opposed the party, in part because of its political platform which, among other things, called for the immediate end of the military draft; the right to vote for all Mexican Americans who were eighteen years of age or older, including those who were immigrants and had felony records; support for the American working class; the release of political prisoners throughout Latin America; freedom for all colonies and territories under U.S. auspices; and support for Palestinians. Though the party did not grow as its founding members would have hoped, its work showed that Mexican Americans could organize politically and resulted in the Democratic and Republican parties paying more attention to the needs of Mexican American communities.

possible when communities organize politically to challenge social inequities. His personal story reveals his lifelong commitment to fighting social injustices, supporting education, and honoring the contributions of near-forgotten social activists.

Richard Mora

FURTHER READING
Gutiérrez, José Ángel. *El Político: The Mexican American Elected Official*. El Paso, Tex.: Mictla, 1972. Offers insights into Gutiérrez's early political thoughts.
_____. *Chicano Manual on How to Handle Gringos.* Houston: Arte Público Press, 2003. An engaging work in which Gutiérrez examines his political experiences to inform a new generation of Chicano organizers and activists.
_____. *A Gringo Manual on How to Handle Mexicans*. Houston: Arte Público Press, 2001. In this updated version of his classic work, Gutiérrez expands his definition of gringos to include anyone who is racist and anti-Mexican, regardless of racial identity.
_____. *The Making of a Chicano Militant: Lessons from Cristal*. Madison: University of Wisconsin Press, 1998. In this autobiography, Gutiérrez details his experience growing up as a Chicano in South Texas and his eventual politicization.
_____. *Making of a Civil Rights Leader*. Houston: Arte Público Press, 2005. A memoir, in which Gutiérrez discusses his participation in the Chicano movement.

See also: Corky Gonzáles; Vilma Socorro Martínez; Reies López Tijerina.

LUIS GUTIÉRREZ

American politician and activist

Gutiérrez is a prominent Latino congressman from Chicago and a leader of progressive causes, such as civil rights for minorities and women, consumer issues, and equality in credit and financial services.

Latino heritage: Puerto Rican
Born: December 10, 1953; Chicago, Illinois
Also known as: Luis Vicente Gutiérrez
Areas of achievement: Government and politics; activism

EARLY LIFE
Luis Vicente Gutiérrez (lew-EES GEW-tee-EH-rehz), of Puerto Rican descent, was born in Chicago, Illinois. Gutiérrez experienced discrimination growing up in Chicago. His family moved back to Puerto Rico when he was a teenager, and because he did not speak Spanish well, he ran into discrimination there. He attended Northeastern Illinois University, graduating in 1977 with a degree in English. He then taught school, drove a taxi, and was a community activist for Latino causes. He worked for the Chicago Department of Family and children's Services and as an adviser to Mayor Harold Washington.

In 1986, Gutiérrez entered politics and was elected an alderman of the Chicago City Council representing the twenty-sixth ward, an area heavily populated by Latinos. In the City Council he led the struggle for affordable housing for the poor and supported ethics reform and legislation outlawing discrimination based on sexual orientation. Gutiérrez married Soraida Arocho, and the couple had two daughters, Omaira and Jessica.

Luis Gutiérrez. (AP Photo)

LIFE'S WORK

In 1992, Gutiérrez won election to the U.S. House of Representatives from Illinois's fourth district, succeeding George E. Sangmeister He was the first Latino to be elected to Congress from the Midwest. Since then, he has won all his reelection bids by landslide victories, garnering more than 90 percent of the vote in 1996. A supporter of liberal causes, he is a member of the Progressive Caucus in the House of Representatives. He fought to establish federal funding for classes in English and citizenship education for new immigrants. He was one of the most prominent spokespersons against the use of Puerto Rico's Vieques Island by the U.S. Navy for artillery practice. The Democratic caucus in the House selected him to be the chair of their immigration task force.

In 2011, Gutiérrez was also on the Financial Services Committee and chaired the Subcommittee on Financial Institutions and Consumer Credit. Gutiérrez has led efforts in Congress to increase minority representation at the nation's banks and other financial institutions. He also sponsored amendments to cap the interest rates that payday lending services charge members of the armed forces and to limit the cost of credit to consumers by championing disclosure of costs and promoting competition in lending.

Gutiérrez has also served on the Committee on Veterans' Affairs and has worked to increase funding for health care for veterans, including the appropriation of millions of dollars for prosthetics. He strongly supports the provision of medical treatment for women members of the military who have suffered sexual abuse during their careers. In 2007, he became a member of the House Judiciary Committee, serving on subcommittees dealing with immigration and international law

Gutiérrez is also interested in public transportation and has obtained federal support in order to improve Chicago's elevated train lines. He has introduced legislation that would give tax breaks to commuters using public transportation. He has also worked with community and business leaders in Chicago to seek ways to improve and maintain the Chicago Transit Authority and to increase its ridership.

Gutiérrez has given the Democratic Hispanic radio address. In 1996, during National Hunger Awareness Week, he helped to deliver food to Chicago's poor residents from the city's food depository mobile units. He had earlier obtained more than $500,000 of federal funding to increase the depository's revenue.

In 2006, Gutiérrez considered running in the Chicago Democratic primary for mayor against incumbent Richard M. Daley, but he opted to maintain his powerful position in Congress. However, in 2010, when Daley announced he would not seek a seventh term, there was speculation that Gutiérrez might be a possible successor, but he did not enter the race.

Gutiérrez has been no stranger to controversy. In addition to participating in the protests at Vieques Island, in May, 2010, he was arrested for taking part in an immigration demonstration in front of the White House protesting Arizona's stringent immigration law. Federal investigators also looked into his dealings with real estate magnate Calvin Boender, who lent him $200,000; Gutiérrez used the money to buy a vacant lot from Boender. Boender, who did not live in Gutiérrez's congressional district, contributed to Gutiérrez's campaign, and Gutiérrez helped Boender meet with Mayor Daley for approval for one of Boender's projects. Boender also hired Gutiérrez's sister-in-law. Gutiérrez insisted he did not do anything unethical, repaid the loan, and was not charged with any violations.

Gutiérrez's influence with controversial Illinois governor Rod Blagojevich enabled his daughter Omaira to obtain a job as a consumer counselor with the Illinois

Commerce Commission in 2004. Additional controversy surrounded Omaira and her husband, both of whom are government employees, over a real estate transaction when they bought an expensive condominium with help from the Gutiérrezes and sold it a year later for a profit of more than 50 percent.

SIGNIFICANCE

Luis Gutiérrez is a leading champion of the rights of immigrants and minority groups and an advocate for financial and consumer reform. He has established workshops in Chicago to help immigrants on the path to United States citizenship in which tens of thousands of people have enrolled. He is also associated with the struggle for Puerto Rican rights, as demonstrated by his opposition to the naval bombardment of Vieques Island.

Frederick B. Chary

FURTHER READING

Carroll's Federal Directory. Bethesda, Md.: Carroll, 2009. Includes a biography of Gutiérrezez.

Gutiérrez, Luis V. "Luis V. Gutiérrez: Representing Illinois' Fourth District." http://www.gutierrez.house.gov. The congressman's official Web site, providing information on his biography, positions, and activities.

Rodriguez, Marissa. "Residential Players." *Hispanic* 21, no. 1 (February, 2008): 49-53. Analyzes the role of Gutiérrez, and others, in the 2008 election campaign.

United States. Congress. House. Office of Congressional Ethics. *Report and Findings: Transmitted to the Committee on Standards of Official Conduct on July 30, 2010, and Released Publicly Pursuant to H. Res. 895 of the 110th Congress as Amended.* Washington, D.C.: U.S. Government Printing Office, 2010. A report on Gutiérrez's activity in an immigration protest in front of the White House.

See also: Joseph Marion Hernández; Ileana Ros-Lehtinen; Edward R. Roybal; Loretta Sánchez; Leticia Van de Putte.

SIDNEY M. GUTIERREZ

American astronaut and pilot

Best known as a shuttle astronaut, Gutierrez trained as a test pilot in the Air Force before entering the National Aeronautics and Space Administration's astronaut training program. Gutierrez was the first Hispanic to fly into space, and he served as a pilot on the Endeavor and commander on the Challenger.

Latino heritage: Mexican
Born: June 27, 1951; Albuquerque, New Mexico
Also known as: Sidney McNeill Gutierrez; Sid Gutierrez
Area of achievement: Science and technology

EARLY LIFE

Sidney McNeill Gutierrez (SIHD-nee MAC-nehl goo-TEE-ahr-ehz) was born in Albuquerque, New Mexico, on June 27, 1951, to Robert and Sarah Gutierrez. He attended Los Ranchos Elementary School, where, in the fifth grade, he was inspired by the American and Soviet space programs, and he decided he wanted to be an astronaut.

Gutierrez went to Valley High School in Albuquerque, graduating in 1969, the year of the Apollo moon landing. After high school, he went to the U.S. Air Force Academy. While there, Gutierrez was a member of the National Collegiate Championship Air Force Academy parachute team and attained the rank of master parachutist. He graduated in 1973 at the top of his class, receiving a bachelor's degree in aeronautical engineering.

After graduation, Gutierrez went to Laughlin Air Force Base in Del Rio, Texas, for pilot training. For two years, from 1975 to 1977, he served as a T-38 instructor pilot at Laughlin. In 1978, he was transferred to Hollomon Air Force Base in Alamogordo, New Mexico, as part of the Seventh Tactical Fighter Squadron, where he flew the F-15 Eagle. While in the Air Force, Gutierrez continued his formal education, and in 1977, he completed a graduate degree program at Webster College, earning a master of arts in management.

In 1981, Gutierrez attended the U.S. Air Force Test Pilot School. After graduation he joined the F-16 Falcon Combined Test Force, where he served as the primary test pilot for the F-16's propulsion system and airframe.

LIFE'S WORK

In May, 1984, Gutierrez was accepted into the National Aeronautics and Space Administration's (NASA) astronaut training program. By June, 1985, he had realized his childhood dream of becoming an astronaut. Gutierrez's first assignment was commander of the Shuttle Avionics Integration Laboratory, in which he flew simulated missions in order to test shuttle flight software.

After the *Challenger* explosion in January, 1986, Gutierrez put his management skills to work when he served as an action officer during the investigation of the accident, coordinating requests for information from a presidential commission and the U.S. Congress.

During 1986 and 1987, Gutierrez was involved with the recertification of the shuttle's engines and propulsion systems, and in 1988 he became the Astronaut Office lead for software development. In 1989, he served as part of the ground support team for five shuttle launches.

In 1991, Gutierrez made his first trip into space. He was the pilot for the *Columbia* for its eleventh mission, STS-40. The flight launched on June 5, 1991, and the mission lasted for nine days. On June 14, Gutierrez piloted the shuttle to a landing at Edwards Air Force Base in California. STS-40 carried the Spacelab Life Sciences (SLS-1) mission, dedicated to biological studies. During the mission, crew members conducted experiments to test the effects of microgravity on humans and other living organisms.

During 1992, Gutierrez was the spacecraft communicator for five shuttle missions, coordinating communications between the shuttle's flight crew and mission control. That year he also became the Astronaut Office branch chief for operations development.

In April 1994, Gutierrez made his second and last flight into space, this time as the commander of *Endeavor*. This flight, STS-59, carried the Space Radar Laboratory (SRL-1) and launched on April 9. The crew used radar to take nearly fourteen thousand photographs of Earth, which would be used to study the planet's geology and ecology. The mission lasted for eleven days, and the shuttle landed at Edwards on April 20, 1994.

Gutierrez retired from the Air Force and NASA with the rank of colonel in September, 1994. With his wife and three children, he moved back to Albuquerque and took a management position at Sandia National Laboratories' Strategic Initiatives Department. In March, 1995, he became the manager of the Exploratory Systems Development Center's Airborne Sensors and Integration Department.

In 1995, Gutierrez was honored by being inducted into the International Space Hall of Fame, located at the New Mexico Museum of Space History in Alamogordo.

The hall of fame was established in 1976 in order to recognize the contributions of those who have added to the knowledge of space exploration and science.

On June 2, 2010, Gutierrez was named as the 2010 Notable New Mexican by the Albuquerque Museum Foundation, an award that celebrates the accomplishments of distinguished New Mexicans who have strong ties to the state and who have served the public good.

Gutierrez has been a member of the boards of directors for Goodwill Industries and the Texas-New Mexico Power Company and served on the New Mexico Space Center's Governor's Commission.

SIGNIFICANCE

Sidney Guiterrez was the first Hispanic to pilot a space mission and, later, to command a space mission. He has earned many special honors, including the NASA Outstanding Leadership Medal, the NASA Exceptional Achievement Medal, the Distinguished Flying Cross, the Air Force Commendation Medal, the 1990 Congressional Hispanic Caucus Role Model Award, the 1991 and 1994 *Aviation Week and Space Technology* Aerospace Laureate in Space and Missiles Awards, and the 1992 Hispanic Engineer of the Year National Achievement Award. Gutierrez has been an ideal role model and actively reached out to young people.

Karen S. Garvin

FURTHER READING

Evans, Ben. *Space Shuttle Columbia: Her Missions and Crews*. Berlin: Springer Praxis Books, 2005. A history of the space shuttle *Columbia*, from the inception of the shuttle program to its final tragic flight in 2003.

Harland, David M. *The Story of the Space Shuttle*. New York: Springer Praxis Books, 2004. A comprehensive history of the space shuttle. Harland explains the shuttle's contributions to science and includes detailed mission descriptions.

Reichhardt, Tony, ed. *Space Shuttle, the First Twenty Years: The Astronauts' Experiences in Their Own Words*. New York: DK, 2002. In first-person accounts compiled by the editors of *Air & Space/ Smithsonian* magazine, seventy-seven shuttle astronauts describe their flights and their personal experiences aboard the space shuttle.

See also: Franklin Ramón Chang-Díaz; Carlos Noriega; Ellen Ochoa.

RITA HAYWORTH

American actor and dancer

Hayworth progressed from being her father's teenage dancing partner to becoming one of the most famous film stars of the 1940's and 1950's.

Latino heritage: Spanish
Born: October 17, 1918; Brooklyn, New York
Died: May 14, 1987; New York, New York
Also known as: Margarita Carmen Cansino; Rita Cansino
Areas of achievement: Acting; dance

EARLY LIFE

Rita Hayworth (REE-tah HAY-wurth) was born Margarita Carmen Cansino, the daughter of Eduardo and Volga Haworth Cansino. Her father's family had been famous as dancers in Spain. Hayworth's mother, who had performed in the Ziegfeld Follies, was descended from a long line of English actors. The family moved in 1927 to Los Angeles, where Eduardo ran a dance studio.

Eduardo decided to resurrect his career with his daughter as his dance partner, and Hayworth left school in the ninth grade to perform with him at a nightclub in Tijuana, Mexico. While they were working at the Mexican resort of Agua Caliente, Hayworth was spotted by a Fox Film Corporation executive who cast her in *Dante's Inferno* (1935) before awarding her a one-year contract.

LIFE'S WORK

Billed as Rita Cansino, Hayworth appeared in a handful of minor films, usually as a dancer of varying ethnicity.

When her Fox contract was not renewed and Columbia Pictures signed her to a seven-year contract, she exchanged Cansino for her mother's maiden name, adding

Rita Hayworth. (AP Photo)

a "y" to ensure its pronunciation. In an effort to avoid the Mexican and Indian roles in which she had been typecast, her husband, Edward Judson, a businessman who became her manager, had her forehead raised by electrolysis and her black hair dyed red.

After several "B" films, Hayworth was finally cast in a leading role, appearing opposite Cary Grant in director Howard Hawks's *Only Angels Have Wings* (1939). The role of a sultry woman with a past served as a template for many subsequent parts. When Columbia could not find a suitable follow-up role for its new star, Hayworth was loaned to Warner Brothers to star opposite James Cagney in *The Strawberry Blonde* (1941), which turned out to be a hit. Hayworth's career received a huge boost when a 1941 *Life* cover photograph of her became the second most-popular pinup, after Betty Grable, among American soldiers in World War II.

Hayworth returned to Columbia to appear with the studio's biggest star, Tyrone Power, in the bullfight drama *Blood and Sand* (1941) and then was cast in a series of musicals that showed off her dancing talent. Her singing was dubbed by others in *You'll Never Get Rich* (1941) and *You Were Never Lovelier* (1942), both with Fred Astaire; *My Gal Sal* (1942) with Victor Mature; *Cover Girl* (1944) with Gene Kelly; and *Tonight and*

Public Perceptions of Hayworth as a Latina Film Star

Early in her film career Rita Hayworth routinely played characters with names such as Carmen Zoro and Angela Gonzales, but it was soon realized that for her career to flourish she could not be limited to a specific ethnic identity. Changing her name and her hair color and style was necessary to expand her roles. Nevertheless, Hayworth's Latina identity kept recurring during her career. She is a Spanish aristocrat in *Blood and Sand* (1941), a wealthy Argentinean in *You Were Never Lovelier* (1942), and a Spanish gypsy in *The Loves of Carmen* (1948), in which she also performs Spanish dances. In *Gilda* (1946) her character sings "Amado Mio" in a nightclub in Uruguay, and she attempts to make Glenn Ford jealous by saying, "I always say there's something about Latin men. For one thing they can dance. For another . . ." *Only Angels Have Wings* (1939), *Gilda, The Lady from Shanghai* (1947), *The Loves of Carmen, They Came to Cordura* (1959), *The Happy Thieves* (1962), and *The Wrath of God* (1972) are all set at least partly in Latin America or Spain. So many such associations helped the public perceive her as Latina.

Every Night (1945) with Lee Bowman. She was Columbia's leading female actor, earning $6,500 a week.

Of these musicals, *Cover Girl*, with the lush color cinematography of Rudolph Maté, best showcased Hayworth in a semiautobiographical story of a dancer transformed into a famous model. Columbia reteamed Hayworth with Maté and *Cover Girl* director Charles Vidor for *Gilda* (1946), her biggest success. A black-and-white film noir love triangle, featuring Glenn Ford as her former lover and George Macready as her mysterious husband and set in a Buenos Aires casino, *Gilda* firmly established Hayworth as a sex goddess. The first shot of Hayworth, as she flips her long hair up to reveal a smiling face, establishes the tone of the film, with the sexual intensity increasing until it culminates in Hayworth's heated performance of "Put the Blame on Mame," her most indelible scene.

Divorced from Judson, Hayworth married actor-director Orson Welles in 1943 and gave birth to their daughter, Rebecca, the following year. Her tempestuous marriage to Welles was winding down when the couple costarred in *The Lady from Shanghai* (1947). Hayworth angered Columbia head Harry Cohen by cutting her famous hair and dyeing it blond for the role. Welles hoped the film would save their marriage, but it was a failure, although its reputation has subsequently improved.

Hayworth next made *The Loves of Carmen* (1948), loosely based on the George Bizet opera, with Vidor and Ford and with her father as assistant choreographer. She then interrupted her career to marry Pakistani diplomat and playboy Prince Aly Khan in 1949, a union which generated even more worldwide publicity than her marriage to Welles. This unhappy marriage, which ended in 1953, produced another daughter, Princess Yasmin Khan. Two more marriages, to singer Dick Haymes and producer James Hill, also ended in divorce. Of her many unhappy romantic relationships, Hayworth famously said that men fell in love with Gilda only to awaken with Hayworth. Hayworth's biographers usually present her as being manipulated by the men in her life and as having a shyness which disappeared only when she was on screen and that contributed to her alcoholism.

Hayworth's return to the screen began ignominiously with two flops. *Affair in Trinidad* (1952), again with Ford, with whom she made five films, is a pale imitation of *Gilda,* and *Salome* (1953) is an empty Biblical epic. Hayworth rebounded from these disappointments with the film in which many feel she gives her best performance. In *Miss Sadie Thompson* (1953), based on a W. Somerset Maugham short story, Hayworth is a vivacious nightclub performer stranded in American Somoa whose checkered past catches up with her, thanks to a religious hypocrite played by José Ferrer.

Hayworth played a supporting role in her final Columbia film, *Pal Joey* (1957), costarring Frank Sinatra and Kim Novak, who was being groomed to replace Hayworth as Columbia's principal female star. Hayworth exhibited a new kind of vulnerability as the former wife trying to rekindle her relationship with Burt Lancaster in *Separate Tables* (1958). Abandoning her usual glamour for world-weariness, she portrayed an American caught up in Pancho Villa's Mexican Revolution in *They Came to Cordura* (1959), the last notable film she made. *Variety* called this the best performance of her career.

On her final film, *The Wrath of God* (1972), set amid a revolution in Central America in the 1920's, Hayworth was blamed for production delays resulting from her inability to remember her lines, thought to be the result of her drinking. Not until 1980 was she diagnosed as having Alzheimer's disease. Her final years were spent in a mostly helpless state under the care of Princess Yasmin Khan. Her daughter raised millions of dollars for the Alzheimer's Association through annual Rita Hayworth galas in New York, Chicago, and Dallas.

SIGNIFICANCE

Rita Hayworth was emblematic of the Hollywood studio system which painstakingly groomed and publicized performers. She is often characterized as the prototype of the manufactured star. Although her acting talent may not have been comparable to that of such contemporaries as Bette Davis or Katharine Hepburn, Hayworth achieved stardom by combining glamour with sensitivity, fieriness with vulnerability. One of the last of the larger-than-life stars, she was always believable, regardless of the role. Generally considered one of the most beautiful stars ever, Hayworth routinely appears on lists of the greatest film performers.

Michael Adams

FURTHER READING

Kobal, John. *Rita Hayworth: The Time, the Place and the Woman.* New York: Norton, 1977. Biography based on interviews with Hayworth and her coworkers.

Leaming, Barbara. *If This Was Happiness: A Biography of Rita Hayworth.* New York: Viking, 1989. Includes considerable information provided by Orson Welles.

Lerner, Barron H. *When Illness Goes Public: Celebrity Patients and How We Look at Medicine.* Baltimore: Johns Hopkins University, 2006. Includes a chapter on the consequences of the delayed diagnosis of Hayworth's illness.

McLean, Adrienne. "'I'm a Cansino:' Transformation, Ethnicity, and Authenticity in the Construction of Rita Hayworth, American Love Goddess." *Journal of Film and Video* 44, no 3/4 (1992): 8-26. Considers her ethnicity in relation to her stardom.

Vincent, William. "Rita Hayworth at Columbia, 1941-1945: The Fabrication of a Star." In *Columbia Pictures: Portrait of a Studio*, edited by Bernard F. Dick. Lexington: University Press of Kentucky, 1992. Examines the process of creating Hayworth's image.

See also: Dolores del Río; José Ferrer; Mel Ferrer; Fernando Lamas; Ricardo Montalbán; María Montez; Anthony Quinn.

ANTONIA HERNÁNDEZ

Mexican-born lawyer and activist

As a former president of the Mexican American Legal Defense and Educational Fund and president of the California Community Foundation, Hernández has enjoyed an illustrious career as a Latino civil rights attorney and community philanthropist. She has worked hard to improve the lives of Latinos in the areas of labor, education, and health.

Latino heritage: Mexican
Born: May 30, 1948; Torreón, Coahuila, Mexico

Areas of achievement: Activism; law

EARLY LIFE

Antonia Hernández (an-TOH-nee-ah ehr-NAN-dehz) was born in Mexico on May 30, 1948, in the town of Torreón, Coahuila. Even before she was born, her family had faced discrimination in the United States. During the Great Depression, her father, Manuel Hernández, an eight-year-old Texas-born Mexican American, was deported to Mexico and sent off with a one-way train ticket.

Hernández emigrated from Mexico to East Los Angeles with her family when she was eight years old. Her parents hoped to provide Hernández and her siblings with more opportunities in the United States. She grew up in the Maravilla Projects, which were situated in a long-standing neighborhood in East Los Angeles. Like many immigrants in Los Angeles, the family lived under conditions of poverty, but it was bolstered by much family love and support. Her father Manuel worked hard to support the family as a gardener and laborer. Her mother, Nicolasa Hernández, supplemented the family income with odd jobs while raising Antonia and her five younger siblings.

Hernández's experience as a poor immigrant child in American public schools helped sharpen her civil rights focus. In school, she learned English through the immersion method, often described as "sink or swim," and she was not given the opportunity to use the Spanish language in an academic setting. Originally, Hernández wanted to become a teacher and school counselor, but she later decided she could be more helpful to her community as an attorney, influencing and shaping the laws that affected Latino families and children.

LIFE'S WORK

Hernández's experiences as an immigrant Latina in the United States led her to take a leadership role in the Latino civil rights movement. She graduated from the University of California at Los Angeles (UCLA) with a degree in history in 1970 and received a teaching credential from UCLA in 1971. While working on her credential, she served as a coordinator of Project Upward Bound. That experience, along with the East Los Angeles high school walkouts of the late 1960's, in which Latino students demanded better educations, inspired her to work toward improving the lives of Latino families.

Upon graduating from UCLA law school in 1974, Hernández accepted a job with the East Los Angeles Center for Law and Justice, which litigated civil and criminal cases involving police violence and brutality. In 1977, she took a position as an attorney with the Legal Aid Foundation in the Lincoln Heights neighborhood of Los Angeles. That same year, she married Michael Stern, the deputy public defender at the Federal Public Defenders' office, whom she had met several years earlier when both worked as staffers with California Rural Legal Assistance, an organization that collaborated with César Chávez's United Farm Workers union. The couple later had three children.

Antonia Hernández. (AP Photo)

In 1978, Hernández was asked to become staff counsel to the U.S. Senate Judiciary Committee chaired by Senator Ted Kennedy. While in Washington D.C., Hernández served two years as staff counsel and as Kennedy's campaign coordinator. In 1981, after the Republicans had gained control of the Senate, she accepted a position as a staff attorney with the Mexican American Legal Defense and Educational Fund (MALDEF) at its Washington, D.C., location. While at MALDEF, Hernández played a key role in the defeat of the 1982 Simpson-Mazzoli Bill, an immigration reform and control measure that was criticized for being anti-Latino.

Hernández spent most of her career at MALDEF. In 1983, she moved to the organization's Los Angeles office to accept the position of employment litigation director, fighting for affirmative action and increased opportunities for Latinos in both the private and public sectors. Two years later, in 1985, she became president of MALDEF and immediately led a strong opposition movement in response to the Immigration Reform and Control Act of 1986. Convinced that the act would lead to further discrimination of Latinos, she persuaded the 1990 Leadership Conference on Civil Rights to support her in repealing the act.

Hernández's training in advocacy and the law came in handy when, in 1987, an executive committee of MALDEF's board of directors terminated her for her alleged poor administrative and leadership capabilities. They immediately hired former New Mexico governor Toney Anaya, promising to pay him $40,000 more than Hernández. Rumors of sexism and political favoritism surrounded the sudden decision. Hernández, determined to stand her ground, appealed to the state of Texas, who ruled that only the full board of directors could terminate her. The full board voted 18 to 14 to retain her.

In 2003, Hernández resigned from MALDEF. In February, 2004, she accepted a position as president and chief executive officer of the California Community Foundation (CCF), one of California's most influential philanthropic organizations. With more than twelve hundred donors, CCF helps fund nonprofit organizations working in the fields of health, housing, human service, community arts, and education.

SIGNIFICANCE

Antonia Hernández is best known for her eighteen-year tenure as president of MALDEF. While in this position, she oversaw the expansion of the organization, ensured its long-term financial stability, and secured a building in downtown Los Angeles. Her many accomplishments include her victory in *Edgewood Independent School District et al. v. Kirby* (1989), in which the Texas Supreme Court granted state lawmakers the authority to require wealthy school districts to share resources with poor districts in order to provide equal educational opportunities. Under Hernández's leadership, MALDEF also successfully mounted a court battle to defeat Proposition 187, a California ballot initiative that would have prohibited the state's illegal immigrants from using health care, public education, and other social services.

Mary Christianakis

FURTHER READING

Hernández, Antonia. "Closing." *Chicano-Latino Law Review* 14, no. 179 (February, 1994) 1-4. Reprints a speech that Hernández delivered at the *Chicano-Latino Law Review* conference in 1993.

Mendoza, Sylvia. *The Book of Latina Woman: 150 Vidas of Passion, Strength, and Success.* Avon, Mass.: Adams Media, 2004. A collection of short biographical essays of influential Latinas.

Telgen, Dian, and Kamp, Jim, eds. *Latinas! Women of Achievement.* Detroit: Visible Ink Press, 1996. Documents the contributions of Latinas in the United States in areas such as art, science, politics, entertainment, and education.

See also: Joaquín G. Avila; Norma V. Cantú; César Chávez; José Ángel Gutiérrez; Vilma Socorro Martínez.

JOSEPH MARION HERNÁNDEZ

American politician and military leader

Hernández was an active participant in the Florida militia and saw action during the Second Seminole War (1835-1842). He became active in national and local politics, and he was the first Hispanic to be elected to the U.S. Congress.

Latino heritage: Minorcan
Born: May 26, 1788; St. Augustine, Florida
Died: June 8, 1857; Matanzas, Cuba
Also known as: José Mariano Hernández
Areas of achievement: Government and politics; military

EARLY LIFE

Joseph Marion Hernández (ehr-NAHN-dehz) was born in St. Augustine, Florida, on May 26, 1788, when Florida was, for the second time in its history, a Spanish possession. His birth name was José Mariano Hernández.

Hernández's parents were Minorcan immigrants who had come to Florida when it was a British possession in the period from 1763 to 1784. The Minorcans were a diverse group of people recruited from the Mediterranean area and brought to Florida by the Scottish doctor Andrew Turnbull. They were contracted to work on Turnbull's indigo plantation for nine years as indentured workers, after which they would receive their freedom and some land. Hernández's father, Martin Hernández, had been leader of the Turnbull Colony in New Smyrna, which was about seventy miles south of St. Augustine.

In 1816, Hernández bought the plantation Mala Compra, which became his residence. He later acquired two other properties: Bella Vista and Buyks Hammock, also known as St. Ann's. The three properties made Hernández wealthy, and he was one of the largest landowners in Florida. Oranges, corn, and sea cotton were among the crops grown at Mala Compra, which was also known for its sugar production.

LIFE'S WORK

During the second Spanish period in Florida, various Indian tribes began moving into unoccupied areas. Escaped slaves who made it to Florida were welcomed by the Spanish, but this began to cause problems for landowners who wanted their slaves back. Initially, Hernández and a neighboring plantation owner, John Bulow, were supporters of Indian rights and attempted to befriend Native Americans.

In 1817, the First Seminole War began and lasted until May, 1818. Although relatively untouched by the First Seminole War, later events would change Hernández's mind about the political situation with the Indians.

In 1821, the United States acquired the territory of Florida from Spain. Hernández changed his allegiance,

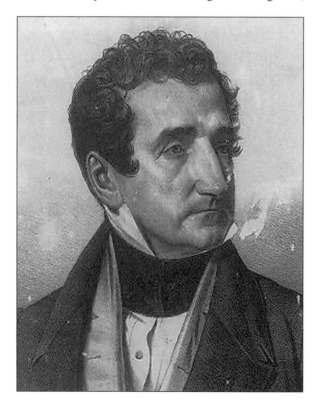

Joseph Marion Hernández. (Library of Congress)

becoming an American citizen and changing his given name from José Mariano to Joseph Marion but keeping his family name unchanged.

From 1821 to1845, Hernández became involved in American politics. On January 3, 1823, he took office as Florida's first delegate to the U.S. Congress. Hernández was the first Hispanic to serve in Congress, completing his service on March 3, 1825. He later made an unsuccessful attempt at reelection. Instead, from 1824 to 1825, Hernández turned to local politics and became the presiding officer of Florida's territorial house of representatives.

The Second Seminole War, also known as the Florida War, was fought from from 1835 to 1842. In 1836, despite Hernández's previous attempts to be a good neighbor to the local Indians, the Seminoles raided and burned his plantation, Mala Compra. Hernández was galvanized into action, and he joined the East Florida Militia, where he soon attained the rank of brigadier general. His property at St. Joseph was used to store the militia's provisions and ammunition, and Mala Compra was used as the military headquarters for his unit.

In 1837, as a brigadier general of the Mounted Volunteers, Hernández served under Major General Thomas Sydney Jesup. During Jesup's Second Seminole War campaign of 1837, Hernández led the eastern force that operated between the St. Johns River and the Atlantic Ocean. Hernández was instrumental in capturing Seminole chief Oceola, who was arrested when he arrived for a purported meeting with Jesup. Hernández also captured several other Seminole leaders.

In 1845, Florida attained its statehood. Making another bid for office, Hernández ran unsuccessfully as the Whig candidate for the U.S. Senate. He again returned to local politics, and in 1848 he served a one-year term as mayor of St. Augustine.

Hernández petitioned Congress over a period of several years for remuneration for the damages sustained to his plantations. The destruction was severe and left the plantations all but worthless. After trying unsuccessfully to restore them, Hernández immigrated to Cuba and became a planter near Matanzas in the Coliseo district, where his family owned a sugar estate.

Hernández lived in Cuba until his death in 1857. He is buried in the Necropolis San Carlos Borromeo in the del Junco family vault.

SIGNIFICANCE

Hernández's history is one of both political and military successes. He was a wealthy plantation owner, possessing three plantations in the St. Augustine area. After Florida became a U.S. territory, Hernández changed his allegiance and became a U.S. citizen. Hernández became actively involved in national politics and was soon elected Florida's first nonvoting delegate to the U.S. Congress, becoming the first Hispanic to serve in Congress. After his term, he returned to Florida where he successfully served in various local political offices.

Hernández was also successful in the military and was recognized for his leadership. He was initially involved with the Florida Militia and then commissioned by the U.S. Army. He served in the Second Seminole War as a brigadier general and led the expedition that captured Seminole chief Oceola.

Karen S. Garvin

FURTHER READING

Mahon, John K. *History of the Second Seminole War, 1835-1842.* Gainesville: University of Florida Press, 2010. Mahon focuses on the Second Seminole War, one of three conflicts that involved the Seminole Indians. His book includes a biography of Hernández.

Peters, Virginia Bergman. *The Florida Wars.* North Haven, Conn.: Archon Books, 1979. A history of the Florida Wars, which are more commonly known as the Seminole Wars. Peters includes an account of Major General Jesup's campaign, in which Hernández played a decisive role.

See also: David G. Farragut; José Antonio Navarro; Juan Seguin.

JUANO HERNÁNDEZ

Puerto Rican-born actor

Hernández starried in films in which he portrayed uncommon, dignified black characters during the 1940's and 1950's, a time when black actors almost always played comic and often demeaning roles. He received critical acclaim as one of the first ethnic actors to play a leading role equal to that of the white actors in the 1949 film Intruder in the Dust. *His work made the next generation of black and Latino actors' work less degrading and ultimately more satisfying.*

Latino heritage: Puerto Rican and Brazilian
Born: July 19, 1896; San Juan, Puerto Rico
Died: July 17, 1970; Trujillo Alto, Puerto Rico
Also known as: Huano G. Hernández; Kid Curley
Areas of achievement: Acting; theater; radio and television; entertainment

EARLY LIFE

Juano Hernández (WAH-noh ehr-NAN-dehz) was born Huano G. Hernández, the son of a Puerto Rican fisherman and a Brazilian mother. While he was still an infant, his father died and his mother took the baby back to Rio de Janeiro. By the time he should have started school, his mother died. To support himself, Hernández started singing for food in the streets. He managed to survive and also learn the skills suitable for a career in entertainment.

Unable to go to school, Hernández taught himself to read and write. He learned acrobatics and joined a Cuban circus, performing as a tumbler, acrobat, and strong man. When he moved to the Caribbean islands,

Juano Hernández. (AP Photo)

he turned professional boxer, fighting under the name Kid Curley. He also sang in a minstrel show. Deciding his future lay in entertainment, he made his way to the United States by the 1920's

Once in the United States, he successfully established his career in entertainment. He worked for a while in vaudeville and performed at the famous Cotton Club and in the theatrical show *Blackbirds*. He worked as a radio scriptwriter and performed in soap operas and other shows, costarring in the first all-black soap opera, *We Love and Learn*. He also acted in such shows as *The Shadow*, *Against the Storm*, and *Mandrake the Magician*. His work in radio was highly successful, and he was the only black actor who was consistently used on radio shows. Because of radio's visual anonymity, Hernández, with his deep strong voice, could play all kinds of roles, regardless of the characters' ethnicity. Consequently, he played Benito Mussolini, Chiang Kai-shek, Haile Selassie I, and Mandrake the Magician, among others. His participation in the popular radio series *The Cavalcade of America* made his name recognizable to the public. In 1927, he was in the chorus of the Broadway production of *Showboat*, which led to film opportunities.

The films in which Hernández first acted were produced by the Foster Photoplay Company of Chicago, the Lincoln Motion Picture Company, and Micheaux Film and Book Company, all black-owned and black-operated firms whose motion pictures starred black actors and were shown in black-owned theaters around the country. Among the films he made with these companies were *The Girl from Chicago* (1932), *Harlem Is Heaven* (1932), and *Lying Lips* (1939). These films helped Hernández hone his acting skills and made the mainstream film companies aware of him.

LIFE'S WORK

The film for which Hernández will likely be most remembered is *Intruder in the Dust*, released in 1949. Although there were a few other dignified black actors at this time, like Paul Robeson, Rex Ingram, Canada Lee, and Leigh Whipper, Hernández's performance as Lucas Beauchamp, a poor southern sharecropper unjustly accused of murder, earned him a Golden Globe Award nomination for New Star of the Year and two foreign film awards.

He performed in more than thirty films, as well as several television shows. In 1950, he made three films: *Young Man with a Horn*, *The Breaking Point*, and *Stars in My Crown*. His role as a judge in *Trial* (1955) was

acclaimed as an outstanding performance. In 1957, he played a Kenyan in *Something of Value*, which also starred up-and-coming black actor Sidney Poitier. In 1960, he and black actor Woody Strode appeared in *Sergeant Rutledge*.

His role of Mr. Smith in *The Pawnbroker* (1964) with actor Rod Steiger was said by film critic Pauline Kael to be "the single most moving performance [she] saw in 1965." His performance as a dispirited, pathetic, lost man was described as brilliant. By the 1960's, the caliber of his roles declined. When he made his last film, *They Call Me MR. TIBBS!*, in 1970, he was playing a more stereotypical role— a toothless old janitor. In the 1950's and 1960's, Hernández also appeared on numerous television programs, including *Studio One in Hollywood*, *Alfred Hitchcock Presents*, *Adventures in Paradise*, *Route 66*, *The Defenders*, and *Naked City*.

Altogether, Hernández's film career lasted from 1932 to the 1970's. When he retired, he moved back to Puerto Rico where, in 1970, he died of a brain hemorrhage.

SIGNIFICANCE

Though Juano Hernández's name is not widely known today, his dignified portrayals of proud, intelligent men made it possible for subsequent black and Latino actors to get roles that were not stereotypically musical, comic, or demeaning. He always played a strong, defiant individualist who met a crisis head on and scorned the rules of white society.

His later roles did not allow him much opportunity to display his ethnic assurance. As a consequence, his impact as a pioneering Afro-Latino actor was lost on subsequent audiences, and his legacy is not as evident as it deserves to be.

Jane L. Ball

FURTHER READING

Bogle, Donald. *Toms, Coons, Mulattoes, Mammies, and Bucks: An Interpretive History of Blacks in American Films*. 4th ed. New York: Continuum, 2001. A discussion of Hernández's role in *Intruder in the Dust* and his subsequent work. Features black-and-white photographs.

Gray, John. *Blacks in Film and Television*. Westport, Conn.: Greenwood Press, 1990. A listing of bibliographical sources that examine the black film experience.

Leab, Daniel. *From Sambo to Superspade: The Black Experience with Motion Pictures*. Boston: Houghton

Mifflin, 1976. Hernández's performance in *Intruder in the Dust* and his subsequent roles are critiqued. Includes black-and-white photographs.

Medrano, Marianela. "Notes on Eusebia Cosine and Juano Hernandez." In *The Afro-Latin Reader: History and Culture in the United States,* edited by Miriam Jimenez Roman and Juan Flores. Durham, N.C.: Duke University Press, 2010. Essay describing Juano Hernández's specific Afro-Latin contributions to American culture.

See also: Leo Carrillo; Dolores del Río; José Ferrer; Mel Ferrer; Rita Hayworth; Fernando Lamas; Beatriz Noloesca; Ramón Novarro; Erasmo Vando.

RAFAEL HERNÁNDEZ

Puerto Rican-born musician and composer

A musician from Puerto Rico, Hernández came to the United States in time to serve with the American Army in World War I. He later became a bandleader and a prolific composer of popular songs while living in New York City, Mexico, Cuba, and his homeland.

Latino heritage: Puerto Rico
Born: October 24, 1892; Aguadilla, Puerto Rico
Died: December 11, 1965; San Juan, Puerto Rico
Also known as: Rafael Hernández Marín
Area of achievement: Music

EARLY LIFE

Rafael Hernández Marín, better known as Rafael Hernández (rah-fah-EHL ehr-NAN-dehz) was born of African-Puerto Rican heritage in the coastal town of Aguadilla, Puerto Rico. He was the son of a poor tobacco farmer, José Miguel Rosa; his mother, María Hernández, was a laundress. Hernández grew up under American occupation and economic domination after Puerto Rico became a U.S. possession following the Spanish-American War. As a young boy, Hernández rolled cigars to supplement the family income, and he became steeped in the songs the other cigar makers sang as they worked. At the age of twelve, he traveled to the capital, San Juan, to study music. Under the tutelage of private teachers, he learned to play a variety of instruments, including clarinet and saxophone, tuba and trombone, piano and guitar. Hernández composed his first tune while still in his teens. By the age of fourteen, he was already performing professionally with the Cocolia Orchestra and with the San Juan Municipal Orchestra.

In the mid-1910's, Hernández left Puerto Rico for the United States and began working as a musician in North Carolina. In 1917, the Jones Act was passed, making all Puerto Ricans U.S. citizens, without voting rights but eligible to be drafted into the American military. Well-known New York bandleader James Reese Europe, commissioned as a lieutenant, began recruiting Puerto Rican musicians. They were enticed to be part of a sixty-five-piece band attached to the segregated 369th Infantry Regiment being recruited to fight in World War I; the regiment would become famous as the "Harlem Hell Fighters" for its ferocity in battle. Hernández and his brother Jesús were two of about twenty Puerto Ricans to become members of the regimental band. In France, Hernández joined such musicians as Noble Sissle (cornet), Buddy Gilmore (drums), Arthur Briggs (trumpet), and dancer Bill "Bojangles" Robinson to perform. Under the direction of Europe, the band toured the country giving rousing, morale-boosting concerts for citizens and soldiers alike. In the process, the musicians introduced jazz, blues, and ragtime to the continent, setting off a craze for American music that would last for decades.

LIFE'S WORK

After the war, Hernández mustered out of the military at the rank of sergeant. He returned to the United States, briefly settling in New York City, where most Puerto Ricans congregated. In 1920, thanks to connections in the music business, he was hired to create musical shows and direct the Fausto Theater orchestra at the Paseo del Prado in Havana, Cuba. During a five-year stay in Cuba, he performed trombone solos as bandleader. He also composed numerous popular tunes, such as "Amor Ciego" (Blind Love). Hernández experimented in a variety of genres drawn from the rich musical heritage of the Caribbean. He wrote *sones*, zarzuelas, *guarachas*, boleros, *danzas*, and rumbas, and he blended other musical forms to create new sounds and styles. Much of his work employed Cuban or Afro-Cuban rhythms and instrumentation or borrowed from Puerto Rican folk traditions.

"Lamento Borincano"

Considered a Puerto Rican anthem and an early song of protest against the miserable economic conditions that existed on the island as a result of American occupation, "Lamento Borincano" was composed in late 1929 or early 1930. Rafael Hernández wrote it soon after the Great Depression began, while he was living in wintry New York City. The composer was inspired to pen the lyrics after sharing a bottle of rum with out-of-work musician friends and with growing nostalgia for the sunny shores of his homeland. The title translates as "Puerto Rican Lament"; Borincano is the Spanish version of Borinquen, the original name given to the island by native Taino Indians.

"Lamento Borincano" follows the form of a slow bolero, with verses in a major key and a chorus in a minor key. The song tells the simple, poignant tale of a *jíbaro*, a peasant farmer from the mountains in Puerto Rico's interior. The farmer has harvested his meager produce and loaded it onto his mare, heading for the city to sell it. He is happy, thinking perhaps he will buy his wife a new dress with the proceeds. When he reaches the city, however, there is no business because of the Depression. He sadly returns home, having sold nothing. He wonders aloud as he travels what will become of him, his wife, his children, and his country, but he cannot imagine the answers to his questions.

In the mid-1920's, Hernández left Cuba to return to New York City. He founded a group, the Trío Borincano (also known as Trío Borinquen, for the Indian name for Puerto Rico, and Trío Quisqueya, for the native name for the Dominican Republic), which played in local ethnic nightclubs and cabarets. He later organized the Victoria Quartet, named for his sister, who opened a music store and musician's booking agency in Harlem in 1927. Under various names the trio and quartet toured widely across the United States and throughout Latin America, playing a selection of standards and Hernández compositions. During the late 1920's, Hernández composed some of his best-known works, including "Preciosa" ("Precious") and "Lamento Borincano" ("Puerto Rican Lament").

In 1932, Hernández was hired to direct an orchestra in Puebla, Mexico. He married a Mexican woman, María Pérez, who gave birth to three of the couple's four children in Mexico. He also studied at the Mexican National Conservatory of Music, earning qualifications to become a teacher of harmony, composition, and counterpoint. Hernández wrote and recorded many of his best-loved songs during stays in Mexico that lasted more than fifteen years, including "Perfume de Gardenia" ("Gardenia Perfume"), "Tabú" ("Taboo"), and "El Ultimo Suspiro" ("The Last Breath"). He also became involved in the Mexican film industry, contributing numerous musical pieces to motion picture soundtracks from the 1930's to the 1950's. In the late 1930's, he returned briefly to Cuba for the opening of the Tropicana Club, where as a producer for RCA Victor he recorded several musical groups. In the late 1940's, he returned to New York to resurrect the Victoria Quartet (also known as Conjunto Victoria and Rico Quartet), which featured singer Myrta Silva, fondly called "La Gorda del Oro"(the golden fat girl).

In the early 1950's, following several tours to great acclaim, Hernández returned permanently to Puerto Rico. There, in addition to maintaining a musical presence, he worked as a consultant and musical director for WIPR, the government-operated radio station. Known throughout Latin America for his compositions, he was named honorary president of the Association of Composers and Authors of Puerto Rico, serving in that capacity from 1953 to 1956. Active in civic and charitable causes, Hernández was instrumental in founding Little League baseball in Puerto Rico. He died at age seventy-three after a long bout with cancer and was buried with great ceremony in San Juan.

SIGNIFICANCE

For his work with the "Harlem Hell Fighters" regimental band during World War I, Hernández and his bandmates all received the Croix de Guerre and the World War I Victory Medal from the French government. Following his death, Puerto Rico named many landmarks in Hernández's honor, including buildings, schools, streets, and the airport in his hometown of Aguadilla. Several states in America followed suit, naming schools in New York, Massachusetts, and New Jersey for the composer. His son, Alejandro "Chalí" Hernández, serves as director at a museum at the Interamerican University of Puerto Rico that celebrates his father's life and work as one of the island's greatest composers.

Hernández's greatest legacy is his music. Decades after their composition, his songs are still tuneful, still relevant. Modern Puerto Rican musical artists like Marc Anthony have recorded several Hernández works, and contemporary films, such as *Don Juan DeMarco* (1994), *Pleasantville* (1998), *Buena Vista Social Club* (1999), *American Pie 2* (2001), *Get Rich or Die Tryin'* (2005), and *Hollywoodland* (2006), have immortalized Hernández by including selections from his oeuvre on their soundtracks.

Jack Ewing

FURTHER READING

Glasser, Ruth. *My Music Is My Flag: Puerto Rican Musicians and Their New York Communities, 1917-1940.* Berkeley: University of California Press, 1997. A detailed study of Puerto Rican music as it evolved in New York during Hernández's time in the city, complete with definitions of musical styles and a discography.

Harris, Stephen L. *Harlem's Hell Fighters: The African-American 369th Infantry in World War I.* Dulles, Va.: Potomac Books, 2005. An account of the exploits of the segregated U.S. Army unit and the associated regimental band, with which Hernández played.

Hernández, Rafael. *Songs/Canciones.* Milwaukee, Wisc.: Hal Leonard, 1999. A compact disc featuring twenty-five Hernández songs with musical notations and lyrics in Spanish and English, including "Lamento Borincano," "Preciosa," and other favorites.

Matos-Rodriguez, Felix V., and Pedro Juan Hernandez. *Pioneros: Puerto Ricans in New York City 1892-1948.* Charleston, S.C.: Arcadia, 2001. Profusely illustrated with period photographs, this brief history in both Spanish and English incorporates oral accounts of immigrants like Hernández who established a vibrant Puerto Rican presence that greatly affected New York's culture.

See also: Jorge Bolet; Noro Morales; Jesús María Sanromá; Claudio Spies.

WILLIE HERNÁNDEZ

Puerto Rican-born baseball player

Hernandez rose from relative obscurity to win the American League's most valuable player and Cy Young awards in his first season with the Detroit Tigers in 1984, establishing himself as one of the premier relief pitchers of his day.

Latino heritage: Puerto Rican
Born: November 14, 1954; Aguada, Puerto Rico
Also known as: Guillermo Hernández Villanueva
Area of achievement: Baseball

EARLY LIFE

Guillermo Hernández Villaneuva (gee-YEHR-moh hur-NAHN-dehz VEE-yah-new-AY-vah) came from a family of softball players on the northwest coast of Puerto Rico, a clan in which the women were as accomplished on the diamond as the men. With eight children, the family could nearly field an entire team; however, the extreme poverty in which Hernández and his siblings lived took an emotional toll on him. It would affect his mental approach to the game of baseball in later years. Once, while waiting in line at a store with a few coins to buy his mother a humble Christmas present, young Willie saw another boy riding a new bicycle. That image would burn into his memory and become a reservoir of motivation, anger, and rage when facing a tough hitter in a key situation as a major-league pitcher.

The son of a factory worker, Hernández played shortstop and third base before becoming a pitcher. By the age of eighteen, he was a local legend in Aguada, signing with the Philadelphia Phillies for a $25,000 bonus. In his early years in professional baseball, however, Hernández relied too much on his strong arm and did not understand the finer points of pitching. He was picked up by the Chicago Cubs, with whom he made his major league debut as a twenty-two-year-old early in the 1977 season.

LIFE'S WORK

Hernández languished in obscurity in the Cubs' bullpen until he joined the Detroit Tigers on March 24, 1984, just a few days before the regular season was about to begin. By that time, he had recorded just twenty-seven saves in seven seasons with the Phillies and Cubs and yearned to find a larger role with another club. He had begun his transformation in 1983, helping Philadelphia to the National League pennant and pitching four scoreless innings in the World Series. That year, he incorporated a screwball into his pitching repertoire— a pitch that breaks in the opposite direction of a curveball and that he learned from former Baltimore Orioles pitcher Mike Cuellar while Willie was getting some extra experience over the winter while pitching in the Puerto Rican League. He coupled his new screwball with another new pitch in his arsenal— a cut fastball, which handcuffed righthanded hitters by breaking in toward them from Hernández's left arm. Yet another legendary pitcher, Ferguson Jenkins, taught Hernández this pitch, as the future Hall of Famer was finishing his own career with the Cubs. The tutelage from Cuellar and Jenkins completed Hernández's new, dominating array of weapons, which he took with him to the American League.

Hernández in 1984 became only the seventh pitcher in Major League Baseball (MLB) history to win both the Most Valuable Player and Cy Young awards in the same season. During the year, Hernández failed to save only one game (a contest in late September, after the Tigers had already clinched a play-off spot), with 18 of his saves requiring two innings of work or more and 6 requiring three innings or more. To illustrate how Hernández immediately stabilized the Tigers' bullpen in 1984, one only need consider that in 1983 the Detroit relief corps failed to hold a lead in the seventh inning or later a total of 27 times.

Hernández proceeded to save the final games that clinched the American League Eastern Division, the American League pennant, and the World Series title for the Tigers as well. When the final out of the World Series was recorded, so many well-wishers had crowded around the pitcher that his chewing tobacco was knocked loose from his cheeks and swallowed, forcing Hernández to make a quick exit from the on-field celebration to head the Tigers' clubhouse with an upset stomach.

Hernández followed his stellar 1984 campaign by becoming the first Tigers pitcher in history to post back-to-back seasons with at least 30 saves in 1985. Soon after, however, Hernández's popularity faded along with his effectiveness on the mound. He was defeated ten times in 1985, leading to a gradual downfall that included his insistence on being called "Guillermo" instead of "Willie" and dumping a full water cooler on the head of columnist Mitch Albom in a clubhouse tirade in spring training of 1988— even though Albom claimed the two men had not spoken with each other in five months. (A year earlier, Albom had written an article in which he criticized Hernández for uttering expletives at the Detroit fans the previous season). Hernández retired at the end of the 1989 season.

Later in life, Hernández needed to have a pacemaker installed to assist with cardiac troubles. He received a scant number of votes for the National Baseball Hall of Fame during his years of eligibility on the ballot.

SIGNIFICANCE

Hernández is an important figure in Detroit Tigers history and has the rare distinction of winning the Cy Young and Most Valuable Player awards in the same season. Relief pitchers often get less recognition than starting pitchers, but Hernández made a name for himself with his dominance, reliability, and competitive nature.

Doug Feldmann

FURTHER READING

Anderson, George "Sparky." *Bless You Boys: Diary of the Detroit Tigers 1984 Season.* New York: Mc-Graw-Hill, 1984. The manager of the Tigers gives an inside look as to how Hernández impacted the team in his first year as a pitcher in Detroit.

Cantor, George. *Wire to Wire: Inside the 1984 Detroit Tigers Championship Season.* Chicago: Triumph Books, 2004. The author describes the day-to-day highlights of the great season enjoyed by Hernández and the Tigers.

Lombardi, Stephen. *The Baseball Same Game: Finding Comparable Players from the National Pastime.* New York: iUniverse, 2005. The author

Willie Hernández. (AP Photo)

describes Hernández's achievements in the context of the accomplishments of other relief pitchers during his era.

See also: Joaquín Andújar; Pedro Guerrero; Juan Marichal; Dennis Martínez; Luis Tiant; Fernando Valenzuela.

AURELIO HERRERA

American boxer

Herrera was the most prominent Mexican American boxer at the dawn of the twentieth century and is credited with helping to popularize cultural identity and involvement with the sport as Southern California became home to large communities of Spanish-speaking immigrants.

Latino heritage: Mexican
Born: June 17, 1876; San Jose, California
Died: April 11, 1927; San Francisco, California
Area of achievement: Boxing

EARLY LIFE

Aurelio Herrera (oh-RAY-lee-oh huh-REH-rah) was born in San Jose, California, on June 17, 1876, the fourth of six children of Anselmo and Asencion Herrera. Herrera and his brothers helped his father, who operated a saloon and worked as a street vendor in Kern City. However, Herrera soon became interested in more active pursuits and found early success in boxing. He was able to develop a local reputation and received support from the Mexican American community. Prominent among his supporters was Frank Carillo, who set up a training facility in the basement of his dance and gambling hall and offered to assist Herrera.

Despite his early successes, Herrera lost a match that temporarily caused him to abandon the sport he had loved. He returned home to be a card dealer, working for five dollars a night. His dedication to enforcing the rules of the house caught the attention of the city marshal, who appointed Herrera a deputy marshal.

Herrera was drawn back to boxing in 1893, three years after his mother's death. He soon became the dominant featherweight fighter in southern California, though he was untested in matches beyond regional competitors.

LIFE'S WORK

In 1896, Herrera began a boxing career that would last for more than thirteen years, losing only 14 times in 94 professional bouts, including 57 knockouts. Interestingly, from his earliest bouts, Herrera was described variously as "a white man," an "Indian," an "Iberian," and a "Mexican," which may have been a part of his appeal to those who followed boxing locally. Now managed by Carillo, Herrera fought and won or tied all of his bouts through 1900, most of which were still in Southern California. In 1901, Herrera lost a controversial eight-round bout to Terry McGovern, world featherweight champion, and soon began to manage himself for future bouts. Herrera trained and fought regularly for the next two years, regularly sparring with his brother, Mauro, but moved away from California in 1903 shortly after their father died. His win that year over the previously undefeated Kid Broad in Butte, Montana, gave him widespread recognition. He was now fighting exclusively outside of California and under the tutelage of Biddy Bishop, from whom he developed a "crouch" style of boxing. Herrera also packed a powerful right punch within his 5-foot, 4-inch frame.

Herrera married Bertha Martensen on May 23, 1904, and continued to tour extensively. He defeated former world featherweight champion Young Corbett II in January, 1906, in Los Angeles before five thousand fans. After he parted ways with Bishop, the manager circulated disparaging stories about Herrera's card-playing, smoking, and drinking habits as he prepared for his fights. Nevertheless, his popularity soared and he was embraced as a hero. However, his image was severely tarnished when a scheduled bout for $20,000 with reigning champion Battling Nelson failed to materialize because of weigh-in protocol; thousands of spectators already were present. In the aftermath, Herrera was cast as the villain in the press.

By July, 1906, Herrera was fighting intermittently and purchased a local saloon, which burned down within a year. Following a short-lived attempt at promoting boxing in Bakersfield, he resumed training and divorced his wife in 1908. He temporarily retired that year and returned to his business interests. However, at age thirty-six, Herrera made one last attempt before officially retiring just as California banned professional boxing.

He spent his remaining years farming and involved in occasional scrapes with the law.

Arrested at least twice for vagrancy, Herrera died destitute in San Francisco, California, on April 12, 1927. By that time, Southern California had absorbed thousands of immigrants from Mexico and boxing was recognized as a part of Mexican American cultural identity, due in no small part to Herrera's notoriety and legendary image.

SIGNIFICANCE

Herrera was a pivotal figure in the emergence of Mexican Americans in boxing and the development of racial stereotypes of early twentieth century Southern Californians. Although born in California to American parents, Herrera was publicly identified with his Mexican heritage. In a sport where few Hispanics found a place, much less success until the mid-twentieth century, Herrera gained national recognition. His career in the ring was quite successful, although his reputation as a self-promoter with casual training habits often overshadowed his achievements in the ring. Nevertheless, his thirteen-year professional career, tumultuous as it may

have been, served as an inspiration for many and he is recognized as the first great fighter of Mexican heritage.

P. Graham Hatcher

FURTHER READING

Nicholson, Kelly Richard. *Hitters, Dancers, and Ring Magicians: Seven Boxers of the Golden Age and Their Challengers*. Jefferson, N.C.: McFarland, 2010. Describes Herrera's career in the context of other great fighters of his era.

Rodriguez, Gregory. "Aurelio Herrera: Southern California's First 'Mexican' Boxing Legend." *The Arizona Report* 4 (1999): 2-4. Chronicles the accomplishments, impact, significance, and last days of Herrera.

VanCourt, DeWitt. *The Making of Champions in California*. Los Angeles: Premier, 1929. The author was a prominent sportswriter and developer of boxing talent in Southern California and includes commentary on Herrera's career.

See also: Art Aragon; Wilfred Benitez; Sixto Escobar; Félix Trinidad.

CAROLINA HERRERA

Venezuelan-born fashion designer and business executive

Herrera transformed herself from jet-setting socialite to astute businesswoman. Her designs set the tone of fashion in the 1980's and continued to offer elite women wearable, elegant, tasteful, yet fun clothes through the end of one century and the beginning of the next. Her business empire includes mid-priced, sportswear, and bridal lines in addition to couture, with sales of some $250 million a year.

Latino heritage: Venezuelan

Born: January 8, 1939; Caracas, Venezuela

Also known as: María Carolina Josefina Pacanins y Niño

Areas of achievement: Fashion; business

EARLY LIFE

Carolina Herrera (kah-roh-LEE-nah eh-RAR-ah) was born into a prominent and wealthy family in Caracas, Venezuela. One of four daughters, she had a protected upbringing. At age eighteen, with the encouragement of her parents, she married. After ten years and two daughters,

the marriage ended in divorce in 1965— a shocking first divorce for her family. In 1968, she remarried, this time to the wealthy and aristocratic Reinaldo Herrera. Herrera was well-known in Venezuela as a media personality. He had traveled widely in Europe before their marriage, and the couple traveled together. They were part of the "jet set" of the glittering 1970's, spending part of each year abroad in England, France, and the United States. Their wealth, good looks, impeccable breeding, and sense of fun made them affable companions for the likes of Princess Margaret of Great Britain, artist Andy Warhol, and other cultural icons of the time. Together they had two daughters.

While nothing in her upbringing trained Carolina Hererra for a career, many things prepared her for a role in fashion. Her mother and grandmother (and later her mother-in-law) prided themselves on their stylishness. By the time she was thirteen, Carolina accompanied her mother and grandmother on visits to the couturiers of France. She had her own clothes custom-made by the talented dressmakers in Caracas. Photographs of her

Carolina Herrera.
(Evan Agostini/PictureGroup via AP Images)

appeared regularly in fashion magazines such as *Vogue*, and she was recognized as "best dressed" year after year. She had little experience in business, but she was familiar with design houses at home, and between her marriages, she held a genteel position in publicity and public relations for designer Emilio Pucci in Venezuela.

LIFE'S WORK
Herrera and her family relocated to New York in 1981. Now past forty, she was casting about for some project to fill her time. Encouraged by Diana Vreeland, editor of *Vogue*, and others, she sketched a collection of twenty dress designs and had samples sewn by her dressmakers in Caracas. She held a small informal showing at the apartment of a friend in New York, and the response was quite positive. The only problem was that she had no idea of how to make the transition from sketch and sample to production line.

In the previous decade, several society women had dabbled in fashion design, but their careers were usually short-lived. (Diane von Furstenberg was a notable exception.) At first, many of Herrera's circle and most

of the press treated her as a dilettante. She was a quick study, however. She received significant financial backing from Armando de Armas of Venezuela, and she soon understood how the fashion business worked. Of course, her social connections helped; her shows were attended by all the "right people." However, as she herself said, if she only dressed her friends, she would have been out of business almost immediately. More important, she completely understood the lives of her clients. Her clothes reflected her own style: cool, elegant and feminine, classic without being stuffy. Her apparel was also influenced by 1930's Hollywood glamour and the tailoring and structure of such designers as Balenciaga and Mainbocher. Her collections highlighted luxurious fabrics and fine finishes, and she is credited with introducing the padded shoulder look so closely associated with fashion in the 1980's. Her designs sold for very high prices.

Herrara's designs were consonant with the luxury of the Ronald Reagan era, when gala social events and opulent costumes represented outward signs of American affluence and dominance. First Lady Nancy Reagan was a client, and Herrera's success was confirmed when former First Lady Jacqueline Kennedy Onassis became a steady customer. Herrera designed the wedding gown for Caroline Kennedy's wedding in 1986. This dress is the epitome of Herrera's taste in the 1980's: a structured and modest bodice appliquéd with symbolic white shamrocks, strong padded shoulders, and a full ball gown skirt of rich silk.

Carolina Herrera, Inc., developed with the times. With herself firmly at the helm, her company became one of the most profitable in the industry. She expanded with the mid-priced CH line in 1986 and the Carolina Herrera Collection II for sportswear in 1989. She opened a bridal couture in 1987, and she dressed many celebrities and socialites for their big day. Her first fragrance was produced in 1988; several more were licensed by 1997; and her flagship store opened on Madison Avenue in New York City in 2000. Much of this expansion was overseen by her daughter and collaborator, Carolina, Jr.

Herrera received many honors in her career, including MODA's Top Hispanic Designer (1987), the Council of Fashion Designers Women's Wear Designer of the Year award (2004), and the Geoffrey Beene Lifetime Achievement Award (2008).

SIGNIFICANCE
Carolina Herrera continued the tradition of excellence in Hispanic fashion design established by such designers

as Balenciaga and Oscar de la Renta. Understanding the needs of stylish, affluent women in America in the late twentieth century, Herrera built a business empire of fashion and fragrance. Her clothes captured the extravagant tone of the Reagan era, but she was also able to adapt her ideas to the more streamlined and practical needs of women in the following decades. A woman of great personal elegance, she offered other women some of that elegance for themselves.

Jean Owens Schaefer

FURTHER READING

Fernandez, Idy. "The Muse." *Hispanic* 21, no. 4 (April, 2008): 22-23. An interview with Herrera's daughter Carolina, Jr., discussing the collaboration of mother and daughter in expanding and diversifying the business.

Garcia-Johnson, Ronie-Richele. "Carolina Herrera." In *Latinas: Women of Achievement*, edited by Diane Telgen and Jim Kamp. Detroit: Visible Ink Press, 1996. Brief but informative; attention is paid to the character of Herrera's designs. Includes a listing of periodical sources.

Kotur, Alexandra. *Carolina Herrera: Portrait of a Fashion Icon*. New York: Assouline, 2004. Some biographical information among the many, many photographs of Herrera. Text is mostly a paean to her personality.

See also: Oscar de la Renta; Narciso Rodriguez.

MARÍA HERRERA-SOBEK

Mexican-born scholar and educator

Herrera-Sobek has published foundational scholarship examining Chicano and Mexican folklore beliefs and practices. Much of her research investigates the use of the oral tradition to share corridos (ballads) expressing community values and/or discourses critiquing dominant ideologies and social injustices. She also has used an ecofeminist framework to examine Chicano writers' development of resistance literature.

Latino heritage: Mexican

Born: January 21, 1942; San Pedro de Las Colonias, Coahuila, Mexico

Also known as: María Díaz Herrera

Areas of achievement: Education; scholarship

EARLY LIFE

María Herrera-Sobek (ehr-EHR-ah-SOH-behk) was born on January 21, 1942, in San Pedro de Las Colonias, Coahuila, but spent much of her early life in Rio Hondo, Texas, and Gilbert, Arizona, after her grandparents, Susana Escamilla and José Pablo Tarango, migrated to the United States. Herrera-Sobek primarily grew up in the care of her grandparents. She attended elementary school and junior high school in Rio Hondo. However, she graduated from Gilbert High School in Arizona, which she began attending after her grandparents were offered employment in the agricultural fields in Gilbert as they traveled to California.

Herrera-Sobek had hoped to graduate from high school in California and complete her undergraduate studies at the University of California at Los Angeles (UCLA) but instead attended Arizona State University and earned a bachelor's degree in chemistry in 1965. In 1971, she earned a M.A. in Latin American studies from UCLA. In 1975, Herrera-Sobek was awarded a Ph.D. in Hispanic languages and literatures from UCLA.

Herrera-Sobek's commitment to promoting social justice through scholarship and service was influenced by her early life experiences. Her grandparents had a major influence on her early understanding of how dominant ideologies nurture systemic oppression, such as heteronormative ideologies informing gender relations within communities. Her grandfather expressed a cautious view of power systems sustained via the social institutions of religion and government. Additionally, Herrera-Sobek's understanding of the ecology of race, class, and gender relations within her community was influenced by her grandmother's feminism. Her awareness of dominant ideologies underlying social injustices also was partly informed by the challenges she had encountered as a student in a segregated school environment in Rio Hondo.

LIFE'S WORK

Herrera-Sobek pursued a career in academia to promote social justice, including racial and ethnic diversity within higher education. From 1975 to 1996, she taught

Spanish first as a lecturer then as a professor at the University of California, Irvine. Moreover, during the 1990's, she taught as a visiting professor at both Stanford University and Harvard University. By 1997, Herrera-Sobek was named the Luis Leal Endowed Chair at the University of California at Santa Barbara (UCSB). Herrera-Sobek helped establish a Ph.D. program in Chicana and Chicano studies at UCSB. She also served as the acting associate vice chancellor for academic policy at the university before assuming the position of associate vice chancellor for diversity, equity, and academic policy in 2003. The title of the position reflects the university's effort to promote diversity in higher education through programs such as a postdoctoral fellowship program designed to recruit minority faculty.

Herrera-Sobek's scholarship in folklore studies and literary criticism has extended Chicano studies. In her first book, *The Bracero Experience: Elitelore Versus Folklore* (1979), Herrera-Sobek introduces the term "elitelore" and engages in a comparative analysis of elitelore and folklore. Using data compiled from oral history interviews with former braceros as well as data collected from thematic analyses of *corridos*, the author

María Herrera-Sobek.
(courtesty of María Herrera-Sobek)

develops a composite bracero to juxtapose elitelore and folklore. By 2006, Herrera-Sobek had published several books, including *The Mexican Corrido: A Feminist Analysis* (1990) and *Chicano Folklore: A Handbook* (2006).

Herrera-Sobek also has edited and coedited several books and anthologies. For example, she co-edited the first edition (1988) and second edition (1996) of *Chicana Creativity and Criticism: New Frontiers in American Literature* with Helena María Viramontes. She also edited *Critical Insights: The House on Mango Street* (2010).

Herrera-Sobek also has engaged in service at the state level and the local level to promote social justice. For instance, she was a committee member on the California Campus Sexual Assault Task Force from 2003 to 2004. She also has served as a mentor and interacted with youths from local schools.

SIGNIFICANCE

Herrera-Sobek uses her roles as folklorist, literary critic, and educator to advance Chicano studies. As a result of authoring foundational works in Chicano and Mexican folklore studies, she was recognized as a fellow of the American Folklore Society. Herrera-Sobek also uses an ecofeminist framework to analyze how Chicano writers develop resistance literature to highlight social injustices. In addition to her contributions in scholarship on folklore and literature, Herrera-Sobek has advanced Chicano studies through her involvement in organizing a Ph.D. program in Chicana and Chicano studies at UCSB and coordinating international conferences on Chicano studies.

Kristina A. Gutierrez

FURTHER READING

Herrera-Sobek, María. *Chicano Folklore: A Handbook*. Westport, Conn.: Greenwood Press, 2006. Herrera-Sobek traces both indigenous and European influences on Chicano folklore.

_____. *The Mexican Corrido: A Feminist Analysis*. Bloomington: Indiana University Press, 1990. Herrera-Sobek uses a feminist archetypal framework to critique examples of the archetypes of good mother, mother goddess, soldier, terrible mother, and lover within *corridos*, particularly *corridos* following conventions of the heroic genre.

Martínez, Elizabeth C. "A Trailblazing Leader: María Herrera-Sobek." *The Hispanic Outlook in Higher Education* 19, no. 3 (2008): 40-41. Martínez overviews Herrera-Sobek's contributions in promoting Chicano studies.

See also: Fernando Alegría; Lourdes Casal; Rigoberto González; Luis Leal; Helena María Viramontes.

EDWARD HIDALGO

Mexican-born Secretary of the Navy, diplomat, and lawyer

A successful attorney with a long and distinguished career in government service, most notably as an expert in naval intelligence and later in diplomatic work, Hidalgo became the first Hispanic to serve as the secretary of the Navy when President Jimmy Carter appointed him to this post in 1979.

Latino heritage: Mexican

Born: October 12, 1912; Mexico City, Mexico

Died: January 21, 1995; Fairfax, Virginia

Also known as: Eduardo Hidalgo

Areas of achievement: Government and politics; military; diplomacy; law

EARLY LIFE

Edward Hidalgo (EHD-wahrd ee-DAHL-goh) was born Eduardo Hidalgo in Mexico City, Mexico. His family moved to New York City when he was six, and his parents anglicized his first name when the family became naturalized citizens four years later. Young Edward was especially adept in school, quickly mastering the difficult transition into English-language schooling. He showed remarkable promise early on, and he later graduated magna cum laude from Holy Cross College in 1933 and earned his doctor of jurisprudence degree from Columbia Law School in 1936. Hidalgo clerked for the U.S. Second Circuit Court of Appeals in New York before going into private law practice until 1942.

With the advent of World War II, Hidalgo, although nearing thirty years old, enlisted in the U.S. Navy, billeted as a lieutenant in the Naval Reserves from 1942 to 1946. Initially assigned legal duties in Montevideo, Uruguay, he went on to serve as an air combat intelligence officer assigned to the storied carrier USS *Enterprise.* Hidalgo saw significant action throughout the Pacific theater, for which he was awarded the Bronze Star.

As the war drew to its close, high-echelon discussions were held concerning strategies designed to maintain the cooperation among the branches of the military that had been necessitated during the multifront international war effort. Headed by lawyer and government policy adviser Ferdinand Eberstadt, a blue-ribbon panel, for which Hidalgo was selected, drew up detailed recommendations for such cooperation. Hidalgo received a meritorious commendation for his advisory service on the Eberstadt Committee. He then completed his tenure in the Navy as special assistant to Secretary of the Navy James Vincent Forrestal.

LIFE'S WORK

Hidalgo returned to private practice in 1945. During a two-year stint with the prestigious New York law firm of Curtis, Mallet-Prevost, Colt and Mosle, Hidalgo was put in charge of its offices in Mexico City. In 1948, he chartered his own law firm in this city and remained there, as a senior partner, for more than two decades, receiving a degree in civil law from the University of

Edward Hidalgo. (Time & Life Pictures/Getty Images)

Efforts to Promote Hispanic Enlistment in the Navy

Long before his historic appointment as President Jimmy Carter's secretary of the Navy, Edward Hidalgo understood the problems facing Hispanics in the Navy. Although Hispanic Americans had served with distinction in every war in the nation's history and Hispanic Americans were a significant presence in the contemporary sea services, Hidalgo recognized four critical areas to address: recruiting interested Hispanics for naval service and promoting English language skills; securing qualified Hispanics for officer training programs; retaining the Hispanic presence through re-enlistment strategies and career counseling; and fostering the growth of the Hispanic presence by developing networking systems for mentoring and educating promising recruits.

Hidalgo's success in promoting Hispanic presence in the peacetime Navy was manifested in two major achievements. He directed the public relations services of the Navy to pursue an unprecedented media campaign, including television commercials featuring Hispanics, in order to provide information about career opportunities in the Navy. These television advertise-

ments were target marketed to air in metropolitan areas, many of them in the Southwest.

Hidalgo's second and long-term achievement was the founding of the Association of Naval Service Officers (ANSO) in 1981. As part of the Navy's larger strategy to meet diversity goals, ANSO worked to provide a network of support and career direction for qualified junior-level Hispanics, as well as access to the Navy's promotion pipeline. As of 2010, active duty Hispanics in the Navy accounted for roughly 15 percent of the enlisted personnel, but only 6 percent of its officers; ANSO aimed to increase the number of officers to 13 percent within the next twenty-five years. In addition to fostering career opportunities, ANSO develops programs through which Hispanic officers return to Hispanic communities in order to provide information about naval careers. Although the practical benefits of Hidalgo's vision are tangible in the expanding influence of Hispanics in the sea services, his advocacy provided a sense of pride and influence for what has emerged as America's dominant minority population segment.

Mexico in 1959. At the request of the administration of President Lyndon B. Johnson, in 1965 Hidalgo returned to Washington, D.C., to serve as special assistant to Paul H. Nitze, the secretary of the Navy. During his one year of service, Hidalgo was instrumental in realizing Nitze's ambitious agenda for securing and retaining qualified personnel through a system of meritorious bonuses.

For the next six years, Hidalgo returned to private practice, living in London and running the European division of the international law firm of Cahill, Gordon and Reindel. At the request of President Richard Nixon's administration, however, Hidalgo returned to Washington in 1972 to serve as the special assistant for economic affairs to the director of the United States Information Agency (USIA), a public policy division responsible for distributing information that clarified the workings of American foreign policy to nations both receptive and hostile to American interests. It was a most challenging time for USIA in the wake of America's military withdrawal from the protracted war in southeast Asia, as well as the Nixon administration's historic China initiative. A year later, Hildago was named USIA's general counsel and its liaison to Congress.

During the tempestuous collapse of the Nixon presidency and the subsequent administration of President

Gerald R. Ford, Hidalgo continued his government service, distinguishing himself as a competent facilitator without partisan leanings. He became known as an affable presence and a reassuringly stable voice for USIA on Capitol Hill, and he was retained as general counsel after the election of President Jimmy Carter in 1976. In 1977, Hidalgo was appointed to serve as the assistant secretary of the Navy in charge of manpower development and reserve affairs. During his two-year stint in this position, he was instrumental in coordinating the Navy's legal strategy in order to settle a massive lawsuit filed by General Dynamics, in which the corporation sought to recover millions of dollars in cost overrun charges for construction problems associated with building the Navy's nuclear submarine force during the previous decade.

Hidalgo's distinguished service, as well as his significant career of both legal and government work, led to his historic nomination on September 13, 1979, to serve as the secretary of Navy, succeeding W. Graham Claytor, Jr. After he received U.S. Senate confirmation on October 19, Hidalgo took the oath five days later and became the first Latino ever to hold that post. Although his tenure was relatively brief, Hidalgo directed the Navy at a time of remarkable activism. Under the aegis of the Carter administration's enthusiastic endorsement of progressive reform and its embrace of diversity, the Navy had begun to pioneer rights for both women and gays. Hidalgo recognized the importance of Latino service in the Navy and set as his goals a bold initiative to encourage Hispanic recruitment and new strategies for retaining and promoting Latino officers. His efforts led directly to the establishment of the Association of Naval Service Officers (ANSO) in 1981, an organization of Hispanic naval officers that would connect the Latino community with the Navy, the Marine Corps, the Coast Guard, and the Merchant Marine in order to recruit qualified Hispanic officers.

In 1981, with the beginning of President Ronald Reagan's administration, Hidalgo retired after more than four decades of public service. During the next decade, he was a government consultant, maintaining a vigorous public presence as an advocate for Hispanic service in the Navy. Hidalgo died in 1995, at the age of eighty-two, from cardiac arrest in Fairfax, Virginia, just outside Washington, D.C.. In recognition of his tireless campaign to build Hispanic presence in the American military, ANSO established the Hidalgo Medal, given annually to a Hispanic who has contributed significantly to the sea services and who has exemplified the core values that defined Hidalgo's own career: leadership, dedication, and commitment.

SIGNIFICANCE

In a divisive era, when conservative critics of affirmative action regularly pointed to minority appointments in both corporations and government as evidence of unearned professional reward, the stellar career ascent of Edward Hidalgo affirmed that minority achievement did not depend on preferential treatment. Hidalgo brought

to the position of secretary of the Navy his four decades of dedicated public service, as well as his legal skills as a negotiator and a facilitator. As the naval secretary, he vigorously pioneered the concept of American military recruitment of a specific minority presence, offering military service as a viable career opportunity for Hispanics, as well as working to guarantee fair access to promotions and career advancement.

Joseph Dewey

FURTHER READING

Asch, Beth J., Paul Heaton, and Bogdan Savych. *Recruiting Minorities: What Explains Recent Trends in the Army and Navy.* Santa Monica, Calif.: RAND, 2009. Comparative study of data concerning the military recruitment of African Americans and Hispanics, specifically the steady increase of Hispanics. Cites recruitment efforts begun by Hidalgo.

Klerman, Jacob Alex, et al. *Military Enlistment of Hispanic Youth: Obstacles and Opportunities.* Santa Monica, Calif.: RAND, 2009. Concise and effective summary of the challenges facing military recruitment of the growing Hispanic population, with particular emphasis on the difficulties with language skills. Includes a survey of the Navy's groundbreaking efforts to expand Hispanic presence.

Zelizer, Julian E. *Jimmy Carter.* New York: Times Books, 2010. Helpful and concise overview of the agenda and the achievements of the Carter administration. Places the historic appointment of Hidalgo within its political perspective.

See also: Henry G. Cisneros; Alberto Gonzales; Manuel Luján, Jr.; Bill Richardson; Ken Salazar; Hilda L. Solis.

HILDA HIDALGO

Puerto Rican-born activist, educator, and social reformer

Hidalgo dedicated her life to social activism on behalf of the Hispanics, homosexuals, and women who often had little access to community or government support while furthering the educational needs of minorities as a well-respected professor at Rutgers University.

Latino heritage: Puerto Rican
Born: September 1, 1928; Puerto Rico
Died: November 8, 2009; Gainesville, Florida

Areas of achievement: Activism; education; social issues; gay and lesbian issues

EARLY LIFE

Hilda Hidalgo (HIHL-dah ee-DAHL-goh) was born in Puerto Rico on September 1, 1928, and lived in Rio Piedras with her family. The family included sisters Elia and Zaida; Elia would later help Hidalgo in her research and would publish works on minority issues in her own right.

As a young woman, Hidalgo taught in a Puerto Rican school for a few years before earning her B.A. from the University of Puerto Rico in 1957. In 1958, she left Puerto Rico to pursue a master's degree from Catholic University of America, which she earned in 1959. By 1968, Hidalgo added a master's degree in social work from Smith College School of Social Work, located in Northampton, Massachusetts, and a Ph.D. from Union Graduate School in Yellow Springs, Ohio. She later credited an episode of racial intolerance during her first two years in the United States with spurring her to concentrate her lifelong efforts on furthering equality.

LIFE'S WORK

In 1960, Hidalgo moved to Newark, New Jersey, to work for the Girl Scouts Council of Greater Essex in the position of district director before serving as director of Child Services from 1965 through 1970. After leaving Child Services, Hidalgo began teaching at the Rutgers School of Social Work in New Brunswick, New Jersey, before moving to the Newark campus to teach in the Department of Public Administration. In her capacity at Rutgers, she served as director of the Master's of Work Bilingual Program and later as the director of the Masters of Public Administration Hispanic, Bilingual, and Bicultural Program. In a position with special relevance to her birthplace, Hidalgo also periodically worked as the coordinator of Puerto Rican studies. Throughout her career, she edited and wrote about the issues to which she devoted her life, including a collection of essays dedicated to other women struggling with being both lesbians and part of the minority population, and a resource manual for the disabled.

In her spare time, Hidalgo helped to organize community groups with emphasis on Hispanic, women's, and gay rights issues, including the women-oriented Aspira, Inc., of New Jersey and La Casa de Don Pedro. She also branched out into organizations with wider appeal, such as the United Community Foundation, the Newark Urban League, and the United Community Corporation. In 1975, she cofounded the Puerto Rican Congress, whose mission was to help coordinate the efforts of area groups for the benefit of the substantial Puerto Rican population in the New Jersey-New York area. In recognition of her significant professional and volunteer efforts, Rutgers University awarded her the Rutgers Presidential Award for Public Service.

Using her academic expertise, Hidalgo conducted a study of the frequency of lesbianism among women in high positions in Puerto Rican organizations. Because of the cultural attitudes of both Puerto Rican and non-Hispanic society, these women overwhelmingly kept their homosexuality private, making the publicly acknowledged lesbian Hidalgo not only a researcher but also a source of inspiration. In 1976, Hidalgo and her sister Elia Hidalgo Christenson published an academic article in the *Journal of Homosexuality* entitled "Puerto Rican Lesbians and the Puerto Rican Community."

Although primarily known for her work as a gay activist and Hispanic leader, Hidalgo's interest in helping others encouraged her to pursue interests in several other areas. She earned certifications as a marriage counselor and in social work. She served on the New Jersey Department of Human Services Advisory Committee and participated in the National Association of Social Workers.

After twenty-three years teaching at Rutgers University, Hidalgo formally retired but continued her public work as the assistant commissioner of education in New Jersey from 1994 through 1995. She left New Jersey for Florida, where she actively participated in the gay rights organizations Wild Iris and Equality Florida.

During her years of activism, Hidalgo garnered several awards and honors. In 1978, Essex County College chose her as the Puerto Rican Woman of the Year. The national publication *Ladies Home Journal* named her one its "50 American Heroines," and New Jersey honored her in 1986 as part of Women's History Week. In 2007, she received the Maria De Castro Blake Community Service Award. Hidalgo died of pancreatic cancer on November 8, 2009, in Gainesville, Florida, survived by her partner, Cheryl Lamey, and her sisters.

SIGNIFICANCE

Hilda Hidalgo used her experience as an openly lesbian Latina to help others who struggled with cultural acceptance and who needed access to programs and organizations that could better their lives. Hidalgo's professional and volunteer work was far-reaching, both in scope and ambition, and provided a pathway for other women who were often overlooked in the latter part of the twentieth century.

Bonnye Busbice Good

FURTHER READING

Hidalgo, Hilda. *Lesbians of Color: Social and Human Services*. Binghamton, N.Y.: Haworth Press, 1995. This collection of essays highlights programs that can benefit minority women with economic, educational, social, and other needs.

Telgen, Diane, and Jim Kamp, eds. *Notable Hispanic American Women*. Detroit: Gale Research, 1993. Includes a concise but thorough biography of Hidalgo, providing a detailed overview of her contributions to Hispanic and gay rights issues, in addition to her social work efforts.

Torres, Andres, and Jose Emiliano Velasquez, eds. *The Puerto Rican Movement: Voices from the Diaspora*. Philadelphia: Temple University Press, 1998. Discusses the community organizations designed to help Puerto Ricans navigate American society, including several in which Hidalgo actively participated.

See also: Helen Fabela Chávez; Antonia Hernández; Dolores Huerta; Felisa Rincón de Gautier.

OSCAR HIJUELOS

American writer

Hijuelos is noted for fiction depicting the lives of Cuban Americans as they try to adapt to a new culture while they are still influenced by the old. His plots and his prose style reflect the importance of Latin American music to his characters. Hijuelos is credited with popularizing Latin American fiction among readers throughout the United States.

Latino heritage: Cuban
Born: August 24, 1951; New York, New York
Area of achievement: Literature

EARLY LIFE

Oscar Hijuelos (AHS-kahr ee-WEHL-ohs) was born in New York City on August 24, 1951, the younger son of Pascual Hijuelos and Magdalena Torrens Hijuelos, who had left their native Cuba for the United States in 1943. After losing the money he had meant to use to start a business, Pascual began working for a hotel, where he remained for the next thirty years. He also held a second job. His hard life, along with an addiction to alcohol, undoubtedly led to his early death.

On one of the family's frequent trips to Cuba, four-year-old Oscar became ill. When his family learned that he had nephritis, a serious kidney disease, his parents took him to a children's hospital in Connecticut. During his year there and at a convalescent home, Oscar forgot his Spanish and learned English. After he returned to his Spanish-speaking family, he continued to use English, even in conversation.

A sickly child, Oscar was often kept home. His mother, who was a talented but uneducated woman, often read him poems she had written, and she also told him stories about her girlhood in Cuba. Hijuelos did complete his education, first attending a Catholic grade school, then going to a public junior high and high school. Meanwhile, he had learned to play guitar and piano, and as a teenager he began earning money by playing in bands that featured both popular tunes and Latin music.

When Hijuelos was seventeen, his father died, leaving the family penniless. It had always been assumed that the Hijuelos boys would go to college. However, they now had to support the family. Though he did try to take some college courses, he always dropped out in order to earn money by picking up odd jobs and playing

Oscar Hijuelos. (AP Photo)

Hijuelos and the Cuban Experience in America

Most of Oscar Hijuelos's immigrants live in New York, far from the Cuban villages where they knew everyone. However, they are so focused on the possibilities that America offers that they do not brood about the past. Instead, they use their traditions, notably music and dance, as a means of expression and a source of joy.

Hijuelos's characters come together in dances, such as the mambo and the rumba, responding to the strong sexual component of the music. In keeping with their culture, the women dance to prove that they are desirable, while the men dance to exhibit their machismo, their power over women. During the sex act, for a brief time they can forget their real problems, their loneliness, which Hijuelos believes is not the result of their being immigrants but simply the mark of their humanity.

with various bands. Finally, he enrolled in the City University of New York (CUNY), majoring in English. At first, he was uncertain about his career goals; however, as soon as he took a course in creative writing, he knew that he wanted to be a writer. After graduating in 1975, Hijuelos remained at CUNY for another year, and in 1976, he received his M.A. in creative writing. Meanwhile, his marriage to an actor he had met in college ended in divorce.

In 1977, Hijuelos was hired by an advertising firm, and for the next eight years he worked there by day and wrote every night. His short fiction brought him some recognition, as well as several small grants. In 1983, his first novel appeared. *Our House in the Last World*, the story of a Cuban American family much like his own, brought Hijuelos a number of awards, including a prestigious fellowship from the National Endowment for the Arts. At last he could quit his advertising job and devote all of his time to his literary career.

LIFE'S WORK

Since his next novel was to be set during the 1950's, when the mambo captured the Latin American musical scene, Hijuelos did extensive research into the period before writing *The Mambo Kings Play Songs of Love*, which was published in 1989. The central characters in the novel are two brothers, Cesar and Nestor Castillo, who decide to move from their native Cuba to New York. There they organize an orchestra specializing in the mambo. In one episode in the book, Hijuelos

introduces the real-life television and film star Desi Arnaz, who has the brothers appear in the popular television show *I Love Lucy*. Although that episode makes them famous, the brothers cannot find happiness or even inner peace. Only in their music and in sporadic sexual encounters do they find release, and in the end, that is not enough to give them the happiness they seek.

The Mambo Kings Play Songs of Love was a best seller and in 1990 was awarded the Pulitzer Prize for fiction. A 1992 film adaptation was highly successful, and a stage musical was scheduled to open on Broadway in 2005, but at the last minute it was canceled. *The Mambo Kings Play Songs of Love* remains Hijuelos best-known work.

The inventiveness that makes that work so memorable is just as evident in the later novels by Hijuelos. For example, though most of his works are about Cuban Americans, the short novel *Mr. Ives' Christmas* (1995) is about a crisis of faith, not about issues of identity. *The Fourteen Sisters of Emilio Montez O'Brien* (1993) is set in rural Pennsylvania, rather than in New York or Cuba. Hijuelos likes to explore various points of view. The title character of *Empress of the Splendid Season* (1999) is a Cuban aristocrat, forced by circumstances to work as a housekeeper. In *Beautiful Maria of My Soul* (2010), Hijuelos features the same characters who appeared in *Mambo Kings*, but the point of view is that of the woman who was the love object in the earlier novel. While Latin American music remains a constant in his works, in *A Simple Habana Melody: From When the World Was Good* (2002), it is not the mambo but the rumba that takes center stage.

Inspired by his wife Lori Marie Carlson, many of whose books were written for younger readers, Hijuelos even ventured into young adult literature. *Dark Dude* (2008) is a realistic, often hilarious story about a teenager living in 1960's Harlem.

SIGNIFICANCE

The Mambo Kings Play Songs of Love is credited with having introduced Cuban American literature to the general public. While earlier books by Cuban Americans had focused primarily on the immigrants' yearning for the past and their search for a new identity, Hijuelos dealt with more universal issues. A reader did not have to be familiar with Latin American music or Cuban culture to relate to characters who fall in and out of love, worry about their families, and seek reassurance from their faith but are often tormented by doubt. Above all, the general reader could identify with people who, even in the midst of success, find themselves desperately lonely. By dealing with such universal human concerns, Hijuelos reached across ethnic lines and attracted readers from throughout the United States and all over the world. His success made it possible for other Latin American writers to enter the literary mainstream.

Rosemary M. Canfield Reisman

FURTHER READING

Herrera, Andrea O'Reilly, ed. *Cuba: Idea of a Nation Displaced*. Albany: State University of New York Press, 2007. Essays on problems associated with the Cuban diaspora, including issues of identity, memory, and cultural change. A discussion of Hijuelos focuses on his novel *The Fourteen Sisters*. Includes notes, bibliographies, and index.

Hijuelos, Oscar. "Words and Music." Interview by Ilan Stavans. *Conversations with Ilan Stavans*. Tucson: University of Arizona Press, 2005. In this 1989 interview, Hijuelos reveals details about his early life and his professional development.

Kevane, Bridget. *Latino Literature in America*. Westport, Conn.: Greenwood Press, 2003. A chapter on Hijuelos provides perceptive comments on his work and an analysis of *The Mambo Kings Play Songs of Love*. Includes bibliography and index.

Pérez Firmat, Gustavo. *Life on the Hyphen: The Cuban-American Way*. Austin: University of Texas Press, 1994. Discusses Hijuelos as a writer who has moved away from his Cuban heritage and into the American mainstream. Includes illustrations, notes, and index.

Smorkaloff, Pamela Maria. *Cuban Writers on and off the Island: Contemporary Narrative Fiction*. New York: Twayne, 1999. An excellent overview. Includes chronology, notes, bibliography, and index.

See also: Julia Alvarez; Reinaldo Arenas; Jimmy Santiago Baca; Giannina Braschi; Sandra Cisneros; Cristina García.

MARIA HINOJOSA

Mexican-born journalist

A broadcast journalist, producer, and author, Hinojosa has won numerous awards during a career that has included stints with National Public Radio, CNN, and CBS. The author of two books, Hinojosa has been recognized as one of America's most influential Hispanic women.

Latino heritage: Mexican
Born: July 2, 1961; Mexico City, Mexico
Also known as: Maria de Lourdes Hinojosa
Area of achievement: Journalism

EARLY LIFE

Maria de Lourdes Hinojosa (EE-noh-HOH-sah) was the fourth child of Raul and Berta (Ojeda) Hinojosa. Raul was a doctor and Berta a social worker. When Hinojosa was eighteen months old, her family immigrated to the United States. At first living in New England and then settling in Chicago, Hinojosa attended the University of Chicago High School, where she founded a group called Students for a Better Environment. With an eye toward being an actor, she enrolled at Barnard College, part of Columbia University.

While at Barnard, Hinojosa landed a job at Columbia's student radio station, WCKR-FM, where she was

producer and host of *Nueva cancion y demas* and later became the station's program director while earning a degree in Latin American studies, political economy, and women's studies. Hinojosa graduated *magna cum laude* from Barnard.

Hinojosa took an internship with National Public Radio (NPR) in Washington, D.C., in 1985 and worked as associate producer on *Enfoque nacional*, NPR's weekly Spanish-language news program, which aired out of San Diego. For this assignment Hinojosa lived in nearby Tijuana, Mexico. NPR's first Latina correspondent, Hinojosa returned to Washington in 1988 to report and produce stories for *Morning Edition* and *All Things Considered*. In 1989, she won a Corporation for Public Broadcasting Silver Award for her report "Day of the Dead."

LIFE'S WORK

In 1990, Hinojosa was the first Latino to host a prime-time public-affairs television show in New York when she hosted *New York Hotline* on WNYC. In 1993, she launched *Latino USA*, an NPR program heard in several U.S. markets. The program introduced Latino issues to the rest of America and helped Latinos learn about topics relevant to themselves and their communities.

María Hinojosa. (Getty Images)

From 1997 to 2005, Hinojosa worked for CNN's New York City bureau, where she reported on urban issues. In 2001, she reported a weeklong series for CNN and *Time* magazine about the United States-Mexico border. Two years later, she covered the *Columbia* space shuttle disaster for CNN as a reporter and anchor.

Hinojosa has authored two books. In 1995, she released the young-adult book *Crews: Gang Members Talk with Maria Hinojosa*, based on a 1990 story she reported for NPR. This book gave a voice to gang members, an element of society whose point of view is rarely explored in the popular media. Hinojosa's 1999 title, *Raising Raul: Adventures Raising Myself and My Son*, is a serious departure from her previous title. In this book, she examined inequalities in the minority community and the disappointments and the happiness involved in conception and childbearing.

As the head of the Futuro Media Group in New York City, Hinojosa leads journalists in developing stories that reflect the rich cultural diversity of the United States. Once the senior correspondent for *NOW* on PBS, Hinojosa became a contributing correspondent to its successor, *Need to Know*. Hinojosa and her husband, artist German Perez, create altars for Day of the Dead observances. This artwork gives the journalist a different outlet for her creativity.

Over the years, many awards and honors have been bestowed upon Hinojosa for her work as a broadcast journalist, including the prestigious Leadership Award from the National Association of Hispanic Journalists. In 2007, she was honored by the Paley Center in a program that recognized women's contributions to media. She also won the 2002 Latino Heritage Award from Columbia University and the Rubén Salazar Award from the National Council of La Raza for outstanding work in her career. *Hispanic Business* magazine has named her among the One Hundred Most Influential Latinos in the United States three times. In 1999, *Working Mother* magazine named her one of the Twenty-five Most Influential Working Mothers in America.

Significance

Hinojosa has covered a wide range of important news stories in her years as a journalist. She provides a positive Latina presence in news media and brings insight and acumen to her work. She also is an accomplished author and advocate for women and Latinos.

Randy L. Abbott

Further Reading

Hinojosa, Maria. *Crews: Gang Members Talk to Maria Hinojosa*. San Diego, California: Harcourt Brace, 1995. Aimed at the young adult market and based on an NPR report for *All Things Considered*, this book presents candid and disturbing interviews with gang members.

_____. *Raising Raul: Adventures Raising Myself and My Son*. New York, N.Y.: Viking, 1999. This book covers the author's conflicting attitudes toward having her own family, the difficulties and complications involved in the process of having and rearing children in modern America.

Rodriguez, Marissa. "The Binds of Marriage: Journalist Maria Hinojosa Travels the World to Document the Shocking Practice of Child Marriage." *Hispanic* 20, no. 11 (November, 2007): 34-36. Discusses Hinojosa's reporting on child brides.

See also: Cristina García; Soledad O'Brien; Rubén Salazar.

ROLANDO HINOJOSA

American writer, scholar, and educator

Internationally renowned as a foremost Chicano novelist, Hinojosa is regarded as a highly influential figure among the first wave of Chicano writers. Best known for his ongoing oeuvre, the Klail City Death Trip*, a panoramic series of award-winning, interlocking, multigenerational works set in the fictional Belken County along the lower Rio Grande Valley of South Texas on the Texas-Mexico border.*

Latino heritage: Mexican

Born: January 21, 1929; Mercedes, Texas
Also known as: Rolando R. Hinojosa-Smith; Rolando R. Hinojosa-S.; Roland Hinojosa-Smith; P. Galindo
Areas of achievement: Literature; education

EARLY LIFE

Rolando R. Hinojosa-Smith, better known as Rolando Hinojosa (roh-LAN-doh ee-noh-HOH-sah), is the youngest of five children born to Carrie Effie Smith, a

Rolando Hinojosa.
(© Marsha Miller/The University of Texas at Austin)

member of one of the earliest Anglo-American families to settle in the valley of South Texas in 1887, and Manuel Guzmán Hinojosa, a descendant of the Escandón colonists who arrived in the area in the late 1740's. Hinojosa, who attended American public schools in Mercedes, Texas, earned a B.S. degree in Spanish literature from the University of Texas at Austin in 1954. He taught Spanish, U.S. government, and world history at Brownsville High School from 1954 to 1956, and it was during these years that he began to commit himself to the task of writing creatively about a border ethos specific to community life in the South Texas valley. In 1962, he enrolled as a graduate student at New Mexico Highlands University, where he received an M.A. in Spanish literature. Hinojosa subsequently earned a PhD in Spanish literature in 1969 from the University of Illinois.

By 1970, while he served as chair of the Modern Language Department at Texas A& M University Kingsville, Hinojosa began to publish short prose pieces in early Chicano and Hispanic journals, such as *Caracol*, *Hispamérica*, *Revista Chicano-Riqueña*, and *The Bilingual Review*. Hinojosa's first novel, *Estampas del valle, y otras obras* (*Sketches of the Valley, and Other Works*, 1973) was awarded the Premio Quinto Sol, and in 1976 he was awarded the prestigious Casa de las Américas Award for his second novel, *Klail City y sus alrededores*, a continuation, both in form and content of *Estampas del valle*. These early works, stylistic blends of collage, folkloric motifs, oral history, and eclectic bilingual vignettes told by multiple narrators, foreshadow Hinojosa's later work. In 1976, Hinojosa accepted an appointment as professor of creative writing and chair of Chicano studies at the University of Minnesota. In 1981, he began teaching in the Department of English at the University of Texas at Austin, where he remained in 2011.

LIFE'S WORK

With the publication in 1978 of *Korean Love Songs*, a collection of poems penned in the tradition of English World War I poetry, Hinojosa firmly established the *Klail City Death Trip* as a series, or one multidimensional metahistory, of the Texas-Mexican border.

Although on the surface Hinojosa's works appear inaccessible, fragmented, and even contradictory, when considered as a whole, which is in keeping with the author's intention as discussed in various interviews, the

Klail City Death Trip comprises a unique voice that resists both closure and what literary critic Mikhail Bakhtin called "monologism." Scholars and critics generally agree that Hinojosa's strength rests on the "dialogic" nature of his work. There are no absolutes, and there is no single voice, or linear history, in Hinojosa's oeuvre. Instead, the author blends ethnopoetics and folkloric techniques to push the limits of postnarrative forms. The result is a collective overlapping narrative of four generations of storytelling in the valley of South Texas. More than a thousand characters populate his series of fictional texts that portray the conflicts and tensions between Hispanics and Anglos on the Texas-Mexico border.

Recurrent themes that speak to the political, socioeconomic, and historical ethos of South Texas inform the individual texts that comprise the *Klail City Death Trip.* Works are presented from the point of view of recurring characters whose stories often overlap. Characters such as Esteban Echevarría, Jehú Malacara, Rafa Buenrostro, and Aureliano Mora appear often, as do themes of the uses and abuses of power in South Texas, the memories of a vanishing Mexican culture, and the transformation of peoples and cultures wrought by changing historical and economic developmentss. The dynamics of integration, especially in terms of oral historicity, are key to acknowledging and appreciating Hinojosa's series. His works challenge individual readings and readers alike in that, like orality, they presuppose engagement with the texts. The texts in the *Klail City Death Trip* represent remembrances, histories, and, ultimately, decentered constructions that capture the changing conditions of the author's fictional Belken County. The fragmented, often disintegrated, intertextual form of the series reflects Hinojosa's literary agenda of representing elusive, alternative histories.

As of 2010, more than a dozen works comprised the as-yet-unfinished the *Klail City Death Trip.* In addition *Estampas del valle, y otras obras, Klail City y sus alrededores,* and *Korean Love Songs,* the series includes *Mi querido Rafa* (1981), *Rites and Witnesses* (1982), *The Valley* (1983), *Partners in Crime: A Rafe Buenrostro Mystery* (1985), *Claros Valores de Belken* (1986), *Klail City* (1987), *Becky and Her Friends* (1990), *The Useless Servants* (1993), *Ask a Policeman: A Rafe Buenrostro Mystery* (1998), and *We Happy Few* (2006).

SIGNIFICANCE

A master of satire, humor, and the use of autobiography, Rolando Hinojosa's highly intertextual works constitute a

Impact on Other Nations: The Casa de Las Américas Award

The Casa de Las Américas Award is among the most prestigious literary competitions in Latin America. The granting organization, Casa de las Américas, is based in Havana and was founded in April, 1959, by the government of Cuba and the Cuban revolutionary Haydée Santamaría, who served as the organization's first president until her death in 1980. A powerful center for the promotion of national cultures, revisionist histories, and the intellectual exchange of ideas central to Third World issues, Casa de Las Américas publishes a bimonthly review guide, and, since its inception, has published the works of winning literary titles under the auspices of its publishing fund. Despite periods of economic crisis in the region, the organization remains a powerful scholarly, cultural, and political force dedicated to promoting and fostering social and cultural relations between Latin America, the Caribbean, and the rest of the world in the genres of poetry, novel, short story, essay, theater, and *testimonio.* Awards alternate annually in various categories, which may include sculpture, theater, and essay, and may be submitted in either English or Spanish. Special prizes and honorary awards are given yearly, and Latin Americans and naturalized citizens of Latin America are invited to apply.

Rolando Hinojosa is the first Chicano author to receive the prestigious Premio Casa de las Américas for his work of fiction, the second installment in the *Klail City Death* series, *Klail City y sus alrededores* (1976).

substantial body of writing that draws readers into a complex 150-year alternate history— told from the Chicano point of view— of the Rio Grande Valley on the Texas-Mexico border in the American Southwest. Through the use of poetry, prose, oral history, epistolary, and diverse linguistic strategies, such as bilingualism, mixed genres, and varying narrative styles, his collective ongoing novel, the *Klail City Death Trip,* has influenced a generation of Chicano scholars, writers, and activists. The diversity of Hinojosa's oeuvre speaks to his legacy, as he boldly interprets and often redefines the varied political, social, cultural, personal, and collective experiences of Mexican Americans of the Rio Grande Valley within a topos of experimental modes. A scholar and writer whose innovative style has widely impacted the shape and direction of Chicano literature, Hinojosa's continuing, still incomplete metahistory of the Rio Grande Valley remains critical to understanding the Chicano experience and history in Texas and the United States.

Cordelia E. Barrera

FURTHER READING
Hinojosa, Rolando. *Estampas del valle, y otras obras.* Berkeley: Quinto Sol, 1973. Seminal first installment in the *Klail City Death Trip* series that contains the seeds of all Hinojosa's subsequent works. A bilinguial edition, with translation by Gustavo Valadez and Jose Reyna and published as *Sketches of the Valley, and Other Works*, was released by Berkeley, California-based Justa Publications in 1980.

_____. *Klail City y sus alrededores.* Havana: Casa de las Américas, 1976. Second installment in the *Klail City Death Trip* series and the winner of Latin America's highest literary award, the Premio Literario Casa de las Américas. A bilingual edition with translation by Rosaura Sanchez, published as *Generaciones y semblanzas*, was issued by Justa Publications in 1977; Hinojosa's own translation, published as *Klail City*, was released by Houston-based Arte Público Press in 1987.

Kaup, Monika. *Rewriting North American Borders in Chicano and Chicana Narrative.* New York: Peter Lang, 2001. A broad study of Chicano literature since the 1960's that examines how Hinojosa and other writers approach ideologies and themes about the United States-Mexico border.

Saldívar, José David, ed. *The Rolando Hinojosa Reader: Essays Historical and Critical.* Houston: Arte Público Press, 1985. One of the earliest critical works in Chicano literature, this collection contains four short essays by Hinojosa, an editor's interview with the author, and nine critical essays by leading Chicano authors that discuss Marxist, feminist, and poststructural approaches to Hinojosa's work.

Zilles, Klaus. *Rolando Hinojosa: A Reader's Guide.* Albuquerque: University of New Mexico Press, 2001. Discusses the *Klail City Death Trip* as one integrated text. Zilles provides a close reading of the series, situating Hinojosa's oeuvre in the context of postmodernism, intertextuality, and the oral history of South Texas.

See also: Isabel Allende; Rudolfo Anaya; Raymond Barrio; Arturo Islas; José Montoya; Tomás Rivera.

LORENZO HOMAR

Puerto Rican-born artist

Homar was a prolific and multitalented artist who produced a wide range of works including woodcuts, silkscreens, calligraphy art, engravings, posters, and political caricatures. Despite his long career and role as the first director of the Graphic Arts Workshop, he remains largely unknown.

Latino heritage: Spanish

Born: September 10, 1913; Puerta de Tierra, San Juan, Puerto Rico

Died: February 16, 2004; San Juan, Puerto Rico

Also known as: Lorenzo Homar Gelabert

Area of achievement: Art

EARLY LIFE

Lorenzo Homar Gelabert (OH-mahr) was born in the barrio of Puerta de Tierra in San Juan, Puerto Rico, to Lorenzo Homar Zampol and Margarita Gelabert. His father was a film distributor and his mother was a pianist; both were immigrants from Majorca and returned to Spain for a brief period during their son's childhood. After returning to Puerto Rico, the Homar family moved to the United States in 1928 in search of work.

After arriving in New York at fifteen years of age and during the Great Depression, Homar abandoned his formal studies to work in a textile factory. He participated in athletics and acrobatics as an adolescent, even working temporarily as a vaudeville gymnast in the 1930's. In 1931, he enrolled at the Art Students League of New York after demonstrating an aptitude for art. There he studied with artist George Bridgman for six years, developing his personal style and honing his artistic talent, which helped him secure an apprenticeship with jeweler Cartier. As a result of this opportunity, he learned engraving skills from Ernest Loth, a master designer at the jewelry company. This ability was integrated into later works featuring Homar's distinctive style of typography and calligraphy. After completing his apprenticeship, Homar began working for Cartier full time.

LIFE'S WORK

Homar's impressive and diverse artistic career was interrupted by his voluntary enlistment in the U.S. Army during World War II. He was wounded in action in the Philippines and received a Purple Heart. Upon returning from his tour of duty, he resumed working at Cartier and began taking art classes at the Brooklyn Museum. His teachers there included accomplished and internationally renowned artists such as Arthur Osver, Gabor Peterdi, Ben Shahn, and Rufino Tamayo. In 1950, he returned to his homeland and had his first exhibition the next year at the Puerto Rican Athenaeum. Homar then established the Center for Puerto Rican Arts and produced significant works for DIVEDCO, a division of the Puerto Rico Department of Education, where he worked as a teacher and artist.

Homar produced hundreds of works of art, ranging from woodcuts to political caricatures depicting the cultural, historical, and political issues prevalent in Puerto Rico. He also created posters and printed engravings with vivid scenes and unique lettering. Homar received numerous accolades for his work. He earned a Guggenheim Fellowship in fine arts in 1956. The next year, he heeded the government's request and established the Graphic Arts Workshop of the Institute of Puerto Rican Culture. He served as director until his retirement in 1973. During his tenure there, Homar taught graphic arts and inspired countless artists, including Myrna Báez and Antonio Martorell.

In 1978, the Ponce Museum of Art presented the first full retrospective exhibit of Homar's work. In 2001, 150 of his posters were displayed in the exhibit "Abra palabra . . . la letra mágica: Carteles de Lorenzo Homar 1951-1990" at the Museum of Art at the University of Puerto Rico. His works have been displayed across the United States and Puerto Rico and are exhibited at the Library of Congress, the Metropolitan Museum of Art, Princeton University Library, and various museums in Puerto Rico.

In 1987, the University of Puerto Rico awarded Homar an honorary doctorate in arts. The Institute of Puerto Rican Culture awarded him a Medal of Honor in 2003. A year later, in 2004, Homar died in San Juan near the same neighborhood where he was born. He was surrounded by his wife, Dorothy, and their two daughters.

SIGNIFICANCE

Homar was a prolific artist who produced hundreds of works, including posters, printed engravings, silkscreens, and caricatures. He was a pioneer in the graphic arts, design, and plastic arts movements during the second half of the twentieth century. He also was a major influence on the Puerto Rican artists known as Generación del Cincuenta (Generation of the 1950's). He widely utilized the *afiche*, a type of commemorative poster with engravings and calligraphy. Although his works are not well-known internationally, Homar received numerous accolades for his art.

Alyson F. Lerma

FURTHER READING

AIGA: The Professional Association for Design. "Lorenzo Homar." http://www.aiga.org/content.cfm/design-journeys-lorenzo-homar. This professional association Web site offers a detailed biographical profile of Homar and his career.

Cotter, Holland. "Art in Review; Between the Lines." *The New York Times*, June 2, 2006. Review comparing Homar and Pedro Pietri and includes a brief discussion of Homar's career. Author claims that Homar was one of the most influential but overlooked modern artists.

Mendez Mendez, Serafín. "Lorenzo Homar." In *Notable Caribbeans and Caribbean Americans: A Biographical Dictionary*, by Serafín Mendez Mendez and Gail A. Cueto. Westport, Conn.: Greenwood Press, 2003. This reference work includes a valuable entry on Homar's early life and career.

Roylance, Dale. "The Art of Lorenzo Homar." *Calligraphy Review* volume 11 (1994): 34-37. Roylance describes the designs that define Homar's distinctive style.

_____. *Lorenzo Homar: A Puerto Rican Master of Calligraphy and the Graphic Arts*. Princeton, N.J.: The Graphic Arts Collection, Princeton University Library, 1983. Twenty-four-page pamphlet focusing on Homar's work in various media.

See also: José Aceves; Olga Albizu; Fernando Botero; Ana Mendieta.

EUGENIO MARÍA DE HOSTOS

Puerto Rican-born activist, educator, and writer

A teacher, journalist, essayist, editor, and moral philosopher, Hostos spent most of his adult life traveling throughout the Western Hemisphere. In his inspirational lectures, writings, and activities, he campaigned for a variety of worthy causes and was an especially strong advocate for the independence of his homeland, Puerto Rico.

Latino heritage: Puerto Rican
Born: January 11, 1839; Rio Cañas, Mayagüez, Puerto Rico
Died: August 11, 1903; Santo Domingo, Dominican Republic
Also known as: Eugenio María de Hostos y Bonilla; The Citizen of the Americas
Areas of achievement: Activism; education; journalism

EARLY LIFE

Eugenio María de Hostos y Bonilla (yew-JEHN-ee-oh mah-REE-ah deh OH-stohs ee bo-NEE-yah) was the descendant of Castilians who migrated to Cuba in the early eighteenth century. He was the sixth of eight children born into a wealthy family, the son of plantation owner Eugenio María de Hostos y Rodriguez and María Hilaria de Bonilla y Cintron.

Hostos attended elementary school in San Juan, Puerto Rico, before being sent to Bilbao, Spain, at the age of thirteen to continue his education. After graduation from high school in 1856, he studied law at the Central University of Madrid, where he became involved in politics with fellow Puerto Rican students who agitated for the independence of Spanish possessions in the Greater Antilles of the Caribbean. While at the university, he published a social-political novel, *La peregrinación de Bayoán* (*Bayoán's Pilgrimage,* 1863), which was critical of Spanish colonialism.

When a new Spanish constitution, adopted in 1869, made no provision for Puerto Rico's independence, Hostos left Spain for New York City. There he worked for Cuban independence, the first strategic step in what he hoped would be a movement for self-determination for all Spanish-controlled islands in the Caribbean. Toward that end, he edited and wrote for *La revolución*, a newspaper that supported Cuban autonomy, and corresponded with Cuban patriot José Martí. Hostos soon became frustrated with Cuban leaders in New York, who preferred for the United States to annex the island, and left the city to undertake an ambitious, solo campaign.

LIFE'S WORK

For the next four years, Hostos traveled through Central and South America, raising awareness and drumming up support for the cause of independence and the abolition of slavery. He lived off the sales of the many essays, articles, and books he wrote, and from stipends earned as teacher, lecturer, or editor. In Peru, he publicly condemned the harsh treatment of Chinese laborers— gaining concessions for them in the process— and was influential in the development of the country's educational system.

In Chile, as a university professor, he was instrumental in persuading the government to permit women to attend college. In Argentina, Hostos argued successfully for the benefits of a trans-Andean railway, and a grateful Argentine government named a locomotive for him.

Hostos returned to New York in 1874 and was involved in organizing several unsuccessful revolutionary schemes in Puerto Rico and Cuba. In 1875, he moved to the Dominican Republic, where he founded several newspapers. The following year, he went to Venezuela to help improve education. While there, he married Cuban native Belinda Otilia de Ayala Quintana; the couple had five children between 1879 and 1892. For ten years, Hostos remained in the Dominican Republic, teaching law at the Professional Institute, founding Santo Domingo's first teachers' college and a night school, and writing and lecturing extensively.

In 1889, following an appeal from the Chilean government, Hostos traveled to Valparaiso to help revamp the country's educational system. For a decade, he worked tirelessly, writing textbooks on law and grammar, teaching law at the University of Chile, and creating curricula. In 1899, after the conclusion of the Spanish-American War, Hostos was selected as a delegate to meet with U.S. President William McKinley to plead for Puerto Rico's independence. His appeal, however, was ignored, and the United States annexed the island as a territory.

Hostos afterward traveled to Puerto Rico for the first time in many years to found the Municipal Institute. In 1900, he returned to Santo Domingo, where he was appointed inspector general of public education. He remained in the Dominican Republic until his death in 1903 and was buried in the National Pantheon.

SIGNIFICANCE

One of the great thinkers of his time, Hostos was both a man of letters and a man of action. Although he did not live to see his dream of Antillean autonomy fulfilled— Puerto Rico remains a U.S. territory to this day— his life and work have greatly affected the philosophy, sociology, and psychology of Latin America. His impact has been most notable in the field of education, in which he encouraged learning for women, forged solid curricula founded on sciences and liberal arts, and emphasized critical thinking rather than rote learning. Many of his writings are still used in Latin American classrooms. His writings (encompassing everything from children's stories to Shakespearean critiques to learned treatises) form the basis for what is known as Hostian thought.

Jack Ewing

FURTHER READING

Burke, Janet, and Ted Humphrey, eds. and trans. *Nineteenth-Century Nation Building and the Latin American Intellectual Tradition*. Indianapolis, Ind.: Hackett, 2007. This is a collection of translated readings from the works of some of the greatest Latin American thinkers of the nineteenth century— including Hostos, Martí and others— regarding such issues as race, economics, education, and international relations.

Mendez Mendez, Serafin, and Gail Cueto. *Notable Caribbeans and Caribbean Americans: A Biographical Dictionary*. Westport, Conn.: Greenwood Press, 2003. This reference work contains a brief but highly detailed biography of patriot, educator, and humanist Hostos, and provides an overview of his work, complete with bibliographical notes.

Ramos, Julio. *Divergent Modernities: Culture and Politics in Nineteenth-Century Latin America*. Durham, N.C.: Duke University Press Books, 1999. Analyzes the links among history, literature, culture, and the development of national identity in the formation of modern Latin America.

See also: Ignacio Manuel Altamirano; Román Baldorioty de Castro; Jesús Colón; José de Diego; José Martí; Lola Rodríguez de Tió.

DOLORES HUERTA

American labor union leader and feminist

Huerta, along with César Chávez, founded the National Farm Workers Association that later became the United Farm Workers (UFW) union. She is best known for her work as the vice president of UFW, as well as a lobbyist, negotiator, and organizer for the farmworkers' rights movement of the 1960's and 1970's.

Latino heritage: Mexican
Born: April 10, 1930; Dawson, New Mexico
Also known as: Dolores Clara Fernández Huerta; Dolores Clara Fernández
Areas of achievement: Activism; women's rights

EARLY LIFE

Dolores Clara Fernández Huerta (doh-LOH-rehs CLAH-rah fehr-NAHN-dehs WEHR-tah) was born on April 10, 1930 in Dawson, New Mexico. Her mother, Alicia Chávez, was from New Mexico, but after her divorce from Huerta's father she moved to Stockton, California, along with Dolores and Dolores's two brothers, John and Marshall. Huerta's mother first worked in canneries and other service-industry jobs before acquiring her own restaurant and hotel, becoming an independent business woman. Huerta's father, Juan Fernández, was a first generation immigrant from Mexico who worked in coal mines in New Mexico and later became a labor organizer for the Congress of Industrial Organizations (CIO). He was elected to the New Mexico state legislature in 1938.

As a young girl, Huerta also lived with her maternal grandfather, who called her Seven Tongues because of her quick thought and verbal dexterity. Because both Huerta's mother and grandfather were strong presences in her early life, Huerta has said that her household was very egalitarian and committed to social justice. Her mother's businesses were prosperous, enabling Huerta to participate in music and dance lessons, various church activities, such as choir, and the Girl Scouts. She excelled in school and eventually obtained a teacher's certificate from the University of the Pacific's Delta Community College, an unusual educational achievement for Chicanas during this era. Huerta's middle-class background, bilingual skills in English and Spanish, and egalitarian upbringing were strong influences for her later volunteer and organizing work.

In 1950, Huerta married her first husband, Ralph Head, who had been her high school boyfriend. She had two daughters with him, Celeste and Lori. However, this marriage ended as Huerta became more involved in community service activities. Her second marriage to Ventura Huerta produced five more children: Fidel, Emilio, Vincent, Alicia, and Angela. As Huerta's involvement with farmworker and community services grew, this marriage soon dissolved, and Huerta became a single mother with seven children. In 1975, she became involved with Richard Chávez (César Chávez's brother), and had four more children with him (Juanita, María Elena, Ricky, and Camilla), although she never formalized their relationship through marriage.

LIFE'S WORK

After working as a teacher for several years, Huerta became involved with Fred Ross and the Stockton branch of the Community Service Organization (CSO) in 1955, first as a volunteer and later as a political lobbyist who advocated for the expansion of services for

Dolores Huerta. (Library of Congress)

the poor. In the late 1950's, Huerta met César Chávez, who was also involved with CSO. After much deliberation, Huerta and Chávez determined that CSO did not prioritize farmworkers' rights, and in 1962, they cofounded the National Farm Workers Association (NFWA), which later evolved into the United Farm Workers (UFW). Chávez was elected the president of the NFWA, and Huerta was elected to serve as vice president. Although Chávez has received much credit for the formation of the UFW, Huerta played an extremely important leadership role within and outside of the union. She was also an adviser and collaborator with Chávez on many union activities.

Because the National Labor Relations Act of 1935 provided protections for most workers in the United States except farmworkers, the need for a farmworker union was important, given that these laborers were paid extremely low wages and had virtually no workplace protections, such as access to toilets, drinking water, and worker safety measures. The purpose of the UFW was to advocate in the state of California and nationally for greater protections and rights for farmworkers. In 1965, the Agricultural Workers' Organization Committee decided to go on strike against grape growers. Although the NFWA was struggling to gain credibility and membership, Huerta and Chávez decided to join the strike, which would attract national publicity and evolve into a years-long boycott of grapes. Huerta was responsible for negotiating contracts with growers during this strike, and she also became the director of the union's East Coast operations in New York City.

The UFW's successful boycott of table grapes led to numerous other successes, such as collective bargaining and union contracts with growers that allowed for greater protection of farmworkers' rights. Through her political lobbying and contract negotiations, Huerta helped lead the union's efforts to improve the lives and working conditions of farmworkers. For example, Huerta's leadership and lobbying was instrumental in passing the 1975 Californian Agricultural Labor Relations Act. In terms of the union as an organization, Huerta also helped develop its credit union, its newspaper (*El malcriado*), and its radio station (Radio Campesina).

Often working eighteen-hour days, Huerta dedicated her life and family to the union. Not only did her children participate in many union activities, but also she took them to protests, meetings, and other organizational activities. Her life was one of self-sacrifice, especially in the 1960's, when she lived on between $5

La Pasionaria of the Farmworkers

Dolores Huerta is well known for her commitment to farmworker rights, among many other causes. She became known as La Pasionaria (the passionate one), Adelita (a Mexican female soldier), and the Grand Lady of Steel because of her passion and outspokenness on social justice issues, particularly those related to poverty and racial and sexual discrimination. Growers also problematically referred to her as the Dragon Lady because she refused to back down during negotiations for union contracts. At protests or on the picket line, Huerta would shout, "Don't be a marshmallow!" Huerta's speeches also closed with *gritos* (shouts), such as *¡Viva la justicia!* (Long Live Justice!), *¡Abajo!* (Down With!), and, most commonly, *¡Sí, se puede!* (Yes, It Can Be Done or Yes, One Can!). Her passion and dedication for social justice is evidenced in her lifelong work for the United Farm Workers and through her own organization, the Dolores Huerta Foundation, that works to further social justice through community organizing.

and $35 a week and relied on family, friends, and union supporters to help care for her children.

Although Huerta was not involved in the women's rights movement early on, she came to realize the sexism that she and other women experienced in labor organizing, social movements, and politics. These experiences led her to appreciate the women's rights movement, even though she was personally opposed to abortion and birth control, key issues in the movement during the 1960's and 1970's.

SIGNIFICANCE

As the cofounder of the UFW, Huerta was one of the top leaders of the union until 2000, when she retired. She made many important contributions to the UFW, the Chicano movement, the women's rights movement, and numerous other social justice causes. Her role as UFW spokesperson, picket and membership organizer, political lobbyist, contract negotiator, and social justice leader was unusual within the UFW, as well as within the Chicano movement, yet her visibility as a leader and spokesperson for the UFW has inspired numerous Chicanas and Latinas to participate in social justice causes.

Stacey K. Sowards

FURTHER READING

García, Mario T., ed. *A Dolores Huerta Reader*. Albuquerque: University of New Mexico Press, 2008. Contains original speeches and letters written by and interviews with Huerta, as well as articles and essays about her.

Griswold del Castillo, Richard, and Richard A. Garcia. *César Chávez: A Triumph of Spirit*. Norman: University of Oklahoma Press, 1995. Chapter four discusses Huerta and Chávez's relationship within the UFW.

Rose, Margaret. "Dolores Huerta: The United Farm Workers Union." In *The Human Tradition in American Labor History*, edited by Eric Arnesen. Wilmington, Del: Scholarly Resources Books, 2004. This chapter provides a biography of Dolores Huerta and discusses her role in the UFW.

_____. "Traditional and Nontraditional Patterns of Female Activism in the United Farm Workers of America, 1962 to 1980." *Frontiers* 11, no. 1 (1990): 26-30. Examines different roles women played in the UFW, specifically focusing on Huerta and Helen Chávez.

Sowards, Stacey K. "Rhetorical Agency as Haciendo Caras and Differential Consciousness Through Lens of Gender, Race, Ethnicity, and Class: An Examination of Dolores Huerta's Rhetoric." *Communication Theory* 20, no. 2. (May, 2010): 223-247. Examines Huerta's public and private discourse to better understand her leadership successes in the UFW.

See also: Luisa Capetillo; César Chávez; Helen Fabela Chávez; Antonia Hernández; Vilma Socorro Martínez; Antonio Orendain.

Julio Iglesias

Spanish-born singer

Best known as a hard-working, award-winning singer, songwriter, and humanitarian, Iglesias has earned the distinction of being one of Guinness Book of World Records' best-selling artists.

Latino heritage: Spanish
Born: September 23, 1943; Madrid, Spain
Also known as: Julio Jose Iglesias de la Cueva
Areas of achievement: Music; philanthropy

EARLY LIFE

Julio Jose Iglesias de la Cueva (HOO-lee-oh ee-GLAY-see-uhs) was born in Madrid, Spain, on September 23, 1943, the son of Dr. Julio Iglesias and Rosario de la Cueva y Iglesias. He attended the College of the Sacred Heart religious school where he became interested in soccer. As a child, Iglesias spent time playing and practicing soccer and played for the Real Madrid soccer club as a teenager. He continued playing soccer as a student at Madrid University, where he studied law, with hopes of playing the position of goalkeeper in the World Cup.

Iglesias's dream of becoming a professional soccer player ended abruptly on the night of his twentieth birthday after he suffered injuries in a car accident. A spinal injury sustained in the accident left him temporarily paralyzed. During his stay in the hospital and as the feeling returned to his extremities, Iglesias was given a guitar to play to help him regain dexterity in his fingers. He began writing songs to accompany his newly acquired ability to play the guitar.

After recovering from near paralysis, Iglesias's parents sent him to Cambridge University in England to study English for a year. Iglesias continued playing the guitar and writing songs and began performing his work in Cambridge pubs, where his music was well received. He returned to Spain a year later with the desire to become a singer. He began writing more songs and shopping them in pursuit of a record deal.

Iglesias entered the Festival de la Cancion (Festival of Singing) in Spain in 1968. He won with a performance of a song he had written, "La vida sigue iqual" ("Life Goes On"). The song became successful in Spain and was later adapted as a film in which Iglesias played the lead role.

LIFE'S WORK

By the 1970's, Iglesias had earned a reputation as a hardworking singer-songwriter. Drawing on the success of his first album *Yo canto* (*I Sing*), he began touring and performing in music festivals across Europe. He traveled extensively across Europe and Latin America. In 1971, he married Isabel Preysler Arrastia, with whom he had three children: Maria; Julio, Jr.; and Enrique.

In 1972, Iglesias recorded the song "Un canto a Galicia" ("A Song for Galicia"). The song was a chart-topper across Europe and Latin America and broadened his global appeal. Iglesias's world travels exposed him

Julio Iglesias (AP Photo)

The 1980's ushered in more success for Iglesias. He became a certified diamond-selling artist, with more than 100 million records sold, which earned him the distinction of being named the *Guiness Book of World Records* best-selling artist. Iglesias also recorded his first English-language album, *1100 Bel Air Place*, released in 1985. This album, best known for the song "To All the Girls I've Loved Before," a duet with country music artist Willie Nelson, sold four million copies.

By 1985, Iglesias was active in numerous humanitarian projects in addition to touring. His numerous philanthropic efforts included appearances at fund-raisers, telethons, and benefit concerts for earthquake victims in Mexico, the American Muscular Dystrophy Association, and Farm Aid. Iglesias received a star on the Hollywood Walk of Fame in 1985. He later won a Grammy Award for Best Latin Pop Artist in 1988.

SIGNIFICANCE

A noted performer and humanitarian, Iglesias's rise to fame and success was marked by his determination and steadfast work ethic. Few artists have achieved the global success of Iglesias, and he has created a legacy of achievement and unwavering dedication to his craft. His award-winning discography, which includes more than seventy albums recorded in six languages, his amiable persona, and his philanthropic spirit demonstrate his ability to reach people of all racial, ethnic, and social groups.

Tamela N. Chambers

FURTHER READING

Acton, Figuera. *Julio Iglesias and Enrique Iglesias*. New York: Rosen, 2004. A short, succinct profile of Julio and his son Enrique, written for young readers.

Billboard. "Julio Iglesias Thirtieth Anniversary." 112, no.22 (May 27, 2000): 72. A comprehensive look at Iglesias's body of work, awards, and accomplishments.

Martino, Elizabeth. *Julio Iglesias*. New York: Chelsea House, 1994. A biography aimed at young adults that includes a chronology of events spanning twenty years in Iglesias's career.

See also: Gloria Estefan; José Feliciano; Jennifer Lopez; Ricky Martin; Linda Ronstadt.

to a variety of cultures and languages. He recorded his first non-Spanish language album, in German, in 1972. As his reputation and appeal as a crossover artist grew, Iglesias's fans responded in kind by making him a top-selling and award-winning artist. He made history when he performed in front of 100,000 Chilean spectators. Iglesias won numerous awards in Latin America and Europe, including artist of the year honors in France and Italy.

Iglesias signed a deal with CBS International and worked toward achieving crossover success in the United States. In 1976, he performed at Madison Square Garden in New York City. This performance was noted for its record-breaking attendance and helped solidify Iglesias's reputation as a global megastar. While his work ethic earned him the admiration of fans, other noted musicians, businessmen, and politicians worldwide, it also played a role in the dissolution of his marriage. Iglesias and his wife Isabel divorced in 1979.

ARTURO ISLAS

American novelist and educator

Islas wrote short stories, poems, and critical essays, but his fame rests mainly on his novels, emphasizing a gay, Chicano subjectivity that deals with issues of race, sexuality, gender, class, and religion; his fiction also is imbued with the pre-Columbian cosmology of the Aztecs. Born in Texas, he wrote about the cultural experience of the borderlands between the United States and Mexico, becoming a powerful voice for Americans of Mexican descent.

Latino heritage: Mexican

Born: May 24, 1938; El Paso, Texas

Died: February 15, 1991; Stanford, California

Also known as: Arturo Islas La Farga; Sonny (nickname); Arturo Islas, Jr.

Areas of achievement: Literature; poetry; education; gay and lesbian issues

EARLY LIFE

Born in El Paso, Texas, to Arturo Islas, Sr., a police officer, and Jovita La Farga, a secretary, Arturo Islas La Farga (ahr-TEW-roh EES-lahs lah FAHR-gah) grew up as the eldest of three sons near the city's El Segundo barrio. Since his paternal grandmother tutored him early in English, he excelled in school, but at age eight, Islas contracted polio, which left him with a limp for life. Despite his physical disability, he became very popular in high school, getting elected as the second Mexican American president of student council.

In his teenage years, Islas struggled with his homosexuality but remained closeted until he got to college. Throughout his childhood, though, he endured a dysfunctional home life— tolerating a hostile and detached father and what he perceived as an acquiescent and martyred saint of a mother. After graduating as the first Chicano valedictorian from El Paso High School (1956), Islas was admitted to Stanford University in Palo Alto, California, receiving an Alfred P. Sloan scholarship. He first studied premedicine, hoping to become a neurosurgeon, but his grades suffered, so he quickly shifted major to the humanities. He was named a member of the Phi Beta Kappa honor society and eventually earned his B.A. with honors in English in 1960. Despite enduring intestinal cancer and a colostomy that left him in discomfort and disfigured, Islas overcame his pain and suffering to persevere and finish his education at a time when he was beginning to explore his homosexuality.

LIFE'S WORK

After leaving El Paso for college on the West Coast, Islas resided in California's San Francisco Bay area for the rest of his life. In 1960, he entered Stanford's graduate school, studying under the auspices of the school's famed literary figures, such as Wallace Stegner, Hortense Calisher, and Yvor Winters. In 1963, he earned an M.A., and in 1976, his Ph.D.— becoming the first Chicano in the United States to earn a doctoral degree in English. Teaching at Stanford, he eventually earned tenure in 1976 and ten years later was promoted to full professorship there.

In the uphill battle to get his first novel in print in the mainstream press, Islas was rejected by more than thirty publishing houses until he finally was accepted by a small, local one. His publications include *The Rain God: A Desert Tale* (1984), its sequel *Migrant Souls* (1990), and two works published posthumously: a third novel, *La Mollie and the King of Tears* (1996), and *Arturo Islas: The Uncollected Works* (2003).

Islas's awards were numerous: Stanford University's Lloyd W. Dinkelspiel Award in 1976 for exceptional contributions to undergraduate education; one of the three best novels of 1984 selected by the Bay Area Reviewers Association; and the best fiction prize from the Border Regional Library Conference in 1985 and a nomination for *The Los Angeles Times* best fiction award for *The Rain God.* Islas's first novel also won the Southwest Book Award for its literary excellence and cultural-heritage enrichment in 1986. The University of Texas at El Paso elected him to its Writers Hall of Fame in 1991.

Islas lived with his partner, Jay Spears, for many years. Suffering from poor health for most of his life, Islas died on February 15, 1991, from pneumonia related to complications of acquired immune deficiency syndrome (AIDS).

SIGNIFICANCE

In literature, Islas crafted fiction whose borderland characters reflect a Chicano ethnicity, intersecting with a gay sexuality, and immersed in symbols/icons from indigenous Aztec culture. He claimed that immigrants from Mexico to the United States should actually be viewed as "migrants," as they mirror migration patterns that their Amerindian ancestors made throughout the Americas during the Mesoamerican era. His claim to fame is most notable: his second literary work, *Migrant Souls,* became in 1990 the first novel by a Chicano author to be published by an East Coast publishing house, a major feat. Celebrating the rich cultural experience of Chicanos in the United States, Islas created fiction with complexity and nuanced characters that shuns ethnic stereotyping.

Itzcóatl Tlaloc Meztli

FURTHER READING

Aldama, Frederick Luis. *Dancing with Ghosts: A Critical Biography of Arturo Islas*. Berkeley: University of California Press, 2005. Provides crucial insights about Islas's childhood and his dysfunctional family, his years at Stanford as an academic, his attempts to get published, and his sexual orientation.

_____, ed. *Critical Mappings of Arturo Islas's Fictions*. Tempe, Ariz.: Bilingual Review/Press, 2005. A collection of seventeen essays and interviews on Islas's works of fiction by scholars and critics.

Islas, Arturo. "Arturo Islas: I Don't Like Labels and Categories." Interview by Hector A. Torres. In *Conversations with Contemporary Chicana and Chicano Writers*. Albuquerque: University of New Mexico Press, 2007. Torres interviewed Islas eight months before the novelist died; Islas discussed his years at Stanford, experiencing racism growing up in El Paso, and expanding American literature to include the literatures of all of the Americas.

_____. *Arturo Islas: The Uncollected Works*. Edited by Frederick Luis Aldama. Houston, Tex.: Arte Público Press, 2003. Recovered from Stanford University's archives, included in this collection are Islas's unpublished works— short fiction, poetry, and essays.

See also: Alurista; Rudolfo Anaya; Gloria Anzaldúa; Reyes Cárdenas; Rigoberto González; Cherríe Moraga; John Rechy.

Cleofas Martinez Jaramillo

American writer, folklorist, and businesswoman

Jaramillo worked to preserve for future generations the folklore, cuisine, dress, and other Hispanic customs that were being eroded by the introduction of Anglo culture. Her books are poignant reminders of the late nineteenth and early twentieth century Hispanic way of life and the cultural richness it so generously offered.

Latino heritage: Spanish and Mexican

Born: December 6, 1878; Arroyo Hondo, New Mexico Territory (now New Mexico)

Died: November 30, 1956; El Paso, Texas

Also known as: Cleofas Martinez

Areas of achievement: Literature; business

EARLY LIFE

Cleofas Martinez Jaramillo (KLEE-oh-fahs mahr-TEE-nehz hah-rah-MEE-yoh), one of seven children, was born in Arroyo Hondo in what is now northern New Mexico into a family of extremely fortunate means. Her parents, Marina Lucero and Julian Antonio Martinez, descendants of the original pioneer families of Arroyo Hondo, operated various successful businesses in the region. Jaramillo's schooling was just as privileged as her family background. She was educated at Loretto Convent School in Taos, New Mexico, and the Loretto Academy in Santa Fe, where her future husband would start courting her.

After her marriage in 1898 to her cousin Colonel Venceslao Jaramillo at the age of twenty, she would go on to negotiate a life fraught with personal tragedies and public triumphs. At the epicenter of her personal sorrow were the untimely deaths of her husband and all three of their children. Two children died at infancy, and her only surviving offspring, her daughter Angelina, was murdered in 1931, at the age of seventeen. Her husband, a businessman and state senator, succumbed to illness in 1920, while the couple was living in Denver, Colorado. After his death she moved back to New Mexico and established residence in Santa Fe. Her deeply religious nature buoyed her through these times of despair.

Her husband's death presented a dual tragedy. His failure to properly designate Jaramillo as a beneficiary of his estate left her facing an arduous battle to exercise her rightful claim over their property. In addition, his businesses were mired in huge debt resulting from a host of unfortunate circumstances, not the least being his inability to exercise proper control because of his long illness. After successfully establishing her legitimacy as heir, Jaramillo, now forty-two years of age, took on the responsibility of consolidating and operating the respective businesses and steering them out of debt. This imposed undertaking afforded her the opportunity to hone her business acumen.

Even though her writing was profoundly influenced by her personal loss, the impetus for Jaramillo to write came from her apprehension of cultural loss. Resentful of what she perceived as an invasion of the Hispanic culture by outsiders, she lamented the dilution of the

La Sociedad Folklórico

Cleofas Martinez Jaramillo was a founding member of La Sociedad Folklórico, an organization that was formed in 1935. The fundamental ethos of this group was the preservation of Hispanic history and folk traditions in New Mexico. To this end, group membership was restricted to people of Hispanic lineage. Another critical imperative of the group was the preservation and promotion of the Spanish language, which was being lost through cultural diffusion. During the late nineteenth and early twentieth centuries, there was much movement of people among the various regions in the United States. The tendency to adopt the language of European Americans, or to develop a unique local dialect that blended the language of the different groups residing in that locale, was prevalent. As a result, the native languages of individual groups were lost to later generations. To ensure that the pure form of the Spanish language was preserved for posterity, La Sociedad Folklórico conducted all its meetings in Spanish only. La Sociedad Folklórico provided members a forum where they could share stories and participate in various activities reminiscent of the Hispanic culture. The organization no longer exists.

traditional customs and community values with which she grew up. This cultural sentiment translated into a fervid desire to preserve Hispanic traditions, history, and cultural artifacts.

LIFE'S WORK

In June, 1935, *Holland's: The Magazine of the South* published an article on Spanish-Mexican cooking. Upon reading the article, the need for culturally authentic literature on the history and traditions of the Hispanic community of New Mexico became distinctly apparent to Jaramillo. She surmised that cultural synchronization and assimilation with the modern age was responsible for gradually eroding the Spanish-Mexican cultural legacy and this loss was being reflected in contemporary literature. She reflected on her rich cultural heritage and resolved to restore authenticity to the way it was being represented. She thus embarked on her literary career, writing *Cuentos del hogar* (*Spanish Fairy Tales*, 1939), *The Genuine New Mexico Tasty Recipes: Potajes sabrosos* (*Delicious Stews*, 1939), *Shadows of the Past* (*Sombras del pasado*, 1941), and *Romance of a Little Village Girl* (1955). These writings represent her most earnest and

enduring endowment to the preservation of the Hispanic legacy. Each book endeavored to remind later Latino generations of the rich heritage they owned and implored them to fiercely guard and nurture their cultural roots. An exposition of each book provides an enlightening synopsis of Jaramillo's life's work.

The manifestation of folk culture through oral traditions is a cherished Hispanic institution. Through folklore, the architecture of daily life and the lived cultural experience is preserved. Folklore thus offers vivid insights into the past. An avid storyteller, Jaramillo's mother regularly narrated stories and tales to Jaramillo and her siblings. In *Cuentos del hogar* (*Spanish Fairy Tales*), Jaramillo translated twenty-five of the stories she's heard from her mother into English. Apart from affording her a familial reminiscence, this book serves as an enduring chronicle of customs, dress, and folk arts of the nineteenth century Spanish-Mexicans of New Mexico.

Because indigenous foods are a venerable cultural indicator, recipe giving, like storytelling, was an important aspect of the Hispanic oral tradition. In *The Genuine New Mexico Tasty Recipes*, Jaramillo endeavors to preserve this facet of her cultural heritage. Even though this book is written with much pride about her native cuisine, it is, however, not merely a collection of recipes but a bold testament to cultural ownership.

In *Shadows of the Past* (*Sombras del pasado*) and *Romance of a Little Village Girl*, Jaramillo provides compelling vignettes of daily life and customs in northern New Mexico from the late nineteenth through the early twentieth century. Nostalgic representations of cultural and social harmony paint a vivid picture of ethnic community and her personal identity. *Romance of a Little Village Girl*, an autobiography, was published a year before she died.

In 1935, Jaramillo founded La Sociedad Folklórico. She was actively sought out by scholars, journalists, and researchers during her later years, obliging them with interviews in which she regaled them with stories that she hoped would contribute to the preservation of her cultural history.

SIGNIFICANCE

Cleofas Martinez Jaramillo's literary endeavors not only provide insight into the cultural traditions, practices, and artifacts of a bygone epoch but also serve as a powerful affirmation of ethnic difference and a censure of cultural appropriation. Her life's work centered on preserving for future generations the Hispanic cultural legacy which was gradually being lost through cultural accommodations. In addition to being an inspired writer, Jaramillo was a businesswoman who was ahead of her time; being a businesswoman went explicitly against the prescribed domestic role of females in the late nineteenth century. Her perseverance and resulting success stand as a forceful testament to her tenacity and boldness in the face of adversity.

Jeff Naidoo

FURTHER READING

Augenbraum, H., and M. F. Olmos, eds. *The Latino Reader: An American Literacy Tradition from 1542 to the Present.* New York: Houghton Mifflin, 1997. Jaramillo's inclusion in this anthology of Latino literature confirms her place in history as an iconic and relevant cultural advocate.

Davis, Kate K. "Cleofas M. Jarmillo." In *American Women Writers, 1900-1945*, edited by Laurie Champion. Westport, Conn.: Greenwood Press,

2000. Highlights Jaramillo's status as a prolific regional women writer who celebrated the many colors of her cultural heritage as it played out in the form of traditions, customs, and folklore that characterized her region.

Jaramillo, Cleofas. *Romance of a Little Village Girl*. San Antonio: Naylor, 1955. This autobiography was published a year before Jaramillo died. It serves as the last vestibule into her life, documenting her complete history and the experiences that defined the person she was.

_____. *Shadows of the Past* (*Sombras del pasado*). Santa Fe, N.M.: Seton Village, 1941. Jaramillo presents nostalgic representations of cultural and social harmony in this penetrating portrait of her ethnic community and personal identity.

See also: Mercedes de Acosta; Julio Arce; Sara Estela Ramírez; Evaristo Ribera Chevremont.

MARÍ-LUCI JARAMILLO

American educator and diplomat

Jaramillo worked hard to finance her education, eventually earning a doctorate and rising to become the U.S. ambassador to Honduras. During a career spanning nearly half a century, she was a grade school teacher, university instructor, and university administrator, as well as a staunch advocate for the power of learning.

Latino heritage: Mexican
Born: June 19, 1928; Las Vegas, New Mexico
Areas of achievement: Education; diplomacy

EARLY LIFE

Marí-Luci Jaramillo (mah-REE LOO-see har-ah-MEE-yoh) was the second of three children born to Mauricio Autuna Jaramillo, the owner of a shoe shop originally from Durango, Mexico, and his wife Elvira Ruiz Jaramillo, a New Mexican native. As a child, Marí-Luci shined the handcrafted shoes in her father's store, and after graduating from high school she worked at a variety of jobs in order to afford college tuition at New Mexico Highlands University. After her freshman year, however, she married a schoolteacher and dropped out of the university. She gave birth to three children—Ross, Richard, and Carla—before eventually divorcing. Eager to continue her education, Jaramillo returned

to the workforce, taking jobs as a waitress, parachute seamstress, and housecleaner, and she saved enough money to return to New Mexico Highlands University, from which she graduated magna cum laude in 1955 with a bachelor's degree in education and minors in English and Spanish.

From 1955 to 1965, Jaramillo taught in elementary schools in Albuquerque and Las Vegas, New Mexico. At the same time, she continued her studies, earning a master's degree with honors from New Mexico Highlands University in 1959. Between 1962 and 1964, she was a language arts consultant to the Las Vegas school system. In 1965, she began teaching at the University of New Mexico, from which she earned her Ph.D. in 1970. At this university she served successively as assistant director of Latin American education (1965-1969), assistant director of minority instruction (1969-1972), chairman of the Elementary Education Department (1972-1975), and professor of education (1976-1977). Under the auspices of the U.S. Agency for International Development, Jaramillo traveled throughout Central and South America during the 1960's and 1970's, presenting teacher training and school development workshops. She also wrote many articles for educational journals, gave countless lectures on the subject of teaching, and participated in the production of several training films.

LIFE'S WORK

In 1977, based on the strength of her work in the Latino community, President Jimmy Carter nominated Jaramillo to be the ambassador extraordinary and plenipotentiary of the United States to Honduras. She and her second husband (they would later divorce) lived in Tegucigalpa, the Honduran capital, until 1980. During her tenure as ambassador, Jaramillo was in charge of six governmental agencies, oversaw five hundred Peace Corps volunteers, and attended to the needs of some two thousand Americans living in Honduras. After Carter left office in 1980, Jaramillo returned to the United States and worked until 1981 as the deputy assistant secretary for inter-American affairs at the U.S. Department of State in Washington, D.C. In 1982, she returned to the University of New Mexico as special assistant to the president and associate dean of the College of Education, and she continued to teach, specializing in English as a second language, women's studies, and minority education with a particular emphasis in Latino learning. In 1985, she became the university's vice president for student affairs.

Two years later, Jaramillo left the University of New Mexico for a job in private industry. Stationed in San Francisco, California, she served as regional vice president for the Princeton, New Jersey-based Educational Testing Services (ETS), a company that develops and administers tests for universities and professional organizations throughout the world. She later was named the company's assistant vice president of field services, administering eight ETS offices throughout the United States. In 1993, under U.S. President Bill Clinton, she worked in the Pentagon as a minority recruiter for the U.S. Department of State. Jaramillo retired in 1995 and returned to live in her hometown of Las Vegas, New Mexico, where she continued to advocate for a variety of educational, minority, and human rights causes.

SIGNIFICANCE

Marí-Luci Jaramillo pursued learning in an era when few Latinas took courses after high school, and she became a staunch advocate of education, particularly for women and minorities. A highly respected teacher and educational author, Jaramillo was associated with many organizations throughout her long career. She was a member of the National Association of Latino Elected and Appointed Officials, the National Association for Bilingual Education, the Latin Americanista Association, Bilingual Children's Television, the Diversity External Advisory Council of the Los Alamos National Laboratory, and the McGraw-Hill Broadcasting

---

Influence of Jaramillo's Travels in Latin America on Her Teaching

During the late 1960's and early 1970's, Marí-Luci Jaramillo was heavily involved in New Mexico University's Cultural Awareness Center. Under the aegis of the United States Agency for International Development, she represented the university's Latin American educational programs and was an informal ambassador for the United States before she became formal ambassador to Honduras in 1977. Fluent in Spanish and English, she visited every Central American country, as well as Venezuela, Colombia, Ecuador, and Argentina. At her stops in each nation she held teacher-training workshops focusing on education in general and school development in particular.

In the course of her career, Jaramillo's concepts of education changed. When she first began, she believed that if people were educated, they would be able to succeed in the world, as she had. However, from her travels she discovered this was not a universal truth: Many highly educated people, for a variety of reasons—primarily political and economic—were denied the opportunity to participate in the social system. She incorporated the information she had obtained from her travels into her lectures, articles, and training sessions. Jaramillo counseled students to learn the importance of economics and to study the business world and the workings of politics and government in order to understand the economic and political systems and make them work to their advantage. She stressed the necessity of voting and the importance of making individual voices heard.

For Jaramillo, understanding cultural differences was as important as knowing teaching techniques or finding the proper educational materials, especially for teachers of English as a second language. Teachers, she maintained, have to be committed to promoting positive activities in and out of classrooms in order to ease cultural conflicts. Educators must become keen cultural observers, divorcing themselves from preconceived notions, while teaching in humanistic ways not only English but also the way of life that the language represents.

Corporation's La Raza Films Coordinating Committee. She has also been a member of the board of trustees of the Tomás Rivera Center at Claremont University in California, the Children's Television Network, and the board of directors of the New Mexico Highlands University Foundation.

Jaramillo has often been honored for her efforts on behalf of education, minorities, and women. In 1986, she received the Harvard Graduate School of Education Anne Roe Award for her contributions to education and women's professional growth. In 1988, the Miller Brewing Company named her one of America's most outstanding Latino educators; *Hispanic Business* magazine named her one of the one hundred most influential Hispanics in the United States. The Mexican American Women's National Association gave Jaramillo its Primera Award in honor of her appointment as the first Latina to serve as U.S. ambassador to Honduras. She also received an award from the American Association for Higher Education for outstanding leadership in education in the Latino community.

Jack Ewing

FURTHER READING

Dorman, Shawn, ed. *Inside a U.S. Embassy: How the Foreign Service Works for America.* Dulles, Va.: Potomac Books, 2009. A general study that lists Foreign Service personnel typically found at U.S. embassies and explores the duties of American diplomats and ambassadors with examples from around the world.

Grogan, Margaret, and Charol Shakeshaft. *Women and Educational Leadership.* Hoboken, N.J.: Jossey-Bass, 2010. An examination of the contributions of women to the field of education, and how they have changed the concept of what it means to be a leader.

Jaramillo, Marí-Luci. *Madame Ambassador: The Shoemaker's Daughter.* Tempe, Ariz.: Bilingual Press, 2002. An autobiographical memoir charting Jaramillo's rise from poverty to U.S. ambassador to Honduras, university teacher and administrator, corporate spokesperson, and respected educational advocate.

_____. *To Serve Hispanic American Female Students: Challenges and Responsibilities for Educational Institutions.* Claremont, Calif.: Tomás Rivera Center, 1987. This brief work encapsulates many of Jaramillo's concepts of minority and Latina education, emphasizing teamwork, cultural integration, and a strong foundation of activities in and out of the classroom.

MacDonald, Victoria-Maria, ed. *Latino Education in the United States: A Narrated History from 1513-2000.* Basingstoke, England: Palgrave Macmillan, 2004. An overview of the domestic state of education for Latinos over five centuries, as told in the words of those who experienced it first hand, and the impact of Latino culture on the United States.

Reardon, Vince. *Legacy: Passing on Cherished Values in a Values-Starved World.* n.p.: L.P., 2010. Presents the stories of twenty-five men and women, including Jaramillo, who have demonstrated particular sets of values and contributed to making the world a better place.

See also: Rodolfo F. Acuña; Lauro Cavazos; Julian Nava; Raul Yzaguirre.

FLACO JIMÉNEZ

American musician

Through an exploration of musical genres, most prominently rockabilly swing and honky-tonk country, five-time Grammy Award-winning accordionist Jiménez, in more than four decades of trailblazing recordings and electrifying stage performances, introduced the distinctive sounds and rhythms of classic Tejano music to a mainstream international audience.

Latino heritage: Mexican
Born: March 11, 1939; San Antonio, Texas
Also known as: Leonardo Jiménez

Area of achievement: Music

EARLY LIFE
Leonardo Jiménez,, better known as Flaco Jiménez (FLAH-coh hee-MEHN-ehz), was born in the working-class barrios of San Antonio in the heart of south central Texas, and he learned early the musical culture of his Mexican ancestry. His father, Santiago, was a local legend of conjunto music, a hybrid of Mexican Tejano music and European dance rhythms, most notably the waltz and the polka, the result of the mass immigration

Flaco Jiménez. (AP Photo)

performer, like his father, playing in San Antonio bars and appearing regularly live on local television.

LIFE'S WORK

Jiménez, however, grew restless. He felt pigeonholed, confined within the relatively narrow market of San Antonio's Tex-Mex music scene. He listened to the groundbreaking rock and roll recordings and the emerging generation of country and blues artists and sensed in those rhythms a new direction for conjunto. The opportunity to expand the sound of conjunto came in the late 1960's, when Jiménez teamed up with fellow Texan Douglas Sahm, a free-spirited rock and roll guitarist known for his energetic contribution to the iconic mid-1960's band the Sir Douglas Quintet, which fused driving Tex-Mex rhythms with the infectious, bouncy sass of British Invasion pop (hence the elaborate name of the band). Sahm encouraged Jiménez to go to New York in 1973 in order to participate in a recording project that was bringing together a wide range of musical talent in a variety of genres, including folk icon Bob Dylan and New Orleans boogie-woogie keyboard great Dr. John. Jiménez loved the cutting-edge feel and loose improvisations of such bold genre-bending. Although the recording would find limited market appeal, it earned critical praise, and Jiménez was invited to recording sessions with other mainstream artists. This free-styled fusion of musical styles from different cultures would be a precursor to what would come to be known as world music.

Over the next decade, Jiménez recorded with more than one hundred artists, most notably the Rolling Stones, Linda Ronstadt, Ry Cooder, Emmylou Harris, The Clash, Carlos Santana, Willie Nelson, Los Lobos, and Dwight Yoakum. It was his experience with eclectic musician Cooder that most impacted Jiménez's emerging perception of fusing musical styles. Jiménez's work on Cooder's landmark 1976 release *Chicken Skin Music* established him among the premier studio musicians of the era. A charismatic stage performer, Jiménez was the first Tejano musician to tour both Europe and Asia. His own recordings during the 1980's garnered critical praise, including his first Grammy Award for a recording of one of his father's songs, a bouncy break-up song, "Ay Te Dejo en San Antonio" ("I'm Leaving You in San Antonio").

Although accounts differ, in the late 1980's, Jiménez was approached by Sahm to participate in a proposed Tex-Mex supergroup project that would feature a number of prominent Tejano studio musicians, as

of Germans and Poles to southern Texas a century earlier. Young Jiménez grew up listening to his father play the two-button accordion and watching him perform in bars, social clubs, and neighbors' homes all around San Antonio. However, the boy was also listening to a rich variety of musical styles, including country (particularly Hank Williams, Sr.), blues, and honky-tonk. He knew he wanted to be a musician, and his father taught him the *bajo sexton*, a twelve-string guitar whose crisp sound was a distinctive element of Tejano music, before the boy was eight. He was performing with his father's band within a year.

Although accomplished on the guitar, Jiménez was drawn to the sound of his father's accordion. He listened to recordings of Cajun zydeco legend Clifton Chenier, relishing how Chenier coaxed the accordion to create a foot-stomping raucous sound that invited dancing. He mastered the accordion, and by sixteen he fronted his own band, Los Caporales (The Cowboys). The band enjoyed a huge following in the San Antonio area and made several recordings that scored radio airplay throughout southern Texas. By the age of twenty, Jiménez, now known by his father's nickname Flaco (Spanish for "skinny"), had established himself as an exciting

well as Sahm; Augie Meyers, keyboardist for the Sir Douglas Quintet; and Freddie Fender, a Louisiana-born country crooner who had enjoyed mainstream pop success a decade earlier with songs such as "Wasted Days and Wasted Nights" and "Before the Next Teardrop Falls." Jiménez happily joined the project. In 1990, the Texas Tornados released its first album—in both English and Spanish versions— to wide critical praise; a track from their debut album, "Soy de San Luis," won the Grammy Award for Best Mexican American Performance. However, it was the group's high-energy stage show that created international buzz. The Tornados released several successful follow-up albums before creative disputes between Sahm and Fender caused irresolvable friction.

Jiménez had never entirely abandoned his own recording career. He won a Grammy Award in 1996 for Best Mexican American Performance for his self-titled solo album, and won another award three years later for Best Tejano Performance for *Said and Done*. When he was approached in late 1998 to be part of a second Tex-Mex supergroup, Los Super Seven, he jumped at the chance. The lineup this time included musicians from the Los Angeles Chicano fusion band Los Lobos, rockabilly guitar legend Joe Ely, Sahm (before his sudden death from a heart attack in late 1999), and Fender. The group's self-titled debut recording won the 1999 Grammy for Best Mexican American Performance.

By the turn of the century, Jiménez, now a five-time Grammy winner, enjoyed an international reputation as a master of musical styles, a sterling studio musician able to add flair and energy to virtually any genre of recording, and an established recording artist of a string of highly successful, critically praised Tejano recordings. Past sixty, he nevertheless maintained a hectic touring schedule. In late 2009, Jiménez was approached by Sahm's son, Shawn, himself an accomplished guitarist and vocalist, to play a tribute concert to the Texas Tornados at South by Southwest, a world-renowned music festival held in Austin, Texas. This performance led to a recording, which featured never-recorded songs by Shawn's father, as well as new songs by Fender, who had died three years earlier from cancer. In addition to the original lineup, horns were added to give the music a wider dimension. The album, *¡Esta Bueno!*, was released in March, 2010. Sales confirmed the short-lived supergroup's status as a groundbreaking Tex-Mex act. Awarded the prestigious Lifetime Achievement Award from *Billboard Latin Magazine*, Jiménez continued to record and perform to enthusiastic audiences around the

world. In 2004, he was inducted into the Conjunto Hall of Fame in San Benito, Texas.

SIGNIFICANCE

Flaco Jiménez was an established conjunto musician by his early twenties, known throughout south Texas for his accomplished virtuosity and technical proficiency on the genre's demanding signature instrument, the button accordion. More important, however, Jiménez expanded the reach—and the audience—for this regionally-defined music by developing conjunto's roots into broader musical languages, including rock and roll, blues, and country, as well as Mexican and Spanish dance genres. He created a body of musical work that transcended genre and engaged fans with its infectious rhythms and percolating instrumentation. Music, he believed, whatever its subject, whatever its genre, should make people happy. Given the critical success of his recordings and the popular response to his performances

---

Jiménez and the Texas Tornados

Unlike similarly storied but short-lived supergroup projects—such as Crosby, Stills, Nash, and Young, the Traveling Wilburys, the Monsters of Folk, and The Highwaymen—the creation of the Texas Tornados was a deliberate effort on behalf of its principal organizer, iconoclastic rock guitarist Douglas Sahm, to bring together a variety of dance and rhythm genres, all loosely associated with the musical styles of band members' common native south Texas heritage. The fusion of styles created a distinctive sound that, while flavored with the rambunctious rhythms of Tex-Mex party music, reflected a sophisticated blend of the syncopations and instrumentation of rockabilly, country, and Cajun swamp music, as well as waltzes and polkas.

Of the musicians who worked on the project, Flaco Jiménez undoubtedly brought the most impressive credentials as a solo musician, but with typical commitment to the music, Jiménez blended his considerable talents to help forge the group's synergy. In addition, he starred in their stage performances, weaving and swaying as he worked the accordion's keyboard, dispensing the stereotype of the accordion as a stodgy instrument appropriate to wedding receptions and amateur talent shows. Jiménez used the genre-busting conception behind the Texas Tornados to bring to their relatively slender body of recordings his own signature riffs and deft chord progressions that enhanced the improvisational party feel of the band's distinctive sound.

that often involved long and energetic jam sessions on stage, Jiménez emerged as the premier Tex-Mex musician of his generation and the de facto ambassador of Mexican-style music for audiences worldwide.

Joseph Dewey

FURTHER READING

Clayton, Lawrence, and Joe W. Sprecht, eds. *The Roots of Texas Music*. College Station: Texas A&M Press, 2005. Collection of essays that survey and define the wide variety of music genres indigenous to Texas, including conjunto.

Reid, Jan, and Shawn Sahm. *Texas Tornado: The Times and Music of Doug Sahm*. Austin: University of Texas Press, 2010. Broad-reaching study of a musician who was seminal in Jiménez's development as a world music artist. Includes lengthy discussions about the Texas Tornados, as well as illustrations.

San Miquel, Guadalupe. *Tejano Proud: Tex-Mex Music in the Twentieth Century*. College Station: Texas A&M Press, 2002. Seminal look at the genre that most defined Jiménez. Includes information about Jiménez and his father. Traces the music's evolution into mainstream success in the last two decades of the twentieth century.

See also: Narciso Martínez; Lydia Mendoza; Linda Ronstadt; Selena.

FRANCISCO JIMÉNEZ

Mexican-born writer, scholar, and educator

Best known for his autobiographical stories on his early years growing up in a family of migrant farmworkers, Jiménez has advanced the study of Latino literature through his numerous articles, books, and edited anthologies, while also contributing to the understanding of the cause of social justice for Latinos.

Latino heritage: Mexican
Born: June 29, 1943; San Pedro, Tlaquepaque, Jalisco, Mexico
Also known as: Francisco Hernández Jiménez
Areas of achievement: Literature; scholarship; education

EARLY LIFE

Francisco Hernández Jiménez (frahn-SEES-koh ehr-NAN-dehz hee-MEHN-ehz) was born in Tlaquepaque, Jalisco, Mexico. Jiménez lived with his family in a small village without electricity or running water. These conditions ultimately prompted his family to migrate to California in search of a more prosperous life. When Jiménez was four, he and his family crossed under a wire and traveled to a migrant labor camp in central California hoping to secure work picking strawberries. Instead of finding prosperity, Jiménez's family entered what he called "the circuit" of migrant farm labor. Jiménez's family moved frequently from one town to another in California's Central Valley, picking strawberries, cotton, and other crops and living in dilapidated housing provided by growers that lacked running water and often lacked electricity. Jiménez would routinely start school two months late; he struggled with English throughout primary school, but he also worked hard to master the language and other school subjects with the limited resources he had. The Jiménez family finally settled in Santa Maria, California, only to be uprooted again by being deported to Mexico when Jiménez was fourteen.

The family was ultimately able to return legally to the United States, and they settled again in Santa Maria, where Jiménez would confront the challenge of working thirty-five hours a week to help support his family while attending high school. Nevertheless, Jiménez managed to perform well in high school and was accepted to Santa Clara University, located near San Jose, California. Through the encouragement of his mentors at college, Jiménez pursued and ultimately earned a Ph.D. in Latin American literature from Columbia University in 1972.

LIFE'S WORK

In 1973, Jiménez was hired as a professor of modern languages at Santa Clara University, a position he continued to hold in 2010. Early in his career, Jiménez helped to establish *The Bilingual Review/La Revista Bilingüe*, an academic journal that has published articles on topics such as language, Latino literature, and bilingual education. Jiménez's research has focused on the study of Chicano and Latino literature, including sole-authored books and two anthologies of Latino literature edited with Gary D. Keller. Jiménez's work has also focused on the cause of social justice for Latinos and the impoverished, as exemplified in his edited anthology *Poverty and Social Justice: Critical Perspectives* (1987) and in *Ethnic Community Builders* (2007), about Mexican American community advocates in San Jose, California.

Notwithstanding his academic contributions, Jiménez is best recognized for his autobiographical work. As of 2010, Jiménez had published three short novels, each of which chronicles different periods of his life through a series of short stories. In *The Circuit: Stories from the Life of a Migrant Child* (1997), Jiménez recounts his journey from a poor village in Mexico, his early experiences living in migrant labor camps, and the challenge of learning and making friends while continuously being uprooted as his family follows "the circuit." In his sequel, *Breaking Through* (2001), Jiménez retraces his high school years, as he works to help support his family, attempts to integrate into the culture of his white peers, and ultimately gains the opportunity to attend college. Finally, in *Reaching Out* (2008), Jiménez reveals his emotional journey of pursuing a college education as his family continues to struggle; he finds support among friends and compassionate mentors, as well as the strength to confront discrimination and inequity. Jiménez has also written two children's books based on his childhood experiences: *La mariposa* (the butterfly; 1998), which was published in both English- and Spanish-language editions, and the bilingual book *The Christmas Gift* (*El regalo de Navidad*, 2000). All three of his novels have also been published in Spanish, and *The Circuit* has been translated into Chinese, Italian, Japanese, and Korean. In addition, *The Circuit*, *La mariposa*, and *Breaking Through* have been adapted as plays.

Jiménez has received many honors during his career. All three of his novels and *La mariposa* have been chosen by *Smithsonian* magazine as Notable Books for Children. Jiménez's novels have also received honors from the American Library Association (ALA); his first two novels were selected for the ALA's list of Best Books for Young Adults, while *Reaching Out* was chosen as an ALA Pura Belpré Honor Book, an award reserved for children's books written by Latinos that best evoke the Latino experience. Jiménez was also chosen the Outstanding Professor of the Year in 2002 by the Council for Advancement and Support of Education and the Carnegie Foundation for the Advancement of Teaching.

SIGNIFICANCE

Francisco Jiménez has dedicated much of his career to exposing the stories of Latinos, whether in the form of literary anthologies or biographical narratives, to a greater audience. By making his own contributions to Latino literature, Jiménez has evoked the experience of many undocumented Latino families, while educating many others about the plight of undocumented immigrants and of farmworkers in particular. His stories highlight the value of compassion toward the underprivileged; the importance of hope, faith, and perseverance; and the role of education in helping marginalized people transcend their circumstances.

Josef Castañeda-Liles

FURTHER READING

Jiménez, Francisco. *Breaking Through*. Boston: Houghton Mifflin, 2001. Jiménez focuses on his junior high and high school experiences and the difficult decision to leave his family to attend college.

_____. *The Circuit: Stories from the Life of a Migrant Child*. Albuquerque: University of New Mexico Press, 1997. Jiménez recounts his early experiences up to the age of fourteen, when his family is deported to Mexico.

_____. *Reaching Out*. Boston: Houghton Mifflin, 2008. Jiménez's third autobiographical novel, which focuses on his college years.

Jiménez, Francisco, Alma M. García, and Richard A. García. *Ethnic Community Builders: Mexican Americans in Search of Justice and Power, the Struggle for Citizenship Rights in San Jose, California*. Lanham, Md.: AltaMira Press, 2007. A compilation of narratives based on oral history interviews with fourteen Mexican American activists whose advocacy helped to improve conditions for people of Mexican-origin in San Jose.

See also: Rudolfo Anaya; Gloria Anzaldúa; Norma Elia Cantú; Denise Chávez; Gary D. Keller; Alejandro Morales; Tomás Rivera; Alma Villanueva; Victor Villaseñor.

LUIS ALFONSO JIMÉNEZ, JR.

American artist

Jiménez pioneered the use of commercial materials, such as fiberglass, neon, and spray paint, to create striking works of art. He is best known for heroic-scale multicultural outdoor sculptures which explore the political and social life, cultures, and legends of both Mexico and the United States.

Latino heritage: Mexican
Born: July 30, 1940; El Paso, Texas
Died: June 13, 2006; Hondo, New Mexico
Area of achievement: Art

EARLY LIFE

Luis Alfonso Jiménez, Jr. (lew-EES al-FON-soh hee-MEHN-ehz) was born July 30, 1940, and was raised in the Segundo Barrio neighborhood of El Paso, Texas. During trips to Mexico the family visited museums and public buildings where they saw Mexico's huge historical murals, and Luis developed an appreciation for the arts of that nation, particularly the works of José Clemente Orozco and the other great muralists. His father, Luis Jiménez, Sr., operated a successful sign shop in El Paso. Although his father once aspired to becoming a professional artist, he poured his creative energies into designing and building the elaborate signs that were known as far away as Las Vegas and New York.

Jiménez began to work in his father's sign shop by the time he was six years old and continued to do so through his high school years. He grew up learning and understanding the use of such industrial materials as metal and fiberglass and the appropriate paints to use with them. He learned such skills as welding, glassblowing, metalworking, and painting. Although he was awarded prizes for sculpture in high school competitions and was offered several art scholarships, he was determined to study architecture. He attended the University of Texas at El Paso, then called Texas Western, for one year, after which he spent four years in the architecture program at the University of Texas at Austin. He eventually dropped out of the architecture school and switched his focus to art, earning his B.S. degree in art in 1964.

LIFE'S WORK

Jiménez spent two years studying art in Mexico City and another year teaching for the El Paso school district before going to New York City, where he worked at various jobs before becoming an assistant to sculptor Seymour Lipton. In 1969, frustrated with the inability to place his work in galleries, he dragged several sculptures through the front doors of the Leo Castelli Gallery. Director Ivan Karp sent him to the Graham Gallery, which gave him his first solo show. His career accelerated when powerful *New York Times* critic Hilton Kramer praised the works in Jiménez's second Graham Gallery exhibit. Jiménez's goal was to create public artworks, and although his career flourished in New York, he felt disconnected from his roots. He returned temporarily to El Paso.

In 1972, art collector Donald Anderson offered Jiménez a position in his private museum in Roswell, New Mexico. Jiménez remained in New Mexico for the rest of his life. He began to win commissions for large public sculptures in southwestern cities. His first public commission was the sculpture *Vaquero* for Houston's Tranquility Park. A cast of *Vaquero* was later installed at the Smithsonian Institution's American Art Museum in Washington, D.C.

Jiménez became widely recognized as a significant American sculptor. His works were purchased by the Museum of Modern Art and Metropolitan Museum of Art in New York and by the Art Institute of Chicago. "Luis Jiménez: Man on Fire," a retrospective, opened at the Albuquerque Museum in New Mexico in 1995 and traveled to the Smithsonian American Art Museum. In 1997, another traveling exhibition, "Luis Jiménez: Working Class Heroes: Images from a Popular Culture," opened at the Dallas Museum of Art, the first venue of a three-year national tour. In 1998 he received a Distinguished Alumni award from the University of Texas in recognition of his artwork.

Jiménez was killed on June 13, 2006, while completing *Mustang*, a 32-foot steel and fiberglass sculpture of a rearing horse commissioned for the Denver airport. The sculpture swung out of control, pinning Jiménez against a beam and severing a major artery.

SIGNIFICANCE

Luis Alfonso Jiménez, Jr., was famous for his large-scale fiberglass and metal sculptures in electric colors that he designed for public spaces where they could be seen and appreciated by a wide variety of people, as well as by sophisticated art collectors. His sculpture reflected his vision of Mexican American culture. His works, such as *Man on Fire* and *Southwest Pieta*, displayed a rough realism and a clear social or political agenda. His themes had commonplace sources, such as popular Indian and Mexican dancers, Aztec warriors, cowboys, horses, and "lowrider" truck decorations. They were frequently controversial, sometimes mythical, occasionally violent, intentionally disturbing, but always innovative.

Jan Statman

FURTHER READING

Carlozzi, Annette. *Fifty Texas Artists*. San Francisco: Chronicle, 1986. Includes a specific selection of painters and sculptors who work or live in Texas, including essays and photo portraits of the artists and their works.

Congdon, Kristin G, and Kara Kelley Hallmark. *Artists from Latin American Cultures: A Biographical Dictionary*. Westport, Conn.: Greenwood Press, 2002. Profiles seventy-five twentieth century artists

working in a variety of genres in clear, concise essays. Quotations from the artists are included.

Crawford, Bill. "Luis Jiménez's Outdoor Sculptures Slow Traffic Down." *Smithsonian Magazine,* March 1, 1993. A photographic essay with descriptions of Jiménez's huge outdoor public sculptures and viewers' reactions to them.

Flores-Turney, Camille. "Howl: The Artwork of Luis Jiménez." *New Mexico Magazine*, December 31, 1997. This review describes Jiménez's portrayals of southwestern life.

Jiménez, Luis, et al. *Man on Fire* (*El hombre en Llamas*). Albuquerque: Albuquerque Museum, 1994. A handsomely illustrated catalog published in conjunction with the "Man on Fire" exhibit organized by the Albuquerque Museum in 1994. The text by several different author-contributors offers insight into Jiménez's life and art.

See also: Tony Labat; Marisol; Ana Mendieta; Amalia Mesa-Bains; Liliana Porter.

RAÚL JULIÁ

Puerto Rican-born actor and activist

Most famous as a Broadway actor, Juliá was a handsome leading man of stage and screen, playing both Latino and non-Latino roles. As a star of both musical theater and dramatic plays, Juliá was an acclaimed performer who often used his work as an avenue to promote social justice.

Latino heritage: Puerto Rican
Born: March 9, 1949; San Juan, Puerto Rico
Died: October 24, 1994; Manhasset, New York
Also known as: Raúl Rafael Carlos Juliá y Arcelay
Areas of achievement: Theater; acting; activism

EARLY LIFE

Raúl Rafael Carlos Juliá y Arcelay, better known as Raúl Juliá (rah-OOL jool-ee-AH), was born to middle-class parents in San Juan, Puerto Rico, on March 9, 1940. His mother was a singer, as were other members of his family, which Juliá claimed was a great influence on his decision to become a performer. His father, owner of a fast-food restaurant, introduced pizza to Puerto Rico, making the family financially secure and allowing Juliá to attend private school. His passion for

acting began in the first grade when he acted in a school play. This was followed by more performances while in elementary school and leading roles in college productions. Although the family intended Julia to study law or medicine, he graduated from college and embarked on a career as an entertainer.

He performed as a part of an acting and singing troupe in Puerto Rico, as well as hosting game shows and teen programs on Puerto Rican television. He starred at the Tapia Theatre in San Juan performing four different plays in 1963. One night, in 1964, while performing in a night club, he was approached by actor Orson Bean, who urged him to move to New York to broaden his opportunities. So, at age twenty-four, Juliá left Puerto Rico and went to New York City, where he landed his first role in *La vida es sueno,* a Spanish-language Off-Broadway production.

In 1966, Juliá had his first big break when he was hired by Joe Papp, director of the New York Shakespeare Festival. This began a decades-long relationship between Juliá and Papp. His first role for Papp was in the Spanish-language version of *Macbeth* in 1966. He performed minor roles and in nonacting jobs for Papp

Raúl Juliá. (AP Photo)

until his breakout performance in *Two Gentlemen of Verona* in 1971 for Shakespeare in the Park.

During this time, Juliá helped to found the Puerto Rican Traveling Theatre, an acting troupe that traveled around New York City performing for free in English and Spanish. Juliá also did some television work, appearing in the soap opera *Love of Life* and as a regular on *Sesame Street* as Rafael the fix-it man for one year.

LIFE'S WORK
Juliá's big commercial break occurred when *Two Gentlemen of Verona* moved to Broadway in 1971 and earned him his first of four Tony Award nominations. The other nominations were for *Where's Charley?* (1974), *The Threepenny Opera* (1976), and *Nine* (1981).

While establishing himself as a major presence on the Broadway stage, Juliá also appeared in many films. Most notably he starred in *Kiss of the Spider Woman* (1985), for which he shared a National Board of Review Best Actor award with costar William Hurt. His performance in this film, in which he played a Marxist political prisoner in a South American jail, was one of many film roles in which Juliá played a Latino leading man, as he did in *La gran fiesta* (1987), the first film produced

solely by the Puerto Rican film industry. He also appeared in the films *Florida Straits* (1987), about Cuban refugees; *Tango Bar* (1988), about an expatriate Argentinean who returns to his home after the government is overthrown; and *Havana* (1990), which takes place on the eve of the Cuban Revolution of the late 1950's. He continued his commitment to presenting powerful Latino figures in *Romero* (1989), about the revolutionary El Salvadoran priest Oscar Romero; *The Plague* (1992), about a breakout of the plague in South America; *The Burning Season* (1994), a biographical film about Chico Mendes, a Brazilian environmental activist; and *Down Came a Blackbird* (1995) about the effects of torture in an unnamed Central American country.

However, he did not limit himself to playing only Latino roles because he felt that actors should never be stereotyped. He starred in the films *The Morning After* (1986), *Presumed Innocent* (1990), and *The Rookie* (1990), among others, playing non-Latinos. He also appeared in comic films, such as *The Addams Family* (1991) and *Addams Family Values* (1993), in which he played Gomez Addams, and *Moon Over Parador* (1988). On stage he starred in plays by Anton Chekhov, George Bernard Shaw, and Nöel Coward, proving his versatility. For all his roles, Juliá extensively researched the backgrounds and experiences that shaped his characters' lives in order to bring authenticity to his portrayals. When playing a hairdresser, for example, he learned to cut hair and spent time in a hair salon so he would be convincing as a hairstylist.

Juliá died on October 24, 1994, the result of complications of a stroke. He was reading scripts for future projects and had just finished filming *Street Fighter* (1994), based on the video game. Following his wishes, Juliá was buried in San Juan, where thousands turned out to honor him.

SIGNIFICANCE
Raúl Juliá was committed to his craft, acting, and to his philanthropic causes, mostly concerned with Latino issues. On stage and on the screen he excelled at playing both Latino and non-Latino characters, never allowing himself to be stereotyped or kept from exploring roles outside of his ethnicity. He helped Latino performers to be perceived as appropriate for all types of roles.

Juliá also used his celebrity to champion philanthropic organizations, such as The Hunger Project, devoted to eradicating global hunger. He was a staunch supporter of Puerto Rican independence and made commercials promoting tourism in Puerto Rico. He helped develop the Latino Playwrights Reading Workshops to

---

Juliá's Portrayal of Archbishop Oscar Romero

Romero (1989), a film written by John Sacret Young and directed by John Duigan, is the story of Oscar Arnulfo Romero's life, from his 1977 promotion to archbishop of San Salvador until his assassination in 1980. It shows his transformation from a scholarly priest with no political agenda to a vocal figure intent on bringing peace and justice to his country.

The government, which was waging a war against Marxist guerrillas, approved his nomination for archbishop because he was not seen as a threat to their regime. However, after witnessing the assassination of two of his priests and the relentless violence against the El Salvadoran people, Romero became an outspoken critic of the government. Simultaneously, Romero condemned the guerrillas, whom he perceived as being equally dangerous. He preached nonviolence, urging soldiers on both sides to defy orders and give up fighting. He was executed while saying mass at the Divine Providence Hospital chapel. His murderers have never been bought to justice.

In the film, Raúl Juliá portrays Archbishop Romero as quiet and dignified, while representing Romero's growing realization of the need to do God's work by confronting violence in his country. Juliá plays Romero as initially timid and introspective, slow to anger, but totally committed to his principles. He accentuates Romero's quiet resolve in the scene in which Romero sits in a chair and silently waits for hours to be seen by the governor. Juliá also shows Romero's will when he calls the governor a liar to his face.

---

encourage Latino writers. He performed using Spanish as well as American and English accents and appeared in both Spanish-language and English-language films.

He was awarded The Hispanic Heritage Award, among other honors, to celebrate his commitment to Hispanic and charitable causes. The Puerto Rican Traveling Theatre honored Juliá by naming their actor-teaching division the Raúl Juliá Traveling Unit. He is also honored by having a charter school named for him, The Raúl Juliá Micro Society, in Bronx, New York. He posthumously earned an Emmy Award, a Cable Ace Award, a Screen Actors Guild Award, and a Golden Globe Award for *The Burning Season*. The National Endowment for Hispanic Arts named an annual award after him, and his family was honored by being awarded the Congressional Gold Medal on his behalf.

Leslie Neilan

FURTHER READING

Berg, Charles Ramiréz. *Latino Images in Film: Stereotypes, Subversion, and Resistance.* Austin: University of Texas Press, 2002. Looks at the role of Latino actors and their depictions of Latinos in Hollywood films, from stereotypes to the more modern portrayals by actors, like Juliá, who broke away from the stereotypes.

Cruz, Bárbara. *Raúl Juliá: Actor and Humanitarian.* Berkeley Heights, N.J.: Enslow, 1998. A no-frills, young-adult biography of Juliá focusing on both his career and his philanthropic activities.

Mott, Gordon. "Only as Good as the Memories." *Cigar Aficionado,* December 1, 1993. A biographical sketch of and interview with Juliá.

Rodriguez, Clara. *Heroes, Lovers, and Others: The Story of Latinos in Hollywood.* New York: Oxford University Press, 2008. Chronicles the history of Latino actors, including Juliá, and their roles in Hollywood films.

See also: Miriam Colón; Linda Cristal; Hector Elizondo; Cheech Marín; Edward James Olmos; Lupe Ontiveros; Martin Sheen; Raquel Welch.

KATY JURADO

Mexican-born actor

Jurado excelled at playing strong women's roles in Mexican and American films for more than fifty years.

Latino heritage: Mexican

Born: January 16, 1924; Guadalajara, Mexico

Died: July 5, 2002; Cuernavaca, Mexico

Also known as: María Cristina Estela Marcela Jurado García

Area of achievement: Acting

EARLY LIFE

Katy Jurado (hoor-AH-doh) was born María Cristina Estela Marcela Jurado García on January 16, 1924, in Guadalajara, Mexico. She came from a wealthy family of Andalucian ancestry. Her mother was an opera singer who gave up her career to raise her three children. Jurado's maternal great-great-grandfather had once owned much of the land that subsequently became Texas. The family moved to Mexico City in 1927, and Jurado lived in luxury until their land, on which cattle were raised and oranges grown, was confiscated by the government and redistributed to the poor. Ironically her cousin, Emilio Portes Gil, had been provisional president of Mexico from 1928 to 1930.

When she was sixteen, Jurado was discovered by Emilio Fernandez, an actor, screenwriter, and director who would later become familiar to audiences in the United States for roles in films such as *The Wild Bunch*. Jurado's family, especially her aristocratic grandmother, objected to her entering show business. To escape their control she married actor Victor Velázquez.

LIFE'S WORK

Jurado made her film debut in *No matarás* (1943) and quickly became a star by playing forceful women who often seduced and dominated men. Her breakthrough role came with *Nostros los pobres* (1948). Too restless to wait around for film roles, Jurado also worked as a radio reporter, a newspaper and magazine columnist writing about films, and a bullfight critic. Actor John Wayne and director Budd Boetticher saw her at a bullfight and cast her opposite Robert Stack and Gilbert Roland in *Bullfighter and the Lady* (1951), produced by Wayne. Her meager English-language skills required her to learn her role phonetically.

Jurado began alternating between work in Mexico, most notably with director Luis Bunuel's *El bruto* (1953), and Hollywood, continuing this practice until her death. Her best-known American film came early on, when she played Gary Cooper's former girlfriend in the Western classic *High Noon* (1952), for which she received Golden Globe Award nominations as Best Supporting Actress and Most Promising Newcomer. Her *High Noon* role was a stereotype, but Jurado carried it off with affecting dignity, showing viewers there was more to her character than appeared on the surface.

Jurado replaced fellow Mexican Dolores del Río in the role of Spencer Tracy's Indian wife in *Broken Lance* (1954) and became the first female Mexican actor to receive an Academy Award nomination, as Best

Supporting Actress. Divorcing Velázquez, the father of her two children, Jurado moved to Hollywood and worked steadily in American films, mostly Westerns, during the 1950's, working with many notable leading men. She costarred with Charlton Heston and Jack Palance in *Arrowhead* (1953), Kirk Douglas in *The Racers* (1955), Glenn Ford in *Trial* (1955), Burt Lancaster and Tony Curtis in *Trapeze* (1956), and her fellow countryman Anthony Quinn in *Man from Del Rio* (1956). After costarring with Ernest Borgnine in *The Badlanders* (1958), she married this Oscar-winning actor in 1959. The couple made headlines by frequently breaking up and reconciling before finally divorcing in 1963.

After she played Karl Malden's wife in *One-Eyed Jacks* (1961), the only film directed by her close friend Marlon Brando, Jurado's Hollywood career declined. She was soon reduced to a negligible role in an Elvis Presley vehicle, *Stay Away, Joe* (1968). Following a suicide attempt in 1968, she moved back to Mexico permanently. Her most notable remaining American films were Sam Peckinpaugh's *Pat Garrett and Billy the Kid* (1973), which reunited her with her mentor, Fernandez; *Under the Volcano* (1984), directed by John Huston; and *The Hi-Lo Country* (1998), directed by Stephen

Katy Jurado. (AP Photo)

Frears. She also costarred with Quinn and del Rio in the Mexican-American production *The Children of Sanchez* (1978).

In addition to her film work, Jurado starred on Broadway in 1956 in *The Best House in Naples*, which closed after three performances. In 1975, she costarred with Quinn and Claire Bloom in Tennessee Williams's *The Red Devil Battery Sign*, but the play closed in Boston before it could open on Broadway. She costarred with Paul Rodríguez and Hector Elizondo in the 1984 situation comedy *a.k.a. Pablo*, which was canceled after six episodes. Her final film was *Un secreto de Esperanza* (2002). Jurado suffered from heart and lung ailments in her final years and died in Cuernavaca, Mexico, on July 5, 2002.

SIGNIFICANCE

Katy Jurado's intense, limpid eyes and thick, full lips made her an exotic beauty, helping her establish a foothold in both Mexico and Hollywood. Her nominations for an Academy Award and a Golden Globe Award were unprecedented for Latinas. Predecessors, such as María Montez and Lupe Velez, had been stereotyped into playing hot-bloodied spitfire roles in Hollywood. After Jurado's triumph in *High Noon*, the range of available roles for Latinas broadened somewhat, though they were still subject to limitations imposed by the era's prejudices.

Jurado won Ariel Awards, the Mexican Oscars, for *El bruto*, *Fe, esperanza, y caridad* (1974), and *El evangelio de las Maravillas* (1998), as well as a lifetime achievement award in 1997. In recognition for her work in the United States, Jurado received a star on the Hollywood Walk of Fame. In 1992, the Motion Picture and Television Fund awarded her a Golden Boot in recognition of her contributions to Western films.

Jurado worked tirelessly to promote the use of her home state, Morelos, by filmmakers. Although she was renowned for her smoldering sexuality in the first part of her career, Jurado made an easy transition to playing more maternal roles. By bringing considerable dignity and grace to all her parts, she helped gain more roles for Latino performers in Hollywood and contributed to the slow break from the stereotyped roles of the past.

Michael Adams

FURTHER READING

Cavallo, John. "The Career of Katy Jurado." *Classic Images* 186 (1992): 18-19. An overview of Jurado's films.

Rainey, Buck. *Sweethearts of the Sage: Biographies and Filmographies of 258 Actresses Appearing in Western Movies*. Jefferson, N.C.: McFarland, 1992. A brief look at Jurado's career, with emphasis on the Westerns in which she appeared.

See also: Dolores del Río; Hector Elizondo; John Gavin; Fernando Lamas; María Montez; Anthony Quinn; Paul Rodríguez; Gilbert Roland; Lupe Velez; Elena Verdugo; Carmen Zapata.

Eugenia Kalnay

Argentine-born scientist, educator, and writer

Kalnay was the first woman to obtain a Ph.D. in meteorology from the Massachusetts Institute of Technology. She served as director of the Environmental Monitoring Center of the National Centers for Environmental Prediction from 1987 to 1997.

Latino heritage: Argentinean

Born: October 1, 1942; Buenos Aires, Argentina

Also known as: Eugenia Kalnay-Rivas, Eugenia Kalnay de Rivas

Areas of achievement: Science and technology; scholarship

Early Life

Eugenia Kalnay (yoo-GEE-nee-uh KAL-nay) originally studied physics in her homeland of Argentina. Her mother convinced her to change her major to meteorology upon learning that scholarships existed in the field. Kalnay made the change after winning a full scholarship from the Argentine National Weather Service and graduated from the University of Buenos Aires in 1965. She took on the post of research assistant that year, but a brutal military coup forced the College of Science to shut down.

With the help of her supervisor, Kalnay applied to the Massachusetts Institute of Technology (MIT). She was accepted to the meteorology program, where she was supervised by Jule G. Charney. Her dissertation focused on research regarding the atmosphere of Venus. After graduating in 1971, she accepted the post of as-sistant professor at the Universidad de Montevideo in Uruguay. She returned to MIT in 1973, then left in 1979 to work at the National Aeronautics and Space Administration (NASA).

Kalnay worked at NASA from 1979 to 1986 as a senior research meteorologist and later branch head for the Goddard Space Flight Center (GSFC) in Greenbelt, Maryland. While in Greenbelt, Kalnay met Dr. Malise Cooper Dick, a leading economist with the World Bank. They were married in 1981. As branch head at the GSFC, Kalnay was responsible for leading an all-male team of scientists working on the Global Modeling and Simulation Project. Her work on the Fourth Order Global Model, the backbone of the agency's numerical weather prediction abilities for over a decade, was recognized in 1981 when she received the NASA Medal for Exceptional Scientific Achievement.

Life's Work

In 1987, Kalnay moved to the National Centers for Environmental Prediction (NCEP), where she worked for ten years as director of the Environmental Modeling Center. While there, she contributed significantly to the improvement of the National Weather Service's forecasting abilities by focusing research on the development of the ETA model of weather prediction. The ETA model is a physics-based system of detecting variations in patterns such as surface pressure, temperature, and wind changes. Kalnay also contributed to NCEP research projects on the breeding method and ensemble forecasting, both of which are mathematical methods of predicting variations in patterns. Her contributions led to the National Weather Service's ability to produce three-day forecasts as accurate as their previous daily forecasts.

Kalnay also pioneered research in the field of data assimilation and copublished a paper titled "The NCEP/NCAR Forty-Year Reanalysis Project." The project created a system of collaboration among multiple countries, including China, Great Britain, and Japan, that supplied global research data to the project. The project also contained data from the Geophysical Fluid Dynamics Laboratory, which provided oceanic observations. The project was hailed as an immediate success and quickly became one of the most quoted sources on climate change and weather predictability.

In 1998, Kalnay was granted the Robert E. Lowry Endowed Chair in Meteorology at the University of Oklahoma. She then joined the University of Maryland in 2000 after accepting a position as chair of the Department of Atmospheric and Oceanic Science. There, Kalnay cofounded the Weather and Chaos Project with fellow distinguished professor Jim Yorke. The project has proved successful in research and development of new theories, including the Local Ensemble Kalman Filter, which applies differential equations to solve geophysical forecasting problems.

Kalnay participated in the 2006 Supreme Court Case of *Commonwealth of Massachusetts et al. vs. U.S. Environmental Protection Agency et al.* The case was petitioned by twelve states; Kalnay, along with thirteen other leading climate change scientists, submitted an amicus curiae brief providing documentation of their research into global warming. The case set an important legal precedent in that it held the Environmental Protection Agency (EPA) and the Alliance of Automobile Manufacturers, among others, accountable for failing to regulate carbon emissions by motor vehicles as required by the Clean Air Act. The EPA was forced to examine the scientists' findings and later publicly recognized carbon as a detriment to the atmosphere. They were then required to come up with a method to systematically regulate automobile carbon emissions.

Kalnay was awarded the Eugenia Brin Endowed Professorship in Data Assimilation in 2008. That same year, Kalnay's name was added, without her permission, to a list of scholars who denied the existence or effects of climate change. The list, produced by the Heartland Institute, was titled "Five Hundred Scientists

---

Kalnay's "Reanalysis" of World Climatic Patterns

Although it was not the first meteorological reanalysis study completed, Eugenia Kalnay's "The NCEP/NCAR Forty-Year Reanalysis Project" was significant in that it assimilated data from meteorological centers around the world and covered a large time frame. Previously, the European Center for Medium-Range Weather Forecasts (CMWF) project covered a period from 1978 to 1994; Kalnay's project covered the span from 1957 to 2002. The project, which is ongoing, focuses on updating historical data using mechanized analysis systems that are free from human error, thus eliminating inconsistencies that occur over time. This method allows for better judgment in potential forecasting, especially in regard to rising atmospheric temperature. Kalnay and others concerned about climate change continue to rely on the project to provide government agencies and environmental groups with accurate and precise data related to global warming.

---

with Documented Doubts of Man-Made Global Warming Scares." Outraged at being linked to a statement directly contradicting her own beliefs and research, Kalnay repudiated her involvement. Heartland senior fellow Dennis T. Avery compiled the list, which included dozens more named individuals who later denied their involvement and denounced their inclusion in the list. Kalnay and the others listed against their will protested the article and called for its immediate correction. A similar event occurred when the novelist Michael Crichton cited Kalnay's work in his anti-global-warming novel, *State of Fear* (2004). The novel references Kalnay's research, but its premise is contradictory of the conclusions of that research.

On July 6, 2007, Kalnay's husband of twenty-six years died of a heart attack. She continues to work in Greenbelt, Maryland, where she lives with her son Jorge Rivas.

SIGNIFICANCE

Kalnay has made important contributions to the male-dominated field of meteorology. As MIT's first female Ph.D. graduate in meteorology, she went on to have a highly successful and inspirational career in environmental engineering. Considered the foremost authority in her field, her own contributions to the study and improvement of weather forecasting cannot be underestimated, and her pioneering research continues through the encouragement of and collaboration with the Ph.D. candidates she advises. Kalnay's work has helped to bring attention to the phenomenon of climate change, and she continues to push for further public awareness of the issue. She also works to encourage governments around the world to pursue research into climate change. In 2009, Kalnay received the Fifty-fourth International Meteorological Prize from the World Meteorological Organization, an agency of the United Nations based in Switzerland. In 2010, she served as a member of the High Level Taskforce for the Global Framework of Climate Services.

Shannon Oxley

FURTHER READING

Jacovkis, Pablo Miguel. "The First Decade of Computer Science in Argentina." *History of Computing and Education* 2 (2006): 181-91. This article discusses the "Night of the Long Sticks" coup of 1966 at the University of Buenos Aires. Kalnay was a subject of and informant for the article.

Kalnay, Eugenia. *Atmospheric Modeling, Data Assimilation, and Predictability*. New York: Cambridge University Press, 2002. A textbook for upper-level university students filled with equations and graphs that help to describe the mathematical processes involved in forecasting.

Kalnay, Eugenia, et al. "The NCEP/NCAR Forty-Year Reanalysis Project." *Bulletin of the American Meteorological Society* 77, no. 3 (March, 1996): 437-471. Kalnay's most prominent contribution to the field of meteorology.

Lahoz, William, Boris Khattatov, and Richard Menard, eds. *Data Assimilation: Making Sense of Observations*. New York: Springer, 2002. This book discusses the concept of data assimilation and describes Kalnay's work.

See also: Daniel Acosta; Margarita Colmenares; Jane L. Delgado; Arturo Gómez-Pompa; Mario Molina.

NICOLÁS KANELLOS

American educator, publisher, and writer

Kanellos founded Arte Público Press, acknowledged as the foremost publisher of Latino literature in the United States. It publishes contemporary literature, as well as recovered literature located under the auspices of the Recovering the U.S. Hispanic Literary Heritage Project. As an educator, Kanellos mentors doctoral students at the University of Houston. Books and articles written by Kanellos on Hispanic theater and Hispanic periodicals in the United States are foundational to any study of those genres.

Latino heritage: Puerto Rican

Born: January 31, 1945; New York, New York

Areas of achievement: Publishing; education; scholarship

EARLY LIFE

Nicolás Kanellos (nihk-oh-LAHS kah-NEH-lohs), the oldest of three boys, was born to a Greek father, Constantinos Kanellos, and a Puerto Rican mother, Inés de Choudens García, in New York City on January 31, 1945. The family moved to Jersey City, New Jersey, in 1950, where they lived until Kanellos graduated from high school in 1962. Both his parents had graduated from high school, but while circumstances did not

permit them to further their studies, they valued and promoted their children's educations. Kanellos's father often worked at two jobs to make ends meet, but living near a bookbindery offered the possibility of obtaining free books discarded as damaged. Presaging his future as a writer and publisher, Kanellos would take the blank sheets, known in the industry as signature pages, and put them together to make his own books. The discarded works of writers, such as Ernest Hemingway, John Steinbeck, and W. Somerset Maugham, served to inspire him and he became a voracious reader.

The family's frequent summer trips to Puerto Rico kept Kanellos close to his Hispanic roots and to his Puerto Rican extended family. Of these family members, he was most influenced by his aunt, Providencia García, affectionately known as Titi Provi. He remembers her as always being over at their house, and she gave the young Kanellos his first guitar. She was instrumental in developing the Latin American music division of Peer Southern Music Company (now Peermusic, Inc.), so she was a valuable example of how to preserve and promote Latino culture.

In school, Kanellos loved sports but was uninspired by his teachers. His fascination with books and reading prompted him to spend time in the school library when

Nicolás Kanellos. (AP Photo)

ever possible. After high school, Kanellos attended Fairleigh Dickinson University in Madison, New Jersey. As an undergraduate he also spent the 1964-1965 academic year at the Universidad Nacional Autónoma de México. He graduated from Fairleigh Dickinson with a B.A. in 1966. Kanellos went on to the University of Texas at Austin to earn his master's degree in Romance languages in 1968. He entered the university's doctoral program and also studied one year, 1970-1971, at the University of Lisbon in Portugal. He earned his doctorate from the University of Texas in 1974. It was during his time in Austin that he became an activist with the Teatro Chicano de Austin, an involvement that would become the initial focus of his life's work. Kanellos married Cristelia Pérez on May 12, 1984, after moving to Houston. They had one son, Miguel José Pérez Kanellos, born April 11, 1989.

LIFE'S WORK

Kanellos left Texas in 1971 and took a position on the faculty of Indiana University in Gary, Indiana, where he taught until 1979. In 1972, he cofounded with Luis Dávila the literary magazine *Revista Chicana-Riqueña*. In 1986, the magazine changed its title to *The Americas*

Review in order reflect its inclusion of Latinos from other regions. It published under that title until 1999, when its final issue appeared. This highly acclaimed and very successful literary magazine represented Kanellos's first foray into the world of publishing.

It soon became clear to Kanellos that there was a need for a publishing house whose primary goal was the publication of works by Latino authors. *Revista Chicana-Riqueña* had already published an anthology, *Nuevos Pasos*, so he knew he could undertake a book-length effort. Thus was born Arte Público Press in 1979. Working outside the realm of the established industry was not easy at first. The nascent publisher had many difficulties to overcome, but in the 1980's, Arte Público was able to obtain funding from the Mellon Foundation.

The publication by Arte Público Press of the novel *Rain of Gold* by Victor Villaseñor in a clothbound edition in 1991 was the turning point for the publisher. This work also represented the company's first attempt at establishing a widespread network of distribution to the public and competing with the industry for classification as a best seller. By successfully scaling the many hurdles of distribution, promotion, and media review, *Rain of Gold* became a best seller. Arte Público eventually sold the rights not only of that book but also of others by Villaseñor to Bantam Doubleday Dell, thus the reputations of both the author and Arte Público Press became established in the industry. Since this first success in the national market, Arte Público has also sold film rights to made-for-television films.

In 1992, under the auspices of Arte Público Press, Kanellos initated the work of the Recovering the U.S. Hispanic Literary Heritage Project, whose purpose is to locate, recover, preserve, index, and publish both in print and electronic media literary works by Latinos living in the United States from colonial times to 1960. The primary audience for these volumes is in academia, as they are intended to broaden universities' curriculum in the humanities. In 1994, Arte Público Press expanded its horizons by launching the imprint Piñata Books in order to address the needs of juvenile bilingual readers. This imprint sought to authentically depict Latino culture to young readers.

Beyond his work in publishing, Kanellos is a professor at the University of Houston. He mentors students in the doctoral program, as well as those who work as research assistants in the Recovering the U.S. Hispanic Literary Heritage Project. His academic work has also produced a wide range of personal publications. His involvement with Chicano theater that began while he

Recovering the U.S. Hispanic Literary Heritage Project

Recovering the U.S. Hispanic Literary Heritage Project was begun in 1992 in order to make accessible literary material produced by Latinos that would otherwise be lost. Working throughout the fifty states, scholars have uncovered valuable literary and historical material. These documents have been published in academic editions by Houston-based Arte Público Press. They are also available on the EBSCO-host computer platform, on which the Arte Público Hispanic Historical Collection: Series I digital collection features almost sixty thousand historical articles and eleven hundred historical books on Latino literature and culture. As the title of the EBSCO collection implies, more articles and books will be added in the future.

While digital availability of documents fills a need, the preservation of the original material is also crucial. The recovery project microfilms and stores all original documents in its possession, as well as documents that have been lent to the project by libraries and private collections throughout the country. These microfilmed documents are made available to scholars, who have used them for research, as well as for the teaching of Latino literature and history.

the definition of American literature by charting works produced by Latinos from the colonial period through the twentieth century. This foundational anthology takes the work he began on theater and adds to it examples from all literary genres to demonstrate the depth of literary contributions by Latinos. Even after a decade of scholarly effort, this work clearly demonstrates the continuing need to research and unearth unpublished and out-of-print manuscripts to attain further understanding of the cultural wealth that Latinos have contributed to the United States.

Kanellos's vision for preserving Latino culture also demonstrated a need to make young Latinos aware of their culture. His imprint Piñata Books attempts to fill that void and instills a cultural awareness that was slowly being eroded, while at the same time fostering bilingual literacy.

Norma A. Mouton

FURTHER READING

Kanellos, Nicolás. "An Interview with Nicolás Kanellos." Interview by Debra D. Andrist. *South Central Review*, 19, no. 1 (Spring, 2002): 15-25. Focuses on Arte Público Press, describing how Kanellos got started in publishing and the success he has had.

Kanellos, Nicolás, et al. "Bilingual Books for Children: An Interview with Nicolás Kanellos, Director of Piñata Press." *MELUS* 27, no. 2, (Summer, 2002): 217-224. Highlights the work of the Piñata Books imprint, an offshoot of Arte Público Press.

Wilson, Wayne. *Careers in Publishing and Communications*. Bear, Del.: Mitchell Lane, 2001. Profiles Latinos who have succeeded in the fields of newspaper, magazine, and book publishing, as well as radio, television, films, and the Internet.

See also: María Herrera-Sobek; Roberto J. Suarez.

studied in Austin, Texas, culminated in his writing *A History of Hispanic Theatre in the United States: Origins to 1940* (1990). He has also written more than eight articles and many chapters on American literature written by Latinos. Another of his books, *Hispanic Immigrant Literature: El Sueño del Retorno*, was scheduled to be published in 2011.

SIGNIFICANCE

As an editor of *Herencia: The Anthology of Hispanic Literature of the United States* (2002), Kanellos changed

JOE KAPP

American football player, coach, and actor

One of the most celebrated Latino football players of all time, Kapp led the University of California to the Rose Bowl, the British Columbia Lions to a Canadian Football League championship, and the Minnesota Vikings to the Super Bowl. He also is remembered for

bringing an antitrust suit against the National Football League that forced a fundamental change in league-player relations.

Latino heritage: Mexican

Born: March 19, 1938; Santa Fe, New Mexico

Also known as: Joseph Robert Kapp; El Cid; Injun Joe

Areas of achievement: Football; acting

EARLY LIFE

Born in Santa Fe, New Mexico, Joseph Robert Kapp grew up in California, the son of a German American laborer. His Mexican American mother played a strong role in his life by raising him to do his best in everything he undertook—a trait that would later foster his indomitable will to win. Despite his German surname, Kapp always proudly acknowledged his Latino roots and regarded himself as a Mexican American.

Kapp started high school in Salinas, California, where his family lived among mostly Latino farmworkers, and finished at Newhall's Hart High School in Southern California. A standout in football and basketball, he was given an athletic scholarship at the University of California at Berkeley (Cal), which he entered in 1955. At that time, Cal's football program under the legendary coach Pappy Waldorf was in decline and its basketball program under Pete Newell was growing in stature. The fact that Kapp would become the best player on weak football teams while riding the bench on strong basketball teams would play an important role in shaping his ideas about team play.

After completing his first college season on Cal's freshman football team, Kapp became the starting quarterback on the varsity in 1956. It was Waldorf's last season, and his Golden Bears won only three games. The following season, Pete Elliott took over as coach and won only one game. The Bears opened the 1958 season dismally with two straight losses, but Kapp was not ready to give up. Under his determined leadership, Cal won seven of its remaining eight games, captured the Pacific Coast Conference championship, and earned a trip to the Rose Bowl.

During Kapp's senior year, he led his team in rushing, passing, and minutes played while playing both offense and defense; led the conference in rushing; won first-team All-Conference and several first-team All-American honors; and was named the most outstanding player on the Pacific Coast. A tough, physical player, he thought nothing of running into and over opposing players, many of whom could not match his 6-foot, 3-inch, 215-pound size. Against Oregon, Kapp scored a touchdown on a 92-yard run that remains among the longest in Cal history. Cal's Rose Bowl contest against a much stronger Iowa team ended in a disappointing loss, but Kapp never gave up until time ran out. Afterward, an assistant coach described Iowa's quarterback as "a good quarterback on a great team," while calling Kapp "a great quarterback on an average team."

Meanwhile, Kapp had earned two varsity letters in basketball at Cal playing the guard position. Although he played limited minutes, Newell and Kapp's teammates respected him for his aggressive play and the leadership he brought to the team. In later years, Kapp would recall what it meant to be treated as an important team member despite receiving limited playing time. Because the Rose Bowl extended his football season, he skipped basketball during his senior year and consequently just missed being on Cal's 1959 national championship basketball team.

LIFE'S WORK

Despite his impressive college football credentials, Kapp was not selected in the National Football League (NFL) draft until the eighteenth round, and the Washington Redskins, who drafted him, never even contacted him. Kapp responded by signing with the Calgary

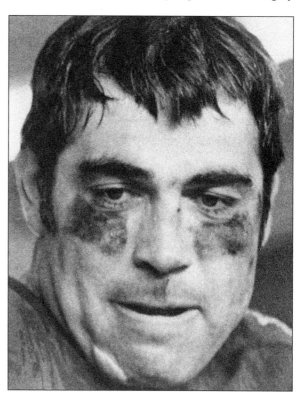

Joe Kapp. (AP Photo)

Stampeders of the Canadian Football League (CFL). He then began a decade-long period of playing football in cold-weather cities. In later years, he would recall his shock on arriving in Calgary, Alberta, and discovering there were no Mexican restaurants in the Canadian town.

Kapp played in the CFL from 1959 through 1966. Despite sustaining several serious injuries and often playing in frigid weather, he never missed a game and developed a reputation for being a fearless brawler. During his first season, he led the Stampeders to their first play-off berth in years. In 1961, he was traded to the British Columbia Lions, an expansion team in Vancouver, for four players. It was a gamble that paid off. Kapp soon led the Lions to their first play-off berth and in 1964 to their first Grey Cup—the CFL championship.

After eight years in Canada, Kapp wanted to play in the United States. This time, many NFL and American Football League (AFL) teams—including California's Raiders and Chargers—wanted to sign him. Eventually, he chose the NFL's Minnesota Vikings, another cold-weather team in the days before covered stadiums. Although he would play for the Vikings for only four seasons, Kapp proved to be an excellent investment. In 1968, his second season as the Vikings' starting quarterback, he led the team to its first play-off berth. The following year, he led it to its first league championship in last season before the NFL and AFL merged. The title placed the Vikings in their first Super Bowl.

Kapp's Super Bowl season was the finest of his professional career. In addition to compiling the best passing statistics and ratings of his NFL career, he led the Vikings to a 13-1 record while dominating opponents by huge margins. Along the way, he tied an all-time NFL record by throwing seven touchdown passes in one game. He also personally knocked out a Cleveland linebacker in a play-off game. However, at the end of the season, he recalled what he had learned at Cal by declining the team's most valuable player award, insisting that no one Viking was more valuable than the rest. The Vikings were heavy favorites in the Super Bowl, but once again the ultimate prize eluded Kapp, who suffered a separated shoulder in his team's loss to the Kansas City Chiefs.

Because the Vikings had not renewed Kapp's contract before the 1969 season, he emerged from the 1970 Super Bowl as a free agent. Now widely recognized as a proven quarterback with an indomitable will to win, Kapp made the cover of the July 20, 1970, issue of *Sports Illustrated*, which dubbed him "The Toughest

Chicano." In September, the Boston Patriots gave him a four-year contract, making him one of the highest-paid players in the NFL. However, after only one, substandard, season with the cellar-dwelling Patriots, Kapp challenged the legality of the league's standard player contract, which contained the equivalent of the Major League Baseball "reserve clause" that already had been overturned in the courts. Kapp's case dragged on for eight years before a federal court finally ruled in his favor. He never played football again. His legal victory did for professional football players what Curt Flood's challenge of the reserve clause had done for baseball players, but Kapp himself received no compensation for his lost earnings.

Meanwhile, Kapp began a second career as a screen actor. Between 1970 and 1982, he had small parts in

---

"The Play"

One of the most famous finishes in football history occurred in the final game of Joe Kapp's first season as coach of the University of California at Berkeley (Cal) Golden Bears. On November 20, 1982, his Bears met traditional rival Stanford in a tough contest in which the lead changed several times until Cal led 19-17 with only 1:27 left on the clock. Stanford had the ball on its own 20-yard line. Stanford quarterback John Elway then led a drive to Cal's 18-yard line, where he let the clock run down before calling time out. Stanford then kicked a field goal to take a 20-19 lead with only four seconds left. When Stanford players rushed onto the field to celebrate, the referee whistled a 15-yard penalty to make Stanford kick off from its 25-yard line. Cal's situation still looked hopeless, but Kapp had trained his players never to give up, and they went out to receive the kickoff with that thought in mind. Kevin Moen caught Stanford's short "squib" kick around Cal's 44-yard line. When he ran into Stanford defenders, he wheeled and overhanded the ball back to a teammate. When that player could go no farther, he lateraled to a third teammate. As the third player collided with three Stanford men on the 27-yard line, he threw the ball back over his head without looking. Moen managed to wheel around, catch the ball, and head for the end zone. By then, Stanford reserves and band members were pouring onto the field, thinking the game had ended, as Moen bulled through the band to reach the end zone. After a long deliberation, the referees ruled a touchdown had been scored, giving Cal a 25-20 win and sending Kapp on his way to becoming coach of the year.

more than twenty television and film productions. His first role was an uncredited part as a football player in the 1970 Korean War film *M*A*S*H*. He also appeared in three other films revolving around football, *The Longest Yard* (1974), *Two-Minute Warning* (1976), and *Semi-Tough* (1977). His television credits include a dozen popular dramatic series.

In December, 1981, after Kapp had been out of football for a decade, the football world was shocked to learn that the former quarterback with no coaching experience had been hired as the University of California's new head football coach. Cal athletic director Dave Maggard hired Kapp because Cal football had fallen on hard times and Kapp was an iconic figure he hoped would revitalize the program. Kapp did just that. Putting in eighteen-hour days, he drove Cal's 1982 team to a surprising 7-4 record and was himself named the conference's coach of the year. Kapp restored excitement to Cal football, but the effect did not last. After a 5-5-1 season in 1983, two losing seasons followed. Maggard let Kapp know toward the end of the 1985 season that it would be his last, but Kapp managed to go out in glory. After his emotionally charged team upset Stanford in his final game, his players carried him off the field

Fiercely loyal to his alma mater, Kapp was devastated by his firing, but he soon bounced back. In 1990, the British Columbia Lions hired him as general manager. His tenure in that position was brief, but he left a lasting legacy when he signed to quarterback Doug Flutie, who would go on to become of the CFL's greatest players.

Over the next twenty years, Kapp turned his attention to raising a family, operating a restaurant in Mountain View, California, and working as a motivational speaker and workshop organizer. In 2008, he reconnected with Cal football when his son Will started playing for his beloved Golden Bears.

Significance

Despite never winning a Rose Bowl or a Super Bowl, Kapp still is revered by fans. His many honors have included induction into the University of California Athletic Hall of Fame, the College Football Hall of Fame, the British Columbia Sports Hall of Fame, the British Columbia

Lions Walk of Fame, the Canadian Football Hall of Fame, and the Laredo Latin American International Sports of Fame. His name is invoked as a model of strong leadership among Latinos, and he maintains an active public career as a speaker and promoter of Latino causes.

R. Kent Rasmussen

Further Reading

Bruton, Jim. *A Tradition of Purple: An Inside Look at the Minnesota Vikings*. Champaign, Ill.: Sports Publishing, 2007. Anecdotal history of the Vikings by a former Kapp teammate that pays considerable attention to Kapp's place in Viking lore. Index.

Erskine, Chris. "Joe Kapp Is Still Full of Fight . . . and Fun." *The Los Angeles Times*, November 14, 2010, p. C1. Interview with Kapp on the eve of the 2010 Cal-University of Southern California game, in which his son Will was to play. Includes anecdotes about Kapp's own college days.

Fimrite, Ron. *Golden Bears: A Celebration of Cal Football's Triumphs, Heartbreaks, Last-Second Miracles, Legendary Blunders, and the Extraordinary People Who Made It All Possible*. San Francisco: Macadam Cage, 2009. Rich history of Cal football by a former San Francisco reporter and *Sports Illustrated* writer offering many details about Kapp's college career.

"Hispanic NFL Players." *The San Antonio Express-News*. September, 9, 2010, p. CX12. Discusses four notable Latino football players: Tony Romo, Jim Plunkett, Joe Kapp, and Tom Flores.

Johnson, George, "Ornery QB Recalls Move to McMahon." *The Calgary Herald*. August 12, 2010, p. F1. Article about the fiftieth anniversary of the Calgary Stampeders' McMahon Stadium that fondly recalls Kapp's CFL playing days.

Renteria, Melissa. "Football Americano." *The San Antonio Express-News*, September 9, 2010, p. CX12. Discussion of the popularity of pro football among Texas Mexican Americans with extensive comments about Kapp's views on Latinos and football.

See also: Tedy Bruschi; Manny Fernández; Jeff Garcia; Tony Gonzalez; Anthony Muñoz; Jim Plunkett; Rich Rodriguez; Eddie Saenz; Danny Villanueva.

GARY D. KELLER

American writer, scholar, educator, and publisher

In addition to being a distinguished professor, Keller is the sole author and editor of twelve books and more than thirty other titles, and he has coauthored or coedited more than one hundred other works. He also founded The Bilingual Review/La Revista Bilingüe, *a groundbreaking journal that was one of the few U.S. publications to feature articles by and about Latinos.*

Latino heritage: Mexican

Born: January 1, 1943; San Diego, California

Also known as: El Huitlacoche; Gary Keller-Cárdenas

Areas of achievement: Literature; scholarship; education

EARLY LIFE

Gary D. Keller (GAR-ee KEHL-ehr) was born in San Diego, California, to Jack and Estela Cárdenas Keller. He grew up living on both sides of the United States' border with Mexico to accommodate his father's employment.

As a child, Keller was required to contribute to the family's support by working for pay while attending school. Despite the work, frequent moves, and school changes, Keller was an ardent reader and excellent student who completed a bachelor's degree in philosophy from the Universidad de las Americas in Mexico City in 1963.

In talks and writings he has noted the importance of his boyhood challenges and the influence of his hardworking parents in shaping his cultural identity, intellectual curiosity, and entrepreneurial courage. These traits led him to pursue graduate studies at Columbia University in New York City, where he studied Hispanic literature and linguistics, receiving a master's degree in 1967 and a Ph.D. in 1971. He simultaneously earned a fourth degree in 1971, a master's in psychology from the New School for Social Research.

LIFE'S WORK

Keller supported himself throughout his studies by teaching. He taught English at the Universidad de las Americas and was a graduate instructor of Spanish, Portuguese, and French at Columbia and Pace University. Appointed to his first full-time faculty position at the City College of the City University of New York (CUNY) in 1970, he was tenured in 1974 and promoted to full professor in 1979. He actively published articles

in scholarly journals, as well as monographs on educational testing, such as *Ambiguous Word Language Dominance Test* (1978) and *Special Education Bilingual Assessment* (1979). He also coauthored the books *España en el siglo veinte* (1974) and *Viva la lengua!* (1975), among others.

His rapid academic development at CUNY included chairing the Department of Humanities, Foreign Languages, and English as a Second Language until 1979, when he accepted an offer from Eastern Michigan University (EMU) in Ypsilanti. At EMU, Keller was appointed tenured professor of Hispanic literature, dean of the graduate school, and chief research officer of the university. Continuing his remarkable career trajectory, he moved to the State University of New York at Binghamton in 1983 to serve as provost for graduate studies and research, with joint appointments as a tenured professor of Hispanic literature in the Department of Comparative Literature and the Center for the Study of United States Hispanics. He was the center's founding director until 1986.

Early in his career, Keller applied his innovative vision to developing institutional programs that reflected the multicultural realities of the nation and world. One of his most important contributions was the establishment of *The Bilingual Review/La Revista Bilingüe* in 1973, which developed into an international journal and one of the few U.S. publications with Latino-themed subjects and bilingual content. The journal eventually expanded into the award-winning Bilingual Review Press. Both the journal and publishing house continued to thrive in the twenty-first century and were widely acknowledged as major resources on bilingualism and U.S. Latino cultures.

In 1986, Keller returned to the Southwest border region of his boyhood to join the Arizona State University faculty in Tempe, Arizona, as a tenured professor of Spanish. With his typical innovative entrepreneurship, he helped establish the university's Hispanic Research Center (HRC) in order to advance Latino scholarship. During two decades the HRC served as a major force in research production and in the recruitment to college of underrepresented minority faculty and students through Project 1000 and the Coalition to Increase Minority Degrees/Doctorates, both initiated and directed by Keller.

Throughout his career Keller continued to produce his own research and creative writing. He published *The*

Flexibility Language Dominance Text (1978) and wrote the Spanish versions of the *Language Assessment Battery for the New York Department of Education* (1975, reprinted 1979). His other books include *Hispanics in the United States: An Anthology of Creative Literature* (coedited 1982), *Leo y entiendo* (1984), *Chicano Cinema: Research, Reviews, and Resources* (1985), *Curriculum Resources in Chicano Studies* (coedited 1989), and numerous others.

His poetry and fiction include the 1977 prize-winning story "The Man Who Invented the Automatic Jumping Bean," selected for inclusion in the prestigious *Best Essays from a Quarter-Century of The Pushcart Prize* (2002). Appearing in 1984, *Tales of El Huitlacoche* introduced Keller's pseudonym, chosen for its double meaning as a Mexican corn delicacy and as the stage name of a famous Mexican boxer known for his generosity to the poor living on the border. El Huitlacoche's poems also appeared in *Five Poets of Aztlán* (1985) under the heading "Real Poetría," capturing Keller's punning bilingual humor. Humor and ethnohistorical insight define his collections of fiction *Zapata Rose in 1992, and Other Tales* (1992) and *¡Zapata Lives!* (1994), both receiving favorable reviews. Another well-received story, "The Raza Who Scored Big in Anáhuac" (1984), was honored by inclusion in *Chicano/Latino Literary Prize: An Anthology of Prize-Winning Fiction, Poetry, and Drama* (2008).

Keller's published research extends to the visual arts and to science and technology. A foremost curator of Chicana/o art, he coedited the stunning coffee table reference works *Contemporary Chicana and Chicano Art: Artist, Works, Culture, and Education* (2002) and the *Triumph of Our Communities: Four Decades of Mexican American Art* (2005). His scholarship on cinema resulted in *The Cisco Kid: American Hero, Hispanic Roots* (coedited, 2008), which was soon followed by "Thirteen Ways to Capture Our Quetzal in Good Faith," an essay for *Camino Real: Estudios de las Hispanidades Norteamericanas* (2009).

SIGNIFICANCE

For more than fifty years Keller has had a major impact on American education and letters. He has received many honors, including the $50,000 Charles A. Dana award for education pioneers in 1992, which he donated to minority student scholarships and scholarly publishing. A highly successful writer, publisher, scholar, and administrator he has broadened the range of knowledge about Latino culture, thereby advancing the scope of American studies and the texture of America itself.

Cordelia Chávez Candelaria

FURTHER READING

Daydi-Tolson, S. "Gary D. Keller." In *Dictionary of Literary Biography*, edited by Francisco Lomelí and Carl R. Shirley. Vol. 82. Detroit: Gale Research, 1989. Provides a brief biography and an overview of Keller's published works.

Keller, Gary D., and Randall G. Keller. "The Literary Language of United States Hispanics." In *Handbook of Hispanic Cultures in the United States: Literature and Art*, edited by Francisco Lomelí and Claudio Esteva-Fabregat. Houston: Arte Público Press and Instituto de Cooperación Iberoamericano, 1993. An example of Gary D. Keller's scholarly writing, this article demonstrates how the Hispanic literary language reflects the multicultural nature of language, the bilingualism and bidialectalism of the U.S. Hispanic population, and the use of "code-switching," or the concurrent use of more than one language.

See also: Juan Bruce-Novoa; Norma Elia Cantú; Denise Chávez; Nicolás Kanellos; Luis Leal.

TONY LABAT

Cuban-born artist and educator

A Cuban émigré, Labat is an art teacher and visual artist, whose nontraditional works often carry a cultural message.

Latino heritage: Cuban
Born: November 14, 1951; Havana, Cuba
Areas of achievement: Art; education

EARLY LIFE

Born in Havana, Cuba, in 1951, Tony Labat (lah-BAHT) immigrated to the United States in 1966. After meeting the entrance requirements for the San Francisco Art Institute, Labat began pursuing an education there, earning his B.F.A. degree in 1978. That same year, before he received his degree, Labat submitted a proposal to Langton Arts (now New Langton Arts) in order to participate in an exhibition at this gallery. Although Labat was familiar with the gallery's standard review and selection process for prospective exhibitors, he did not follow the usual procedure. Instead of an art portfolio and résumé, Labat submitted a dozen plastic roses to the panel of judges; his attached note read only "Trust me." Although Labat's actions bypassed convention and might have been subject to misunderstanding, the panel received his approach well and allowed him to exhibit. The plastic roses later were placed on a display stand at the entrance to the show.

Labat received public attention in 1978 for another action: his "gonged" appearance on *The Gong Show*, a popular television program. Performers on this show would have to leave the stage if the judges banged a

Tony Labat.
(© Katy Raddatz/San Francisco Chronicle/Corbis)

504

gong during their routines. Labat would later create an innovative video based on his performance.

Labat's continued his training at the San Francisco Art Institute, earning his M.F.A. degree in 1980.

LIFE'S WORK

After completing his education, Labat converted his art studio into a combination gym and training facility in order to make a statement about the public's preference for primarily purist art, including traditional photographic documentation. After training for months in this newly established gymnasium, Labat challenged rival realist artist and former jockey Tom Chapman to a regulation boxing match at Kezar Pavilion. To publicize the fight, Labat commissioned not the typical photograph but a chaotic painting by artist Katherine Sherwood. This publicity also served as a critical appraisal of the sole use of photographic documentation. To further heighten the buildup for the event, Labat scheduled San Francisco topless entertainer Carol Doda to be the card girl marking the round count.

In 1985, Labat joined the faculty of the San Francisco Art Institute, and he eventually became faculty director of the school's M.F.A. program.

In 2005, New Langton Arts presented a survey of Labat's work to celebrate its thirtieth anniversary. The exhibit highlighted Labat's performances, films, paintings, and drawings, demonstrating his proficiency and talent in many media. Labat's 1978 appearance on *The Gong Show* and his 1981 video *Fight, P.O.V. (Point of View)* were shown at this exhibit. Labat inserted commercials and televised news reports dating from 1978 and 1981, respectively, into these videos, creating a deliberately irregular record of events. In his 2006 article in *Artforum International*, Bruce Hainley argued that these two videos were precursors of reality television.

In 2006, Labat completed *Day Labor: Mapping the Outside*, a popular but controversial video installation. For three months he had secretly filmed Hispanic workers waiting for employment. This frequently exhibited video demonstrates the passivity of the Hispanics and California's dependence upon the labor of illegal immigrants.

Regardless of the medium in which he works, Labat helps his viewers to identify with the experiences he presents to them. Never hesitant to incorporate culture, fashion, and politics into his artworks, he depicts people as heroes and as villains and objects as both trash and treasure.

SIGNIFICANCE

Tony Labat's innovative artwork draws upon many styles and media, including film, painting, and drawing. Labat has sought both to raise public consciousness of the differences and similarities among various cultures—particularly between the Cuban and American cultures—and to publicize marginalization and displacement of various peoples.

Between 1980 and 2007, Labat contributed work to 383 national and international exhibits, developed more than 30 videos, and placed his work in more than 20 collections, including the Museum of Modern Art. He has received several awards and fellowships from the National Endowment for the Arts, the Institute of Contemporary Art, and other organizations.

Anita Price Davis

FURTHER READING

Hainley, Bruce. "Tony Labat: New Langton Arts." *Artforum International* 44, no. 5 (January, 2006): 227. Hainley notes that Labat uses media—particularly video and television—to construct social, aesthetic, and political narratives. This brief biographical sketch also calls attention to Labat's focus on Cuban-American relations.

Kuenstler, Emily. "Objects Collected, Images Understood." *Afterimage*, January-February, 2006, 42. This biographical sketch, published after Labat's 2005 exhibit at New Langton Arts, recounts his work in various media, his influences, and his successes. The article also comments on the exhibit itself.

Labat, Tony, and Carlo McCormick. *The Strange Case of T. L.* San Francisco: Artspace Books, 1995. Artist Labat and critic McCormick wrote this nontraditional portrait of Cuban immigrant T. L., who may be Labat himself. Each time T. L. speaks, McCormick responds and analyzes T. L.'s words and photos.

See also: Olga Albizu; Juan Boza; Barbara Carrasco; Ana Mendieta.

FERNANDO LAMAS

Argentine-born actor, director, and singer

Lamas was a distinguished Argentinian film star who immigrated to the United States to become a celebrity playing numerous "Latin lover" roles. He often was paired with Hollywood's most glamorous women on-screen and off.

Latino heritage: Spanish and Argentinian
Born: January 9, 1915; Buenos Aires, Argentina
Died: October 8, 1982; Los Angeles, California
Also known as: Fernando Álvaro Lamas y de Santos
Areas of achievement: Acting; radio and television; music

EARLY LIFE

Fernando Álvaro Lamas y de Santos (LAH-muhs) was born on January 9, 1915, to Emelio and Maria Lamas. Lamas's parents originally were from Spain, but they emigrated to and settled in Buenos Aires, Argentina. Lamas's father, an electrical engineer, died when he was one year old; his mother died three years later. Lamas was raised by his paternal grandmother, Carmen, and maternal grandmother, Generosa, who encouraged him to swim competitively. At twenty-five, he represented Argentina at the Pan American Games in Buenos Aires and was ranked as one of the five fastest male swimmers in the world.

Lamas married Perla Mux in 1940 and had a daughter, Cristina, but the couple divorced over his political opposition to Nazism. He married Lydia Babacci, a Uruguayan heiress, in 1946. They had a daughter, Alexandra, and moved to Beverly Hills in 1950 after Lamas signed a contract with film studio Metro-Goldwyn-Mayer (MGM). He and Lydia divorced in 1952.

LIFE'S WORK

By the 1940's, Argentina had developed the most successful film industry in South America, and during World War II, Lamas became a star. He appeared in numerous films in the 1940's, including *Stella* (1943), *Villa rica del Espiritu Santo* (1945), *The Poor People's Christmas* (1947), *The Story of a Bad Woman* (1948), *La rubia Mireya* (1948), *The Unknown Father* (1949), and *Vidalita* (1949). In the United States, Lamas played Andre LeBlanc in *The Avengers* (1950) and had his first major film credit in *Rich, Young and Pretty* (1951). *The Merry Widow* established Lamas's star power, and he struck up a romance with costar Lana Turner.

In 1953, Lamas starred in *The Girl Who Had Everything*, *Sangaree*, and *Dangerous When Wet*. He left Turner for actor Arlene Dahl, whom he married in 1954. They had a son, Lorenzo, before divorcing in 1960. Lamas met his future fourth wife, swimmer and actor Esther Williams, when they costarred in *Dangerous When Wet*. For this film, Williams had Lamas's role rewritten to enlarge his part, as he wanted to act only in "important pictures" and was extremely careful about his strong, masculine image. Their attraction was immediate and mutual, but Williams remained married to Ben Gage until 1959, after which she and Lamas began a relationship.

Lamas was truly an international star who spoke five languages: Spanish, English, Italian, French, and Portuguese. He could convincingly play European, Mediterranean, and Latino characters in various film genres. He was in constant demand to play suave, handsome leading men in films such as *The Diamond Queen* (1953), *Jivaro* (1954), *Rose Marie* (1955), and *The Girl Rush* (1955). In the late 1950's, he began to

Fernando Lamas. (AP Photo)

take on roles outside the film industry, appearing on television in *The Lucy-Desi Comedy Hour* (1958) and on Broadway in 1957-1958 in *Happy Hunting* with Ethel Merman. For the latter role, Lamas was nominated for a Tony award for Best Actor in a Musical.

In the early 1960's, Lamas starred in the films *The Lost World* (1960), *Duel of Fire* (1962), and *Revenge of the Musketeers* (1963). He also appeared in a television special, *Esther Williams at Cypress Gardens* (1960), in which they swam together and their spark was rekindled. He took Williams on a trip to Spain while she was filming *The Big Show* (1961) in Germany.

Lamas, as an American film star, was lavished with attention from European dignitaries, especially in Madrid, Spain, where he and Williams were entertained by General Francisco Franco and Prince Juan Carlos and his wife, Sophia. On one occasion, he and Williams were co-guests of honor with the Duke and Duchess of Windsor. Lamas often entertained by singing popular tango songs by Carlos Gardel of Argentina, reciting poetry, performing flamenco dancing, or telling stories. Lamas could sing by heart all the parts in the operas *Rigoletto*, *Tosca*, *La Traviata*, *Aida*, and *La Boheme* in his well-trained baritone voice.

In 1961, Lamas played the lead in *The Magic Fountain* opposite Williams, who insisted he direct the film as well. Lamas was a success as a director, always meeting deadlines and budget. They returned from Rome in the fall of 1962 to live in Bel-Air, California, in a home of his own design, and Lamas began directing for television series. He directed episodes of *Run for Your Life*, *The Rookies*, *Mannix*, *Starsky and Hutch*, and *Alias Smith and Jones*. He would later direct episodes of *Falcon Crest*, starring his son, Lorenzo.

Lamas starred in *The Violent Ones* (1967) and *Kill a Dragon* (1967), then returned to Spain in 1968 to film *100 Rifles* (1969) with Burt Reynolds, Raquel Welch, and Jim Brown. He married Williams on December 31, 1969, and they remained married until his death from lymphoma and pancreatic cancer in 1982. His ashes were scattered off the California coast.

SIGNIFICANCE

Lamas was an excellent character actor and, as a director, opened doors in the American film industry to

Lamas as an Archetype of the "Latin Lover"

The "Latin lover" film character originated in the era of the silent films, when Antonio Moreno began playing suave seducers. Moreno was followed by actors including Rudolph Valentino, Ramón Novarro, Ricardo Montalbán, and Roland Gilbert. By the 1950's, Fernando Lamas had come to personify the Latin lover character.

The Latin lover was viewed as radiating sexual magnetism, mystery, and intrigue, representing forbidden temptations and passionate encounters. The character was ultramasculine, virile, well-traveled and well-connected, debonair, and charismatic. Lamas fit this profile perfectly. His Casanova reputation was well-deserved in reality as it was on screen. Although many other actors have played Latin lover types onscreen, including César Romero, Anthony Quinn, Pedro Armendariz, Perry Lopez, and José Ferrer, Lamas remains one of the men most commonly associated with that image.

Latinos, allowing them to move into prominent positions behind the camera. He was known for his sex appeal and his forceful, competent intelligence.

Barbara Bennett Peterson

FURTHER READING

Berg, Charles Ramírez. *Latino Images in Film: Stereotypes, Subversion, and Resistance.* Austin: University of Texas Press, 2002. Includes a historical discussion of the "Latin lover" character as a stereotype that eventually was challenged by a new generation of Latino filmmakers.

Reyes, Luis, and Peter Rubie. *Hispanics in Hollywood: A Celebration of One Hundred Years in Film and Television.* Hollywood, Calif.: Lone Eagle, 2000. Describes the history of Spanish-language filmmaking in Hollywood and the rise of Hispanic actors, including Lamas.

Williams, Esther. *The Million Dollar Mermaid.* New York: Simon & Schuster, 1999. Lamas's life story is related in Williams's autobiography.

See also: José Ferrer; Ricardo Montalbán; Ramón Novarro; Anthony Quinn; César Romero.

OCTAVIANO LARRAZOLO

Mexican-born politician

In an often controversial public career that spanned more than four decades in both Texas and New Mexico, Larrazolo tirelessly championed the political rights of Hispanics. His long, distinguished career was capped in 1928, when Larrazolo became the first Mexican American elected to the U.S. Senate.

Latino heritage: Mexican

Born: December 7, 1859; El Valle de San Bartolo (now Allende), Chihuahua, Mexico

Died: April 7, 1930; Albuquerque, New Mexico

Also known as: Octaviano Ambrosio Larrazolo

Area of achievement: Government and politics

EARLY LIFE

Octaviano Ambrosio Larrazolo (ahk-TAY-vee-ah-noh ahm-BROH-see-oh lahr-ah-ZOH-loh) was born in central El Valle de San Bartolo, Mexico, the largest city in Chihuahua, the country's largest state. The son of a wealthy landowner, Larrazolo was born to privilege. Recognized for his devotion to his Catholic faith and his desire to enter the priesthood, eleven-year-old Octaviano was sent to live in Tucson, Arizona, under the tutelage of the bishop. Despite his young age, he showed tremendous promise in theological study and, when, five years later, the bishop accepted a posting as archbishop in Santa Fe in the New Mexico Territory, Larrazolo followed, completing his studies at St. Michael's College (now Santa Fe University) in 1877. In 1884, he became a U.S. citizen. Abandoning the priesthood, Larrazolo turned instead to teaching, accepting an appointment as a high school principal in San Elizaro in El Paso County at the westernmost tip of Texas along the New Mexico border. He was only nineteen at the time.

Over the next seven years, Larrazolo completed his duties as a school administrator, and he also became interested in politics, working with the local Democratic Party to help advance his interest in better funding for public schools. In 1886, he was elected clerk of the U.S. district and circuit courts in El Paso. He took advantage of the opportunity to study law and was admitted to the bar in 1888. The following year he was elected (and subsequently reelected) district attorney for western Texas, his meteoric rise as much a measure of his legal acumen as of his mesmerizing power as an orator on the stump. In 1895, Larrazolo relocated to Las Vegas in the New Mexico Territory to open his own law practice.

LIFE'S WORK

Once in New Mexico, Larrazolo became a fixture in Democratic Party politics. In 1900, 1906, and 1908, he was the party's nominee as the territory's delegate to the U.S. House of Representatives, but he lost each time. However, he was a force in party politics, he wrote tirelessly for regional newspapers, and his voice helped shape public opinion. In the years leading up to New Mexico's statehood in 1912, Larrazolo pressured the committees meeting to shape the state's constitution to guarantee that the state would protect both the bilingual status of its education system and the voting rights of its Hispanic population. A dispute with party leadership over the representation of Hispanics on the party's state ballots led Larrazolo to leave the party in 1911. Because Hispanics accounted for nearly two-thirds of the state's population, Larrazolo argued passionately that half the party's nominees for state offices should be Hispanic. When the Democrats refused to support his request, Larrazolo left the party.

Larrazolo decided to seek the state's governorship, running as a Republican. Given his accomplished

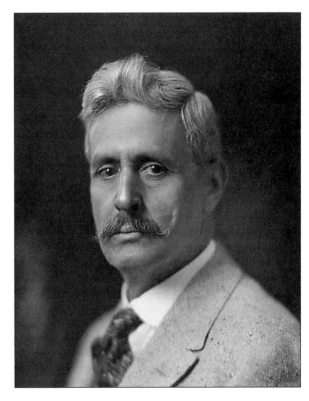

Octaviano Larrazolo. (Library of Congress)

Larrazolo's Role in Protecting the Civil Rights of New Mexico's Hispanics

Given his own cultural roots, Octaviano Larrazolo understood that New Mexico, as it made its application for statehood, was essentially bicultural, an experiment in which two different cultures and two different languages sought to exist side by side and forge a united state, a single free government with neither culture sacrificing its integrity. During the three years in which New Mexico shaped its state constitution, Larrazolo, although not a delegate to the constitutional convention, exerted tremendous influence through his public speeches and his widely circulated writings geared to guarantee that the state's large population of Mexicans and Spaniards would not forfeit their cultural identity or their language. The state's Bill of Rights became a template for biculturalism, particularly targeting public education and voting rights.

Larrazolo, with other prominent Hispanic political leaders, sought to guarantee that New Mexico's public school teachers would be bilingual, thus protecting the rights of children of first-generation immigrants to have access to public schooling. Larrazolo worked to eliminate language requirements for voting privileges and for holding public office; he even delivered many of his stump speeches in Spanish. Despite Larrazolo's own political record of working for both women and the state's considerable population of Native Americans, New Mexico's Bill of Rights addressed only Hispanics.

Larrazolo faced stinging criticism from conservative anti-immigrant coalitions, who saw his efforts to protect the civil rights of "non-Americans" as a form of reverse discrimination that inevitably pitted Anglos and Hispanics against each other. His opponents argued that assimilation was the only workable strategy for New Mexico. Larrazolo, however, perceived that New Mexico was unique among the American states and eloquently argued that preserving its unique bicultural identity could only strengthen the state and ensure its long-term socioeconomic stability.

oratory abilities and his wide appeal among Hispanic voters, Larrazolo was elected the state's fourth governor in November, 1918. His campaign was heated and ugly, turning on his opponent's xenophobic assertions that Larrazolo's foreign birth made it impossible for him to understand the needs of his constituents. Larrazolo won a narrow victory, even though East Coast political pundits had written off his candidacy, but he would serve only a single term. In that time, Larrazolo successfully shepherded landmark legislation that protected children from harsh labor practices, guaranteed state aid to distressed farmers, established the state's first Board of Health in response to the influenza pandemic, and promoted medical benefits and job opportunities for the state's World War I veterans. However, he fell out of favor with his own party because of his advocacy of a controversial state income tax bill, his veto of a bill that denounced the League of Nations, his passionate defense of bilingual education, and his promotion of the Nineteenth Amendment, which would guarantee women's suffrage. In 1920, the Republicans did not renominate him. Larrazolo briefly returned to El Paso to practice law before returning to New Mexico in 1922.

Larrazolo ran unsuccessfully for the state's Supreme Court in 1924 but did serve two terms in the state's House of Representatives in 1927 and 1928. However, his career changed dramatically when Andrieus A. Jones, a Tennessee-born lawyer in the last year of his second term as New Mexico's junior senator, died suddenly in Washington, D.C., at the age of sixty-five on December 27, 1927. A special election was called to fill out the unexpired term. Larrazolo ran as a Republican and was elected. Larrazolo would serve barely six months in the U.S. Senate, from December 7, 1928, to March 3, 1929, but he was the first Hispanic to serve in this body. It was a cause of great celebration for New Mexico's Hispanic population and a personal vindication for Larrazolo and the many controversial stands he had taken in his long public career. Concerned over his own failing health and the intemperate climate of Washington, he opted not to run for a full term. He returned to Albuquerque and for the next several years maintained a limited law practice until his death on April 7, 1930.

SIGNIFICANCE

Octaviano Larrazolo defied the caricatures of a career politician of his era. Neither a crusading quixotic idealist, nor a close-minded party toady, nor an ambitious self-serving egoist, Larrazolo was a pragmatic populist. His ambitious agenda was driven by his deep compassion for Hispanics and for safeguarding their opportunity to succeed in their adopted land, as well as by his humanitarian concern for all marginalized people—women, the poor, tenant farmers, forgotten veterans, the uneducated, and children—whose concerns the political establishment of his era seldom acknowledged. Trained to be a priest, he more often followed his conscience than political expediency. Such concern, of course, made for an uneven record of political success. However, through his gift of stirring eloquence and his charismatic persona—handsome and vigorous, he was the epitome of Spanish aristocratic gentility—Larrazolo became a force in New Mexico politics at the crucial time when, through the process of its admission to the union, it was initially defining itself as a bilingual state.

Joseph Dewey

FURTHER READING

Chavez, Thomas E. *An Illustrated History of New Mexico*. Albuquerque: University of New Mexico Press, 2002. Authoritative and comprehensive look at the cultural and political context of Larrazolo's long career of public service. Particularly helpful in summarizing the contentious debate over bilingual education and voting rights.

Cordova, Alfred G. *Octaviano Ambrosio Larrazolo, the Prophet of Transition in New Mexico: An Analysis of His Political Life*. Albuquerque: University of New Mexico Press, 1950. Still considered the seminal look at Larrazolo's evolving political sensibility and his impact on shaping New Mexico.

Prince, L. Bradford. *New Mexico's Struggle for Statehood*. 1910. Reprint. Santa Fe, N.M.: Sunstone Press, 2010. A reissue of a landmark study, first published in 1910, by one of early New Mexico's most distinguished and controversial politicians. Provides a helpful introduction.

Zannos, Susan. *Octaviano Larrazolo*. Hockessin, Del.: Mitchell Lane, 2003. Although designed for young adult readers, this slender volume is an effective look at Larrazolo's Catholicism and his passionate defense of Hispanic causes.

See also: Toney Anaya; Jerry Apodaca; Dennis Chavez; Manuel Luján, Jr.; Joseph M. Montoya; Bill Richardson.

LUIS LEAL

Mexican-born writer, educator, and scholar

Best known for his literary criticism of the Latin American short story, Leal also was a professor and an advocate for the dissemination of Mexican literature, Chicano literature, and the literature of Latin America in the United States. Leal helped define the term "Magical Realism" as it is used in Latin American fiction.

Latino heritage: Mexican
Born: September 17, 1907; Linares, Mexico
Died: January 25, 2010; Santa Barbara, California
Areas of achievement: Literature; scholarship; education

EARLY LIFE

Luis Leal (lew-EES LEE-ahl) was born on September 17, 1907, to a prominent and influential rancher family in Linares, Mexico. He grew up in a large Spanish-style house with his parents, four brothers and sisters, and a host of aunts, uncles, and cousins. From a very early age, Leal had been interested in literature and was always reading different types and genres of literature. In May, 1927, he came to the United States, where he had been accepted as a student at Northwestern University in Chicago. Although he originally planned to study mathematics, Leal soon discovered that his academic interest was in Spanish, particularly in the literature of Latin America. In 1940, he earned his B.S. degree in Spanish from Northwestern. In 1941, he received his M.A. in Spanish from the University of Chicago, and in 1950, after serving in the U.S. military from 1943 to1945, he received his Ph.D. in Spanish and Italian from the same university.

While studying at Northwestern, Leal met Gladys Clemens, who tutored him in English and whom he married in 1936. They had two children, Antonio and Luis Alonso, and two grandchildren and four great grandchildren.

LIFE'S WORK

Leal distinguished himself as a professor at various universities in the United States, among them the University of Mississippi (1952-1956), Emory University (1956-1959), and the University of Illinois, Urbana-Champaign (1959-1962), and he was a visiting professor at the University of California at Santa Barbara for many years. At the latter university, Leal taught graduate courses in Latin American and Chicano literature, held various research fellowships, and served as the director of the Center for Chicano Studies.

Leal was a popular teacher and scholar who taught many graduate students, mentored many professors, and directed forty-four Ph.D. dissertations. As a professor and researcher, he championed the dissemination of Chicano, Mexican, and Latin American literature in the United States and encouraged American universities to incorporate these literatures into their curricula.

Leal was a prolific scholar, who, in his fifty years as an academic, wrote more than four hundred scholarly articles and forty-five books. His scholarship was focused primarily on Mexican literature, as well as Latin American literature and later on Chicano literature. His scholarly publications, his conference presentations, and his teaching popularized Chicano literature in the United States and led to the development of the first graduate degree in Chicano studies in the United States, pioneered by the University of California at Santa Barbara.

Leal's scholarship was as diverse as it was prolific. His initial academic fame originated with the publication of his seminal text *Brief History of the Mexican Short Story*, originally published in Spanish in 1956. In this text, he demonstrates his attention to careful and precise research; it became a popular academic book not only for its use of research methods but also for its historical content. Some of his other works, such as his book *Juan Rulfo* (1983), demonstrate Leal's scholarly ability to systemically analyze literary texts written by other authors.

Leal also popularized the legitimacy of oral traditions as an accepted literary venue by conducting conference presentations on this topic and by the publication of his short story collection *Myths and Legends of Mexico* (2003), in which he recounts a number of stories, all based on oral traditions from the Mexican culture.

Although Leal was a naturalized U.S. citizen, he never forgot his Mexican culture and roots and made every effort to popularize knowledge of Chicano literature in American and Mexican colleges. As a student in Chicago, he worked successfully with the Mexican American Council to make university scholarships available to Chicano students. In 1973, he published "Mexican-American Literature: A Historical Perspective" in the journal *Chicana-Riqueña*, in which he postulated, convincingly, that Chicano literature has its roots in the Spanish civilization and colonization of the Southwest. He followed this with his book *No Longer Voiceless* in 1995, in which he affirms that Chicanos in the United States now have a literary forum through which their voices can be heard and their academic accomplishments showcased.

In addition to being a professor and a scholar, Leal established a literary journal, *Ventanas Abiertas*, which served as an academic venue for the publication of literary articles on Chicano and Latin American literature. Because of his pioneering work in the promulgation of Chicano, Mexican, and Latin American culture and literature, the University of California at Santa Barbara in 2003 created the competitive Luis Leal Award for Distinction in Chicano/Latino Literature, presented annually to deserving scholars.

Leal received many prestigious awards, among them the Distinguished Scholarly Award from the National Association of Chicano Studies in 1988, the Aguila Aztec Award presented to him by Mexican president Carlos Salinas de Gortari in 1991, and the National Humanities Medal presented to him by President Bill Clinton in 1997.

Leal died on January 25, 2010, predeceased by his wife, Gladys, and his son Luis Alonso.

SIGNIFICANCE

Leal was one of the principal figures in disseminating and popularizing the study of Mexican, Chicano, and Latin American literature in universities in the United States. Because of his tireless efforts, U.S. universities developed graduate programs in these literary areas, giving students the opportunity to specialize in these fields. In addition to his scholarly achievements, Leal helped forge, through an awareness of literature and culture, a closer and more meaningful academic relation between Mexico and the United States.

Víctor Manuel Durán

FURTHER READING

García, Mario T. *Luis Leal: An Auto/Biography*. Austin: University of Texas Press, 2000. A concise biography of Leal, emphasizing his literary formation.

Leal, Luis. *Brief History of Latin American Literature*. New York: Knopf, 1971. A synopsis of the development of Latin American literature from its origins to the time of its publication.

_____. *A Luis Leal Reader*. Edited by Ilan Stavans. Evanston, Ill.: Northwestern University Press, 2007. A collection of Leal's selected writings.

_____. *Myths and Legends of Mexico*. Santa Barbara, Calif.: Center for Chicano Studies, 2003.

A collection of twenty well-known Mexican myths related by Leal.

See also: Juan Bruce-Novoa; Lourdes Casal; Gary D. Keller.

LOLITA LEBRÓN

Puerto Rican-born activist

Notorious for orchestrating and leading an attack on the U.S. Congress, Lebrón was an ardent advocate for Puerto Rico's independence from the United States. While condemned as a terrorist by many, Lebrón's supporters honor her for giving Puerto Rico a voice with which to determine its own identity.

Latino heritage: Puerto Rican

Born: November 19, 1919; Lares, Puerto Rico

Died: August 1, 2010; San Juan, Puerto Rico

Also known as: Dolores Lebrón Sotomayor; Dolores Lebrón de Perez; Doña Lolita

Area of achievement: Activism

EARLY LIFE

Lolita Lebrón (loh-LEE-tah lay-BRON) was born in Lares, Puerto Rico, on November 19, 1919, to Gonzalo Lebrón Bernal and Rafaela Soto Luciano. While the mountain town of Lares was known for its history of political rebellion, Lebrón's father did not have time for political involvement. As the foreman of a coffee farm in the Pezuelas barrio of Lares, her father worked hard to support her and her four siblings. As a small child, Lebrón attended a small community school where she received a rudimentary education. However, her father eventually relocated his family to Mirasol, where Lebrón had access to a better education at the local public school.

As a teenager in Lares, Lebrón was renowned for her beauty, winning her the local Queen of the Flowers of May beauty contest. During this time, she moved to San Juan in pursuit of her first love and to learn the art of sewing. However, unable to find the man with whom she had fallen in love, Lebrón moved back to Lares to care for her father, who had contracted tuberculosis. After her father's death, Lebrón earned a living by sewing and making clothing.

While registered with the Liberal Party at a young age, Lebrón's interest in politics did not surface until she was eighteen years old. In 1937, seventeen Puerto Rican nationalists were killed during a peaceful protest on orders of the American-appointed governor. Angered by what became known as the Massacre of Ponce, Lebrón became a nationalist.

During this time, Lebrón had her first child, Gladys. Seeking work and a better life, she left Gladys with her mother and moved to New York in 1940. While in New York, Lebrón worked in sweatshops as a machinist. On more than one occasion, she was fired for protesting the unfair discrimination against Puerto Ricans. The prejudice Lebrón experienced led her to officially join the Puerto Rican Nationalist Party. While working in New York, she took night classes in an effort to further her education. At twenty-two, Lebrón briefly married and gave birth to her son, who was sent to Puerto Rico to live with her mother.

LIFE'S WORK

In 1943, disgusted by the poverty Puerto Rican immigrants faced in the United States, Lebrón increased her

Lolita Lebrón. (AP Photo)

involvement in the Puerto Rican Nationalist Party. As a party member, she familiarized herself with the ideas of its president, Pedro Albizu Campos. Inspired by his ideas, Lebrón began integrating feminist and socialist principles into the party's work. Her hard work and passion earned her a number of powerful positions in the party, including that of vice president.

Albizu Campos was arrested in 1950 and found guilty of orchestrating a plot to assassinate President Harry S. Truman. After his imprisonment, Lebrón continued to promote his ideas by spreading the message of Puerto Rican liberation. In 1952, Puerto Rico's governor signed a commonwealth pact that granted Puerto Ricans self-government but kept the nation subject to the United States. Angered by this decision, Albizu Campos chose Lebrón and three others to carry out an attack on the United States. Lebrón immediately took leadership by studying the plan and choosing the location of the attack.

Lebrón chose the day of the attack to coincide with the Interamerican Conference in Caracas, Venezuela. She hoped that an attack on this date would demonstrate the seriousness of Puerto Rican liberation to the Latin American countries at the conference. On March 1, 1954, Lebrón and her fellow nationalists, Andrés Figueroa Cordero and Irving Flores Rodríguez, took the train from New York to Washington, D.C., where they met Rafael Cancel Miranda. Expecting to die, Lebrón and her companions had purchased one-way tickets. Arriving at the visitor's gallery in the chambers of the House of Representatives, the nationalists listened while Congress debated an immigration bill. Lebrón gave the order for the attack, shouting "Viva Puerto Rico Libre!"and unfurling a Puerto Rican flag. The attackers fired twenty-nine shots, injuring five congressmen; Lebrón fired eight of these shots directly at the ceiling.

Lebrón was convicted of five counts of assault with a dangerous weapon, as well as conspiracy, and sentenced to serve from sixteen years and eight months to fifty-six years in the Federal Correctional Institute for Women in Alderson, West Virginia. During her first two years in prison, Lebrón's son and mother died. On two occasions she was offered parole, which she refused, using the offer as an opportunity to make political statements in protest of U.S. foreign policy. Lebrón spent her time in prison studying and writing poetry.

In 1977, Lebrón was given furlough to attend the funeral of her daughter, Gladys, who had died in a car

---

Attack on the U.S. Congress

On March 1, 1954, Lolita Lebrón, Andrés Figueroa Cordero, Irving Flores Rodríguez, and Rafael Cancel Miranda fired twenty-nine shots in the chambers of the U.S. House of Representatives in protest of the United States' control of Puerto Rico. This attack was instigated shortly after Puerto Rico's governor signed a commonwealth agreement. Pedro Albizu Campos, who was serving time in prison for conspiring to assassinate President Harry S. Truman, contacted Lebrón and advised her to lead and orchestrate an assault on the United States.

After mapping out the attack, Lebrón and her nationalist collaborators purchased one-way tickets from New York to Washington, D.C., where they had lunch at Union Station and then walked to the U.S. Capitol. As members of the House of Representatives debated an immigration bill, the nationalists began firing bullets from the Ladies Gallery. Lebrón unfurled the Puerto Rican flag and shouted "Viva Puerto Rico Libre!" ("Long live a free Puerto Rico"). Five congressmen were injured during the assault, including one who was badly injured with a bullet to the chest. Lebrón did not expect to survive the attack, and after her arrest, police found a handwritten note in her purse that read, "My life I give for the freedom of my country."

Lebrón was sentenced to sixteen to fifty-six years in prison. After serving twenty-five years, she was pardoned by President Jimmy Carter in 1979 in a suspected prisoner swap with Cuba.

---

accident. Two years later, Lebrón and her collaborators were pardoned and released from prison by President Jimmy Carter. The pardon is suspected to have been part of a prisoner swap with Cuba. After their release, she and the other nationalists toured the U.S., visiting Puerto Rican communities and rallies. Arriving back in Puerto Rico, she was greeted by crowds of supporters.

Back in Puerto Rico, Lebrón married Sergio Irizarry Rivera, a doctor who had monitored her health in prison. Even after twenty-five years in prison, her passion for Puerto Rican independence had not wavered. Having renounced violence and embraced civil disobedience, Lebrón participated in protests against the U.S. military's use of the island of Vieques. In 2001, at the age of eighty-one, she was arrested and sentenced to sixty days in jail for trespassing on the military base there.

In 2008, Lebrón began to experience health complications because of a fall that resulted in a fractured hip and arm. In 2009, she suffered a series of heart and respiratory problems that would contribute to her death on August 1, 2010.

SIGNIFICANCE

While thought of as a terrorist by many people, Lebrón's extreme actions for independence had a tremendous impact on many Puerto Ricans. Even though she was unsuccessful in securing independence for Puerto Rico, Lebrón's actions brought attention to the issue. Her position as a woman leader underscored her uniqueness and visibility. She did not fit the stereotypes of revolutionary male leaders, but her long years in prison gave her similar stature. After her release from prison, Lebrón continued to inspire many young Puerto Ricans advocating for independence, only this time she inspired civil disobedience. Many Puerto Ricans continue to feel a sense of national pride when they think of Doña Lolita.

Erin E. Parrish

FURTHER READING

Ribes Tovar, Federico. *Lolita Lebrón, La Prisonera*. New York: Plus Ultra Educational, 1974. This book, written in Spanish, is perhaps the most complete biography available on Lolita Lebrón and includes many details from her childhood.

_____. "1954." In *A Chronological History of Puerto Rico*. New York: Plus Ultra Educational, 1973. Not only provides chronological details of Lebrón's attack on the U.S. Congress and her court trial but also offers historical context by discussing events occurring simultaneously in Puerto Rico.

Roig-Franzia, Manuel. "A Terrorist in the House." *The Washington Post Magazine*, February, 24, 2004, W12. While this article provides biographical details of Lebrón's life, it also imparts stories of Roig-Franzia's personal interactions with her.

Vilar, Irene. *The Ladies Gallery: A Memoir of Family Secrets*. New York: Other Press, 2009. Formerly published as A Message from God in the Atomic Age, this memoir by Lebrón's granddaughter includes family details from three generations, beginning with Lebrón's life. Lebrón contested many of the stories in her granddaughter's book.

See also: Pedro Albizu Campos; Rubén Berríos; José de Diego; Luis Gutiérrez.

JOHN LEGUIZAMO

Colombian-born comedian, actor, and writer

Leguizamo is a multifaceted entertainer whose credits include author, screenwriter, actor, voiceover artist, producer, director, and comedian. Leguizamo's upbringing and ethnicity influenced his desire to succeed and give voice to the Latino culture. His one man shows portray Latinos beyond their stereotypical characteristics while often reflecting elements of his personal experiences.

Latino heritage: Colombian and Puerto Rican
Born: July 22, 1964; Bogotá, Colombia
Also known as: John Alberto Leguizamo
Areas of achievement: Entertainment; acting; radio and television; theater

EARLY LIFE

John Alberto Leguizamo (jon ahl-BEHR-toh leh-gee-ZAH-moh) was born in Bogotá, Colombia, on July 22, 1964. He is the oldest son of Alberto and Luz Leguizamo, his Puerto Rican father and Colombian mother.

Leguizamo's parents moved to the United States when he was three years old. They later brought him and his younger brother Sergio to Queens, New York, and relocated in the same vicinity several times throughout the years. Fighting bitterly throughout their marriage, Leguizamo's parents divorced in 1978. Leguizamo and his brother lived with their mother after the divorce.

Leguizamo's penchant for writing and performing originated during his childhood. He often used humor to prevent or delay his father's punishments. He also employed wit and sarcasm to fit in at school and in the ethnically diverse neighborhoods in which he was raised. Leguizamo was frequently in trouble for his behavior. He was arrested a few times, the first at age fourteen after breaking into a subway conductor's booth and performing impressions.

Leguizamo attended Murray Bergtraum High School in New York City and then spent one year at a private school in Colombia, where he was sent as a punishment after his first arrest. He also briefly attended

John Leguizamo. (AP Photo)

New York University, and while there he acted in the student film *Five Out of Six*. He also studied acting at Sylvia Leigh's Showcase Theater, HB Studio, and the Lee Strasberg Theatre Institute.

While growing up, Leguizamo observed discriminatory treatment toward the Latino community. He was conscious of how hard his parents worked to establish themselves in the United States. He was affected by his father's bitterness resulting from forgoing his dreams of becoming a director, which led to his father's subsequent harsh and controlling nature toward his children. These factors influenced Leguizamo's desires to attain his self-expression and create his own path and contributed to his strong work ethic.

Leguizamo was divorced from his first wife, Yelba Matamoro (also known as Yelba Osorio), in 1996 after two years of marriage. He married Justine Maurer in 2003. Leguizamo and Maurer have two children: a daughter, Allegra, and a son, Ryder.

LIFE'S WORK

Leguizamo has credited his high school math teacher, Mr. Zufa, as the catalyst for his entertainment career. His first acting jobs were in children's theater in New York. He worked the comedy-club circuit and was a member of the First Amendment Comedy Troupe. Leguizamo first appeared on television in the mid-1980's in episodes of *Miami Vice*. His initial professional film appearance was as an extra in *Mixed Blood* (1984), followed by a speaking role in *Casualties of War* (1989). He made his first onstage appearances when he performed in *La Puta Vida Trilogy* (1987) and *A Midsummer Night's Dream* (1988).

Leguizamo produced and starred in *House of Buggin'* (1995), a comedy show featuring a Latino cast. He directed and acted in the 2003 film *Undefeated*. Leguizamo has also written books and starred in one man stand-up comedy shows, such as *Mambo Mouth*, *Freak*, and *Klass Klown*. He provided voiceover talent for animated television programs, including *Dora the Explorer*, and was the voice of Sid in the *Ice Age* films.

By 2011, Leguizamo's list of credits included more than sixty roles. These roles include a gangster, drag queen, boxer, thief, doctor, clown, video game character, and broadcast journalist. Many of the personalities featured in his live shows are rooted in or based on his experiences as a Latino.

Leguizamo has received numerous honors for his varied achievements, including Outer Critics Circle Awards for *Mambo Mouth* (1991) and *Freak* (1998), an Obie Award for *Mambo Mouth* (1994), and three Cable Ace Awards for *Spic-O-Rama* (1994). He also won a Drama Desk Award in 1998 and an Emmy Award in 1999, both for *Freak*. Leguizamo has been nominated for several American Latino Media Arts (ALMA) Awards and has won for Outstanding Performance by an Individual or Act in a Variety or Comedy Special (1999), Outstanding Host of a Variety or Awards Special (2001), Entertainer of the Year (2002), and Best of the Year in Film—Actor (2009). He has also been nominated for Golden Globe, Tony, Screen Actors Guild, and Emmy Awards. In 2010, Leguizamo hosted the Poetry Out Loud Finals competition and Nickelodeon's Mega Music Fest.

SIGNIFICANCE

Leguizamo uses his talents and drive for realism to depict Latinos as complex beings, a change from the way in which they had been previously conceived and portrayed. His skill at creating relatable characters, as well as his ability to improvise and perform with a direct and unapologetic style, have resulted in his creation of personalities with depth and often with a message about humanity and perception. Leguizamo has used a variety of media to hone his acting, writing, producing, and performing skills and to connect with audiences from similar backgrounds, as well as those from other cultures who are interested in his stories and the Latino culture.

Caprice Nelson de Lorm

FURTHER READING

Leguizamo, John. *Pimps, Hos, Playa Hatas, and All the Rest of My Hollywood Friends: My Life*. New York: HarperCollins, 2006. Covers many aspects of Leguizamo's experiences. Writing candidly, Leguizamo provides insight into the impact of his childhood on his drive, self-perception, and commitment to portraying Latinos with depth.

_____. *The Works of John Leguizamo*. New York: HarperCollins, 2008. Contains content from his one-man shows *Freak, Spic-O-Rama, Mambo Mouth*, and *Sexaholic: A Love Story*; these shows feature stories and characters based on his life.

Leguizamo, John, and Kathleen McGowan. "One-Man Firebrand: John Leguizamo Turns His Tumultuous Personal Life into Street-Smart Comedy—and Dishes out Sharp Insights About Love, Family Disasters, and the Shaky Male Ego." *Psychology Today* 38, no.2 (March/April 2005): 48. Leguizamo discusses aspects of his work, his childhood, and his views on family and marriage.

Rodriguez, Marissa. "Being John Leguizamo." *Hispanic*, April, 2008, 48. Discusses some of Leguizamo's acting experiences, his upbringing, being a father, and his belief about being provocative while entertaining.

See also: Benjamin Bratt; Emilio Estevez; George Lopez; Cheech Marín; Esai Morales; Paul Rodríguez; Charlie Sheen.

JOSÉ ARCADIO LIMÓN

Mexican-born dancer and choreographer

A dancer, choreographer, and founder of his own dance company, Limón established the role of the male dancer in modern dance.

Latino heritage: Mexican
Born: January 12, 1908; Culiacán, Sinaloa, Mexico
Died: December 2, 1972; Flemington, New Jersey
Areas of achievement: Dance

EARLY LIFE

José Arcadio Limón (ahr-KAH-dee-oh lee-MOHN) was born in Culiacán, Sinaloa, Mexico. His father was a musician and teacher; his mother was a homemaker. The couple had eleven children, of which Limón was the oldest. Limón's mother was a devout Catholic and raised her children in the ways of the church.

When Limón was young, the Mexican Revolution forced his family to move often in attempts to avoid violence. When he was seven, the family crossed the border into the United States. The move immediately lowered their standard of living. In Mexico, musicians often were supported by the government, but in the United States, his father found work scarce. The family moved often before settling in Los Angeles when Limón was twelve years old. He was interested in art when he was in high school and showed talent in that area.

José Arcadio Limón.
(AP Photo)

When Limón was eighteen, his mother died in childbirth. Limón blamed the church and his father for her death and distanced himself from both. He studied art in California for a while, but friends persuaded him to move to New York City in 1928. He was disillusioned with art, since he idolized El Greco and knew that he could never reach that level of proficiency. By chance, Limón attended a dance performance of Harald Kreutzberg and was so moved that he felt that dance was his calling. He began taking classes with Doris Humphrey and Charles Weidman; when they saw his promise, they became his mentors and champions.

Amazingly, within a year of his first dance class, Limón was performing with a professional company. Most people begin training to become dancers in childhood, but he was nineteen when he discovered modern dance. By age twenty, he was performing for audiences.

Limón began living with Humphrey, Weidman, and Pauline Lawrence. All were immersed in the American modern dance movement. Limón became a part of their company and performed in works that they choreographed and produced.

LIFE'S WORK

Limón began choreographing around 1930 with others from the Humphrey-Weidman company. Company members also often worked and performed at Bennington College in the summers. Limón was named a Bennington College choreography fellow in 1937. In 1938, he choreographed _Danzas Mexicanas_, his first major work. It was influenced by Mexican themes.

In the early 1940's, Limón moved to California, expressing discomfort with Broadway and its lack of creativity; however he moved back to the East Coast soon after and married Pauline Lawrence, one of the colleagues he had lived and worked with while a part of the Humphrey-Weidman company. During this period, he choreographed _Chaconne in D Minor_ (1942), a dance solo to the music of Johann Sebastian Bach.

Limón was drafted into the U.S. Army in 1943 but was able to continue dancing and choreographing for Army shows while he served. On weekends and on leaves, he choreographed for a small company that eventually became the José Limón Dance Company. Doris Humphrey, one of Limón's early teachers and mentors, retired from dancing because of a hip injury. She became the artistic director for his company and also choreographed many numbers to highlight Limón's talents as a male solo dancer.

Ties to Mexico After Becoming an American Citizen

Although José Arcadio Limón never returned to Mexico to stay, it was obvious that he had strong ties to his homeland's history and culture. He choreographed a number of dances with Mexican themes, including _Danzas Mexicanas_ (1938), _La Malinche_ (1949), and 1951's _El grito, Los cuatros soles_, and _Tonantzintla_.

Limón's most famous Mexican-themed dance, _La Malinche_, tells the story of an indigenous Mexican woman caught up in the Spanish conquest of Mexico. The title character is familiar to Mexicans and Mexican Americans alike. Many dance critics find it interesting that Limón chose a woman as the main character rather than a man, since war is most often seen as the province of men. Some feel Limón may have been empathic toward La Malinche, a woman torn between two allegiances (to the conquistadors and the conquered), as he may have been torn between his Mexican and American roots.

Spanish and Mexican works of art also influenced many of Limón's costumes and set designs, and memories of Mexican music of his childhood seemed to have inspired some of the music he commissioned. The dance _Tonantzintla_ is inspired by a church, Santa Maria Tonantzintla, in a small Mexican town. It was decorated by sixteenth-century Indian artists, so the artwork is unlike that of most Spanish-influenced churches.

In 1949, Limón choreographed _La Malinche_, a work based on a major figure in Mexican history. Shortly after, he developed _The Moor's Pavane_ (1949), one of his best-known dances. This latter work was based on William Shakespeare's _Othello, the Moor of Venice_ (pr. 1604, rev. 1623). It is one of Limón's most famous works.

In 1950, Limón (by this time an American citizen) and his company traveled to Mexico City, where he was invited to establish a school and company. He created several new works for the Ballet Mexicano, including _El grito, Los cuatros soles_, and _Tonantzintla_ in 1951. He soon returned to his company in New York and accepted a faculty position in the Dance Department at the Juilliard School of Music, where he taught for the rest of his life. In 1954, he became a cultural ambassador for the U.S. government, and his company was the first to participate in the State Department's Cultural Exchange Program. In that year, they made a tour of four South American cities. In 1957, the company went on a five-month tour of Europe, including Poland and Yugoslavia, The company went to South America in 1960 and to the Far East in 1963, with sponsorship of the United States' State Department. Limón died in Flemington, New Jersey, on December 2, 1972. The next year, his company continued its State Department duties with a performance tour to the Soviet Union.

SIGNIFICANCE
Limón was a key figure in the history and development of modern dance. He choreographed a number of pieces that have become classics. He was a guest at the White House in 1962 and performed *The Moor's Pavane* at a White House state dinner in 1967 for President Lyndon Johnson and King Hassan II of Morocco.

M. C. Ware

FURTHER READING
Dunbar, June, ed. *José Limón: The Artist Re-Viewed*. Amsterdam: Harwood Academic, 2000. Collection of essays about Limón by a number of individuals who knew him personally.

Limón, José. *José Limón: An Unfinished Memoir*. Edited by Lynn Garafola. Hanover, N.H.: University Press of New England, 1998. This memoir, begun by Limón when he was near death, offers much detail about his life through 1942.

Mazo, Joseph H. *Prime Movers: The Makers of Modern Dance in America*. 2d ed. Hightstown, N.J.: Princeton Book Company, 2000. A basic history of modern dance that covers all the major figures in its development, including Limón.

Pollack, Barbara, and C. H. Woodford. *Dance Is a Moment: A Portrait of José Limón in Words and Pictures*. Pennington, N.J.: Princeton Book Company, 1993. A detailed biography of Limón's life and work, based on extensive research.

See also: Fernando Bujones; Evelyn Cisneros; Royes Fernández; Rita Moreno; Chita Rivera.

VICENTE JOSÉ LLAMAS
American educator and scientist

Throughout his professional career, Llamas has been an active mentor to Latino professionals in the sciences, mathematics, and engineering. He established or cofounded a number of organizations designed to increase opportunities for disadvantaged minorities in scientific and technical fields.

Latino heritage: Mexican
Born: February 14, 1944; Los Angeles, California
Areas of achievement: Education; science and technology

EARLY LIFE
Vicente José Llamas (vee-SEHN-tee hoh-ZAY YAH-mahs) was born on February 14, 1944, in Boyle Heights, a Chicano neighborhood in East Los Angeles, to parents from Mexico. As a child, Llamas enjoyed family life with his two siblings. Interested in science and mathematics at a young age, Llamas built a stereo receiver with his father from used electrical parts and often took apart electrical appliances to determine how they worked. After graduating from high school, he elected to major in physics at Loyola Marymount University in Los Angeles, graduating with his B.S. in 1966. With the help of his professors, he obtained a full scholarship to the University of Missouri at Rolla in south central Missouri. He was one of only two Latinos in the physics department and one of very few Latinos on campus. He obtained his M.S. in 1968 and his Ph.D. in 1970, focusing on solid-state physics and air pollution. During graduate school, Llamas taught physical science at Cuba Middle School, as well as serving as an instructor in the University of Missouri at Rolla's Department of Physics. As graduation neared, Llamas had applied to more than 250 colleges and universities for an assistant professor position. The only offer he received was to join the faculty of New Mexico Highlands University in Las Vegas, New Mexico, a small state university serving almost exclusively residents in northern New Mexico.

LIFE'S WORK
During his career at New Mexico Highlands University, Llamas focused his research on alkali halides, the most well known of which is sodium chloride, common table salt, using the infrared part of the spectrum. He also continued his studies of atmospheric pollutants. He was promoted to associate professor in 1973 and was made a full professor in 1984. He retired in 1994 as an emeritus professor of physics. During his years at the university,

he was a visiting professor at United World College of the Southwest in 1984. As in his graduate school days, Llamas also made time to teach the physics class at West Las Vegas High School from 1978 to 1980.

Active in serving the needs of secondary-school science teachers, Llamas was associate director and then director of the New Mexico Highlands Science Education Resources Center from 1987 to 1990. The center provided regular workshops for classroom teachers and loaned science equipment and materials to area schools. From 1989 to 1991, Llamas also served as assistant director and then director of a large-scale scholarship program for minority students at New Mexico Highlands University funded by the National Science Foundation. As a companion to this effort, in 1989 he founded the New Mexico Alliance for Science Education and served as its chairperson from 1989 to1991, when the organization was formally dissolved. He then became copresident of the New Mexico Partnership for Mathematics and Science Education. The partnership works with kindergarten through twelfth-grade schools, colleges, universities, corporations, and nonprofit groups across New Mexico to advance teaching, learning, and career exploration in science, technology, engineering, and mathematics (STEM). This organization has received state appropriations, as well as long-term support from the National Science Foundation. In 1991, Llamas ran the Los Alamos Summer Science Student Program, which provided opportunities for students to work and learn at the Los Alamos National Laboratory of the U.S. Department of Energy.

Not content to just focus on New Mexico, Llamas served on the National Science Foundation Minority Institutes for Excellence Blue Ribbon Committee (1994-1999), the National Advisory Board of the National Urban League (1995-1997), and the National Association of State Science and Mathematics Coalitions (1995-2007).

SIGNIFICANCE

Llamas was an early pioneer in advancing the interests, involvement, and achievement of Latinos in science, technology, engineering, and mathematics through advocacy, programs, and mentoring. He inspired other professionals to involve themselves in similar activities in New Mexico and across the nation.

Dennis W. Cheek

FURTHER READING

Heil, Diana. "Committee to Begin Work on Education Reform This Week." *Santa Fe New Mexican*, October 20, 2003, p. A1. Reports about the efforts of a committee of one hundred New Mexicans, including Llamas, who were scheduled to meet in order to help determine the course of education in the state.

Llamas, Vicente. SACNAS Biography Project. http://bio. sacnas.org/beta/pdf/llamasHS.pdf. Llamas provides a brief but informative overview of his life and work.

Newton, David E. *Latinos in Science, Math, and Professions*. New York: Facts On File, 2007. This encyclopedia includes an entry about Llamas.

Propp, Wren. "Indian Science Education Gets Boost." *Albuquerque Journal*, November 29, 1995, p. 1. Discusses the work of the Utah, Colorado, Arizona and New Mexico Rural Systemic Initiative. This project, directed by Llamas, sought to increase science, math, and technology education for Native American and other minority students in four Southwestern states.

See also: Luis W. Alvarez; Ralph Amado; Albert V. Baez; Manuel Cardona; José D. García.

REBECCA LOBO

American basketball player, activist, and journalist

Lobo's success as a talented female basketball player transformed a traditionally male sport. Her ability to balance academics, athletics, and family made Lobo a role model for women and men alike.

Latino heritage: Cuban

Born: October 6, 1973; Hartford, Connecticut

Also known as: Rebecca Rose Lobo-Rushin; Rebecca Rose Lobo

Areas of achievement: Basketball; journalism; activism

EARLY LIFE

Rebecca Rose Lobo-Rushin, better known as Rebecca Lobo (ree-BEHK-ah LOH-boh), was born in Hartford,

Connecticut, on October 3, 1973 and grew up in South-wick, Massachusetts. The youngest daughter of two teachers, Lobo's parentage was quite diverse. Her mother, RuthAnn Hardy Lobo, is of German and Irish heritage; her father, Dennis Joseph Lobo, is of Cuban and Polish descent. Lobo received an early exposure to basketball. Her older siblings played on their collegiate basketball teams, and her father was a basketball coach.

From a young age, Lobo established herself as an exemplary basketball player. During her basketball career at Southwick-Tolland High School, she scored a total of 2,470 points—the state record for almost two decades. With her evident and remarkable athletic ability, Lobo was courted by more than one hundred colleges and universities upon graduation from high school. After much deliberation, she chose the University of Connecticut.

LIFE'S WORK

At the University of Connecticut, Lobo continued her career of athletic excellence. During her senior year, she greatly contributed to her college team, the Huskies, who won the 1995 national championship with a record of 35-0. For her efforts, Lobo was named the Naismith college player of the year.

Indeed, 1995 proved to be a pivotal year for Lobo. She also received the 1994-1995 Honda-Broderick Cup, which recognizes superb female collegiate athletes. In addition, she was named 1995 Sportswoman of the Year by the Women's Sports Foundation. However, Lobo was not simply a superb basketball player. Because her parents were teachers, she knew the value of an education and strove to keep a balance between athletics and academics. In 1995, Lobo received her B.S. in political science.

Upon graduation from the University of Connecticut, Lobo joined the U.S. Olympic Women's Basketball Team in time to play at the 1996 Olympic Games in Atlanta, Georgia. Her team won the Gold Medal after defeating Brazil in the final rounds of play.

After the 1996 Olympic Games, Lobo briefly considered traveling to Europe to play professional women's basketball. However, the Women's National Basketball Association (WNBA) was organized during 1997. Lobo joined the association when she became a member of the New York Liberty team. One of the most high-profile players in the WNBA, some critics stated that Lobo received more recognition than she deserved, despite her strong performance for the Liberty from 1997 through 1999. However, Lobo was highly

Rebecca Lobo. (AP Photo)

regarded by fans and teammates alike, and that popularity translated into greater recognition and higher television ratings for the WBNA.

In 1999, Lobo suffered a debilitating injury when the anterior cruciate ligament in her knee was torn at the beginning of the season. A subsequent reinjury caused Lobo to further sit out the 1999 and 2000 seasons. After a long recovery, Lobo played for the New York Liberty during the 2001 season. She was traded to the Houston Comets in April, 2002, and to the Connecticut Suns for the 2003 season. She retired from professional basketball after the 2003 season.

Since her retirement, Lobo has worked as a sports analyst for ESPN, with a natural focus on women's basketball, both collegiate and professional. In addition to sports commenting, Lobo has campaigned extensively to raise awareness about breast cancer. Her mother, RuthAnn Hardy Lobo, suffered through excruciating rounds of treatment during her ordeal with breast cancer. After witnessing the experience, RuthAnn and Rebecca cowrote their book *The Home Team: Of Mothers, Daughters, and American Champions* (1996), which details the ordeal in order to elevate national awareness about the disease. The two also established the RuthAnn and Rebecca Lobo Scholarship for students enrolled in the School of Allied Health at the University of Connecticut; preference is given to students of Hispanic and African descent.

SIGNIFICANCE

In 2010, Rebecca Lobo was inducted into the Women's Basketball Hall of Fame. Located in Knoxville, Tennessee, the organization honors both men and women who have contributed to the sport of women's basketball. The selection of Lobo for the Class of 2010 reflects her great impact on female athletes and the game of basketball.

Rebecca M. Marrall

FURTHER READING

Heaphy, Leslie. "Rebecca Lobo." In *Great Athletes: Basketball*, edited by the editors of Salem Press. Pasadena, Calif.: Salem Press, 2010. Recounts Lobo's career and her contribution to women's basketball.

Kilmeade, Brian. *It's How You Play the Game: The Powerful Sports Moments That Taught Lasting Values to America's Finest.* New York: HarperCollins, 2007. Includes a chapter about the impact and contribution of Lobo to women's basketball.

VanDerveer, Tara, and Joan Ryan. *Shooting from the Outside: How a Coach and Her Olympic Team Transformed Women's Basketball.* New York: Avon Books, 1997. Recounts the history of the 1996 U.S.Olympic Women's Basketball Team, which won the Gold Medal.

See also: Carlos Arroyo; Rolando Blackman; Eduardo Nájera; Diana Taurasi.

EVA LONGORIA

American actor, entrepreneur, and philanthropist

Longoria is an actor best known for her role of Gabrielle Solis on the television show Desperate Housewives. *Along with a successful career in television and film, she is an accomplished entrepreneur and advocate for the Latino community.*

Latino heritage: Mexican

Born: March 15, 1975; Corpus Christi, Texas

Also known as: Eva Jacqueline Longoria; Eva Longoria Parker

Areas of achievement: Radio and television; acting; business; philanthropy

EARLY LIFE

Eva Jacqueline Longoria (lahn-GOH-ree-ah) was the last of four daughters born to Ella Eva Mireles and Enrique Longoria, Jr., both of whom are of Mexican descent. Longoria was raised on the family's ranch in Corpus Christi, Texas and grew up in modest circumstances. Her parents taught her to work and farm the land, and she grew vegetables and learned to hunt on the weekends with her father.

Longoria's father was an army engineer and her mother was a special education teacher. Although they had relatively good jobs, family finances were tight. As a teenager, Longoria took a job at Wendy's, the local fast-food restaurant, to contribute to the expenses of her quinceñeara (fifteenth birthday party), a Latin American tradition celebrating a young woman's coming of age. The family's financial circumstances instilled in Longoria a strong work ethic and a sense of self-sufficiency that persisted throughout her life.

Longoria attended local schools and went on to earn her B.S. degree in kinesiology from Texas A&M Kingsville, a small community college forty miles from her home. At the age of twenty-three, Longoria was crowned Miss Corpus Christi, an accomplishment superseding moments in her early childhood and adolescence when she was referred to as the "ugly duckling" in her family because of her dark hair and skin. Her pageant prize included an opportunity to travel to Los Angeles. Rather than return to Texas to get a master's degree in sports medicine, she stayed in Los Angeles to pursue a career in acting.

LIFE'S WORK

Longoria's early acting jobs included small roles on *Beverly Hills 90210*, *The Bold and the Beautiful*, and *General Hospital.* From 2001 to 2003, she had a recurring role as Isabella Braña Williams on *The Young and the Restless*, making her the first Latina actor contracted with the popular daytime soap opera. In 2002, this performance earned her an American Latino Media Arts Award (ALMA). That same year, she

Eva Longoria. (AP Photo)

married actor Tyler Christopher; the couple divorced in 2004.

After leaving *The Young and the Restless*, Longoria starred in a number of films, including *Snitch'd* (2003), *Senorita Justice* (2004), and *Carlita's Secret* (2004). On television Longoria joined the series *L.A. Dragnet* (2003) as Detective Gloria Duran.

In 2004, Longoria landed the role of Gabrielle Solis on ABC's *Desperate Housewives*. The popularity of the show, with a worldwide audience of 120 million viewers, established Longoria as the most recognized Latina on broadcast and cable television that year. In 2005, the National Hispanic Foundation for the Arts recognized her with the organization's first Horizon Award. That same year, she signed a lucrative endorsement deal with L'Oreal Paris, becoming the company's first Latina spokeswoman.

Because of Longoria's popularity, she was asked to host and coproduce the National Council of La Raza's ALMA Awards in 2006. The awards recognize Latino artistic achievement in television, film, and music.

On July 7, 2007, Longoria married San Antonio Spurs player Tony Parker. She adopted her husband's last name, and during the marriage she was known as Eva Longoria Parker.

With an established career in acting and production, Longoria ventured into the restaurant business. In 2008, she partnered with chef Todd English to open the Mexican cuisine restaurant Beso in Hollywood. In 2010, she opened a second restaurant in Las Vegas's CityCenter complex, becoming the first female restaurant owner on the Las Vegas Strip.

Longoria used her prominence in the entertainment industry to advocate for issues important to the Latino community. She partnered with civil rights organizations, like the Mexican American Legal Defense and Educational Fund (MALDEF), the United Farm Workers (UFW), the Dolores Huerta Foundation, and the National Council of La Raza, to champion the rights of immigrants and workers.

In 2005, Longoria became the national spokesperson for Padres Contra El Cáncer (Parents Against Cancer), an organization working with children and their families affected by the disease. Inspired by her sister's ability to live with Down's syndrome, she founded Eva's Heroes in 2006, offering services to special-needs children in San Antonio, Texas. In 2010, Longoria partnered with A Home in Haiti, an organization providing temporary shelter to the country's citizens devastated by an earthquake.

In 2009, Longoria enrolled at California State University, Northridge, to pursue a degree in Chicano studies and political science in order to further her understanding of the history of Mexican Americans living in the United States. In November, 2010, Longoria filed for divorce from Parker and requested that her maiden name be restored. The divorce was finalized on January 28, 2011.

Significance

Eva Longoria has remained committed and connected to her Mexican American roots throughout her rise to stardom. She has used her influence in the entertainment industry as a foundation from which to champion efforts to improve the lives of others and to advocate at the national level for issues affecting Latinos in the United States. She has received numerous awards for her philanthropy, including Philanthropist of the Year (2009) and the 2010 Medallion of Excellence for Leadership and Community Service from the Congressional Hispanic Caucus Institute. In 2009, she was selected by Speaker of the House Nancy Pelosi to serve on the National Museum of the American Latino Commission.

Karina Cervantez and Aída Hurtado

FURTHER READING

Merskin, Debra. "Three Faces of Eva: Perpetuation of the Hot-Latina Stereotype in *Desperate Housewives*." *Howard Journal of Communications*, 18 (2007): 133-151. Provides an analysis of the first season of Longoria's hit show, *Desperate Housewives*, demonstrating the persistence of Latina stereotypes on television.

Ocaña, Damarys. "Eva in Charge." *Hispanic* 23, no 2 (April/May, 2010): 35-38. Profiles Longoria's business accomplishments, including her restaurant on the Las Vegas Strip and her commitment to environmental sustainability.

Schulte, Mary. *Eva Longoria: Overcoming Adversity, Sharing the American Dream.* Broomall, Pa.: Mason Crest, 2009. A biography of Longoria written for children ages nine through twelve, which highlights some of the challenges she has overcome in her life.

See also: Jessica Alba; Cameron Diaz; America Ferrera; Zoë Saldana.

GEORGE LOPEZ

American actor and entertainer

While Lopez was not the first Latino to become a successful stand-up comic, he is one of the most successful. He was one of the first Latinos to successfully star in a television situation comedy and the first to host a network talk show.

Latino heritage: Mexican

Born: April 23, 1961; East Los Angeles, California

Also known as: George Edward Lopez; G. Lo

Areas of achievement: Radio and television; entertainment; acting

EARLY LIFE

George Edward Lopez (LOH-pehz) and his mother Frieda were deserted by his father, Anastasio Lopez, when George was two months old. His mother remarried when he was ten, but she left him to start a new family. Lopez was raised by his maternal grandparents, Benita, a factory worker, and Refugio Gutierrez, a laborer, in a Mexican neighborhood in the Mission Hills section of Los Angeles. Decades later, Lopez based the character of Benny in his television show *George Lopez* on his grandmother and took the title of his autobiography, *Why You Crying? My Long, Hard Look at Life, Love, and Laughter*, from a favorite phrase of hers.

Lopez was a latchkey child; when he got home from school, there were no adults in the house, so he watched television by himself. He especially liked talk shows hosted by Mike Douglas, Merv Griffin, Dinah Shore, and others and featuring comedians, such as Jimmie Walker and George Carlin, as well as situation comedies, like *The Brady Bunch* and *The Partridge Family*. In 1974, he discovered his idol Freddie Prinze, star of *Chico and the Man,* one of the most popular situation comedies of the decade. When Prinze committed suicide in 1977, Lopez was heartbroken, and on many occasions he has visited Prinze's grave in the Forest Lawn cemetery and the hotel where Prinze shot himself. Lopez then discovered comedian Richard Pryor in 1979 after seeing the film *Richard Pryor: Live in Concert* (1979) on cable

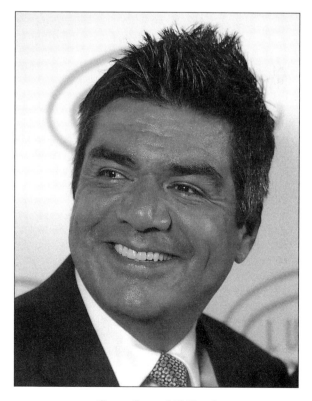

George Lopez. (AP Photo)

television; Lopez purchased all Pryor's books and albums and saw all his films. Inspired by Prinze and Pryor, Lopez decided to become a stand-up comic.

LIFE'S WORK

Lopez graduated from San Fernando Valley High School in 1979. That same year, he first performed stand-up comedy at the Comedy Store Annex in the Westwood neighborhood of Los Angeles on open microphone nights, when amateurs were given the opportunity to appear. However, he gave up comedy between 1980 and 1982 and worked a series of dead-end jobs.

In 1982, Lopez returned to stand-up comedy, performing at night while working other jobs during the day. By 1987, he was making enough money as a performer of comedy to give up his day job. He began appearing on *The Arsenio Hall Show, MTV's Half Hour Comedy Hour, The Tonight Show,* and other television programs in 1989, and starred in his first film, *Ski Patrol,* in 1990. Over the next several years, he turned down many film roles because he felt the characters were stereotypes. One of the few exceptions was the role of a murder investigator in *Fatal Instinct* (1993).

Lopez made three significant breakthroughs in 2000. First, he earned critical success as the villain in the film *Bread and Roses* (2000). He then began hosting a morning radio show for Clear Channel Communications

---

Latino Themes in Lopez's Standup Routines

George Lopez learned from comedian Richard Pryor that he could find material for comedy in his own life experiences. For instance, when ABC sent him a plant as a gift, he added the incident to his stand-up routine, joking that many Latinos, like his grandparents, do not water their lawns, so they do not have to cut the grass.

Latinos, according to Lopez, raise their children by saying no to every request. This was how his grandmother raised him to make sure that life would never disappoint him. However, Lopez adds, Latino children never move out of their homes, which explains the absence of homeless Latinos.

He also observes that Latinos never congratulate each other and never wish each other good luck because they are afraid that by doing so, it will cause bad things to happen. Similarly, Latinos do not draft wills because they fatalistically feel it will hasten their deaths.

---

in Los Angeles, which made him the first Latino to be featured in a valuable morning radio time slot on an English-language station in that city. Finally, Lopez was approached by actor Sandra Bullock, who asked him to produce and star in a television situation comedy. Bullock had formed her own production company with Jonathan Komack Martin, the son of James Komack, who had produced *Chico and the Man.* They had observed the lack of Latino-oriented situation comedies on television and thought there was an opportunity for a show that starred Latinos without being exclusively about Latinos. They also recruited Bruce Helford, who had been head writer on *Roseanne* and had created *The Drew Carey Show,* to become one of the executive producers. *George Lopez* ran for 118 episodes on ABC from 2002 to 2007, and Lopez was the cocreator, cowriter, coproducer, and star.

Lopez's film career took off after his television show went on the air. Critics praised his performance as a teacher in *Real Women Have Curves* in 2002; his other films include *Outta Time* (2002), *Frank McCluskey, C.I.* (2002), *The Adventures of Sharkboy and Lavagirl* (2005), *Where's Marty?* (2006), *Tortilla Heaven* (2007), *Balls of Fury* (2007), *Henry Poole Is Here* (2007), *Swing Vote* (2008), and *Valentine's Day* (2010). He has also provided voices for characters in the animated films *South of the Border* (2008), *Beverly Hills Chihuahua* (2010), and *Marmaduke* (2010). In 2004, he starred in the ABC Christmas television film *Naughty or Nice,* in which he played a controversial radio personality who learns that miracles can happen.

Lopez performed before President George W. Bush and his wife Laura at Ford's Theater in Washington, D.C., in 2003, and he was a commentator for *Inside the NFL* on Home Box Office (HBO) for the 2003-2004 football season. In 2009, Lopez began hosting a late night talk show, *Lopez Tonight,* on TBS.

SIGNIFICANCE

The numerous awards George Lopez has obtained attest to his influence on American culture.

In 2003 and 2004, *George Lopez* received an Image Award for Best Primetime Comedy Series from the National Association for the Advancement of Colored People (NAACP), and Lopez himself received an Image Award for Best Actor in a Television Comedy in 2004. He has also received the Latino Spirit Award for Excellence in Television, the National Hispanic Media Coalition Impact Award, the Manny Mota Foundation Community Spirit Award, the 2004 Artist of the Year and Humanitarian Award from Harvard University, and the 2004 Spirit of Liberty Award from People for the American Way. He has been named an honorary mayor of Los Angeles in recognition of his fund-raising efforts on behalf of earthquake victims in El Salvador and Guatemala.

His compact disc *Team Leader* was nominated for a Grammy Award in the Best Comedy Album category in 2004. Lopez has also been included on the list of America's favorite television personalities and in 2005, *Time* magazine listed him as one of its twenty-five most influential Latinos in the United States. *Forbes* magazine included him on its 2006 list of the one hundred celebrities who earned the greatest amount of money. In 2006, he received a star on the Hollywood Walk of Fame, and the following year, he was named one of the one hundred most influential Latinos by *People en Español.*

Thomas R. Feller

FURTHER READING

Diaz, Jaime. "George Lopez Had a Tough Start in Life and in Golf." *Golf Digest,* 59, no.2 (February, 2008): 104. Focuses on Lopez's interest in golf.

Garron, Barry. "Lopez Tonight." *Hollywood Reporter* 424, no.14 (November 12, 2009); 20. Review of Lopez's talk show on TBS.
_____. "Stand-up Guise: *George Lopez* and the Comic Creator Behind It Celebrate Reaching One Hundred Episodes." *Hollywood Reporter,* 393, no.38 (March 29, 2006): 13-14. Commemorates the one hundredth episode of *George Lopez.*
Guzmán, Lila, and Rick Guzmán. *George Lopez: Comedian and TV Star.* Berkeley Heights, N.J.: Enslow, 2006. Biography of Lopez aimed at children.
_____. *George Lopez: Latino King of Comedy.* Berkeley Heights, N.J.: Enslow, 2009. Biography aimed at young adults.
Koseluk, Chris. "You the Hombre." *Hollywood Reporter* 390, no.20 (December 27, 2006): G-1-2. Interview with Lopez.
Lopez, George, with Armen Keteyian. *Why You Crying? My Long, Hard Look at Life, Love, and Laugher.* New York: Touchstone, 2004. Lopez's autobiography.

See also: Benjamin Bratt; Emilio Estevez; John Leguizamo; Cheech Marín; Esai Morales; Freddie Prinze; Paul Rodríguez; Charlie Sheen.

JENNIFER LOPEZ

American singer, actor, and entrepreneur

Lopez is a renowned singer, actor, fashion designer, film producer, and entrepreneur. Recognized as the highest paid Latina in Hollywood, her triumphs in the entertainment industry have been fueled by her risqué fashion choices, high-profile relationships, and reputation as a diva.

Latino heritage: Puerto Rican
Born: July 24, 1969; Bronx, New York
Also known as: Jennifer Lynn Lopez; J.Lo
Areas of achievement: Music; acting; radio and television; business

EARLY LIFE

Jennifer Lynn Lopez (LOH-pehz) was born to Guadalupe Rodriguez, a kindergarten teacher, and David Lopez, a computer specialist, on July 24, 1969. Both her parents had immigrated to the Bronx, New York, from Ponce, Puerto Rico. Lopez's parents encouraged her and her two sisters to participate in extracurricular activities, such as dance and theater, in order to keep them off the streets of their rough Bronx neighborhood, Castle Hill. Growing up with dreams of being a dancer and admiring Puerto Rican actor Rita Moreno, Lopez dropped out of Baruch College in New York after only one semester to the dismay of her parents, who did not consider performing to be a wise career path.

Her big break came in 1990, when she was cast to be a dancer on the television show *In Living Color.* After the show's cancellation in 1993, Lopez went on to star in several short-lived television series, such as *South Central, Second Chances,* and *Hotel Malibu,* as well as appearing in Janet Jackson's music video for "That's the Way Love Goes." In 1995, she had her first leading role in director Gregory Nava's film *My Family,* an epic that follows a Mexican American family's struggle in the United States. Leading roles in the films *Money Train* (1995), *Jack* (1996), and *Blood and Wine* (1996) followed. Although *Jack* was not favorably received by critics, the film marked the

Jennifer Lopez. (Frederick M. Brown/Getty Images)

first time Lopez was cast in a role not written specifically for a Latina.

Lopez and Nava teamed up again for the film *Selena* (1997), based on the life and tragic murder of the Tejano singer. Despite having already worked with Nava, Lopez had to undergo an intense audition process to prove she was suited for the role. Although Lopez's performance in the film received rave reviews, the decision to have a woman of Puerto Rican descent portray the "Queen of Tejano Music" angered many in the Mexican American community. Despite these tensions, Lopez was quickly becoming an important figure in the Latino community and graced the first cover of the newly created magazine *Latina* in 1996.

In 1997, Lopez proved her ability as a box office draw by starring in the action film *Anaconda*. Although she married Ojani Noa in 1997, she continued to work relentlessly, appearing in director Oliver Stone's film *U Turn* (1997) and director Steven Soderbergh's *Out of Sight* (1998). As Lopez's film career rose, the press begun to take notice of her remarkable figure. Often clad in risqué ensembles, Lopez became as renowned for her body as for her work, and she was included on *People*

magazine's 1997 list of the "Fifty Most Beautiful People in the World."

LIFE'S WORK

Having become established as an actor, Lopez set her sights on a music career. The idea of recording an album came to Lopez when she performed live for audiences while shooting *Selena*. She signed a deal with Sony Music and set to prepare the album materials. She began working with producer and rapper Sean Combs (also known as Puff Daddy or Diddy), but their relationship quickly became personal. After much media speculation, Lopez and Noa divorced in March, 1998. Lopez garnered criticism for her personal relationships, as well as for interviews in which she criticized several of her former costars and other Hollywood actors, earning her a repuation as a diva. Her presence at a shooting involving Combs's entourage in a New York City club led to even more criticism.

The release of Lopez's first album *On the 6* (1998) coincided with the height of the Latin pop invasion, which also catapulted performers Ricky Martin and Enrique Iglesias to fame. Although the album was not a critical success, *On the 6* made history by hitting number one on the Hot 100, Hot 100 Singles Sales, and R&B (rhythm and blues) Singles Sales charts simultaneously. While "If You Had My Love," the album's first single, headed to the top of the pop charts, Lopez continued to make films, working on *Antz* (1998), *The Cell* (2000), and *The Wedding Planner* (2001). Her second album, *J.Lo*, was released in 2001 and debuted at number one on the Billboard 200 chart; the album included the hits "Love Don't Cost a Thing" and "I'm Real."

Shortly after her break-up with Combs, Lopez married her second husband, dancer Cris Judd, but the marriage was dissolved less than a year later when Lopez began dating actor Ben Affleck. Her relationship with Affleck received constant media attention and contributed to the failures of their costarring films *Gigli* (2003) and *Jersey Girl* (2004). After the dissolution of her engagement to Affleck, Lopez married singer Marc Anthony and retreated from the public eye. She produced and starred in the films *El Cantante* (2007) and *Bordertown* (2007) and also produced the MTV reality television series *Dancelife*.

In 2007, Lopez released her first all-Spanish-language album *Como ama una mujer*. The video for the album's lead single "Que hiciste" became the first

Lopez's Business Enterprises

After having firmly established herself as a successful film actor and singer, Jennifer Lopez ventured into other projects. In 2002, she opened Madre's restaurant in Pasadena, California, which remained in business until 2008. She began her incursion into the world of fashion in 2003 with the launch of her clothing line for young women, JLO by Jennifer Lopez, which included clothing, accessories, lingerie, and jewelry. Another clothing line, Sweetface, was launched in 2005, and a juniors line called JustSweet followed in 2007. Lopez's presence in the world of fashion has been sustained by the steady production of designer perfume lines, which started with her debut fragrance, Glow by J.Lo, and has continued with several spin-offs of the original perfume, as well as the release of a fragrance for men.

Beyond this, Lopez has formed her own television and film production company, Nuyorican. The company has produced some of her films, such as *El Cantante* and *Bordertown*, as well as the TV series *South Beach* and *Dancelife* and the soap opera *Como ama una mujer*. Lopez's success as an entrepreneur has been recognized by *Forbes* magazine, which in 2007 named her one of the twenty richest women in entertainment, thanks to her multimedia enterprises.

Spanish-language video to peak at number one on the popular MTV show *Total Request Live*. Lopez then took some time off from her hectic film schedule to care for her twins, born in February, 2008. Three years later, Lopez became one of the judges on the popular television program *American Idol*, and she was contracted to be the "celebrity face" of several products, including the L'Oreal beauty firm, Venus razors, and Gucci children's clothes. In April, 2011, *People* magazine named Lopez the most beautiful woman in the world.

Significance

As one of the most visible and highest paid Latina performers, Jennifer Lopez has broken down barriers in the entertainment industry. Her success as an artist has been as inspirational as the unashamed display of her voluptuous body, both of which have provided the

entertainment industry with a much-needed diversity. She was named the most influential Hispanic entertainer in the U.S. in *People en Español*'s 2007 list of the "100 Most Influential Hispanics." Her work as a singer and actor has continuously been recognized for promoting positive representations of Latinos by the American Latino Media Arts Awards (ALMA). Her work as producer and star of the film *Bordertown*, which brought attention to the ongoing murders of women in the border city of Ciudad Juárez, Mexico, earned her an Artists for Amnesty International Award. Lopez's achievements as a talented performer in the entertainment industry and as a successful businesswoman have made her a key figure for the Latino community.

Georgina Chinchilla-Gonzalez

Further Reading

Cottrell, Robert C. *Icons of American Popular Culture: From P. T. Barnum to Jennifer Lopez*. Armonk, N.Y.: M. E. Sharpe, 2009. Traces the evolution of American popular culture over the past two centuries and includes a chapter detailing the struggles of Michael Jordan and Jennifer Lopez to become cultural icons in the late 1990's.

Duncan, Patricia J. *Jennifer Lopez: An Unauthorized Biography*. New York: St. Martin's Press, 1999. Spanish/English bilingual account of Lopez's early life and career.

Lockhart, Tara. "Jennifer Lopez: The New Wave of Border Crossing." In *From Bananas to Buttocks: The Latina Body in Popular Film and Culture*, edited by Myra Mendible. Austin: University of Texas Press, 2007. Analyzes Web postings and fan club discussions to study how audiences of different ethnic constituencies come to consider Lopez a "Latina."

Tracy, Kathleen. *Jennifer Lopez: A Biography*. Westport, Conn.: Greenwood Press, 2008. Up-to-date and thorough biography. Discusses the most important personal and career events of Lopez's life and contains an extensive bibliography.

See also: Benjamin Bratt; Mariah Carey; Cameron Diaz; Emilio Estevez; Ricky Martin; Rosie Pérez; Selena.

NANCY LOPEZ

American golfer

Lopez is credited with increasing the profile and popularity of women's golf and the Ladies Professional Golf Association. Her likable personality and gracious accessibility has charmed the fans and the public alike. When she joined the professional tour, she created a media buzz and wide interest in a sport that had previously been ignored.

Latino heritage: Mexican

Born: January 6, 1957; Torrance, California

Also known as: Nancy Marie Lopez; Nancy Knight; Nancy Lopez-Melton

Area of achievement: Sports

EARLY LIFE

Nancy Marie Lopez (NAN-cee MAH-ree LOH-pehz) was born in Torrance, California, the second daughter of Mexican immigrant Domingo Lopez and Marina Griego Lopez. The family moved to Roswell, New Mexico, where Lopez and her sister Delma grew up. At age eight, she was playing golf with her parents. Domingo Lopez saw that his daughter had a natural ability for

Nancy Lopez. (AP Photo)

the game and became her coach and most enthusiastic promoter.

At the age of nine, she entered her first pee-wee tournament, a children's competition, and finished the three-day, nine-holes-a-day event 110 strokes ahead of her nearest competitor. In fact, she was so far ahead that she had the time to help other children tee their balls. When she was twelve, she played better than her father, and she won her first New Mexico Women's Amateur championship. Already a golfer to be reckoned with, Lopez became the first girl to play on a boys' high school golf team, as there was no girls team in her school. The boys had no reason to complain, especially after she led the team to two state championships.

The Lopez family was not poor, as Domingo owned an automobile repair shop, but they were not rich either. However, they willingly made the sacrifices that were necessary to finance Nancy's lessons and her time on the links. One of these sacrifices was driving her two hundred miles to play in Albuquerque; because they were Mexican Americans, the Lopezes were not allowed to play at the Roswell Country Club. Domingo even built a backyard sand trap in order for Nancy to practice at home. Nancy herself had the discipline to practice and maximize her natural talent, but she still had a normal childhood. Along with the golf lessons, she tap danced, swam, and played volleyball and basketball. She lived a typical Mexican American, Catholic life in a tight-knit family.

After high school, Lopez went to the University of Tulsa on a golf scholarship. She dropped out of college after her second year and turned professional in 1977. That same year, she was named Rookie of the Year by *Golf Digest.* One of Lopez's disappointments is that her mother died of a heart attack shortly before she turned professional and never saw her daughter win a professional championship.

Lopez married her first husband, Tim Melton, in 1978. The couple met when Melton, a Pennsylvania sportscaster, interviewed her. The marriage ended in divorce three years later, in part because he wanted her to retire from golf.

LIFE'S WORK

Lopez became a media sensation during her rookie year on the Ladies Professional Golf Association (LPGA) Tour when she won eight tournaments, five of which

Lopez's Books on Golf

It stands to reason that the little girl who helped her opponents tee up their balls in her very first pee-wee tournament would grow up to be someone who still wants to help others enjoy the sport she loves. Toward that end, Nancy Lopez wrote two books on golf, and wrote forewords for at least two more. Both of her books, *The Education of a Woman Golfer* and *Nancy Lopez's the Complete Golfer* (reprinted as *The Complete Golfer*), offer golfing anecdotes for the trivia buff, recount the author's personal experiences, and provide her opinions of other golf greats, in addition to instructing readers on the proper technique and equipment. The books are accessible and friendly, just like the author. The reader and/or golf student will finish these books with the feeling of having sat down for a chat about the ins and outs of the sport, although that conversation just happened to be with one of the legends of the game.

were consecutive. She was named LPGA rookie of the year. The following year she was named player of the year, following that with the receipt of the prestigious Vare Trophy. In 1979, she played in nineteen tournaments and won eight, an achievement *Sports Illustrated* magazine heralded as "one of the most dominating sports performances in the last fifty years." She can also boast of three career holes-in-one. Among her many firsts, she was the first woman golfer to earn $1 million; in 1997, she earned $5 million.

In 1982, Lopez married Major League Baseball player Ray Knight. During Knight's career, he played third base for the Cincinnati Reds, the Houston Astros, the New York Mets, and the Baltimore Orioles. The couple had three daughters, Ashley Marie, Erinn Shea, and Torri Heather, and settled in Knight's hometown, Albany, Georgia. Never a prima donna, Lopez never lost sight of the fact that golf is only a game. However, she was serious about the game, continuing to practicing and having the discipline for an extensive exercise regime that included five hundred crunches a day.

Among Lopez's forty-eight tournament wins are the Sarasota Classic, Mazda Championship, LPGA Championship, Coca-Cola Classic, Women's Kemper Open, and Elizabeth Arden Classic; she received some of these wins multiple times.

Lopez was inducted into the LPGA Hall of Fame in 1989 and at that time was the youngest person to achieve that honor. She easily met the requirements (the

most stringent in professional sports halls of fame) of thirty tournament wins, with two of those being major titles. She has said that her only professional disappointment is that she never won the U.S. Women's Open, although she came in second four times.

On her farewell tour in 2002, Lopez played in only fourteen tournaments. She decided to retire because of health issues and to spend more time with her family. Her painful arthritis had required several knee surgeries over the years, and in 2000, she underwent gallbladder surgery. Lopez enjoyed her long run as a professional golfer, but she has often said that as much as she liked being a professional athlete, she enjoys being a wife and mother more. She has credited a happy marriage with her success. Her supportive husband has been known to caddy for her, and he always gave her career the same respect he gave his own.

Some critics have noted that Lopez's golf swing is awkward. She agrees, but she has said that her swing worked for her, so she never tried to change it. The only real weakness of her game was her chip shot. She was not a good chipper because she seldom missed the green, so she had little chipping experience. Lopez founded the Nancy Lopez Company in order to market a line of golfing equipment and clothing for women. In addition, she has written two books on the sport. To keep busy in retirement, Lopez and Knight opened Ashbrook Quail Preserve in southern Georgia, a hunting and fishing lodge where the couple are hands-on owners and where Lopez, an avid cook, enjoys pulling kitchen duty.

Significance

Nancy Lopez has remained true to her Latino roots, and in 1997 received the Hispanic Heritage Award. The Nancy Lopez Elementary School in Roswell, New Mexico, where she grew up, was named in her honor. This was done partly in recognition of her phenomenal athletic success but also because as the hometown girl who made good, she has been a role model for girls in general and for Latinas in particular. Whether winning or losing, Lopez maintained the grace and innate goodness that made her one of America's sports sweethearts. The annual Nancy Lopez Award honors the world's best female amateur golfer.

Norma Lewis

Further Reading

Dye, Alice, with Mark Shaw. *From Birdies to Bunkers: Discover How Golf Can Bring Love, Humor, and Success into Your Life.* New York: HarperCollins, 2004.

Lopez wrote the foreword, and the book discusses the greatest golfers, including Lopez, Tiger Woods, Arnold Palmer, and Babe Didrickson Zaharias.

Lopez, Nancy. *The Complete Golfer.* Reprint. New York: Galahad Books, 2000. Packed with instruction about golfing technique and geared toward woman. Lopez also provides her impressions of other women golfers. Originally published in 1979 as *Nancy Lopez's the Complete Golfer.*

_____. *The Education of a Woman Golfer.* New York: Simon & Schuster, 1979. Lopez writes about golf technique, her personal experiences, and golf lore,

Reid, Cindy, with Steve Eubanks. *Cindy Reid's Ultimate Guide to Golf for Women.* New York: Atria Books, 2003. Reid and Eubanks thoroughly cover every aspect of the sport in order to help the aspiring woman golfer improve her game.

Vaughan, Roger. *Golf: The Woman's Game.* New York: Henry N. Abrams, 2001. Lopez wrote the forward for this book that covers one hundred years of women's golf and discusses the greatest players, herself included.

See also: Chi Chi Rodriguez; Lee Trevino.

Rafael López

Mexican-born artist

Known for his vibrant murals and artwork imbued with surrealism and Magical Realism, López has enjoyed a successful career as an award-winning children's book illustrator and sought-after artist. His list of clients have included Oprah Winfrey, President Barack Obama, the United States Postal Service, and Amnesty International, to name a few.

Latino heritage: Mexican
Born: August 8, 1961; Mexico City, Mexico
Areas of achievement: Art; literature

Early Life
Rafael López (rah-FAY-ehl LOH-pehz) was born in Mexico City to architects Rafael López Recendez and Guadalupe "Pillo" Acosta Viderique. The oldest of four children and the only boy, he spent his formative years immersed in the bright, native colors and rich cultural heritage of Mexico. At an early age, López expressed a voracious interest in art, which was assiduously supported by his parents and teachers. Often he would spend hours drawing on large rolls of paper that his uncle brought home from his job at a paper factory. When López ran out of paper, his mother allowed him to sketch on the walls of their house and assisted him with mixing bold paints to add to his drawings, many of which were inspired by Mexican artist José Guadalupe Posada.

As a young child, López studied at the Manuel Bartolome Cossio, a school in Mexico City which subscribed to the pedagogy of French educator Célestin Freinet and placed a strong emphasis on the investigation of a topic in lieu of grades. At the age of eleven, he

was sent to Exeter, England, to live on a commune and study printmaking with Mexican artist Felipe Ehrenberg. During this time, López's artistic interests began to resonate with elements of the Spanish *dichos* (sayings) and the Mexican surrealism around him.

About a decade later, López was among the first group of Latino students enrolled in the prestigious Art Center College of Design in Pasadena, California, where he studied to be an illustrator. In 1985, he graduated with honors and began his illustration career in Los Angeles before moving to San Diego in 1987. It was at this time that he claimed acrylic Mexican paints on textured wood as his signature medium for creating the graphics in his artwork.

Life's Work
Although López had been creating blazing images steeped with Latino cultural elements for magazines, book covers, calendars, and broadsides for almost fifteen years, he did not break into the larger world of children's book publishing until the publication of his first children's picture book. Around the year 2000, he was approached by the publisher Luna Rising and asked to create illustrations for its picture-book biography about salsa singer Celia Cruz written by Latina children's author Monica Brown. In 2004, *My Name is Celia: The Life of Celia Cruz (Me llamo Celia: La vida de Celia Cruz)* was published and López's artwork received critical acclaim, winning the Pura Belpré Illustrator Honor Award. The award, named after a Puerto Rican-born librarian and storyteller, announced to the literary and artistic communities that López's work was exceptional in its depiction of Latino culture. The book also received the prestigious Américas Award, touting both

López and Brown as distinguished contributors in the area of Latino children's literature.

Soon López's career was soaring with opportunities. In 2005, he created a merengue stamp for the United States Postal Service, and two years later he designed the commemorative stamp for the sixtieth anniversary of the groundbreaking legal case for education equality, *Mendez vs. Westminster*. In 2007, López published his second collection of illustrations in Pat Mora's book *¡Yum! ¡Mmmm! ¡Qué rico!: America's Sproutings*, which also received the Américas Award for its lively illustrations of children all across the Americas enjoying varieties of native foods. The following year his poster *Voz Unida* was selected by the Barack Obama presidential campaign as an official poster at Artists for Obama and was used to create national awareness about the candidate among the Latino population. That same year, López published his third set of book illustrations in Pam Muñoz Ryan's *Our California*.

Continuing on this upward trajectory, López was contracted in 2009 by Oprah Winfrey to create a series of three paintings for her schools in South Africa. In 2010, López received the Pura Belpré Illustrator Award for his energetic, colorful images in Pat Mora's *Book Fiesta! Celebrate Children's Day/Book Day* (*Celebremos El día de los niños/El día de los libros*). In addition, his work with the Postal Service was so well received that he was commissioned to fashion a series of five additional Latino-themed stamps in 2010.

When asked about the greatest influence in his artwork and career, López has identified his son Santiago as the energetic and driving force whose fresh ideas and amazing talents challenge the artist every day.

SIGNIFICANCE

Suffused with elements native to his Mexican roots, López's artwork transcends cultures, races, and ages while celebrating America's pluralistic society and the importance of lifelong literacy. One of the most talented U.S. artists and muralists of the 21st century, he has received numerous awards and recognition for his work and has created both national and international pieces. At the same time, the work of López has opened doors for Latino artists across the U.S. not only in the area of children's book publishing but also in the larger artistic community.

Jamie Campbell Naidoo

FURTHER READING

Colorin' Colorado. Meet the Author: Rafael López. http://www.colorincolorado.org/read/meet/lopez. An informative series of streaming videos describing López's artistic influences as a child, how he became an illustrator for children, and the various ways he interprets text in his mural-styled illustrations. A transcript of all the videos is also available.

López, Rafael. "Pura Belpré Illustrator Award Acceptance Speech Connecting Children to Books." *Children and Libraries* 8, no. 2 (Summer/Fall, 2010): 12, 14. One of the first published articles to examine any aspect of López's life, this speech describes his childhood artistic experiences.

See also: Judith F. Baca; Barbara Carrasco; Daniel DeSiga; Yolanda M. López; Leo Tanguma; Jesse Treviño.

RAMON E. LOPEZ

American scientist

Lopez is a prominent research scientist in the field of space weather and studies of Earth's magnetosphere and solar-terrestrial interactions. He is also well known for his work aimed at advancing science education.

Latino heritage: Puerto Rican

Born: September 7, 1959; Aberdeen, Maryland

Also known as: Ramon Edgardo Lopez II

Areas of achievement: Science and technology; education

EARLY LIFE

Ramon Edgardo Lopez II (rah-MOHN ehd-GAHR-doh LOH-pehz) was born in 1959, the son of Ramon E. and A. Esther Lopez. Lopez's parents were originally from Puerto Rico. His father was a doctor in the U.S. Army, and thus the family moved frequently during his early childhood. He attended a number of elementary schools in El Paso, San Antonio, and at Fort Hood, Texas. He often went with his family to visit relatives in Puerto Rico, sometimes for as long as a month. By attending school in Texas, as well as interacting with family members in

Puerto Rico, Lopez became fluent in both English and Spanish; his bilingualism would prove to be useful in his scientific career. Lopez's father encouraged him in his studies and gave him a telescope as a child. However, it was watching the Gemini and Apollo space missions that motivated him to study space physics.

Lopez's father left the Army when Lopez was in sixth grade and established a medical practice in Freeport, Illinois. Eventually, the family moved to Pearl City, Illinois, where Lopez attended Pearl City High School. At this time, the University of Illinois-Champaign had a program allowing advanced high school students to enter the university without finishing high school. Lopez took advantage of this program and did not graduate from high school. At first, he found college challenging, but he learned to study and excelled, graduating in 1980 with a B.S. degree in physics. Besides physics, Lopez learned to love history, literature, and writing while in college. He went to Rice University for graduate study, receiving an M.S. degree in 1984 and a Ph.D. in 1986, both in space physics.

LIFE'S WORK

After receiving his Ph.D., Lopez took a postdoctoral position with Applied Research Corporation, working at the Johns Hopkins University Applied Physics Lab. While there, he volunteered to work in Linda Chavez's campaign for U.S. Senate, an experience that led to his meeting his future wife, Ellen Ann. The couple had two children, Ramon E. Lopez III and Nancy Lopez.

Seeking a position with a greater educational component, Lopez took a job at the University of Maryland at College Park. While there, he also served as the director of education and outreach programs for the American Physical Society. Lopez helped develop inquiry-based educational activities for elementary school science students, and he worked with several public school systems in the area. In 1999, Lopez took a position as department chair in physics at the University of Texas at El Paso. Three years later, Lopez was awarded the Nicholson Medal for Humanitarian Service in recognition of his efforts to improve precollege science education and to encourage underrepresented minorities to study physics. From 2004 to 2007, Lopez was a professor at the Florida Institute of Technology before taking a position as a professor at the University of Texas at Arlington.

Lopez conducted space physics research, studying Earth's magnetosphere and interactions between the magnetosphere and the solar wind, a field of study called space weather. In particular, he has worked on mathematical models of the magnetosphere in an attempt to predict the effects of both solar storms and disruptions called geomagnetic storms on the magnetosphere. Associated with these studies, Lopez has also researched the dynamics of auroral (natural light) displays in the sky.

In addition to his space physics research, Lopez has remained active in education. His involvement gradually evolved from working with precollege science education to attempting to further physics education among college students. He helped secure a grant to fund scholarships that will enable community college students to major in physics and chemistry at the University of Texas at Arlington. By 2010, Lopez was also working with the National Academy of Sciences to develop recommended standards for college readiness for students entering college who were interested in science, technology, engineering, or mathematics (STEM).

SIGNIFICANCE

Most scientists, even college professors, focus either on research or teaching. Few are like Lopez, who is able to be effective in both education and scientific research. Lopez is a prominent figure in space physics research, but he has also played an extremely important role in science education, particularly in the field of physics. He has actively encouraged minority students interested in pursuing careers in science and engineering fields, particularly students of Latino backgrounds. Lopez's influence in science education spans the range of instruction, from elementary and high schools to college and postgraduate programs. In 2010, Lopez was recognized for his work when the Society for the Advancement of Chicanos and Native Americans in Science (SACNAS) named him a distinguished scientist.

Raymond D. Benge, Jr.

FURTHER READING

Carlowics, Michael J., and Ramon E. Lopez. *Storms from the Sun: The Emerging Science of Space Weather*. Washington, DC: Joseph Henry Press, 2002. An excellent explanation of the nature and significance of space weather, Lopez' area of research.

Lopez, Ramon E. Dr. Ramon E. Lopez. http://www.uta.edu/ra/real/editprofile.php?onlyview=1&pid=1926. Lopez's profile on the University of Texas at Arlington's Web site, with information about his professional and educational activities, publications, and seminars.

Lopez, Ramon E., and Ted Schultz. "Two Revolutions in K-8 Science Education." *Physics Today* 54, no.

9 (September, 2001): 44-49. A discussion of the importance of professional scientists working with educators in elementary and secondary school science education.

McCray, Richard A., Robert L. DeHaan, and Julie Anne Schuck, eds. *Improving Undergraduate Instruction in Science, Technology, Engineering, and Mathematics.* Washington, D.C.: National Academies Press, 2003. A report on undergraduate education strategies and initiatives of the Steering Committee on Criteria and Benchmarks for Increased Learning from Undergraduate STEM Instruction, of which Lopez was an active member.

See also: Franklin Ramón Chang-Díaz; France Anne Córdova.

TRINI LÓPEZ

American singer, musician, and actor

Using a Latin-inspired dance beat, López transformed Spanish and English-language folk music and introduced it to a large and diverse international audience. As a singer and a guitarist, he traveled the world popularizing folk music and Spanish-language songs. He paved the way for Latino musicians with his Tex-Mex, folk-rock fusion.

Latino heritage: Mexican
Born: May 15, 1937; Dallas, Texas
Also known as: Trinidad López III
Areas of achievement: Music; acting

EARLY LIFE

Trinidad López III (LOH-pehz) was born in Dallas, Texas, on May 15, 1937. His father had been a singer, dancer, and actor in Mexico, but he left to raise his family in the United States so that they could have a better future. However, the family lived in dire poverty in the Barrio, a poor, mostly African American community in Dallas.

When López was twelve years old, his father caught him associating with local youths known to be troublemakers and punished him severely. This incident was the defining moment of López's young life. His father felt so bad about spanking him that he bought López a secondhand guitar for twelve dollars, a very large sum for the family at the time. From that day on, music became the motivating force in López's life.

López began performing locally as a teenager. A Dallas record producer offered to release López's first single, "The Right to Rock," on Volk Records. However, when López went to sign the deal, he was asked to change his name to Trini Roper to hide his Chicano ethnicity. Having been subjected to relentless anti-Mexican prejudice in Texas, López refused to change his name. The producer relented, and López's first single was released in 1958. He was signed to a three-year contract singing cowboy songs; only one single reached the charts.

About a year later, Buddy Holly introduced López to his producer, who tried to hire López's band without López. After recording a few instrumentals and not being allowed to sing, López fired everyone and went home. Holly's death a few months later left a vacancy in his group, the Crickets, and they invited López to take his place. López moved to Hollywood, California, to begin

Trini López. (AP Photo)

López's Musical Style

Trini López came from a musical background: His father had been an amateur singer and guitar player in Mexico. López was taught Mexican folk songs and *rancheras*–songs sung by a solo vocalist accompanied by a guitar–by his father. When López received his first guitar at the age of twelve, he learned to accompany himself while singing these songs. As he continued to learn to play guitar, López also was exposed to African American musical styles such as Delta blues and rhythm and blues. He particularly liked T-Bone Walker and Jimmy Reed. However, his musical style was not fully realized until he discovered American folk music and rock and roll. He loved the melodies and lyrics of folk music and the rock-and-roll sound of Buddy Holly and Elvis. He also idolized Frank Sinatra's smooth singing style.

Taking English-language classics such as "If I Had a Hammer," Spanish folk songs such as "Cielito lindo," and cross-cultural songs such as "La Bamba" and "Lemon Tree," López played them with a swinging, Latin-infused beat, creating folk music that people could dance to. He added rock-and-roll drumming and guitar playing and created his signature "Trini Beat." According to López, one could put on his albums and dance to them all the way through without stopping.

He has produced albums in many genres–folk, Spanish- and German-language, Latin, Broadway, Tex-Mex, and pop–all in his signature danceable, cheerful style. His music had a great impact on the folk-rock movement in general and the California rock scene in particular.

recording with the Crickets, but when he got there, he found that they did not plan to record for a while. Needing to earn money to get back home, López become a solo performer in Los Angeles.

Life's Work

In 1960, López got a two-week gig at Ye Little Club playing acoustic guitar and singing. He was so popular that the club extended his contract to a year. Next, the more prestigious PJ's offered him a three-month contract and immediately extended it to eighteen months. This would prove to be López's big break, because he caught the attention of Frank Sinatra, who arranged for López to be signed to an eight-year contract by Don Costa of Reprise Records, Sinatra's label.

López's first album, *Live at PJ's*, was released in 1963. It sold more than one million copies and produced such hits as "If I Had a Hammer" and "Kansas City." "If I Had a Hammer" charted at number one in more than twenty countries, making it more successful than Peter, Paul and Mary's earlier version. The hit was followed by 1964's "Lemon Tree," which became his signature song. In 1963, López made his New York City debut and played a two-week engagement with the Beatles in Paris.

In 1966, López released his version of "La Bamba," a song made famous by Ritchie Valens in 1958. According to López, who never met Valens, his version of the song was not at all similar to Valens's. López's popularity grew with the rise of folk music, but his appeal was more directed at adult record buyers. Rather than singing in the folk clubs that young listeners frequented, López tended to perform in nightclubs, and he soon became a popular Las Vegas performer.

His career includes fourteen Top 100 singles, more than twenty albums, and many years as a major Las Vegas attraction. López also has had success as an actor, most notably in *The Dirty Dozen* (1967).

López's generous nature and winning personality led to his being named a goodwill ambassador for the United Nations. The United States Congress honored him for his years of work on behalf of international relations. He has received many other accolades, including induction into the Las Vegas Casino Legends Hall of Fame (2002) and the International Latin Music Hall of Fame (2003). His popularity was so great that guitar maker Gibson produced two Trini López signature guitar models for many years; they were reissued in the 2000's.

López continues to record and to promote folk and Latin music. In 2002, he released *Legacy: My Texas Roots*, an album of Chicano-Texan music. He also devotes much of his time to charity, including a performance in 2004 to raise funds for victims of the Indian Ocean earthquake and tsunami.

Significance

López helped to make folk music popular with a large and diverse audience. Using his characteristic singing and guitar-playing style, he infused classic American songs with a Latin flavor. He always included Spanish-language songs on his albums and released some albums totally recorded in Spanish. He fought prejudice and ignorance, refusing to change his name or to alter his accent to sound less Mexican. The pride he has shown in his ethnic background has made him a role model for other Latino musicians.

Leslie Neilan

FURTHER READING

Alegre, César. *Extraordinary Hispanic Americans*. New York: Scholastic, 2007. This book provides short biographies of famous Hispanic Americans, including López. It is intended for young-adult readers.

Cohen, Ronald D. *Rainbow Quest: The Folk Music Revival and American Society, 1940-1970*. Amherst: University of Massachusetts Press, 2002. Provides a comprehensive look at the renewed interest in folk music in the middle of the twentieth century. The forces that shaped López's love of the genre are explored, and he is mentioned in context of the greater folk music scene of the times.

Jones, Mickey. *That Would Be Me: Rock and Roll Survivor to Hollywood Actor*. Bloomington, Indiana: AuthorHouse, 2007. This autobiography by López's drummer of eight years includes a chapter on Jones's experiences in López's band.

Roberts, John Storm. *The Latin Tinge: The Impact of Latin American Music on the United States*. 2d ed. New York: Oxford University Press, 1999. This book looks at the various types of Latin American music, including folk, and shows its influence on music in the United States. López is mentioned in the text.

Unterberger, Richie. *Turn! Turn! Turn!: The 60's Folk-Rock Revolution*. San Francisco, Calif.: Backbeat Books, 2002. Using interviews and research, this book explores the rise of folk music and its impact on 1960's culture.

See also: Joan Baez; Mimi Fariña; José Feliciano; Jerry Garcia; Ritchie Valens.

YOLANDA M. LÓPEZ

American artist

An artist who works in a variety of media, including watercolors, mixed-media collage, posters, printmaking, video, and installations, López is an activist whose work challenges stereotypes. She is best known for her Virgin of Guadalupe paintings, a series that uses this icon to uplift the image of women of Mexican descent.

Latino heritage: Mexican
Born: November 1, 1942; San Diego, California
Areas of achievement: Art; women's rights

EARLY LIFE

Yolanda M. López (yoh-LAHN-dah LOH-pehz) was born in San Diego, California, to a struggling, working-class family. Her grandfather, Margarito Senebio Franco, a tailor, and his wife Victoria emigrated from Mexico to the United States in 1918. In 1942, when López was born, factories and shipyards that produced and distributed war goods were a growing industry in San Diego. Many of those jobs were closed to nonwhites, a factor that added to the city's ethnic and economic segregation.

López grew up in a Mexican community near the border. During her early years, she lived with her mother, grandparents, and two younger sisters. Her mother, Margaret, made a meager living as a presser and seamstress. As a working mother in a conservative community, Margaret was prounion and relegated to cook for others, but she approached her work with passion and inventiveness. Her behavior helped to dispel stereotypes and influenced López's attitudes toward traditional gender expectations.

After earning an associate's degree at the College of Marin, López enrolled in San Francisco State College, joined the Student Nonviolent Coordinating Committee, and became actively involved in anti-Vietnam War activism and in the Third World Strike, a struggle to integrate the student body and to diversify the curriculum. This 1968 rebellion resulted in a violent confrontation in which demonstrators were beaten by police. While the resulting media attention was intrusive, it helped the students achieve their goals and gave López a greater sense of the power of the image. López went on to earn a B.A. from San Diego State University in 1975 and a M.F.A. from the University of California, San Diego, in 1978. After graduating, she returned to the San Franciso Bay Area with René Yáñez, and their son Rio was born in 1980.

LIFE'S WORK

As an activist in the late 1960's, López's early work was influenced by the revolutionary spirit of the time, including her interaction with Emory Douglas, whose graphic art appeared in the low-budget Black Panther newspaper. Some of her earliest work included posters and graphic art designed to create an awareness of injustices committed against Latinos. Her poster art reflects an irony that increasingly infuses López's work. In *Free Los Siete*, a poster created in 1969 to defend seven Central American youths accused of killing a police officer, the text of the Pledge of Allegiance frames and imprisons the black-and-white images of the youths.

The 1978 piece *Who's the Illegal Alien, Pilgrim?* was produced as both a poster and a mixed-media collage. It features an Aztec warrior standing in the pose of Uncle Sam while crumpling papers with the heading "Immigration Plans." López's biographer, Karen Mary Davalos, argues that this work admonishes the concept of manifest destiny and that its reference to actor John Wayne spins and undermines the iconic figure's statement. She maintains that López's art routinely uses pre-Columbian and Catholic iconography in an effort to analyze and investigate how images function in popular culture.

López's formal education and burgeoning feminism contributed to her growing interest in the politics of representation, resulting in work that progressively examined the social and cultural invisibility of women. Her Virgin of Guadalupe series, which gained her international recognition, uses vivid oils and mixed-media collages to celebrate ordinary Mexican American women and includes images of her mother, grandmother, and herself. The series, which includes photographs by artist and colleague Susan Mogul, was completed between 1978 and 1988.

After returning to the Bay Area, López began to further hone her photographic talents, often serving as a photographer for hire. During this period, she created her Life in the Mission series, which captured compelling images of Chicanos in the Mission District of San Francisco, and a sequence of documentary photographs on the Day of the Dead. Her work also began to venture further into video and installations.

When You Think of Mexico: Images of Mexicans in the Media, a video López created in the late 1980's, began as a satirical slide show designed to parody the negative images of Mexicans in contemporary culture. During the 1990's, it was included as a component of the *Cactus Hearts/Barbed Wire Dreams* exhibit, an installation which circulated throughout California art galleries and organizations.

SIGNIFICANCE

In 1990, a *New York Times* article that discusses "quality" in art cites López's installation piece *Things I Never Told My Son About Being Mexican* as a work that conveys both innovation and an awareness of aesthetic standards. Some critics argue that López is an artist whose work challenges form and whose power is in her willingness to do so. Others assert that López's vision is transformative and that her work merges the past into the future.

Her works spans several decades and incorporates a variety of media from the traditional oil on canvas and printmaking to collage, installations, and film. Activism is inherent in her work. In creating art that exposes sexism and racism, López has received worldwide acclaim, as well as threats of violence.

Although most of López's solo exhibits have been held at galleries and museums in California, her work has been included in exhibitions throughout the United States and Europe. She has been the recipient of numerous awards and fellowships, including the National Lifetime Achievement Award in the Visual Arts, which was presented at the 2008 Women's Caucus for Art in Dallas, Texas.

Esperanza Malavé Cintrón

FURTHER READING

Cockcroft, Eva Sperling. "From Barrio to Mainstream: The Panorama of Latino Art." In *Handbook of Hispanic Cultures in the United States: Literature and Art*, edited by Thomas Weaver and Claudio Esteva-Fabregat. Houston: Arte Público Press, 1994. A history of Latino art and artists from a sociopolitical perspective.

Cotter, Holland. "Through Women's Eyes, Finally." *The New York Times*, May 16, 1999, p. SM92. Examines the traditional image of women in art and how the inclusion of women artists is changing these images.

Davalos, Karen Mary. *Yolanda M. López*. Los Angeles: UCLA Chicano Studies Research Center Press, 2008. A thorough and reverent biography of the artist with an intense analysis of her work.

See also: Carmen Lomas Garza; Tony Labat; Rafael López.

FRANK LORENZO

American airline executive

Lorenzo built an airline empire in the 1970's and 1980's through a series of mergers and takeovers. His low-cost, low-fare management philosophy proved financially successful, but his efforts to cut wages and benefits and break the powerful pilots and mechanics unions resulted in costly strikes and his forced departure from the airline industry.

Latino heritage: Spanish

Born: May 19, 1940; New York, New York

Also known as: Francisco Anthony Lorenzo

Areas of achievement: Business; philanthropy

EARLY LIFE

Francisco Anthony Lorenzo (loh-REHN-zoh) was born on May 19, 1940, in New York City to Spanish immigrant parents. He grew up in Queens and attended Forest Hills High School. After graduation, he earned degrees from Columbia College and Harvard Business School. He then worked as a financial analyst for Trans World Airlines and Eastern Air Lines. In 1966, Lorenzo and Robert Carney founded Lorenzo, Carney and Company, which specialized in financial consulting for airlines and related businesses. In 1969, he and Carney launched a second consulting firm, Jet Capital Corporation. Jet Capital began raising capital for Texas International Airlines (TIA) and purchased a controlling interest in the company in 1972. Lorenzo was named president.

LIFE'S WORK

At the helm of Texas International, Lorenzo embarked on mission to save the troubled airline. He began TIA's turnaround by cutting costs, upgrading obsolete planes, getting rid of routes on which the company was losing money, and attracting customers with "half-price" fares. By 1978, Texas International was a profitable company, and Lorenzo was attracting the attention of the larger airlines.

The Airline Deregulation Act of 1978 gave Lorenzo an opportunity to expand. This legislation, designed to increase competition within the airline industry, allowed companies to expand their routes and set prices without government interference. The result was a wave of takeovers and mergers. Lorenzo made a bid for National Airlines and then for the even larger Trans World Airlines. Both of these takeovers failed but proved profitable, leaving Texas International with $60 million in cash. In 1980, Lorenzo formed Texas Air Corporation. The company launched New York Air, which initially offered shuttle flights between New York City and Washington, D.C. To compete with Eastern Air Lines and Pan American World Airways, Lorenzo hired nonunion pilots and workers at substantially lower pay than union employees at TIA received.

In 1981, Lorenzo set his sights on a bigger target. Continental Airlines was faltering badly and vulnerable to a takeover. TIA began buying shares of the company's stock, and by the end of year, Lorenzo was on the board of directors. After a rough year in which Continental continued to lose money, Lorenzo became chairman and once again launched a transformation, which included the merger of TIA and Continental and the creation of a hub-and-spoke routing system with Houston as the hub. Both companies operated under the Continental name.

Labor relations turned out to be a major problem with the refurbished airline. Negotiations with Continental's mechanics union dragged on for almost two years as the merger plans went forward but ended in a strike in late 1983. As part of his strategy to keep his growing empire competitive with smaller airlines, Lorenzo sought to break the powerful unions by declaring Chapter 11 bankruptcy. As part of the company's reorganization plan, the bankruptcy judge allowed Lorenzo to cancel all union contracts. Lorenzo fired eight thousand union workers and offered sharply reduced wages to pilots and other employees who chose to stay. Continental emerged from bankruptcy with a nonunion workforce; employees worked longer hours for reduced benefits and sharply reduced wages. As he had done at New York Air and TIA, Lorenzo offered cut-rate fares to fill seats. The company also introduced successful innovations such as self-service ticketing. Although these measures turned Continental into a profitable business, employee morale and customer satisfaction plummeted.

With Continental turning a profit, Lorenzo began to seek further expansion opportunities. He acquired struggling Eastern Air Lines for $640 million in November, 1986, tripling the size of Texas Air. In December, Texas Air also snapped up PEOPLExpress Airlines, along with its subsidiary, Frontier Airlines. PEOPLExpress

Frank Lorenzo. (AP Photo)

new owners ordered him to step down. In the aftermath of these public struggles, Lorenzo tried to rebuild. In 1990, he sold his holdings in Continental Airlines and founded Savoy Capital, a private investment firm that manages his family's holdings and those of other investors. Lorenzo also turned to philanthropy. He served as trustee of the Hispanic Society of America and the Woodrow Wilson National Fellowship Foundation and became involved in other arts and chartable organizations.

SIGNIFICANCE

Praised by industry experts and vilified by union leaders, Lorenzo left a lasting mark on the airline industry. Consumers benefited from his companies' lower fares and innovations such as self-service ticketing. Lorenzo's management practices, although considered ruthless and harsh by his critics, saved several airlines from collapse during a difficult period for the industry as a whole. However, his experience also shows that businesses cannot succeed without the support of their workers.

Robert E. McFarland

FURTHER READING

Berstein, Aaron. *Grounded: Frank Lorenzo and the Destruction of Eastern Airlines.* New York: Simon & Schuster, 1990. Critical in-depth study of Lorenzo's battle with Eastern's unions that ultimately blames both management and the unions for the airline's demise.

Lawrence, Harry. *Aviation and the Role of Government.* Dubuque, Iowa: Kendall/Hunt, 2004. Examines the history and impact of government regulation (and deregulation) of the airline industry, including discussion of Lorenzo's dealings and their fallout.

Peterson, Barbara Sturken, and James Glab. *Rapid Descent: Deregulation and the Shakeout in the Airlines.* New York: Simon & Schuster, 1994. Records the consequences of airline deregulation, which created an environment in which Lorenzo and other executives fought to build empires and remain profitable.

Petzinger, Thomas, Jr. *Hard Landing: The Epic Contest for Power and Profits That Plunged the Airlines into Chaos.* New York: Three Rivers Press, 1996. Chronicles the history of the airline industry from the 1930's to the 1990's, focusing on the period of the 1970's and 1980's during which Lorenzo was a major figure.

See also: Linda Alvarado; Ralph Alvarez; Arte Moreno; Samuel A. Ramirez, Sr.; Joseph A. Unanue.

and Frontier were absorbed by Continental in 1987, but trouble was brewing at Eastern. Cost-cutting efforts such as increased firings, decreased maintenance, and intentional violations of Federal Aviation Administration regulations had brought the airline negative publicity, safety concerns, and increased federal scrutiny.

In March, 1989, a major strike by machinists, pilots, and flight attendants crippled the company as thousands of flights were canceled at a time when cash was desperately needed. Six days later, Eastern filed for bankruptcy. It began operating on a reduced schedule with nonunion pilots as it struggled to meet the demands of its creditors. By November, the pilots and flight attendants had ended their strike, but the machinists' strike persisted as Eastern continued to lose money. In April, 1990, a federal bankruptcy court, acting on behalf of Eastern's creditors, ruled that Lorenzo was unfit to run the airline and appointed a trustee to take his place. Eastern limped along for another year but closed for good in January, 1991.

Lorenzo endured bitter attacks from the press and union leaders, accusing him of acquiring companies in order to raid their assets, including their pension funds. He sold his holdings in Continental, and the company's

MANUEL LUJÁN, JR.

American politician

Luján served for more than twenty years as a member of the U.S. House of Representatives from New Mexico, concentrating largely on issues concerning public lands and American Indians. He then was appointed to head the Interior Department under President George H. W. Bush, where he served a controversial four-year tenure.

Latino heritage: Mexican
Born: May 12, 1928; near San Ildefonso, New Mexico
Area of achievement: Government and politics

EARLY LIFE

Manuel Luján, Jr. (loo-HAHN) was born on May 12, 1928, in a rural area near San Ildefonso, about twenty miles northwest of Santa Fe, New Mexico. The son of Manuel and Lorenzita Romero Luján, Luján was raised in and around Santa Fe, attending Catholic schools before graduating from St. Michael's High School. On November 18, 1948, he married Jean Couchman, with whom he would have four children.

Luján earned his bachelor's degree in business administration in 1950 at the College of Santa Fe. He then joined his father's insurance and real estate business, the Manual Luján Agency. His father, a moderate Republican, also served as mayor of Santa Fe and had run for both the governorship of New Mexico and the U.S. House of Representatives. Manuel, Sr.'s love of Republican politics was passed down to his son.

After working at the insurance agency for fourteen years, Luján decided to run for the New Mexico State Senate in 1964. He was defeated; however, four years later, he was successful in his candidacy for New Mexico's First District seat in the U.S. House of Representatives, joining Joseph M. Montoya as New Mexico's second Hispanic congressman.

LIFE'S WORK

Luján served for twenty years in the House, helping to establish the Congressional Hispanic Caucus (he also was its first Republican member) and serving on numerous committees. He was a conservative Republican in many ways, supporting the position of the so-called Sagebrush Rebellion of the early 1980's, which called for the opening of federal lands in the West to mining, grazing, and logging. In other cases, he strayed from the party line, opposing immigration reform efforts that he feared would result in discrimination against Latinos and advocating the return of ancestral lands to Indian tribes, especially the Pueblo groups in New Mexico, among whom he had been raised. He was an instrumental supporter of President Richard Nixon's efforts that led to the return of Blue Lake to the Indians of Taos Pueblo, who consider the lake a sacred site. He also was appointed to the Mexico-United States Interparliamentary Group, which encouraged an ongoing dialogue between legislatures of the two neighboring nations.

During his years in Congress, Luján's primary area of interest related to his service on the Interior and Insular Affairs Committee. Although he supported some environmental regulations, such as the Clean Air Act and the Clean Water Act, of which he was a sponsor, he fought against others. He was an ardent supporter of nuclear power and was not opposed to development along the borders of national parks, even when it might adversely impact the park ecosystems. Regardless, Luján

Manuel Luján, Jr. (AP Photo)

served on the Interior and Insular Affairs Committee long enough that he was the ranking member of the committee until 1985. That year, he gave up the seat to join the Science, Space, and Technology Committee. The addition of a third congressional district in New Mexico had changed his district from primarily rural to predominantly urban, and his new constituency had a vital interest in the booming technology sector in and around Albuquerque.

Luján's congressional career came to an end when he decided to retire in 1988. However, his retirement was short-lived. His years of service on the Interior and Insular Affairs Committee would lead directly to his next position, when President George H. W. Bush asked him to serve as secretary of the interior. Luján accepted, and his appointment was ratified by the U.S.

Lujan's Positions on Environmental Issues

First as a member of the House Interior and Insular Affairs Committee and later as secretary of the interior, Manuel Luján, Jr., would have liked to have been known as a moderate, supporting what he termed "balance between environmentalism and economic development."

However, he was torn between his Republican sensibilities, which favored development over preservation of natural resources, and growing public sentiment in favor of conservation. In addition, the 1989 *Exxon Valdez* oil spill drove more support to the environmental movement. Luján supported legislation that protected clean air and water but opposed across-the-board environmental impact studies for oil and gas development; his positions could be seemingly at odds with each other.

Even after the oil spill, Luján remained opposed to restrictions on offshore oil drilling, and he continued to support mining, timber, and ranching interests. However, he might have been best known for his opposition to the 1973 Endangered Species Act, which he described as "too tough." Luján exempted lands from its provisions when he deemed it economically necessary, endangering species such as the northern spotted owl. His public statements often drew criticism for what seemed to be a callous disregard for creatures his department was charged with protecting, such as his comment regarding the endangered Mount Graham red squirrel: "Nobody's told me the difference between a red squirrel, a black one, or a brown one."

Senate in 1989. During his tenure, Luján tried to walk the thin line between the Republican position of advocating for development and the cultural momentum in favor of environmental protection, which had been growing steadily since he took office during the 1960's.

As interior secretary, Luján often ran afoul of the growing environmental movement. He openly discussed his doubts about Charles Darwin's theory of evolution. Although his particular policies might have been considered moderate, his public statements reminded many observers of James Watt, who had been interior secretary under President Ronald Reagan. When discussing his long-standing opposition to the Endangered Species Act, Luján said in an interview: "I just look at an armadillo or a skunk or a squirrel or an owl or a chicken, whatever it is, and I consider the human being on a higher scale. Maybe that's because a chicken doesn't talk." He described the 270 million acres administered by the Bureau of Land Management as "a place with a lot of grass for cows."

Other constituencies looked upon Luján more favorably. He made the education of American Indians a priority, increasing funding for programs through the Bureau of Indian Affairs. The Interior Department as a whole hired more minorities during his tenure than it ever had before. He found a popular public issue when Matsushita Electric Industrial, a Japanese company, acquired MCA, which contracted to run the public concessions in Yosemite National Park. Many supported his crusade against the "incursion," and public pressure forced Matsushita to give up the concession. Luján's tenure as interior secretary ended when President Bill Clinton took office in January, 1993.

After his term in office, Luján returned to Albuquerque, where he worked as a lobbyist. In 2004, he founded the Hispanic Alliance for Prosperity Institute, a conservative think-tank focusing on issues affecting the Hispanic community.

SIGNIFICANCE

Although he was not the first Hispanic American to be elected to Congress or nominated to a cabinet post, Luján was one of the few Hispanic Republicans to achieve these positions. By winning reelection consistently for twenty years, he became the ranking member of two different committees. As interior secretary, he was one of the highest ranking Hispanics in the U.S. government at the time.

Steven L. Danver

FURTHER READING

Cargo, David Francis. *Lonesome Dave: The Story of New Mexico Governor David Francis Cargo*. Edited by Dennis Domrzalski. Santa Fe, N. Mex.: Sunstone Press, 2010. Cargo's autobiography offers a colorful history of New Mexico politics, including the roles played by Luján and his father. Also discusses Luján's support for the return of Blue Lake to the Taos Pueblo Indians.

Gómez-Quiñones, Juan. *Chicano Politics: Reality and Promise, 1940-1990*. Albuquerque: University of New Mexico Press, 1990. This overview of Hispanic politicians mostly during the second half of the twentieth century presents much information about Luján's tenure both as a congressman and as interior secretary.

Gup, Ted. "Manuel Lujan: The Stealth Secretary." *Time*, May 25, 1992. Largely critical of Luján's term as interior secretary, this article presents information on his environmental views and his public pronouncements, many of which resulted in criticism from environmentalists.

Plevin, Nancy. "Ex-Interior Boss Lujan Defends His Stewardship of Public Lands." *The Los Angeles Times*, May 9, 1993. This article presents Luján's perspective on his tenure as interior secretary.

Vigil, Maurilio E. *Hispanics in American Politics: The Search for Political Power*. Lanham, Md.: University Press of America, 1987. Much of Luján's early life and his years in Congress are profiled in this work.

See also: Dennis Chavez; Alberto Gonzales; Mel Martínez; Joseph M. Montoya; Bill Richardson; Ken Salazar.

M

EDUARDO MACHADO

Cuban-born playwright

Machado's semiautobiographical plays examine the legacy of exile among Cubans in America. His work has been produced at several major theaters across the country.

Latino heritage: Cuban
Born: June 11, 1953; Havana, Cuba
Also known as: Eduardo Oscar Machado
Area of achievement: Theater

EARLY LIFE

Eduardo Oscar Machado (mah-CHAH-doh) was born into an affluent family in Havana, Cuba, and raised in Cojimar. His paternal grandfather, Fernando Machado, was an official at the docks, while his maternal grandfather, Oscar Hernandez, was a self-made businessman who owned a major bus company. Oscar particularly influenced the young Machado, exposing him to the working-class world of bus drivers, factory workers, and boat builders, as well as the poverty of street children and the beauty of rural Cuba.

Machado was anxious and troubled as a child by conversations about the Cuban Revolution. Like many wealthy families, his family was at first divided between Fidel Castro and the U.S.-backed dictator Fulgencio Batista, but in 1959, after Castro's forces triumphed, the family discovered that the communists were worse for them than any previous government. Machado's grandfather Fernando lost his job at the docks. Soon after, Oscar lost his bus company when it was nationalized.

In 1961, Machado and his brother Jesus became two of the fourteen thousand children who were airlifted from Cuba as part of Operation Peter Pan, a program

Eduardo Machado. (Time & Life Pictures/Getty Images)

coordinated by the Roman Catholic Archdiocese of Miami and the United States government to weaken support for Castro in Cuba. Machado was bitter about the separation from his parents. He and his brother went to live with an uncle and attempted to adjust to their new immigrant poverty. Although they were told that they would never see their parents again, Machado was relieved when they arrived in Florida six months later, just before the Cuban Missile Crisis put an end to flights between Cuba and the United States.

Machado's father became an accountant, but with scant work in Miami, the family relocated to California. Machado, who never felt that he fit in, began to find solace in theater and music. He gained attention at Porter Junior High School for his singing and received an award for acting at Van Nuys High School. This led to escalating fights with his father, who vehemently opposed Machado's wish to become an actor.

LIFE'S WORK

Machado left home at sixteen, and by age seventeen, he was working professionally as an actor. In 1979, he attended the Padua Hills Playwrights Festival and Workshop, where he met fellow Cuban playwright Maria Irene Fornes, who became a major influence on him. Unsure about his English, Machado had been reluctant to pursue writing, but with Fornes's encouragement, he enrolled in her writing workshop at Padua Hills and wrote his first play, *Embroidery*. He read the play at the Ensemble Studio Theatre in Los Angeles and was persuaded to submit the play to the National Endowment for the Arts. To his surprise, he received a $12,500 grant.

Machado moved to New York City in 1981. He continued to act, appearing in Fornes's *A Visit* (1981) at Theater for the New City that year, but he began to focus more of his attention on playwriting. He participated in Fornes's writing workshop at International Arts Relations (INTAR), where he wrote his first full-length play, *Fabiola* (1985). At the workshop, he also wrote parts of *Rosario and the Gypsies* (1982), *The Modern Ladies of Guanabacoa* (1983), and *Broken Eggs* (1984), all of which later were produced by Ensemble Studio Theatre in New York City. Machado received glowing reviews in *The New York Times* for these works.

In 1994, with a grant from the Pew Charitable Trusts, Machado to become a playwright-in-residence at the Mark Taper Forum in Los Angeles, where his plays *The Modern Ladies of Guanabacoa*, *Fabiola*, *Broken Eggs*, and *In the Eye of the Hurricane* (1991) were presented as an epic series. Set between 1928 and 1979, the plays depict four generations of a bourgeois Cuban family from their rise to affluence to a bittersweet wedding in Los Angeles after their exile. Subject to extensive rewrites, the series received mixed reviews but brought Machado's work to a wider audience.

Machado returned to Cuba for the first time in thirty-eight years in 1999. The visit coincided with the international custody battle surrounding Elián González. Machado's nervousness about the visit and his mixed feelings over the González debate led to the play *Havana Is Waiting* (2001). Originally titled *Where the Sea Drowns in Sand*, it was a hit at the Actors Theatre in Louisville. Rehearsals for a subsequent production at the Cherry Lane Theater in New York began on September 11, 2001, the day the World Trade Center and Pentagon were attacked by terrorists. Despite the anti-American sentiments in the play, which Machado refused to rewrite, *Havana Is Waiting* was warmly reviewed in *The New York Times*.

Machado's *The Cook* (2003), inspired by his second visit to Cuba, was produced at INTAR, the Goodman Theatre, and Seattle Repertory Theatre. He served as the head of playwriting at Columbia University from 1995 to 2007 and as the artistic director of INTAR from 2004 to 2010. In 2007, he was named head of playwriting at New York University's Tisch School of the Arts.

SIGNIFICANCE

Machado's work most often reflects his personal experience as an upper-middle-class Cuban exile. Unlike the work of many other Latino writers, his plays are not peopled with working-class laborers, nor are there moments of Magical Realism. Machado perhaps most closely resembles Anton Chekhov in his heightened naturalistic style, the familial conflicts in his plays, and characters haunted by the past. He also often explores homosexuality and gender roles in Latino society. Machado's feelings about Cuba are complex, and his plays have divided the Cuban American community. He continues to explore the impact of the Cuban Revolution and the American embargo on Cuba through plays that are sensitive, nuanced, and charged with the pain of exile.

Victoria Linchong

FURTHER READING

Machado, Eduardo. *The Floating Island Plays*. New York: Theatre Communications Group, 1991. A collection of Machado's plays *The Modern Ladies* of *Guanabacoa*, *Fabiola*, *In the Eye of the Hurricane*, and *Broken Eggs*, which depict a Cuban family's rise to affluence in the 1920's and their displacement after Castro's takeover.

———. *Havana Is Waiting, and Other Plays*. New York: Theatre Communications Group, 2011. A collection of four of Machado's plays: *Havana Is Waiting*, *The Cook*, *Crocodile Eyes* (1999), and *Kissing Fidel* (2005).

Machado, Eduardo, and Michael Domitrovich. *Tastes Like Cuba: An Exile's Hunger for Home*. New York: Gotham Books, 2007. A memoir by Macha-

do that poignantly presents his life experiences as a culinary adventure, complete with recipes.

Ortíz, Ricardo L. "Beyond All Cuban Counterpoints: Eduardo Machado's *Floating Island Plays*." In *Cultural Erotics in Cuban America*. Minneapolis: University of Minnesota Press, 2007. Scholarly examination Machado's four-play cycle and its presentation of Cuban history and identity.

See also: Mercedes de Acosta; Reinaldo Arenas; Denise Chávez; Maria Irene Fornes; Cristina García; Oscar Hijuelos; Luis Miguel Valdez.

ARTURO MADRID

American educator and social reformer

Madrid, an educator, scholar, and advocate for social reform in the Latino community, was the founding president of the Tomás Rivera Center, a national institute for policy studies on Latino issues. Among his many accomplishments, Madrid directed the U.S. Department of Education's Fund for the Improvement of Postsecondary Education, and he was involved in, and a director of, numerous organizations, including Arte Público Press, the National Hispanic Cultural Center, and the National Center for Public Policy and Higher Education.

Latino heritage: Mexican
Born: January 20, 1939; Tierra Amarilla, New Mexico
Also known as: Arturo Madrid-Barela
Areas of achievement: Education; social issues

EARLY LIFE

Arturo Madrid (ahr-TOR-oh muh-DRIHD) grew up in Tierra Amarilla, New Mexico, a small town in the northern part of the state. He was the eldest of three children born to Arturo Teófilo Madrid and Gabriela Barela Madrid. The pietism of his maternal, agrarian grandparents was a strong influence on his early life. Madrid's grandfather also set an example of public service through his work as a justice of the peace, a probate judge, and the majordomo of his water district. Madrid's mother similarly provided public service as both an elected and an appointed public official. Madrid's young life was informed by the Presbyterian Church, the dynamics of the county courthouse in which his mother served, and the school in which his father worked as a teacher and subsequently as an administrator.

In his boyhood, Madrid ran errands for various officials in his mother's office and later earned pocket money by microfilming deeds and titles and proofreading copies of official documents. However, his favorite activities were trout fishing, shooting, and hunting. Madrid was sent to the Menaul School of the Presbyterian Church in Albuquerque to finish his senior year as a boarding student. He later lived at this school while attending the University of New Mexico.

These academic environments thrust him fully into an Anglo world. He dated Anglo women who were members of the Presbyterian university fellowship, and he only came into regular contact with other Latinos in his Spanish classes. During the first three years of his undergraduate education, Madrid was a candidate for the Presbyterian ministry and immersed in church-related activities. However, he eventually decided to focus on the study of literature and attended graduate school at the University of California, Los Angeles (UCLA), where he studied Spanish. In 1961, while he was a graduate student, Madrid married Robin Wilstach; they had three children and eventually divorced in 1983.

LIFE'S WORK

After obtaining his master's degree in 1964 and while working on his doctorate from UCLA, Madrid began his teaching career at Dartmouth College in Hanover, New Hampshire. He completed his Ph.D. in 1969, and from 1970 to 1973 he taught at the University of California, San Diego. He later served as director of the Ford Foundation Graduate Fellowships Program for Mexican Americans, Native Americans, and Puerto Ricans from

1975 to 1976 and as the program's national director from 1976 to 1980. Concurrently, he was an associate professor at the University of Minnesota from 1973 to 1979 and a full professor from 1979 to 1986. He was the chair of this university's Department of Spanish and Portuguese from 1976 to 1978, the associate dean of humanities and fine arts from 1978 to 1979, and dean and executive officer from 1979 to 1980. He subsequently worked at the U.S. Department of Education, directing both the Fund for the Improvement of Postsecondary Education and the Minority Science and Engineering Improvement Program from 1980 to 1981.

In 1984, Madrid became the founding president of the Tomás Rivera Center, a national institute for policy studies on Latino issues based at the University of Southern California. He married Antonia Castañeda, a historian and Chicano studies specialist, two years later. In 1993, he left the Tomás Rivera Center and accepted a job teaching Spanish at Trinity University in San Antonio, Texas, where, as of 2010, he was the Murchison Distinguished Professor of the Humanities. As a Spanish professor, Madrid acquired a reputation for mentoring students and faculty. He has been a particularly effective role model because of his participation in legal, educational, and cultural affairs related to Latinos. From the beginning of his career, Madrid felt a need to be involved in something historically important and socially significant. He has been driven by the challenge of alleviating inequity and marginalization, and he derives great satisfaction from developing intellectual resources for the Latino community.

SIGNIFICANCE

The numerous contributions made by Madrid to the Latino community are reflected in the awards and honors he has received. In 2002, he was presented the Matt García Public Service Award of the Mexican American Legal Defense and Education Fund (MALDEF). In the same year, he was recognized with the Tomás Rivera Lifetime Achievement Award. In 1996, Madrid was awarded the Charles Frankel Prize by the National Endowment for the Humanities, which acknowledged his role in developing the field of Latino studies in the United States.

Norma A. Mouton

FURTHER READING

Madrid, Arturo. "Because I Like the Questions." In *The Condition of American Liberal Education: Pragmatism and a Changing Tradition*, edited by Robert Orrill. New York: College Entrance Examination Board, 1995. This commentary responds to an essay by Bruce A. Kimball on pragmatic liberal education. Madrid, speaking in personal terms, gives insight into his professional life.

_____. "Diversity and Its Discontents." In *Understanding Inequality: The Intersection of Race/Ethnicity, Class, and Gender*, edited by Barbara A. Arrighi. 2d ed. Lanham, Md.: Rowman and Littlefield, 2007. This essay, written in the first person, gives Madrid's perspective on growing up as a Mexican American in a village in New Mexico. He also discusses the paradoxes of diversity and the challenges faced by the United States as it comes to terms with diversity.

Moyers, Bill D., and Betty S. Flowers. *A World of Ideas: Conversations with Thoughtful Men and Women About American Life Today and the Ideas Shaping Our Future*. New York: Doubleday, 1989. Includes an interview with Madrid focusing on why it was important for him to found the Tomás Rivera Center and his vision for its future. Madrid relates his work for the center in terms of his personal experiences growing up in New Mexico.

See also: Edna Acosta-Belén; Rodolfo F. Acuña; Lauro Cavazos.

SONIA MANZANO

American actor, entertainer, and writer

Manzano's greatest contribution is her gift for eloquence, charm, and simplicity in language, both written and spoken, as evidenced by her lengthy career as an actor, her scriptwriting for Sesame Street, *and her publication of two children's books.*

Latino heritage: Puerto Rican
Born: June 12, 1950; New York, New York
Also known as: Sonia Reagan
Areas of achievement: Radio and television; education; theater; literature

Sonia Manzano. (AP Photo)

EARLY LIFE

Sonia Manzano (SOHN-ah mahn-SAHN-oh) was born in New York City on June 12, 1950, to Puerto Rican immigrants, Bonifacio Manzano, a roofer, and Isidra Rivera Manzano, a seamstress. One of four children, Manzano was raised in a family-like Puerto Rican community in the South Bronx. As a child, Manzano loved to watch television, but she was frustrated by the fact that the shows were mediocre in content and contained no Latino characters who looked like herself. Manzano attended the exclusive High School for the Performing Arts in Manhattan, made famous in the film *Fame* (1980). In her junior year in high school, she began acting, and in 1968, she entered Carnegie Mellon University in Pittsburgh on a scholarship, studying drama and becoming fascinated with experimental theater.

Manzano left Carnegie Mellon in 1971 to join the cast of the original Off-Broadway musical *Godspell*. While performing in *Godspell*, she sang the premier rendition of "Turn Back, O Man," later to become a hallmark when the show was produced on Broadway. An agent who attended a performance of *Godspell* was so impressed with Manzano's theatrical talent that he offered to represent her at an audition for a Public

Broadcasting Service (PBS) children's television series, *Sesame Street*. Manzano auditioned for the role of a new character, Maria, to be introduced on the show, and in 1971, she joined the show's cast.

LIFE'S WORK

On *Sesame Street*, Manzano was asked to contribute fully to her role as Maria, a Latina teenager. For almost ten years, she made regular suggestions to the writers and producers about how to make Maria's character and surroundings more authentic and believable for Latino audiences, especially viewers living in urban environments. Manzano's ideas were incorporated, but after she complained in the late 1970's that an episode depicting Latinos seemed fake, *Sesame Street* executive producer Dulcy Singer insisted that Manzano begin writing material for the show, as well as performing. For more than thirty years, Manzano has written scripts for *Sesame Street*, entwining elements from her own personal life and Puerto Rican American heritage into the show. By 2010, Manzano and the rest of the writing staff at *Sesame Street* had won 15 Emmy Awards for their screenwriting.

As a child watching television and films in the South Bronx, Manzano was greatly influenced by Hollywood musicals, especially grand stage show productions starring dancers Fred Astaire and Ginger Rogers, the pair she considered particularly glamorous. Some of Manzano's most memorable scripts for *Sesame Street* involve song or dance numbers, directly inspired by musicals from the big screen. One of the most popular *Sesame Street* episodes of all time, episode 2164, features the song "You Say Hola and I Say Hola" (1984), which she both wrote and produced. Manzano and actor Emilio Delgado dressed as Ginger Rogers and Fred Astaire, singing and dancing in a festive tribute to the the classic musical *Top Hat* (1935). Another Manzano tribute to Hollywood musicals, "Muppets Rhyme in School" (1987), from episode 2291, includes a classroom of muppets learning to rhyme words like "nose," "toes," and "rose," a parody of the song "Moses" in *Singin' in the Rain* (1952).

In Manzano's musical number "Thirteen" (1993), from episode 3142, muppet character Telly sings of his love for the newly discovered number thirteen. "Don't Be a Tough Nut to Crack" (1994), from episode 3281, and "Yell" (1994), from episode 3259, further illustrate Manzano's talent for writing musical compositions in which she interweaves song, dance, plot, and dialogue in a style reminiscent of Hollywood musicals.

Evolution of *Sesame Street*'s Maria Character

When Sonia Manzano joined *Sesame Street* as Maria in 1971, she portrayed a young teenager who had just moved into the neighborhood, living in a second-story apartment located above owners Gordon and Susan's fix-it shop. After applying for a job at the lending library, Maria became the *Sesame Street* librarian, encouraging children to read, while introducing them to new letters, words, and books.

Viewers of *Sesame Street* were given the opportunity to grow up with Maria, watching her metamorphose from a librarian to a babysitter, best friend, confidant, and adult. Children shared in Maria's first schoolgirl crush, her first date, and her falling in love. Maria's marriage to Luis, played by Emilio Delgado, in 1988 closely resembled Manzano's real-life falling in love with and marriage to Richard Reagan in 1986. In 1988, Manzano's real-life daughter, Gabriella, was born, and she played Maria's daughter Gabi, who was ostensibly born on *Sesame Street* in 1989 to proud parents Maria and Luis. Just as Manzano's husband frequently read books aloud to her, likewise Maria's husband, Luis, read books aloud to her on *Sesame Street.*

The development of the character of Maria was largely autobiographical in its social, cultural, and political themes. Throughout the 1970's and 1980's, for example, as Manzano became immersed in feminism and the women's movement, Maria expressed a desire to work in the fix-it shop with the men and become part-owner of the business. Maria dreamed of becoming a construction worker, and although she was told that only men could perform this work, she learned to build things and achieved her goal of working with a construction crew. Manzano also introduced distinctly Latino cultural elements into *Sesame Street* by incorporating Puerto Rican food, music, clothing, traditions, and celebrations into Maria's character.

Manzano has also written extensively for *Sesame Street* videos, most notably *Sesame Street Visits the Hospital* (1990), *Big Bird's Birthday* (1991), and *Plaza Sezamo: Bienvenida la primavera* (2006). A huge fan of Charlie Chaplin and a devotee of the art of pantomime, Manzano has created her own recurring Chaplin look-alike character for *Sesame Street*. First appearing in 1982, Manzano, dressed as Chaplin, mimicked his silent film antics, waddling like a penguin with cane in hand and performing Chaplin-inspired pantomime skits.

In addition to her work on *Sesame Street,* Manzano has appeared in Off-Broadway theater productions of *The Vagina Monologues* (1996) and *The Exonerated* (2004*)*, as well as starring briefly as Barbara Benitez in a 2004 episode of the television series *Law and Order.* Manzano has also contributed as a writer to *Little Bill,* the award-winning television series for children on the Nickelodeon network.

In 2004, Manzano became a critically acclaimed children's book author, publishing *No Dogs Allowed!*, followed by *A Box Full of Kittens* in 2007. Both books draw extensively from her own childhood. *No Dogs Allowed!* was adapted as a musical play in 2006 and produced at the Actor's Playhouse in Coral Gables, Florida.

In 2004, Manzano was inducted into the Bronx Hall of Fame, and in 2005, Notre Dame University awarded her an honorary doctorate degree. In 2007, she was named one of the most influential Hispanics in America by *People en Español* magazine.

S<small>IGNIFICANCE</small>

Manzano is significant because she provided millions of children an image which she was unable to find on television when she was a child: a positive Latina character whom children could watch, identify with, and emulate. Manzano's greatest gift is in her service as a role model for children, particularly minority children. As a child, Manzano believed that Latinos were invisible, unrepresented by the media, except in rare appearances, when they were cast as negative, often violent stereotypes. By watching Manzano on *Sesame Street*, Latino children receive validation and inclusion, recognizing in the voice and actions of Puerto Rican American character Maria their own ability to make a difference and be heard someday.

Mary E. Markland

F<small>URTHER</small> R<small>EADING</small>

Cramer, Kathryn, and Hank Wasiak. *Change the Way You See Everything Through Asset-Based Thinking.* Philadelphia: Running Press, 2006. Manzano talks about her first book, *No Dogs Allowed!*, describing it as largely autobiographical and teaching the values of family, loyalty, and sharing she learned as a child in her South Bronx, Puerto Rican American neighborhood.

Davis, Michael. *Street Gang: The Complete History of Sesame Street.* New York: Penguin Group, 2008. Discusses *Sesame Street* character Snuffy and his longtime crush on Maria, explaining it was written into the show because Snuffy's creator, puppeteer Martin Robinson, had a real-life crush on Manzano.

Gikow, Louise. *Sesame Street: A Celebration of Forty Years of Life on the Street.* New York: Black Dog & Leventhal, 2009. Manzano addresses the absence of Latinos in the media when she was a child and

her desire to provide a positive image for children on *Sesame Street* by creating a Latina character who is an integral part of her community.

See also: María Conchita Alonso; Lynda Carter; America Ferrera; Eva Longoria; Elizabeth Peña; Bob Vila.

MICHAEL A. MARES

American mammalogist

Mares is the world's leading expert on desert rodents. He is credited with discovering three new species.

Latino heritage: Mexican
Born: March 11, 1945; Albuquerque, New Mexico
Also known as: Michael Allen Mares
Area of achievement: Science and technology

EARLY LIFE

The son of Ernesto Gustavo Mares and Rebecca Gabriela Devine, Michael Allen Mares (MAH-rehs) grew up in New Mexico amid deserts and the life that inhabits them. He enrolled in 1963 at the University of New Mexico in Albuquerque, intending to major in biology as prerequisite to studying medicine. By 1965, he had shifted his focus to zoology, and he went to Mexico on his first research trip a year later to study bats. Despite contracting a near-fatal infection in the bat caves, Mares continued his work in field biology.

Mares married Lynn Ann Brusin, an attorney, on August 27, 1966, after his junior year; their union resulted in two children, Gabriel Andres and Daniel Alejandro. Mares was drafted to serve in the Vietnam War, but his military service was deferred because of damage his lungs had suffered from the Mexican infection. After graduating with a bachelor of science degree in biology in 1967, he enrolled in the graduate zoology program at Fort Hays State University in Kansas, receiving his master of science degree in 1969. He then moved to the University of Texas at Austin, where he earned his Ph.D. in zoology in 1973, specializing in mammalogy. Mares's fluency in Spanish and proficiency in Portuguese and French positioned him well for the extensive field trips and research collaborations in South America that would characterize his career. He focused his doctoral thesis on desert rodents' adaptations to climates, other mammalian communities, and their evolutionary

convergence, studying rodent populations in Argentina. During his doctoral studies he became an adjunct professor of zoology at the Universidad Nacional de Cordoba (1971) and the Universidad Nacional de Tucumán, Instituto Miguel Lillo (1972) in Argentina, where he undertook his field work and where his sons were born.

LIFE'S WORK

Mares accepted an appointment as assistant professor of biological sciences at the University of Pittsburgh in 1973 and became an associate professor in 1981. In 1976, he won a Fulbright-Hays Postdoctoral Research Fellowship, which took him back to Argentina. In 1978, he received a National Chicano Council on Higher Education Research Postdoctoral Fellowship in Arizona, and in 1980, he won a Ford Foundation Minority Postdoctoral Fellowship, which allowed him to serve as a visiting professor of ecology and evolutionary biology at the University of Arizona at Tucson in 1980-1981. Throughout this period, he established himself as a global expert on the evolution and adaptation of desert mammals, especially rodents. His work led to his appointment as associate professor of zoology and associate curator of mammals at the Stovall Museum of Science and History at the University of Oklahoma from 1981 to 1985. Mares was elevated to full professor of zoology in 1985 and then named presidential professor of zoology in 2003. He became director of the Oklahoma Museum of Natural History at the University of Oklahoma in 1983 and dramatically improved the museum's facilities, public outreach, and educational programs. When he stepped down as director in 2003, he was designated distinguished research curator of the (newly renamed) Sam Noble Oklahoma Museum of Natural History.

Throughout his career, Mares has specialized in desert and neotropical environments with a particular focus on Argentina, Chile, and Brazil. His work has led to major breakthroughs in the identification of mammalian species and understanding of South American biology, population biology, zoogeography, conservation, and desert ecology. Three different types of living creatures are named in his honor: a Bolivian rodent genus, a subspecies of neotropical bat, and a parasitic mite that is found on neotropical rodents. Mares also has identified and named three new rodent species as part of his lifetime of work exploring desert habitats throughout North America, South America, Egypt, and Iran.

An extremely able administrator, fund-raiser, mentor, teacher, consultant, and adviser, Mares has been appointed to numerous prestigious advisory boards and councils, including the Smithsonian Institution Council (2000), the U.S. Department of the Interior's advisory board for the Center for Biological Diversity (1994), board of directors of the Council for the International Exchange of Scholars (1988-1991), numerous panels of the National Science Foundation, as well as national and international scientific boards relating specifically to South America. He has spoken widely as a keynote speaker at major biological meetings and consulted with the World Wildlife Fund and international organizations. He has edited or served on the editorial boards of numerous professional journals in his field, including *Journal of Mammalogy*, *Current Mammalogy*, and the *Revista Chilena de Historia Natural*.

In 2002, Mares was elected a fellow of the American Association for the Advancement of Science for his contributions to mammal biogeography and conservation and his support of natural history museums as centers for helping to preserve biodiversity. He has received numerous awards for teaching, mentoring, service, and leadership. His involvement in major biological, conservation, and educational efforts in South America has improved public understanding, government leadership, and university teaching of matters related to biodiversity and conservation. In 2002, Mares wrote and produced the film *Behind the Rain: The Story of a Museum* to chronicle the development of the Sam Noble Oklahoma Museum of Natural History and help other museums improve their collections, outreach, and impact.

SIGNIFICANCE

A world-renowned expert on desert rodents, Mares has made an indelible imprint on the fields of biodiversity, biogeography, and conservation of desert and neotropical ecosystems. He also has set an important example for how natural history museums can improve conservation and biodiversity efforts and advanced Latinos' formal study of the natural environment.

Dennis W. Cheek

FURTHER READING

Mares, Michael A. *A Desert Calling: Life in a Forbidding Landscape*. Cambridge, Mass.: Harvard University Press, 2002. Mares presents an introduction to the world's major deserts and the life that inhabits them, mixing personal stories with discussion of local politics and policies and the importance of preserving these unique environments.

_____, ed. *A University Natural History Museum for the New Millennium*. Norman: Sam Noble Oklahoma Museum of Natural History, 2001. Discusses the important role natural history museums can play in conservation and how Mares advanced the art and science of such efforts in Oklahoma and globally.

Newton, David E. "Michael A. Mares." In *Latinos in Science, Math, and Professions*. New York: Facts On File, 2007. Succinct overview of Mares's life, career, and importance to the field of mammalogy.

See also: Anne Maino Alvarez; Walter Alvarez; Francisco Dallmeier; Arturo Gómez-Pompa; Elma González; Eugenia Kalnay.

JUAN MARICHAL

Dominican-born baseball player

Marichal's distinctive high leg kick, excellent strikeout-to-walk ratio, and competitive attitude made him the winningest pitcher in baseball in the 1960's. He was named to the National League All-Star team numerous times, threw a no-hitter in 1963, and had his uniform number retired by the San Francisco Giants.

Latino heritage: Dominican
Born: October 20, 1937; Laguna Verde, Monte Cristi, Dominican Republic
Also known as: Juan Antonio Marichal Sánchez; Dominican Dandy; Manito; Mar
Area of achievement: Baseball

EARLY LIFE

Juan Antonio Marichal Sánchez (MAHR-ih-shahl) was born on October 20, 1937, in Laguna Verde, Monte Cristi, Dominican Republic. As a teenager, he became a legend as a starting pitcher for the Dominican Air Force baseball team.

Marichal was signed by the New York Giants of Major League Baseball (MLB) as a free agent in 1957 and sent to the team's Class A minor-league affiliate in Michigan City, Michigan, in 1958. He had a record of 21-8 and an earned run average (ERA) of 1.87. The next year, Marichal played for the Class A team in Springfield, Massachusetts, where he went 18-13 with a 2.39 ERA. He credited his distinctive high leg kick with helping him throw an intimidating fastball and hard slider with pinpoint accuracy—in his first minor league season, for example, Marichal recorded 246 strikeouts in 245 innings and only 50 walks, a high strikeout-to-walk ratio that he would maintain throughout his career.

In the late 1950's, the Class AAA Pacific Coast League (PCL) lost some of its premier cities in San Francisco and Los Angeles as the New York Giants and Brooklyn Dodgers relocated to those two cities, respectively. In 1960, Marichal was promoted to the now-San

Juan Marichal. (AP Photo)

Francisco Giants' PCL franchise in Tacoma, where he had an 11-5 record in 18 starts before being called up to the parent club in midseason. Marichal made his major-league debut on July 19, 1960, against the Philadelphia Phillies. He threw a no-hitter through 7 2/3 innings, finished with a 1-hit shutout, striking out 12 while walking only one batter. He finished the 1960 season with a 6-2 record and 2.66 ERA. Meanwhile, the Giants were assembling a legendary team (Willie Mays, Willie McCovey, Orlando Cepeda, Felipe Alou, and Matty Alou, among others) to contend with the Dodgers.

LIFE'S WORK

Marichal's extraordinary starting pitching for the Giants throughout the 1960's made him a celebrity in the Spanish-speaking portions of the Western Hemisphere as well as a feared competitor throughout baseball. Although the Dodgers and Giants continued their epic rivalry, now relocated to the West Coast, the Dodgers generally prevailed. After the two teams' relocations, the Dodgers won the National League (NL) pennant in 1959, 1963, 1965, and 1966, and went on to win the World Series in all but the 1966 season. The Giants won 103 games and the NL pennant in 1962 but lost the World Series to the New York Yankees in seven games.

Marichal, having completed only his second full season with the Giants in 1962, was fourth in the starting-pitcher rotation, even though he had won eighteen games. He started only game four of the World Series, pitched a shutout for four innings, and recorded a no-decision as the Giants lost the game, 4-3. Marichal's only other postseason experience came in 1971 when the Giants played the Pittsburgh Pirates in the National League Championship Series and lost, three games to one. Marichal pitched a complete game 4-hitter in game three but lost, 2-1, after allowing two solo home runs. It is ironic that one of the dominating pitchers of his era was only 0-1 with a 1.50 ERA in his scant two postseason appearances.

One of Marichal's signature games came against the Milwaukee Braves and future Hall of Fame left-hander Warren Spahn on July 2, 1963. Spahn was known for his own high leg kick, although his did not approach the height of Marichal's. Marichal pitched sixteen scoreless innings, and Spahn matched him until the bottom of the sixteenth inning, when Mays hit a solo home run. Given the rise in the use of relief pitchers in the 1970's and 1980's and the concern about long-term damage to pitchers' arms, it is unlikely that Marichal's and Spahn's feat ever will be duplicated.

Marichal's Confrontation with Roseboro

In the midst of five-team National League pennant race that would soon narrow to the Los Angeles Dodgers and San Francisco Giants, the Giants hosted the Dodgers at Candlestick Park on August 22, 1965. Juan Marichal was pitching against Dodgers ace Sandy Koufax. In the early innings of the game, Marichal threw intimidating brushback pitches at Maury Wills and Ron Fairly. When Marichal went up to bat in the bottom of the third inning, catcher Johnny Roseboro called for Koufax to throw a high, inside pitch at Marichal, but Koufax refused to do so. Roseboro's return throws to Koufax came close to Marichal's face, and the latter, incensed, hit Roseboro on the head three times with his bat. A melee ensued between the two teams, and Roseboro needed fourteen stitches in his head. Marichal was suspended for nine games and fined $1,750. The Giants won the game, 4-3, but the Dodgers won the pennant and the World Series in 1965. Roseboro later sued Marichal for $110,000 but settled out of court for an undisclosed amount. The two players eventually reconciled. Dodger fans remained angry at Marichal for years. When he signed with the Dodgers at the start of the 1975 season, fans reacted with venom until Roseboro spoke publicly on Marichal's behalf. Roseboro's forgiveness also likely swayed the opinions of voters who had previously denied the pitcher induction into the Baseball Hall of Fame. Marichal was enshrined in the Hall of Fame in 1983.

Marichal's notorious 1965 fight with the Dodgers' Johnny Roseboro occurred during one of the pitcher's extraordinary seasons, in which he went 22-13 with a 2.13 ERA and 10 complete games. Marichal's stamina and resilience were legendary; he pitched more than 300 innings in a season three times and more than 250 innings in a season seven times.

In 1970, Marichal received a penicillin injection that resulted in a violent reaction, causing back pain and arthritis. His final four seasons in San Francisco paled in comparison with his first decade as a professional. His contract was sold to the Boston Red Sox before the 1974 season, and he pitched well as a spot starter (5-1, 4.87 ERA in eleven games). Marichal signed with the Los Angeles Dodgers before the 1975 season and had two mediocre outings that April before retiring from professional baseball. That year, his number, 27, was retired by the Giants.

After his retirement, Marichal worked as a broadcaster and served as minister of sport in the Dominican Republic. He was inducted into the Baseball Hall of Fame in 1983, and in 2005, the Giants erected a statue of him outside their ballpark in San Francisco.

SIGNIFICANCE

Marichal was only the second pitcher from the Dominican Republic to play in the major leagues, and his stunning statistics (243-142, 2.89 career ERA, 191 wins in the 1960's, ten All-Star team selections) likely would have merited his membership in the Baseball Hall of Fame in his first (rather than his fifth) year of eligibility were it not for negative publicity generated by his fight with Roseboro.

Richard Sax

FURTHER READING

Burgos, Adrian. *Playing America's Game: Baseball, Latinos, and the Color Line.* Berkeley: University of California Press, 2007. A definitive study of Latinos in professional baseball from the 1880's through the middle of the first decade of the twenty-first century.

Fost, Dan. *Giants, Past & Present.* London: MVP Books/Quayside, 2010. More than two hundred photographs, including some of Marichal and others from his 1960's teams, are included in this extensive history of the team.

Murphy, Brian. *San Francisco Giants: Fifty Years.* San Rafael, Calif.: Insight Editions/Palace Press, 2008. Liberally illustrated text traces the path of the Giants from their first days in San Francisco, playing at the old San Francisco Seals ballpark, through four decades at Candlestick Park and the move to AT&T Park.

Nan, Chuck. *Fifty Years by the Bay: The San Francisco Giants.* Bloomington, Ind.: AuthorHouse, 2006. Bay Area journalist and teacher Nan relies heavily on interviews to provide firsthand accounts of Giants players, including Marichal and others from the 1960's teams.

Schott, Tom, and Nick Peters. *The Giants Encyclopedia.* 2d ed. Champaign, Ill.: Sports Publishing, 2000. This definitive encyclopedia of the baseball team includes an extensive profile of Marichal.

See also: Felipe Alou; Joaquín Andújar; Dennis Martínez; Pedro Martinez; Johan Santana; Luis Tiant; Fernando Valenzuela.

CHEECH MARÍN

American actor and comedian

Best known for his irreverent, slapstick, cultural satire as part of the comedic duo Cheech and Chong, Marín has enjoyed success as a comedian, actor, writer, director, and art collector. His body of work intervenes in mainstream representations of Latinos, but broadly offers humor and satire as alternative means in the creation of social and political change.

Latino heritage: Mexican
Born: July 13, 1946; Los Angeles, California
Also known as: Richard Anthony Marín
Areas of achievement: Acting; entertainment

EARLY LIFE

Richard Anthony Marín (mah-REEN) was born in Los Angeles, California, to Mexican American parents, Elsa and Oscar Marín. He was raised in Granada Hills, a suburb in the San Fernando Valley, and was given the nickname "Cheech" as an infant. Marín's uncle saw the newborn asleep in his bassinet and joked that he

Cheech Marín. (AP Photo)

resembled a *chicharrón*, a Mexican snack made from deep-fried pieces of pigskin. The family nicknamed him "Chicharrón," which later was shortened to "Cheech."

As a teenager, Marín was a good student who earned top grades, particularly in subjects related to art and art history. He also showed a talent for music at an early age. Later, Marín studied English at California State University, Northridge. However, in 1967, only eight credits shy of earning his degree, he decided to leave the university. At an antiwar rally hosted by Muhammad Ali, Marín burned his draft card and fled to Vancouver, British Columbia. He was twenty-one years old at the time.

In Canada, Marín met his comedic counterpart, club owner and fellow musician Tommy Chong. Marín was working as a music reviewer for a Canadian magazine when a mutual acquaintance recommended him for Chong's improvisational theater group. This group and newfound friendship gave Marín the opportunity to develop his improvisational skills and hone his musical talent. The troupe, established in 1969, was called City Works and offered a unique brand of counterculture comedy that quickly gained popularity. In 1970, Marín and Chong decided to move to Los Angeles together to pursue careers in entertainment. Gaining a following among Los Angeles's counterculture youths, Marín and Chong toured small venues as "Cheech and Chong," performing skits and playing music. In 1971, after impressing music industry guru Lou Adler with their act, Marín and Chong signed a deal to record a comedy album.

LIFE'S WORK

Between 1972 and 1985, Marín and Chong collaboratively produced nine comedy albums, including *Cheech and Chong* (1971), *Big Bambú* (1972), *Sleeping Beauty* (1976), *Up in Smoke* (sound track, 1979), and *Get Out of My Room* (1985). Six of their albums went gold, and four were nominated for Grammy Awards, including *Los cochinos* (1973) which won the Grammy for best comedy album of that year. Their records and films brought Marín and Chong's drug-themed comedy to the forefront of youth culture in the United States. Together, they released eight full-length feature films, including *Up in Smoke* (1978), *Cheech and Chong's Next Movie* (1980), *Still Smokin'* (1983), and *Cheech and Chong's The Corsican Brothers* (1984). *Up in Smoke* was the highest-grossing comedy of 1978.

Although he was not formally credited, Marín codirected all of the films with Chong. While the films were popular at the box office, they drew criticism within the Latino community for reinforcing negative stereotypes of Latinos. Some Chicano film scholarship, however, suggests interpretations of their comedic style as complex images of self-affirmation and as possessing keen awareness of comedy as political resistance—characteristics also present in Marín's later solo work.

In 1985, the comedy duo decided to go their separate ways, and Marín pursued his own cinematic endeavors. His first major solo film, *Born in East L.A.* (1987), displayed his writing, acting, and directing abilities. Marín created and embodied the character of Rudy Robles, a third-generation Mexican American living in East Los Angeles. Robles is accused of being in the country illegally and is consequently deported. The film employs comedy, music, and political satire to comment on the status of Chicanos in the United States and attack the Simpson-Rodino Immigration Reform Act of 1986. At the 1987 Havana Film Festival, *Born in East L.A.* won the Grand Coral Prize for Best Picture, as well as awards for Best Production Design and Best Screenplay. Furthermore, the film was heralded as being part of a new wave of Latino films in the 1980's referred to as "Hispanic Hollywood," which included the films *La Bamba* (1987), *The Milagro Beanfield War* (1988), and *Stand and Deliver* (1988).

By 2010, Marín had appeared in more than twenty films, including *Desperado* (1995), *From Dusk Till Dawn* (1996), *Tin Cup* (1996), *Once Upon a Time in Mexico* (2003), and *Machete* (2010). In the realm of children's cinema, Marín lent his voice to the animated films *Oliver and Company* (1988) and *The Lion King* (1994) and appeared in Robert Rodriguez's *Spy Kids* (2001) and *Spy Kids 2: Island of Lost Dreams* (2002). His work in television included *The Golden Palace* (1992), *Nash Bridges* (1996-2001), and appearances on the popular television series *Lost* (2007-2009).

Marín's career has not been limited to playing characters on television and in film. In 1992, he released an album of children's songs, *My Name Is Cheech the Bus Driver*. In 2005, he extended his directing repertoire to include the Broadway production of *Latinologues*, a collection of monologues depicting Latino life in the United States. In 2008, Marín reunited with Chong and toured the United States and Canada with *Cheech and Chong Light Up America/Canada*. The tour revived the characters, skits, and music that made the duo famous and cemented their place in popular culture. In 2010,

---

Marín's Collection and Exhibitions of Chicano Art

By 2010, Cheech Marín possessed one of the largest private collections of Chicano art in the United States. It contains art by some of the most prominent Chicano artists as well as Marín's personal favorites: Patssi Valdez, Frank Romero, and Carlos Almaraz. Pieces in his collection examine issues such as racism, sexism, sexuality, politics, and family. Much of Marín's collection toured the United States from 2001 to 2007 with the exhibition *Chicano Visions: American Painters on the Verge*. Selections from his collection also were displayed in 2008 at the Los Angeles County Museum of Art (LACMA), an institution that once refused to display the work of Chicano artists. From 2008 to 2009, Marín contributed pieces from his collection to the touring exhibit *Papel Chicano: Works on Paper from the Collection of Cheech Marín*. Marín's goal is to bring Chicano art into the mainstream and expose people to the unique style and commentary produced by these artists.

---

they reunited again for their *Get It Legal* tour. They used this tour and its accompanying press as a platform to discuss the legalization of marijuana in the U.S.

SIGNIFICANCE

Through his work writing, directing, and acting (both alone and with Chong), Marín produced some of the first mainstream representations of Latinos that satirized established stereotypes and moved Chicano film from serious social realism into a medium that employed parody and humor as politically charged cinematic tools. As a part of "Hispanic Hollywood" in the 1980's, Marín put mainstream film success within reach of Latino filmmakers. In the decades that followed, he extended this influence to younger Latino filmmakers such as Robert Rodriguez. Marín demonstrated the successful use of alternative media to create complex representations and positive social change.

Marlene Galvan

FURTHER READING

Chong, Tommy. *Cheech and Chong: The Unauthorized Autobiography.* New York: Simon Spotlight Entertainment, 2009. Offers a firsthand account of the career of Marín and Chong, from their first meeting to their first reunion in 2008.

Fregoso, Rosa Linda. "*Born in East L.A.* and the Politics of Representation." *Cultural Studies* 4, no. 3

(October, 1990): 264-280. Scholarly assessment of Marín's *Born in East L.A.* and its contributions to the genre of Chicano film.

List, Christine. "Self-Directed Stereotyping in the Films of Cheech Marín." In *Chicanos and Film: Representation and Resistance*, edited by Chon A. Noriega. Minneapolis: University of Minnesota Press, 1992. Scholarly evaluation of Marín's contributions to his films with Chong. Discusses positive stereotypes and places him within the context of Chicano cinema.

Marín, Cheech, Max Benavidez, Constance Cortez, and Terecita Romo. *Chicano Visions: American Painters on the Verge.* Boston: Bulfinch, 2002. A collection of reprinted paintings from Marín's touring exhibition of the same name accompanied by essays that discuss Chicano art's contribution to the mainstream art world.

Noriega, Chon A. "Chicano Cinema and the Horizon of Expectations: A Discursive Analysis of Film Reviews in the Mainstream, Alternative, and Hispanic Press, 1987-1988." *Aztlán: A Journal of Chicano Studies* 19, no. 2 (1988): 1-32. Analyses of film reviews that originally appeared in magazines and newspapers during 1987-1988 about films considered part of "Hispanic Hollywood."

See also: Catherine Bach; Edward James Olmos; Rosie Pérez; Freddie Prinze; Paul Rodríguez; Robert Rodriguez; Charlie Sheen; Danny Trejo.

MARISOL

French-born artist

Marisol has created imaginative, masterfully crafted, figurative sculptures out of wood, metal, plaster, and found materials. These sculptures range from ironic critiques of society to self-portraits and portraits of personalities from the arts, history, and politics.

Latino heritage: Venezuelan
Born: May 22, 1930; Paris, France
Also known as: Marisol Escobar
Area of achievement: Art

EARLY LIFE

Marisol Escobar (mah-ree-SOHL EHS-coh-bahr) was born on May 22, 1930, in Paris, France to Venezuelan parents, Gustavo and Josefina Hernández Escobar. Since the 1950's she has been known professionally by her first name, Marisol, which in Spanish means "sea and sun." Her earliest years were spent commuting with her parents and her brother, Gustavo, between Europe, the United States, and Caracas, Venezuela. After her mother died in 1941, she was sent to boarding school. In 1946, her father took her to Los Angeles to support her early interest in becoming an artist, and here she attended the Westwood School for girls and took evening classes with artist Howard Warshaw at the Jepson School.

In 1949, Marisol went to Paris to study at the École des Beaux-Arts, but she left after a year because she was disappointed with the training there. In 1950, she moved to New York, where she studied painting with Yasuo Kuniyoshi at the Art Students League. Marisol then transferred to Hans Hoffman's Painting School,

Marisol. (AP Photo)

where she was a student from 1950 to 1954. She later commented that Hoffman was the one teacher who taught her something useful.

By the mid-1950's, Marisol was a part of the art culture of New York's Greenwich Village, meeting artists such as Jackson Pollack, Willem de Kooning, Franz Kline, and Robert Motherwell at the Cedar Bar at 24 University Place. At the artist-run Tanager Gallery (where she also exhibited), Marisol saw an exhibition of founding member William King's pseudoprimitive sculptures. During this period, she also had seen an exhibition of pre-Columbian sculptures. Both of these influences can be seen in her sculpture in terra cotta and bronze, titled *Queen*, created in 1957. In the mid-1950's, Marisol also began exhibiting at the Stable Gallery's annual exhibitions. However, in 1958 she had her first solo exhibition at the prestigious Leo Castelli Gallery.

In 1960, after discovering a sack full of wooden hat forms at a friend's house on Long Island, Marisol created the first wooden sculpture that reflected her mature style. In this sculpture, titled *Self-Portrait* (1961-1962), she transformed the hat forms into seven carved and painted heads with a variety of hairstyles and expressions. The heads sat upon bodies of connected painted wooden blocks from which six bare wooden legs stuck out.

LIFE'S WORK

In the early 1960's, Pop Art was beginning to develop and the art of assemblage flourished, exemplified in the work of Robert Rauschenberg. Marisol's sculptures of the 1960's reflect aspects of both of these trends. Echoing the art of assemblage, she incorporated objects that she found in the street into her sculptures, as in *The Family* (1963), where a baby carriage was recycled into the work. This sculpture also reflected Pop Art's concerns with consumer culture, although an element of satire and critique existed that was more typical of the artist. Her whimsical, yet satirical, sculpture of actor John Wayne (1963), who looks like he is riding a hobby horse, also contains the references to mass media culture that are an element of Pop art.

Marisol's art could also be personal and introspective. She often included images of her face in her sculptures, suggesting a search for self-identity. In *Dinner Date* (1964), two wooden figures dine with each other. *The Party* (1965-1966) features fashionable women wearing elegant, abstract evening gowns, but they all have the facial features of the artist. Influenced by an old family photograph and made of steel and aluminum,

Mi mama y yo (1968) is a particularly moving image of the artist as a child with her mother. In the early 1970's, after returning from a year of travel in Asia, where she viewed art and learned to scuba dive, Marisol produced a series of elegant wood fish sculptures with plaster masks of her own face. However, in 1975, she stopped incorporating her face into her sculptures.

In the late 1970's and early 1980's, Marisol made a number of wood sculptures of older, seated artists in her Artists and Artistes series. These included Willem de Kooning (1980), Georgia O'Keeffe (1977), Louise Nevelson (1981), and the dancer Martha Graham (1977). Exhibited at the Sydney Janis Gallery in New York in 1983, these sculptures of wood and plaster exude a dignity and timelessness. Through the late 1990's, Marisol continued to create and exhibit her sculptures that included social critiques, such as *Poor Family I* (1987), a magnificent group of wood sculptures of American Indians, and tributes to artists she admired, such as a series of sculptures of the surrealist artist René Magritte (1998).

SIGNIFICANCE

Marisol was one of the few American women artists—and the only Latina artist—to gain recognition in the 1960's. She was included in the pivotal museum exhibitions at the Museum of Modern Art, "The Art of Assemblage" (1961) and "The Americans" (1963). From 1966 through 1968, her work was featured in more than twelve exhibitions, and she was becoming known internationally. In 1968 she represented Venezuela at the XXXIV Venice Biennale (she could not represent the United States, as she was not a citizen). She would continue to exhibit regularly at galleries and museums through the 1990's. While Marisol's work shared some affinities with Pop Art, such as an interest in popular culture, her sculptures also incorporated a wit, satire, and irony that did not characterize this movement. In her beautifully crafted sculptures, Marisol used images of women and the family that drew on both personal elements and social critique.

Sandra Rothenberg

FURTHER READING

Grove, Nancy, and National Portrait Gallery (Smithsonian Institution). *Magical Mixtures: Marisol Portrait Sculpture*. Washington, D.C: Smithsonian Institution Press, 1991. Catalog for an exhibition of Marisol's portrait sculpture at the National Portrait Gallery.

Heartney, Eleanor, et al. *Marisol*. Purchase, N.Y: Neuberger Museum of Art, 2001. Catalog for an exhibition spanning Marisol's career, including her portrait and nonportrait sculpture.

Kuspit, Donald. "Two Versions of Marisol, Overlapping and Underlapping." *Art Criticism* 16, no.1 (2001): 71-95. Observes the complexities of Marisol's art, including the self-references in her work and her depictions of families and other artists.

Pacini, Marina. "Tracking Marisol in the Fifties and Sixties." *Archives of American Art Journal*. 46, no.3/4 (2007): 60-65. A chronological look at Marisol's career in the 1950's and 1960's based on documents from the collections at the Archives of American Art.

Ratcliff, Carter and Neuhoff Edelman Gallery. *Marisol: Works, 1960-2007*. New York: Neuhoff Edelman Gallery, 2007. Catalog for an exhibition of Marisol's work that featured sculptures from her entire career, with a special emphasis on the late works created in the 1990's.

Whiting, Cécile. *A Taste for Pop: Pop Art, Gender, and Consumer Culture*. New York: Cambridge University Press, 1997. Examines Marisol's position as a women artist in the 1960's, as well as her sculpture and its relation to Pop Art.

See also: Luis Alfonso Jiménez, Jr.; Tony Labat; Ana Mendieta; Amalia Mesa-Bains; Liliana Porter.

José Martí

Cuban-born activist, poet, and journalist

Best known as Cuba's national hero and as the author of verses used in the song "Guantanamera," Martí spent most of his adult life in the United States and wrote extensively about life there.

Latino heritage: Cuban
Born: January 28, 1853; Havana, Cuba
Died: May 19, 1895; Dos Ríos, Cuba
Also known as: José Julián Martí y Pérez; Pépé; the Apostle of Cuban Independence; the Martyr of Cuban Independence
Areas of achievement: Activism; journalism; literature

Early Life

José Julián Martí y Pérez, better known as José Martí (hoh-ZAY mahr-TEE), was born in Cuba when it was still a Spanish colony. He was the oldest child and only son of Mariano Martí, a sergeant in the Spanish army, and Leonor Pérez. The elder Martí was a strong proponent of Spanish rule, but at high school the young José came under the influence of Rafael María de Mendive, the school's director and a strong supporter of Cuban independence.

At the age of fifteen Martí published a poem in a local newspaper, and the next year, after the outbreak of an uprising against Spanish rule, he published or worked for two short-lived journals calling for Cuban independence, *El diablo cojuelo* (*The Limping Devil*) and *La patria libre* (*The Free Homeland*). In the latter, he pub-

lished a verse drama, *Abdala*, about a young man leading a revolt in the ancient land of Nubia against the wishes of his family. That same year, 1869, both he and his mentor, Mendive, were arrested by the Spanish authorities.

José Martí. (Library of Congress)

In 1870, at the age of seventeen, Martí was sentenced to a term of hard labor at a stone quarry in San Lázaro, Cuba, where he spent six months, after which he was exiled to Spain.

Martí spent four years in Spain, during which time he completed degrees in philosophy and law at the Central University of Madrid and the University of Zaragoza. He also published two political works on the situation in Cuba, *El presidio político en Cuba* (*The Political Prison in Cuba*), in which he described abuses and mistreatment, and *La república Española ante la revolución Cubana* (*The Spanish Republic and the Cuban Revolution*), in which he called on the new Spanish Republic to extend democratic rule to Cuba.

His family having moved to Mexico, Martí joined them there in 1875, but after the coup by Porfirio Díaz, he found it impossible to stay and moved to Guatemala. He worked as a teacher in both countries and also began writing for the newspapers. He made a brief return to Cuba in 1877 under an assumed name, and then after an amnesty was issued he moved there more permanently in 1878. However, his political activities got him arrested and exiled again in 1879. He went first to Spain, but then made his way to New York City, arriving in January, 1880.

LIFE'S WORK

Martí spent most of the rest of his life in New York, working as a journalist, writing poetry, and promoting the cause of Cuban independence. He lived briefly in Venezuela in 1881, but he ran into difficulties with the Venezuelan government and returned to live in New York.

In New York he found work as a translator and teacher of Spanish, but he devoted most of his time to journalism, writing in English for the New York paper *The Hour* and also contributing reports to a large number of newspapers in Latin America, including *La nación* in Argentina. He became the interpreter of the United States to Latin America, writing on a wide range of topics from Coney Island and the Brooklyn Bridge to American elections, natural disasters, the racial situation, immigration, and labor issues. He also wrote many profiles of leading American politicians and writers, such as Ulysses S. Grant and Ralph Waldo Emerson.

Martí also became a diplomatic representative for several Latin American countries, including Paraguay, Uruguay, and Argentina, and he represented Latin American interests at two international conferences, the Pan-American Conference of 1889 and the International Monetary Conference of 1891, at both of which he

warned Latin Americans against letting themselves fall under the sway of the United States.

Falling ill after the 1889 conference, he went to the Catskill Mountains to recuperate, and there he wrote a collection of poems published in 1891 as *Versos sencillos* (*Simple Verses*). He had earlier published a collection of poems, *Ismaelillo* (1882), about his son, and after his death another collection of his poetry was published as *Versos libres* (*Free Verses*). In 1891, however, he stopped writing poetry and journalism, gave up his diplomatic posts, and turned his full attention to the struggle for Cuban independence.

In the 1880's Martí had distanced himself from the two generals, Máximo Gómez and Antonio Maceo, most involved in raising forces to invade Cuba to free it from Spain, fearing they would institute military rule on the island. He believed that an independent Cuba would have to be a democratic republic under civilian rule. He later reconciled with the generals and began working with the various proindependence groups in Cuban exile communities, eventually succeeding in unifying them in 1892 into the Cuban Revolutionary Party, of which he became the leader.

Over the next three years, he made visits to the Cuban communities in Florida, notably in Tampa and Key

Martí's Long Residence in the United States

The day before he died, José Martí wrote a letter warning against the designs of the United States on Cuba and describing the United States as a monster. Left-wing commentators focus on this description, arguing that Martí became increasingly anti-American over the years. Other commentators dispute this claim, maintaining that during his long stay in the United States Martí continually expressed mixed views on the country.

While he lived in the United States, Martí expressed a wide range of attitudes to it, from wonder at the construction of the Brooklyn Bridge to shock at the anarchist bombings at Haymarket Square in 1886 and from a celebration of its many poets to disapproval of its treatment of African Americans, Indians, and Chinese immigrants. Martí made himself a commentator on American life, mostly for his Latin American compatriots, and it may be that the complexity of his responses to what he saw in the United States reflects not only the complexities of his own views but also the complexities of the country he was observing.

West, and began publishing *Patria*, the organ of the Cuban Revolutionary Party. He also met with Gómez and Maceo in various locations in the Caribbean, and early in 1895 he and Gómez issued the Montecristi Manifesto in the Dominican Republic. The uprising against Spanish rule began in February that year, and Martí landed in Cuba to join it in April. He was shot and killed in a skirmish at Dos Ríos on May 19 after ignoring orders from General Gómez to stay away from the front lines.

SIGNIFICANCE

After his death, Martí became a Cuban national hero, claimed by all sides in Cuba's various political conflicts. In the first half of the twentieth century, he was known as the Apostle and the Martyr of Cuban Independence, seen as almost saintly and commemorated with various statues. Hailed by Fidel Castro as the inspiration for Castro's 1959 revolution, Martí continued to be honored in Castro's Cuba but as an anti-imperialist, anti-American revolutionary. At the same time, the anti-Castro Cuban community in the United States continued to revere Martí, using his name for their radio station and calling him a defender of liberal democracy and human rights.

In the 1990's, some American academics began to see him as a promoter of transnationalism and Latin Americanism in opposition to what they termed American imperialism. Other scholars pointed to Martí's complexity and elusiveness, noting that in his large body of works could be found praise for the ingenuity, industriousness, and democratic traditions of the United States, as well as criticism of its emphasis on the accumulation of wealth, its political corruption, and its expansionism. Most agreed, however, that he had perceptive things to say about life in nineteenth-century America.

Martí perhaps became best known to an English-speaking audience through his association with the popular song, "Guantanamera," which is based in part on poetry from his *Versos sencillos*.

Sheldon Goldfarb

FURTHER READING

Abel, Christopher, and Nissa Torrents. *José Martí, Revolutionary Democrat*. London: Athlone Press, 1986. Collection of articles looking at such things as Martí's situation in the United States and his views on class struggle.

Gray, Richard Butler. *José Martí, Cuban Patriot*. Gainesville: University of Florida Press, 1962. Includes a brief biography and an examination of Martí's ideas.

Kirk, John M. *José Martí, Mentor of the Cuban Nation*. Tampa: University Presses of Florida, 1983. Includes a brief biography, followed by analysis of Martí's ideas. Aims at neutrality and has been criticized by both left and right.

López, Alfred J. *José Martí and the Future of Cuban Nationalisms*. Gainesville: University Press of Florida, 2006. Sophisticated analysis of the complexities of Martí's character and thought.

Montero, Oscar. *José Martí: An Introduction*. New York: Palgrave Macmillan, 2004. Study of various aspects of Martí's journalism, including his writing on Coney Island, on women, and on race.

Ronning, C. Neale. *José Martí and the Emigré Colony in Key West: Leadership and State Formation*. New York: Praeger, 1990. Detailed study of Martí's role in organizing and uniting the Cuban exile groups in Key West.

Turton, Peter. *José Martí: Architect of Cuba's Freedom*. London: Zed Books, 1986. Provides detailed biographical information. Marred by repeated criticisms of Martí for not being a Marxist.

See also: Ignacio Manuel Altamirano; Julio Arce; Tomás Estrada Palma; Eugenio María de Hostos.

RICKY MARTIN

Puerto Rican-born singer and actor

A versatile musical artist who has performed on recordings, the concert stage, Broadway, and in television and films, Martin arguably was the the world's leading Puerto Rican performer in the late 1990's. Before crossing over to mainstream pop music, he was very successful throughout most Spanish-speaking countries in the Western hemisphere.

Latino heritage: Puerto Rican
Born: December 24, 1971; San Juan, Puerto Rico
Also known as: Enrique José Martín Morales IV; Kiki
Areas of achievement: Music; radio and television; gay and lesbian issues

Ricky Martin. (AP Photo)

EARLY LIFE

Ricky Martin was born Enrique José Martín Morales IV on December 24, 1971, in San Juan, Puerto Rico. His father and namesake is a psychologist, and his mother, Nereida Morales, is an accountant. They were divorced when Martin was very young. Although the only child of that marriage, he has several half-siblings. Martin took singing and dancing lessons as a child and began acting at the age of eight in Spanish-language television commercials. At the age of twelve, he became a member of the popular Latino boy band Menudo, and he adopted the stage name "Ricky Martin" while touring with that group. Following his stint with Menudo, he finished high school in Puerto Rico and then moved to New York City.

LIFE'S WORK

Looking to establish an adult career, Martin moved to Mexico City in 1992 and was cast in a daytime serial called *Alcanzar una estrella* (*Reach for a Star*). The previous year, he had released his first Spanish-language solo album. In 1993, he released a second Spanish-language album and began appearing in a Los Angeles-based television series called *Getting By*. It was on the

air very briefly. That same year, Martin won the *Billboard* Video Award for Best New Latin Artist and Mexico's Heraldo Award for best actor for his role in the film version of his Mexican daytime drama.

The next year, Martin was cast in the long-running American soap opera *General Hospital* as singing bartender Miguel Morez. In 1998, he came to widespread attention singing "La copa de la vida" ("The Cup of Life") at the World Cup soccer championships. The following year, Martin successfully crossed over into the mainstream American pop market with his performance of "La copa de la vida" at the Grammy Awards. This appearance introduced Martin to American audiences; he already was well-known to fans of Latin music through his Spanish-language albums as well as for his onstage charisma.

As a performer, Martin is known for his sex appeal, including tight clothing and suggestive dance moves. In 1999, he released his first English-language album, which was self-titled. It featured the single "Livin' la Vida Loca," which became a breakout hit worldwide. His subsequent albums in English and Spanish performed well but could not match the success of *Ricky Martin*; they produced singles such as "Shake Your Bon Bon," "She's All I Ever Had," "Tal vez," and "She Bangs."

Martin's fame and highly sexualized onstage persona led to intense media speculation about his personal life. In 2000, television host Barbara Walters asked him in an interview whether he was gay, a question he declined to answer. In 2008, he became the father of twin boys, Matteo and Valentino, who were born to a surrogate mother. Although Martin was romantically linked for many years with a female television personality, he announced in 2010 that he is gay. Later that year, he released a memoir titled *Me*.

SIGNIFICANCE

Martin's crossover to the American market considerably increased the visibility of Latino musicians at the end of the twentieth century. His success helped pave the way for such singers as Enrique Iglesias, Jennifer Lopez, and Marc Anthony. He has received numerous awards, including the Ritmo Latino Music Awards for Male Pop Artist of the Year, Album of the Year, and Video of the Year; Best Selling Latin Artist at the World Music Awards; Latin Pop Album of the Year at the *Billboard* Latin Music Awards; and a Grammy for Best Latin Pop Performance. Martin also appeared on Broadway in 1994 in the long-running musical *Les Miserables* (1980). As one of Puerto Rico's most famous citizens, he became an official spokesman for tourism to his native land. His Ricky Martin Foundation, established in 2000, targets social problems such as child labor and human trafficking. For his charitable work, he has been honored by the Congressional Hispanic Caucus Institute and received *Billboard's* Spirit of Hope Award.

Roy Liebman

FURTHER READING

Duncan, Patricia J. *Ricky Martin: La Vida Loca*. New York: Grand Central, 1999. A fairly brief and lavishly illustrated book intended for fans.

Martin, Ricky. *Me*. New York: New American Library, 2010. An intimate and revelatory memoir about Martin's career, struggles, and relationships.

_____. "Ricky Martin on Coming Out and Coming into His Own." Interview by Nkesa Mumbi Moody. The Associated Press, November 3, 2010. Martin discusses his decision to publicly reveal his sexual orientation and how he was influenced by factors such as the media and Latin American culture.

Sheldon, Harvey. "Ricky Martin." In *The History of Afro-Cuban Latin American Music: Singers, Musicians, Composers*. Charleston, S.C.: BookSurge, 2010. Discusses Martin's career in Latin music and his crossover success.

See also: Mariah Carey; Gloria Estefan; Jennifer Lopez; Jon Secada; Selena; Jaci Velasquez.

Menudo

Ricky Martin became a member of the Latino boy band Menudo (a Spanish slang term for small or diminutive) at the age of twelve and performed with the group from 1984 to 1989. At the time he joined, he was Menudo's youngest member, and he remains its most famous alumnus. The band was founded by Edgardo Diaz in Puerto Rico in the late 1970's and remained active off and on, with ever-changing membership, until 2009. Like many of the boy bands of that era, Menudo was put together to attract young female fans. When band members began to look too mature, younger boys would take their places. Martin was one such replacement, becoming a member of the group after he had auditioned three times. Because he was small for his age, he was able to remain with Menudo for several years.

Reportedly rehearsing up to sixteen hours a day, the group recorded many albums and toured extensively throughout the world while singing in Spanish, English, and Portuguese. Not only did this experience give Martin valuable experience and discipline, but it also made him a wealthy teenager. Although at least one former Menudo member openly complained that the band's management had exploited its youthful members, Martin has expressed no such extreme feelings. He has said, however, that boys' creativity was stifled, particularly when it came to writing their own songs.

ANTONIO JOSÉ MARTÍNEZ

American religious leader

Martínez was a popular administrator of a parish in Taos, New Mexico Territory, a priest and educator who worked mostly independently of his diocese. However, after a series of conflicts with a bishop who had been appointed his superior, he was excommunicated from the church.

Latino heritage: Mexican

Born: January 7, 1793; Santa Rosa de Abiquiú, northern New Mexico, New Spain (now New Mexico)

Died: July 27, 1867; Taos, New Mexico Territory (now New Mexico)

Also known as: Antonio José Martín

Areas of achievement: Religion and theology

EARLY LIFE

Antonio José Martínez (mahr-TEE-nehz) was born on January 7, 1793, in Santa Rosa de Abiquiú in what is now New Mexico. In 1804, when he was eleven years old, the Martín family—as they originally were known—moved to Taos, which was the third largest settlement in the New Mexico territory at the time. When the family moved, they they changed their name to Martínez.

At age eighteen, Martínez married Maria de la Luz, who died giving birth to their first child, also named Maria de la Luz. After this tragedy, Martínez thought about becoming a priest. He wrote to the bishop of Durango, and in 1817, he entered the seminary. Martínez excelled as a student and was ordained a priest five years later. While he was away, his young daughter died. He returned to New Mexico, served in a few parishes in Santa Fe, then went back to Taos, where he became known as Padre Martínez.

LIFE'S WORK

During Martínez's lifetime, there were vast stretches of open land in what is now the states of California, Nevada, Utah, and parts of Colorado, Arizona, New Mexico, Texas, and Wyoming. These areas were sparsely occupied by a mixture of Spanish, Mexican, and Indian peoples. At the time of Martínez's birth in 1797, the area was a colony of Spain. After the Mexican War of Independence (1810-1821), the territory was governed by Mexico, and it was not until after the Mexican-American War and the Treaty of Hidalgo in 1848 that the area was brought under the government of the United States. By the time Martínez died in 1867, New Mexico had yet to become an official state of the United States (1912).

Franciscan friars had come from Spain during the colonial period, starting in the 1500's. These friars worked with the native people, and by the 1600's, the New Mexicans had built churches and developed their own religious and indigenous art. However, when the area came under the control of the Mexican government, all Spanish citizens were expelled, including the

---

Death Comes for the Archbishop

Willa Cather's 1927 novel *Death Comes for the Archbishop* concerns the problems the Catholic Church faced when New Mexico became a part of the United States. It is based on the life of Jean-Baptiste Lamy, the bishop who excommunicated Antonio José Martínez. Martínez is depicted in the novel as self-serving, disorderly, gluttonous, and dismissive of the authority of Rome or his bishop. He tells the bishop, "If you try to introduce European civilization here and change our old ways, . . . I foretell an early death for you." Although Cather depicts him as dishonest, Martínez was devoted to the Indians. He took upon himself their education and their spiritual guidance in the days when native-born priests were few and their bishops were remote and of little help. In one incident in the novel, Martínez's character promises that he will intercede on behalf of seven Indians if they deed their lands to him. The Indians cede their land but are hanged anyway. The bishop in the story, a Frenchman like Lamy, is unfamiliar with the culture of the people he leads and unsure how to deal with Martínez. Ultimately, Martínez is excommunicated.

---

friars. This left only twelve native-born Mexican priests to serve this vast area; Martínez was one of them. The diocesan center was in Durango, fifteen hundred miles away from Santa Fe, with no transportation except horses and mules. Many of the churches were neglected and fell into ruin. A group of laypeople known as *penitentes* took on the duties of the absent priests. This group would later be problematic for the future diocese.

It was in this atmosphere that Martínez began his life as a pastor in Taos. He opened a school for boys and girls with the idea of preparing the boys for the seminary. Because he needed books for the school, he bought a printing press and set about producing his own textbooks, catechisms, and missals. Since his superior was far away, he became independent and began to build up his own realm of authority. Martínez was popular and revered in the parish. People celebrated his birthday. He soon had a small library. Martínez was a close friend of Bishop Zubiría, his superior in Durango, who had empowered him to give the sacrament of confirmation, a power normally reserved for bishops.

Like most New Mexicans, Martínez opposed any authority that came from the United States. However, by 1851, the border between the United States and Mexico had been established and a new bishop appointed for the Santa Fe area. This was Bishop Jean-Baptiste Lamy, a Frenchman who had a different mind-set than the native-born Martínez. A culture clash ensued. Because communications were so slow, even Bishop Zubiría in Durango did not at first accept the new appointment.

As time went on, Lamy became aware of scandals in the Taos parish. Martínez had fathered children with a married woman. Lamy insisted that all parishes collect tithes from their parishioners, but Martínez refused, claiming that the natives were too poor to pay. When Martínez wrote to the bishop asking for a helper priest, Lamy sent Father Damasco Taladrid, a Spaniard who looked down on Mexicans, to replace Martínez as pastor of Taos. Martínez said that he had been tricked by the bishop, and the friction between Martínez and Taladrid grew. Finally, Martínez set himself up in a private oratorio and conducted services there. When Lamy ordered him not to do this, Martínez continued anyway, which forced Lamy to excommunicate him. Still, Martínez did not back down. He protested the decree and quoted church law, saying that excommunication had to be preceded by a certain number of warnings in order for it to be valid. Lamy tried to suppress the Penitente Brotherhood, but Martínez had been given faculties as chaplain of the Brotherhood by

Zubiría, a task he kept for himself and did not share with Taladrid.

Throughout his years at Taos, Martínez allegedly became active in several minor rebellions against the United States government. He is reported to have been active in the 1847 insurrection in which New Mexicans along with Pueblo, Apache, Comanche, and Kiowa natives fought against the American occupation of northern New Mexico. At the time of his death in 1867, the New Mexico Territorial Legislative Council formally proclaimed Martínez as "The Honor of His Homeland," and in July, 2006, a life-sized statue was erected in the center of the Taos Plaza in his honor.

SIGNIFICANCE

Martínez lived at a time of crossroads and conflict in Mexican American history. The story of his life affords a brief look into the lives of the people of the time. These were people who were caught between Spain, Mexico, and the westward expansion of the United States. Martínez took up his duties in good faith, but forces beyond his control changed his plans.

Win Whelan

FURTHER READING

Horgan, Paul. *Lamy of Santa Fe: His Life and Times.* New York: Farrar, Straus and Giroux, 1975. The book is principally about Lamy but includes many references to Martínez.

Lavender, David. *The Southwest.* New York: Harper & Row, 1980. Recounts the history of Martínez and his efforts to defend the Indians and natives of the Santa Fe area.

Lucero, Donald. "Padre Antonio José Martínez." In *The Adobe Kingdom: New Mexico, 1598-1958, as Experienced by the Families of Lucero de Godoy y Baca.* 2d ed. Santa Fe, N. Mex.: Sunstone Press, 2009. Brief section on Martínez detailing his life and his influence on the New Mexico Territory.

Mares, E. A. *I Returned and Saw Under the Sun: Padre Martínez of Taos, a Play.* Albuquerque: University of New Mexico Press, 1989. A one-man play in which Martínez returns from the dead to defend himself against the accusations that have been lodged against him.

Peterson, Iver. "Priest Willa Cather Assailed Finds a Defender." *The New York Times,* June 29, 1985. This brief article reviews Mares's play and compares the man he finds there with Willa Cather's depiction of him in *Death Comes for the Archbishop.*

See also: Elfego Baca; Fray Angélico Chávez; José Policarpo Rodríguez.

DENNIS MARTÍNEZ

Nicaraguan-born baseball player

Martínez became the first Nicaraguan-born Major League Baseball player when he was signed to the Baltimore Orioles in 1973. By the end of his career, he had racked up the most wins of any Latin American pitcher in major league history, winning 245 games, while losing 193.

Latino heritage: Nicaraguan
Born: May 14, 1955; Granada, Nicaragua
Also known as: José Dennis Martínez Emilia; El Presidente
Area of achievement: Baseball

EARLY LIFE

On May 14, 1955, José Dennis Martínez Emilia, better known as Dennis Martínez (DEHN-ihs mahr-TEE-nehz), was born in Granada, Nicaragua, where he also attended high school. The Baltimore Orioles signed Martínez as a free agent when he was an eighteen-year-old amateur athlete, thus making him the first Nicaraguan-born player in Major League Baseball.

LIFE'S WORK

Martínez's major league debut with the Orioles came on September 14, 1976. Because it was late in the season, he only appeared in four games, but his 2.60 earned run average (ERA) hinted at future success for the slim right-hander nicknamed "El Presidente." In 1977, Martínez pitched in forty-games, winning fourteen and losing seven, the second-best winning percentage of any of Baltimore's fourteen pitchers that season. Martínez's success continued the next year, as his win-loss record was 16-11, with a 3.52 ERA. In 1979, Martínez pitched 292 innings, the most in his twenty-four-year career. Although his ERA was a respectable 3.66, he lost one more game than he won (15-16). However, he did win his game against the California Angels in the 1979 American League play-offs, but the Pittsburgh Pirates shelled him in his only two innings of that year's World Series, which the Orioles lost.

The 1980 season was a poor one for Martínez. Slowed by injuries, he pitched only ninety-nine innings, the fourth-lowest total of his career. Martínez rebounded in 1981, however, pitching 179 innings with a win-loss record of 14-5 and a 3.32 ERA. He finished fifth in the voting for the Cy Young Award, given to the league's top pitcher, and ranked twenty-third in the balloting for the league's Most Valuable Player.

Martínez had another strong year in 1982, pitching 252 innings with a win loss record of 16-11. His ERA, however, ballooned to 4.21, which signaled an impending decline. Martínez also struggled with alcohol addiction, and during the next three seasons his average win-loss record was 8-12, with an ERA of 5.23. In 1983, the Orioles won the World Series, but Martínez's win-loss record was 7-16, with a 5.53 ERA, and he did not even appear in that year's postseason games.

Martínez's career seemed over, and in 1986, after pitching in just four games with a 6.75 ERA, the Orioles traded him to the Montreal Expos of the National League. This change rejuvenated Martínez, and from 1987 to 1993, he won an average of 60 percent of the games in which he played. For three consecutive years, 1990-1992, he made the National League All-Star Team, and in 1991 he finished fifth in the voting for the National League Cy Young Award. That year, he had a solid 2.39 ERA and pitched five shutouts, two more than in any other year of his career. The highlight of that season, and perhaps Martínez's career, was his perfect game against the Los Angeles Dodgers, in which no batter reached base, on July 28, 1991. He was the first Latin American player in Major League Baseball history to pitch a perfect game.

Martínez's next two years were also exemplary, as he won thirty-one games, while losing twenty. The 1992 season marked his third appearance on the All-Star Team. After an excellent 1993 season, in which he won 62 percent of his games, Martínez, despite being thirty-eight years old, had become a valuable commodity on the free-agent market. The Cleveland Indians signed him to a $4.5 million dollar contract, $1.2 million more than he had made in any previous season.

Over the next three years, Martínez's win-loss record was 32-17, with a 3.58 ERA. He made the American League All-Star Team in the 1994 season, and in

Dennis Martínez. (AP Photo)

1995, he helped the Indians to the World Series with wins over Boston and Seattle in the American League play-offs. Martínez pitched well (3.48 ERA) against the Atlanta Braves in the 1995 Series, but the Indians lost in six games.

The 1996 season brought the final decline for Martínez's professional career. His win-loss record was 9-6, but he pitched just 112 innings. Again a free agent, the Seattle Mariners picked him up in February, 1997, but released him seven weeks into the season after his win-loss record was 1-5 with a 7.71 ERA. Martínez was not done yet, however. At the age of forty-three, the Atlanta Braves signed him for one more season. Although he only pitched ninety-one innings that year, Martínez did have a win for three innings of work in the National League play-offs against the San Diego Padres.

SIGNIFICANCE

While Dennis Martínez may never be elected to Major League Baseball's Hall of Fame, in 2002, the Baltimore Orioles enshrined him in the team's hall of fame, and his fellow Nicaraguans renamed the baseball stadium in Managua after him. He overcame his struggle with alcohol, and as of 2010 was one of only nine Major League pitchers with one hundred wins in both leagues. He also racked up the most wins of any Latin American pitcher in major league history. His Dennis Martínez Foundation supports needy children in Nicaragua.

John E. Thorburn, Jr.

FURTHER READING

Coffey, Michael, and Bill James. "El Presidente: Dennis Martínez." In *Twenty-seven Men Out: Baseball's Perfect Games*. Updated ed. New York: Atria Books, 2005. Describes Martínez's 1991 shut-out against the Dodgers and places it within the context of other players who pitched "perfect games."

Fordin, Spencer. "Notes: Martínez Sharing His knowledge." February 25, 2006. http://baltimore.orioles. mlb.com/news/article.jsp?ymd=20060225&content_ id=1322491&vkey=spt2006news&fext=.jsp&c_ id=bal. This article, from the official Web site of the Baltimore Orioles, provides a brief overview of Martínez's career and his attempts to obtain a job as a roving pitching instructor for the Orioles.

Freedman, Lew H. *Latino Baseball Legends: An Encyclopedia*. Santa Barbara, Calif.: Greenwood Press, 2010. Includes a lengthy entry on Martínez.

O'Brien, Richard, and Kostya Kennedy. "Nicaragua's Number One Export." *Sports Illustrated*, June 30, 1997, 20. A profile of Martínez and an overview of his career in baseball.

Washburn, Gary. "'El Presidente' Happy in New Job: Former Orioles Star Coaching Pitchers at Camp." February 20, 2005. http://baltimore.orioles.mlb. com/news/article.jsp?ymd=20050220&content_ id=946722&vkey=news_bal&fext=.jsp&c_id=bal. This article, from the official Web site of the Baltimore Orioles, reports on Martínez's new job as a spring training pitching instructor for this team.

See also: Joaquín Andújar; Willie Hernández; Luis Tiant; Fernando Valenzuela.

ELIZABETH MARTÍNEZ

American activist, feminist, and writer

Martínez wrote several books and articles on human rights and social justice. Focused on issues of race and ethnicity, her works urge people of color, especially women, not only to unite to combat racial oppression but also to preserve the history of Chicano people. She is best known for her book 500 Years of Chicano History in Pictures *(1991).*

Latino heritage: Mexican

Born: December 12, 1925; Washington, D.C.

Also known as: Elizabeth Sutherland Martínez; Betita Martínez; Elizabeth Sutherland

Areas of achievement: Activism; women's rights; literature

EARLY LIFE

Elizabeth Martínez (mahr-TEE-nehz) was born in 1925 to Manuel Guillermo Martínez and Ruth Phillips. While Martínez remembered experiencing discrimination as a child, she never attributed discrimination to her parent's interracial marriage. She felt her father's prominent secretarial position at the Mexican embassy was the reason her parents' relationship did not cause problems for her family. However, when she was five years old and segregation was still in effect in Washington, D.C., Martínez remembers being sent to the back of the bus after boarding with her father. In addition, she remembers feeling isolated in a mostly white public school and other children being forbidden to play with her because her father was Mexican. The combination of firsthand discrimination and her father's experiences during the Mexican Revolution no doubt influenced Martínez's future as a civil rights activist.

In 1946, Martínez graduated from Swarthmore College with an English degree. Motivated by the atrocities of World War II, she went to work at the United Nations after graduation. Working as a researcher in the Department of Trusteeship in Non-Self-Governing Territories, she began to see a connection between colonialism and racism. In a foiled effort to leak negative information about the effects of colonialism to a progressive delegation in the United Nations, Martínez lost her job as a researcher.

During this same time and after a brief marriage to Leonard Berman, Martínez met and married author Hans Koning. In 1954, she gave birth to their daughter, Tessa Koning Martínez.

LIFE'S WORK

After losing her job at the United Nations, Martínez went to work as an editor at Simon & Schuster and *The Nation*. In the early 1960's, her activism in the Civil Rights movement increased and she joined the Student Nonviolent Coordinating Committee (SNCC). Inspired by the passion and work of this group, Martínez published her first book, *The Movement* (1963), through Simon & Schuster. Outraged by the bombing of a Birmingham, Alabama, church in 1963 that resulted in the deaths of four girls, Martínez quit her job at Simon & Schuster to dedicate her time organizing for the SNCC. In 1964, she went to Mississippi for the Freedom Summer project. During this time, she directed the New York SNCC office and published a book called *Letters from Mississippi* (1965), a collection of letters that volunteers in Mississippi had written home.

Martínez was sent to California to represent the SNCC at the United Farm Workers march in 1965. Having previously worked in the African American Civil Rights movement, this was her first time working with individuals who shared her ancestry, which influenced her decision to focus her organizing efforts on the Chicano movement.

By 1968, Martínez was living in New Mexico, where she helped found and edit *El grito del norte,* a newspaper dedicated to the Chicano land movement. While in New Mexico in 1973, she also helped found and direct the Chicano Communications Center, an organization dedicated to teaching Chicanos about their history as well as contemporary issues.

In 1976, Martínez published *450 Years of Chicano History in Pictures*, which would later be reprinted as *500 Years of Chicano History in Pictures*. The book's association with the socialist movement made it difficult for her to work in New Mexico. As a result, she relocated in 1976 to California, where she taught women's and ethnic studies at California State University, joined the women-led Democratic Workers Party, and unsuccessfully ran for governor in 1982.

Martínez founded the Institute for Multi-Racial Justice in 1997 and edited a newsletter, *Shades of Power,* that was dedicated to uniting people of color. Her dedication and work in social justice, race

relations, and feminism made her a nominee for the activist group 1,000 Women for the Nobel Peace Prize in 2005. In 2008, Martínez published *500 Years of Chicana Women's History*, a pictorial documentation of Chicana women.

SIGNIFICANCE

In *500 Years of Chicano History in Pictures* and *500 Years of Chicana Women's History*, Martínez not only documents Chicano history but also reflects on the revolutionary struggle for equal rights in America. These books as well as her other works stress the need for people of color to build alliances with each other in order to overthrow oppression. Furthermore, Martínez's work has contributed to an increased exploration of women's roles in social justice movements and the absence of Chicana voices in feminism.

Erin E. Parrish

FURTHER READING

Martínez, Elizabeth. *500 Years of Chicana Women's History*. New Brunswick, N.J.: Ruetgers University Press, 2008. Demonstrates Martínez's passion for feminism and the Chicano movement as well as her dedication to teaching the revolutionary history of the Chicano people.

_____. "History Makes Us, We Make History." In *Feminist Memoir Project: Voices from Women's Liberation*, edited by Rachel Blau DuPlessis and Ann Snitow. New York: Three Rivers Press, 1998. In this essay, Martínez recalls pivotal points in her life that contributed to her passion for feminism and social justice. The chapter includes biographical information as well as Martínez's poetry.

_____. *Voices of Feminism Oral History Project: Elizabeth (Betita) Martínez*. Interview by Loretta Ross. Northampton, Mass.: Sophia Smith Collection, Smith College, 2006. Part of an oral history project, this transcribed interview with Martínez is an in-depth look at her life.

See also: César Chávez; Corky Gonzáles; Reies López Tijerina; Helena María Viramontes.

MEL MARTÍNEZ

Cuban-born politician and lawyer

During the early twenty-first century, Martínez served as a U.S. senator, chairman of the Republican National Committee, and secretary of the Department of Housing and Urban Development.

Latino heritage: Cuban
Born: October 23, 1946; Sagua La Grande, Cuba
Also known as: Melquíades Rafael Martínez Ruiz
Areas of achievement: Government and politics; law

EARLY LIFE

Melquíades Rafael Martínez Ruiz (mehl-KEE-ah-dehs mahr-TEE-nehz) was born into a large middle-class family near the northern coast of Cuba. His father, Melquíades C. Martínez, was a hard-working veterinarian who charged his customers according to their ability to pay. As a child, Martínez worked with his father as well as at his uncle's dairy farm and his grandfather's soda factory. The family was devoutly Catholic, and Martínez would remain committed to the religion. When

Mel Martínez. (AP Photo)

Fidel Castro took over the Cuban government in 1959, the Martínez family opposed the new regime. When the government instituted anti-religious policies and closed Martínez's Catholic school, he was openly defiant, resulting in threats that his parents took seriously.

In 1962, when Martínez was sixteen years old, he was one of more than fourteen thousand children taken to the United States as part of a Catholic humanitarian project called Operation Peter Pan. Martínez first stayed in two youth facilities, then lived with English-speaking foster families. In his autobiography, Martínez highly praises the families' hospitality and kindness. Although he entered the country without any knowledge of English, he was not given any special training in English, and he wrote in his memoirs that he felt overwhelmed and alienated. By the time he was reunited with his biological family in 1966, he was fluent in English and able to help the other family members adapt to new circumstances.

Influenced by his father's emphasis on the value of education, Martínez was an excellent student. In 1967, he was awarded an associate's degree from Orlando Junior College, and he then majored in international affairs at Florida State University. While taking an anthropology course during his senior year, he met an Anglo student, Kitty Tindal, whom he married in 1970. After completing his B.A., he entered the law school of the university, from which he graduated with a juris doctorate in 1973.

LIFE'S WORK

After earning his license to practice law, Martínez began working as a trial attorney for an established law firm in Orlando. Within a few years, he became a partner in the firm, where he stayed for more than a decade. During his twenty-five year career, he actively participated in a variety of civil and business organizations. Among other positions, he served as the vice president of the board of Catholic Charities of the Orlando Diocese. He also served as chairman of the Orlando Housing Authority and as president of the Orlando Utilities Commission.

Martínez was elected to his first elective office, Orange County chairman, in 1988. When he ran for lieutenant governor of Florida in 1994, he finished fifth in the Republican primary, receiving less than 10 percent of the vote. In the presidential election of 2000,

Cuban Americans and the Republican Party

Since the 1960's, most Latinos in the United States have strongly identified with the Democratic Party. The overwhelming majority of Cuban Americans, in contrast, have remained loyal to the Republican Party, primarily because they have agreed with the Republicans' strong opposition to communism and the Fidel Castro regime. In addition, about 85 percent of Cuban Americans classify themselves as "white," and their average family incomes and educational levels both tend to be significantly higher than those of other Latino groups. A significant percentage of Cuban Americans, nevertheless, have supported social policies more liberal than those of most Republicans.

By the end of the 2000's, Cuban Americans were becoming increasingly diverse in their political opinions. Their anger at the Democratic Party because of the Bay of Pigs fiasco (1961) and the Elián González controversy (2000) were gradually diminishing. In the presidential election of 2004, about 68 percent of Cuban Americans supported the Republican candidate, compared with 78 percent in 1988. When Democrat Barack Obama ran against Republican John McCain in 2008, Obama received about 38 percent of the Cuban American vote; among those age forty-five or younger, 51 percent voted for him. In 2009, when the Obama administration announced a loosening of travel restrictions to Cuba, 67 percent of Cuban Americans indicated that they approved of the change.

Martínez was co-chairman of George W. Bush's campaign in Florida, and he proved to be a highly successful fund-raiser. That year, he also was one of Florida's twenty-five Electoral College voters. From 2001 to 2003, Martínez was a member of President Bush's cabinet as the nation's secretary of housing and urban development, and in this capacity, he was a strong defender of public housing for poor people. During this period, he was also an ex-officio member of the President's Advisory Commission on Education Excellence for Hispanic Americans.

In 2003, Martínez resigned from his cabinet post in order to run for the U.S. Senate, and the following year he prevailed in a close election, becoming the first Cuban American to serve as a senator. In November, 2006, he became the first Latino to serve as chairman of the Republican National Committee. Some conservatives objected to his selection, primarily because of his nuanced positions on immigration policy. Commentators suggested that Republican leaders made the choice in order to improve the party's image among Latino voters.

In the Senate, Martínez's policies were moderately conservative. For example, he unambiguously indicated his moral opposition to abortions, even in cases of rape or incest, but he also said that he did not favor criminal prosecutions for those involved in the practice, even if the Supreme Court were to rule that abortion was not a constitutional right. He spoke out against federal legislation to expand civil rights protections to gays and lesbians and opposed same-sex marriage, even favoring a constitutional amendment to define marriage as a relationship between one man and one woman. However, he employed two openly gay men in his Senate campaign of 2004.

In economic policy, Martínez generally was a supporter of free trade, low taxes, and fewer regulations on business. On education, he approved of the No Child Left Behind Act, particularly its emphasis on standardized testing. He also endorsed English-only education and advocated the expansion of school vouchers for private schools. One major area in which Martínez disagreed with most Republicans was his opposition to ceilings in medical malpractice awards. In foreign relations, he usually defended Bush's policies, although he advocated closure of the Guantanamo Bay detainment camp. Despite his generally conservative views on constitutional interpretation, he voted in 2009 to confirm President Barack Obama's nomination of Sonia Sotomayor to the Supreme Court.

Because of his Latino background, Martínez's views on immigration attracted considerable attention. In his 2004 campaign, he stated his opposition to amnesty for illegal immigrants, but he also insisted that it was necessary to provide a path to citizenship for law-abiding persons who were residing illegally in the country. He helped to design the Comprehensive Immigration Reform Bill of 2006, which many Republicans denounced as an amnesty program. His disagreement with most Republicans on the issue was a source of considerable distress to him,

Despite his reputation for honesty and integrity, Martínez faced a potentially serious scandal. In August, 2006, the Citizens for Responsibility and Ethics in Washington filled a complaint alleging that the Martínez campaign had illegally accepted more than $600,000 from the Bacardi beverage company, which had solicited funds in ways that violated the Federal Election Campaign Act. An audit by the Federal Election Commission found that the campaign had accepted

$313,235 that exceeded legal donation limits from 186 contributors. In October, 2008, the Martínez campaign agreed to pay $99,000 in fines.

In the presidential election of 2008, Martínez endorsed the Republican nominee, John McCain, and he was disappointed by the Democratic victories of that year. A few months after the election, he resigned from the Senate, effective September 9, 2009. In a press conference, he explained that his decision was motivated by a desire return to private business and to have more time with his family. He then became a lobbyist and partner at the international firm DLA Piper, and he was later named chairman of JP Morgan Chase Bank's operations in Florida, Mexico, the Caribbean, and Central America.

SIGNIFICANCE

After immigrating to the United States as a teenager without financial means and without any knowledge of English, Martínez advanced to become a successful lawyer, the first Cuban American senator, and the first Latino chairperson of the Republican National Committee. His impressive career demonstrated the extent to which Cuban Americans were becoming an entrenched part of the U.S. mainstream.

Thomas Tandy Lewis

FURTHER READING

Eckstein, Susan. *The Immigrant Divide: How Cuban Americans Changed the U.S. and their Homeland.* New York: Taylor and Francis, 2009. Historical analysis of the cultural, economic, and political adaptation of the immigrants from Cuba, and their impact on both U.S. and Cuban societies.

Foglesong, Richard. *Immigrant Prince: Mel Martínez and the American Dream.* Gainesville: University Press of Florida, 2011. A scholarly and readable biography by a well-recognized historian.

Marcovitz, Hal. *Cuban Americans.* Philadelphia: Mason Crest, 2009. A concise introduction to Americans of Cuban ancestry, including biographies of Martínez and six other outstanding individuals—written primarily for young adults.

Martínez, Mel. *A Sense of Belonging: One Man's Pursuit of the American Dream.* New York: Three Rivers Press, 2008. Memoirs with very interesting discussions of his early life in Cuba, his immigration to the United States, and his assimilation into U.S. society.

See also: Henry G. Cisneros; Robert Martinez; Bill Richardson; Ileana Ros-Lehtinen.

NARCISO MARTÍNEZ

Mexican-born musician

A first-generation pioneer in the rousing instrumental dance music known as conjunto, Martínez, an accomplished accordionist, introduced this regional style to an international audience through hundreds of pre-World War II recordings that in the Tejano revival of the 1980's were recognized as classics of the genre.

Latino heritage: Mexican
Born: October 29, 1911; Reynosa, Tamaulipas, Mexico
Died: June 5, 1992; San Benito, Texas
Area of achievement: Music

EARLY LIFE

Narciso Martínez (nahr-SEE-soh mahr-TEE-nehz) came from humble roots. He was born in the rural village of Reynosa on the east coast of Mexico along the Rio Grande. His parents, migrant farmworkers, immigrated to the United States the year he was born. Narciso grew up largely in the tiny town of La Paloma, outside Brownsville in south Texas. Because of the peripatetic life of migrant workers, Martínez attended school sporadically, more often working the fields alongside his family. At gatherings of families, however, Martínez listened attentively and was enthralled by the vibrant dance music of small ensembles of instrumentalists, called *conjuntos.* These ensembles would play lively, often improvised, music that drew on the bold rhythms and brassy melodies of Mexican music, as well as on the European dance rhythms familiar to German, Czech, and Polish immigrants who were also part of the Texas rural culture. Martínez was particularly drawn to the button accordion. Like most aspiring Latino musicians in 1920's rural Texas, Martínez was self-taught. He watched accomplished adults (in his case, an older brother) and patiently worked his way through the dance repertoire, teaching himself rhythmic pacing and fingering.

By the early 1930's, now married with children and living in Bishop, Texas, Martínez was determined to make a living as a musician, taking advantage of opportunities to play dance halls and wedding receptions, social clubs, and even fandangos in private homes. In 1935, he met and began playing with Santiago Almeida, a guitarist with a flair for the *bajo sexto*, a demanding twelve-string Mexican guitar. The two collaborated with a drummer to create the sound combination that would over the next decade come to define *conjunto* music.

LIFE'S WORK

For the next several years, Martínez earned a regional reputation for both his accomplished playing and his energetic performances; he was known as "El Huracan del Valle," or the "Rio Grande Valley Hurricane." Martínez did not read music, but he would hear a melody that he liked and work out the instrumentation on his own. He taught himself a wide repertoire of Mexican folk music, as well as European dances, such as boleros, polkas, waltzes, mazurkas, and tarantellas, whatever his working-class dance hall audience would enjoy. He made little money because his audiences, largely migrant farmworkers at the height of the Depression, had little to give. At the suggestion of a Brownsville store owner who heard him play at a dance hall, Martínez went to San Antonio to seek a recording contract.

Fortuitously, Martínez's rise to area prominence coincided with the growing interest by major East Coast recording companies in capturing the folk music of the Tex-Mex culture, much as a decade earlier the same companies had "discovered" African American roots music as part of the jazz explosion and in the 1950's they would "discover" Native American music. In 1936, Martínez made his first recording for RCA/Bluebird, "La Chicharronera," whose title was a Spanish word meaning "pork burnt to a crackling crisp." This infectious, rippling instrumental featured Martínez's fierce staccato playing. The recording sold well, and Martínez became the sound of the *conjunto* musical style. Over the next decade, he proved ferociously productive, and he and his ensemble would record dozens of songs in a single marathon recording session. These recordings, without elaborate studio dubbing, captured the improvisational energy of live *conjunto*. His records sold, despite establishment critics who dismissed the accordion-based music as low brow and accordionists as competent minor talents.

Martínez saw little financial remuneration from royalties. He was most often paid by the session, and given his remarkable stamina, a single studio fee of

Narciso Martínez. (© Philip Gould/Corbis)

$150 could net the recording company dozens of saleable tracks. Even at the height of his recording career in the mid-1940's, Martínez received $35 for each completed track. Because Martínez was not confident in his range as a singer, these landmark recordings were largely dance instrumentals, many of them revamped traditional folk melodies set to the irresistible cadences and shimmering rapid-fire melody lines of Martínez's accordion. These recordings sold well in the American Southwest, where they were given heavy rotation on rural radio stations that also broadcast to northern Mexico, but Martínez's music also found its way to juke boxes and radio stations in San Francisco, with its burgeoning Hispanic market; Chicago, with its long interest in American folk music; and New York, a ready market for cutting-edge roots music.

During the 1940's, Martínez toured tirelessly and was a much sought-after studio musician, often providing accompaniment for vocal work. Martínez recorded Cajun-style music under the name Louisiana Pete and polkas under the name Polski Kwartet. However, by the 1950's, with the advent of rock and roll, commercial interest in *conjunto* significantly dropped. Recording labels were more interested in vocal-centered Tejano

Martínez and Tejano Music

Seldom does an entire musical genre have a single inventor. Jazz, blues, folk—the signature sound of each is the collaborative effort of many artists. However, this is not the case with the genre of Tejano music known as *conjunto*. Much like the acoustic guitar in folk music or the bass in the blues or the trumpet in be bop jazz, the boxy diatonic button accordion became the defining instrument in *conjunto*. Pulsing, irrepressible, and animated, the accordion establishes an accessible melody and then riffs improvised variations designed to keep dance halls energized: This signature sound is the invention of Narciso Martínez.

Certainly *conjunto* existed before Martínez picked up the accordion in the mid-1920's. However, the accordion music he learned was far different from the accordion music he would play. The accordion, as he learned it, had long emphasized the left hand, providing the ensemble its grounding in chord progressions, its rhythmic foundation. This style of playing gave the accordion a heavy feel and seldom allowed it to dominate the sonic effect. Martínez, however, shifted the focus to the right hand, his fingers flying furiously over the keys to command the melody, leaving the bass foundation to the guitar, played by his longtime partner Santiago Almeida. This technique gave the accordion, and by extension the ensemble, a brighter, louder, crisper, kinetic feel that quickly became the dominant sound of *conjunto* music. Although Martínez often acknowledged that he was not the most technically proficient nor the flashiest among the accordionists on the circuit in Texas, he was certainly the most popular, and given the range of his recording career, his sound and his style of playing, at once spirited and robust, came to define the genre during its most popular period between the world wars.

genres. In addition, as newer instrumentalists emerged, Martínez and his generation of musicians, despite essentially inventing *conjunto*, became increasingly marginalized. Martínez himself continued to play when he could find play-for-pay gigs, often at birthday and anniversary parties. By the early 1970's, however, despite being past sixty, Martínez turned to manual labor to make a living, initially as a field hand in Florida and then as a truck driver in Ohio. In 1971, he finally found long-term employment on the maintenance crew at the Gladys Porter Zoo, a newly opened botanical park in downtown Brownsville.

With the revival of interest in Tejano music in the 1980's, most prominently associated with the crossover success late in the decade of the singer Selena, Martínez's landmark recordings were rediscovered. In 1983, he was awarded a National Heritage Fellowship Award by the National Endowment for the Arts in recognition of his contribution to the nation's musical heritage. In 1989, an album of new material earned Martínez his first Grammy Award nomination for Best Mexican American Recording. Martínez continued to tour the Southwest until he was diagnosed with leukemia in late 1991. He died on June 5, 1992, in San Benito, Texas. A decade later, he was among the second class of musicians inducted into the National Conjunto Hall of Fame.

SIGNIFICANCE

It is tempting to reshape the life of Narciso Martínez into some cautionary tale about original visionary artists who are often relegated to the margins by a crass consumer culture that cannot appreciate innovative creativity. Although Martínez did lapse into obscurity for a time, he never stopped playing, his signature keyboard work attracting fans to an instrument dismissed as a working-class amusement. Drawn to the energy and vibrancy of the dance hall music of the migrant workers with whom he grew up, Martínez developed the raw elements of that music—the heavy rhythms, the brassy accordion riffs, the guitar counterpoint, and the raucous feel of improvisation—into a distinct musical genre that, in turn, came to define both the emerging Latino culture of the Tex-Mex borderlands and, like blues and jazz, American multiculturalism itself.

Joseph Dewey

FURTHER READING

Hartman, Gary. *The History of Texas Music.* College Station: Texas A & M Press, 2008. Comprehensive account of the genres of immigrant music in Texas that represented Mexican and European influences. Includes information about *conjunto* and Martínez. Illustrated.

Martínez, Narciso. *Father of the Texas Mexican Conjunto.* El Cerrito, Calif: Arhoolie Records, 1993. This compact disc provides an indispensable introduction to the *conjunto* sound that Martínez pioneered. A compilation of the best of Martínez's work, it includes comprehensive discography and helpful liner notes.

Peña, Manuel. *The Texas-Mexican Conjunto: History of a Working-Class Music*. Austin: University of Texas Press, 1985. Considered the seminal work on the genre and its roots by a respected commentator on the genre, himself a 2010 inductee in the Conjunto Hall of Fame.

See also: Flaco Jiménez; Lydia Mendoza; Selena.

PEDRO MARTINEZ

Dominican baseball player

Martinez was one of the most dominant starting pitchers of the 1990's and 2000's, winning three Cy Young Awards and leading the National League in earned run average and opponents' batting average five times. In 2004, he helped the long-suffering Boston Red Sox win their first World Series in eighty-six years.

Latino heritage: Dominican
Born: October 25, 1971; Manoguayabo, Dominican Republic
Also known as: Pedro Jaime Martinez; Petey
Area of achievement: Baseball

EARLY LIFE

Pedro Jaime Martinez (mahr-TEE-nehz) was born on October 25, 1971, in Manoguayabo, Dominican Republic, the son of Paulino Martinez, a school janitor, and Leopoldina Martinez, a homemaker. His parents divorced when he was nine years old. Martinez grew up in poverty with three brothers and two sisters. Two of his brothers, Ramon and Jesus, later pitched professionally.

Martinez, a righthanded pitcher, was signed by the Los Angeles Dodgers organization in June, 1988, at age sixteen. After two seasons in the Dominican Summer League, he spent 1990 with the Dodgers' minor-league team in Great Falls, Montana. *The Sporting News* named Martinez minor league player of the year in 1991, when he won a combined eighteen decisions with Bakersfield of the California League, San Antonio of the Texas League, and Albuquerque, New Mexico, of the Pacific Coast League.

Martinez spent most of 1992 at Albuquerque, striking out 124 batters in 125 1/3 innings. He made his major-league debut on September 24, in relief against the Cincinnati Reds. Martinez thrived in the Dodgers bullpen in 1993 with a 10-5 record and 2.61 earned run average (ERA), pacing National League relievers with 10 victories and recording 119 strikeouts in 107 innings. The Dodgers traded him to the Montreal Expos in November, 1993.

LIFE'S WORK

With Montreal, Martinez flourished as a starter under manager Felipe Alou and pitching coach Joe Kerrigan. He compiled a 11-5 record with a 3.42 ERA and 142 strikeouts in 144 2/3 innings in 1994. Although he led the National League with 11 hit batters in 1995, Martinez won fourteen of twenty-four decisions with a 3.51 ERA and 174 strikeouts in 194 2/3 innings. On June 3, he pitched nine perfect innings against the San Diego Padres but was relieved after allowing a leadoff double in the tenth inning.

Martinez encountered difficulty controlling his fastball early in his career, but Kerrigan taught him a four-seam fastball that was easier to control. Martinez

Pedro Martinez. (AP Photo)

also mastered the curveball and changeup. His remarkable repertoire, improved control, and ability to change speeds enhanced his effectiveness. He pitched inside in an era when pitchers typically worked around the outside corner of the strike zone. Opposing teams often have accused him of deliberately throwing at hitters, and he was involved in several on-field altercations.

In 1996, Martinez made the National League (NL) All-Star team and finished with a 13-10 record and 3.70 ERA., striking out 222 batters in 216 2/3 innings. He continued to improve in 1997, finishing with a 17-8 record. He led the major leagues with a superb 1.90 ERA and 13 complete games and struck out 305 batters, becoming the first ERA leader with more than 300 strikeouts since Steve Carlton in 1972. Opponents batted a major-league-low .184 against him. No right-hander since Walter Johnson in 1912 had registered an ERA under 2.00 and more than 300 strikeouts in the same season. Martinez became the first Dominican to win the NL Cy Young Award and earned *The Sporting News* NL pitcher of the year honors.

In November, 1997, Montreal traded Martinez to the Boston Red Sox. Martinez signed a $75 million, six-year contract, making him baseball's highest-paid player. Numerous Latino fans came to Fenway Park with Dominican flags when Martinez pitched. Martinez posted a 19-7 record in 1998, along with a 2.89 ERA and 251 strikeouts, lifting Boston into the play-offs. An American League (AL) All-Star selection, he placed second in the Cy Young Award balloting. He captured Boston's lone victory in the AL Division Series against the Cleveland Indians.

Martinez won the AL Cy Young Award unanimously in 1999 with a sparkling 23-4 record, leading the league in victories, ERA (2.07), and strikeouts (313). His average of 13.2 strikeouts per 9 innings set a major-league record. Martinez started the All-Star game at Fenway Park that season, striking out five of the six batters he faced and earning most valuable player (MVP) honors. Boston earned a wild-card berth in the play-offs. Despite a sore back, Martinez threw six hitless relief innings against Cleveland to win the decisive game five of the AL Division Series. Next, he held the New York Yankees scoreless for seven innings in game three for Boston's sole triumph in the AL Championship Series. He finished second in the AL MVP award balloting and earned *The Sporting News* AL pitcher of the year honors.

In 2000, Martinez compiled 18 wins and 6 losses with an AL-leading 1.74 ERA. He paced the AL with 284 strikeouts and four shutouts and became the first AL pitcher to win successive unanimous Cy Young Awards. After an injury-plagued 2001 season, Martinez strengthened his shoulder with extensive weight training. He returned in 2002 and went 20-4 with a 2.26 ERA, 239 strikeouts, and just 40 walks in 199 1/3 innings, finishing second in the AL Cy Young Award balloting.

In 2003, Martinez led AL starting pitchers with a 2.22 ERA, ranked second with 206 strikeouts in just 186.2 innings, and won fourteen of eighteen decisions, helping the Red Sox capture the AL wild card. He won a game in the AL Division Series against the Oakland Athletics but lost game three of the AL Championship Series to New York. Martinez squandered a three-run lead in the eighth inning of decisive game seven at Yankee Stadium.

The 2004 season brought Martinez his first World Series appearance. Martinez finished the season 16-8 with a 3.90 ERA and 227 strikeouts in 217 innings, helping potent-hitting Boston reach the play-offs. Martinez beat the Anaheim Angels (now known as the Los Angeles Angels) in game two of the AL Division Series,

---

Martinez vs. Zimmer

The altercation between Boston Red Sox pitcher Pedro Martinez and New York Yankees bench coach Don Zimmer occurred in the fourth inning of game three of the 2003 American League Championship Series at Fenway Park. Bitter rivals, Boston and New York had split the first two games at Yankee Stadium.

Martinez faced fellow pitching ace Roger Clemens. After Yankee Hideki Matsui broke a 2-2 tie with a fourth-inning double, Martinez threw behind Karim Garcia's head. The umpire ruled the ball had hit Garcia in the back and awarded him first base. On Alfonso Soriano's grounder, Garcia slid hard past second base and knocked down Boston infielder Todd Walker. Garcia and Walker shoved each other. Both teams emerged from their dugouts, with Zimmer especially vocal.

Later that inning, Clemens threw a pitch that nearly hit Red Sox slugger Manny Ramirez. When both benches cleared again, Zimmer lunged at Martinez. Martinez sidestepped, grabbed Zimmer by the head with both hands, and threw the elderly coach to the ground, where he cut the bridge of his nose. Nobody was ejected.

Right-fielder Garcia cut his hand in a ninth-inning skirmish involving a Boston groundskeeper in New York's bullpen. The Yankees triumphed, 4-1, and went on to win the series in seven games.

then lost to rival New York, 3-1, in game two of the AL Championship Series. However, the Red Sox overcame a 3-0 deficit in the AL Championship series (the first time that feat had been accomplished) to reach the World Series. Martinez shut out the St. Louis Cardinals for seven innings while striking out six batters in a 4-1 triumph in game three, and the Red Sox went on to win their first World Series in eighty-six years.

In December, 2004, the New York Mets signed Martinez to a $52 million, four-year contract. Martinez went 15-8 with a 2.82 ERA and 208 strikeouts in 217 innings the next season. His final three seasons with the Mets, however, were riddled with injuries, resulting in only 17 victories.

In July, 2009, the Philadelphia Phillies signed Martinez as a free agent. Martinez won five of six decisions to help the Phillies capture the NL East title and hurled seven shutout innings against the Los Angeles Dodgers in the NL Championship Series but lost his two World Series contests to New York.

SIGNIFICANCE

In eighteen major league seasons, Martinez appeared in 476 games, recording 219 wins and 100 losses, a 2.93 ERA, 3,154 strikeouts, and only 760 walks in 2,827 innings. The three-time All-Star intimidated hitters with an array of pitches and was one of the few pitchers to win Cy Young Awards in both the American and National leagues. He compiled a 4-0 record and 2.84 ERA in four Division Series and a 1-2 record in four Championship Series and two World Series. Martinez led his league in ERA and opponents' batting average five times, strikeouts three times, winning percentage twice, and victories, complete games, and shutouts once each. He paced his contemporaries in career winning percentage, ERA, strikeout-to-walk ratio, hits per 9 innings, and opponents' batting average.

David L. Porter

FURTHER READING

Gallagher, Jim. *Pedro Martinez*. Hockessin, Del.: Mitchell Lane, 1999. Excellent young-adult biography highlighting Martinez's earlier life.

Golenbock, Peter. *Red Sox Nation: An Unexpurgated History of the Boston Red Sox*. Chicago: Triumph Books, 2005. Comprehensive oral history of the storied team from writers' and players' perspectives.

Olin, Stewart, and Stephen King. *Faithful*. New York: Scribner, 2004. Colorfully describes the roller-coaster ride of the 2004 Red Sox, highlighting their heated rivalry with the Yankees. Includes analysis of games Martinez started.

Shaughnessy, Dan. *Reversing the Curse*. Boston: Houghton Mifflin, 2005. Profiles the 2004 Red Sox, including Martinez. Describes Boston's dramatic AL Championship Series comeback and first World Series title in 86 years.

Stout, Glenn, and Richard A. Johnson. *Red Sox Century*. Boston: Houghton Mifflin, 2005. Exhaustively researched history of the Red Sox through 2004. Contends Martinez's 1999 season might have been the best ever by a major-league pitcher.

Verducci, Tom. "Duel Exhaust." *Sports Illustrated* 94, no. 24 (June 11, 2001). Compares Martinez with former great major-league pitchers.

_____. "The Power of Pedro." *Sports Illustrated* 92, no. 13 (March 27, 2000). Profiles how Martinez became the most dominant pitcher in the late 1990's.

See also: Juan Marichal; David Ortiz; Manny Ramirez; Johan Santana; Luis Tiant; Fernando Valenzuela.

ROBERT MARTINEZ

American politician

In 1987, Martinez became only the second Republican governor elected in the state of Florida since Reconstruction. The state's first elected governor of Hispanic descent and the first Catholic, Martinez was a two-term mayor of Tampa from 1979 to 1986.

Latino heritage: Spanish

Born: December 25, 1934; Tampa, Florida

Also known as: Bob Martinez

Area of achievement: Government and politics

EARLY LIFE

A third-generation American whose four grandparents immigrated from Spain to work in the cigar factories of West Tampa, Robert Martinez (mahr-TEE-nehz) was the only child of Sarafin Martinez, a waiter, and his wife, Ida Carreno Martinez, a garment worker. Martinez met his future wife, Mary Jane Marino, at Jefferson High School in Tampa. The couple married in 1954, while Martinez was a sophomore at Tampa University. At the time, he also played semiprofessional baseball.

After graduating from Tampa University with a bachelor of science degree in social science, Martinez became a teacher. Seeking a higher salary to support his wife and two young children, he left his job in teaching in 1962 to move his family to the University of Illinois, where Martinez pursued a master's degree in labor and industrial relations. Upon earning that degree in 1965, he returned with his family to Tampa and to teaching. He soon became involved in the local teachers' union, the Hillsborough Classroom Teachers Association (HCTA), and was named its executive director in 1966.

Martinez supported the Florida Education Association's call for a statewide teacher strike in 1968, a strike designed to agitate for better funding and bargaining rights. Martinez held his position as union leader until 1975. He took over his uncle's family business, the Café Sevilla restaurant in West Tampa, but stayed active in public life. Florida governor Reubin Askew named Martinez vice chairman of the Southwest Florida Water Management District. Management of Florida's natural resources became an important issue in Martinez's nascent political career. While he operated his restaurant, the Café Sevilla became an important meeting place for local politicians. In late 1978, Martinez decided to run for mayor of Tampa, a nonpartisan office. He became the first mayor of Tampa to have a Hispanic last name.

LIFE'S WORK

When he took office as Tampa's mayor, Martinez inherited a city in need of improvements. During his tenure, he spearheaded the development of one of America's first refuse-to-energy plants, oversaw the construction of a performing arts center and a convention center, revamped the city's zoo, led the restoration of Tampa's 1915 city hall, and annexed thousands of acres of undeveloped land for the city. Martinez slashed property taxes and invested money in improvements to the city's infrastructure. He gained national recognition as a trendsetter among mayors of small American cities.

While in his second term as mayor, Martinez attended a ceremony at the White House. He became acquainted with President Ronald Reagan, Vice President George H. W. Bush, and Florida entrepreneur and future governor Jeb Bush. Martinez changed his party affiliation from Democrat to Republican in 1983. The Tampa

Robert Martinez. (AP Photo)

mayor was chosen to speak at the Republican National Convention in 1984 and again in 1988.

Elected Florida's governor in 1987, Martinez was seen as a rising star in Republican politics. He was named conservationist of the year by the National Parks Conservation Association for his leadership in Preservation 2000, a program that allowed the state of Florida to buy and protect lands from development. Under Martinez, Florida became the first state to pass legislation on the management of solid waste. While his passion for conservation earned him supporters, other decisions during his administration were considerably less popular.

Martinez introduced a tax on services that would affect small businesses. Although the legislation was never enacted, it met with strong opposition inside and outside the state, and Martinez was forced to call for its defeat. He adopted a hard line on drugs, building more prisons and funding fewer drug treatment facilities. Martinez also took a strong stand against abortion and sex education, seeking to stop Miami's public schools from spending money on birth-control information. In 1990, Martinez sought to bring racketeering and obscenity charges against the rap group 2 Live Crew for its album *As Nasty as They Wanna Be* (1989).

Martinez's handling of the matter—including the arrests of the group's members—led to allegations of racism that helped tilt the 1991 election for governor to his opponent, Lawton Chiles.

After his governorship, Martinez was named by George H. W. Bush as the second director of the Office of National Drug Control Policy, or "drug czar," as the position came to be known. Martinez's tenure lasted only two years, as the office was plagued by disorganization and claims of a lack of experience on the part of Martinez and his staff.

SIGNIFICANCE

Martinez was an important player in the Republican Party in the late 1980's, early 1990's. As governor of Florida, Martinez was a valuable friend of the Reagan and Bush administrations and especially the Bush family, bringing future Florida governor Jeb Bush into his cabinet. A significant fund-raiser for the party and its nominees, Martinez left politics in the mid-1990's in order to pursue international business consulting in the United States and Latin America.

Randy L. Abbott

FURTHER READING

Garcia, John A. *Latino Politics in America: Community, Culture, and Interests*. Lanham, Md.: Rowman & Littlefield, 2003. Includes an overview of Martinez's career in the context of Latino politicians' growing visibility and influence.

Keil, R. "Bob Martinez: A Czar Is Born." *Mother Jones* 16, no. 4. (July/August, 1991): 42-43. Offers speculation as to how Martinez will perform as "drug czar."

Silva, Mark. "Early Challenges to Test Martinez." *The Miami Herald*, November 9, 1986, p. A1. Outlines the political challenges facing Martinez as the newly elected Republican governor of Florida.

Treaster, Joseph B. "New Drug Chief Turns to Softer Side of Issue." *The New York Times*, April 15, 1991, p. A12. Examines Martinez's approach to the drug crisis in his new role as "drug czar" in comparison with his record as Florida governor on the same issue.

See also: Toney Anaya; Jerry Apodaca; Joseph Marion Hernández; Manuel Luján, Jr.; Mel Martínez; Ileana Ros-Lehtinen.

VILMA SOCORRO MARTÍNEZ

American lawyer, activist, and ambassador

Martinez was the first female president of the Mexican American Legal Defense and Educational Fund (MALDEF) and has enjoyed an illustrious career as a Latino civil rights attorney, labor attorney, and the first female ambassador to Argentina.

Latino heritage: Mexican
Born: October 17, 1943; San Antonio, Texas
Also known as: Vilma Martínez
Areas of achievement: Law; activism; diplomacy

EARLY LIFE

Vilma Socorro Martínez (soh-KOH-roh mahr-TEE-nehz) was born to Salvador, a construction worker, and Marina Martínez in San Antonio, Texas, on October 17, 1943. She grew up in a Spanish-speaking household and did not learn English until she entered school. Her family served as a source of strength and support throughout her youth.

During Martínez's childhood, Texas was openly segregated. As a result, she faced blatant discrimination in many public and private institutions. In her youth, Martínez was denied entry into some public parks, and at movie theaters, she and other Mexican Americans were relegated to seats in the back. Throughout her schooling, she weathered insults from other children about her Mexican heritage. Martínez even experienced discrimination from her high school counselor, who encouraged her to go to a trade school rather than a university, even though she was an honors student.

At age fifteen, while still in high school, Martínez had the opportunity to volunteer at the law firm of Alonso Perales, a well-known Texas civil rights attorney, who became a role model for her. This internship, coupled with her experience of discrimination, influenced her decision to enter the law profession so that she might improve the lives of other Latinos.

LIFE'S WORK

In 1964, Martínez earned an undergraduate degree in political science from the University of Texas at Austin. At the suggestion of a professor, Martínez applied to

East Coast law schools in order to escape the discrimination she faced in Texas. She earned her L.L.B., a professional law degree, in 1967 from Columbia University School of Law.

Upon graduation, Martínez took a position with the National Association for the Advancement of Colored People (NAACP) Legal Defense Fund. In that capacity, she served as counsel for the petitioner in the landmark employment-discrimination case *Griggs v. Duke Power Company* (1971), which was heard before the U.S. Supreme Court, and informed former President Richard M. Nixon's Executive Order 11625, mandating nationwide affirmative action. In *Griggs v. Duke Power Company*, the Supreme Court ruled that employers could not use aptitude tests as the sole criterion for employment or advancement if those tests disproportionately affected minorities.

In 1970, Martínez took a position as an equal-opportunity counselor with the New York State Division of Human Rights. There, she was instrumental in drafting employee-rights legislation. After a year, she joined Cahill Gordon and Reindel, a prestigious New York City firm, where she specialized in labor law. During these early years of her career, Martínez married Stuart Singer, a fellow attorney, and they had two sons, Carlos and Ricardo.

After six years, Martínez had established a reputation as an excellent attorney and an advocate for underrepresented minorities. In 1973, at just twenty-nine

years old, she was offered the position of general counsel and president of the Mexican American Legal Defense and Educational Fund (MALDEF), a move that would define her career for the following nine years and make MALDEF one of the most powerful civil rights organizations in the country for years to come. At MALDEF, she litigated precedent-setting cases before the Supreme Court and established a fund-raising platform that allowed the organization to expand its client base in the years following her presidency.

Martínez's expertise was highly prized in the political realm. Between 1975 and 1981, she volunteered her consulting services to the U.S. Census Bureau, which subsequently added "Hispanic" as an ethnic category. This addition to the census helped reconfigure electoral districts and empower Latino voters. In 1976, California governor Jerry Brown invited Martínez to join the board of regents of the University of California, and she served as a board member and chairperson through 1990. From 1977 to 1981, she also served on an advisory board to President Jimmy Carter's administration reviewing ambassadorial appointments around the world.

In addition to her work on labor and civil rights issues, Martínez served as an adviser on many boards and committees, including President Bill Clinton's Advisory Committee for Trade Policy and Negotiations. She was appointed to the advisory boards of Columbia University School of Law and the Los Angeles Philharmonic Association. Martínez also served on the boards

Martínez and MALDEF

Vilma Socorro Martínez was the first female president of the Mexican American Legal Defense and Educational Fund (MALDEF) and the first woman in the nation to lead a civil rights organization. Under her leadership, MALDEF focused on fund-raising so that the organization could grow and expand in scope.

Martínez also brought Chicana issues out into the open by encouraging MALDEF to work beyond the male-dominated agendas. Within MALDEF, she instituted the Chicana Rights Project (CRP), which operated from 1974 through 1983 and was funded by the Ford Foundation. The CRP advocated on behalf of women on issues related to employment, education, immigration, housing, reproductive rights, and childcare.

During Martínez's presidency, she fought to include Mexican Americans in the Voting Rights Act. In spite of protests from the conservative groups and the National Association for the Advancement of Colored People

(NAACP), Martínez and MALDEF convinced Congress in 1975 to extend to Mexican Americans the protections and provisions guaranteed by the Voting Rights Act.

Under Martínez's leadership, MALDEF filed the *Plyler v. Doe* (1982) case, which challenged a Texas law that denied free public education to children of parents who lacked legal documentation. Martínez and fellow attorneys argued that children who grew up and lived in the United States for years were, in effect, American. In June, 1982, the court ruled that the Texas law was unconstitutional and that the state must extend free public education to children of undocumented immigrants.

By the time of Martínez's departure in 1982, MALDEF had established relationships with corporate sponsors and been awarded many grants. Martínez's leadership created a strong foundation for MALDEF, which eventually became one of the nation's largest nonprofit organizations.

of corporations such as Anheuser-Busch and Shell Oil Company.

In 1982, Martínez left MALDEF to become a partner with Munger, Tolles, and Olson, a well-known Los Angeles firm. She specialized in labor disputes and commercial litigation. While in Los Angeles, she was hired in 1994 by the Los Angeles Unified School District to fight Proposition 187, which sought to deny public education to children of undocumented immigrants. Martínez halted Proposition 187 at the state level, and after the intervention of MALDEF and other civil rights organizations, in 1998, the federal courts deemed nearly all of Proposition 187 unconstitutional.

On July 24, 2009, the U.S. Senate confirmed Martínez as the ambassador to Argentina. She was both the first woman and the first non-career ambassador appointed to the position.

SIGNIFICANCE

Committed to civil rights, Martínez used her legal training to create and promote legislation that would improve the lives of Latinos and other minorities, particularly in the areas of education, labor, and political participation. By serving as MALDEF's first female president and turning it into one of the most influential civil rights

organizations in the United States, Martínez proved herself to be a trailblazer for all women as well as Latinos.

Mary Christianakis

FURTHER READING

Flores, Lori A. "A Community of Limits and the Limits of Community: MALDEF's Chicana Rights Project, Empowering the 'Typical Chicana,' and the Question of Civil Rights, 1974-1983." *Journal of American Ethnic History* 27, no. 3 (July, 2008): 81-110. A detailed historical account of the Chicana Rights Project and Martínez's role in Chicana feminism.

Meier, Matt S., and Margo Guttierez. *The Mexican American Experience: An Encyclopedia*. Westport, Conn.: Greenwood Press, 2003. Martínez is profiled and her work with MALDEF is discussed in this useful reference work.

Telgen, Dian, and Jim Kamp, eds. *Latinas!: Women of Achievement*. Detroit, Mich.: Visible Ink Press, 1996. This volume documents the contributions of Latinas in the United States, including Martínez.

See also: Joaquín G. Avila; Norma V. Cantú; Dolores Huerta; Reies López Tijerina.

MARÍA MARTÍNEZ-CAÑAS

Cuban-born artist

Martínez-Cañas is an accomplished photographer and mixed-media artist. Her work—which employs innovative techniques—often reflects her Cuban heritage.

Latino heritage: Cuban
Born: May 19, 1960; Havana, Cuba
Area of achievement: Art

EARLY LIFE

María Martínez-Cañas (mahr-TEE-nehz-CAHN-yahs) was born in Havana, Cuba, on May 19, 1960. Her family left the country three months after her birth to escape Fidel Castro's Cuban Revolution. After a stop in Miami, Florida, they settled in 1964 in Puerto Rico, where she was raised. Encouraged in her interest in photography by her parents, Martínez-Cañas attended the Philadelphia College of Art, receiving a B.A. in photography in 1982. She then studied at the School of the Art Institute in Chicago and received her M.F.A. in 1984.

In 1983, Martínez-Cañas traveled to Spain as part of a foreign study class, and remained there afterward to travel widely. She returned to live in Spain in 1985 as a result of being awarded a Fulbright Hays grant. Her family's memories of Cuba and her experiences in Spain led her to develop iconographies in her photographic work that revolve around Cuban imagery and artifacts. Her first negatives that made use of Cuban maps were created in 1986 and printed the following year. In the autumn of that year, Martínez-Cañas moved to Miami, Florida, which became her home. In 1988, she received photography fellowships from the National Endowment for the Arts and the Cintas Foundation.

LIFE'S WORK

For much of her photographic career, Martínez-Cañas's work has reflected her identity and history. Whether the references are to her Cuban lineage, as seen in her use of Cuban maps, documents, and stamps, or to events in her family's experiences, her iconography often is personal. To explore these themes, she makes use of diverse techniques, both traditional and innovative. She creates negatives by drawing, cutting, and assembling collages of materials onto film-covered sheets of acetate. Throughout her career, she has invented new techniques, experimenting with multistep processes that made use of everything from scanners and computer software to sand-blasting, images of bacteria, and piles of dust.

Some of Martínez-Cañas's works are very large, possibly reflecting the influence of Latin American mural traditions. At the same time, her work frequently is characterized by a density of detail that invited close inspection. Although objects are identifiable in her prints, the relationship of one form to another often is obscured. Forms lose their representational moorings until the composition has an essentially abstract visual appeal.

One of Martínez-Cañas's largest compositions, *Años continuos* (1996), is a "photo sand-blasted" mural on glass measuring forty feet by forty feet. It was commissioned for the Miami International Airport. Divided into a series of panels, it made extensive use of map imagery, abstracted forms, and dense detailing. It also coincided with her involvement in public service and community outreach for the arts when she served on the Miami-Dade Art in Public Places Commission,

In the late 1990's, Martínez-Cañas explored new subjects and techniques. Inspired by botanical illustrations, she began a series of nature prints, with foliage and plants the main objects. These were produced using the photogram method that had been used in the nineteenth century for botanical prints. Photograms do not use cameras; rather, they are created by placing objects—in this case, plant materials—on light-sensitive paper, then exposing the collage to a light source. For these unique images, she employed diazo paper, which is traditionally used to make architectural blueprints.

In the early years of the twenty-first century, a new theme entered Martínez-Cañas's art when she began creating images that explored ideas of truth and falsehood and the ability of art to alter reality. For these prints she uses software programs to manipulate photographic images. By 2006, she also had begun creating mixed-media installation art.

Martínez-Cañas's art can be found in major museum collections, including the Museum of Modern Art in New York, the San Francisco Museum of Art,

and the Smithsonian American Art Museum. Her work has been exhibited in major art galleries throughout the United States. She has received numerous awards and taught and lectured at several colleges and universities.

SIGNIFICANCE

A daughter of Cuba's post-revolution diaspora, Martínez-Cañas has created imagery related to her culture that embodies a longing for identity in a land out of reach. For her, Cuba is almost a mythical land because she learned of it primarily through the memories and stories of her parents and through historical artifacts. Her work is admired for its strong compositions, technical experimentation and precision, and its graphical qualities. Although categorized as a photographer, her prints are inventive expansions on traditional photographic media and provide distinct, personal, and sophisticated examples of art produced by a United States artist steeped in Latin American culture and history.

Madeline Cirillo Archer

FURTHER READING

Kuspit, Donald. "Cuba of Her Mind: María Martínez-Cañas' Photographic Constructions." Los Angeles, Calif.: Iturralde Gallery, 1994. Catalog essay for exhibition "María Martínez-Cañas: Cronologias, 1990-1993." Kuspit analyzes Martínez-Cañas's work from the early 1990's, in particular the totem images through which she constructed memories of a Cuba she never saw. He identifies Wilfredo Lam as an important influence on her art.

Martínez-Cañas, María. "Historia rota (Broken History)." In *Remembering Cuba: Legacy of the Diaspora*, edited by Andrea O'Reilly Herrera. Austin: University of Texas Press, 2001. The artist discusses the influence of her Cuban birth and culture on her art.

Spring, Justin. "María Martínez-Cañas." *Artforum* 3 (November, 1999): 146. Spring discusses Martínez-Cañas's botanical prints in terms of technique and aesthetics.

Thall, Larry. "Visual Folktales of an Artist in Search of Her Homeland." *The Chicago Tribune*, May 3, 1991. Discusses the influence of Martínez-Cañas's Cuban heritage on her imagery and themes.

See also: Olga Albizu; Tony Labat.

NORMA MARTINEZ-ROGERS

American nurse and educator

A bilingual nurse, Martinez-Rogers is an advocate for the Latino nursing community and the elimination of healthcare disparities. She served as president of the National Association of Hispanic Nurses.

Latino heritage: Mexican

Born: 1943; San Antonio, Texas

Also known as: Norma Rogers

Areas of achievement: Medicine; education; social issues

EARLY LIFE

Norma Martinez-Rogers (NOR-mah mahr-TEEN-ehz RAH-jehrs) came from a poor background, growing up in the Alazan-Apache Courts, a public assistance housing project in San Antonio, Texas. Despite this challenge, her Mexican parents instilled in her a strong sense of education and a connection to community service. Martinez-Rogers was raised in a bilingual household in which both English and Spanish were spoken. She attended Ursuline Academy with her sisters, and in 1965 she received her bachelor of nursing degree from Incarnate Word College (now University of the Incarnate Word) in San Antonio. She subsequently obtained two master's degrees, one in counseling from St. Mary's University in 1968 and another in psychiatric/mental health nursing from the University of Texas Health Science Center in San Antonio in 1978.

LIFE'S WORK

Martinez-Rogers initially worked as a staff nurse at Santa Rosa Medical Center from 1965 to1968. She then became a case worker for Catholic Family and Children's Services (now the Catholic Charities of the Archdiocese of San Antonio, Inc.) from 1968 to 1970. In 1970, she accepted a position as a nurse coordinator for the University of Texas Health Science Center, which she held until 1972, when she began a four-year stint teaching through the Edgewood Independent School District in San Antonio.

Still wanting to play a greater role in her community, Martinez-Rogers returned to nursing, and she would practice this profession for more than thirty years. She worked at several hospitals in Texas, specializing in psychiatric nursing, and during this time she also directed several psychiatric nursing departments. From 1978

to 1987, Martinez-Rogers was an associate professor of the Department of Family Nursing at San Antonio College. She served in the U.S. Army during Operation Desert Storm at William Beaumont Army Medical Center in Fort Bliss, earning two U.S. Army Commendation Medals in 1987 and 1991 and one U.S. Army Achievement Medal in 1991 for her work.

Wanting to expand her nursing career in order to incorporate her Hispanic culture and strong ties to the community, Martinez-Rogers became the quality assurance coordinator and manager of the sexually transmitted diseases program at the Austin/Travis County Health and Human Services Department. She held this position from 1993 to 1995, and during this time she also completed a doctorate in cultural foundation in education from the University of Texas at Austin in 1995. She returned to academia as an instructor in the Department of Family Nursing at the University of Texas Health Science Center from 1995 to 1996. She

Norma Martinez-Rogers.
(courtesy of the UT Health Science Center San Antonio)

subsequently completed two postdoctoral fellowships at Indiana University School of Nursing, one in cultural aspects of learning (1996-1997) and one in research for community health (1997-1998).

Martinez-Rogers became an assistant professor at the University of Texas in 1999 and was promoted to associate professor and full clinical professor in 2005 and 2009, respectively. At the university she combined her nursing and cultural experience to create several programs for minority populations. Some examples of these programs include Juntos Podemos (Together We Can), a mentoring program for nursing students; Nueva Fronteras (New Frontiers), a support group for female prisoners returning to society; the Martinez Street Women's Center, an educational program for adolescent and adult females; and Avanzar (To Advance), a prenursing society.

In 2008, Martinez-Rogers was elected president of the National Association of Hispanic Nurses, an organization that aims to improve health care in the Hispanic community and serve the professional needs of Hispanic nurses and nursing students. Under Martinez-Rogers's leadership, the association began offering scholarships for bilingual and bicultural nursing students and raised awareness about the financial issues preventing Hispanic nurses from entry into the profession.

Martinez-Rogers has received numerous honors for her work. She was named National Hispanic Nurse of the Year by the National Association of Hispanic Nurses in 2004, was appointed an inaugural member of the Medicaid and CHIP Payment and Access Commission in 2010, and received the Diversity Health Care and Leadership Award from the Association of Healthcare Executives in 2010. She was elected a fellow of the American Academy of Nursing in 2006, one of only ten Latino nurses to receive this honor. In 2008 she began serving as a consultant for the Bexar County Ryan White Program in San Antonio, Texas, and she has been a member of the board of directors of the National Coalition of Ethnic Minority Nurses Association, the advisory board of the pharmaceutical company Pfzier, Inc., and the Department of Health and Human Services Nonprescription Drugs Advisory Committee.

Martinez-Rogers was married, and she and her husband had two sons, Sean and Scott, before her husband was killed in the Vietnam War.

SIGNIFICANCE

Martinez-Rogers overcame poverty to become a prominent nurse and an advocate for other Latinos in her profession. By some estimates, only about 1.7 percent of nurses are Latinos, and Martinez-Rogers has worked to increase this number. A native of San Antonio, she spent almost her entire career devoted to serving the community where she was raised. She also stayed true to her roots by fighting to reduce health and educational disparities among minorities, specifically Latinas.

Janet Ober Berman

FURTHER READING

Rogers, Norma, and Cantu, Adelita G. "The Nurse's Role in the Prevention of Cervical Cancer in Underserved and Minority Populations." *Journal of Community Health* 34, no. 2 (April, 2009): 135-143. Outlines the role of nurses in educating minority patients about the availability of vaccinations and other medical care.

Trapp, Doug. "Medicaid, CHIP Payments to Be Reviewed by New Federal Commission." *American Medical News*, January, 2010. http://www.ama-assn.org/amednews/2010/01/25/gvsc0125.htm. Explains how the new commission, of which Martinez-Rogers is a member, will determine if Medicaid patients receive equal access to care.

University of Texas Health Science Center. "Dr. Rogers to Lead National Association of Hispanic Nurses." August 14, 2008. http://www.uthscsa.edu/hscnews/singleformat.asp?newID=2835. Discusses Martinez-Rogers's plans for her presidency and her concerns about healthcare disparities among Latinos. Provides background information about her life and career.

See also: Martha Bernal; Teresa Bernardez; Richard Henry Carmona; Antonia Novello.

JORGE MAS CANOSA

Cuban-born entrepreneur and activist

*A Cuban refugee who rose from dishwasher to mul-
timillionaire businessman and political activist, Mas
Canosa is best known for his tireless advocacy of Cuban American interests in the United States and as one
of the most visible, vocal, and controversial opponents
of Fidel Castro's regime.*

Latino heritage: Cuban

Born: September 21, 1939; Santiago de Cuba, Oriente,
Cuba

Died: November 23, 1997; Miami, Florida

Areas of achievement: Business; activism

EARLY LIFE

Jorge Mas Canosa (mahs cah-NOH-sah) was born in
Santiago de Cuba, a mid-sized city in the southeast of
Cuba, to Ramon Mas Cayado, an army veterinarian, and
Josefa de Carmen Canosa Aguilera. Mas Canosa wrote
in his autobiography that he developed an interest in
politics as a young man and was involved in student
groups opposing the dictatorship of Fulgencio Batista.

Jorge Mas Canosa. (AP Photo)

Fearing for his safety, his parents sent him to Maxton,
North Carolina, where he studied at Presbyterian Junior
College. After his return to Cuba, Mas Canosa studied
law. He was living in Santiago in 1959 during Batista's
overthrow by Fidel Castro, and upon Castro's drift toward communism, found himself again in opposition to
the Cuban government. The Castro regime issued a war-
rant for Mas Canosa's arrest, and he was forced to flee
the island in 1960.

After his arrival in Miami, Mas Canosa worked a
series of low-paying jobs: stevedore, shoe salesman,
and milkman. He married his high school girlfriend,
Irma Santos, and eventually had three sons with her.
When the Central Intelligence Agency (CIA) came to
Miami seeking Cuban exiles to fight in an excursionary
force that would attempt to topple Castro's regime, Mas
Canosa volunteered, joining Brigade 2506, as the group
of volunteers came to be known. He did not participate
in the fight, serving on a decoy ship instead. The excur-
sion, later known as the Bay of Pigs, failed.

Following his return to the United States, Mas
Canosa enlisted in the U.S. Army, eventually graduating from Officer Training School at Fort Benning, Georgia, as a second lieutenant. After his service, he went to
work for a small construction firm and later purchased
the company, changing its name from Iglesias and Torres to Church and Tower of Florida. He built the firm
into a multimillion-dollar business with more than
four hundred employees and changed its name again,
to MasTec. The company provides construction and
telecommunications services to clients in business and
government. The success of MasTec also allowed Mas
Canosa to amass a large personal fortune, which he used
to finance his lobbying and political activities.

LIFE'S WORK

While Mas Canosa did not become an American citizen
until 1982 and never ran for public office, his lobbying
activities in the United States on behalf of the interests
of Cubans in exile and Cuban Americans began well before then and continued for the rest of his life. More than
any other individual, Mas Canosa was responsible for the
U.S. government's hardline stance in its Cuban foreign
policy, and he influenced the policies of presidents Ronald Reagan, George H. W. Bush, and Bill Clinton.

During the 1970's, Mas Canosa became known as
someone who could deliver the Cuban American vote

to politicians, making him a much-sought-after political ally. He hoped to create an organization that would focus and harness that influence for the betterment of Cuban exiles and Cuban Americans; eventually, in cooperation with Raul Masvidal, a fellow member of Brigade 2506, Mas Canosa became a founder and chairman of the Cuban American National Foundation (CANF) in 1981. Under his leadership, CANF spawned an array of political action committees (PACs), such as the Free Cuba PAC and the Cuban American Foundation, the primary lobbying arm of CANF.

The foundation also was successful at fund-raising, which increased its influence—as well as that of Mas Canosa—through generous donations to presidential and congressional candidates. One of CANF's greatest successes was the Cuban Democracy Act, signed into law in 1992, which prohibited the foreign subsidiaries of American companies from doing business with Cuba and prohibited travel to Cuba by U.S. citizens. Another triumph was the Helms-Burton Act of 1996, which prohibits foreign companies from engaging in any business with Cuba and penalizes them by denying their corporate leaders entry to the United States.

Under Mas Canosa, CANF also was instrumental in the founding of Radio Martí and TV Martí, which broadcast Spanish-language news and information to Cuba. During the 1970's, Mas Canosa began to study the possibility of a radio station based in the United States that would broadcast news and information to Cuba and sought the backing of legislators in Congress. With Ronald Reagan's election in 1980, Mas Canosa gained a powerful ally in his quest, and in 1985, Radio Martí began broadcasting, with TV Martí following in 1990. In 1986, Reagan appointed Mas Canosa chair of the advisory committee that now supervises both radio and television stations; as the chair, Mas Canosa wielded tremendous influence over the broadcasts' content.

During the 1990's, Mas Canosa's reputation as a petty tyrant and a grudge holder grew with his influence in Washington and Miami. Under his leadership, CANF became in effect his megaphone and cudgel, as he used the organization's funds and personnel to strong-arm his critics into submission. His detractors in the press found themselves the targets of investigations by the Immigration and Naturalization Service and other federal bureaus, as well as Miami city agencies. Journalists, media company owners, and others who failed to support his opinions wholeheartedly or who dared to offer alternative viewpoints received death threats, and in some

cases, their offices were firebombed and their families threatened. He was famously involved in a feud with the publishers of *The Miami Herald*, whose newspaper had accused him of fraud, even challenging one of the editors to a duel. Even Mas Canosa's colleague and cofounder of CANF, Masvidal, left the foundation in 1985 in a dispute with Mas Canosa over his authoritarian leadership style. Mas Canosa brushed off all criticism of his activities as the slurs of Castro's agents seeking to discredit him, calling his critics communists, traitors,

The Cuban American National Foundation After Mas Canosa

Jorge Mas Canosa served as chair of the Cuban American National Foundation (CANF) until his death in 1997. Under his leadership, the foundation was the preeminent Cuban American lobbying group in Washington, and wielded enormous influence over American foreign policy toward Cuba. In many instances, CANF members took an active and direct role in the crafting of legislation. CANF is a grant-giving organization as well as a lobbying group and sponsors an array of organizations that advance the interests of Cuban Americans, including Cuban refugee resettlement and scholarships for Cuban Americans through the Cuban Exodus Relief Fund. Additionally, the foundation has a prodigious publishing record, including an extensive numbered pamphlet series on various topics pertaining to Cuba and United States-Cuba relations. The foundation also published the collected speeches and position papers of Mas Canosa.

After Mas Canosa's death, CANF suffered from a leadership vacuum, as Mas Canosa's authoritarian style had left little room or opportunity for the mentoring of a new generation of leaders. The foundation splintered in 2001 when no agreement could be reached among the membership on its direction, with one breakaway group forming the rival Cuban Liberty Council. CANF has since adopted a far more conciliatory stance toward Cuba. In 2009, it issued a series of press releases arguing for strengthened ties between the United States and Cuba and an opening of trade barriers between the two countries. And in January, 2011, after President Barack Obama significantly eased travel restrictions to and from Cuba for religious organizations and educators and allowed non-family members to make remittances to Cubans for the encouragement of enterprise development, the foundation issued a press release in support of the new policy.

and racists. Whenever he drove anywhere in Miami, he rode in a bulletproof limousine, claiming that Castro's agents were trying to assassinate him.

Mas Canosa was widely considered to be a possible successor to Castro as president of Cuba, once the regime had been toppled. Under his direction, CANF created a new constitution and economic recovery plan for Cuba, and Mas Canosa often was addressed in public by his supporters as "Señor Presidente" (Mr. President), a title he did not reject. While he insisted that he had no definite plans to run for the presidency of Cuba, he also stated that he would not give up his right to run. However, any plans Mas Canosa might have had to run for Cuban office were derailed when he developed Paget's disease, a painful inflammation of the bones, then lung cancer. He died of complications from lung cancer and congestive heart failure in 1997.

SIGNIFICANCE

As the most vocal and persistent of Cuban exiles and the foremost advocate for the U.S. government's hardline stance on Cuba throughout the second half of the twentieth century, Mas Canosa secured a place in history. He is widely acknowledged not only as the primary influence on that stance but also as its architect. However, Mas Canosa's legacy is somewhat tarnished by his bellicosity, his combative approach to politics, and his dictatorial stance with regard to CANF.

Olivia Olivares

FURTHER READING

Bardach, Ann Louise. "Our Man in Miami." *The New Republic*, December 3, 1994. An excellent overview of Mas Canosa's life and works.

Eckstein, Susan. "The Personal Is Political: The Cuban Ethnic Electoral Policy Cycle." *Latin American Politics and Society* 51 (Spring, 2009): 119-148. An examination of attempts by CANF and other Cuban American organizations to influence politicians through campaign donations and promises of votes.

Haney, Patrick Jude, and Walt Vanderbush. *The Cuban Embargo: The Domestic Politics of an American Foreign Policy.* Pittsburgh, Pa.: University of Pittsburgh Press, 2005. A well-researched and well-written overview of the policies behind the American embargo of Cuba, describing in detail the players in the formation of those policies, including Mas Canosa and others in the Cuban American National Foundation.

Mas Canosa, Jorge. *Jorge Mas Canosa: A Life in Search of Freedom.* Miami, Fla.: Cuban American National Foundation, 1997. Mas Canosa's life, beliefs and struggle, in his own words in this collection of speeches. One of the few resources featuring Mas Canosa's words available in English.

Rieff, David. *The Exile: Cuba in the Heart of Miami.* New York: Simon & Schuster, 1994. An interesting examination of Cubans and Cuban Americans living in Miami, with particular attention to the divide between older Cuban "exiles" longing for the fall of Castro and the return home and younger Cuban Americans born in the United States with a thoroughly American sensibility.

Rohter, Larry. "A Rising Cuban-American Leader: Statesman to Some, Bully to Others." *The New York Times*, October 29, 1992. Part of a series on Mas Canosa, CANF, and life among Cuban exiles in Miami.

See also: Ángel Ramos; Lionel Sosa.

EDUARDO MATA

Mexican-born conductor and musician

Mata is best known for his tenure as conductor of the Dallas Symphony Orchestra and his formidable production of high-quality recordings that included an impressive array of Latin American symphonic works.

Latino heritage: Mexican
Born: September 5, 1942; Mexico City, Mexico
Died: January 4, 1995; Cuernavaca, Morelos, Mexico
Also known as: Jaime Eduardo Vladimiro Mata Asiaín; Eduardo Mata Asiaín

Area of achievement: Music

EARLY LIFE

Jaime Eduardo Vladimiro Mata Asiaín (MAH-tah) was the youngest of three children born to Federico Mata Sarmiento and Ana María Asiaín de Mata. His father served as head of finance in Oaxaca under Mexican president Miguel Alemán Valdés. Mata became enamored with music at an early age and began memorizing the family's collection of 78 rpm records. He also

Eduardo Mata. (AP Photo)

played guitar and sang with his siblings. Mata studied music casually with an uncle who encouraged formal music lessons and introduced him to classical works such as Edvard Grieg's *Piano Concerto*, as well as assorted sonatas by Ludwig van Beethoven. As a youth, Mata also became a regular fixture at performances of the Banda de Oaxaca and befriended its director, Amador Pérez Torres.

At age eleven, Mata entered the Conservatorio Nacional de Música de México, where he began studying theory with Francisco Moncada and Teodoro Campos Arce, piano with Amelia Torres de Espinosa, voice with Matilde Ladron de Guevara, and harmony with Carlos Jiménez Mabarak. His interest in modern composition led him to found El Grupo Berlioz with José Antonio Alcaraz, Salvador Reyes, Domingo Borrego, and Jesus Villaseñor. Between 1956 and 1959, the student group, encouraged by composer and conductor José Pablo Moncayo, performed their original works. Mata made his conducting debut at the group's first concert with his own composition, *Trío a Vaughan Williams* (1957), for clarinet, drums, and cello. Their second concert notably included a performance of Mata's *Cantata fúnebre* (1957)—an homage to composer Manuel Ponce—sung by a teenage Plácido Domingo.

When Carlos Chávez formed an independent composition workshop within the conservatory, Mata interviewed with the elder composer for a spot in the program. In 1960, Mata became one of seven students to gain admission to Chávez's studio. *Piano Sonata*, written in an atonal style, marks his transition to a more mature—if short-lived—compositional style. In 1964, Mata won a Koussevitzky Fellowship to study conducting with Max Rudolph and Erich Leinsdorf, and composition with Gunther Schuller at the Berkshire Center in Tanglewood, Massachusetts. At the opening concert of the Contemporary Music Festival at Tanglewood, Mata conducted Loren Rush's *Nexus 16*, a work that required Mata to imitate the second-hand sweep of a stopwatch—first with his left arm moving downward and then with his right moving upward.

LIFE'S WORK

Mata began his professional conducting career in 1965 with the Orquesta Sinfónica de Guadalajara (later renamed Filharmónica de Jalisco). The following year, he was appointed artistic director of the Orquesta Sinfónica (later Filharmónica) de la Universidad Nacional Autónoma de México (UNAM). In 1972, Mata left Mexico to become music director for the Phoenix Symphony Orchestra at Symphony Hall, the newly constructed cultural arm of Phoenix's massive convention center. As his conducting career grew, however, his compositional output shrank. In 1970, he completed *Improvisaciones no. 3* for wind and horns. The work contains recurring leitmotifs, dominant ninth chords, parallel chords, and other impressionistic devices in conjunction with extended techniques such as playing the highest audible pitch on the violin and pizzicato Bartók slaps in the high register while playing as fast as possible. Film scores for a romantic comedy, *Ya se quién eres (te he estado observando)* (1971) directed by José Agustin, and a drama, *El señor de Osanto* (1974) directed by Jaime Humberto Hermosillo, mark the end of his compositional output.

In 1977, the troubled Dallas Symphony Orchestra (DSO) lured Mata to Texas to take on the role of artistic director and resident conductor. Just three years before, Max Rudolph had resigned midway through his first and only season with the orchestra, and the organization suspended performances nearly one million dollars in debt. Mata's appointment drew some controversy based on his relatively limited experience in the United States; however, his tenure proved to be a golden age for the DSO, as he led the orchestra to international stature

---

Mata's Advocacy for Latin American Music

Eduardo Mata recognized the appeal, accessibility, and quality of Latin American symphonic works that were unfairly neglected in favor of Eurocentric fare. The inclusion of works by Latin American masters such as Carlos Chávez and Silvestre Revueltas played an important role in his revitalization of the Dallas Symphony Orchestra.

Mata produced more than seventy recordings of symphonic works in his lifetime and contributed significantly to the growing Latin American repertory. A complete set of Chávez's six symphonies recorded with the London Symphony Orchestra in 1982 represented the first digital recording of the Mexican maestro's music. More important, Mata embarked on a series with the Dorian label devoted to recording Latin American orchestral music with the Orquesta Sinfónica Simón Bolívar. Cut short by his untimely death, the series included works by Revueltas, Julián Orbon, Alberto Ginastera, and Antonio Estevez.

---

and worldwide acclaim. Mata's aggressive resuscitation spawned two Carnegie Hall performances, a Kennedy Center appearance, the orchestra's first European tour, three concerts in Mexico City, and three concerts in Singapore. His campaigning, combined with public enthusiasm for the revitalized organization, earned the orchestra a new home in 1989 at the Morton H. Meyerson Symphony Center. Designed by architect I. M. Pei and acoustician Russell Johnson, it set a benchmark for concert halls.

Moreover, during his first year in Dallas, Mata secured a recording contract with RCA and produced an album of works by Aaron Copland (including his 1936 *El salón México*), and a collaboration with pianist Tedd Joselson performing piano concerti by Sergei Prokofiev and Maurice Ravel. Between 1978 and 1993, Mata produced an impressive thirty-two recordings with the DSO and earned a Grammy nomination for his 1982 recording of *Don Juan* (1888), *Salome* (1905), and *Death and Transfiguration* (1889) by Richard Strauss.

In addition to selections from the traditional European and Russian symphonic fare, Mata embraced works by composers from the Americas. His dedication to Latin American composers such as Carlos Chávez, Silvestre Revueltas, and Julian Orbón introduced new and exciting rhythms to audiences and greatly expanded the orchestra's repertoire. Mata's symphonic

interpretations were well-studied readings that stayed true totempo with attention to rhythmic precision, instrumental balance, and melodic clarity. From subtle glances and nods to broad gestures, his conducting style revealed an array of successful communication techniques. Mata's reputation earned him myriad guest-conducting roles, recording opportunities, and artistic advisory responsibilities with leading performance organizations throughout the world, including the Baltimore Symphony Orchestra, the BBC Northern Symphony Orchestra, the London Sinfonietta and Chorus, the London Symphony Orchestra, the National Arts Centre Orchestra of Canada, the New Philharmonia Orchestra, the Opera Nacional de México, the Orquesta Sinfónica Simón Bolívar, the Orquesta Sinfónica Nacional de México, and the Solistas de México.

When Mata ended his sixteen-year run with the Dallas Symphony Orchestra in 1993—the longest tenure of any conductor in the orchestra's history—he was named conductor emeritus. Mata returned to his childhood home of Oaxaca with multiple goals in mind, including the establishment of a new music school and library, restoration of the Teatro Macedonio Alcalá, and promotion of modern Latin American compositions. On January 4, 1995, Mata, an instrument-rated pilot, boarded his Piper Aerostar at Cuernavaca Airport bound for Dallas. Upon takeoff, the aircraft suffered an engine failure and crashed. Both Mata and his companion, Maria Anaya, were killed.

SIGNIFICANCE

A well-regarded interpreter of music with high professional standards, Mata ranks among the most important and influential conductors of the twentieth century. He played a pivotal role in reviving the Dallas Symphony Orchestra, establishing the Morton H. Meyerson Symphony Center, and securing a world-class reputation for the organization. He actively promoted and premiered works of Latin American composers that were otherwise neglected, supported cultural growth in Mexico, and contributed significantly to the recorded legacy of Latin American symphonic music.

Gary Galván

FURTHER READING

Chism, Olin. "Crescendo of a Century: Symphony Celebrates One Hundred Years in Dallas, Ten in Meyerson." *The Dallas Morning News*, September 5, 1999. This retrospective on the Dallas

Symphony Orchestra notes Mata's importance to the organization.

"Eduardo Mata." In *UXL Hispanic American Biography*, edited by Sonia G. Benson, Rob Nagel, and Sharon Rose. Detroit, Mich.: UXL, 2003. Brief, informative biography describing Mata's life and music career.

Kozinn, Allan. "Eduardo Mata Is Dead at Fifty-two; Conducted Dallas Symphony." *The New York Times*, January 5, 1995. This obituary offers an overview of Mata's life and work, focusing on his years in Dallas.

See also: Justino Díaz; Lalo Schifrin; Claudio Spies.

HAROLD MEDINA

American federal judge, lawyer, and educator

A successful lawyer and respected legal scholar and educator, Medina became the first Latino federal judge when he was appointed to the U.S. District Court in 1947. During his tenure, he presided over several volatile cases of national significance, and he later served for more than twenty-five years as an appellate judge.

Latino heritage: Spanish
Born: February 16, 1888; Brooklyn, New York
Died: March 14, 1990; Westwood, New Jersey
Also known as: Harold Raymond Medina, Sr.
Areas of achievement: Law; education

EARLY LIFE

Harold Raymond Medina, Sr. (meh-DEE-nah) was descended from Spanish conquistadors. His father, Joaquin Adolfo Medina, grew up on a prosperous plantation on the Yucatan Peninsula in Mexico before becoming a naturalized American citizen and a successful importer. His mother, Elizabeth Fash Medina, was of Dutch heritage and from a prominent New York family. The elder of two boys, Harold grew up in a middle-class neighborhood. He attended public school in Brooklyn, where during the Spanish-American War he absorbed insults for his Hispanic ancestry. He later graduated in 1905 from a private institution, Holbrook Military Academy, in Ossining, New York.

A brilliant student, Medina in 1909 graduated tenth in his class from Princeton University with a degree in modern languages. He then attended Columbia Law School, rather than Princeton, so he could be closer to his future wife, beautiful socialite Ethel Forde Hillyer, whom he married in 1911. The couple had two sons, Harold Raymond, Jr., and Standish Forde Medina, who both graduated from Princeton and became lawyers. Medina obtained his law degree in 1912, winning a prize for the highest standing in his class. He went into

private practice, ultimately rising to senior partnership in the New York firm Medina and Sherpick.

Ambitious and energetic, Medina achieved financial and critical success on three interrelated fronts. Early in his career, he created a comprehensive cram course to assist aspiring attorneys in passing the bar exam. For thirty years, nine out of ten New York lawyers paid $35 apiece to take Medina's course, which helped make them lawyers and helped make Medina wealthy. He started earning a second source of income in 1915, when he was appointed special lecturer at Columbia Law School, and for

Harold Medina. (AP Photo)

years afterward he taught the New York Code of Civil Procedure to a generation of students that included such legal lights as future Supreme Court Justice William O. Douglas. A third and major source of income was his law practice. During the height of his career, Medina earned more than $100,000 annually, thanks to his willingness to accept—and usually win—difficult, often controversial appeal cases. Between 1912 and 1947, Medina argued more than 1,300 appeals, triumphing in the great majority of cases because of his excellence in strategy, thoroughness of preparation, and dynamic courtroom presence. Medina's earnings from all sources allowed him to purchase To Windward, a fifty-six-acre country estate at Westhampton, Long Island, where he maintained a plush mansion; houses for his aged widowed mother, his sons, and their families; a separate library; a boathouse; and other amenities.

LIFE'S WORK

In 1947, Medina sacrificed his luxurious lifestyle to take on a more prestigious and, at a salary of just $15,000 per year, much lower-paying role. President Harry S. Truman nominated Medina to be a judge in New York's busy Southern District, and the U.S. Senate confirmed him unanimously, making Medina the first Hispanic federal judge. During his tenure on the U.S. District Court, from 1947 to 1953, Medina presided over numerous high-profile cases. One of the most contentious and longest lasting was the so-called Communist Conspiracy Case of 1949, which revolved around the issue of free political speech. Another was the yearlong *United States v. Morgan, et al.*, also known as the Investment Bankers Case, which charged that seventeen leading Wall Street banking investment companies—including Morgan Stanley & Co., Goldman Sachs, Smith Barney & Co., and Lehman Brothers—had conspired to manipulate and monopolize the market for U.S. securities.

Based on Medina's masterful handling of such highly publicized cases, President Truman subsequently nominated him as judge of the U.S. Court of Appeals for the Second Circuit. Confirmed in 1953 to replace semiretiring chief judge Learned Hand, Medina served actively from 1951 to 1958 and held senior status until 1980, at age ninety-two the oldest person on the federal bench. Medina and his circuit court colleagues—thirteen active judges and various senior-status judges stationed throughout the court's venue—maintained jurisdiction over the district courts of New York, Connecticut, and Vermont. Medina served alongside such luminaries as future U.S. Supreme Court Justices John M. Harlan II and Thurgood Marshall.

After retiring from public service, Medina returned to his estate to enjoy the remaining years of his life in comfort. Though his wife died at age eighty-three in 1971, he had the constant company of his sons and their children on his Long Island compound. He attended annual reunions at his alma mater, was an avid billiard player, read and collected rare books in several languages for his personal library, and was a bright, enthusiastic conversationalist to the end of his days. The last surviving member of the Princeton graduating class of 1909, Medina died at the age of 102.

Medina's Role in the 1949 Trial of Communist Conspirators

As a judge in the U.S. District Court for the Southern District of New York, Harold Medina heard what became popularly known as the Communist Conspiracy Case. Formally known as *United States v. Foster* (1949) and later on appeal as *Dennis v. United States* (1950-1951), the case involved individuals prominently associated with the Communist Party USA. Eleven men (a twelfth was tried separately) were charged with violation of the Smith Act of 1940, also known as the Alien Registration Act, as members of a group that advocated the overthrow of the United States government.

Medina presided over what became the longest, most boisterous, and most controversial federal criminal case in American history to that point. The trial cost the government more than $1 million; trial transcripts consumed more than two thousand pages. Phalanxes of picketers marched outside the courthouse and sent Medina thousands of insulting telegrams. Inside, disorder threatened to reign, with reporters occupying half the spectator seats, defendants making frequent vocal outbursts, and their attorneys practicing various disruptive and delaying tactics. The case featured the testimony of undercover agent Herbert Philbrick, whose story served as the basis for the 1950's television series *I Led Three Lives*. Medina became a heroic figure, denying frivolous motions, verbally sparring with lawyers, and handing out contempt citations en masse. Ultimately, the jury found all defendants guilty and they were sentenced to prison and fined. The U.S. Supreme Court later upheld the convictions.

This landmark case was a precursor of the anticommunist furor of the early 1950's. *United States v. Foster* would become a precedent for later conspiracy cases. For his fair and balanced handling of a volatile situation, Medina became a national figure representing the triumph of reason over chaos.

SIGNIFICANCE

A fixture in the New York legal community for nearly seventy years, Harold Medina built his early reputation by advocating for unpopular causes in defense of civil rights and personal freedom. He often took on authoritarian forces, such as banks (*People v. Marcus*, 1932-1933) and governmental agencies (*MacAdams v. Cohen*, 1932). In one of his most famous cases, *Cramer v. United States* (1942-1945), Medina risked public condemnation and personal safety to go before the U.S. Supreme Court in defense of Anthony Cramer, a naturalized German convicted of treason for associating with Nazi saboteurs in World War II. One of the first Supreme Court decisions involving treason, and a precedent-setter in constitutionally limiting governmental powers during wartime, the case was a victory for Medina and his client, whose conviction was overturned.

Highly esteemed among colleagues for his superb courtroom manner (he vigorously practiced his court presentations before a mirror) and his superlative memory (he argued extemporaneously before juries without notes), Medina served as vice president of the Association of the Bar of the City of New York. He was also director of the American Judicature Society and president of the Manhattan Lawyers Club. Featured on the cover of *Time* magazine in 1949 following the Communist Conspiracy Case, Medina received the Columbia Law School Alumni Association Medal for Excellence in 1965. In addition, a chair in procedural law at Columbia Law School was named in his honor.

Jack Ewing

FURTHER READING

Howard, J. Woodford, Jr. "Advocacy in Constitutional Choice: The Cramer Treason Case, 1942-1945." *American Bar Foundation Research Journal* 11, no. 3 (Summer 1986): 375-413. A detailed examination of one of Medina's most significant cases, which has contemporary implications in the use of legal weapons when defending national security against perceived political criminals.

Medina, Harold R. *Important Features of Pleading and Practice Under the New York Civil Practice Act.* Florence, Ky.: Gale Cengage, 2010. This reference book lists about twenty thousand treatises, casebooks, manuals, and other works that Medina compiled regarding American and British domestic and international law.

Vile, John R. *Great American Judges: An Encyclopedia.* Santa Barbara, Calif.: ABC-CLIO, 2003. Contains brief biographies of one hundred state and federal judges, including Medina, who greatly influenced American law.

See also: Joaquín G. Avila; Lourdes G. Baird; Norma V. Cantú; José Ángel Gutiérrez; Antonia Hernández; Vilma Socorro Martínez; Alonso Perales; Sonia Sotomayor.

BILL MELENDEZ

Mexican-born animator of *Peanuts* cartoons

The only person Charles Schulz would permit to animate his Peanuts *comic strip characters, Melendez directed, produced, and provided voices for 63 half-hour* Peanuts *television shows, 5 one-hour specials, 4 feature films, and more than 370 commercials. During a career that spanned seventy years, Melendez won six Emmy Awards and two Peabody Awards and was nominated for an Oscar.*

Latino heritage: Mexican
Born: November 15, 1916; Hermosillo, Sonora, Mexico
Died: September 2, 2008; Santa Monica, Californi
Also known as: José Cuauhtémoc Melendez; J. C. Melendez; C. Melendez
Areas of achievement: Art; animation

EARLY LIFE

The son of a Mexican cavalry officer who gave his children Aztec names, Bill Melendez (meh-LEHN-dehz) was born José Cuauhtémoc Melendez on November 15, 1916, in Hermosillo, Sonora, Mexico. He was twelve years old when his family moved to Arizona so that the children could learn English. Melendez found himself in a kindergarten class, where the embarrassment of having classmates half his age encouraged him to learn English quickly. He demonstrated his artistic ability at an early age and could quickly sketch animals and people. The family soon moved to Los Angeles, where Melendez hoped to become an engineer.

The Great Depression prevented Melendez from achieving his dream, but he was encouraged by a friend to show his drawings to Walt Disney. Disney recognized his talent and advised Melendez to attend art school. Melendez studied at the Chouinard Art Institute, and he was hired by Disney in 1938. The Disney studio was enjoying the success of its first full-length animated feature, *Snow White and the Seven Dwarfs* (1937). During his years with the studio, Melendez worked on the films *Pinocchio* (1940), *Fantasia* (1940), *Dumbo* (1941), and *Bambi* (1942). Melendez wanted his name to appear in credits as Cuauhtémoc Melendez, but Disney said the name was too long and credited him as "Bill" Melendez instead.

One of the few Hispanic animators at Disney, Melendez helped to organize a strike to improve the wages and rights of animators. In 1941, he left the company and went to work for Leon Schlesinger Productions, which was later purchased by Warner Bros. At Warner Bros., Melendez worked on Bugs Bunny, Daffy Duck, and Porky Pig cartoons. In 1948, he left Warner Bros. to work for United Productions of America, a company that was doing innovative work in animation, especially for commercial advertisements.

It was during his work for United Productions of America that Melendez first met Charles Schulz, creator of the classic comic strip *Peanuts*. Ford Motor Company was interested in featuring the *Peanuts* characters in its advertising, but Schulz was reluctant to have other artists animate his characters until he saw Melendez's drawings. Melendez did not try to embellish the *Peanuts* characters but maintained the same style as Schulz. This initial collaboration eventually led to a string of highly successful television programs, a cartoon series, films, and more commercials, including those for MetLife, an insurance company that began featuring *Peanuts* characters in 1985.

LIFE'S WORK

His association with Schulz allowed Melendez to open his own studio in 1964, Bill Melendez Productions. In 1965, Melendez, Schulz, and Lee Mendelson created the first *Peanuts* television special, *A Charlie Brown Christmas*. Created in eight months, the program, which was sponsored by Coca-Cola and aired by CBS, was a radical departure from traditional primetime programming or children's programming of its day.

First, Melendez, Schulz, and Mendelson all agreed that the voices of the young characters should be provided by actual children instead of adults imitating children, which was the common practice. Furthermore, Schulz insisted that there be no laugh track.

Bill Melendez. (AP Photo)

The music for *A Charlie Brown Christmas*, provided by Brazilian pianist Vince Guaraldi and his trio, was fast-paced, swinging jazz, unlike anything a network had previously chosen for a children's program. Finally, Schulz argued for the Christmas story in the Gospel of Luke from the King James Bible to be the highlight of the twenty-five-minute program. When CBS executives previewed the rough cut before it aired, they were less than impressed. However, the night it first aired, *A Charlie Brown Christmas* was viewed in 50 percent of American homes. Reviewers loved the show, and *A Charlie Brown Christmas* has aired on network television at least once every year since then.

Because Schulz did not believe that Snoopy, a beagle, should speak English, Melendez dubbed nonsense sounds in his own voice and sped them up to represent Snoopy's "language." In all subsequent *Peanuts* productions, Melendez provided the voice of Snoopy, Woodstock, and later Spike, Snoopy's brother. Melendez received residual payments for his voice work until his death.

In addition to his *Peanuts* work, Melendez animated television specials such as Jean de Brunhoff's *Babar Comes to America* (1971), the C .S. Lewis classic *The*

Lion, the Witch, and the Wardrobe (1979), Jim Davis's *Garfield on the Town* (1983), and *Cathy* (1987) based on Cathy Guisewite's comic strip.

Melendez was married in 1940 to Helen Huhn, and they had two sons: Steven Cuitlahuac, the president of Bill Melendez Productions, and Rodrigo Cuauhtemoc, a retired rear admiral of the United States Navy. Melendez died on September 2, 2008, in Santa Monica, California.

SIGNIFICANCE

Melendez was responsible for producing, directing, writing, or animating dozens of *Peanuts* television shows and specials, including *It's the Great Pumpkin, Charlie Brown* (1966), *A Boy Named Charlie Brown* (1969), and several specials after Schulz's death in 2000, including *Lucy Must Be Traded, Charlie Brown* (2003). The *Peanuts* characters have been involved in every major American event and holiday, from the nation's bicentennial and the National Football League's Super Bowls to programs celebrating Thanksgiving, Christmas, Easter, Halloween, Valentine's Day, New Year's, and even Arbor Day. *A Charlie Brown Christ-*

mas is one of a handful of seasonal chestnuts that mark the yuletide.

Randy L. Abbott

FURTHER READING

Melendez, Bill. "Maestro of the Acetate, Champion of the Old Style." Interview by Gloria Goodale. *Christian Science Monitor* 87, no. 252 (November 24, 1995): 10. Melendez discusses his devotion to a good story and criticizes cartoons that seem to have nothing to say.

Nichols, Bill. "The Christmas Classic That Almost Wasn't." *USA Today*, December 6, 2005, p. 1A. Outlines how *A Charlie Brown Christmas* differed from the usual children's programming of its day.

Schulz, Charles, Lee Mendelson, Bill Melendez, and Antonia Felix. *"A Charlie Brown Christmas": The Making of a Tradition*. New York: HarperCollins, 2000. This is a behind-the-scenes account includes the story of how the program was developed and includes segments of the original score and production notes.

See also: Alma Flor Ada; Lalo Alcaraz; Monica Brown; Yuyi Morales.

MARGARITA BRADFORD MELVILLE

Mexican-born activist and anthropologist

Melville has made significant contributions to the fields of anthropology and Chicano studies. She was one of the first anthropologists to examine the intersections of race, class, and gender in the Mexican American community. When the field of Chicano studies emerged, she served as a role model because of her unique blend of scholarship and activism.

Latino heritage: Mexican
Born: August 19, 1929; Irapuato, Guanajuato, Mexico
Also known as: Marjorie Bradford; Sister Marian Peter; Marjorie Bradford Melville
Areas of achievement: Activism; anthropology; religion and theology

EARLY LIFE

Margarita Bradford Melville was born Marjorie Bradford in Irapuato, Guanajuato, Mexico in 1929, one of five children. Her father was an American and her mother was of Mexican and English descent. When Melville was eight years old, her family relocated to the northern

Mexican state of Chihuahua, where they lived in an American colony. For high school, Melville was sent to El Paso to attend the Loretto Academy, an all-girls Catholic school. It was at Loretto that Melville made the decision to become a nun. She joined the Maryknoll religious order, an order whose missionaries at the time worked primarily in Asia, Africa, and South America.

In the fall of 1949, Melville was assigned to the Maryknoll novitiate training program in Valley Park, Missouri. After two and a half years of training, she took her initial vows and the name Sister Marian Peter. Melville attended Maryknoll's Mary Rogers College in New York, graduating with her bachelor's degree in education in 1954. In the late summer of that year, the Maryknoll order assigned Melville to Guatemala, a new mission for Maryknoll sisters, where she would serve as a teacher.

LIFE'S WORK

Melville's work as a missionary and teacher in Guatemala was one of the most formative experiences of her life. Although she wanted to work among the poor, Melville was assigned to teach at the elite Monte Maria girls school in Guatemala City. After witnessing the stark disparities between rich and poor in Guatemala, Melville embarked on a series of projects to educate the elite young women of Guatemala about poverty in their own country and attempted to instill in them a sense of obligation to serve disenfranchised communities. These early efforts resulted in the establishment of a Girl Scout troop in 1956 and a Junior Red Cross in 1961 at Monte Maria.

In 1962, Melville's service gained a broader social and political context when she met Father Aguirre, a Venezuelan Jesuit who was promoting his Cursillos de Capitación Social—courses designed to promote social awareness. With the help of a local Jesuit seminarian, Melville organized similar courses for high school and some college students. These courses brought together activists from urban and rural areas to promote social justice for the poor in Guatemala. Through this undertaking, Melville became acquainted with many activists, including leftist guerrillas. She soon became involved with members of left-wing activist groups such as Fuerzas Armadas Rebeldes (FAR).

In 1967, Melville and other members of the Maryknoll religious order and laity—including Thomas Melville, a priest in the order—were expelled from Guatemala because of their subversive activity; they went into hiding in Mexico. While planning their return to Guatemala, they learned that the right-wing extremists had issued warrants for their deaths. Because of the threat to the students involved, Melville returned to the United States.

While in Mexico, Melville married Thomas Melville, and the two moved to Washington, D.C. Shortly thereafter, they were arrested for their radical protest of the Vietnam War, which the Melvilles saw as parallel to the United States' intervention in Guatemala. They both were sentenced to one year in jail. Melville was released after nine months for good behavior.

After her release from prison, Melville and Thomas pursued their doctoral degrees in anthropology at American University in Washington, D.C., and conducted research on the social organization of Mapuche Indians in Chile. After completing her doctorate in 1976, Melville accepted a position as assistant professor of anthropology at the University of Houston. In her career as an academic, Melville's research interests broadened to include women's and Chicano issues. She is the editor of two important books in the field of Chicano studies—

Twice a Minority: Mexican American Women (1980) and *Mexicanas at Work in the United States* (1988)—and numerous articles about Chicanos in the United States.

Melville accepted a position as an associate professor at the University of California at Berkeley in 1986, where she served as coordinator of Chicano studies and associate dean of the Graduate Division. Melville also served on the editorial board of *Aztlán* and was an active member of Mujeres Activas en Letras y Cambio Social (MALCS). She is the recipient of an award from the National Association of Chicano Studies in 1992 for significant contributions to the field. Melville retired from UC Berkeley in 1995.

SIGNIFICANCE

Melville is a key figure among Latinos in the United States because of her unique position as a scholar and activist. Her early years as a nun in Guatemala inspired her career as an academic to go beyond the production of knowledge; she engaged in scholarship that would result in positive social change for disenfranchised members of society. Melville was one of the first anthropologists to study the intersections of race, class, and gender in the Chicano community and served as an important role model in the development of Chicano studies as a field of academic inquiry and activism.

Jennifer R. Nájera

FURTHER READING

Fitzpatrick Behrens, Susan. "From Symbols of the Sacred to Symbols of Subversion to Simply Obscure: Maryknoll Women Religious in Guatemala, 1953 to 1967." *The Americas* 61, no. 2 (October, 2004): 189-216. Scholarly article examining the feminist implications of Melville's actions as a nun in Guatemala. This piece details the process by which Melville became aligned with leftist guerrillas in Guatemala.

Melville, Margarita B., ed. *Mexicanas at Work in the United States*. Houston, Tex.: Mexican American Studies Program, University of Houston, 1988. Melville's edited volume about Mexican women and labor in the United States. Various scholars explore issues of systematic class oppression of Mexican origin women.

_____, ed. *Twice a Minority: Mexican American Women*. St Louis, Mo.: Moby Press, 1980. Melville's best-known edited volume about Mexican American women in the United States. This collection of articles was one of the first of its kind examining the intersections of race, class, and gender.

Melville, Marjorie, and Thomas Melville. *Whose Heaven, Whose Earth?* New York: Knopf, 1971. Autobiography cowritten by Melville and her husband. It chronicles their respective paths toward radical-ization in Guatemala and ends with their arrest for protesting the Vietnam War.

See also: Edna Acosta-Belén; Corky Gonzáles; María Herrera-Sobek; Vilma Socorro Martínez; Reies López Tijerina.

José Méndez

Cuban-born baseball player

Known in his native Cuba as El Diamante Negro (the Black Diamond), Méndez's pitching prowess in the Cuban League made him a legend in his homeland. He also was a pitcher, shortstop, and manager in the American Negro Leagues.

Latino heritage: Cuban
Born: March 19, 1887; Cárdenas, Matanzas, Cuba
Died: October 31, 1928; Havana, Cuba
Also known as: José de la Caridad Méndez; Black Diamond; El Diamante Negro
Area of achievement: Baseball

Early Life

José de la Caridad Méndez, better known as José Méndez (hoh-ZAY MEHN-dehz), was born in Cárdenas, Matanzas, Cuba, in 1887. In 1907, an official of the Almendares Blues, a team in the Cuban League, recruited Méndez.

In January, 1908, Méndez, a right-handed pitcher with a rising fastball and a snapping curve, made his professional debut, compiling a record of fifteen wins against six losses and leading the Almendares Blues to capture the league's pennant during his first season with the team. In the summer of 1908, Méndez played his first game in the American Negro Leagues, pitching for the Brooklyn Royal Giants.

Life's Work

Méndez became a baseball legend as the result of his performance in the fall of 1908, when the Cincinnati Reds competed against Cuban League teams in Havana. Méndez dominated the Reds, pitching twenty-five consecutive scoreless innings in three appearances. In three of his games with the Reds, Méndez allowed no runs and racked up twenty-four strikeouts. His dominance continued during the following six seasons, in which he led the Cuban League in wins three times and had win-loss records of 15-6, 7-0, 11-2, 9-5, 1-4, and 10-0, consecutively. His team, the Almendares Blues, won pennants in three of these six years. Méndez pitched equally well when other American Major League teams, such as the Detroit Tigers, Philadelphia Athletics, and Brooklyn Dodgers, visited Havana and when the Cuban League played in the United States during the summers of 1909, 1911, and 1912.

In 1913, Ira Thomas, a catcher with the Philadelphia Athletics, wrote an article for *Baseball Magazine* in which he described Méndez as "a remarkable man" and a pitcher who "ranks with the best in the game,"

José Méndez. (Getty Images Sport/Getty Images)

displaying "terrific speed, great control" and "excellent judgment." Thomas added that if Méndez "were a white man [he] would command a good position on any Major League club in the circuits."

From 1912 to 1916, Méndez played for All-Nations, an American team founded by the Hopkins Brothers, who owned sporting goods stores. All-Nations was named for its racially mixed roster, which included black, white, Japanese, Hawaiian, Native American, and Latin American players. The team, based out of Kansas City, Kansas, and Des Moines, Iowa, toured the Midwest from 1912 to 1918. One day, however, the team's manager ran off after he had stolen the daily gate proceeds.

J. L. Wilkinson, one of the team's players, replaced him as manager and later became the team's owner. Wilkinson transported the team to its games in a $25,000 Pullman car, which held portable bleachers that would be set up for the games. He did not pay for hotel rooms but arranged for his players to sleep in tents that were set up on the playing fields.

In late 1914, Méndez developed trouble with his arm. An able fielder, he was moved to shortstop for All-Nations and only pitched occasionally. After his stint with All-Nations, he played for the Chicago American Giants (1918) and the Detroit Stars (1919).

In 1920, Méndez signed on with a new professional baseball league, the Negro National League, becoming a player and manager with Wilkinson's Kansas City Monarchs. While with the Monarchs, he divided his time between pitching and playing shortstop, and his management led the Monarchs to win pennants in 1923, 1924, and 1925. He eventually was able to resume pitching, although his pitching load was lighter than it had been during his prime years, from 1908 to 1914.

From 1923 through 1926, Méndez's win-loss records were 12-4, 4-0, 2-0, and 3-1, consecutively. His performance was particularly impressive during the first Negro League World Series in 1924, when the Monarchs competed against the Hilldale Club of the Eastern Colored League. Méndez pitched in four games, with a shutout victory in the deciding final game.

During the winters, Méndez returned to his homeland to play for the Cuban League. He was the pitcher for the Santa Clara Leopards, considered the most dominant team in the history of Cuban baseball, from 1923 to 1924. He won his last game in Cuba on January 21, 1927. On October 31, 1928, Méndez died in Havana at the age of forty-one.

SIGNIFICANCE

José Méndez pitched year-round in the Cuban Winter Leagues and in the U.S. Negro Leagues in the summer. In exhibition games, he defeated Hall of Famer Eddie Plank and won one of two games against legend Christy Mathewson. His career win-loss record in the Cuban League was 76-28, and he ranks first in all-time career winning percentage with .731.

Méndez was one of the first players elected to the Cuban Baseball Hall of Fame in 1939; in 2006, he was elected to the U.S. National Baseball Hall of Fame. He is generally considered to be one of the greatest Cuban ballplayers who did not play in the American major leagues.

Michael J. Bennett

FURTHER READING

Echevarría González, Roberto. *The Pride of Havana: A History of Cuban Baseball.* New York: Oxford University Press, 1999. This definitive cultural history of Cuban baseball from 1860 to the late twentieth century includes numerous references to Méndez.

Holway, John B. *The Complete Book of Baseball's Negro Leagues: The Other Half of Baseball History.* Fern Park, Fla.: Hastings House, 2001. Holway provides a complete statistical accounting of the leagues' accomplishments, with a brief overview of statistics attained by African American players from 1859 to 1882 and an annual accounting for subsequent years through 1948, the year after Jackie Robinson broke the "color barrier" by entering the major leagues.

See also: Mel Almada; Minnie Minoso; Sandy Nava.

ANA MENDIETA

Cuban-born artist

Mendieta's brief career was marked by increasing recognition for her artwork, which combined feminist, ecological earthwork, and performance interests. She died under suspicious circumstances in 1985, and her husband's arrest, trial, and acquittal for her murder divided the New York art world.

Latino heritage: Cuban
Born: November 18, 1948; Havana, Cuba
Died: September 8, 1985; New York, New York
Also known as: Ana Maria Mendieta Oti
Area of achievement: Art

EARLY LIFE

Ana Maria Mendieta Oti (AHN-ah mah-REE-ah mayn-DYAY-tah OH-tee) was born in Havana, Cuba, the younger daughter of wealthy parents. Her father, Ignacio Mendieta, was an early supporter of Fidel Castro's rise to power in 1958. Soon, however, he fell under suspicion and life for the family became dangerous. The girls, Ana and her sister Raquelin, were sent to safety in the United States in 1961, but their life there was difficult. They lived in Iowa in foster care until joined by their mother and brother in 1966. Mendieta's father was imprisoned in Cuba until 1979, when he immigrated to the United States.

Mendieta attended the University of Iowa, majoring in indigenous arts and cultures. In 1969, she began graduate studies in studio art at the same university. Under the mentorship of one of her professors, Hans Breder, she began her performance and intermedia studies. With Breder, she made the first of several trips to Mexico. These trips were a significant source of inspiration for her. Mendieta received her master's of fine arts degree in 1972.

LIFE'S WORK

"Body" was a key concern to Mendieta as an artist. In the Silueta series, which she created from 1972 to 1981, she used her own body in a variety of performance pieces to investigate her relationships with nature, Hispanic culture, and homeland. Her body, or rather the silhouette of her absent body, combined with blood, grass, flowers, or fire, was the medium for exploring the divine rituals of burial and rebirth, her ties to the Earth. In 1980, Mendieta returned to Cuba for the first time; there, in 1981, she completed the Silueta series.

This series had precedents in work by other artists, including the earlier work of Yves Klein. However, unlike her male contemporaries, such as artist Robert Smithson, Mendieta's work is nonmonumental and even self-effacing. While other earthwork artists tended to extreme formalism, Mendieta's work was raw and immediate. Much of this work is now only known through her photographic documentation, which was organized and became available for research in the mid-1990's.

From the late 1970's until her death, Mendieta's opportunities for exhibition, teaching, and visiting artist awards increased. She joined the feminist A.I.R. Gallery in New York in 1979 and had her first solo show there. She left that gallery, however, in 1981, saying that feminism created too simplistic a reading of her work. She began developing a network of patronage that allowed her to create works of greater permanence. Her visiting artist positions give evidence of her growing prestige. In 1983, she received the Rome Prize enabling her to live at the American Academy for a year, but she extended this residency into 1985. Her career was in ascendence.

Mendieta had met Carl Andre, a sculptor, at the A.I.R. Gallery. They traveled together in Europe during her residency and married on January 17, 1985. On September 8 of that year, Andre called New York police to report that Mendieta had fallen to her death from their apartment window.

SIGNIFICANCE

At her death, Mendieta was still developing as an artist. No assessment can ever be given to works that were not created. In her surviving works and the documentation which exists for her ephemeral pieces, she enacted postmodernism before that critical discourse had been invented. She showed herself to be capable of negotiating between and among the divisions by which the art of her times was classified. She was a feminist, but not merely a feminist, and she crossed between dominant and subdominant cultures. Similarly, she transgressed the borders of abstract, performance, political, ecological, and mainstream modernism. Only after her death was it recognized that such transgression of categories was a hallmark of postmodernist work.

Jean Owens Schaefer

FURTHER READING

Adler, Esther. "Ana Mendieta." In *Modern Women: Women artists at the Museum of Modern Art*, edited by Cornelia Butler and Alexandra Schwartz. New York: Museum of Modern Art, 2010. Brief but critically informative essay providing an opportunity to understand Mendieta's work in relation to other women artists in the museum's collection.

Katz, Donald. *Naked by the Window: The Fatal Marriage of Carl Andre and Ana Mendieta*. New York: Atlantic Monthly Press, 1990. Detailed and journalistic biography of Mendieta that focuses on her suspicious death in 1985 and the subsequent trial and acquittal of her husband, Carl Andre, for murder.

Moure, Gloria. *Ana Mendieta*. Barcelona: Ediciones Polígrafa, 1996. Catalog containing several essays and many photographs that accompanied a 1996 exhibit of Mendieta's work, the first exhibition benefitting from access to her archives, which were collected and organized after her death. Includes a bibliography.

Viso, Olga. *Mendieta: Earth Body, Sculpture, and Performance, 1972-1985*. Washington, D.C.: Hirshhorn Museum and Sculpture Garden, Smithsonian Institution, 2004. A catalog documenting one of Mendieta's exhibitions, with essays placing her work within the criticism of late twentieth century art.

_____. *Unseen Mendieta: The Unpublished Works of Ana Mendieta*. Munich, Germany: Prestel Verlag, 2008. A thematic presentation of Mendieta's work. Includes many photographs and a bibliography.

See also: Juan Boza; Luis Alfonso Jiménez, Jr.; Yolanda M. López; Liliana Porter.

LOUIS MENDOZA

American educator and writer

Mendoza is a university professor whose specialities include Chicano literary and cultural studies, Latino immigration, and the experiences of immigrants in U.S. prisons. In 2007, he took a bicycle trip through the U.S., interviewing hundreds of people for a major study of immigration.

Latino heritage: Mexican
Born: August 25, 1960; Houston, Texas
Also known as: Louis Gerard Mendoza; Jerry Mendoza
Area of achievement: Education; scholarship

EARLY LIFE

Louis Gerard Mendoza (LOO-ihs JEHR-ahrd mehn-DOH-sah) grew up in an inner-city neighborhood of Houston, Texas, called Denver Harbor. He was the sixth of eight children born to Joe Mendoza, Jr., and Mary Concepción Mendoza. He attended local schools, graduating from St. Thomas High School in 1978. He then worked as a mechanic and a contractor's manager and had a job at a home equipment rental store before enrolling in evening classes, initially at San Jacinto Junior College and later at the University of Houston-Downtown. In 1987, he received his B.A. degree in English with a minor in Mexican American studies from the University of Houston's University Park campus.

Mendoza went on to earn a master's degree in English from the University of Texas at Austin in 1990 and a Ph.D. in English, with a concentration in ethnic and third world literatures and a minor in philosophy, from the same university in 1994. His Ph.D. dissertation was entitled *Making History: Generational Constructs, National Identity, and Critical Discourse in Twentieth Century Chicana/o literature*.

LIFE'S WORK

In 1992, Mendoza began his teaching career at the University of Texas at San Antonio, where he was an assistant professor of English in the Division of English, Classics, Philosophy, and Communication. He subsequently taught English at the University of Houston-Downtown during the 1994-1995 academic year and was a visiting professor of English at Brown University in the 1995-1996 academic year.

In 2001, he became the interim director of the Hispanic Research Center at the University of Texas, San Antonio, and the following year he was associate dean of this university's College of Liberal and Fine Arts. In 2004, he came to the University of Minnesota-Twin Cities to teach in and chair the Chicano Studies Department; four years later, he was this university's associate vice provost for equity and diversity and the interim chair of the Department of Spanish and Portuguese.

Mendoza has published several books, including one he has written, *Historia: The Literary Making of Chicana and Chicano History* (2001). He also has edited *Raúl Salinas and the Jail Machine: My Weapon Is My Pen, Selected Prison Writings, 1963-1974* (2006) and coedited *Crossing into America: The New Literature of Immigration* (2003) and *Telling Tongues: A Latin Anthology on Language Experience* (2007). In 2011, he was the lead adviser for a projected PBS documentary about Raúl R. Salinas, a poet who had been incarcerated for many years.

As a professor, Mendoza's specialities include Chicano literary and cultural studies and Latino immigration. In regard to the latter, in 2007 he embarked on his Journey Across Our America research project, driving his bicycle around the perimeter of the United States to visit Latino communities.

He went to thirty-four states during a period of six months, interviewing hundreds of people about the subject of immigration. He planned to write two books based upon his research: *A Journey Across Our America: Observations and Reflections on the Latinization of the U.S.*, a travel memoir, and *Voices from A Journey Across Our America: Interviews and Oral Histories from the Front Lines and Fronteras of Latinization in the U.S.*, a compilation of firsthand accounts. Mendoza also has made many keynote addresses and presentations on the subject of immigration, speaking on the growing Latino population in Minnesota and the rest of the United States.

SIGNIFICANCE

Mendoza's research has provided new insight into the literature and culture of Latinos in the United States. His Journey Across Our America research project will similarly provide significant information about Latino immigrants. Mendoza has compiled a list of fifteen emerging themes from the project. Among them is the conclusion that "cultural adaptation and exchange is ongoing," with most immigrants experiencing "neither complete assimilation nor simple accommodation" to the mainstream culture but rather living biculturally.

Sandra W. Leconte

FURTHER READING

Mendoza, Louis Gerard. "Emerging Research Themes Derived from A Journey Across Our America." http://minnesotahumanities.org/resources/Research%20Themes%20from%20A%20Journey%20Across%20Our%20America.pdf. Provides preliminary information about the data Mendoza uncovered while conducting this project.

_____. *Historia: The Literary Making of Chicana and Chicano History*. College Station: Texas A & M University Press, 2001. Examines the contributions of literature to the creation of Mexican American identity.

Mendoza, Louis Gerard, and Toni Nelson Herrera, eds. *Telling Tongues: A Latin Anthology on Language Experience*. Austin, Tex.: Calaca Press and Red Salmon Press, 2006. Collection of essays, in which contributors counter simplistic stereotypes about Latino immigrants and demonstrate how the language used by Latinos reflects the complexities of life.

Mendoza, Louis Gerard, and Subramanian Shankar, eds. *Crossing into America: The New Literature of Immigration*. New York: New Press, 2003. An anthology of thirty-one literary works by writers and poets of various ethnic backgrounds, including Hispanic, Asian, Romanian, African, South African, and American-born sons and daughters of immigrants. Provides insight into the immigrant experience in the United States.

Minnesota Humanities Center. "Where in the World Are Minnesota's Latinos?" http://minnesotahumanities.org/outreach/lunchLatinos. Based on Mendoza's speech 2009 speech at the center, this Web page provides information about his Journey Across Our America research project.

See also: Edna Acosta-Belén; Pura Belpré; María Herrera-Sobek; Gary D. Keller; Luis Leal.

LYDIA MENDOZA

American singer

Mendoza was a trailblazing star of Tejano and Norteño music. She played a twelve-string guitar and sang in a voice known for its distinctive mix of sultriness and strength. In the 1940's, she began a career that stretched into the 2000's.

Latino heritage: Mexican

Born: May 21, 1916; Houston, Texas

Died: December 20, 2007; San Antonio, Texas

Also known as: La Alondra de la Frontera; la Cancionera de los Pobres; la Gloria de Tejas; the Lark of the Border

Areas of achievement: Music

EARLY LIFE

Lydia Mendoza (mehn-DOH-zah) was born on May 21, 1916, in Houston, Texas to Leonor Zamarripa Mendoza and Francisco Mendoza. She was the second oldest of seven children. Mendoza's father was opposed to his daughters' formal schooling, but her mother stepped in to teach them what she could, even purchasing school supplies for their use at home.

During the late 1920's and early 1930's, the Mendoza family collectively made a meager living, mainly through street performances. They performed under the name El Cuarteto Carta Blanca (the Carta Blanca Quartet) and performed throughout Texas's Lower Rio Grande Valley.

It was also during this time that the Mendoza family joined the mass migration of agricultural workers who traveled north for work. They went as far north as Michigan, where the family gained fame among the other migrant workers for their musical talents.

By the end of the Great Depression, the Mendoza family had left Michigan and returned to Houston and eventually San Antonio. They continued to perform in various public squares.

Soon, Lydia Mendoza herself began entering and winning singing contests and even gained some early popularity with radio performances. In the 1930's, Mendoza recorded her first solo song, "Mal hombre," on RCA Victor's Bluebird label. The song became a hit and her signature song.

LIFE'S WORK

With the recording and ensuing popularity of "Mal hombre," Mendoza was well on her way to becoming a star. Her subsequent recordings also became wildly popular. She toured as a solo singer but was accompanied by her family's variety show. In 1937, they were able to gain acceptance outside of Mexico and Texas and were booked to perform in California for the first time.

In 1935, Mendoza married Juan Alvarado, and together they had three daughters: Lydia, Yolanda, and Maria Leonor. In the 1940's, Mendoza found it difficult to tour because of gasoline rationing during World War II. Mendoza continued to record with her family's variety show. During this time she released other popular recordings of "Celosa," "Amor de madre," "Pajarito herido," "Al pie de tu reja," "Besando la cruz," "Joaquin Murrieta," all of which became hits. In 1954, Mendoza's mother died, ending the variety show's long run.

Mendoza continued to tour in the United States, Mexico, and throughout Latin America. She also recorded with various companies. From the 1940's through the 1960's, she continued to perform in theaters and at festivals. That she also performed at the Smithsonian

Lydia Mendoza. (Michael Ochs Archives/Getty Images)

Festival of American Folklife in Montreal and on university campuses attests to her broad appeal.

After the death of Juan in 1961, Mendoza married Fred Martínez in 1964. In 1977, she performed at the inauguration of President Jimmy Carter. In 1982, Mendoza, whose father had eschewed her formal education, was invited to be a guest lecturer at California State University at Fresno. She became one of the first recipients of the National Heritage Fellowship Award from the National Endowment for the Arts.

Mendoza's indefatigable pace was halted in 1987, when she suffered a stroke that left her incapacitated; however, her popularity never waned, particularly in her home state of Texas. In San Antonio she was inducted into the Conjunto Hall of Fame by the Guadalupe Cultural Arts Center. In 1999, President Bill Clinton awarded her a National Medal of Arts, the highest national award given to performers. Mendoza died in San Antonio on December 20, 2007.

SIGNIFICANCE

Mendoza's many monikers reveal her effortless connection to the common person. The working class and poor appreciated the relatable singer's talents and cheered her crossing over into a mainstream world that likewise recognized her musical genius. From her hometown to the White House, she received numerous awards and lasting popularity.

Yvette D. Benavides

FURTHER READING

Broyles-González, Yolanda. *Lydia Mendoza's Life in Music: Norteño Tejano Legacies/La historia de Lydia Mendoza*. New York: Oxford University Press, 2001. An invaluable work based on extensive research into Mendoza's family and music.

_____. "Ranchera music(s) and the Legendary Lydia Mendoza: Performing Social Location and Relations." In *Chicana Traditions: Continuity and Change*, edited by Norma Elia Cantú and Olga Nájera-Ramírez. Urbana: University of Illinois Press, 2002. Scholarly examination of Mendoza's music and its place in Latino culture.

Mendoza, Lydia, Chris Strachwitz, and James Nicolopulos. *Lydia Mendoza: A Family Autobiography*. Houston, Tex.: Arte Público Press, 1993. Autobiography based on a number of interviews with Mendoza and her family.

See also: Celia Cruz; Carmen Miranda; Selena.

AMALIA MESA-BAINS

American artist and writer

A leading voice of the Chicano movement and a cultural critic who has written on feminism, education, and multiculturalism, Mesa-Bains is an artist whose works incorporate the memories, images, and materials of her Chicano heritage, giving perspectives on the lives of Chicanas as they have negotiated their identities both within a patriarchal community and as outsiders to the dominant culture of the United States.

Latino heritage: Mexican
Born: July 10, 1943; Santa Clara, California
Also known as: Maxine Amalia Mesa; Amalia Mesa
Areas of achievement: Art; literature

EARLY LIFE

Amalia Mesa-Bains (ah-MAHL-ee-ah MEH-sah baynz) was born in 1943 to immigrants from Mexico. During her youth in Santa Clara, California, she experienced the rich traditions of her family's Chicano culture, including the religious ideas of the Catholic faith and the social expectations among and for Chicanos that would later form the basis for her art and writings. After attending junior college, she moved to San Jose State University in California, from which she graduated in 1966. Her formal education later included a master's degree in interdisciplinary education from San Francisco State University and a Ph.D. in clinical psychology from the Wright Institute in Berkeley, California.

Mesa-Bains spent twenty years working in the San Francisco public school system. At the same time she was developing as an artist and activist. Her participation in the Chicano movement during the late 1960's preceded her eventual feminist activism, and she has written that her interest in feminism evolved out of issues regarding patriarchy in the Chicano movement itself.

In the mid-1970's, she began making the altars that would bring her to national prominence as an artist. Her first large-scale altar, exhibited in 1976, included among its images reference to the Mexican artist Frida Kahlo, with whose work Mesa-Bains had become familiar. Mesa-Bains was instrumental in reviving interest in and study of Kahlo among Chicanos through this and other exhibits, such as the Day of the Dead exhibition of 1978. However, she wrote that the popularity of Kahlo that developed in subsequent decades was an example of the dominant culture appropriating, trivializing, and depoliticizing the icons of minority cultures.

LIFE'S WORK

According to Mesa-Bains, her altars and other works of art were acts of "cultural reclamation." When critics used the word "kitsch" to describe Chicano altar art because the altars consist of an assemblage of often tacky objects of everyday life, Mesa-Bains explained that the altars instead are forms of *rasquachismo*, or the practice of making something from almost nothing, a common practice in the Mexican American experience because of economic necessity. Derived from the altars often present in Mexican and Chicano homes, her altars were not religious in intention and sometimes did not make use of religious iconography, but they did not deny spirituality, which is a common element in Chicano art. Mesa-Bains's altars also became the means by which she referenced the visual culture of her community in order to comment and critique upon feminine identity within the context of cultural memory and historical social practices. Not intended as mere records, these artworks were instead imbued with imagery that made them not only reflections of identity but also activist statements about it. She further explored these subjects in pioneering exhibitions that she helped mount during her career, in which she highlighted the social issues being explored by Chicano and feminist artists.

By the mid-1980's, her altars evolved to include references to cross-cultural spiritual practices. By the early 1990's, in the first two chapters of her series Venus Envy, the altars transformed into installation assemblages that transcended the concept of altar as object, or as a recognizable construct . Later in that decade, her *Venus Envy, Chapter Three* continued the expansion to larger installations.

In addition to these visual analyses, Mesa-Bains wrote critical essays on social and artistic issues. Several of her important essays were published subsequent to her receiving a highly prestigious fellowship from the John D. and Catherine T. MacArthur Foundation in 1992. Her essays were wide-ranging in their topics and positioned her own art and that of her colleagues in the broader questions of the relationship of a cultural minority, whether based on ethnicity or gender, to a dominant culture. Mesa-Bains addressed how this affected not only art related to her heritage but also education and other cultural manifestations of the tensions that the relationship engendered.

SIGNIFICANCE

Mesa-Bains was one of the most important and well-respected voices to emerge in the Chicano community in the 1960's, and she became a prominent articulator of Chicana feminism in particular. Through her art and her writings, she addressed multifaceted cultural issues that affected society and politics in the United States in the late twentieth and early twenty-first centuries. Rejecting the tradition of silent resistance prevalent among Chicanas of prior generations, she used art and critical writing to open discourses on important issues of class, ethnicity, patriarchy, multiculturalism, and education.

Madeline Cirillo Archer

FURTHER READING

Barnet-Sanchez, Holly. "Tomás Ybarra-Frausto and Amalia Mesa-Bains: A Critical Discourse from Within." *Art Journal* 64, no. 4 (Winter, 2005): 91-93. A brief but succinct analysis of Mesa-Bains's critical work, positioning her as one of the important theorists of Chicano art.

Gonzalez, Jennifer. "Rhetoric of the Object: Material Memory and the Artwork of Amalia Mesa-Bains." *Visual Anthropology Review* 9, no. 1(March, 1993): 82-91. A discussion of Mesa-Bains's altars.

Hooks, Bell, and Amalia Mesa-Bains. *Homegrown: Engaged Cultural Criticism.* Cambridge, Mass.: South End Press, 2006. Presented as a conversation between the two authors, this book addresses Mesa-Bains's background, influences, and formative experiences. It also gives her perspectives on a wide range of social issues, including educational concerns and the "cultural strip-mining" of ethnic experiences by a dominant culture that trivializes what it appropriates.

Mesa-Bains, Amalia. "Domesticana: The Sensibility of Chicana *Rasquache.*" In *Distant Relations: Chicano, Irish, Mexican Art and Critical Writings*, edited by Trisha Ziff. Santa Monica, Calif.: Smart Art Press, 1995. Mesa-Bains discusses her assemblages and altars and places them within the context of her themes and influences.

Pérez, Laura E. *Chicana Art: The Politics of Spiritual and Aesthetic Altarities*. Durham, N.C.: Duke University Press, 2007. Contains repeated references to Mesa-Bains as an artist and theorist, placing her within a broader, scholarly analysis

of Chicana art. The Venus Envy series is analyzed in detail.

See also: Judith F. Baca; Carmen Lomas Garza; Yolanda M. López; Liliana Porter.

MINNIE MINOSO

Cuban-born baseball player

After a successful stint in the Negro Leagues, Minoso joined the Chicago White Sox in 1951. His consistent hitting, aggressive base-running, and enthusiasm made Minoso enormously popular with fans and fostered the acceptance of Latino ballplayers in the major leagues.

Latino heritage: Cuban
Born: November 29, 1922; El Perico, near Havana, Cuba
Also known as: Orestes Minoso; Saturnino Orestes Arrieta Armas
Area of achievement: Baseball

EARLY LIFE

The son of workers in the sugarcane fields of Cuba, Orestes Minoso (mih-NOH-soh) grew up in poverty and with little education. He was born Saturnino Orestes Arrieta Armas; after his father left the family, he adopted the surname of his mother's first husband, Minoso. He followed in the athletic footsteps of older brother Francisco in learning how to play baseball. Both excelled in the sandlots, and the game ultimately provided Minoso an escape from school and life in the sugarcane fields.

Minoso advanced through semiprofessional teams in Cuba. He played catcher and pitcher, but to secure a spot on one team, he claimed to be a third baseman. By 1945, he was starring for the Mariano Tigers of the Cuban Professional League. One of his childhood heroes was Martin Dihigo, who had left Cuba to play in the Negro Leagues in the United States. In 1946, Minoso rejected a lucrative offer to play for the outlaw Mexican Leagues and instead signed a contract with baseball executive Alex Pompez of the New York Cubans, Dihigo's former team, in the Negro Leagues. Minoso now had the opportunity to compete at a higher level for more money and escape the poverty of Cuba; however, he had to deal with the rampant discrimination against people of color in American society. He did not regret his decision, since his burning desire was to become the best baseball player he could.

From 1946 to mid-1948, Minoso excelled for the New York Cubans. He played a crucial role in winning the Cubans' only Negro League championship. With a month left in the 1948 season, Pompez sold Minoso's contract to the Cleveland Indians, who shipped him to their minor-league club in Dayton, Ohio. His play led to a promotion to the Indians' highest minor league team in San Diego, where he played the 1949 and 1950 seasons.

LIFE'S WORK

Minoso felt he earned a position on the Cleveland's major-league squad in 1951, but on April 30, he was traded

Minnie Minoso. (AP Photo)

Minoso and the New York Cubans in the Negro Leagues

The Negro League team that lured Minnie Minoso from Cuba in 1946 had a colorful and important history. The origins of the New York Cubans stretched back to the turn of the century, when an all-Hispanic team arrived to challenge Negro League teams. After various financial reorganizations, new team owner Alex Pompez officially entered the New York Cubans in the Negro National League for the 1935 and 1936 seasons. The Cubans' most famous player was Martin Dihigo. In 1939, the Cubans reentered the league and competed until they disbanded. In 1947, with Minoso starring at third base and as a leadoff hitter, the Cubans won their only Negro League World Series, defeating the Cleveland Buckeyes of the Negro American League.

Despite their name, the New York Cubans included natives of Mexico, Puerto Rico, the Dominican Republic, and Cuba, as well as African Americans. The team served as a valuable conduit of Hispanic players to baseball teams in the United States. For Minoso, who knew no English, the appeal of the team was undeniable. His salary was twice what he received in Cuba. With the integration of Major League Baseball (MLB), the New York Cubans sent many Latino ballplayers, such as Minoso, to MLB teams. To survive, Pompez maintained an informal working relationship with the New York Giants, whose ballpark the Cubans used. Eventually, the Cubans ran out of marketable talent and folded in 1950.

to the Chicago White Sox. Chicago's new manager, Paul Richards, had seen Minoso play for San Diego and strongly encouraged the owner to acquire him. Minoso was the first black player on the White Sox. Whatever reservations Chicago fans might have had, however, they likely were alleviated when Minoso hit a home run in his first at-bat against the hated New York Yankees. The White Sox in 1951 were a rapidly improving team blessed with speed and youth. As a twenty-eight-year-old rookie, Minoso's enthusiasm, base stealing, and competitive spirit made him a perfect fit. The team's reputation as the "Go-Go White Sox," with leftfielder Minoso and second baseman Nellie Fox leading the way, reflected a strategy that was difficult for the opposition to contain.

In his first three years with the White Sox, Minoso led the American League in stolen bases. He hit over .300 in eight of his first ten seasons in Major League Baseball. He led the American League in hits in 1960.

In 1951 and 1954, Minoso led the major leagues in triples; he led the American League in doubles in 1957. From 1956 to 1960, he averaged almost 20 home runs a year. This combination of speed and power made Minoso a special talent and very popular. Off the field, Minoso reinforced his celebrity status with fancy cars, stylish clothes, and jewelry. Minoso always returned to Cuba to play winter baseball. On those fields just as in the ballparks in the United States, Minoso played with an intensity that Cuban spectators admired. When the Fidel Castro regime tightened its grip in 1961, however, Minoso retired from winter ball and refused to return to Cuba.

Perhaps Minoso's greatest disappointment came after the 1957 season, when he was traded to Cleveland in exchange for future Hall of Fame pitcher Early Wynn. In 1959, the White Sox captured their first league pennant since 1919. It was bittersweet for Minoso and the White Sox, and owner Bill Veeck brought him back to Chicago the following season and gave him a championship ring. Minoso, however, would never appear in a World Series. In the early 1960's, Minoso's talents waned significantly, but his will to play baseball remained strong. In 1965, he joined a team in the Mexican Leagues where he was a star until he retired in 1973. From 1976 to 1980, Minoso served as a coach for the White Sox. Team owner Veeck convinced Minoso to play in a couple games in 1976 and 1980, which made Minoso a five-decade player in the major leagues. He has remained involved with baseball as a goodwill ambassador.

SIGNIFICANCE

Minoso worked hard to excel at his profession. He was a star in Cuba and the Negro Leagues, but his acceptance in the newly integrated major leagues was not a given. Manager Paul Richards noted that Minoso was "completely fearless," and in ten seasons, Minoso led the American League in being hit by pitches. His inexhaustible good humor and enthusiasm and his distinctive combination of talents helped show baseball fans and owners that Latino players belonged in the major leagues. The Chicago White Sox retired Minoso's jersey number, 9, and in 2005, a statue of him was unveiled outside the team's new stadium.

M. Philip Lucas

FURTHER READING

Heaphy, Leslie A. *The Negro Leagues, 1869-1960*. Jefferson, N.C.: McFarland, 2003. Solid history of the

Negro Leagues that covers the New York Cubans and Latino ballplayers. Bibliography.

Lanctot, Neil. *Negro League Baseball: The Rise and Ruin of a Black Institution.* Philadelphia: University of Pennsylvania Press, 2004. Thoroughly documented history that establishes the context of the dying league in which Minoso flourished before signing with Cleveland.

Minoso, Minnie. *Just Call Me Minnie: My Six Decades in Baseball.* Champaign, Ill.: Sagamore, 1994. Minoso's autobiography offers insights into his experiences as a Latino ballplayer in the United States in the early years of desegregation.

_____. "Minnie Minoso Added an Unforgettable Touch to the Game." Interview by John Kuenster. *Baseball Digest* 64, no. 1 (January/February, 2005): 17-20. Minoso's engaging personality and humor shine throughout this brief interview that reviews his career accomplishments and disappointments.

Peterson, Robert. *Only the Ball Was White.* New York: Oxford University Press, 1992. This seminal study of the Negro Leagues includes brief player biographies and league records.

Vanderberg, Bob. *Minnie and the Mick: The Go-Go White Sox Challenge the Fabled Yankee Dynasty, 1951 to 1964.* South Bend, Ind.: Diamond Communications, 1996. Review of the games between Minoso's White Sox and their hated rivals that conveys the excitement of the pennant races.

See also: Mel Almada; Felipe Alou; Luis Aparicio; Orlando Cepeda; Roberto Clemente.

CARMEN MIRANDA

Portuguese-born actor and singer

An adopter and adapter of lower-class Afro-Brazilian samba musical styles, Miranda became an American film sensation during World War II, embodying a caricature of the South American woman as colorful, fiery, kinetic, and often comical, with flamboyant headgear usually containing fruit as part of her signature apparel.

Latino heritage: Portuguese and Brazilian

Born: February 9, 1909; Marco de Canaveses, Portugal

Died: August 5, 1955; Beverly Hills, California

Also known as: Maria do Carmo Miranda da Cunha; The Brazilian Bombshell; the Lady with the Tutti-Frutti Hat

Areas of achievement: Entertainment; acting; music

EARLY LIFE

Maria do Carmo Miranda da Cunha—better known as Carmen Miranda (mih-RAN-duh)—was born on February 9, 1909, in Marco de Canaveses in the north of Portugal. She was the second daughter born to José Maria Pinto Cunha and his wife, Maria Emilia Miranda. Her father soon relocated his family to Rio de Janeiro, Brazil, where he sought work as a barber. He loved comic opera and music, sentiments he passed on to Miranda, who decided early that she desired the life of an entertainer. Her father did not approve, however. He once beat her mother for allowing Miranda to audition for a radio performance.

Four younger siblings joined the family, and when Miranda's older sister, Olinda, was sent back to Portugal for medical reasons, fourteen-year-old Miranda was required to work to help provide for the family. She started in a tie shop, progressed to a hat boutique, and eventually started her own small business making hats. Meanwhile, she continued singing at parties and festivals, and her persistence paid off when, at the age of twenty, she was discovered by composer Josué de Barros. He recognized her potential and talent and guided her first to Brunswick, a German recording company, and then to the more influential Victor Records.

Miranda's appropriation of the samba musical stylings and vivid fashions of working-class women of color in Bahia quickly made her a star in Brazil. She became a radio and recording celebrity, acquiring a rare two-year contract in 1933 with Rádio Mayrink Veiga. That same year, Miranda made her film debut in *A voz do Carnaval.* She spent most of the 1930's as a musical entertainer in Brazil, with a highly successful 1934 appearance in Buenos Aires, Argentina, broadening her international appeal. Miranda made five more films in Portuguese before Broadway theatrical producer Lee Schubert recognized her talent and box office potential and took her to New York City. Schubert arranged for Miranda to be showcased in his 1939 production of *The Streets of Paris.* At Miranda's request, her backup band, Bando da Lua, came with her.

Carmen Miranda. (Silver Screen Collection/Getty Images)

LIFE'S WORK

The diminutive (only 5 feet tall) and dynamic Miranda won many fans in her Broadway run from June, 1939, through February, 1940, among them the film studio heads at Twentieth Century-Fox. Miranda took offense when she returned to Brazil in 1940 and critics there accused her of having become Americanized; this reception made her Hollywood opportunities all the more attractive.

Miranda became one of the major film stars of World War II, and in 1946, she was Hollywood's highest paid entertainer, garnering a salary of over $200,000. In her first American film, *Down Argentine Way* (1940), she played herself; in this and her subsequent American film roles, she would regularly convey, along with vivacious Latin rhythms, an omnipresent underlying sensuality, exotic beauty (which offered an excellent opportunity to promote Technicolor advancements), and playfulness. Although she often was relegated to playing quirky and amusing secondary characters, Miranda stole scenes with her flamboyance and energy. She made a total of fourteen feature films in Hollywood from 1940 through 1953, and as the first three film ti-

tles indicate—*Down Argentine Way* was followed by 1941's *That Night in Rio* and *Week-End in Havana*—for American audiences she came to personify not only the women of Brazil but also, more generally, those of all nations south of the United States. Similarly, her performance numbers incorporated a range of different Latin traditions from South America and the Caribbean.

Miranda's hats and jewelry inspired some American fashion fads during the war years, and she often was parodied in 1940's cartoons, indicating her swift and significant rise to iconic status. In 1947, Miranda married Dave Sebastian, an assistant to the producer on *Copacabana* (1947), a film she made with comedy legend Groucho Marx that offered her the opportunity to satirize the stereotypes of the day for female singers from Latin America. She joined bandleader Xavier Cugat for some lavish Latin music performances in *A Date with Judy* (1948), an MGM production to promote the beauty of adolescent Elizabeth Taylor, and after that only appeared in two more films: *Nancy Goes to Rio* (1950), another MGM musical featuring Jane Powell, and *Scared Stiff* (1953), a comedy starring the popular team of Dean Martin and Jerry Lewis. Nevertheless, Miranda remained busy in this period, regularly performing in nightclubs and appearing as a guest on television variety shows.

Following her marriage Miranda became increasingly depressed. Her husband's abusive behavior and her use of alcohol and drugs accentuated her problems. After she suffered a physical breakdown in 1954, on doctor's orders she returned to Rio de Janeiro for a rest. After some months, she returned to the United States and began anew her strenuous schedule. In August, 1955, while performing a musical number live on *The Jimmy Durante Show*, Miranda suffered a heart attack, stumbled, and fell. Durante stepped in to help and replace her, but she waved him away, got back up, and finished the number. Later that night at home, she had a second heart attack and died at the age of forty-six. Her body was returned to Rio de Janeiro for burial; a national day of mourning was declared there, and more than a half-million Brazilians turned out to walk in her funeral procession.

SIGNIFICANCE

Through radio and recordings, Miranda popularized the samba music of lower-class people of color. The Hollywood film personas she created in the 1940's made her a dominant symbol of Latin American culture for filmgoers in the United States. Her roles reflect

Miranda as an American Icon of Latino Culture

In 1940, Carmen Miranda arrived in Hollywood. At the time, World War II was under way in Europe, cutting off a major market for film distribution. President Franklin D. Roosevelt was eager to strengthen his Good Neighbor Policy through increased commerce with Latin America, so the film studios and the federal government both had an incentive to promote positive public awareness of and interest in Latin American culture. The success of Miranda throughout the war years made her the representative figure of this process. It also, however, meant she came to be a broad, general Latina icon; her image as "the Lady with the Tutti-Frutti Hat" encapsulated not only all things Brazilian but also the dance, music, language, cultural behaviors, and traditions of all Spanish- and Portuguese-speaking nations south of the United States.

contemporary stereotypes and perceptions of Latinos: She played women who were exotic, beautiful, passionate, and fiery—but also often bumbling with English, a bit silly, headstrong, and childlike. Miranda blazed a trail for a generation of Latina actors in the United States, such as Rita Moreno, who often found themselves

relegated to secondary roles as hot-tempered women; her cultural influence also extends to drag queens, many of whom identified with Miranda's strength, resiliency, flamboyance, and inherent sensuality.

Scot M. Guenter

F<small>URTHER</small> R<small>EADING</small>

Freire-Medeiros, Briana. "Hollywood Musicals and the Invention of Rio de Janeiro, 1933-53." *Cinema Journal* 41, no. 4 (Summer, 2002): 52-67. Discusses Hollywood representations of the city and Brazilian culture.

Gil-Montero, Martha. *Brazilian Bombshell.* New York: Dutton, 1989. An English-language biography sympathetic to Miranda notes how her American success stereotyped her, causing both personal trauma and resentment in Brazil.

Mandrell, James. "Carmen Miranda Betwixt and Between, or Neither Here nor There." *Latin American Literary Review* 29, no. 57 (2001): 26-39. Deconstructs Miranda as a representative of Latin American culture.

See also: Desi Arnaz; Dolores del Río; José Ferrer; Mel Ferrer; Rita Hayworth; Ricardo Montalbán; Rita Moreno; Beatriz Noloesca; Chita Rivera; Lupe Velez.

N<small>ICHOLASA</small> M<small>OHR</small>

American writer and artist

Mohr is a fine artist who is known for writing and illustrating books about growing up poor, female, and Puerto Rican in New York. Her novels and short stories describe some of the injustices endured by Puerto Rican immigrants.

Latino heritage: Puerto Rican
Born: November 1, 1935; Spanish Harlem, New York
Also known as: Nicholasa Golpe
Areas of achievement: Art; literature; theater

E<small>ARLY</small> L<small>IFE</small>

Nicholasa Mohr (nih-koh-LAH-suh) was born on November 1, 1935, to Pedro and Nicholasa (Rivera) Golpe in Spanish Harlem, New York. Her parents and four of her brothers had migrated to the United States from Puerto Rico. Once in the United States, two more sons

were born before the last child, Mohr, arrived. Before she entered school, the family moved to the Bronx. Mohr grew up in a traditional Puerto Rican home where, as the only female child, she had more household responsibilities than her six brothers and less freedom to explore areas outside the home.

Mohr's father died when she was eight years old, leaving her mother, who often was ill, to take care of the family. Mohr admired her mother's strength and ingenuity as she struggled to keep the family together. Eventually, despite her efforts, they went on welfare. Mohr's mother encouraged her to work hard in school and often gave her paper, pencils, and crayons to keep her busy. Mohr used the materials to create art, which served as a means of escape. Her drawings garnered praise from her mother, who hoped she would eventually use her talent to support herself. Her mother died when Mohr was fourteen, and the family was separated. Mohr went to live with her mother's sister but never really felt welcome there.

Mohr was an avid reader who enjoyed works by Bernard Shaw, Eugene O'Neill, and Carson McCullers. She wanted to attend a college preparatory high school, but a guidance counselor—who saw her only as a poor Latina—encouraged her to attend a trade high school and learn to sew rather than draw. Not one to be discouraged, Mohr continued to pursue her dream of becoming an artist through courses in fashion illustration. Unsatisfied with four years of high school training, Mohr enrolled in the Art Students League of New York in 1953. While there, she studied painting and drawing in a program that was deeply grounded in European culture. Like most of her classmates, Mohr began saving money for a trip to Europe before she found books in the public library that featured Mexican art. She was inspired to travel to Mexico City, where she studied art and printmaking at the Taller de Gráfica Popular (People's Graphic Workshop). While there, Mohr admired the work of Diego Rivera, David Alfaro Siqueiros, Frida Kahlo, and others. When she returned to New York, she studied at the New School for Social Research. It was there that she met Irwin Mohr, a doctoral student in clinical psychology; the couple married in 1957. They raised two sons, David and Jason, together in Teaneck, New Jersey, where Mohr set up a studio in their home.

LIFE'S WORK

By 1972, Mohr had spent eighteen years using visual art—oil paintings, drawings, and prints—to tell stories about her community. She had exhibited her work and was supported by a number of galleries. One of her collectors, the head of a publishing company, approached her agent about a possible book project after noticing that her art contained words and phrases. There was an untapped market for books written about Puerto Ricans at the time; however, Mohr was not interested, even though she realized that she had an aptitude for writing. After a while, she relented. She wrote fifty pages of short vignettes about growing up Puerto Rican with few financial resources. The publisher liked Mohr's work but was not interested in the type of stories she had written. She suspected that the publisher might have been looking for sensational stories.

With the vignettes filed away, Mohr continued to produce art. Publishing house Harper & Row asked if she would provide the art for a book of poetry, but when she showed them her work, they decided against using

Mohr's *Nilda*

Nicholasa Mohr's first novel, *Nilda* (1973), was influenced by events in her life. Early drafts of the coming-of-age story were written in the first person, but Mohr decided first-person pronouns were too conversational. Instead, she preferred third person because it allowed her distance from the character.

Nilda is the story of a young girl growing up, from ages ten to thirteen, in New York's Spanish Harlem during World War II. The novel shows how people in authority, from teachers to police officers, are cruel to Nilda's poor Puerto Rican family. When her parents die, Nilda's siblings are separated; she is sent to live with an aunt in the Bronx. Through all of the pain and disappointments, however, Nilda finds solace in art, just as Mohr did while growing up.

Nilda was lauded by critics and earned several awards, including the Society of Illustrators citation of merit, which was given to Mohr for the book's jacket and eight illustrations.

it. While there, Mohr asked Ellen Rudin to read her vignettes; a few weeks later, she was offered a book contract. Mohr had received a fellowship to reside at the MacDowell Colony in New Hampshire during the summer, so she used the time to write *Nilda*. The novel was published in 1973. *Nilda* earned Mohr *The New York Times*'s Outstanding Book Award for juvenile fiction in 1973 and the Jane Addams Children's Book Award in 1974.

The success of her first novel encouraged Mohr to shift her focus from art to writing. One of her older brothers, Vincent, who worked in publishing, helped Mohr achieve her goal. Her second book, *El Bronx Remembered: A Novella and Stories*, was published in 1975 with Mohr's own cover art. It was cited as a best book in 1975 by *School Library Journal* and received *The New York Times*'s Outstanding Book Award in teenage fiction. *El Bronx Remembered* also was a National Book Award finalist for most distinguished book in children's literature in 1976. The following year, *In Nueva York* (1977) was published. *In Nueva York* was named a Notable Trade Book in Social Studies by the National Council for the Social Studies and the Children's Book Council, a Best Book by *School Library Journal*, and a Best Book for Young Adults by the American Library Association.

Mohr cites American authors, especially Southern women such as Eudora Welty and Carson McCullers, as influences. Mohr, who has been labeled a children's author, argues that she writes for all ages. She maintains that the only books she wrote specifically for children are *Felita* (1979) and its sequel, *Going Home* (1986). Mohr's other books include *Rituals of Survival: A Woman's Portfolio* (1985) and *A Matter of Pride, and Other Stories* (1997). In 1994, she published a memoir, *In My Own Words: Growing Up Inside the Sanctuary of My Imagination*. Two years later, she wrote the foreword for *Latinas!: Women of Achievement* (1996).

Mohr also has written for television, radio, and the stage. She was the head creative writer and coproducer of the television series *Aquí y ahora* (*Here and Now*). Her plays include *Zoraida* (1988) and *I Never Even Seen My Father* (1995), based on a short story from *In Nueva York* (1995). She also received a grant from the New York State Council on the arts to create a play based on *Nilda* (1973). Mohr has taught at various universities, such as Queens College, Richmond College, and American International University in London. She received the Hispanic Heritage Award in 1997.

SIGNIFICANCE

A novelist and playwright, Mohr is one of the pioneers of fiction about Latinos in the United States. During the 1970's, she was one of the few writers of color who illustrated her own work, providing readers with images and narratives. Since then, she has spoken and written repeatedly about her position as a Puerto Rican born in the United States who fully embraces the use of mainstream American English in her work. She has inspired many writers to tell their own stories of growing up talented and hopeful, despite disenfranchisement.

KaaVonia Hinton

FURTHER READING

Mohr, Nicholasa. "An Interview with Nicholasa Mohr." Interview by Myra Zarnowski. *Reading Teacher* 45, no. 2 (October 1991): 100-106. Mohr describes her writing process.

_____. "Pa'lante: An Interview with Nicholasa Mohr." Interview by Bridget Kevane and Juanita Heredia. In *Latina Self-Portraits: Interviews with Contemporary Women Writers*, edited by Bridget Kevane and Juanita Heredia. Albuquerque: University of New Mexico Press, 2000. A candid interview about Mohr's life and work, particularly her eight-year (1986-1994) absence from the world of publishing.

Rico, Barbara Roche. "'Rituals of Survival': A Critical Reassessment of the Fiction of Nicholasa Mohr." *Frontiers: A Journal of Women Studies* 28, no. 3 (2007): 160-179. This article offers an extensive look at the lack of attention to Mohr's work and includes a critical discussion of several of Mohr's books.

Vasquez, Mary S. "Borderspaces in Nicholasa Mohr's *Growing Up Inside the Sanctuary of My Imagination*." *Bilingual Review* 26, no. 1 (January-April 2001/2002): 26-33. Provides a close examination of Mohr's memoir in the context of autobiographical work or testimonials by Latinas.

See also: Alma Flor Ada; Miguel Algarín; Julia Alvarez; Marie Arana; Giannina Braschi; Monica Brown; Esmeralda Santiago.

GLORIA MOLINA

American politician

As a county supervisor, Molina oversees many government services provided to Los Angeles's First District, including public health, law enforcement, assessment and tax collection, and social services. She is one of the most influential politicians in Los Angeles.

Latino heritage: Mexican

Born: May 31, 1948; Los Angeles, California

Also known as: Jesus Gloria Molina

Area of achievement: Government and politics

EARLY LIFE

Jesus Gloria Molina (moh-LEE-nuh) was born on May 31, 1948, to Mexican American parents. The oldest of ten children, she grew up and attended community college in Pico Rivera, a city within the county of Los Angeles. As a young adult, Molina was inspired to enter politics in the early 1970's by the Chicano movement in Los Angeles. The Latino community had long been underserved in terms of educational and economic opportunities, but its political consciousness was growing.

Molina began by working on the campaigns of Latino representatives in Los Angeles. Recognizing the absence of Latinas in city politics, she began to take on greater roles at the local level in Los Angeles and soon thereafter at the state level in Sacramento.

When Molina won election to the state assembly in 1982 representing the Fifty-sixth District, she became the first Latina representative to join the California Legislature. After serving in Sacramento from 1982 to 1987, she returned to local politics in her home city of Los Angeles. In 1987, she was elected to the Los Angeles City Council, and once in office, she began implementing programs to address issues important to working-class neighborhoods in neglected areas of the city.

LIFE'S WORK

From the beginning of her tenure on the city council, Molina steadily improved delivery of a range of services to her constituents. Her proactive stance led to anticrime programs and improved policing that lowered crime rates throughout her district. In 1991, Molina was elected to the Los Angeles County Board of Supervisors.

Gloria Molina. (AP Photo)

As a county supervisor, Molina represents more than two million residents living in East Los Angeles and twenty-two other surrounding cities. She has placed a high priority on improving life for underprivileged families in that area. She improved resources and support for families and children, including the development of child-care services, expansion and improvement of public parks, and greater funding for one of the principal medical facilities in Los Angeles County, the medical center at the University of Southern California.

As supervisor, Molina oversees the commercial and economic development of the First District of Los Angeles County, and her accomplishments include numerous projects and programs to promote business, commercial, and economic growth in the East Los Angeles area. She has implemented plans to extend Los Angeles Metro service into East Los Angeles, an area where working families rely heavily on public transportation. Molina also coordinated the East L.A. Works initiative to support local businesses in the area.

Los Angeles has the largest Latino population of any major city in the United States; in 2004, in recognition of the enormous economic and cultural contributions of Latinos to the area, Molina approved funds for construction of a Latino museum and cultural center. From the beginnings of her political career in Los Angeles, Molina also worked to support other Latinos, such as Mayor Antonio Villaraigosa. *Hispanic Business* magazine recognized Molina's achievements and contributions to public service by naming her its woman of the year in 2006. As of 2011, Molina served on the boards of the Southwest Voter Registration Education Project and the Mexican American Legal Defense and Educational Fund.

SIGNIFICANCE

Molina paved the way for increased Latina involvement in California politics. She served as the first president of the Comisión Femenil de Los Angeles (Los Angeles Feminine Commission), a network and advocacy group for Latinas. She worked for President Jimmy Carter as deputy director of the Office of Presidential Personnel and then as a congressional liaison to the U.S. Department of Health and Human Services. In 1982, she was the first Latina elected to the California State Legislature, and in 1991, she became the first Latina elected to the Los Angeles County Board of Supervisors. Molina also serves as a vice chair of the Democratic National Committee.

Molina's career reflects her deep commitment to serving her constituents. She is highly respected locally and nationally for her dedication, leadership, and commitment to improving the quality of life in the First District of Los Angeles County, as well as for opening doors to greater political representation for Latinos throughout the United States.

William A. Teipe

FURTHER READING

Bonilla-Santiago, Gloria. *Breaking Ground and Barriers: Hispanic Women Developing Effective Leadership*. San Diego, Calif.: Marin, 1992. This examination of Hispanic women in positions of power includes a profile of Molina and discussion of her significance in California politics.

Garrison, Jessica. "L.A. County OKs Mexican American Cultural Center." *The Los Angeles Times*, September 15, 2004. Describes Molina's role in promoting a cultural center reflecting the city's Latino population and heritage.

Russell, Joel. "A Day in the Life of the Woman of the Year." *Hispanic Business* 4, no. 170 (April, 2006). Laudatory profile covering Molina's career and accomplishments in local and state politics.

See also: Cruz Bustamante; Edward R. Roybal; Loretta Sánchez; Hilda L. Solis.

MARIO MOLINA

Mexican-born scientist

Molina's work in atmospheric science, particularly in explaining the deleterious effect of chlorofluorocarbons on the ozone layer, earned him a share of the 1995 Nobel Prize in Chemistry. It vindicated environmental science, which previously had been belittled by mainstream science.

Latino heritage: Mexican

Born: March 19, 1943; Mexico City, Mexico

Also known as: José Mario Molina-Pasquel Henríquez; Mario J. Molino

Areas of achievement: Science and technology; education; social issues

EARLY LIFE

José Mario Molina-Pasquel Henríquez (moh-LEE-nah-pahs-KEHL hehn-REE-kehz) was born in Mexico City, Mexico, to Roberto Molina-Pasquel and Leonor Henríquez de Molina. His father was a lawyer who taught at Mexico City's Universidad Nacional Autónoma de Mexico (UNAM) and later was the Mexican ambassador to Ethiopa, Australia, and the Philippines. Inspired by his aunt, chemist Esther Molina, young Molina performed experiments in a home laboratory. After attending elementary and high school in Mexico City, at age eleven he attended a boarding school in Switzerland.

In 1960, Molina entered the chemical engineering program at UNAM, where he took mathematics-oriented courses not open to chemistry majors and earned his B.S. degree in 1965. He spent two years working on polymerization kinetics at the University of Freiburg, Germany, where he earned a master's degree in 1967. Returning to UNAM as an assistant professor, he established the first graduate program in chemical engineering.

In 1968, Molina joined George C. Pimentel's research group at the University of California at Berkeley. He studied the distribution of internal energy in the products of chemical and photochemical reactions using lasers and other instruments. During his years in Berkeley, near the end of the free-speech movement, he realized the impact of science and technology on society and began his lifelong opposition to the application of research for weapons and other potentially destructive purposes. Molina earned his Ph.D. in 1972 and continued his research on chemical dynamics at Berkeley for another year. On July 12, 1973, he married fellow graduate student Luisa Y. Tan, with whom he collaborated on environmental and other scientific topics.

In 1973, Molina joined Professor F. Sherwood Rowland at the University of California at Irvine as a postdoctoral fellow. He studied the accumulation in the atmosphere of inert chlorofluorocarbons (CFCs), then thought to have no effect on the environment. At Irvine, where he was an assistant professor and associate professor from 1975 to 1982, he studied the chemical and spectroscopic properties of unstable atmospherically important compounds.

LIFE'S WORK

CFCs—nontoxic, nonflammable, inexpensive compounds widely used in industrial products as

Mario Molina. (AP Photo)

refrigerants, aerosol propellants, and solvents—can persist in the atmosphere for forty to fifty years because of their inertness. In 1970, James E. Lovelock showed that these gases had spread throughout the atmosphere; the next year, he found that a CFC, trichlorofluoromethane, had spread through the troposphere (the lowest layer of the atmosphere) over the north and south Atlantic Ocean. Molina and Rowland began their search for a "sink"—the reactions by which CFCs are decomposed and where this decomposition occurs. The process through which these particles decompose yields chlorine atoms, which break down ozone molecules and deplete the ozone layer that protects the Earth from the sun's harmful ultraviolent rays.

Molina and Rowland calculated by reaction rate measurements that continued use of CFCs for several decades would deplete the ozone layer by several percent. A 5 percent depletion would produce an additional forty thousand cases of skin cancer in the United States after 2050. CFCs also contribute to the greenhouse effect and global climate change. In the June 28, 1974, issue of *Nature*, Molina and Rowland warned of the deleterious effects of CFCs on the atmosphere. Their article initially was ignored by the academic commu-

nity, so they reported their results on September 11, 1974, at the American Chemical Society's national meeting in Atlantic City, New Jersey, where they held a press conference. Their subsequent appearances before legislative committees urging a complete ban on CFCs garnered them extensive coverage in the popular press and alerted the public to the danger. Despite opposition of anti-environmentalists and commercial manufacturers, a consensus emerged that industrially manufactured gases were responsible for destroying the ozone layer. The U.S. Environmental Protection Agency (EPA) banned the use of CFCs in aerosols in 1978, and some companies developed nonchlorine-containing products as refrigerants and aerosol sprays. The 1987 Montreal Protocol and subsequent provisions restricted atmospheric release of manufactured ozone-destroying gases.

Molina worked in the Molecular Physics and Chemical Section at the National Aeronautics and Space Administration's Jet Propulsion Laboratory in Pasadena, California, from 1982 to 1989. After learning of Joseph Farman's discovery of the seasonal depletion of ozone over Antarctica, Molina showed that this effect could be attributed to chlorine-activation reactions under polar stratospheric conditions. Molina, Rowland, and the Dutch-born Paul J. Crutzen received the 1995 Nobel Prize in Chemistry for their work in atmospheric chemistry, particularly in the area of ozone depletion, an award widely regarded as a vindication of environmental and atmospheric science.

Molina was professor of chemistry and atmospheric chemistry from 1989 to 1997 and institute professor of earth, atmosphere, and planetary sciences from 1997 to 2004 at the Massachusetts Institute of Technology (MIT). He was elected to the U.S. National Academy of Sciences in 1993 and the U.S. Institute of Medicine in 1996. On July 1, 2004, he assumed joint appointments with the Department of Chemistry and Biochemistry at the University of California at San Diego and the Center for Atmospheric Sciences at the Scripps Institution of Oceanography in La Jolla, California. In 2005, he founded a center for strategic studies in energy and environment in Mexico City. Molina holds a number of honorary degrees and has served on the President's Council of Advisors in Science and Technology, the Secretary of Energy Advisory Board, National Research Council Board on Environmental Studies and Toxicology, and the boards of the U.S.-Mexico Foundation for Science and other nonprofit environmental organizations. An asteroid was named in his honor. After

Environmental Chemistry Comes of Age

Chemical compounds called chlorofluorocarbons (CFCs) once were widely used as aerosol propellants and refrigerants because they are nontoxic, inert, and nonflammable. However, the inertness that made them commercially useful permits them to persist for as long as five decades in the atmosphere, where their slow breakdown depletes the ozone layer and creates an environmental disaster.

The scientific work of Mario Molina, F. Sherwood Rowland, and Paul J. Crutzen, who collectively earned the 1995 Nobel Prize in Chemistry, demonstrated that CFCs were harmful to the environment. They discovered that insoluble CFCs could not be removed by rainfall or the oceans but would rise into the stratosphere and be decomposed by ultraviolet radiation to yield chlorine atoms. Through a chain reaction, one chlorine atom reacts with and destroys as many as ten thousand ozone molecules and regenerates the active chlorine-containing compounds to repeat the cycle, breaking down the ozone layer that blocks the sun's harmful ultraviolet rays.

This decrease in the ozone layer has far-reaching environmental consequences, the most publicized of which is an increase in skin cancer. The 1987 Montreal Protocol and more recent regulations have banned the use of CFCs and recommended suitable replacements.

his divorce from Luisa, in February, 2006, Molina married Guadalupe Álvarez.

SIGNIFICANCE

Molina was the first Mexican-born citizen to receive a Nobel Prize in Chemistry. His work brought atmospheric chemistry into the mainstream by demonstrating that human activities can adversely affect the Earth's fragile environment. He donated $200,000 of the prize money to fund a fellowship program to provide advanced training at MIT for young environmental researchers from developing countries. In the PBS television program *Breakthrough: The Changing Face of Science in America* (1996), he was one of twenty African American, Latino, and Native American scientists who discussed their research and careers. Molina has collaborated with colleagues from many disciplines on the chemistry of atmospheric pollution and issues of global climate change, especially in rapidly growing cities. He also has significantly improved the air quality of Mexico City.

George B. Kauffman

FURTHER READING

Cullen, Katherine. "Mario J. Molina." In *Weather and Climate: The People Behind the Science.* New York: Facts On File, 2006. Describes Molina's career and impact on the environmental movement and the field of atmospheric science. Aimed at younger readers.

Kauffman, George B., and Laurie M. Kauffman. "Atmospheric Chemistry Comes of Age." *Today's Chemist at Work* 5, no. 10 (November, 1996): 52-58. An account of the award of the 1995 Nobel Prize in Chemistry to Crutzen, Molina, and Rowland and details of their lives and work.

Molina, Mario J. "Polar Ozone Depletion." In *Nobel Lectures Including Presentation Speeches and Laureates' Biographies: Chemistry, 1991-1995*, edited by Bo G. Malmström. River Edge, N.J.: World Scientific Publishing Company, 1997. Nobel lecture account of Molina and Rowland's research and results. Molina's portrait and autobiography also are included.

Molina, Mario J., and F. Sherwood Rowland. "Stratospheric Sink for Chlorofluoromethanes: Chlorine-Atom Catalysed Destruction of Ozone." *Nature* 249 (June 28, 1974): 810-814. This frequently cited paper described what many have called a "planetary time bomb" and "invisible menace."

See also: Albert V. Baez; Margarita Colmenares; Arturo Gómez-Pompa; Adriana C. Ocampo; Severo Ochoa.

AMALIA MONDRÍGUEZ

Puerto Rican-born educator and writer

A well-respected professor of Spanish in San Antonio, Mondríguez has written books and created classes that aim to teach Spanish to professionals. She also has edited other authors' Spanish-language works, including children's books.

Latino heritage: Puerto Rican

Born: December 15, 1953; Humacao, Puerto Rico

Areas of achievement: Education; literature

EARLY LIFE

Amalia Mondríguez (ah-MAHL-ee-ah mon-DREE-gehs) was born in Humacao, Puerto Rico, to Víctor Mondríguez and Celia Torres. She was raised in Las Piedras and educated in that city's public school system. Through community mobilization, her mother established El Centro de Envejecientes de Las Piedras, a home for older adults eventually renamed in her mother's honor. Her mother was an important influence in Mondríguez's life. At age nine, Mondríguez began her career in education at her mother's suggestion when she tutored a younger neighborhood boy.

Mondríguez obtained her masters degree in Spanish literature from the University of Puerto Rico in 1980. Her hundred-page master's thesis provided what she described as "four approaches" to Gabriel García Márquez's novella *El coronel no tiene quiene le escriba* (1961; *No One Writes to the Colonel*, 1968), and she defended the thesis as if it were a doctoral dissertation. After receiving her degree, she was an instructor and head of tutorial services for three years at Turabo University in Gurabo, Puerto Rico. Meanwhile, she developed a successful Spanish for business class and was an editor for *Vanguardia*, a publication of the Méndez education Foundation.

LIFE'S WORK

Mondríguez completed her second masters degree at Harvard University, where she met Scott Chaiken, a California native working toward his doctorate in psychology. They married in 1987, and in 1996, Mondríguez gave birth to a son.

While a graduate student, Mondríguez provided editorial assistance to other writers and published literary analyses in several peer-reviewed journals. In 1988, she received Harvard University's certificate of distinction in teaching and completed her Ph.D. in Spanish. Her doctoral dissertation examined the depiction of women in literary works in "erotic narratives" by several Spanish-language writers, including José Donoso, Carlos Fuentes, and García Márquez.

Mondríguez joined the faculty of Incarnate Word College (now University of the Incarnate Word) in San Antonio, Texas, in 1988. In her first years there, she created innovative courses that tailored Spanish instruction for specific disciplines and wrote a textbook for each: *Introduction to Spanish in the Media*, *Spanish I for Pharmacists*, and *Spanish II for Pharmacists*. In addition, she developed a course on Spanish radio and on Spanish for the health professions. She frequently included service learning as part of her Spanish courses. For example, in 2006, she assigned students to write and produce a series of radio programs about health issues that was broadcast to indigenous people in Peru. In 1993, Incarnate Word College nominated her for the Piper Professor of Texas award. Mondríguez's interest in teaching is captured in a collection of essays she edited with Melissa Anne Walschak, *Toward the Twenty-first Century: The Future of Teaching and Learning* (1994).

Mondríguez edited *Soñar no cuesta nada: Escritos creativos* (2004), a collection of creative writing, which included three of her original works, primarily focused on children and mothers, as well as writings by students. In 2005, she wrote the lyrics and music for a set of original Spanish lullabies that was recorded on a compact disc. In addition to publishing her own original works, Mondríguez assists others in editing Spanish-language children's books. She helped edit two books written by Carmen Tafolla: *Baby Coyoto and the Old Woman* (*El coyotito y la viejita*, 2000) and *That's Not Fair: Emma Tenayuca's Struggle for Justice* (*No es justo: La lucha de Emma Tenayuca por la justicia*, 2008), the latter of which was cowritten by Sharyll Teneyuca and Terry Ybanez. From 2007 to 2009, Mondríguez was an editor of Spanish children's books at the Intercultural Development Research Association. She also developed a course focusing on children's literature in Spanish. In 2009, she was one of the Spanish-language curators of *Revolution and Renaissance, Mexico and San Antonio, 1910-2010*, an exhibit at The Museo Alameda, a Smithsonian Institution affiliate.

Mondríguez has made numerous community and national presentations, organized children's book fairs and events celebrating Puerto Rican culture, and mentored or supported Latino writers. She was a member of the Modern Language Association from 1984 to 1996, the Southwest Conference on Latin American Studies from 1988 to 1996, and the Society of Children's Book Writers and Illustrators from 2007 to 2010. The Guadalupe Cultural Arts Center in San Antonio recognized Mondríguez as Volunteer of the Year in 1992, and in 2009, she received the Sisters of Charity of the Incarnate Word's Sr. Margaret Rose Palmer Award for Education.

SIGNIFICANCE

Amalia Mondríguez has been a guardian of the Spanish language, writing her own Spanish-language works, as well as editing works in Spanish by other authors. She has developed innovative courses in Spanish that involve her students in service learning and support professionals in their attempts to serve Spanish speakers. Her own original works transport one into a world that responds lovingly to children and a place in which women control their destinies despite life's misfortunes. Her support of Spanish-language children's literature has ensured that a new generation of Latin Americans will enjoy the beauty of the Spanish language, even as they learn English. Her legacy as a Spanish professor also includes service to many protégés for whom she was their quiet and helpful educator.

María Félix-Ortiz

FURTHER READING

Mondríguez, Amalia. *Desde el otro lado*. San Juan, Puerto Rico: Edil, 1991. A collection of Mondríguez's short stories. In Spanish.

_____, ed. *Soñar no cuesta nada: Escritos creativos*. San Antonio, Tex.: University of the Incarnate Word, 2004. Translated as "It Costs Nothing to Dream," this is a collection of work by students in the university's Spanish program. Mondríguez edited the book, which includes some of her original work. In Spanish.

Walschak, Melissa, and Amalia Mondríguez, eds. *Toward the Twenty-first Century: The Future of Teaching and Learning*. San Antonio, Tex.: University of the Incarnate Word, 1994. Collection of essays examining future trends in education.

See also: Gwendolyn Díaz; Louis Mendoza; Pat Mora.

CAROLINA MONSIVÁIS

American poet and activist

A native of El Paso, Texas, Monsiváis is a poet who cofounded a women's collective of activist writers. Her dedication to poetry and her activism to end sexual and domestic violence mark her as one of the Southwest borderlands writers who move between the two worlds of Mexico and the United States.

Latino heritage: Mexican
Born: May 12, 1973; El Paso, Texas
Area of achievement: Poetry; women's rights; activism

EARLY LIFE

Carolina Monsiváis (cah-roh-LEE-nah mohn-see-vah-EES) was born on May 12, 1973, in El Paso, Texas, to Maria Estela Monsiváis and Jose Jesus Monsiváis and grew up in El Paso's East Side neighborhood. During her childhood in the 1980's, her parents divorced, and her mother remarried, becoming Maria Estela Monsiváis Ibarra. Monsiváis attended Eastwood High School in El Paso, graduating in 1994. She moved to Houston, Texas, in 1994 and in 1998 received a bachelor's degree in English/creative writing with a minor in history from the University of Houston. While at the university she began writing poetry, studying with writer Lorna Dee Cervantes in 1994, while Cervantes was a visiting scholar at the university's Mexican American Studies Center.

While Monsiváis was at the university, she also began working at the Houston Area Women's Center with women and children who had been victims of domestic violence and sexual assault. During her time as a student and after her graduation, she was a residential advocate at the center and then a youth outreach counselor in the Houston schools, working with juvenile survivors of sexual and domestic violence. It was during her time in Houston that she became truly engaged with efforts to stem the violence against women and the poor and indigenous peoples of Mexico. Poetry and the fight to end violence against women and children have been the twin passions of her life.

LIFE'S WORK

Several years after Monsiváis's graduation from the University of Houston, she cofounded the Houston chapter of Amigas de las Mujeres de Juárez in order to bring attention to the hundreds of women killed and missing in Juárez, Mexico. Monsiváis went on to work with violence survivors in Juárez, which is directly across the Mexican border from her hometown of El Paso. She would later offer creative writing as therapy workshops to other activists in the cause of violence against women.

At the same time, Monsiváis continued to write poetry. In 2000, she received an Individual Artist Grant from the city of Houston/Harris County. In that same year, her first book, *Somewhere Between Houston and El Paso: Testimonies of a Poet* (2000), was published by Wings Press and won the Premio Poesia Tejana. The poems in this collection are filled with the lives, concerns, and pain of women. Many describe in great detail the difficulties faced by a young woman activist who constantly confronts the damage done to other young women and girls and how her work on behalf of these women is draining, yet necessary.

In 2001, Monsiváis moved back to her hometown, El Paso, to work as an outreach advocate at Sexual Trauma and Assault Services, and she continued to write poetry. She later moved to Santa Teresa, New Mexico, in 2002 to work as a writing teacher in the schools and pursue an M.F.A. in creative writing/poetry from New Mexico State University, graduating in 2004. While in New Mexico, she cofounded The Women Writers Collective, a community of women activist writers that worked to raise awareness of local women's issues and to promote female artists and writers, partnering with Las Amigas de las Mujeres de Juárez and Nuestra Palabra: Latino Writers Having Their Say.

Back in El Paso once more, Monsiváis began teaching at El Paso Community College and married Chicano writer Richard Yañez. She gave birth to her first child, Pablo, in December, 2008. Monsiváis gave dozens of public readings; was featured in several key anthologies of Latino writers, such as *U.S. Latino Literature Today* (2005) and *The Wind Shifts: New Latino Poetry* (2007); and was a Macondista (a member of the Macondo Writers Community). She published another book of poetry, *Elisa's Hunger* (2010), which won the Nuestra Voz Prize. *Elisa's Hunger* focuses on family and its demands and gifts to women through the lens of a young woman starting a family who is remembering and imagining her dead grandmother's life and emotional journey.

SIGNIFICANCE

Monsiváis has been in the forefront of the emerging generation of U.S. Latino writers and activists. Like a number of her peers, she was a writer of the *frontera* (border), and her work moves back and forth across the border between Mexico and the United States as easily as the populations of El Paso and Juárez surge back and forth daily across the bridge that connects the two cities, and just as Monsiváis has moved back and forth between the darkness of society's violence and the healing of poetry.

Linda Rodriguez

FURTHER READING

Monsiváis, Carolina. *Elisa's Hunger*. El Paso, Tex.: Mouthfeel Press, 2010. This chapbook contains poems in which Monsiváis uses her late grandmother, much beloved and partially invented in memory, to try to make sense of a woman's life, then and now. Monsiváis ultimately deals with family, both the family one is born into and the larger family composed of all humankind.

_____. *Somewhere Between Houston and El Paso: Testimonies of a Poet*. With Spanish translations by Estela Monsiváis. San Antonio, Tex: Wings Press, 2000. This book of poems won the Premio Poesia Tejana in 2000 and reflects Monsiváis's experiences working in the areas of domestic violence and sexual assault. Her poems focus on women's lives, the injuries so often done to women by their closest and dearest, and the damage that trying to heal women can do to those who work with them.

Rojas, Raymundo Eli. "Poetry Details Life in Houston to El Paso Area." *El Paso Times*, April 27, 2003. Review of Monsiváis's first book of poetry by the editor of a Latino literary journal, *Pluma Fronteriza*.

See also: Lorna Dee Cervantes; Sandra Cisneros; Carmen Tafolla; Alma Villanueva.

RICARDO MONTALBÁN

Mexican-born actor and activist

Montalbán overcame many stereotypes about Latino actors to achieve success in film, on stage, and in television. Best known for the television series Fantasy Island, *he was active in the entertainment world from the 1940's until his death.*

Latino heritage: Mexican

Born: November 25, 1920; Mexico City, Mexico

Died: January 14, 2009; Los Angeles, California

Also known as: Ricardo Gonzalo Pedro Montalbán y Merino

Areas of achievement: Radio and television; acting; theater; activism

Ricardo Montalbán. (Michael Ochs Archives/Getty Images)

EARLY LIFE

Born in Mexico City to parents who had emigrated from Spain, Ricardo Gonzalo Pedro Montalbán y Merino (MOHN-tahl-BAHN) was born in Mexico City on November 25, 1920, and raised in Torreón, where his father managed a dry goods store. The family moved to Torreón because of the unstable political and economic situation in the capital. Montalbán's parents had four children—three boys and one girl. From his family, Montalbán learned the importance of a happy marriage, family ties, and a deep and profound faith in God. These values remained with him his whole life.

LIFE'S WORK

In his late teens, Montalbán moved to Los Angeles to live with his older brother Carlos, an actor; they later moved to New York. In 1940, he had a minor role in the play *Her Cardboard Lover* (1927), starring Tallulah Bankhead; in 1941, he worked in films produced in New York until his mother's serious illness forced him to return to Mexico. While in Mexico, he became a film star before returning to the United States in 1943.

Because of his dark good looks, Montalbán was typecast as a "Latin lover," a concept and term he abhorred. In 1947, he starred in *Fiesta,* a film in which he and Esther Williams played twins born to an upper-class Mexican family. The anomaly of twins with different accents left Hollywood undaunted. Montalbán and Williams worked together in two other films: *On an Island with You* (1948) and *Neptune's Daughter* (1949). Montalbán was cast as a Latin film star in *On an Island with You* and a South American polo player in *Neptune's Daughter.* In 1950, he costarred with Jane Powell in the musical *Two Weeks with Love* as a sophisticated older man attracted to a young woman at a family resort. In 1953, he costarred with Lana Turner in the film *Latin Lovers.* Montalbán also worked with Cyd Charisse in several films, including *Fiesta* and *On an Island with You.* Because he could dance and sing, he was successful in the era of Hollywood musicals, but those roles dried up in the early 1950's. Metro-Goldwyn-Mayer (MGM), the leading studio for musicals, dropped Montalbán in 1953.

Montalbán thought of himself as a dramatic actor but was not hired for leading roles in major dramas during his early years in Hollywood; however, he did have featured dramatic roles in B films such as *Mystery Street* (1950). In the 1950's, he played Latinos, Indians, Japanese, and even Afro-Caribbean characters. In *Across the Wide Missouri* (1951), starring Clark Gable, Montalbán played an Indian chief; during the filming in 1950, he was seriously injured when his horse was startled by a prop cannon and he was thrown against a large rock. It proved to be a life-changing injury; he was in constant pain for the rest of his career.

In the 1950's, Montalbán moved to the stage. In 1957, he starred on Broadway opposite Lena Horne in the musical play *Jamaica,* winning a Tony Award in 1958. Montalbán and Horne broke a racial taboo of the era when they shared a kiss on stage. Despite his injury, he was able to dance in the play. Also in 1957, he played a Japanese actor in the Marlon Brando film *Sayonara.*

While his career was developing, Montalbán found personal happiness with model Georgiana Belzer, the half-sister of Loretta Young. The two met, fell in love, and were married for more than sixty years until her death in 2007. The couple had four children—two boys and two girls. In his personal life, Montalbán was a devout Roman Catholic and given the high honor of Knight of the Order of St. Gregory in 1998 by

Pope John Paul II. In his memoir, *Reflections: A Life in Two Worlds* (1980), the setting is a Catholic retreat where he reflects on his life after the death of his older brother Pedro.

Over a successful career that spanned seven decades, Montalbán always was conscious of the struggle that Latino actors faced. In 1970, he cofounded the Nosotros Foundation to advance the cause of Latino actors and to honor their work. *Nosotros* means "we" and signifies the unity of all Latino actors. As first president of the foundation, Montalbán was an advocate for Latino actors, which hurt his own career for several years.

In the 1970's, Montalbán's career entered a new phase when he became the spokesman for the Chrysler Cordoba. His commercial might have been more famous than the car itself. Suave and well-groomed, speaking in a charming voice, Montalbán praised the "soft Corinthian leather" of the car's interior, a phrase that was frequently mentioned and often parodied. A major turning point in his later career occurred when he was selected to play Mr. Roarke in the television series *Fantasy Island*, which ran for seven seasons. One of the best roles of his later career was Khan Noonien

Living a Dream on *Fantasy Island*

Although Ricardo Montalbán was successful in several entertainment genres, he is best remembered for the television series *Fantasy Island*. The show was set on a tropical resort island where visitors paid huge fees to realize their dreams. Montalbán played Mr. Roarke, the mysterious proprietor of Fantasy Island, who assisted in fulfilling clients' fantasies. Roarke was charming and sometimes arrogant. Hervé Villechaize played Tattoo, Roarke's diminuitive assistant. The popular series ran from 1978 to 1984. Many Hollywood film and television luminaries appeared in the show, including Robert Goulet, Lorraine Day, Theodore Bikel, and Leslie Nielsen. Each episode typically featured three separate fantasies, and most had an unexpected twist. Rarely did a fantasy turn out the way the protagonist hoped, but often the result was better than anticipated. Roarke controlled events and situations on his island with grace and insight, occasionally disguising himself as one of the characters in an episode. Montalbán's slight accent added a touch of exotic mystery to the character of Mr. Roarke, complementing the show's fantastical setting.

Singh in *Star Trek II: The Wrath of Khan* (1982), in which he reprised a role he had created in an episode of the *Star Trek* television series in 1967.

Montalbán's spinal injury worsened as he aged, and in his seventies he underwent major surgery that left him paralyzed below the waist. He continued to perform in films in a wheelchair. During his last years, he had a number of voice roles in animated series and films. He also remained dedicated to the work of the Nosotros Foundation. In 1999, the foundation and the Ricardo Montalbán Foundation bought the Doolittle theater from the University of California at Los Angeles. In 2004, the theater was renamed the Ricardo Montalbán Theater. In his speech at the time the theater was dedicated, Montalbán spoke of his dual loyalties to Mexico and to the United States, calling Mexico his mother and the United States his friend. He died on January 14, 2009, in Los Angeles.

SIGNIFICANCE

As one of few Latino actors to play starring roles in American films in the 1940's and 1950's, Montalbán transcended the sidekick roles typical of that time but detested being typecast as a Latin lover. He appeared opposite famous leading ladies such as Lana Turner and Esther Williams and costarred with Marlon Brando and Clark Gable, among others. As he aged, Montalbán performed a variety of character roles ranging from Latinos to Japanese to the extraterrestrial Khan. He also did important and influential work on behalf of Latinos that established him as a major activist in the entertainment industry.

Norma C. Noonan

FURTHER READING

Dederer, Claire, and Bruce Weber. "Ricardo Montalbán, Early Latino Leading Man, Dies." *The New York Times*, January 15, 2009. Lengthy obituary detailing Montalbán's career and impact on the entertainment industry.

Montalbán, Ricardo, and Bob Thomas, *Reflections: A Life in Two Worlds.* Garden City, N.Y.: Doubleday, 1980. Montalbán reflects on his life and career in this memoir.

Reyes, Luis, and Peter Rubie. *Hispanics in Hollywood: An Encyclopedia of Film and Television.* Hollywood, Calif.: Lone Eagle Press, 2000. Reference work containing a biography of Montalbán and examination of his career from an ethnic perspective.

Rodriguez, Clara. *Heroes, Lovers and Others: The Story of Latinos in Hollywood.* New York: Oxford University Press, 2008. In-depth examination of the treatment of Latino actors and depictions of Latino characters in the entertainment industry; contains discussion of Montalbán's career and influence.

DIANA MONTES DE OCA LOPEZ

Cuban-born cancer researcher and educator

Montes de Oca Lopez's research has made significant contributions to the understanding of tumor immunology. She has worked to advance the education and support of Latinos within the national and global cancer research community.

Latino heritage: Cuban
Born: August 26, 1937; Havana, Cuba
Also known as: Diana Montes de Oca; Diana M. Lopez
Areas of achievement: Medicine; education

EARLY LIFE

Diana Montes de Oca Lopez (di-AHN-ah MOHN-tes day OH-cah LOH-pehz) was born in Havana, Cuba. After graduating from high school she entered the University of Havana, from which she received her doctorate in natural sciences in 1960. Immigrating to the United States after the Cuban Revolution, she earned an M.S. in microbiology in 1968 and her Ph.D. in microbiology in 1970 from the University of Miami. She remained at the university for a postdoctoral fellowship in immunology and then became an assistant professor of microbiology and immunology at the University of Miami's Miller School of Medicine, where she remained throughout her career.

LIFE'S WORK

As a teacher, Montes de Oca Lopez was promoted to full professor and became director of the undergraduate program and leader of the tumor immunology program at the Miller School of Medicine. Her rapport with and support of students, including Latinos, was recognized by a faculty appreciation award from the microbiology and immunology undergraduate students at the University of Miami and a teaching award from the university's Miller School of Medicine. Montes de Oca Lopez also has been a visiting professor at the University of South Florida and the University of the West Indies.

Her research interests have focused on peptides with antitumor properties that show potential for future treatments, how breast tumors affect the development of the thymus and its functioning, and tumor regulation. She has written more than eight-five technical papers and more than twenty-five book chapters and edited five major textbooks in her specialized field.

Montes de Oca Lopez is a two-time president and former member of the senior council of the International Association for Breast Cancer Research. She won the Merit Award of the National Cancer Institute of the National Institutes of Health and the Excellence Award in Health and Science from *Hispanic Magazine* and Johnson & Johnson. She was appointed to the National Cancer Advisory Board of the National Cancer Institute at the National Institutes of Health in 2004. She has played various roles in the Minorities in Cancer Research Group of the American Association for Cancer Research and has participated in the association's Women in Cancer Research Group.

SIGNIFICANCE

Montes de Oca Lopez's research on tumor growth, metastasis (tumor spread), and treatment draws on her extensive knowledge of both microbiology and immunology, and her work has advanced the understanding and treatment of cancer. As a professor, she has mentored many undergraduate students and prospective physicians over her long and distinguished career.

Dennis W. Cheek

FURTHER READING

Kalte, Pamela M., and Katherine H. Nemeh, eds. *American Men and Women of Science: A Biographical Directory of Today's Leaders in Physical, Biological, and Related Sciences.* Detroit: Thomson/Gale, 2003. Includes an entry about Montes de Oca Lopez.

Kanellos, Nicolás, ed. *The Hispanic American Almanac: A Reference Work on Hispanics in the United States.* Detroit: Gale, 1997. Includes a biographical entry about Montes de Oca Lopez.

Unterburger, Amy L., ed. *Who's Who Among Hispanic Americans.* Detroit: Gale Research, 1994. Includes

See also: Desi Arnaz; Hector Elizondo; José Ferrer; Mel Ferrer; Fernando Lamas; Anthony Quinn; César Romero.

an entry providing bibliographic information about Montes de Oca Lopez.

Wei, Wei-Zen, and Diana M. Lopez, eds. *Immunology of Breast Cancer.* Ann Arbor, Mich.: OCSL Press, 2005. Montes de la Oca Lopez is one of the editors of this collection of research findings that present new directions in the treatment of breast cancer.

See also: Baruj Benacerraf; Jose Alberto Fernandez-Pol; David Domingo Sabatini.

MARÍA MONTEZ

Dominican-born actor

Montez was the biggest Universal Studios box office attraction during World War II, playing goddesses, gypsies, and other exotic characters in highly popular films designed to help international audiences escape the horrors of war.

Latino heritage: Dominican
Born: June 6, 1912; Barahona, Dominican Republic
Died: September 7, 1951; Paris, France
Also known as: María Africa Antonia Gracia Vidal de Santo Silas; La Reina del Technicolor; Technicolor Queen; El Ciclón Caribeño; Caribbean Cyclone; Dinamita Dominicana; Dominican Dynamite; La Tempestuosa Montez; Sirena de Hollywood; Hollywood's Mermaid
Area of achievement: Film

EARLY LIFE

María Montez (mah-REE-ah MON-tehz) was born to Isidoro Gracia García, a Spaniard born in the Canary Islands, and Regla Teresa María Vidal, a native Dominican woman. Her father exported woods and textiles, in addition to holding the title of honorary viceconsul of Spain. Montez came from a family of ten siblings. She taught herself English by listening to American songs and by reading American magazines and newspapers. She graduated with an eighth-grade education from a Catholic convent school in the Canary Islands, Spain.

In 1932, Montez married William McFeeters, a banker who worked at the First National City Bank of New York. They were married for seven years. In New York, she worked as a model, and photographs of her appeared in magazines and newspapers. Her modeling career and other public appearances helped to establish her reputation as an exotic beauty. She was twenty-seven years old but looked much younger. She adopted her stage name, María Montez, to honor a famous dancer favored by her father. Eventually, Montez became bored with New York and her marriage ended in 1939.

LIFE'S WORK

Montez's film career began in 1940, when she was under contract to Universal Studios. Because of her Dominican accent, she began by playing small parts in such "B" films as *Boss of Bullion City* (1940), *The Invisible Woman* (1940), *Lucky Devils* (1941), *That Night in Rio* (1941), and *Raiders of the Desert* (1941). In *Invisible Woman*, she spoke only one phrase. Upset at her meager roles, she became her own public relations manager and organized her own fan club, the

María Montez. (Time & Life Pictures/Getty Images)

Montez for Stardom Club, sending scantily clad photographs of herself to members. In *That Night in Rio,* her first technicolor film, she starred with Carmen Miranda, Don Ameche, and Alice Faye. *Life* magazine published an article about this film that praised all of the stars' performances, and Montez's beauty and ability to dance the rumba were not lost on an international audience. *South of Tahiti* (1941), Montez's first starring role, was another romantic, adventurous film designed to help audiences escape from the horrors of World War II. She dyed her hair blond for *Moonlight in Hawaii* (1941) and gained popularity among soldiers as a pin-up girl.

In 1942, Montez played Scheherazade in *Arabian Nights* and starred in *The Mystery of Marie Roget,* based on Edgar Allan Poe's work. The publication of one of her own poems, *Crepúsculo,* at this time provided favorable press. She repeatedly requested that she not be placed in stereotypical roles that were stifling her career. Universal, however, continued to star her in escapist fare, such as *Bombay Clipper* (1942), *White Savage* (1942), *Ali Baba and the Forty Thieves* (1944), *Bowery to Broadway* (1944), *Gypsy Wildcat* (1944), *Cobra Woman* (1944), and *Sudan* (1945).

Montez married actor and writer Jean-Pierre Aumont in 1943, and in 1946, she gave birth to a daughter, Maria Christina, who later became a film actor known as Tina Aumont. Montez continued to make films for Universal, including *Tangier* (1946), *The Exile* (1947), and *Pirates of Monterrey* (1947). When Universal did not allow her to produce eight films in which she would be featured, Montez sued the studio for discrimination and was awarded $250,000.

At the end of World War II, Montez and her husband moved their family to France. She and Aumont were invited to the Cannes Film Festival and they acted together in *The Siren of Atlantis* (1949) and *Wicked City* (1949). The couple also pursued their individual careers, with Aumont appearing in plays and Montez traveling to Italy to film *The Thief of Venice* (1950) and *Amore e sangue* (1951). After her stint in Italy, she starred in *L'Ile Hereuse,* a play written by her husband. She and Aumont starred in *Revenge of the Pirates* (1951), and that same year saw the release of her final film, the German-made crime story *Schatten über Neapel.*

Montez suffered from an erratic heart. On September 7, 1951, she suffered from a heart attack while in the bathtub, where she died at the age of thirty-nine.

Montez's Other Talents

María Montez, the glamor girl, is famous, but few know her as a dedicated wife, mother, and friend. Even fewer people know her as the writer of books, poems, and songs. In her biography of Montez, Margarita Vicens de Morales states that Móntez wrote three books, two of which were published: *Forever Is a Long Time* and *Hollywood Wolves I Have Tamed.* The unpublished title is "Reunion in Lilith." Montez also wrote articles in four languages that were published in the magazines *Páginas Barilejas* (Dominican Republic) and *Baho Rueco.* Two of her songs were also published and performed, "Doliente" and "Midnight Memories."

SIGNIFICANCE

Although Montez was not a particularly talented actor, her films were immensely popular during World War II. In these low-budget adventure stories, which some critics have dubbed "sand and scandal epics," Montez triumphed over all manner of adversity, and audiences could temporarily escape their troubles and enjoy the spectacle.

Montez's roles alluded to many of the war era's stereotypical views of Latinas as exotic beauties with fiery temperaments, and Montez tried unsuccessfully to transcend these stereotypes. Despite these limitations, Montez remains one of the most popular and successful Latino stars of the 1940's.

María Eugenia Trillo

FURTHER READING

Claqueta. María Montez. http://www.claqueta.es/actrices/maria-montez.html. A biography of Montez, written in Spanish.

Evans, Peter W. "From Maria Montez to Jasmine: Hollywood's Oriental Odalisques." In *"New" Exoticism: Changing Patterns in the Construction of Otherness,* edited by Isabel Santaolalla. Amsterdam: Rodopi, 2000. Examines the depiction of women in Hollywood fantasies set in ancient Baghdad, describing how Montez and other actors reflect changing ideas of femininity.

Smith, Jack. "The Perfect Filmic Appositeness of Maria Montez." In *Historical Treasures,* edited by Ira Cohen. New York: Hanuman Books, 1990. Smith, an underground filmmaker, explains why he idolizes Montez as an "icon of camp style."

Vicens de Morales, Margarita. *María Montez: Su vida.* 3d ed. Coral Gables, Fla.: Vicens and Morales, 2003. A comprehensive biography, written in Spanish.

See also: Desi Arnaz; Dolores del Río; José Ferrer; Rita Hayworth; Fernando Lamas; Beatriz Noloesca; Anthony Quinn; César Romero.

JOSÉ MONTOYA

American poet, artist, and musician

Montoya is considered one of the most influential poets of the Chicano renaissance. His poetry and artwork epitomize the intersection of fine art, scholarship, and social activism that have influenced generations of Chicano artists and scholars.

Latino heritage: Mexican
Born: May 28, 1932; Escoboza, New Mexico
Areas of achievement: Poetry; art; activism

EARLY LIFE

José Montoya (hoh-ZAY mon-TOY-ah) is a third-generation Mexican American who was born in Escoboza, a rural town south of Albuquerque, New Mexico. When he was a young boy, his mother Lucia painted decorative motifs and borders in local homes. She often brought Montoya to work with her, exposing him to color, pattern, and texture.

In 1941, his family briefly moved to the Sierra Vista Ranches in California. Montoya suffered heat stroke while passing out water to the migrant farm workers. The family moved again, to Oakland, California, in search of factory work during World War II. Montoya later used his poetry and art to recount his experiences as a child laborer and his observations about growing up in the aftermath of the Great Depression and World War II.

Montoya's parents separated in 1945. His mother permanently moved the family to Fowler, California, in the San Joaquin Valley. Feeling alienated by the substandard educational system, Montoya often found creative inspiration and hope in popular dime-store comic books, and he began experimenting with the graphic artwork he saw. He graduated from high school in 1951, and he began writing poetry after his high school teacher, Adrian Sanford, encouraged him.

Montoya served four years in the Korean War on a Navy minesweeper. He married his first wife, Mary Ellen Prieto, in 1954, and the couple had six children. In 1979, he remarried and had three more children with Juanita Jue. Montoya earned his associate's degree from San Diego City College in 1956, and in 1959 he won an arts scholarship to Oakland's College of Arts and Crafts. He graduated with a B.A. in education in 1962. The Chicano civil rights movement and César Chávez's United Farm Workers' rallies inspired Montoya to dedicate his life to Chicano social justice. He also joined the San Francisco Bay Area arts scene.

Montoya taught high school in Wheatland, California, until 1969 and then attended California State University, Sacramento. During his years at this university, he studied a variety of American and European authors and philosophers, including Walt Whitman and the Beat poets. He soon cultivated an interest in Mexican American poetry and social activism. During this period, he wrote one of his signature poetry pieces, "The Sell Out."

LIFE'S WORK

Montoya is well known for his work in the anthology *El Espejo* (*The Mirror*), published in 1969 by the influential Chicano editor Octavio Roman. This collection included Montoya's much-beloved classics "La Jefita" (*The Dear Mother*) and "Los Vatos" (*The Dudes*). Montoya's masterful use of code-switching and *calo*, the interplay of English and Spanish in colloquial Chicano speech, endeared him to generations of Chicano readers.

After he earned his M.A. from California State University, Sacramento, in 1971, Montoya taught art and Chicano studies at this university for more than twenty-five years and initiated the first of many community art initiatives. Montoya was among the first wave of Latino American professors hired by universities in the wake of student protests for educational reform in the 1960's.

Montoya is well known for his Barrio Art Program, a community arts education initiative in Sacramento's Washington area neighborhood. This program provides curriculum training for students at California State University, Sacramento, and makes fine art and social expression accessible to local Chicano youth and elderly adults. In addition, in 1971 Montoya founded the Royal Chicano Air Force, a popular Chicano art collective.

Montoya is perhaps most famous for his poem, "El Louie" (1972). This poem expertly depicts the pachuco,

Montoya and the Royal Chicano Air Force

José Montoya cofounded the nonprofit arts collective Rebel Chicano Arts Front with his friend Esteban Villa in 1971. The group later changed its name to the Royal Chicano Air Force (RCAF) as a play on words after people confused it with the Royal Canadian Air Force. Born against the backdrop of El Movimiento, the Chicano civil rights movement, RCAF's mission is to share ideas and resources and to give back to the Chicano community.

The RCAF is the longest-operating arts collective run by trained fine artists who have dedicated their lives and work to transforming the Chicano community. Its well-known murals, posters, and silk screens often use satire to convey a political message or advance a social cause. RCAF's whimsical creations were initially inspired by the pulp-fiction covers, comic books, and art books of the post-World War II era. The group's artists intentionally mix various art traditions in order to make art that is accessible to the general public. Through RCAF's efforts, many Sacramento parks and public facilities became community spaces for self-expression, artistic inspiration, picnics, music festivals, and fund-raising events for the Chicano community.

the Chicano antihero reminiscent of the 1940's zoot suiter, as a redeemable and misunderstood individual worthy of empathy and respect. "El Louie" is a Chicano studies classic and has been extensively critiqued and anthologized. Montoya's poetry collection *El sol y los de abajo* (1972; *The Sun and the Underdog*), represents his full flowering as a distinctly Chicano poet. The collection includes three ancient Mayan-inspired poems, written completely in Spanish, serializing the Chicano experience of oppression and ultimate redemption and hope. In 1991, he published another poetry collection, *Information: Twenty Years of Joda*. One of this collection's poems, "The Movement Has Gone for Its Ph.D, over at the University," speaks to Montoya's ever-present status as an unapologetic champion of the Chicano experience.

As a graphic artist, Montoya's body of work ranges from watercolors, murals, posters, and silk screens to wood carvings and sketches. Many of his poetry collections featured his own cover artwork. For Montoya, art is political, and his visual art, like his poetry, serves as a clarion call for Chicano social justice. His influences were Mexican engraver José Guadalupe Posada and the muralists Diego Rivera, José Clemente Orozco, and David Aflaro Siqueiros. His artwork has appeared in exhibitions nationwide and in Cuba, Mexico, and Paris and is included in the art collections of Yale University, the California State Library in Sacramento, and the Academia de San Carlos in Mexico City. In September, 2010, he was featured in the San Francisco-based exhibit *Rehistoricizing Abstract Expressionism in the San Francisco Bay Area: 1950's-1960's*. In addition to his poetry and artwork, Montoya in 1983 cofounded El Trio Casindio, a musical group that sets poetry to music.

Montoya has been honored with a 1981 National Endowment for the Arts Writing Fellowship grant, a 1995 City of Sacramento Mayor's Award for poetry, and a 1997 California Arts Council award.

SIGNIFICANCE

Throughout his life, Montoya has maintained close ties with the barrio community. His poetry and artwork convey a unique cultural tradition, neither Mexican nor American but distinctly Chicano. His poem "El Louie" represents a shift in Mexican American consciousness from a 1950's quest for assimilation to a 1960's desire to rediscover and embrace a cultural identity that had been marginalized and denigrated since the end of the Mexican Revolution in 1920. His work is a departure from the Chicano movement literature and art that glorified Mexican and Latin American revolutionary heroes of a bygone era. Instead, his work raises the controversial question of who is, and who is not, a true Chicano. Critics have accused Montoya of remaining mired in the 1960's struggle for social justice. Others, however, have lauded his steadfast adherence to his original mission: to challenge the status quo.

Latanya West

FURTHER READING

Gonzalez, Ray. "Information: Twenty Years of Joda." *The Nation* 258, no.4 (1994): 131. Helpful review of Montoya's poetry collection that clarifies his place in the Chicano literary tradition.

Leal, Luis. "José A. Montoya." In *A Luis Leal Reader*, edited by Ilan Stavans. Evanston, Ill.: Northwestern University Press, 2007. This anthology of Leal's critical essays on Mexican and Chicano literature includes an essay on Montoya.

Limón, José Eduardo. "My Old Man's Ballad: José Montoya and the Power Beyond." In *Mexican Ballads, Chicano Poems: History and Influence in*

Mexican-American Social Poetry. Berkeley: University of California Press, 1992. Insightful analysis of the origins of Montoya's pachuco poetry.

Montoya, José. *Information: Twenty Years of Joda*. San Jose, Calif.: Chusma House, 2002. Quintessential collection of Montoya's poetry spanning two decades, from 1969 to 1989. Contains his classics "El Louie," "Eslippng and Esliding," and "Until They Leave Us a Loan."

Villa, Raul. *Barrio-Logos: Space and Place in Urban Chicano Literature and Culture*. Austin: University of Texas Press, 2000. Scholarly book explores the Royal Chicano Air Force, Montoya's body of work to 2000, and his contributions to the Chicano barrios in Sacramento, California.

_____. "'El Louie' by José Montoya: An Appreciation." In *A Companion to Latina/o Studies*, edited by Juan Flores and Renato Rosaldo. Malden, Mass.:Wiley-Blackwell, 2007. Villa, a contemporary Montoya scholar, provides an in-depth analysis of Montoya's impact within the Chicano academic community.

See also: Rudolfo Anaya; Gloria Anzaldúa; Jimmy Santiago Baca; Lorna Dee Cervantes; Ernesto Galarza; Gary Soto; Alma Villanueva.

JOSEPH M. MONTOYA

American politician and lawyer

Montoya served in the New Mexico legislature and as lieutenant governor before his election to Congress. His career in government spanned four decades.

Latino heritage: Spanish and Mexican
Born: September 24, 1915; Peña Blanca, New Mexico
Died: June 5, 1978; Washington, D.C.
Also known as: Joseph Manuel Montoya
Areas of achievement: Government and politics; law

EARLY LIFE

Joseph Manuel Montoya (mahn-TOY-yah) was born in Peña Blanca, New Mexico, on September 24, 1915. His father was the sheriff of Sandoval County; his mother was descended from eighteenth-century Spanish immigrants who settled in what became New Mexico.

Montoya attended Regis College in Denver, Colorado, and later enrolled at Georgetown University law School.

As a full-time student, Montoya worked for the Department of the Interior. In 1936, at age twenty-two and still a law student, he was elected to represent Sandoval County in the New Mexico House of Representatives. He earned his law degree in 1938, the same year he was reelected. In 1939, Montoya was admitted to the New Mexico Bar. Not only was he the youngest member of the New Mexico House, he became its majority leader. The next year, Montoya won a seat in the state senate, where he was once again the youngest member. During his tenure in the New Mexico Senate, Montoya was both majority whip and chairman of the Judiciary Committee. From 1947 to 1957, he served three terms as lieutenant governor.

Montoya married Della Romero on November 9, 1940, and fathered two sons, Joseph M. and Patrick James, and a daughter, Linda Jean. In addition to his

Joseph Montoya. (Time & Life Pictures/Getty Images)

621

political career, Montoya practiced law in Santa Fe and owned and managed a variety of business enterprises that included Western Freight Lines. His only political setback came in 1950 when he lost a bid for the U.S. House of Representatives in the Democratic primary.

LIFE'S WORK

Montoya's opponent in the Democratic primary, incumbent congressman Antonio Fernandez, died in 1956, and Montoya was chosen by the New Mexico Democratic Party to run in a special election for the seat. He defeated his Republican opponent by seven thousand votes and went on to win four consecutive congressional terms with more than 60 percent of the vote. Montoya served on the House Judiciary Committee and gained a reputation for bringing substantial federal monies back to New Mexico. Montoya sponsored legislation that provided New Mexico residents with farm subsidies, increased agricultural support for wheat and cotton, and vocational retraining for unemployed farmworkers. He was a strong supporter of programs for people in poverty, such as low-cost public housing, food stamps, and federal loans for economically depressed rural and urban areas. Montoya helped institute federal aid to urban rapid transit systems, increased aid to education, and pollution controls for the nation's drinking water.

In 1964, Montoya ran for the U.S. Senate seat left vacant by the death of Senator Dennis Chavez and defeated his conservative opponent by almost thirty thousand votes. He spent his Senate years, from 1964 to 1977, working hard for his constituents, which included large populations of Native American and Hispanic voters. New Mexico's largest newspapers received daily reports from Montoya's Senate office detailing his activities. In the Senate, he continued to support legislation benefiting factory workers and farmers. Montoya was a significant contributor to the passage of the Wilderness Act (1964) that designated 9.1 million acres in thirteen states, including New Mexico, as wilderness preserves. He opposed President Richard Nixon's nomination of Earl Butz to be secretary of agriculture because he saw Butz as a supporter of agribusiness, not the small farmer.

Montoya was a strong supporter of the Office of Economic Opportunity and voted to increase the minimum wage, extend jobless benefits, and offer migrant workers unemployment compensation. He actively campaigned to bring industry to New Mexico to increase employment opportunities. Montoya sponsored legislation that included regulations on truth in

Montoya's Legislative Efforts to Benefit Hispanic Americans

During Joseph M. Montoya's political career, he used his influence to benefit Latinos throughout the United States and especially in his home state of New Mexico. He encouraged young Latinos to pursue law degrees and enter the legal profession. In the Senate, Montoya was responsible for the creation of the cabinet-level Committee on Opportunities for Spanish-Speaking People, which sponsored national symposiums to find ways to provide more employment and educational opportunities and improve housing and medical coverage for minorities. Montoya sponsored the Bilingual Education Act (1968), which provided federal educational funds for students learning English as a second language. In 1974, the Bilingual Education Act was strengthened as bilingual education became mandatory in elementary and secondary schools.

advertising, fair packaging, and proper labeling on products, and the registration of products containing toxic or corrosive substances. He also supported gun control, legal counsel for the poor, the Equal Rights Amendment prohibiting gender discrimination, and lowering the voting age to eighteen. Successful bills that Montoya steered into law included the Wholesome Meat Act (1967), the Wholesome Poultry Act (1968), and the Clean Hot Dog Act (1974). During his Senate career, Montoya served on the Appropriations Committee, the Public Works Committee, the Joint Committee on Atomic Energy, and the Senate Select Committee on Presidential Campaign Activities (the Senate Watergate Committee). He was responsible for forcing Nixon to pay for his own legal expenses in the Watergate scandal.

In the era of Watergate and an increasing national suspicion of the government, Montoya became the target of a series of financial investigations that tarnished his image. He was habitually late filing his income tax returns, he was investigated for creating dummy committees to launder campaign contributions, and he failed to report out-of-state campaign contributions. A late filing of his net worth in 1975 indicated that he was a millionaire with extensive real estate investments that included a substantial number of lease agreements for United States post offices and federal buildings. Whether or not he used his political office to obtain these federal lease agreements could never be proved. Montoya was not convicted of any wrongdoing, but the suspicions probably helped kill his bid for reelection in 1976. After Montoya's return to private life in 1977, he was implicated in the Koreagate scandal for accepting a cash campaign contribution from an unregistered foreign agent. He died in Washington, D.C., from liver and kidney failure on June 5, 1978.

SIGNIFICANCE

Montoya is remembered for improving and expanding economic opportunity for the working poor, particularly minorities within his state; his support of Medicare and Medicaid legislation; and his social activism. His papers are held at the Center for Southwest Research at the University of New Mexico Law School. In 1986, the General Services Building, South Complex, in Santa Fe, New Mexico, was named for him. There is a small museum dedicated to his memory in the building.

William A. Paquette

FURTHER READING

Axford, Roger W. *Spanish-Speaking Heroes.* Midland, Miss.: Pendell, 1973. Montoya is featured in this reference work's section on politicians.

Montoya, Joseph M. "The Silent People No Longer." In *Ripples of Hope: Great American Civil Rights Speeches*, edited by Josh Gottheimer. New York: Basic Civitas Books, 2003. Transcript of an address Montoya delivered before Congress in November, 1967, in support of the civil rights of Latinos.

Vigil, Maurilio, and Roy Lujan. "Parallels in the Career of Two Hispanic U.S. Senators," *Journal of Ethnic Studies* 13 (Winter, 1986): 1-20. A study of New Mexico's Democratic senators Joseph M. Montoya and Dennis Chavez, who quietly and effectively promoted opportunities for Hispanic Americans.

See also: Toney Anaya; Jerry Apodaca; Dennis Chavez; Bill Richardson.

PAT MORA

American writer

Best known for her children's books and poetry collections celebrating Latino culture, Mora has flourished as both an educator and award-winning author. Drawing upon her experiences as a Mexican American living on the United States-Mexico border, her rich, expressive writing emphasizes the necessity and importance of cultural, linguistic, and gender equality.

Latino heritage: Mexican
Born: January 19, 1942; El Paso, Texas
Also known as: Patricia Estella Mora
Areas of achievement: Literature; poetry

EARLY LIFE

Patricia Estella Mora (MOH-rah) was born on the United States-Mexico border in El Paso, Texas, to Raúl Antonio Mora and Estela Delgado Mora. She was raised in a bilingual home but mainly spoke Spanish, given that both sets of her grandparents came to El Paso during the Mexican Revolution and did not speak English. Mora attended Catholic schools in El Paso, where she rarely saw reflections of her Mexican culture and Spanish language in the curriculum. Instead, she spent her childhood in two disparate worlds: one filled with beautiful Spanish words and rich Mexican traditions and culture, the other filled with the language of necessity and strict rules.

After Mora graduated high school, she attended Texas Western College (now the University of Texas at El Paso, UTEP), from which she graduated in 1963 with a bachelor of arts degree. In July, 1963, Mora married William H. Burnside, Jr., with whom she would have three children: William Roy, Elizabeth Anne, and Cecilia Anne. She then became an English and Spanish teacher for the El Paso Independent School District, where she worked until 1966. A year later, More earned a master of arts degree in English from UTEP.

From 1971 to 1978, Mora worked as a part-time instructor for El Paso Community College and then moved to UTEP, where she was an English instructor. In 1981, she transitioned into university administration. She and her husband divorced that year, and she began to focus her energy on exploring her cultural heritage through her writing.

Mora published poems in various magazines throughout the late 1970's, but it wasn't until 1984 that she published her first book of poetry, *Chants,* which explored gender roles and inequalities within the Chicano culture. In May, 1984, she married her second husband, Vernon Lee Scarborough, a professor and archeologist. Two years later, Mora published *Borders* (1986), her second collection of poetry, drawing upon many of her experiences growing up on the border between two countries, two cultures, and two languages. The collection also continued to explore her feminist perspective, addressing borders that society constructs between genders.

Immediately, Mora began receiving honors and recognition for her poetry. Both *Chants* and *Borders* were acknowledged with Southwest Book Awards from the Border Regional Library, and she was named to *The El Paso Herald-Post* Writers Hall of Fame in 1988. The same year that she published *Borders*, Mora received a fellowship from the W. K. Kellogg Foundation to explore culture preservation around the world.

In 1989, Mora left academia to begin writing full time. Two years later, she published her third poetry collection, *Communion* (1991), describing the lives of women around the world and further exploring the chasm between the sexes. This was followed by *Nepantla: Essays from the Land in the Middle* (1993), an autobiographical collection of poignant reflections on what it means to be a woman in the United States and in various countries in Latin America. Critics have said that both of these books demonstrated a newfound depth in her writing and were greatly influenced by Mora's research funded by the Kellogg Foundation.

Although Mora would publish a few more works for adults, these writings mark a noticeable end to her early writing career, making way for her life's work as a literacy advocate and children's author.

LIFE'S WORK

Growing up on the border surrounded by Spanish-speakers and attending a school where she rarely heard the language or saw representations of Latinos in her school books greatly influenced Mora's childhood experiences. As a result, she made it her life's work to provide reflections of the Latino cultural experience in children's literature in order to strengthen the ethnic identity of Latino children and foster the intercultural understanding of non-Latino children and educators.

In 1992, Mora published her first book for children, *A Birthday Basket for Tía*. Based on experiences from Mora's own family involving her daughter and aunt, this picture book signified the beginning of the author's work for children celebrating Latino culture, family, strong female characters, and the Spanish language. The publication also marked Mora's journey to promote literacy and spread "bookjoy"—a term she

---

Empowering Cultural and Family Literacy

In 1996, Pat Mora envisioned combining a world celebration of children with the love of reading and books to create a family literacy program connecting children from all linguistic and cultural backgrounds. This literacy program known as El día de los niños/El día de los libros, or Día for short, was Mora's way of ensuring that children had the opportunity to be exposed to books representing their cultures and home languages.

With assistance from REFORMA, the National Association to Promote Library and Information Services to Latinos and the Spanish-Speaking, Día became a reality in 1997, when libraries debuted Día programs. Through the financial support of Dr. Dan Moore at the W. K. Kellogg Foundation, Día began to evolve into a national celebration. Eventually, Día planning initiatives were housed at the American Library Association and states such as Texas and California became "Día States," committing to statewide Día programming every year.

A few years later, Mora and her family established the Estela and Raúl Mora Award in an effort to promote Día celebrations in public libraries. In 2009, Mora, along with Mexican American muralist and illustrator Rafael López, created the bilingual picture book *Book Fiesta!* as a way to further promote the literacy celebration and emphasize Día's role in helping libraries serving multicultural and multilingual populations.

---

coined to describe the deeply emotional and joyful response that readers have to books that they identify with and enjoy.

Two years later, in 1994, Mora published three more children's picture books—*Listen to the Desert/Oye al desierto*; *Agua, Agua, Agua*; and *Pablo's Tree*—and a collection of children's poetry, *The Desert Is My Mother/El desierto es mi madre*. Many of these works celebrate the beauty of Southwestern landscape and pay tribute to the desert. Over the next two years, Mora published two more children's poetry books and two children's folktales, all imbued with elements of Latino culture and Spanish.

In 1997, Mora published one of her most notable children's books, *Tomás and the Library Lady*, an illustrated biography highlighting the importance of the books in the life of famous Mexican American educator Dr. Tomás Rivera. While many of her other children's books received literary honors, this was

Mora's first title to receive two awards specifically for Latino children's literature: the 1998 Tomás Rivera Mexican American children's Book Award, administered by Texas State University at San Marcos, and a 1997 Américas Award for children's and Young Adult Literature Commended Title, administered by the Consortium of Latin American Studies Programs.

Mora's book *The Rainbow Tulip* (1999) highlights her mother's experiences as a bilingual, bicultural immigrant child in first grade working to forge harmony between her home and school lives. She published numerous other works for children over the next decade. Each of these books celebrates the contributions of Latinos or intercultural connections between Latino and non-Latino children.

In addition to writing, Mora has worked tirelessly to establish the family literacy celebration known as El Día de los Niños/El Día de los Libros (The Day of Children/The Day of Books) or Día for short. Her intent was to create a holiday that would encourage families, educators, and other child advocates to celebrate children as well as linguistic and cultural diversity through the use of high-quality, multicultural children's books.

Throughout her career as an author, literacy advocate, and educator, Mora has received numerous awards. She was named an honorary member of the American Library Association and has been granted honorary doctorates by North Carolina State University and the State University of New York at Buffalo. She also has received the University of Southern Mississippi's Medallion for Outstanding Contributions to Children's Literature.

SIGNIFICANCE

In a time when Chicano writers and poets were beginning to add to the cultural fabric of twentieth-century American literature, Mora emerged as one of the most diverse and distinguished Latino writers, creating poetry and books for children and adults. Her work paved the way for future generations of Latino children's authors, helped to establish the field of Latino children's literature, and solidified the importance of creating cultural works for children that represent one of the largest ethnic minority groups in the United States. Mora has also been an assiduous advocate for promoting bicultural, bilingual literacy in schools and libraries.

Jamie Campbell Naidoo

FURTHER READING

Marcovitz, Hal. *Who Wrote That? Pat Mora*. New York: Chelsea House, 2008. An accessible biography highlighting Mora's childhood, writing, accomplishments, and Latino identity. Includes color photos, time line, and suggested readings.

Mora, Pat. "Confessions of a Latina Author." *The New Advocate* 11 (Fall, 1998): 279-290. Thoughtful article in which Mora addresses her purpose and passion for writing children's literature that celebrates the Latino cultural experience.

_____. *House of Houses*. Boston: Beacon Press, 1997. Mora's nontraditional memoir examines the concept of houses (and the secrets they hold) as well as family. Using her own unique style, the author allows her deceased relatives to share their stories with readers, providing biographical information in an engaging narrative format.

_____. "Pat Mora." Interview by Bruce Dick. In *A Poet's Truth: Conversations with Latino/Latina Poets*. Tucson: University of Arizona Press, 2003. Interview with Mora placing her poetry within the larger context of American literature, emphasizing the influence of the author's Latino heritage on her body of work.

Rowlands, Kathleen Dudden. "The Influence of Pat Mora: How—and Why—Literacy Becomes Political." *Children and Libraries* 5 (Spring, 2007): 20-25. Article describing Mora's passion for promoting cultural and bilingual literacy through her Día initiative.

See also: Alma Flor Ada; Pura Belpré; Monica Brown; Ana Castillo; Nicholasa Mohr.

CHERRÍE MORAGA

American playwright, scholar, and feminist

Known for her autobiographical works that explore the multifaceted aspects of her Chicana lesbian identity and multigenerational familial relationships, Moraga is also a prolific playwright and community activist. Her works explore the complex connections of sexuality, race, gender, and class and the inequities and challenges experienced by women of color.

Latino heritage: Mexican

Born: September 25, 1952; Whittier, California

Also known as: Cecilia Lawrence; Cherríe Moraga
 Lawrence; Cherríe L. Moraga

Areas of achievement: Scholarship; theater; social
 issues; gay and lesbian issues

EARLY LIFE

Cherríe Moraga (cheh-REE moh-RAH-gah) was born Cher'rie Cecilia Lawrence in the Los Angeles area, California, to parents Elvira and Joseph. Moraga is the youngest of three children born to a Chicana mother and an Anglo father, and Moraga's work is influenced by the relationship between her parents and by her struggles to integrate the different aspects of her racial identity. When she was nine, Moraga and her family relocated to San Gabriel, California, where she was daily exposed to her mother's extended family and Chicano familial connections. The influence of family, the style of her family's oral storytelling, and the significance of female familial bonds are apparent in Moraga's works.

Moraga and her siblings were the first generation in her family to pursue college degrees, and Moraga completed her teaching degree in English at Immaculate Heart College in 1974. Moraga began to write creatively and grappled with her lesbian consciousness while attending college. In 1975, Moraga came out as a lesbian and began to write openly about her sexuality. In 1977, she relocated to the San Francisco area. Influenced by the racism and heterocentrism in the largely white feminist movement and the sexism and heterocentrism within the Black Power and Chicano movements, her writing became focused on the matters affecting women of color because of societal oppressions based on class, race, and sexuality. She received her M.A. from San Francisco State University in 1980.

LIFE'S WORK

Moraga's experiences with her identities and her desire to pursue a career as a writer and playwright led her to New York City after she received her M.A. degree. In 1981, Moraga cofounded Kitchen Table: Women of Color Press, whose primary goal was to publish works by women of color. Moraga also coedited, along with Gloria Anzaldúa, the foundational feminist text, *This Bridge Called My Back: Writings by Radical Women of Color* (1983). This anthology contains essays, poems, and narratives by a multitude of writers, including Moraga, on various subjects that impact the lives of women of color.

Cherrie Moraga. (courtesy of Cherrie Moraga)

Moraga's autobiographical text, *Loving in the War Years: Lo que nunca pasó por sus labios,* was published in 1983 and considered groundbreaking for its exploration of lesbian identity, the potential violence that impacts the lives of lesbians of color, the critique of Chicana familial relationships and histories, and Moraga's use of Spanish in her prose and poetry throughout the text.

Giving up the Ghost (1986) became the first of many plays written by Moraga and confronts issues of sexual violence, the oppression felt by women of color because of societal injustices, and lesbian sexuality and love. This work was followed by *Shadow of a Man* (1992), *Heroes and Saints, and Other Plays* (1994), *Heart of the Earth: A Popol Vuh Story* (2000), *The Hungry Woman: A Mexican Medea* (2000), *Watsonville: Some Place Not Here* (2000), *Circle in the Dirt: El Pueblo de East Palo Alto* (2002), *Waiting for Da God* (2004), *The Mathematics of Love* (2009), and *Digging up the Dirt* (2010). Her plays have considered issues of oppressive mythologies, community activism, and the lived experiences of women of color.

In 1993, Moraga published *The Last Generation,* a collection of poems and essays that analyze the loss of culture in Chicano communities and the inclusion of homosexual-identified individuals in a Chicano future. She later published *Waiting in the Wings: Portrait of a Queer Motherhood* (1997), an autobiographical text sharing her experiences in becoming a mother.

Moraga has spent much of her career as an educator, serving as the artist-in-residence in the Department of Drama at Stanford University and teaching courses such as Creative Writing and Latino/Queer Performance. She has received numerous awards for her works and community activism.

Significance

In *Loving in the War Years*, Moraga articulated her experiences in coming to consciousness as a Chicana lesbian struggling to find her identity in the liminal spaces between white and Chicano cultures, between her sexuality and a homophobic society, and between her generation and those of Chicanas before her. These personal revelations about sexuality and racial identity, as well as commentary on the oppressions experienced by women of color everywhere, have impacted the evolution of homosexual, Chicana, and feminist studies. Her consistent efforts to address these issues as a playwright, essayist, poet, activist, and educator are Moraga's legacy.

Erin Ranft

Further Reading

Kevane, Bridget A., and Juanita Heredia. *Latina Self-Portraits: Interviews with Contemporary Women Writers.* Albuquerque: University of New Mexico Press, 2000. Contains an interview with Moraga in which she shares her insights and opinions about connections between the Chicano community and academia, about writing, and about the utility and importance of language.

Moraga, Cherríe, and Gloria Anzaldúa. *This Bridge Called My Back: Writings by Radical Women of Color.* Berkeley, Calif.: Third Woman Press, 2002. This third edition of the text includes the original introductions and preface, an introduction by Moraga in which she reflects on the publication of *This Bridge*, and commentary on the political, economic, and social issues that continue to impact women of color.

Sternback, Nancy Saporta. "'A Deep Racial Memory of Love:' The Chicana Feminism of Cherríe Moraga." In *Breaking Boundaries: Latina Writing and Critical Readings*, edited by Asunción Horno-Delgado, Eliana Ortega, Nina M. Scott, and Nancy Saporta Sternbach. Amherst: University of Massachusetts Press, 1989. An examination of Moraga's *Loving in the War Years* and its influential and groundbreaking Chicana lesbian feminist content.

Yarbro-Bejarano, Yvonne. *The Wounded Heart: Writing on Cherríe Moraga.* Austin: University of Texas Press, 2001. A close reading of Moraga's work on the body, sexuality, and desire.

See also: Mercedes de Acosta; Julia Alvarez; Gloria Anzaldúa.

Alejandro Morales

American writer

Morales is best known for his novels that depict the urban experience of Chicanos in the barrios of late-twentieth-century California. His fiction interweaves myth, history, and the fantastic to examine the rural and urban discord between Chicanos and Anglos along the United States-Mexico border in California and Texas.

Latino heritage: Mexican
Born: October 14, 1944; Montebello, California
Also known as: Alejandro Dennis Morales
Area of achievement: Literature

Early Life

Alejandro Dennis Morales (ah-leh-HAHN-droh moh-RAH-lehs) was born and raised in the Simons barrio of Montebello, California. The son of Delfino Morales Martínez and Juana Contreras Martínez, Mexican immigrants from Guanajuato, Morales received his earliest education in the insular barrio built around the Simons Brick Factory. When the Simons barrio schools closed, Morales transferred to Montebello Junior High and subsequently graduated from Montebello High School in 1963. He attended California State University at Los Angeles from 1963 to 1967, earning a bachelor's degree in English in 1967, and a master's degree in 1973. He completed a Ph.D. in Spanish in 1975 from Rutgers University in New Brunswick, New Jersey.

During his senior year in high school and his first year at California State University, Morales flirted briefly with drugs and alcohol in East Los Angeles. It was a low point in his life. He harnessed these early, often violent experiences in a series of personal journals. His first novel, *Caras viejas y vino nuevo* (*Old Faces and New Wine*, 1982; also known as *Barrio on the Edge*, 1998), published in Spanish in 1975 by Editorial Joaquín Moritz in Mexico City, is a fictional account of the Simons barrio milieu of his formative years.

Morales married Rohde Teaze on December 16, 1967, and they had two children, Alessandra Pilar and Gregory Stewart. In 1974, he was a finalist for the Mexico Press Literary Prize for *Caras viejas y vino nuevo*. Morales received a Ford Foundation Fellowship (1972-1973); ITT International Fellowship (1973-1974); Mellon Foundation Fellowship (1975); and the Luis Leal Literature Award (2007) for distinction in Chicano/Latino literature.

LIFE'S WORK

Morales became a professor of Spanish and Portuguese in the School of Humanities at the University of California at Irvine. In the 1980's, 1990's, and 2000's, he published several novels and numerous critical articles. His first novel, *Caras viejas y vino nuevo*, is violent, fragmented, unconventional work that weaves fact with fiction to depict the disillusionment of the working poor wrought by the contemporary urban experience of the barrio. A polemic that presents an often hostile, negative image of the Anglo world—"el otro lado" (the other side)—the novel was met with critical acclaim as well as consternation.

The veiled historicity, awkward syntax, and ambiguous language of Morales's first novel are hallmarks of the innovative, often disjointed narrative style that he continues to hone in later novels, such as *La verdad sin voz* (1979; *Death of an Anglo*, 1988); *Reto en el paraíso* (1983), a mix of Spanish and English; *The Brick People* (1988); *The Rag Doll Plagues* (1992); *Waiting to Happen: Volume One of the Heterotopian Trilogy* (2001); *Pequeña nación* (2005), a collection of three novellas; and *The Captain of All These Men of Death* (2008). Each of these works entwines literary theory and a postmodern sensibility with an intimate, perspicacious knowledge of Chicano life at the turn of the millennium.

Morales's firsthand knowledge of the Chicano experience—existing and even embracing a liminal existence in the borderlands between Mexican and Anglo cultures—has positioned him as a key player in what has been called the Second Wave of Latino/Chicano writing. In moving from experiential, often biographical modes of narrative to neonaturalist, social realist modes, Morales's works often mix stories, characters, and circumstances

to transcend space and time. Ideas about destruction and creation, questions of space, memory, and movement, and elements of eroticism and the fantastic interweave in works such as *The Rag Doll Plagues* and *The Brick People*. *Waiting to Happen* is a hybrid form that intermixes poetry, essay, and epistle within the multilayered spaces of Mexico City and Los Angeles.

SIGNIFICANCE

A pioneer of Chicano literature, Morales skirts conventional lines of form and content in his novels. He consistently produces challenging works that question the fundamental tenets of Chicano life and rural and urban borderland identities while providing few simple answers. One of a handful of Chicano writers to engage with ecological issues related to industrial development of the U.S.-Mexico borderlands, he has characterized and reinterpreted history through unique explorations of the landscape central to the Chicano experience in the American Southwest. Recurrent themes in his work involve disease, medicine, science, and technology, as well as the often socially exclusionary aspects of modernity. These concerns make Morales a distinctive and compelling voice in Chicano literature.

Cordelia E. Barrera

FURTHER READING

Gurpegui, José Antonio, ed. *Alejandro Morales: Fiction Past, Present, Future Perfect*. Tempe, Ariz.: Bilingual Press, 1996. Seven critical essays on Morales's fiction, an essay by Morales, an interview, a bibliography, and family photos. Essays are in Spanish and English.

Kaup, Monika. "From Hacienda to Brick Factory: The Architecture of the Machine and Chicano Collective Memory in Alejandro Morales's *The Brick People*." In *U.S. Latino Literatures and Cultures: Transnational Perspectives*, edited by Francisco A. Lomelí and Karin Ikas. Heidelberg, Germany: Carl Winter Universitätsverlag, 2000. Critical study of collective memory and industrialized capitalism in the novel.

López-Lozano, Miguel. "Cultural Identity and Dystopia in Alejandro Morales's *The Rag Doll Plagues*." In *Utopian Dreams, Apocalyptic Nightmares: Globalization in Recent Mexican and Chicano Narrative*. West Lafayette, Ind.: Purdue University Press, 2008. The author argues that the novel plays a role in situating Morales at the forefront of Chicano writers who engage twenty-first century questions of industrial development, urbanization, and environmental degradation in the shadow of the North American Free Trade Agreement.

Morales, Alejandro. *Barrio on the Edge/Caras viejas y vino nuevo*, translated by Francisco A. Lomelí. Tempe, Ariz.: Bilingual Press, 1998. A bilingual edition with light corrections that maintains the narrative sequence of the original Spanish edition. Contains a critical introductory essay and a bibliography.

See also: Rudolfo Anaya; Norma Elia Cantú; Reyes Cárdenas; Martha P. Cotera; Francisco Jiménez; Mary Helen Ponce.

ESAI MORALES

American actor and activist

Morales has built a career in film, television, and theater, although he is best known for his work in courtroom and crime. He also has made a name for himself as a celebrity activist for political, social justice, and environmental causes.

Latino heritage: Puerto Rican

Born: October 1, 1962; Brooklyn, New York

Also known as: Esai Manuel Morales, Jr.; Manny

Areas of achievement: Acting; radio and television; theater; activism

EARLY LIFE

Esai Manuel Morales, Jr. (EE-si moh-RAH-lehs) was born in Brooklyn, the son of two immigrants from Puerto Rico. His father was a welder, while his mother, Iris Margarita Morales, advocated for the International Ladies' Garment Workers' Union. Through her influence, Morales developed his empathy for the concerns of the working classes and the disadvantaged. His parents divorced when he was still quite young, and he grew up only speaking Spanish until he entered the school system.

Seeing Al Pacino's performance in *Dog Day Afternoon* (1975) motivated Morales to seek a career as an actor, and he eventually applied for and was admitted to the prestigious School of the Performing Arts, a public alternative high school in Manhattan where young thespians could receive professional guidance while honing their craft. Morales drew upon this experience when he landed his first dramatic role as Francisco Esteban in *El Hermano*, a one-act play by Romulus Linney that debuted at the Ensemble Theatre Studio in February, 1981. A choice role as Ariel in *The Tempest* (pr. 1611, pb. 1623) at New York's Shakespeare Festival in the Park soon followed.

LIFE'S WORK

Morales made the jump from stage to cinema in 1982, appearing as Mitchell in Paul Morrissey's seedy tale of a gay hustling scam, *Forty Deuce*. He then landed the significant part of Paco Moreno in *Bad Boys* (1983), a role that gave him the opportunity to play Sean Penn's Latino nemesis. The film that truly brought him widespread recognition and attention, however, was Luis Miguel Valdez's biography of Ritchie Valens, *La Bamba* (1987). In this successful film, Morales played Bob, the biker half-brother of the young rock star, a part that called for considerable range and the confluence of machismo, sensitivity, self-doubt, and cultural pride. With these latter two films, Morales established himself as an actor who left a strong impression in macho roles; this

Esai Morales. (AP Photo)

629

quality led to a career in which he often was cast as a criminal or law-enforcement official, although he also has made several films focusing on Latino family life.

Morales's work on stage and in cinema was supplemented by regular appearances on television. A teen heartthrob part on the ABC Afterschool Special *The Great Love Experiment* in 1984 led to subsequent work on *The Equalizer*, *Fame*, and *Miami Vice* in 1985, and later performances on a range of programs such as *The Twilight Zone* (1989), *Tales from the Crypt* (1994), *The Outer Limits* (1997), and *L.A. Doctors* (1999). He was a series regular on shows including *American Family* (2002), *Resurrection Blvd.* (2000-2002), *Vanished* (2006), and *Jericho* (2008). However, Morales probably is best known to television viewers for his performance as Lieutenant Tony Rodriguez on *NYPD Blue* from 2001 to 2004. In 2009, he starred in the SyFy Network's *Caprica*, a spinoff of the popular *Battlestar Galactica* series.

Morales describes himself as an "actorvist," which he defines as someone who combines art and activism to build bridges of understanding. He demonstrated such commitment in 1997 when, along with Jimmy Smits, Sonia Braga, and attorney Felix Sanchez, he cofounded the National Hispanic Foundation for the Arts, an organization that offers Hispanic artists and professionals graduate scholarships at prestigious universities and also seeks to expand career opportunities in entertainment and performance. By 2010, more than $1 million in scholarships had been distributed to more than 350 recipients. Morales is a committed environmentalist as well; he is a vegetarian and a founding board member of Earth Communications Office, a nonprofit organization dedicated to using celebrity recognition to promote ecologically sustainable living.

SIGNIFICANCE

In 2005, accepting the Rita Moreno Award from the Hispanic Organization of Latin Actors, Morales praised the strong sense of community in Latino culture and called upon Latinos to use their money and power to improve representation of their heritage and culture in popular entertainment. In his life, he balances artistic performance with a serious commitment to social and environmental justice, and even after achieving considerable professional success he continues to advocate forcefully for his dream of a better society.

Scot M. Guenter

FURTHER READING

Berg, Charles Ramirez. *Latino Images in Film: Stereotypes, Subversion, and Resistance.* Austin: University of Texas Press, 2002. A critical reflection on popular film conveying negative Latino images and the way some works challenge that.

Kent, Gary. *Shadows and Light: Journeys with Outlaws in Revolutionary Hollywood.* Austin, Tex.: Dalton, 2009. A filmmaker's memoir on the evolution of indie films includes his collaborations with Morales.

Rodriguez, Clara. *Heroes, Lovers, and Others: The Story of Latinos in Hollywood.* New York: Oxford University Press, 2008. Excellent overview of history of Latino roles in American film contextualizes Morales's personal contributions.

See also: Luis Alfaro; Benjamin Bratt; Emilio Estevez; Andy Garcia; John Leguizamo; George Lopez; Edward James Olmos; Charlie Sheen.

NORO MORALES

Puerto Rican-born pianist, composer, and bandleader

Morales was a pioneering musician in New York and Puerto Rico. He excelled in the Afro-Caribbean, tropical, and Latin jazz music genres; he was a trailblazer as a pianist, composer, arranger, and bandleader. In the New York of the 1940's, he was known as the "Rumba Man."

Latino heritage: Puerto Rico
Born: January 4, 1911; Puerta de Tierra, Puerto Rico
Died: January 14, 1964; Santurce, Puerto Rico

Also known as: Norosvaldo Morales Sanabria
Area of achievement: Music

EARLY LIFE

Norosvaldo Morales Sanabria (NOH-rohs-VAHL-doh moh-RAH-lehs SAH-nah-BREE-ah) was born on January 4, 1911, in the Puerta de Tierra section of San Juan, Puerto Rico. His father was Luis Morales and his mother was Mercedes Sanabria y Ellinger. Originally trained as a trombonist, then as a pianist, Morales was raised in the predominantly black neighborhood where he grew up listening to the Afro-Puerto Rican genres of *bomba* and *plena* that influenced his future musical style.

The Morales family produced several musicians. Morales's father was a violinist and his brothers and sister played various instruments: Ismael (Esy) played the flute and saxophone; Humberto was a percussionist; José (Pepito) was a saxophonist; Luis played the violin; and Alicia was a pianist. When Morales was thirteen years old, the family moved to Caracas, Venezuela, because his father had been invited by Venezuelan president Juan Vicente Gómez to join the official government band. After five years, the family returned to Puerto Rico in 1930.

During his youth, Morales played with several outstanding bands in San Juan, including those led by Ralph Sánchez, Augusto Rodríguez, Carmelo Díaz Soler, and Rafael Muñoz. Morales moved to New York in 1935; two years later, he organized a band that featured his brothers. Los Hermanos Morales (the Morales Brothers) played in clubs such as the famed El Morocco. Not long after that, Morales moved to an apartment near that of legendary composer Rafael Hernández. They developed a relationship, and Hernández often asked Morales to play his most recent works on piano. Morales also recorded several Hernández compositions with his band, which now carried his name: Orquesta de Noro Morales.

LIFE'S WORK

In 1938, Morales began his recording career in earnest with *Ahora sí somos felices* for Columbia Records. After that came many studio sessions. In 1942, *Serenata rítmica* was a major hit for him; famous Mexican singer and actor Jorge Negrete recorded the composition. Morales's popularity came as a result of his syncopated style on the piano. He was described as the Latin Duke Ellington. One of his biggest fans was the great Xavier Cugat, who was impressed with Morales's improvisational skills. According to Latin music historian Max Salazar, Morales's recordings were among the best sellers in the 1940's. This gave Morales opportunities to play in the most popular nightclubs of the period and to appear in films. He performed regularly at the Stork Club, Copacabana, La Conga, Palladium, and China Doll nightclubs. At one point, he was dubbed the "King of Latin music" by the Spanish-language New York newspaper *La prensa*.

Extremely popular in New York, Morales was asked to perform for the 1949 inauguration of Puerto Rico's first elected governor, Luis Muñoz Marín.

Morales played several of his biggest hits, including "Isla verde," "Puerta de tierra," and "Capullito de alelí." His performance gained him a recording contract with MGM Records. On his first MGM album, Morales recorded "Rum and Soda," which he dedicated to the governor and a campaign to popularize the island's rum.

In 1960, Morales returned to his homeland with his wife, Vilma Curbelo. Although he was suffering from acute diabetes, he became music director for the prestigious La Concha Hotel in the Condado section of San Juan, not far from where he was born and raised.

Many significant Latin music artists performed with the Orquesta de Noro Morales, including singers Machito, Tito Rodríguez, Pellín Rodríguez, Vicentico Valdéz, Dioris Valladares, and Vitín Avilés. He also worked with percussionists Tito Puente, Ray Romero, Sabú Martínez, Manny Oquendo, and Willie Rosario; saxophonist and arranger Ray Santos; and bassist Julio Andino. Morales died on January 14, 1964, in Santurce.

SIGNIFICANCE

Morales was a precursor to the salsa movement of the 1960's, which blended Caribbean music with jazz, blues, and other genres. A similar blending can be appreciated in Morales's compositions such as "Bim Bam Boom," "Indiferencia," "María Cervantes," "No puede ser," "Oye Negra," and "What Happened, Baby." He released a number of albums on various labels and influenced numerous musicians throughout his career.

Basilio Serrano

FURTHER READING

Figueroa, Frank. *Noro Morales: Latin Piano Man.* Tampa, Fla.: Pillar, 2007. Biographical essay written by a Morales colleague who is a musician, music historian, and college professor.

Gerard, Charley, Marty Sheller, and Larry Smith. *Salsa!: The Rhythm of Latin Music.* Rev. ed. Tempe, Ariz.: White Cliffs Media, 1998. Describes the evolution of salsa music from its roots in Cuba, Puerto Rico, and New York. Pioneers of salsa such as Morales are described in detail.

Morales, Noro. *The Rumba King: Noro Morales Demonstrates His Original Authentic Method.* New York, Rivoli Music Books, 1950. Morales describes his piano style and how to reproduce his unique sound.

Salazar Primero, Max. *Mambo Kingdom.* New York: Schirmer, 2002. Written by a Morales contemporary and Latin music historian, this book offers useful perspective on Morales's place in the Latin music historical continuum of New York

See also: Claudio Arrau; Ray Barretto; Celia Cruz; Tito Puente.

SYLVIA MORALES

American filmmaker

Recognized as a documentary film writer, editor, producer, and director, Morales also has written essays and taught production courses at several higher education institutions in Southern California. In her film and video work, she has created resources that have increased American understanding of Chicano culture.

Latino heritage: Mexican
Born: July, 1943; Phoenix, Arizona
Area of achievement: Filmmaking

EARLY LIFE

Sylvia Morales (SIL-vee-uh moh-RAH-lehs) was born in Phoenix, Arizona, and raised by her mother. She attended school in Culver City, California. In her youth, she and other family members enjoyed *teatro* (theater), dancing, and singing for family entertainment. After completing high school, Morales earned a bachelor of arts, cum laude, and then a master of fine arts in film from the Motion Picture Department at the University of California, Los Angeles (UCLA). Through connections at UCLA Morales became acquainted with another UCLA graduate, Jose Luis Ruiz, who hired her to do some camera work for KABC-TV, a local affiliate of American Broadcasting Company. The television program *Unidos* focused on the local Chicano community; Morales filmed thirteen short documentaries for *Unidos*. Two years later, in 1973, Morales helped direct portions of a *Sesame Street* production on Cinco de Mayo.

In the late 1960's and early 1970's, documentaries were beginning to appear on Chicano television programming in California. Morales and several other UCLA graduates were among those creating this new genre of film. Using a style and setting similar to that employed by Luiz Valdez in his 1969 documentary *Yo soy Joaquin* (*I Am Joaquin*), Morales directed, produced, and edited *Chicana!* The twenty-three-minute documentary, with script written by Ana Nieto-Goméz, gives a feminine perspective of history. The film begins with stereotypes of Mexican and Chicana women; reviews their history and experiences since pre-Columbian times in Mexico and in southwest-

ern United States; and features women of historical significance.

LIFE'S WORK

Chicana! (1979) is considered to be a milestone Latino documentary as it was among the first in its field. In that same year Morales also created a cultural series entitled *El Espejo* (*The Mirror*) for local television. Over the next decade Morales produced many other mostly Public Broadcasting Service (PBS) documentaries. These documentaries include *Myths and Visions in Film* (1982); *The Art and Magic of Rufino Tamayo* (1983); *Ballad of an Unsung Hero* (1983); *Los Lobos: And a Time to Dance* (1984); *MALDEF* (1983), a program on the Mexican American Legal Defense and Education Fund; *Esperanza* (1985; *Hope*); *Vaya con Dios* (1985; *Go, with God*); *SIDA Is AIDS* (1988); and *Values, Sexuality, and the Family* (1989). Morales's films explored current and historical issues in Hispanic American society.

During the 1980's demand grew for Latino programming, and several Southwestern television stations, in states ranging from Texas to California, united to form the Latino Consortium intended to help reduce programming costs. This consortium eventually grew to include more than fifty stations. From 1981 to 1985 Morales was the executive director of the consortium, overseeing the Latino-themed programs on PBS and also hosting *Presente*, a weekly national line-up. While serving as director, Morales published a book of her photography, *A New View of a Women's Body* (1981); her article "Chicano-Produced Celluloid Mujeres" was published in *Bilingual Review* (1985); and she coproduced a Latino Consortium talk show, *An Interview with . . .* (1985). A couple of years later, Morales wrote a screenplay, *Hearts on Fire* (1987), and formed her own company, Sylvan Productions (1988).

In the early 1990's, Morales's work included *Faith Even to the Fire* (1990-1991); *Life and Times* (1992); *A Century of Women: Work and Family* (1994); and *Struggles in the Fields* (1996), an hour-long episode in a four-hour PBS series *Chicano! The Mexican Civil*

Rights Movement. Morales wrote and produced a short documentary on date violence, *La Limpia* (1996; *The Clean One*); *Women: Stories of Passion, Angel from the Sky* (1997); and *Tell Me Again . . . What Is Love?* (1998). She also directed several episodes of the televised series *Reyes y Rey* and *Resurrection Blvd.* and cowrote the screenplay *Real Men and Other Miracles* (1998) with Carmen Tafallo.

Thirty years after producing *Chicana!* Morales produced a fifty-eight-minute sequel, *A Crushing Love: Chicanas, Motherhood, and Activism* (2009). Morales interviewed five Latina rights movement women, Dolores Huerta, Elizabeth Martinez, Cherríe Moraga, Alicia Escalante, and Martha P. Cotera, who told how they balanced their roles as activist with single parenthood. Morales included responses from some of the activists' children and added herself and her daughter into the film. Morales, the mother of two children, settled in Los Angeles.

In honor of her work, Morales received the Rockefeller Fellowship Award in Media, the VESTA Award for contributions to art in Southern California, and a fellowship from the National Endowment of the Arts. She also earned participation in the American Film Institute's Directing Workshop for Women. In 2009, the Boyle Heights Latina Independent Film Festival honored Morales for her film and video work.

SIGNIFICANCE

Morales was one of the original Chicana filmmakers. Her documentaries have explored stereotypes, religion, sexism, violence, and feminism and have focused on gender and race. In her films she has strived to present accurate images of Mexican American women. Her work began in the early 1970's, continued for over three decades, and influenced her successors.

Her film and production courses also have enhanced education in the field. In 2010, Morales became an associate professor in production film and television at Loyola Marymount University.

Cynthia J. W. Svoboda

FURTHER READING

Hidalgo-de la Riva, Osa. "Stone Chicana Rap: An Interview with Sylvia Morales. *Spectator* 19, no. 1 (Fall/Winter, 1998): 92-96. Summarizes Morales's work and focuses specifically on her work with race and gender in television.

Maciel, David R., Isidro D. Ortiz, and Mariá Herrera-Sobek. *Chicano Renaissance: Contemporary Cultural Trends.* Tucson: University of Arizona Press, 2000. Collection examines the changes that have occurred in the Chicano community in cultural forms, including art, literature, music, cinema and television, radio, and theater. Discusses the important work of Morales.

Noriega, Chon A. *Shot in America: Television, the State, and the Rise of Chicano Cinema.* Minneapolis: University of Minnesota, 2000. Discusses Chicano cinema in the United States and features Morales as one component in the process.

See also: Elizabeth Avellán; Martha P. Cotera; Dolores Huerta; Cherríe Moraga; Robert Rodriguez; George Romero.

YUYI MORALES

Mexican-born artist and writer

Best known for her vibrant artwork infused with magical realism and distinctive elements from the Mexican culture, Morales has enjoyed a lucrative career as an award-winning children's book author and illustrator. Her artwork and storytelling serve as a form of personal cultural preservation, conveying elements of her native Mexico to English-speaking children.

Latino heritage: Mexican
Born: November 7, 1968; Xalapa, Veracruz, Mexico
Also known as: Maria de Lourdes Morales O'Meara
Areas of achievement: Art; literature

EARLY LIFE

Yuyi Morales (JEW-jee MOHR-al-ehz) was born Maria de Lourdes Morales O'Meara in Xalapa in Mexico to parents Eloina and Eligio. The oldest of four children, Yuyi (as she was nicknamed by her family) spent many hours in her childhood drawing and writing stories that resembled the extraordinary tales shared by her extended family. Her early drawings were copies of family portraits, comic book pictures, and sketches of her reflection in the mirror.

Although she exhibited potential as an artist, Morales was also proficient in swimming and spent her teen years as a competitive swimmer. The sport became her passion, and after she graduated from high school in 1985 from Colegio Preparatorio de Xalapa, she enrolled in the Universidad Veracruzana in the physical education program to achieve her dream of becoming a swimming coach and teacher. Upon graduation, Morales worked as a swimming coach, and she met her future American husband Tim. In 1994, she, Tim, and their two-month-old son Kelly emigrated from Mexico to the United States, where Morales and Tim were married.

Originally, Morales's trip to the United States was to meet Tim's family with the intent to return to Mexico. Because of a misunderstanding, the couple was forced to stay in the United States. Morales's first months in her new country were difficult, because she did not speak English or understand the culture. While her husband worked, she spent time at home with their son and her husband's family. Her mother-in-law introduced her to the public library, which was a life-changing experience. At the public library, Morales learned to read English using children's picture books, and she became interested in the artwork of book illustrators. She spent the next few years creating books for her young son and taking creative writing and illustration classes. Many of the stories she wrote were based upon those she had heard as a child in Mexico. In 1997, she started a job as a host for a weekly Spanish-language children's radio program in San Francisco, for which she told various folktales and stories from Latin America, all the while continuing to hone her abilities as a writer and an artist. The show ran for three years.

In 2000, the Society of Children's Book Writers and Illustrators (SCBWI) presented her with the Don Freeman Memorial Grant for her book illustrations. During this time period several people strongly influenced Morales's future: her mother, Latina authors Alma Flor Ada and F. Isabel Campoy, and illustrator Ashley Wolff. Each of these strong female role models played a unique role in leading Morales to her eventual career path. With the help of these role models she was hired to illustrate her first book for Harcourt School Publishers. With a twenty-two-day deadline, she created the illustrations for Campoy's Spanish book *Todas las buenas manos*, which was published in 2002 for the school market. Morales's livelihood as an illustrator had begun.

LIFE'S WORK
After the publication of her first set of illustrations, Morales's career began to change rapidly. She was approached by Harcourt publishers to create illustrations for a book in its trade market line about César Chávez. At the same time, Morales began submitting her original manuscript about Señor Death to various publishers. This manuscript, which she wrote and illustrated in one of her creative-writing classes, was rejected continuously on the grounds that the American children's market was not ready for images of death and the various cultural elements that resonated of Morales's Mexican heritage. Eventually she placed the manuscript with Chronicle Books.

In 2003, both books were published, receiving the highest critical acclaim. Morales's illustrations for Kathleen Krull's picture book *Harvesting Hope: The Story of Cesar Chavez* received thirteen literary honors and awards and was named best book of the year on fourteen national book lists. Among these awards were the Pura Belpré Illustrator Honor Award, named after the Puerto Rican librarian and storyteller Belpré, and the Américas Award, both given for excellence in the representation of Latino cultures. During this same time period, Morales's text and illustrations for *Just a Minute: A Trickster Tale and Counting Book* received thirteen literary honors and awards and was ranked on eight national book lists. Of particular significance is the fact that Morales won the Pura Belpré Illustrator Award the same year that she also received the Belpré Illustrator Honor Award for her other title; she was the first Latino children's book creator to have received this dual distinction. Her book also received four literary awards specifically related to her positive depiction of Latino cultures.

With the publication of these two books, Morales had placed her work prominently in the forefront of Latino children's book publishing and secured a stronghold in her career as author and illustrator. She has written and illustrated two published books and illustrated six other books for various authors. Most all of these books have received multiple literary distinctions, including several Latino children's book awards.

SIGNIFICANCE
By 2010, Morales's work had received more awards for Latino youth literature than any other author or illustrator in the United States. Her humble beginning as an immigrant searching for purpose and belonging allowed Morales to use her life experiences and cultural knowledge to become one of the most talented children's book artists in the twenty-first century. Her work resonates with strong imagery of her native roots and bridges cultural gaps between Latino and non-Latino children and

educators. At the same time, she has paved the way for aspiring Latino authors and illustrators struggling for recognition in U.S. children's publishing.

Jamie Campbell Naidoo

FURTHER READING

Huerta, Mary Esther Soto, Jesse Gainer, and Jennifer Battle. "Finding Voice, Defining Self: An Interview with Yuyi Morales." *Language Arts* 87, no. 4 (March, 2010): 296-307. Describes Morales's artistic style and techniques, explores the symbolism embedded within her illustrations, and details her challenges publishing culturally authentic books reflecting her Mexican heritage.

Morales, Yuyi. "Pura Belpré Illustrator Award Acceptance Speech: An Ongoing Love of Colors and Stories." *Children and Libraries* 7, no. 3 (Winter, 2009): 6-7. Morales details the use of color in her books and the importance of bright hues in her Mexican culture and life.

Naidoo, Jamie. "Just a Minute with Yuyi Morales: Reflections on Libraries, Libros, y Familia." In *Celebrating Cuentos: Promoting Latino Children's Literature and Literacy in Classrooms and Libraries*, edited by Jamie Campbell Naidoo. Santa Barbara, Calif.: Libraries Unlimited, 2011. Examines the influences of the public library in Morales's work, describes the artist's immigration experience, and explores the imagery behind her original character Señor Calavera.

See also: Alma Flor Ada; Monica Brown; César Chávez; Jesse Treviño.

ARTE MORENO

American entrepreneur and baseball team owner

Although he came to national attention in the 1980's for his entrepreneurial savvy in developing a billboard business in Phoenix, Moreno made history in 2003 when he became the first Hispanic majority owner of a major sports franchise in the United States when he purchased the Angels of Major League Baseball.

Latino heritage: Mexican

Born: August, 1946; Tucson, Arizona

Also known as: Arturo Moreno

Areas of achievement: Business; baseball

EARLY LIFE

Arturo Moreno (ahr-TEW-roh moh-REH-noh) was born in August, 1946, in Tucson, Arizona. He is the oldest of eleven children, a fourth-generation American, and the son of a newspaper publisher. Moreno's grandfather started a successful weekly Spanish-language newspaper for Tucson's sprawling Spanish population. Moreno worked in the newspaper's office during high school, developing an exemplary work ethic while discovering the importance of his Mexican heritage.

After graduating from high school in 1965, even as the turmoil over American involvement in the Vietnam War escalated, Moreno enlisted in the U.S. Army. His two-year stint included a tour of duty in Vietnam, where he experienced fierce combat around Da Nang—it was an experience that would shape his conservative political beliefs and his unwavering patriotism. He returned to Arizona committed to a business career. With the help of the G.I. Bill, Moreno enrolled in the University of Arizona, graduating with a degree in marketing in 1973. Throughout his university time, Moreno worked selling shoes, learning firsthand how to appeal to customers.

After graduation, recognizing the potential of billboard advertising given the open expanses around the Phoenix area, Moreno joined Eller Outdoor Advertising Company in the sales division. He struggled initially in the small but highly competitive billboard industry, but his charisma and ability to easily relate to customers quickly established him as a force in the Phoenix business community.

After seven years learning the business, making key contacts, and networking with advertising firms across the country, in 1984 Moreno joined Outdoor Systems, at the time a midsized marketing firm worth about $500,000. Moreno quickly rose within the corporate structure and within three years became the company's chief executive officer (CEO). Under his direction, Outdoor Systems grew exponentially. By the mid-1990's, the company was worth an estimated $90 million and Moreno had become a nationally recognized entrepreneur, profiled in news magazines. In 1996, Outdoor Systems's stock went public, and Moreno became one of the richest entrepreneurs in America.

Arte Moreno. (AP Photo)

LIFE'S WORK

By 1999, Moreno was growing restless in the billboard industry, which was facing competition from the growing cable-television and Internet advertising markets. Moreno always had been interested in sports (an alumni benefactor of the University of Arizona, he was a proud supporter of its athletic programs), particularly baseball. He had coached his sons' Little League baseball teams for ten years. From 1985 to 1992, Moreno was one of seventeen partners (including actor Bill Murray) who owned the Salt Lake City Trappers, a successful minor-league baseball franchise. Moreno loved the intimate atmosphere of the ballpark—he relished time he spent with the fans and devised innovative marketing techniques to attract fans to games. Helped by the team's winning records, Moreno developed his own sense of baseball marketing. It was a remarkable run—the partnership purchased the team for a paltry $150,000 and sold it in 1992 for $1.5 million.

In a bold move, in 1999, Moreno sold Outdoor Systems to Infinity Broadcasting for $8.3 billion. After testing a few projects, including a used car franchise and a golf course, Moreno was determined to buy a Major League Baseball (MLB) team. He already had

purchased a 5 percent stake in the Phoenix Suns of the National Basketball Association. In 2000, he became a minority shareholder (5.3 percent) in the Arizona Diamondbacks of the National League and was part of its World Series championship over the Yankees in 2001. In one of the few missteps in Moreno's career, he attempted to purchase the team outright and assume the role of managing general partner but was outmaneuvered by a consortium of the team's partners. Although he made a second attempt, in the end Moreno was bought out.

Moreno did not have to wait long for another opportunity. In 2002, he showed interest in acquiring the Anaheim Angels, then owned by Disney. The franchise had just won its first World Series but lacked an identity and had only a slender share of the highly competitive sports market in the Los Angeles area. In the spring of 2003, Moreno made his offer—$180 million for a team that at the time had a market value of $250 million. The club was struggling; despite its championship, the franchise attracted only 2.3 million people in annual attendance (14,000 season ticket holders) and generated a thin $100 million in revenue. MLB owners quickly approved the sale, and on May 15, Moreno became the first Hispanic majority owner of a major league franchise in American professional sports history.

Moreno immediately made his mark on the Angels operations. Attendance in the first year of his tenure leaped by more than a million. By 2009, annual attendance exceeded 3.5 million. From 2004 to 2009, the Angels won the highly competitive American League Western Division. By 2009, the franchise was valued at $500 million. In 2006, Moreno negotiated a lucrative exclusive contract with Fox Sports Network to televise all the Angels home games, a deal responsible for generating on average $500 million each year.

However, despite such success, Moreno faced a firestorm of criticism in 2005 when he moved to change the franchise name to the Los Angeles Angels of Anaheim in an attempt to broaden the team's appeal to the lucrative Los Angeles market. Some saw the move as a bid to reach the large Latino population in Los Angeles; Moreno insisted that he was entirely motivated by economics. Although Moreno faced a lawsuit from Anaheim city officials and a backlash of criticism from residents who had long regarded their baseball team as distinct from Los Angeles, Moreno prevailed.

SIGNIFICANCE

Before his move into sports ownership, Moreno made his mark as a self-made millionaire, the consummate

Moreno's Efforts to Attract Hispanic Fans to Angels Games

Determined to fill seats after taking control of a franchise that had just won a World Series but had one of the lowest attendance records in Major League Baseball, arte Moreno initiated a number of risky price cuts for tickets (most notably for children under age twelve); revamped the souvenir and concession operations (in addition to cutting beer prices, he approved the $44 family special: four tickets, four drinks, and four hot dogs for $44); and approved ticket incentive packages for families. All of these moves, some observers speculated, were geared to attract lower-income Latino fans in the Los Angeles area. That argument extended as well to Moreno's bold player personnel moves. In his first year, he made headlines when he invested more than a $140 million to bring four superstar free agents to the Angels: pitchers Bartolo Colon and Kelvim Escobar and outfielders Vladimir Guerrero and Jose Guillen. That the new players were all Latino ignited further controversy–but fans responded. Moreno himself dismissed insinuations that his moves were racially motivated, claiming he had simply acquired the best talent in positions the team needed. The team's success on the field and in the stands amply proved his point.

American success story. Moreno brought to the Angels franchise his business acumen and charisma. Ultra-competitive, Moreno shaped a business plan centered on two simple goals: fill the seats and win games. He has done both. During home games, he often leaves the owner's box to mingle among fans. That populist style, which endeared him to the Angels' fan base, was further enhanced when he turned down more than $3 million in potential yearly revenue when he opted to name the team's new stadium Angels Stadium instead of securing a corporate sponsorship. That mix of business savvy and unaffected populism has defined Moreno's signature success.

Joseph Dewey

FURTHER READING

Basten, Fred E. *Great American Billboards: 100 Years of History by the Side of the Road.* Berkeley, Calif.: Ten Speed Press, 2007. An accessible and helpful history of the rise and fall of the billboard industry and its impact on marketing and on American culture. Important context for understanding Moreno's business achievements.

Bernstein, David. *Advertising Outdoors: Watch This Space.* London: Phaidon Press, 2004. A look at the complex psychology of billboard advertising and the marketing strategy in creating effective billboards.

Burgos, Adrian, Jr. *Playing America's Game: Baseball, Latinos, and the Color Line.* Berkeley: University of California Press, 2007. Although primarily concerned with the impact of Latino players, provides an important historic perspective of Moreno's achievement in becoming the first Latino majority owner.

Lewis, Michael. *Moneyball: The Art of Winning an Unfair Game.* New York: W. W. Norton, 2004. Focused primarily on the Oakland Athletics, this highly readable work presents a compelling description of twenty-first century baseball, the role of the general manager. and the impact of business decisions and front office management in the sport.

Travers, Steven. *Angels Essentials: Everything You Need to Know to Be a Real Fan.* Chicago: Triumph Books, 2007. A handy and thorough history of the team Moreno purchased, includes a full account of the Moreno era.

See also: Linda Alvarado; Ralph Alvarez; Samuel A. Ramirez, Sr.; Joseph A. Unanue.

RITA MORENO

Puerto Rican-born actor, dancer, and singer

A veteran of stage and screen, Moreno was the first woman to win each of the major entertainment awards, including an Oscar in 1962 for Best Supporting Actress for her role as Anita in West Side Story *(1961) and a Tony in 1975 for her performance in* The Ritz.

Latino heritage: Puerto Rican

Born: December 11, 1931; Humacao, Puerto Rico

Also known as: Rosa Alverio; Rita Cosita; Rosita Moreno

Areas of achievement: Acting; theater; dance; music

EARLY LIFE

Rita Moreno (moh-RAY-noh) was born Rosa Dolores Alverio in Humacao, Puerto Rico, to Maria Rosa Marcáno and Paco Alverio. Her parents divorced soon after she was born, and her mother immigrated to the United States. Maria settled in Manhattan, New York, where she worked as a seamstress and eventually married Edward Moreno. Once she saved enough money, Maria returned to Puerto Rico to retrieve five-year-old Moreno. Moreno attended public school in New York and studied dance with Paco Cansino, Rita Hayworth's uncle. At six years old, she began dancing with Cansino at nightclubs and participating in Macy's department store's children's theater. Using the stage name Rita Cosita, she made her Broadway debut at age thirteen as Angelina in Harry Kleiner's *Skydrift* (1945). In her first film, *So Young So Bad* (1950), in which she played a homeless teenager who is sent to reform school, she was billed as Rosita Moreno. She dubbed the Spanish for actors such as Elizabeth Taylor and Margaret O'Brien for films shown in Spanish-speaking countries and continued to work in clubs and at parties until she met Louis B. Mayer, the head of Metro-Goldwyn-Mayer (MGM). He offered the eighteen-year-old a contract and suggested that she change her name. She became Rita Moreno.

LIFE'S WORK

While under contract with MGM, Moreno took dance and acting lessons and played a Cajun woman in *The Toast of New Orleans* (1950), a romantic musical, and a Tahitian in *Pagan Love Song* (1951), also a musical. These roles seem to mark the beginning of her typecasting in stereotypical roles. She often played a provocative or barefoot woman, an Arab, or an Indian. Her beginnings in nightclubs, where she donned fruit and elaborate costumes while singing and dancing, led to the nickname Rita the Cheetah, and Moreno hoped to shed the image of a sultry performer.

Although her contract with MGM was not renewed, Moreno managed to secure roles in several musicals and Westerns: *Singin' in the Rain* (1952), *The Fabulous Señorita* (1952), *Cattle Town* (1952), *The Ring* (1952), and *Latin Lovers* (1953). During the 1950's, Moreno began to receive favorable publicity when she danced with Ray Bolger on *The Ray Bolger Variety Show*. She appeared on the cover of *Life* magazine on March 1, 1954. The cover renewed Hollywood's interest in Moreno, helping her to win a contract with Twentieth Century-Fox and roles in several films, including *Untamed* (1955), *Seven Cities of Gold* (1955), and *The Vagabond King* (1956).

Rita Moreno. (AP Photo)

She also acted in the military comedy *The Lieutenant Wore Skirts* (1956), and the successful musical *The King and I* (1956). Moreno sang two songs in *The King and I* and narrated the film's ballet, which was choreographed by Jerome Robbins. Her performance in *The Deerslayer* (1957) marked the end of her contract with Twentieth Century-Fox.

Many of Moreno's film roles were stereotypical, often requiring her to speak in exaggerated, broken English. To avoid such roles, she turned her attention to television stage performances but returned to film as Anita in *West Side Story* (1961). The film earned ten Oscars, one of which went to Moreno for Best Supporting Actress. She hoped the award would bring her new opportunities to play challenging characters, but it did not. As a result, Moreno appeared in very few films during the 1960's. She left the United States briefly for London, where she performed on stage as Ilona Ritter in Hal Prince's production of *She Loves Me* in 1964.

In 1965, Moreno married Leonard Gordon, an internist and cardiologist who later became her manager. While her career continued to progress, the couple had a daughter, Fernanda Luisa. Moreno played Serafina in Tennessee Williams's *The Rose Tattoo* (1950) in 1968

West Side Story

The musical *West Side Story*, written by Arthur Laurents, debuted on Broadway in 1957. In 1961, it was made into an award-winning film. Influenced by William Shakespeare's classic play *Romeo and Juliet*, the musical is about two rival gangs divided by race—the white Jets, led by Riff, and the Puerto Rican Sharks, led by Bernardo. When Maria, Bernardo's sister, and Tony, Riff's close friend, fall in love, the animosity between the gangs ignites, resulting in violence and murder. In the film, most of the main Puerto Rican characters are portrayed by white actors (Bernardo is played by George Chakiris, Maria by Natalie Wood). One exception is Anita, played by Moreno.

The Puerto Rican characters in the musical have been labeled stereotypical by some critics. Maria is a pious, virginal young woman who has just immigrated to the United States, while Anita is an earthy, sexual "spitfire." Both women are controlled to some degree by the paternalistic Bernardo. The depiction of the Sharks seems to suggest Puerto Rican youths are violent criminals whose existence threatens white Americans. Songs such as "America," led by Moreno, suggest an anti-Puerto Rican sentiment that celebrates assimilation. However, the central theme of the story speaks to the tragedy of hate, violence, and racism.

at the Ivanhoe Theatre in Chicago. The performance earned her the Joseph Jefferson Award. In 1970, Moreno accepted a role on the television series *The Electric Company*, starring Bill Cosby and Morgan Freeman. Later, in 1972, she was awarded a Grammy for the show's sound track. The next year, Moreno starred in *Carnal Knowledge* (1971) with Jack Nicholson, and in 1974, she agreed to perform in Terrence McNally's play *The Ritz* as Googie Gomez, a role based on a performance McNally saw Moreno give at a party. *The Ritz*, which debuted on Broadway in 1975, earned Moreno a Tony Award. Moreno reprised the role in the film version of *The Ritz* in 1976.

Over the next few decades, Moreno's work in television and films encompassed a wide range of experiences. Her performance in *The Muppet Show*'s fifth episode in 1976 won her an Emmy the following year. Moreno earned a second Emmy in 1978 when she guest starred in *The Rockford Files*. Two years later, she appeared in the film *Happy Birthday, Gemini* (1980) as Lucille Pompi. Next, Moreno costarred in *The Four Seasons* (1981) alongside Carol Burnett and Alan Alda. From 1982 to 1983, Moreno appeared on

television as Violet in the series *Nine to Five*. Other television roles followed, including *The Love Boat*, *The Cosby Mysteries*, and *The Cosby Show*. She returned to Broadway in 1985 as Olive Madison in the female version of Neil Simon's *The Odd Couple*. She supplied the voice of the title character in the children's series *Where on Earth Is Carmen Sandiego?* from 1994 to 1999 and guest starred in *Ugly Betty*, the HBO series *Oz*, and the Showtime series *Resurrection Blvd*. She also appeared in films such as *Blue Moon* (2000) and *Play It By Ear* (2006).

Moreno sits on the board of directors of Third World Cinema and the Alvin Ailey American Dance theater. She also is a member of the theater panel of the National Foundation of the Arts. In 1995, Moreno received a star on the Hollywood Walk of Fame. President George W. Bush awarded Moreno the Presidential Medal of Freedom in 2004, and in 2010, President Barack Obama awarded her a National Medal of Arts.

SIGNIFICANCE

Moreno's career has been long and prolific. She entered the entertainment business during a time when Latinas often were resigned to stereotypical roles. Active in the civil rights movement, Moreno spoke out against this practice, helping to improve the types of roles offered to women of color. She was the first woman to win each of the four major entertainment industry awards: Oscar, Tony, Grammy, and Emmy. She also was the first Latina to receive an Academy Award.

KaaVonia Hinton

FURTHER READING

Ada, Alma Flor, and F. Isabel Campoy. *Steps: Rita Moreno, Fernando Botero, Evelyn Cisneros*. Miami, Fla.: Alfaguara/Santillana, 2000. Aimed at younger readers, this book offers illustrated biographies of Moreno, Botero, and Cisneros.

Beltrán, Mary. C. "A Fight for 'Dignity and Integrity': Rita Moreno in Hollywood's Postwar Era." In *Latinoa/o Stars in U.S. Eyes: The Making and Meanings of Film and TV Stardom*. Champaign: University of Illinois Press, 2009. Argues that Moreno was typecast early in her career and struggled to prove she could perform demanding and versatile roles.

Peña Ovalle, Priscilla. "Rita Moreno, the Critically Acclaimed 'All-Around Ethnic.'" In *Dance and the Hollywood Latina: Race, Sex, and Stardom*. New Brunswick, N.J.: Rutgers University Press, 2011.

Examines Moreno's roles and how she has been perceived by Hollywood casting directors and audiences.

See also: Miriam Colón; Dolores del Río; Rita Hayworth; Katy Jurado; Carmen Miranda; Beatriz Noloesca; Chita Rivera.

CARLOS MORTON

American playwright, poet, and educator

Morton is recognized as a pioneer of Latino theater, and his work stands out for his unique blend of language and humor. In various interviews he has reiterated his commitment to his audiences, his students, and aspiring dramaturges by declaring that the basic philosophy of his life's work is to educate and to entertain.

Latino heritage: Cuban
Born: October 15, 1947; Chicago, Illinois
Also known as: Charles Morton
Areas of achievement: Theater; poetry

EARLY LIFE

Carlos Morton (KAHR-lohs MOHR-ton) was born Charles Morton on October 15, 1947, in Chicago, Illinois, to Ciro and Helen Morton. His father was a noncommissioned officer in the U.S. military. Because of the nomadic nature of his father's profession, Carlos Morton lived in various Midwestern states, Ecuador, and Panama. Upon returning to the United States, Morton attended school and graduated from Battle Creek Central High School in Michigan. As an adolescent, he displayed an interest in the same career path as that of his maternal grandfather, a Cuban newspaper publisher living in Corpus Christi, Texas; Morton began writing for his high school paper.

At the age of seventeen he moved to Chicago, where he attended Morton College. He worked as a copyboy and teletypist at the *Chicago Tribune, City News Bureau of Chicago*, and the *Daily News*. Morton also took acting classes and acquired comedic writing experience at the renowned improvisational theater company, Second City. In 1968, he was working as a gofer with a camera crew assigned to Peter Jennings, who was covering the Democratic National Convention. The crew was sent out to cover the clash between protesters and the Chicago Police Department at Lincoln Park. Morton witnessed police officers using their clubs to beat down protesters and innocent bystanders alike. The disparity between the narratives disseminated by politicians at the convention and what Morton had witnessed that day led him to become distrustful of authorities. The week's

events became the impetus that led Morton to drop out of college and to embark on a journey of self-discovery.

In a 1993 essay, Morton recounts how his paternal grandfather, named Carlos Pérez, had reinvented himself when he arrived in the United States from Mexico in 1917. Confronting racial inequality and unable to secure work, Pérez decided to use the name he had seen on a billboard advertizing Morton salt on a job application; he was promptly offered the position. Seeking to redefine himself and to reconnect with his Latino heritage, at the age of twenty-one, Charles Morton changed his name to Carlos Morton. He felt that this name more aptly reflected both his American and Latino roots.

LIFE'S WORK

Morton returned to his studies at the University of Texas, El Paso in the early 1970's, where, he was introduced to the works of other Chicanos, such as theater scholar Jorge Huerta and playwright Luis Valdez. Inspired by their message, Morton began his own playwriting career at this time. In 1975, he directed his first play, *El jardín* (1974; *The Garden*), at Harvard University for the Movimiento Estudiantil Chicano de Aztlán (MEChA), a student organization dedicated to raising cultural, political, and social awareness. He earned his M.F.A. at the University of California at San Diego (1978) and his Ph.D. in drama at the University of Texas at Austin (1987). He is a former Fulbright Lecturer to Mexico (1989) and Distinguished Fulbright Lecturer to Poland (2006). He took a job teaching theater at the University of California at Santa Barbara.

Recognized for his signature linguistic blend of English and Spanish (based on Chicano argot), Morton creates exaggerated, stereotypical characters who use satire and wit to highlight cultural conflicts Latinos face in American society. He tackles a variety of subject matter; religious themes and the struggle between good and evil are dominant in *El jardín* and *Pancho Diablo* (1976). His concern with police brutality prevails in *The Many Deaths of Danny Rosales* (1986), a documentary-drama inspired by the 1974 murder of Richard Morales at the hands of the police chief in Castorville, Texas.

Morton has gained considerable recognition for his work: In 1986, he was awarded first prize for *The Many Deaths of Danny Rosales* in the National Latino Playwriting Contest by the New York Shakespeare Festival. Other awards include the Southwestern Playwriting Contest (1977), second prize at the James Baldwin Playwriting Contest (1989), and the Premio Nebrija de Creadores (2010) given by the Franklin Institute at the University of Alcalá de Henares of Spain. Among the most widely anthologized Latinos, Morton has a fine body of published works, including *The Many Deaths of Danny Rosales, and Other Plays* (1983), *Johnny Tenorio, and Other Plays* (1992), *Rancho Hollywood y otras obras del teatro Chicano* (1999), and *Dreaming on a Sunday in the Alameda, and Other Plays* (2004).

SIGNIFICANCE

Morton has become an ambassador of sorts for his efforts to incorporate Latino theater into the American and the international theater scene. In addition to his treatment of social injustices and religious themes, Morton's use of myths, icons, and stereotypes underscore social problems that resonate with all audiences. His contribution to Latino theater has secured the Chicano and

Latino subjects as integral parts of the world's citizenry. *The Many Deaths of Danny Rosales* and *Johnny Tenorio* have been produced across the United States and in France, Spain, and West Germany.

Yolanda Godsey

FURTHER READING

Huerta, Jorge A. *Chicano Drama: Performance, Society, and Myth.* Cambridge, England: Cambridge University Press, 2000. Huerta shares firsthand knowledge of various Morton productions and treatment of serious social injustice themes and biblical tropes through humor.

Lomelí, Francisco A., and Donaldo W. Urioste. *Chicano Perspectives in Literature: A Critical and Annotated Bibliography.* Albuquerque, N.M.: Pajarito, 1976. Gives an extended bibliographical guide to accessing and locating Morton's early writings, including essays and poetry.

Tatum, Charles M. *Chicano and Chicana Literature: Orta voz del pueblo.* Tucson: University of Arizona Press, 2006. Discussion focuses on dramatic techniques such as language that establishes rapport with audiences; also describes themes of lesser known plays.

See also: Denise Chávez; Maria Irene Fornes; Eduardo Machado; Luis Miguel Valdez.

ANTHONY MUÑOZ

American football player

Muñoz was the most dominant offensive lineman in the National Football League during his thirteen-season career with the Cincinnati Bengals, and he is considered one of the best left tackles ever to play the position. He has used his star status to engage in philanthropic work around the Cincinnati area through the Anthony Muñoz Foundation.

Latino heritage: Mexican
Born: August 19, 1958; Ontario, California
Also known as: Michael Anthony Muñoz
Areas of achievement: Football; philanthropy

EARLY LIFE

Michael Anthony Muñoz (MEW-nyohz), a second-generation Mexican American whose grandparents were natives of Chihuahua, Mexico, was born August 19, 1958, in Ontario, California. The small town east of Los Ange-

les, which boasted a large, close-knit, Latino community. One of five children, Muñoz was raised by his mother, Esther; despite suffering from arthritis, she sorted and packed eggs at a chicken ranch to make ends meet. Muñoz and his brother worked weekends at the factory when the family needed extra money, but Esther actively encouraged him to spend his weekends playing ball.

Muñoz grew up on the Ontario facilities maintained by the Parks and Recreation Department. He was so large for his age that he was not allowed to play Pop Warner football to protect the other children. He turned to Little League baseball, but his coach had to carry Muñoz's birth certificate to each game to prove that the boy was young enough to play.

At Ontario's Chaffey High School, Muñoz was a three-sport star. In baseball, his size and strength allowed him to be a dominant pitcher. In football, he excelled as an offensive and defensive lineman and punter. He also played basketball. Muñoz began to attract national attention after being named a Scholastic All-American as a senior.

Muñoz was heavily recruited by college coaches. He finally decided to play for the University of Southern California (USC) because the coaching staff agreed to allow him to miss spring football practice to play for the baseball team. Although injuries limited him to only one season of baseball, that season was a fateful one as Muñoz anchored the pitching staff of USC's 1978 national championship team.

Injuries shaped much of Muñoz' football career at USC. He was named starting left tackle as a freshman, but only nine games into that campaign, torn ligaments in his right knee ended the season for him and started him on a long period of rehabilitation. Similar knee injuries ended Muñoz's junior season in the seventh game and appeared to have ended his senior season during the first game. Muñoz, however, wanted to play in a Rose Bowl. His rehabilitation program moved along so swiftly that, by the time the Trojans had earned a berth in the Rose Bowl, he was ready to play. It was his block that cleared the path for tailback Charles White to score the winning touchdown against Ohio State University. What Muñoz did not know at the time was that three men named Brown were watching the game on television, and their opinion of his work would change Muñoz's life.

LIFE'S WORK

Those three men watching were Paul Brown, the founder, owner, and former coach of the Cincinnati Bengals, and his sons Mike, the assistant general manager, and Pete, the team's player personnel director. Brown's Bengals held the third pick in the 1980 National Football League (NFL) draft. The Bengals' leadership was very interested in Muñoz but wanted to be certain that he had fully recovered from his injuries. While Muñoz's dominating performance in the Rose Bowl was spectacular; the Browns were not gamblers, so they sent head coach Forrest Gregg out to put Muñoz through a workout. Gregg, a Hall of Fame defensive lineman, put Muñoz through his paces as a blocker. When Gregg attempted to rush past him, Muñoz knocked Gregg to the ground.

Following Gregg's positive report, the Bengals drafted Muñoz. Many football experts promptly derided the Bengals' decision as too risky because of Muñoz's history of injury. However, despite a brief training camp holdout because of a contract dispute, the Bengals and the entire NFL quickly discovered that Muñoz was on his way to becoming the irresistible force at tackle.

Anthony Muñoz. (AP Photo)

In his first preseason game with the Bengals, Muñoz blocked the Denver Broncos' veteran defensive end Brison Manor completely off the field. By continuing to demonstrate such raw dominance, especially as a rookie, Muñoz earned a job as the starting left tackle by opening day. In that first season, despite making his share of rookie mistakes, Muñoz was a consensus choice for the All-Rookie team of 1980. He spent the year working on perfecting his blocking technique while protecting quarterback Ken Anderson's blind side and opening enormous holes for Bengal running backs. As a team, though, Cincinnati only managed to win six of sixteen games that season.

In 1981, Bengals line coach Jim McNally switched Muñoz from a right-handed stance (in which the player begins the play with his right hand on the ground) to a left-handed stance that, for Muñoz, gave him better balance and allowed him to be more explosive. As a result, he held blocks longer, giving quarterback Anderson more time to throw. When the Bengals ran left, the ball carriers found much larger holes through which to run. Muñoz was named NFL lineman of the year in 1981 as he and the Bengals racked up twelve wins in the regular season, powered their way through the play-offs, and reached the franchise's first Super Bowl, Super Bowl XVI.

The Anthony Muñoz Foundation

The Anthony Muñoz Foundation was founded in 2002 to engage the Cincinnati metropolitan area and influence youths "mentally, physically, and spiritually," according to its mission statement. The foundation raises funds to provide the kind of activities that Anthony Muñoz took part in while growing up in Ontario, California—activities that are aimed at providing positive experiences for the young people in the Cincinnati metropolitan area.

Muñoz also provides a great deal of "sweat equity" for the foundation by hosting leadership seminars and the foundation's annual Hall of Fame football Academy. The academy is a football camp that brings together young people from all races and socioeconomic backgrounds to improve their football skills. The foundation's goal is to start dialogues that will break down social and racial barriers while offering services to as diverse a community as possible. The foundation also supports the region's top scholar-athletes with college scholarships.

Muñoz and the Bengals would return to the pinnacle of the NFL once more after the 1988 season, in Super Bowl XXII. That season, Muñoz was blocking for the left-handed quarterback Boomer Esiason. As a result, the Bengals were a left-handed team, running left behind their strong left tackle, and Esiason threw and scrambled most often to the left.

In his thirteen seasons in the NFL, Muñoz was the master of the three primary aspects of blocking. He was unequalled as a straight-ahead run blocker as his strength, speed, and dexterity allowed him to move defenders out of his way. Muñoz had the balance and speed to excel as a pulling blocker, moving laterally down the line, ahead of the play, to clear the way for the ball carrier. He also used exceptional pass-blocking technique and footwork to keep pass-rushers at bay. Muñoz even was utilized occasionally as a receiver, catching four touchdown passes over the course of his career.

Muñoz was considered the premier lineman of his era. He was selected to play in eleven Pro Bowls, named first team All-Pro nine times, and was named the starting left tackle by the NFL for its 1980's All-Decade Team. He retired in 1993 but continues to be called one of the best players ever at his position. He was named starting left tackle on the NFL's Seventy-fifth Anniversary All-Time Team in 1994, was seventeenth in *The Sporting News'* 1999 rankings of the one hundred greatest players of all time, and in 1998 became the first Bengal inducted into the Pro Football Hall of Fame.

Muñoz also has been honored for his philanthropic work; he recieved the 1991 NFL Man of the Year Award, given to the player who most excels as a role model on and off the field. Muñoz, and his wife, DeDe, are highly visible philanthropists in the Cincinnati metropolitan area and have founded the Anthony Muñoz Foundation.

SIGNIFICANCE

As one of the best left tackles ever to play in the National Football League, Muñoz became not just a star but a role model. Muñoz was one of the most visible Hispanic role models for young aspiring Latino football players. He and fellow Bengals lineman Max Montoya certainly were the most high-profile Hispanic linemen to play in the NFL. Muñoz himself has said that, in the 1980's, he symbolized what young Hispanic men were capable of and how they could positively affect their communities.

B. Keith Murphy

FURTHER READING

Gregg, Forrest, and Andrew O'Toole. *Winning in the Trenches: A Lifetime of Football.* Cincinnati, Ohio: Clerisy Press, 2009. A Hall of Fame lineman and Muñoz's first professional coach, Gregg offers behind-the-scenes insight into the pre-draft scouting of Muñoz as well as the Bengals' first Super Bowl season.

Ludwig, Chick. *The Legends: The Cincinnati Bengals, the Men, the Deeds, the Consequences.* Wilmington, Ohio: Orange Frazer Press, 2004. Ludwig's work recounts Muñoz's career and establishes his place in the Bengal pantheon.

Silverman, Steve. "Anthony Muñoz." In *Who's Better, Who's Best in Football? Setting the Record Straight on the Top Sixty NFL Players of the Past Sixty Years.* New York: Skyhorse, 2009. Insightful analysis of Muñoz's playing style and approach to the game.

See also: Tedy Bruschi; Manny Fernández; Tom Flores; Tony Gonzalez; Joe Kapp; Rich Rodriguez; Danny Villanueva.

LUIS MUÑOZ MARÍN

Puerto Rican-born governor of Puerto Rico (1949-1965), journalist, and poet

The first democratically elected governor of Puerto Rico, Muñoz Marín held office from 1949 to 1965. Initially an ardent supporter of Puerto Rican independence, he formed the Popular Democratic Party (PPD) in 1938 and adopted a political platform that advocated accommodation with the United States and enhanced rights for Puerto Ricans.

Latino heritage: Puerto Rican

Born: February 18, 1898; San Juan, Puerto Rico

Died: April 30, 1980; San Juan, Puerto Rico

Also known as: José Luis Alberto Muñoz Marín

Areas of achievement: Government and politics; journalism; poetry

EARLY LIFE

José Luis Alberto Muñoz Marín (MEW-nyohz mah-REEN) was born on February 18, 1898, to Luis Muñoz Rivera and Amalia Marín Castilla in San Juan, Puerto Rico. His father, a prominent politician who advocated political autonomy for Puerto Rico, was the Puerto Rican resident commissioner in the U.S. House of Representatives from 1911 to 1916. Muñoz Rivera was instrumental in the formation of the Jones Act (1917), which enhanced Puerto Rican political autonomy and granted Puerto Ricans U.S. citizenship.

Because of his father's political activities, Muñoz Marín's early years were divided among San Juan, New York City, and Washington, D.C. Unlike his father, Muñoz Marín learned English as a child and was comfortable speaking the language. Prompted by his father, he began his university studies at Georgetown University in 1915, but returned to Puerto Rico in 1916 when his father became ill. After his father's death, he returned to the United States, briefly serving as secretary to his father's replacement in the House of Representatives. Uninterested in continuing his studies at Georgetown University, he abandoned his academic career and devoted his efforts to writing. He published his first book, *Borrones*, a collection of short stories, in 1917. Hoping to pursue a career as a freelance journalist, Muñoz Marín contributed articles to *The New York Herald Tribune* and *La democracia*, a newspaper established by his father in 1889.

In 1920, Muñoz Marín returned to Puerto Rico and joined the Puerto Rican Socialist Party, led by labor leader Santiago Iglesias. However, Muñoz Marín quickly became disillusioned with Iglesias's political tactics and returned to the United States to continue his writing career. He published a collection of his father's writings and wrote numerous newspaper articles and poems.

By 1925, Muñoz Marín's political commentaries were lambasting Iglesias's insistence on immediate Puerto Rican independence as detrimental to the well-being of the masses. Notwithstanding his sharp criticism of the American sugar and coffee corporations that dominated the Puerto Rican economy, he adopted a position that advocated a limited association with the United States and a gradual path toward independence.

LIFE'S WORK

By 1932, Muñoz Marín realized that the only way to achieve the political and economic reforms that he advocated was to become a politician. In 1932, he joined Antonio Barceló's newly formed Liberal Party, which advocated gradual independence. Muñoz Marín was elected to the Puerto Rican senate in the 1932 elections

Luis Muñoz Marín. (AP Photo)

and became the editor of *La democracia*. An ardent supporter of U.S. President Franklin D. Roosevelt's New Deal, Muñoz Marín lobbied for a massive infusion of federal funding, which earned him the support of Puerto Rico's landless peasants. Following a dispute with Barceló, Muñoz Marín established the Popular Democratic Party (PPD) in 1938. The party's platform, which advocated political and economic rights for the rural poor, earned the PPD a solid base of support.

The PPD won a slight majority in the senate in the 1940 elections and Muñoz Marín became the president of the Puerto Rican senate. Muñoz Marín had an easy working relationship with Governor Rexford Tugwell, the last non-Puerto Rican governor appointed by a U.S. president. Rather than actively seeking independence, Muñoz Marín, assisted by Tugwell, sought greater political autonomy for Puerto Rico. During the 1940's, the Puerto Rican Land Authority redistributed tens of thousands of acres of land to the island's peasants. In the 1944 legislative elections, the PPD won a landslide victory. By 1945, Muñoz Marín began to push actively for industrialization, convinced that it was the best way to improve the standard of living of the Puerto Rican people. Members of the PPD who disagreed with Muñoz Marín's new agenda subsequently formed the Puerto Rican Independence Party (PIP) in 1946.

Muñoz Marín's Poetry

Like his father, Luis Muñoz Marín began to write poetry at an early age. Although he is most noted for his political career, Muñoz Marín initially sought a career as a journalist and poet. He was encouraged in his literary endeavors by his first wife, Mississippi-born writer Muna Lee. In 1917, after abandoning his legal studies at Georgetown University, he published his first collection, *Borrones* (*Blemishes*). Puerto Rico and Puerto Ricans do not appear in this book. The stories, which debate the superiority of the noble savage over modern man, take place in Atlantis and the North Pole. After 1920, Muñoz Marín abandoned the sophomoric and romantic poetry of his youth. As he became more politicized, he found a new theme: the life of the *jíbaro*, the rural Puerto Rican peasant. Interspersed with portraits of beautiful landscapes and honorable peasants were darker images. Muñoz Marín related the deplorable working conditions faced by the rural peasants and their mistreatment by the landed aristocracy and American corporations. In 1920, he published one of his most famous poems, "Panfleto," in which he proclaimed himself to be God's agitator.

After the U.S. Congress granted Puerto Rico the right to elect its own governor in 1947, Muñoz Marín won the 1948 gubernatorial elections and became the first democratically elected governor of Puerto Rico. He was subsequently reelected in 1952, 1956, and 1960. Politically, he supported a constitution in 1952 that made Puerto Rico a freely associated commonwealth with the United States. Socially, Muñoz Marín launched Operation Serenity, legislation geared toward promoting education and appreciation of the arts. Economically, Muñoz Marín supported Operation Bootstrap, which transformed the Puerto Rican economy from an agrarian society based on sugarcane into an industrialized economy based on manufacturing and tourism. The Puerto Rican government enticed U.S. companies to establish industry in Puerto Rico by offering cheap labor, access to U.S. markets without import duties, and profits free of federal taxation.

Although it was successful in creating an industrial base in Puerto Rico, Operation Bootstrap was unable to generate sufficient employment opportunities for Puerto Rico's rapidly growing population. Thousands of Puerto Ricans fled the island to the American mainland during the 1950's in search of economic opportunities. Puerto Rican industrialization also laid the basis for a new middle class of urban professionals, which altered the political landscape. Puerto Rican industrialist Luis A. Ferré formed the New Progressive Party (PNP), which challenged Muñoz Marín's PPD. After 1970, the Puerto Rican manufacturing sector shifted from labor-intensive industries such as the manufacturing of food, tobacco, leather, and clothing, to more capital-intensive industries such as pharmaceuticals, chemicals, machinery, and electronics.

Following a series of violent attempts by independence supporters in 1950 to end Puerto Rico's relationship with the United States, Muñoz Marín initiated censorship laws against Puerto Rican nationalists and independence supporters. In 1964, Muñoz Marín declined to run for a fourth term and supported the candidacy of Roberto Sánchez Vilella. Muñoz Marín held a seat in the senate until he retired in 1970. He died in 1980 after suffering a stroke in San Juan.

SIGNIFICANCE

Muñoz Marín is the architect of Puerto Rico's current political and economic relationship with the United States. His political platform, which argued that economic reforms were more important than political independence to Puerto Rico's future, earned him the enmity of pro-independence and pro-statehood movements. In the early twenty-first century, Muñoz Marín's PPD remains a powerful political force in Puerto Rico. The international airport in San Juan, the largest in the Caribbean, was renamed in his honor in 1985.

Michael R. Hall

FURTHER READING

Aitken, Thomas. *Poet in the Fortress: The Story of Luis Muñoz Marín.* New York: New American Library, 1965. Although dated, this book remains a strong biography of Muñoz Marín's career.

Aranda, Elizabeth M. *Emotional Bridges to Puerto Rico: Migration, Return Migration, and the Struggles of Incorporation.* Lanham, Md.: Rowman and Littlefield, 2006. An informative study that contends that, in spite of structural incorporation, many Puerto Ricans do not feel like they fully belong in mainland society.

Ayala, César J., and Rafael Bernabe. *Puerto Rico in the American Century: A History since 1898.* Chapel Hill: University of North Carolina Press, 2007. A detailed study that will be of great value to students searching for new topics to research on Puerto Rican history.

Maldonaldo, A. W. *Luis Muñoz Marín: Puerto Rico's Democratic Revolution.* San Juan: University of Puerto Rico, 2006. An unbiased study supported by historical documents.

Norris, Marianna. *Father and Son for Freedom: The Story of Puerto Rico's Luis Muñoz Rivera and Luis Muñoz Marín.* New York: Dodd, Mead, 1968. Excellent overview of the attempts to achieve political autonomy by both father and son.

See also: Pedro Albizu Campos; José Celso Barbosa; Rubén Berríos; José de Diego; Luis A. Ferré; Lolita Lebrón; Luis Muñoz Rivera.

LUIS MUÑOZ RIVERA

Puerto Rican-born activist, politician, and writer

Muñoz Rivera was a major figure in the struggle for Puerto Rican political autonomy both before and after the Spanish-American War. As Puerto Rico's resident commissioner in the U.S. House of Representatives, he was instrumental in the drafting of the Jones Act, which enhanced Puerto Rican political autonomy and granted Puerto Ricans U.S. citizenship.

Latino heritage: Puerto Rican
Born: July 17, 1859; Barranquitas, Puerto Rico
Died: November 15, 1916; Luquillo, Puerto Rico
Areas of achievement: Activism; government and politics; journalism; literature

EARLY LIFE

Luis Muñoz Rivera (moon-YOHZ rih-VEH-ruh) was born to Luis Muñoz Berrios and Monserrate Rivera in Barranquitas, Puerto Rico. After completing his primary education in 1869, Muñoz Rivera was educated at home by private tutors. He excelled at literature, French, and music. By the time he was an adolescent, he was working for his father's business. Muñoz Rivera's desire to study law at a Spanish university was stymied by his father, who wanted the young man to continue working for him.

During the 1880's, Muñoz Rivera began to dedicate more time to writing. Previously interested in writing love poems, he began publishing essays and poems supporting political autonomy for Puerto Rico. His writings attracted the attention of the leaders of the Liberal Party, and Muñoz Rivera was invited to join their ranks despite his father's close ties to the Conservative Party. In 1877, the Liberal Party held a meeting in Coamo to discuss the future of the party. Several members, including Muñoz Rivera, supported the creation of the Autonomist Party, which was dedicated to political autonomy for Puerto Rico within the Spanish Empire.

LIFE'S WORK

Muñoz Rivera's writings, many of which were directed at the masses, increased support for the Autonomist Party. The growing support for the Autonomist Party angered the Conservative Party and the colonial governor, who attempted to curtail the appeal of the Autonomists by closing newspapers that published pro-Autonomist essays and articles. In 1890, Muñoz Rivera founded *La democracia*, a pro-Autonomist newspaper. Because of his political articles, Muñoz Rivera was arrested and released only after his father paid a substantial bond.

In 1893, Muñoz Rivera went to Spain to form a political alliance with Práxedes Mateo Sagasta, the leader of Spain's Liberal Party. Sagasta promised Muñoz Rivera that he would support political autonomy for Puerto Rico if his party came into power. When he returned to Puerto Rico, Muñoz Rivera helped draft the Plan de Ponce, which detailed the plan for Puerto Rican autonomy. In 1897, after Sagasta was elected prime minister of Spain, he granted Puerto Rico political autonomy. Muñoz Rivera, who renamed the Autonomist Party the Liberal Party of Puerto Rico, was selected to serve as the chief of the Puerto Rican cabinet. The experiment in political autonomy, however, was disrupted by the Spanish-American War.

In July, 1898, the United States military invaded Puerto Rico. Despite the belief held by many prominent members of the Liberal Party that the United States would allow the island to remain autonomous, Muñoz Rivera was skeptical. Unable to work with the new military government, he resigned from the cabinet on February 4, 1899. The U.S. military governor subsequently disbanded the cabinet and ended universal suffrage. The military government was replaced by civilian government following the passage of the Foraker Act in 1900. While providing for a unicameral House of Delegates, the Foraker Act curtailed the political autonomy that had been granted to Puerto Rico by Spain.

In 1901, Muñoz Rivera moved to New York City and established *The Puerto Rican Herald*, a bilingual newspaper advocating greater political autonomy for the island. In the newspaper's first issue, he wrote an open letter to U.S. President William McKinley criticizing the Foraker Act.

Muñoz Rivera became a founding member of the Union of Puerto Rico Party and won a seat in Puerto Rico's House of Delegates in 1904. He served until 1910, when he was elected Puerto Rico's resident commissioner to the U.S. House of Representatives. Muñoz Rivera held that title from 1911 until his death in 1916. His conciliatory stance, which sought increased autonomy without independence and increased rights without statehood, earned him the political support of several members of Congress. In 1916, Muñoz Rivera, who suffered from gallbladder problems, returned to Puerto Rico, where he died.

SIGNIFICANCE

Because of Muñoz Rivera's efforts in the U.S. House of Representatives, on March 2, 1917, Congress passed the Jones Act, which granted U.S. citizenship to Puerto Ricans and created a bicameral legislative assembly elected by universal male suffrage. However, the executive and judicial branches of Puerto Rico's government still were controlled by the United States. The quest for Puerto Rican political autonomy was continued by his son, Luis Muñoz Marín, who became Puerto Rico's first democratically elected governor.

Michael R. Hall

FURTHER READING

Davila, Arlene. *Sponsored Identities: Cultural Politics in Puerto Rico*. Philadelphia: Temple University Press, 1997. Examines how local and transnational forces forge national identity.

Norris, Marianna. *Father and Son for Freedom: The Story of Puerto Rico's Luis Muñoz Rivera and Luis Muñoz Marín*. New York: Dodd, Mead & Company, 1968. Excellent overview of the attempts to achieve political autonomy by both father and son.

Reynolds, Mack. *Puerto Rican Patriot: The Life of Luis Muñoz Rivera*. New York: Crowell-Collier Press, 1969. This well-documented biography, which makes copious use of Spanish-language sources, is an excellent starting point for further research.

Suárez Findlay, Eileen J. *Imposing Decency: The Politics of Sexuality and Race in Puerto Rico, 1870-1920*. Chapel Hill, N.C.: Duke University Press, 2000. Emphasizing the impact on the masses, the author exposes the race-related double standards of sexual norms and practices in Puerto Rico during the period that saw the shift from Spanish to American colonialism.

See also: Pedro Albizu Campos; José Celso Barbosa; Rubén Berríos; José de Diego; Lolita Lebrón; Luis Muñoz Marín.

JOAQUÍN MURIETA

Mexican-born outlaw and folk hero

Murieta is a legendary bandit who terrorized California during the mid-1800's. The legend of Murieta was popularized by John Rollin Ridge's biographical novel, The Life and Adventures of Joaquin Murieta, the Celebrated California Bandit *(1854), which erroneously portrayed the outlaw as a vigilante avenging the injustices faced by Mexicans living in California.*

Latino heritage: Mexican

Born: 1830; Sonora, Mexico

Died: July 25, 1853; Coalinga, California

Also known as: Robin Hood of El Dorado; Joaquín Murrieta

Area of achievement: Crime

EARLY LIFE

According to church records, Joaquín Murieta (wah-KEEN MYEW-ree-EH-tuh) was born in 1830 in the Sonora region of Mexico. His mother, Rosalia, had been previously married. Murieta occasionally used the last name of her first husband, Carrillo, as an alias.

Murieta married Rosa Feliz and moved to California along with his brother Jesus and three of Rosa's brothers shortly after the beginning of the gold rush. The couple moved to Niles Canyon in Northern California, where Murieta worked as a mustang catcher and cowboy. He eventually followed his brother-in-law, Claudio, into a life of crime. Court records show that Claudio was arrested in 1849, escaped custody, and formed a gang. Murieta had joined the gang by 1851. They specialized in robbing and killing travelers, miners, and anyone vulnerable—whether they were Anglo, Chinese, or Hispanic.

According to Ridge's novel, Murieta was a mild-mannered, pleasant young man, who became disillusioned by Americans after they whipped him and raped his girlfriend for being Mexican. This event and the lynching of his brother caused Murieta to seek vigilante justice. However, there are no records of any assault on his wife or any of his girlfriends, and his brother reportedly moved back to Mexico. The novel asserts that Murieta only killed Anglos out of revenge for the way he, his family, and all Mexicans were treated; however, historical evidence clearly disputes this claim.

LIFE'S WORK

When Claudio was killed in 1851, Murieta took over control of the gang of bandits. Murieta was living in Los Angeles with one of his girlfriends, Ana Beniter, when he and Reyes Feliz were implicated as suspects in the murder of General Joshua Bean, a member of California's militia. Feliz was arrested along with some other Mexican bandits, while Murieta fled back to the gold mining camps. While it was unclear which of the two men killed the general, Feliz was executed for the crime.

Shortly after Feliz's death, in January, 1853, Murieta began a brief, bloody crime spree through California. He often attacked Chinese miners, most likely because they were rarely armed, but possibly because of his own racism. Twenty-two men from the mining camps were found with their throats slit in one month. Murieta and his gang were protected by the Hispanic community but were well-known in the camps. The men were tracked by a group of California Rangers led by Harry Love. The Rangers were paid $150 a month and had been offered a bonus for capturing the bandits.

In order to avoid capture, the Murieta gang retreated into the San Joaquin Valley in March, 1853. Love and his men managed to capture Jesus Feliz, Murieta's youngest brother-in-law. Feliz was still angry at Murieta for abandoning his brother Reyes, holding Murieta responsible for Reyes's death. Feliz gave the Rangers the location where Murieta was hiding out. The Rangers captured the gang near dawn on July 25, 1853. Murieta was killed in a gunfight with the lawmen. After the surviving members of the gang were arrested, Feliz was released from custody.

In order to verify that the dead Mexican bandit was in fact Murieta, the Rangers cut off his head and preserved it in a jar of alcohol. The head was shown to people living in the mining camps, who signed statements that it was Murieta's. In his novel, Ridge claims that the Rangers only collected seventeen signed statements because Murieta always wore disguises during his raids. In reality, a large number of people could identify him, and some 167 Hispanics, Chinese, and Anglos signed statements. Murieta's head was displayed in San Francisco and other cities before touring the state of California. Spectators could pay a dollar to see it. The head eventually was destroyed in the 1906 San Francisco earthquake and fire. Several claims were made in

Murieta as a "Hero of the People"

Joaquín Murieta was an outlaw—a thief and murderer—and led one of the most violent gangs in California during the mid-1800's. After John Rollin
Ridge published his fictionalized account of Murieta's life, the legend of Murieta as a righteous avenger
of injustices against Mexicans spread around the
world. The character of Zorro was partly based on
Murieta; he also is the main character in the 1936
film *The Robin Hood of El Dorado*. There are also several songs, plays, musicals, and books based on his
life. In the legends, Murieta is a Robin Hood figure,
fighting to right wrongs, robbing and killing as a
form of social protest, not out of greed. The Murieta-
Feliz gang has been compared by historians to the
James-Young gang led by Jesse James. Both groups
were started by relatives, lived during times when
society was disrupted by war, and were protected by
law-abiding citizens who were threatened by social
and economic changes. Newspapers also portrayed
both gangs as sympathetic, heroic figures fighting for
the greater good. In California, several roads, parks,
and businesses bear Murieta's name. A brand of
tequila and a winery are named after the bandit. His
name has also been used for political movements
such as the Chicano movement in the 1970's, which
protested Anglo oppression.

the years following his death that the head was not really Murieta's. Some newspapers in 1853 claimed that
Murieta was alive, and that the Rangers had bribed witnesses into signing false statements.

Ridge's novel depicts the Murieta gang as horse
thieves and blames Claudio Feliz for the brutal kill-
ings. The gang would lasso a traveler on horseback,
pull him down, rob him, and kill him in the bushes
along the road. While hiding out in the mountains
along the coast, Murieta and his gang enlisted the help
of local Native Americans to steal horses and mules
from nearby towns. During this time, they were rumored to be involved in the disappearances of several
prospectors.

Ridge describes Murieta's ranch hideout, Arroyo
Cantova, as a 7,000- to 8,000-acre ranch, surrounded by
mountains and accessible only through a narrow pass,
making it easy to defend. The ranch was reportedly
located between Tejon and the Pacheco passes, to the

west of Tulare Lake. Ridge does portray Murieta as a
murderer in his novel but also includes anecdotes about
the Murieta gang sparing those willing to help them.
Ridge's novel was plagiarized five years after its publication, with minor changes to names, such as that of
Murieta's wife. Copies of the books were soon spreading throughout Spain, France, and Chile. The legend became more confused as the books were translated into
and out of the different languages.

SIGNIFICANCE

Murieta was an outlaw who became a folk hero because
of misconceptions that his crimes were aimed at avenging mistreatment of Hispanics by Anglos. Even though
the majority of historians agree that this was not the
case, and there is little if no evidence to support the legend, Murieta remains a beloved figure. The site where
Murieta was killed has been deemed a historical landmark; in sharp contrast, protests by Mexican Americans
have prevented any type of marker from being erected
at Love's gravesite.

Jennifer L. Campbell

FURTHER READING

Ridge, John Rollin. *The Life and Adventures of Joaquin Murieta, the Celebrated California Bandit.*
San Francisco, Calif.: W. H. Cook, 1854. Reprint.
Norman: University of Oklahoma Press, 1977. Published within a year of Murieta's death, Ridge's novel was responsible for the popularizing the erroneous
legend of Murieta.

Secrest, William. *The Man from the Rio Grande.* Norman, Okla.: Arthur H. Clark Company, 2005. A biography of Harry Love, the California Ranger who
tracked down Murieta. Also includes a brief history
of the Rangers and myths surrounding Murieta as
a Robin Hood figure. Extensively researched and
well written.

Thornton, Bruce. *Searching for Joaquín.* New York:
Encounter Books, 2003. A biography of Murieta,
that examines the history and myth surrounding
the bandit. The author also discusses the lasting
impact of Murieta's legend. Includes an extensive
bibliography.

See also: Gregorio Cortez; Juan Cortina; Tiburcio
Vásquez.

EDUARDO NÁJERA

Mexican-born professional basketball player

Nájera discovered basketball late during his childhood in Chihuahua, Mexico. Nevertheless, he quickly distinguished himself as a player and went on to a successful collegiate career at the University of Oklahoma. He became the first Mexican-born player drafted into the National Basketball Association.

Latino heritage: Mexican

Born: July 11, 1976; Ciudad Meoqui, Chihuahua, Mexico

Also known as: Eduardo Alonso Nájera Pérez

Areas of achievement: Sports

EARLY LIFE

Eduardo Nájera (ehd-WAHR-doh NAH-hur-ah) was born Eduardo Alonso Nájera Pérez on July 11, 1976, in the northern municipality of Meoqui in Chihuahua, Mexico. He was the seventh child of Servando Nájera and Rosa Irene Pérez. A laborer at a water treatment plant, Eduardo Nájera's father impressed upon his children the value of hard work. Although the sport was more popular in Chihuahua than in the rest of Mexico, Nájera did not begin playing basketball until he was in high school. He honed his skills playing for hours each day with his five brothers. His considerable height—he was already six feet, eight inches tall—and potential caught the attention of a local coach, who encouraged him to join his team. Nájera worked his way up from water boy to starting line-up during his first season. By the time he

was seventeen, he was receiving offers to play basketball professionally. However, he resolved first to move to the United States to continue his education.

Eduardo Nájera. (AP Photo)

LIFE'S WORK

At age nineteen, Nájera moved to Texas and enrolled in the Cornerstone Christian Academy High School in San Antonio. Averaging twenty-seven points per game, Nájera played well enough to attract the interest of National Collegiate Athletic Association (NCAA) powerhouses, such as Duke University, Indiana University, and University of California at Los Angeles. In 1996, he accepted an offer to play for the University of Oklahoma, located in Norman. In college, Nájera primarily viewed basketball as a hobby; he focused on finishing his degree rather than preparing for a career as a professional athlete. Before graduating in 2000 with a degree in sociology, he had led his team to four consecutive NCAA tournament berths and averaged 18.4 points and 9.2 rebounds per game in his final season. Additionally, by the end of his college career, he ranked among the University of Oklahoma's all-time best players in nine different categories: third in minutes played (3,853), fourth in steals (193), fifth in rebounds (910), sixth in blocked shots (89), seventh in field-goal attempts (1,423), eighth in points scored (1,646), ninth in field goals (612), tenth in free-throw attempts (504), tenth in free throws (337). A standout in his division, he was named Second Team All-Big 12 in 1999 and First Team All-Big 12 in 2000. His performance garnered attention from the National Association of Basketball Coaches and the Associated Press; he was named Third Team All-American by both organizations during his senior year. He also played for the Mexican national team in the World University Games, leading them to a fourth-place finish in 1999. The Basketball Hall of Fame honored him in 2000 with the Chip Hilton Player of the Year Award, recognizing Nájera for his personal and athletic integrity.

In the 2000 National Basketball Association (NBA) draft, Nájera was selected by the Houston Rockets in the second round. From 2000 to 2004, Nájera played with the Dallas Mavericks. Chronic knee injuries marred his performance in the 2002-2003 and 2003-2004 seasons. During the 2004 NBA Summer of Goodwill, he took part in the inaugural Basketball Without Borders Americas tournament in Brazil. He was traded to the Golden State Warriors on August 24, 2004.

After a modest season with that Oakland, California, team, he was traded on February 24, 2005, to the Denver Nuggets. With the Nuggets, Nájera had his most impressive seasons in the NBA. Between 2004 and 2008, he averaged 6.2 points and 4.6 rebounds over the course of 243 games.

After mulling offers from the Oklahoma City Thunder and New Orleans Hornets, Nájera signed a four-year, twelve-million-dollar contract with the New Jersey Nets on July 11, 2008. In his forty games with the Nets, he averaged 3.4 points and 2.7 rebounds per game.

Subsequently, he was traded to the Dallas Mavericks on January 11, 2010. During his second tenure with the Mavericks, he played thirty-three games and averaged 2.3 rebounds and 3.3 points per game. On July 13, 2010, he was traded once again, this time to the Charlotte Bobcats.

Nájera also has made a substantial impact off the court. His antidrug stance resulted in his selection as a 2001 Goodwill Ambassador for Sports Against Drugs by the United Nations Drug Control Program. A lifelong proponent of higher education, in 2004 he began the Eduardo Nájera Foundation for Latino Achievement in Frisco, Texas. The organization provides financial assistance to Latino students who would otherwise be unable to attend college. His charitable contributions to the Denver community were recognized with the Chopper Travaglini Award in 2006.

SIGNIFICANCE

Nájera was the first Mexican-born person to be drafted by the National Basketball Association and the second to play in the league, after Horacio Llamas. Nájera's success in the league has helped popularize the sport in his native Mexico and among Mexican Americans. A skilled rebounder, he helped lead the Dallas Mavericks to five playoff appearances and the Denver Nuggets to four.

Leon James Bynum

FURTHER READING

Friedman, Ian C. *Latino Athletes.* New York: Facts On File, 2007. Noting his defensive and rebounding abilities, Friedman argues that Nájera is the most accomplished and influential Mexican-born player in the history of basketball.

Jozsa, Frank P. *Sports Capitalism: The Foreign Business of American Professional Leagues.* Burlington, Vt.: Ashgate, 2004. Jozsa attests to the increasing importance of Nájera and other Latino players as the NBA expands its brand for Latin American audiences.

Sommers, Michael A. *Basketball in the Big 12 Conference.* New York: Rosen, 2008. Sommers discusses Nájera's popularity, emphasizing his precollegiate development, NCAA achievements, early NBA career, and significance to the Latino community.

See also: Carlos Arroyo; Rolando Blackman; Manu Ginóbili; Rebecca Lobo; Diana Taurasi.

JULIAN NAVA

American educator and politician

A respected career academic who had published groundbreaking works on Mexican American identity and culture, Nava emerged as an influential mediating figure in Los Angeles politics during the late 1960's, when young Chicanos en masse vigorously agitated for cultural recognition, education reform, and economic and civil rights.

Latino heritage: Mexican
Born: June 19, 1927; Los Angeles, California
Areas of achievement: Education; government and
     politics; diplomacy

EARLY LIFE

Julian Nava (NAH-vah) was born on June 19, 1927, to Mexican immigrants who spoke little English. The middle child of eight children, Nava grew up in the impoverished barrios of East Los Angeles. Raised during the height of the Great Depression, he learned firsthand to respect the dignity of the poor and the desperate straits of those who worked long hours just to provide the basic necessities for their families.

Nava excelled academically despite attending public schools that were poorly funded, with out-of-date textbooks and crowded classrooms. Education inspired Nava. He dreamed of college, but economic realities directed him to join the military after high school. As World War II was winding down, Nava volunteered for the Navy Air Corps.

When Nava returned to Los Angeles two years later, he was determined to pursue his dream of a college education, specifically to study history, culture, and the interactions between people of different ethnicities inevitable in a melting-pot culture such as the United States. Using the resources of the G.I. Bill, Nava started classes at East Los Angeles Community College. Recognizing Nava's gifts in the classroom, his intellectual acumen, and his academic ambition, his teachers encouraged him to transfer to nearby Pomona College. There, Nava completed his undergraduate work in history. He was immediately accepted for graduate study at Harvard University and there completed his doctorate in Latin American history in 1955.

LIFE'S WORK

For the next several years, Nava held teaching appointments in a number of prestigious foreign universities, most notably in Venezuela, Puerto Rico, Colombia, and Spain. In 1957, he returned to Los Angeles and accepted a teaching position in the history department at the San Fernando Valley State College (now California State University at Northridge), where he would remain until his retirement in 2000. Nava loved the classroom; in addition to his work with students, however, he began the scholarly work of investigating the place of the Mexican American in American culture and the economic and social pressures that shaped the Chicano culture. He established a reputation for his vigorous investigations into Chicano traditions and history, and he began what would become a stellar record of publications in the field.

Nava's university work was dramatically altered in 1967 when the Congress of Mexican American Unity asked Nava to run for a seat on the powerful Los Angeles Unified School District Board of Education. Nava was elected and became the first Hispanic to sit on the board. His election, however, coincided with a wave of protests conducted by Chicano high school students citywide, a loosely organized campaign designed to compel the

Julian Nava. (AP Photo)

board to consider a variety of pressing issues that faced financially strapped inner-city schools. Agenda items put forward by the Chicano student protestors included granting local communities control over their own schools, introducing bilingual education options, promoting more Hispanic teachers into administrative positions, reducing class size, introducing textbooks that covered Mexican history and culture, introducing Mexican dishes to the cafeteria fare, and ending corporal punishment.

Nava sympathized with most of these demands but could not condone the extreme measures the more radical elements of the student movement advocated. At a time when college campuses were routinely interrupted by sit-ins and violent demonstrations, the student leaders in the Chicano community called for students to boycott classes. The strident call for action spread, and by March, 1968, more than twenty thousand students—almost all Latino—participated in the walkouts. Nava met with student leaders repeatedly during this contentious time—he could not advocate the walkouts and encouraged the students to return to class and to use the system, although frustrating in its slow pace, to realize their agenda. Although such diplomatic care and measured response earned Nava respect in the greater community, within the Hispanic community many reviled him, dismissing him as a "coconut": brown-skinned but white on the inside.

Nava's Scholarly Contributions to Mexican American History

Between 1970 and 1976, Julian Nava published four well-respected histories that explored the Mexican American culture and its people, most notably the landmark *The Mexican American in American History* (1973). The studies each became cornerstone texts in the developing curricula for Chicano studies. He also produced a series of documentaries that explored different aspects of Latin American culture, including films on the struggle for freedom in Fidel Castro's Cuba and on the tense border war between the United States and Mexico over the incendiary issue of illegal immigration. He is, however, best known for his autobiography, *Julian Nava: My Mexican-American Journey* (2001), written specifically for young-adult readers, which related his own improbable rise from second-generation immigrant poverty. In casting himself as a kind of hero in an American Dream drama, Nava perceived his autobiography as a way to inspire a generation of Mexican American youths to believe that great achievement was possible.

Over that summer, tensions only escalated as teachers sympathetic to the students were "reassigned" and thirteen student leaders were arrested on trumped-up charges ranging from disturbing the peace to conspiracy. Over the next several months, negotiations eventually eased the conflicts, and Nava established a reputation as a diplomat and careful negotiator. He served on the Board of Education for the next twelve years, at times as its director. Indeed, Nava's reputation secured him an appointment in 1980 to serve as ambassador to Mexico; he was the first Chicano to hold that post. He served until March, 1981.

In October, 1992, at the age of sixty-five, Nava announced plans to run for the Democratic nomination for mayor of Los Angeles in a wide-open primary field created when Democratic Mayor Tom Bradley decided not to run for reelection after twenty years in office. Nava ran as a kind of anti-candidate (he promised to serve only one term), citing his own background in academia and stressing his lack of political obligations to any special interests. He promised to fight street crime (the Los Angeles Police Department had gone through more than a decade of harsh criticism and scandals, and the city had been rocked by race riots) and to rebuild the city's deteriorated job base. His bid was unsuccessful. Nava returned to California State University at Northridge until he retired in 2000. He continued to lecture and publish on the subject of multicultural education, immigrant policy, and Chicano urban culture. Edward James Olmos portrayed Nava in a 2006 HBO television film about the protests, *Walkout*.

SIGNIFICANCE

During the heady times in the late 1960's when Chicano demands for educational reform triggered volatile confrontation, Nava—a career academic and scholar with little direct experience in managing civil affairs—stood out as a singular voice of reason, measured and thoughtful, sympathetic to all sides. He was fiercely dedicated to preserving the integrity of the education process by introducing important changes that would acknowledge the cultural status of Southern California's significant population of Hispanic Americans. Throughout his career, Nava extolled the value of communication among people of different ethnicities and advocated mutual respect and tolerance for every culture's aspirations.

Joseph Dewey

FURTHER READING

Arevan, Alex Moreno. *Mexican Americans in Los Angeles*. Mt. Pleasant, S.C.: Arcadia, 2010. Helpful survey of the historic evolution of Mexican culture in Los Angeles.

Stresses the often difficult economic conditions and the challenge of maintaining a cultural identity.

Chavez, Ernesto. *"Mi Raza Primero!" (My People First): Nationalism, Identity, and Insurgency in the Chicano Movement in Los Angeles, 1966-1978.* Berkeley: University of California Press, 2002. Indispensable look at the decade of the Chicano movement in which Nava played a key role. Includes an account of the student walkouts in 1968 and Nava's role in mediating the crisis.

Nava, Julian. *Julian Nava: My Mexican-American Journey.* Houston, Tex.: Arte Público Press, 2001. Nava's own account of his rise from poverty, his pursuit of education, and subsequent public career as an educator. The book clearly seeks to encourage young Mexican Americans to rise to the challenge of their complex ethnic identity.

Romo, Richardo. *East Los Angeles: History of a Barrio.* Austin: University of Texas Press, 1983. A broad picture of the culture of the barrio community in which Nava grew up.

See also: Edna Acosta-Belén; Rodolfo F. Acuña; Juan Bruce-Novoa.

SANDY NAVA

American baseball player

Nava, a catcher, was the first known Mexican American and second Hispanic baseball player to play in the National League. In an era when defense won low-scoring games, Nava was an aggressive catcher, highly durable, and skilled at throwing out base stealers.

Latino heritage: Mexican

Born: April 12, 1860; San Francisco, California

Died: June 15, 1906; Baltimore, Maryland

Also known as: Vincente Simental; Vincente Irwin, Vincent P. Nava, Irwin Sandy, Vincent Irwin

Area of achievement: Sports

EARLY LIFE

Sandy Nava (NAH-vah) was born Vincente Simental on April 12, 1860, to Josefa Simental, a Mexican single mother living in San Francisco. He gained a reputation playing baseball in San Francisco as Vincente Irwin and Vincente "Sandy" Nava. He made his major league debut for the 1882 Providence Grays.

Nava's history in professional baseball highlighted the arbitrary nature of color lines in baseball. Historian Adrian Burgos asserts that Nava was among the first, if not the first, to openly straddle the line between races in the major leagues—clearly identified by the fans and all in the game as "nonwhite." It also explains the confusion over his name. Although the identity of Nava's father is left to conjecture, he may have been a next-door neighbor named Nava. Shortly after Sandy Nava's birth, his family returned to Mexico; when Nava was seven years old, his family returned to San Francisco. His mother soon married an Englishman named William Irwin, and her son became Vincent Irwin.

LIFE'S WORK

When he began playing baseball, Nava tried to hide his Mexican heritage and often went by such names as "Irwin Sandy" or "Vincente Irwin." Nava played in California's first professional league, the Pacific Base Ball League, which was formed in 1878. Nava played in the league from 1878 to 1881 for the Renos, the Stars, the Athletics, and the Oakland Knickerbockers. Though only eighteen, Nava gained a reputation for working with the hardest throwers on the West Coast, such as Charlie Sweeney.

It was a far different game in the 1880's. The number of pitched balls required for a walk was seven. The game was more violent, with fights on the field and in the stands. The catcher also served as enforcer. In an era of rudimentary gloves and masks, a tough, durable catcher was valuable. At the time, the catcher typically played well back of home plate, perhaps upward of twenty feet. In an 1881 twelve-inning game between the Renos and the Nationals, Nava recorded nineteen put-outs and six assists without an error. In 1881, Jerry Denny, who grew up in a San Francisco orphanage, joined the Providence Grays of the National League. The following winter, he returned west on a barnstorming trip with several other major leaguers, including one of Providence's aces, John Montgomery Ward. Ward had been with the club since 1878 and was one of the main reasons Providence won its first championship in 1879. In January after seeing Nava play, Ward petitioned the club directors on behalf of Nava and a couple other California players to join the Grays.

The Providence directors had to mull over the subject. Some believed a Latin player would be a liability; others cited Nava's potential drawing power. Providence had witnessed an influx of thirty-one thousand Portuguese immigrants over the previous decades. The team finally agreed and brought Nava and Sweeney east for tryouts. The club wired its potential new catcher fifty dollars to cover his expenses. The team capitalized on Nava's heritage and advertised him as "the little Spaniard."

Nava made his major-league debut on May 5, 1882, in a 17-2 victory over Worcester. He went 3 for 6 with a double and two runs scored but made two errors. He broke his finger in the sixth inning and left the game. Nava had difficulty negotiating the tougher expectations of the major leagues. On May 26, club directors fined Nava ten dollars for pulling out as the game neared with an undisclosed injury. On July 27, Nava was fined one hundred dollars by the club for "conduct prejudicial to the interests of the association." It was rumored that the excessively large fine was for drunken behavior at the club's hotel. Public drunkenness was a chronic problem for major-league players during the 1880's.

In 1882, Nava served as a backup catcher and appeared in only twenty-eight games. He also hit a meager .206. His defensive work behind the plate was still impressive, and Providence signed a contract with him for the following year before the season ended. Nava stuck with the club the entire 1883 season but appeared in only twenty-nine games, batting .240. During the off season, Henry Lucas courted Nava for his new Union Association, offering the catcher $2,500 to jump leagues. Nava turned down the offer and rejoined Providence in March 1884. In 1884, Nava caught for thirty-four games, many of them for pitcher Sweeney. Sweeney was one of the fastest pitchers in baseball history. On June 7, 1884, Sweeney, with Nava catching, struck out nineteen Boston batters to set a major-league record. This record would stand for 102 years. However, on July 21, 1884, Sweeney was released from the team after a drunken refusal to leave the mound. He then left for the St. Louis Maroons of the Union Association. On August 22, Nava received a telegram from Lucas offering the catcher six hundred dollars to join St. Louis. The message even carried a personal plea, "Sweeney says come." Nava rejected the offer. Nava then proceeded to hit an anemic .095, managing only eleven hits, all singles, in 116 at bats.

Providence won the pennant by 10.5 games, but Nava missed it. With Sweeney gone and Nava's weak hitting,

he had become expendable. His last appearance occurred on September 5. Instead of telling Nava of its decision, the team left him behind when it took off on September 13 for a month-long road trip. Nava joined the Fort Monroe, Virginia, military team at the beginning of October.

Nava also played some games for the Old Point Nationals, a Norfolk, Virginia, club. During one exhibition contest, the Nationals loaned him to the Baltimore Orioles. Nava impressed the Orioles, and in December he joined the Baltimore squad of the American Association for the 1885 season. Nava quickly became a favorite in Baltimore in 1885 but was released in July after appearing in only eight games. In August, he was driving a taxi. He also found a slot playing for a local amateur club called Patterson. Unsigned as the 1886 season approached, Baltimore needed a catcher at the end of June, so Nava joined the club for two games. With that, his professional baseball career ended.

In February, 1887, Nava was signed by Danbury of the Eastern League but was released before the season started. He settled down in Baltimore where he worked as a bouncer at a saloon located near Hamilton Pier, a tough part of town. On June 15, 1906, Nava passed away at age forty-six from uremia, an illness accompanying kidney failure, at City Hospital. He was interred at the local Trinity Cemetery, a segregated "nonwhite" burial ground.

S<small>IGNIFICANCE</small>

In the late nineteenth century, Nava became the first known Mexican American and second Hispanic baseball player to play in the National League. A brilliant catcher, he was noted for holding onto the ball, even when aggressive runners were trying to throw him off balance as they slid into home plate.

Michael J. Bennett

F<small>URTHER</small> R<small>EADING</small>

Burgos, Adrian. *Playing America's Game: Baseball, Latinos, and the Color Line.* Berkeley: University of California Press, 2007. Burgos examines an era in baseball history largely ignored by historians and sports fans until now: Latinos in professional baseball pre-1947.

Regalado, Samuel O. *Viva Baseball! Latin Major Leaguers and Their Special Hunger.* Urbana: University of Illinois Press, 2008. Thoroughly researched and well written history of Latinos in baseball from the 1800's to the 1990's.

See also: Mel Almada; José Méndez; Minnie Minoso.

JOSÉ ANTONIO NAVARRO

American statesman, merchant, and revolutionary

Navarro favored Mexican independence from Spain and supported the Anglo settlements in Texas. He later supported independence for Texas in 1835-1836 and annexation to the United States in 1845. He helped to write the state's constitution and served two terms in the Texas Senate.

Latino heritage: Mexican

Born: February 27, 1795; San Antonio de Béxar, New Spain (now San Antonio, Texas)

Died: January 13, 1871; San Antonio, Texas

Areas of achievement: Government and politics; law

EARLY LIFE

José Antonio Navarro (hoh-ZAY ahn-TOH-nee-oh nah-VAH-roh) was born into a prominent noble family in San Antonio de Béxar, Texas, a small frontier community that was part of Spanish colonial Mexico. His father, Angel Navarro, an immigrant from Corsica, became a successful merchant and served several terms as mayor (*alcalda*) of the town. The Navarro family included nine children. José Antonio Navarro studied law and business for a short time in Saltillo, Mexico, although he acquired most of his education from reading books and working with the family business.

While in his late teens, Navarro supported the Mexican Revolution against Spanish rule. In 1912 and 1913, he participated in the filibuster expedition led by Lieutenant Augustus Magee and the revolutionary agent, José Bernardo Gutiérrez. Although Navarro was never a soldier, he acquired the title of "colonel." Following the defeat of the rebels at the battle of Medina, he and his family went into exile in Louisiana, where they remained until the king of Spain granted a pardon to the insurgents in 1815. After returning home, Navarro established a personal friendship with Stephen F. Austin and helped him to acquire his first Mexican contract to bring Anglo settlers into Texas. The two men shared a vision of Texas as a place where both Anglos and Tejanos would be able to prosper together.

LIFE'S WORK

When Coahuila y Texas became a Mexican state in 1824, Navarro was elected to its legislature. He was a strong defender of the liberal Federal Constitution of 1824, and he continued to work with Austin to increase Anglo immigration. When Mexico made slavery illegal,

he helped preserve the institution by supporting a law that classified slaves as "indentured servants" with life-long contracts. In 1831, the state governor appointed him commissioner of Green DeWitt's colony of Anglo settlers. In this capacity, he supervised the organization of the colony, including the issuance of surveys and of land titles. Somewhat later he also served as land commissioner in the Béxar district.

In 1935, Navarro was elected to the National Mexican Congress as representative from Coahuila y Texas, but he resigned later that year in order to support the movement for Texas independence, which was growing in popularity. On March 2, 1836, he was one of the three Spanish-speakers (called Tejanos) who helped draft the Texas Declaration of Independence. After Texas became an independent republic, Navarro was elected a member of the national Congress, where he worked with Juan Seguin to encourage legislation favorable to Tejano interests. Navarro's law practice was successful, and he acquired large ranches in several parts of Texas. In 1838, he settled his family on a 6,000-acre ranch about twenty miles west of San Antonio.

A political ally of President Mirabeau Lamar, Navarro strongly encouraged the movement to expand the border of Texas westward to the Rio Grande River. In 1841, he accompanied General Hugh McLeod's ill-conceived expedition to Santa Fe, with the goal of persuading the residents of the region to secede from Mexico and join Texas. Unfortunately, Navarro and other members of the expedition were captured, and he was sentenced to death as a traitor to his native country. When President Antonio de Santa Anna offered Navarro a pardon and a government position if he would recant and pledge allegiance to Mexico, he rejected the offer, against the advice of his family. Soon thereafter, his sentence was commuted to life imprisonment. After staying in the Acordada prison and the dungeon of San Juan Ulloa, he finally escaped in 1845 with the aid of Vera Cruz army officers.

Returning to San Antonio, Navarro was given a hero's welcome, and he was the only Tejano to be elected to the Statehood Convention of 1845, which accepted the U.S. offer of annexation and drafted the state's constitution. At the convention he successfully prevented the word "white" from being added as a requirement for the right to vote, but he was unable to obtain recognition of ancestral lands granted to Tejanos during the Spanish

Tejanos and Texas Independence

Although the Spanish word Tejanos literally denotes all Texans, it has long been used to refer only to the state's Spanish speakers of Mexican ancestry. In 1821, at the end of the Mexican War for independence, about four thousand Tejanos lived in what is now Texas, and by 1830 about thirty thousand settlers from the United States had moved into the region, outnumbering the Tejanos by a ratio of six to one. At the time, the majority of the Tejanos were of pure Spanish ancestry, but they also included a minority of Mestizos and mulattos (persons partially of Indian or African background). While Tejanos generally opposed slavery, a small number of the larger ranchers were small slaveholders.

During the Texas Revolution of 1835 and 1836, most soldiers and volunteers fighting for independence were Anglo settlers from the United States. Numerous Tejanos had divided loyalties. Although proud of their ethnic heritage, a significant percentage of them wanted Texas to become an independent country. In 1836, eight Tejanos were among the 189 men who died at the Alamo. Although Colonel Juan Seguin also was at the Alamo, he crossed enemy lines in order to seek reinforcements, and later he led his volunteers to fight at the decisive Battle of San Jacinto. Navarro and two other Tejanos risked death when they signed the Texas Declaration of Independence. Following independence, Tejanos were increasingly marginalized and victims of invidious stereotypes.

colonial period. After serving as a member of the state senate from 1846 to 1849, he spent the next two decades working on his several ranches. He continued to participate in local politics and was elected to the office of San Antonio alderman in 1853. Distressed to observe the growing discrimination against Latinos, he openly criticized the Anglo nativism and anti-Catholicism of the American (or Know-Nothing) Party.

Always a strong advocate of states' rights, Navarro supported the secession of Texas from the United States in 1861. All four of his sons served in the army of the Confederacy, and two were promoted to the rank of captain. When the early accounts of Texas history ignored the role of the Tejanos, Navarro wrote and published *Apuntes históricos* (1869, *Historical Notes*), which traced Tejano struggles and achievements beginning with the movement for independence from imperial Spain. When he died in 1871, the people of San Antonio held an unusually large funeral procession.

SIGNIFICANCE

Recognized as one of the preeminent founders of Texas, Navarro was a leading participant in the revolution that resulted in the independence of Texas in 1836, and he made valuable contributions to its subsequent development as an independent republic and then as a state within the United States. Despite the anti-Latino prejudices at the time, he was well known and respected by Anglo citizens throughout Texas.

Thomas Tandy Lewis

FURTHER READING

Alonzo, Armando. *Tejano Legacy: Rancheros and Settlers in South Texas, 1734-1900.* Albuquerque: University of New Mexico Press, 1998. History of Latinos in the lower Rio Grande Valley, showing how they adapted to changes, resisted Anglo encroachments, and maintained a sense of community.

Dawson, Joseph Martin. *José Antonio Navarro: Co-creator of Texas.* Waco, Tex.: Baylor University Press, 1969. A relatively brief account, emphasizing Navarro's significance in the creation of the state's political institutions.

MacDonald, L. Lloyd. *Tejanos in the 1835 Texas Revolution.* Gretna, La.: Pelican, 2009. Detailed discussions of the roles of individual Tejanos in battles and conventions that brought about independence from Mexico.

Matovina, Timothy. *The Alamo Remembered: Tejano Accounts and Perspectives.* Austin: University of Texas Press, 1995. Collection of all known accounts by Tejanos, demonstrating that many were allied with Anglo rebels, sharing a common history and a common plight.

McDonald, David. *José Antonio Navarro: In Search of the American Dream in Nineteenth Century Texas.* Denton: Texas State Historical Association, 2010. The standard biography that corrects a number of misconceptions and includes a wealth of details.

McDonald, David, and Timothy Matovina, eds. *Defending Mexican Valor in Texas: José Antonio Navarro's Historical Writings, 1853-1857.* Austin, Tex.: State House Press, 1995. In the first Tejano publication of Texas history, Navarro emphasized achievements and contributions of his ethnic group.

Reséndes, Andrés, ed. *A Texas Patriot on Trial in Mexico: José Antonio Navarro and the Texan Santa Fe Expedition.* Dallas: DeGolyer, 2005. A scholarly and detailed account of the fiasco and resulting trial.

See also: Pío Pico; Juan Seguin.

BEATRIZ NOLOESCA

American comedian and actor

Nolesca was one of the great vaudeville actors, known throughout the United States, Mexico, and the Caribbean for her self-produced working-class Latin American theatrical productions. She performed for more than four decades, entertaining and inspiring several generations of Hispanic Americans.

Latino heritage: Mexican
Born: August 20, 1903; San Antonio, Texas
Died: April 4, 1979; San Antonio, Texas
Also known as: Beatriz Escalona Pérez; La Chata
Areas of achievement: Theater; film

EARLY LIFE

Beatriz Noloesca (BEE-ah-trihs noh-loh-EHS-kah) was born Beatriz Escalona Pérez on August 20, 1903, to parents Escalona and Simona Pérez. A child of working-class Mexican American immigrants, Noloesca spent her formative years between her birthplace San Antonio, Texas, and her parents' place of origin, Galeana, Nuevo Leon, Mexico. She spent most of her childhood with her relatives in Monterrey, Nuevo Leon, Mexico, which is where she cultivated a proclivity for the theater. At the age of ten, she was already absorbed with theatrical entertainment, and she sold bouquets of flowers just to make enough money for admission to Teatro Independencia. Her work in the field of theatrics as "La Chata," a sassy and strong-willed yet sweet Mexican American maid, was undoubtedly tempered by her job selling food and drinks as a young child to working-class Mexican Americans in San Antonio. She picked up the dialect and replicated the mannerisms of those she encountered on the railways while helping to support her family as an adolescent.

LIFE'S WORK

At the age of sixteen, Noloesca worked at the Teatro Zaragoza, which was located in the Mexican American community in San Antonio. At the age of eighteen, she was hired to be an usherette and box-office attendant in the newly built Teatro Nacional in 1920. It was during this time that Noloesca was spotted on stage at the Teatro Nacional competing in a local hosiery company-sponsored beautiful legs contest, which she won, and she was offered a position in the Cuban Spanish dance troupe Los Hermanos Areu. Noloesca debuted with the

company at the Teatro Colón in El Paso, Texas, the same year and began developing the endearing comedic character "La Chata" Noloesca. José Areu, the Cuban American owner of the company, met Noloesca and eventually married her. Shortly after, Noloesca had her only child, Belia Areu, in Mexico City on October 31, 1921. Belia went on to become an accomplished performer in her own right. Noloesca toured with Areu throughout Mexico and the Southwest of the United States, performing everything from dramatic performance to risqué burlesque and comedy. As she became seasoned as a thespian, she began to favor comedy more than other popular genres of stage. Her role as "La Chata" was so revered among the working class in the communities in which the troupe toured that it became a lucrative source of income, and she and her husband were able to rent their own theater in Los Angeles.

In 1930, Areu and Noloesca divorced, and she subsequently left Los Hermanos Areu. She formed her own company, Atracciones Noloesca, which survived for six years in the midst of the Great Depression, which significantly decreased the audiences and consequently decreased the number of Spanish-speaking theaters in the Southwest. During this time, she performed, managed, and hired for the company, normally hiring local Spanish-speaking women from the San Antonio area and periodically hiring men. A famous thespian of note she hired was Mexican actor Eusebio Pirrin, who is known for his role as Don Catarino. Noloesca eventually decided to seek out other cities with enlarging Spanish-speaking populations, such as Chicago and New York, where she found a receptive community of Hispanic Americans.

In 1936, Noloesca met and married immigrant worker José de la Torre. That same year, she revamped her company, changing the name to Beatriz Noloesca "La Chata" Compania Mexicana. She traveled with her new husband, daughter, and four San Antonian actors, performing sketches consisting of singing, dancing, and comedy. The staple of the show was the character "La Chata" Noloesca, reciting comedic dialogue with a male counterpart, most times performed with her husband. Noloesca was able to travel and sustain her career throughout the 1940's, performing throughout the United States, Mexico, and Cuba. In the early 1950's, after Noloesca's divorce from her second husband, she returned with her daughter to her native

San Antonio, Texas, where she worked in radio and television programs, on KCOR and KWEX-TV. She then married Ruben Escobedo, a San Antonio musician. She continued to perform as "La Chata" Noloesca throughout the 1970's, doing her last show at a benefit performance in August, 1977. She died in San Antonio on April 4, 1979.

SIGNIFICANCE

Noloesca was a trailblazer for Latinas in the field of entertainment. She was justly honored by the Mexican National Association of Actors in 1975 for her creation and performance of the character "La Chata" (an endearing term which means "button nose") Noloesca (an anagram of her last name "Escalona"), which has been considered a personification of the Latin American working class. This is one explanation for her popularity among underclass Latin Americans in major urban centers throughout her career.

Derrick J. Jenkins, Sr.

FURTHER READING

Arrizon, Alicia. *Latina Performance: Traversing the Stage.* Bloomington: Indiana University Press, 1999. This book examines Latina performances, including theatrical personalities such as "La Chata" Noloesca.

Ramirez, Elizabeth. *Chicanas/Latinas in American Theatre: A History of Performance.* Bloomington: University of Indiana Press, 2000. This book studies the Latino Theater's transformation from its pre-Spanish origins to the current American theater history.

Ybarra-Frausto, Tomás. "La Chata Noloesca: Figura del Donaire." In *Mexican American Theatre: Then and Now*, edited by Nicolas Kanellos. Houston, Tex.: Arte Publico Press, 1983. This book is a collection of works about the Mexican American influence on American theatre.

See also: Ramón Novarro; Gilbert Roland; Lupe Velez; Elena Verdugo.

CARLOS NORIEGA

Peruvian-born astronaut

Recognized for his expertise and leadership in space operations, Noriega served a distinguished career as a U.S. Marine Corps pilot prior to serving as an astronaut. As a mission specialist and computer scientist, he visited the Russian space station Mir and helped assemble the International Space Station.

Latino heritage: Peruvian

Born: October 8, 1959; Lima, Peru

Also known as: Carlos Ismael Noriega; Carlos I. Noriega

Area of achievement: Science and technology; military

EARLY LIFE

Carlos Ismael Noriega (NOH-ree-AY-gah) was born to Rodolfo and Nora Noriega in Lima, Peru, and reared in Santa Clara, California. He became a naturalized U.S. citizen in 1969 and graduated from Wilcox High School in 1977. A serious student with a keen interest in science and technology, he earned a bachelor's degree in computer science from the University of Southern California (USC) in 1981. While at USC, Noriega was a member of the Navy Reserve Officers' Training Corps (ROTC) unit and was commissioned in the United States Marine Corps in 1981.

Between 1983 and 1985, Noriega flew CH-46 helicopters at the Marine Corps Air Station in Kaneohe Bay, Hawaii. After participating in peacekeeping missions to Beirut, Lebanon, he served as the aviation safety officer and instructor pilot at the Marine Corps Air Station in Tustin, California between 1986 and 1988. Upon his selection to attend the Naval Postgraduate School in Monterey, California in 1988, Noriega proceeded to earn a master's degree in computer science, as well as a master's degree in space systems operations.

LIFE'S WORK

During his flying career, Noriega logged more than 2,200 hours of flying in a variety of fixed-wing and rotary-wing aircraft. In 1990, he was assigned to the United States Space Command in Colorado Springs, Colorado. While serving as a Space Surveillance Center commander, he also oversaw numerous computer hardware and software development projects. Eventually, he was selected to manage the development and integration of the space and missile warning computer system upgrades for Cheyenne Mountain Air Force Base, near Colorado Springs.

In December, 1994, Noriega was selected by the National Aeronautics and Space Administration (NASA)

Carlos Noriega. (AFP/Getty Images)

(NASA) for astronaut training. After a year of training and evaluation at the Johnson Space Center in Houston, Texas, he was assigned as a mission specialist in May, 1996. His first space shuttle flight, STS-84, took him on a nine-day mission on *Atlantis* to the Russian Space Station Mir in May, 1997. During this mission, the Atlantis crew conducted several secondary experiments and transferred about four tons of supplies and equipment to Mir.

In December, 2000, Noriega ventured into space again on the STS-97 mission. He made three space walks from the space shuttle *Endeavor* and helped install and unfold a pair of 110-foot solar panels on the International Space Station. He also helped deliver supplies and equipment to the first resident crew of the station. During STS-84 and STS-97, Noriega logged more than 480 hours of space flight time, and traveled more than eight million miles.

After the STS-97 mission, Noriega trained as the backup commander for the STS-121space shuttle mission to the International Space Station. Because of a temporary medical condition, he was replaced on the crew of STS-121 and assigned to serve as commander of the Exploration Systems Engineering Division at Johnson Space Center. He retired as an astronaut in 2005.

During his distinguished flying career, Noriega received numerous honors in recognition of his valued service to the United States Marines and as an astronaut. Included in his awards are the Defense Superior Service Medal, the Defense Meritorious Service Medal, the Strike Flight Award Air Medal, the Navy and Marine Corps Achievement Medal, the Hispanic Engineer National Achievement Award, the NASA Exceptional Service Medal, and two NASA Space Flight Medals.

Noriega and his wife, Wendy, have five children. When he has the opportunity to speak to the youths of the younger generation, he stresses the importance of doing well in school and excelling in math and science.

SIGNIFICANCE

Through his accomplishments as a U.S. Marine and an astronaut, Noriega has become a role model for achievement, particularly among Latinos. He has rendered invaluable service to the United States in the advancement of flight and space shuttle technology. His leadership and expertise in the computer modernization program for flight command has helped support space combat centers and numerous critical special-access programs. His involvement with the International Space Station helped advance the understanding of how the human body reacts in a weightless environment. Through the efforts of Noriega and other astronauts, knowledge and technology have greatly advanced about how to work in the extraterrestrial environment and how to move forward in conquering the frontier of space.

Alvin K. Benson

FURTHER READING

Bond, Peter. *The Continuing Story of the International Space Station*. New York: Springer, 2002. Describes the history and development of the station, including Noriega's role in various missions there.

Harland, David M., and John Catchpole. *Creating the International Space Station*. New York: Springer, 2002. Documents the early years of the International Space Station, including Noriega's involvement.

Newton, David F. *Latinos in Science, Math, and Professions*. New York: Infobase, 2007. A biogrpahy of Noriega is included in this useful reference work.

See also: Franklin Ramón Chang-Díaz; Sidney M. Gutierrez; Ellen Ochoa.

RAMÓN NOVARRO

Mexican-born actor

Novarro achieved his greatest fame in the 1920's during the silent era of Hollywood filmmaking. His classical good looks, sensuality, and natural talent led to his positioning as a rival to Rudolf Valentino for the "Latin lover" roles of the day. Novarro's greatest film performance was the starring role in the 1925 film Ben-Hur: A Tale of the Christ.

Latino heritage: Mexican

Born: February 6, 1899; Durango, Mexico

Died: October 30, 1968; North Hollywood, California

Also known as: José Ramón Gil Samaniego; Ramón Zerreco

Area of achievement: Acting

EARLY LIFE

Ramón Novarro (noh-VAH-roh) was born José Ramón Gil Samaniego in Durango, Mexico, on February 6, 1899. His father was a wealthy dentist whose family origins may have been Spanish or even Greek. Novarro's mother, Leonor Gavilan, was the daughter of a wealthy landowner who claimed descent from an Aztec prince. The Samaniego family was influential and well-respected with contacts in the presidential palace in Mexico City.

Novarro was the fourth child of thirteen born to his parents. The family was extremely religious, and three of Novarro's sisters became cloistered nuns. Novarro even considered entering the priesthood. However, it was his interest in the theater, opera, and acting that convinced him to not take holy orders. Novarro was extremely artistic, with considerable talent in dance, singing, and playing the piano. His athletic ability earned him a track scholarship.

Civil war plagued Mexico from 1913 to the end of the decade as Pancho Villa repeatedly tried to overthrow the government. Durango was invaded by Villa's forces, and the family's economic well-being was threatened. Parents and children frequently were separated and feared for their lives.

Mexico's political instability convinced Novarro that he could more safely establish a career in the United States. He and a younger brother moved to Los Angeles, where Novarro waited tables, worked as a movie theater usher, and posed nude for an art school to earn money to send to his family in Mexico. He achieved some success with bit parts in films and stage acting.

LIFE'S WORK

Novarro's sensuality, physicality, and exceptional good looks gained him the attention of Hollywood's rising class of film stars and directors. He reportedly appeared in more than one hundred films between 1916 and 1921 as an extra. Novarro was featured in small parts in nine films for the same time period. His persistence and patience eventually earned rewards with a starring role in the 1922 film *The Prisoner of Zenda.* Both he and the film quickly became successful. Believing his unusual last name was a hindrance to future film success, he changed it to Novarro. It remains unclear why he chose Novarro. Navarro (with two *a*'s) is a common Spanish name; his name might have been rendered as Novarro because of a typographical error or because studio executives altered the spelling to make it unique.

During the 1920's, Novarro was recruited for leading roles in silent film classics that included *Scaramouche* (1923), *The Arab* (1924), *Lovers?* (1927), *The Student Prince in Old Heidelberg* (1927), and *The Pagan* (1929). In 1929, he became bored with acting.

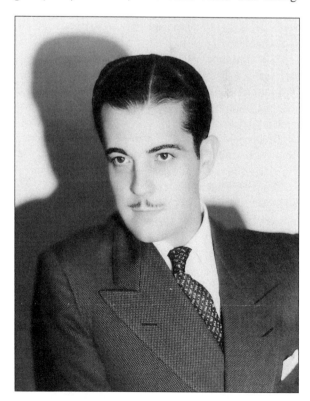

Ramón Novarro. (Moviepix/Getty Images)

Novarro's Rivalry with Rudolph Valentino

The rivalry between Ramón Navarro and Rudolph Valentino was based on publicity shrouded more in rumor than in fact. Both actors often portrayed "Latin lover" characters, stereotypically suave foreigners who appeared in many Hollywood films of the interwar period. Valentino came to epitomize this archetype. He and Novarro briefly worked together on the 1921 film *The Four Horsemen of the Apocalypse*—Valentino as the star and Novarro as an extra—however, they were deemed too handsome to share scenes, and Novarro's part was considerably reduced. Valentino's success in that film convinced him to leave Metro-Goldwyn-Mayer (MGM) for Paramount Studios. Novarro was subsequently promoted as MGM's replacement for Valentino. When the film *Ben-Hur: A Tale of the Christ* (1925) was being cast, Valentino was rumored as a competitor with Novarro for the coveted lead role. In reality, Valentino had no interest in starring in the film and frequently expressed the fear that his career would decline if he took the part because no future film role could surpass that of Ben-Hur. That did not stop the press from casting the two men as rivals, however. Rumors also abounded in Hollywood that Valentino and Novarro were secretly lovers. If true, the relationship might have doomed both their careers. Friends and family of Valentino and Novarro never confirmed that the two men even knew each other, and there is no proof that the men had a sexual relationship. Modern scholarship indicates Valentino's preference was for women and Novarro's for men. In any case, speculation about the relationship between the two ended with Valentino's sudden death in 1926.

His investment of time and money in singing as an alternative career led to a nervous breakdown. The stock market crash of 1929 wiped out his fortune, which had been poorly invested by the brother of a close friend. The death of his own younger brother drove Novarro to alcoholism. His personal life was complicated by his deep devotion to Catholicism, which conflicted with his homosexuality.

The film industry's transition from silent to sound films caused Novarro concern because of his accent. His musical skills along with his considerable acting talent kept him a much sought-after actor, but Novarro typically was cast as a foreigner from an exotic country. He never was allowed to play a Mexican. Novarro's most successful sound film was *Mata Hari* (1931), in which he costarred with Greta Garbo.

By 1932, the film industry's use of "Latin lover" characters was in decline. Novarro's contract with Metro-Goldwyn-Mayer (MGM) was not renewed in 1936. He split from the company by mutual agreement; Novarro had refused the request of the head of MGM, Louis B. Mayer, to get married to cover up his homosexuality. Novarro moved on to Republic Studios, but by this time, his career was in decline. Many of his later films failed to make a profit. During the decade of the 1940's, Novarro made only six films, and his last starring role was the 1944 film *The Saint That Forged a Country*, which was in Spanish with English subtitles.

The advent of television gave Novarro's career a temporary reprieve. From 1952 to 1968, he appeared in twelve different television series. He also occasionally acted in regional theater. Novarro's life came to an abrupt end on October 30, 1968, when he invited the Ferguson brothers, Tom and Paul, into his home. The brothers were seeking money that allegedly was hidden in Novarro's house. They pretended to be interested in Novarro sexually to gain entry, then tortured and beat him to death when no money could be found. Both men served prison time with each accusing the other of the brutal crime.

SIGNIFICANCE

Novarro's talent and looks helped him build a lucrative career; he had the featured role in forty-five films. Throughout his life, however, he was troubled by his inability to reconcile his Catholicism with his homosexuality. He became increasingly depressed and dependent on alcohol. Novarro was further conflicted by his belief that he was a better singer than actor, although he never had any great success in the former career. Regardless, he was a memorable actor whose portrayal of Ben-Hur has been called one of the great performances in film history.

William A. Paquette

FURTHER READING

Berumen, Frank. *Ramón Novarro: The Life and Films of the First Latino Hollywood Superstar.* New York: Vantage Press, 2001. A biography of Novarro that offers some useful information but seems to place more emphasis on rumors than documented facts.

Ellenberger, Allan R. *Ramón Novarro*. Jefferson, N.C.: McFarland, 1999. This biography remains the most authoritative one on Novarro and contains a complete listing of his film, stage, and television roles.

Slide, Anthony. *Inside the Hollywood Fan Magazine: A History of Star Makers, Fabricators, and Gossip Mongers*. Jackson: University Press of Mississippi, 2010. Offers an interesting examination of how the press covered closeted film stars such as Novarro.

Soares, Andre. *Beyond Paradise: The Life of Ramón Novarro*. New York: St. Martin's Press, 2002. A straightforward and insightful biography of Novarro that encompasses his entire life.

See also: Leo Carrillo; José Ferrer; Mel Ferrer; Juano Hernández; Fernando Lamas; Ricardo Montalbán; Anthony Quinn.

ANTONIA NOVELLO

Puerto Rican-born physician and U.S. surgeon general (1990-1993)

As a public health advocate for women, children, and minorities, Novello became the first Hispanic and first woman to serve as United States surgeon general. Her policies aimed to decrease the incidence of pediatric acquired immunodeficiency syndrome (AIDS) and eliminate health-care disparities, particularly in the Latino community.

Latino heritage: Puerto Rican

Born: August 23, 1944; Fajardo, Puerto Rico

Also known as: Antonia Coello Novello; Antonia Coello

Areas of achievement: Medicine; government and politics

EARLY LIFE

Antonia Coello Novello (noh-VEH-loh) was born on August 23, 1944, in Fajardo, Puerto Rico. She was the oldest of three children born to Ana Delia Flores Coello, a schoolteacher, and Antonio Coello. Her parents later divorced, and her mother remarried. Her father died when Novello was eight years old.

Novello was born with megacolon, a birth defect affecting the large intestine. She was not able to receive surgical treatment until she was eighteen years old because her family could not afford transportation to the surgical hospital. Medical treatments at her local hospital instilled in Novello an empathy for patients and inspired her medical career. Novello credits her mother with modeling strong educational values by teaching her math and science and encouraging her to overcome obstacles such as her illness.

Heeding her mother's advice, Novello graduated from high school when she was only fifteen years old. She attended the University of Puerto Rico at Río Piedras on a scholarship and earned a bachelor of science degree (1965). Novello pursued a medical education at the University of Puerto Rico School of Medicine at San Juan, from which she graduated in 1970. During medical school, Novello's favorite aunt died of renal failure, thus stimulating Novello to study renal diseases. She moved to the University of Michigan Medical Center in Ann Arbor for her internship, residency, and a fellowship

Antonia Novello. (AP Photo)

in nephrology in the Department of Internal Medicine (1970-1973). She was the first woman at the medical center to be named intern of the year. Novello relocated to Georgetown University School of Medicine to complete another fellowship in the Department of Pediatrics from 1973 to 1976.

LIFE'S WORK

After the fellowship, Novello entered pediatric private practice in Springfield, Virginia, and became a staff physician at Georgetown University Hospital. In 1978, she joined the Public Health Service Commission Corps (PSCHH) and became project officer at the National Institute of Arthritis, Metabolism, and Digestive Diseases. Novello completed a master's degree in public health at Johns Hopkins University's School of Hygiene and Public Health (later renamed the Bloomberg School of Public Health) in 1982. She was promoted to assistant surgeon general of PSCHH in 1986 and also served as the deputy director and coordinator for AIDS research at the National Institute of Child Health and Human Development, where she published research on pediatric AIDS.

Novello was appointed fourteenth surgeon general of the United States by President George H. W. Bush in 1990. She was both the first Hispanic person and first woman to hold this position. As surgeon general, Novello focused on health care for women, children, and minorities. She raised awareness regarding the maternal transmission of AIDS to newborns, created a workshop that led to the formation of the National Hispanic/Latino Health Initiative, spearheaded the removal of cartoon images from cigarette advertisements, mandated identification checks for the purchase of tobacco products, and discouraged alcohol distribution to minors. She resigned from the position in 1993.

In 1993, Novello was named the PSCHH's special representative for health and nutrition to the United Nations Children's Fund (UNICEF), a position she held until 1996. She subsequently accepted a position as visiting professor of health policy and management at the Johns Hopkins University School of Hygiene and Public Health. New York governor George Pataki then appointed Novello state commissioner of health in 1999. She served for seven years, but was later charged with governmental fraud and theft for using state funds for personal errands. She pleaded guilty to one lesser charge and paid a restitution fee and a fine and completed community service with low-income patients at a New York health clinic.

Novello has received the Public Health Service Commendation Medal, Public Health Service Outstanding Service Medal, Hispanic Heritage Award for Leadership, James Smithson Bicentennial Medal, and Legion of Merit Medal. In 2006, she was a finalist for *Hispanic Business* magazine's woman of the year award (2006).

In 2008, Novello was named vice president of women and children health and policy affairs at Disney Children's Hospital at Florida Hospital in Orlando, where she concentrates on family health and preventing illness. She married Joseph R. Novello, a former U.S. Navy flight surgeon and psychiatrist, in 1970, but the couple eventually divorced.

SIGNIFICANCE

Novello overcame childhood illness and poverty to become one of the country's most successful public health leaders. She turned what could have been a discouraging medical diagnosis into motivation to help others gain equal access to health care. Novello is one of the most influential Latino role models in health care and continues to work to improve care for minorities.

Janet Ober Berman

FURTHER READING

Novello, Antonia C. "Cancer, Minorities, and the Medically Underserved: A Call to Action." *Journal of Cancer Education* 21, no. 1 Supplement (Spring, 2006): S5-S8. Transcript of a lecture detailing Novello's approach to eliminating health disparities in minorities.

Novello, Antonia C., et al. "Final Report of the United States Department of Health and Human Services Secretary's Work Group on Pediatric Human Immunodeficiency Virus Infection and Disease: Content and Implications." *Pediatrics* 84, no. 3 (September, 1989): 547-555. Influential paper on pediatric AIDS that brought attention to Novello's work and led to her appointment as surgeon general.

Olmstead, Mary. *Antonia Novello*. Chicago: Raintree, 2004. Basic biography for younger readers, focusing on Novello's tenure as surgeon general.

Wade, N. A., et al. "Decline in Perinatal HIV Transmission in New York State (1997-2000)." *Journal of Acquired Immune Deficiency Syndromes* 36, no. 5 (August, 2004): 1075-1082. Article detailing the success of public health policies in declining rates of newborns with human immunodeficiency virus (HIV).

See also: Richard Henry Carmona; Norma Martinez-Rogers; Marian Lucy Rivas.

Soledad O'Brien

American broadcaster

O'Brien is a reporter and news anchor who has appeared on several major cable and broadcast networks, including CNN and MSNBC. She has made several award-winning reports, including investigations into the aftermath of 2005's Hurricane Katrina and an exploration of Latinos in the United States.

Latino heritage: Cuban
Born: September 19, 1966; St. James, New York
Also known as: María de la Soledad Teresa O'Brien
Areas of achievement: Radio and television; journalism

Early Life

María de la Soledad Teresa O'Brien (SOH-leh-dad oh-BRI-uhn) was the fifth of their six children born to Edward and Estella O'Brien. Her father was an Australian of Irish descent who became a professor of mechanical engineering after having studied at Johns Hopkins University in Baltimore. Her mother was of Afro-Cuban origin and met her husband while also studying at Johns Hopkins. She later became a teacher of French and English.

The O'Brien family settled in St. James, a Long Island community. All of the children did well at school, and all attended Harvard University, although Soledad did not obtain her bachelor's degree until 2000. Several of her siblings became lawyers; others entered the medical profession.

O'Brien's first job was as an associate producer and news writer for WBZ-TV, a NBC affiliate in Boston in 1989. She then moved on to NBC News in New York in 1991 as a field producer for *Nightly News*

Soledad O'Brien.
(Ben Hider/Picturegroup via AP Images)

and *Today.* Again, she held this position for a couple years, gaining experience in the field of news broadcasting.

O'Brien then relocated to the West Coast to become a local reporter and bureau chief for KRON, a San Francisco affiliate of NBC. She reported particularly for the station's program *The Know Zone.* At the same time, she also appeared on the Discovery Channel in a series titled *The Next Step.* In 1995, she married Bradley Raymond, an investment banker, with whom she went on to have four children, two girls and twin boys.

LIFE'S WORK

One year later, in 1996, O'Brien became an anchor for the award-winning MSNBC technology series *The Site.* She also anchored the cable network's weekend morning show until 1999. O'Brien's work for NBC included anchoring the *Weekend Today* program with David Bloom. She also contributed reports to *Today* and weekend editions of *Nightly News.* During this period, she covered such stories as the 1999 Columbine High School shooting in Colorado, and the plane crash of John F. Kennedy, Jr.

O'Brien is best known for her work with CNN, the cable network she joined in July, 2003. She coanchored the flagship morning program *American Morning* with Miles O'Brien (no relation). During this period, she memorably covered the December, 2004, South Asian tsunami and Hurricane Katrina in 2005, which devastated New Orleans and the Gulf Coast. After the latter disaster, she had an in-depth interview with former Federal Emergency Management Agency chief Michael Brown that exposed the many flaws in the federal government's response to the crisis. O'Brien and Miles were replaced in April, 2007.

O'Brien moved on to making documentaries on newsworthy events or people, starting with two films on the aftermath of Hurricane Katrina. She has remained committed to covering the slow and difficult rehabilitation of the city of New Orleans. In 2008, CNN undertook a major project to review the state of African Americans in America forty years after the death of Martin Luther King, Jr. The result was the special reports *Black in America* and *Black in America 2.* In both of these, O'Brien played a major part, as she did in *Words that Changed a Nation*, a report covering the King assassination based on recently uncovered diaries, letters, and other papers.

In 2009, O'Brien took part in the special report *Latino in America,* covering the history and cultural influence of Latino Americans. She also has reported on children affected by the 2010 Haiti earthquake.

O'Brien has won several prestigious awards for her reporting. The South Asian tsunami coverage won her an Alfred duPont Award and the Katrina coverage a George Foster Peabody Award. For the same coverage, she also won the Goodermote Humanitarian Award from Johns Hopkins University. Her reporting of the Israel-Hezbollah conflict from the island of Cyprus won her a Gracie Allen Award in 2007, while in the same year the National Association for the Advancement of Colored People gave her its President's Award for her humanitarian efforts. In 2008, the Morehouse School of Medicine named an award after her, the Soledad O'Brien Freedom's Voice Award. She was its first recipient as a "catalyst for social change."

SIGNIFICANCE

O'Brien's mixed heritage has given her a compassionate and humanitarian view of minority and oppressed groups not only in the United States but also around the world. Many groups have recognized her for this: She has appeared on *Black Enterprise* magazine's 2005 Hot List and *Irish American Magazine*'s Top 100 Irish Americans list twice. She was named journalist of the year in 2010 by the National Association of Black Journalists, and in 2005, she was named Groundbreaking Latina of the Year by *Catalina* magazine. O'Brien was awarded an honorary doctorate by Bryant University in 2007.

David Barratt

FURTHER READING

Edelhart, Courtenay. "CNN's O'Brien Embraces Her Own Diversity." *The Indianapolis Star,* October 24, 2005. An article on O'Brien's diverse background and how it has shaped her career and concerns.

O'Brien, Soledad. "The Church Across the Street." *Guideposts,* April, 2004. O'Brien shares some of her early Catholic connections.

O'Brien, Soledad, and Rose Marie Arce. *The Next Big Story: My Journey through the Land of Possibilities.* New York: Celebra, 2010. O'Brien reflects on her many special reports and assignments to assess the state of America and its direction.

Robson, David. *Soledad O'Brien: Television Journalist.* Broomall, Pa.: Mason Crest, 2009. A straightforward biography of O'Brien aimed at younger readers.

See also: Ron Arias; Maria Hinojosa; Maggie Rivas-Rodriguez; Geraldo Rivera.

ADRIANA C. OCAMPO

Colombian-born planetary geologist

Ocampo has excelled in three areas of science: space, earth, and education. She has been involved in vital aspects of several space projects for the National Aeronautics and Space Administration (NASA). She was the first to relate the sinkholes in Mexico to the Chicxulub crater. She has developed the pattern for science education meetings and workshops given in many countries of the world.

Latino heritage: Colombia

Born: January 5, 1955; Barranquilla, Colombia

Also known as: Adriana Christian Ocampo Uria

Areas of achievement: Science and technology; education

EARLY LIFE

Adriana Christian Ocampo Uria (oh-KAHM-poh) was born to Victor Alberto Ocampo, a Columbian electrical engineer, and Teresa Uria do Ocampo, a teacher from Argentina. She was the second of three daughters. A few months after Adriana was born, the family moved to Buenos Aires, Argentina. In 1969, the family moved to Los Angeles, California.

Even before that move, Ocampo exhibited an interest in space and a vivid imagination. She had so much imagination that schoolwork was boring to her and her grades were not outstanding. In 1972, she joined the Explorer Scouts' Space Exploration Post. This allowed her to spend time at NASA's Jet Propulsion Laboratory (JPL) and to see the launch of *Apollo 17*. She also worked part-time at JPL during her high school years.

When Ocampo graduated from South Pasadena High School, she started working nearly full time at JPL. In 1976 she joined the imaging team of the *Viking* mission to Mars. Her involvement was in sequence planning and data analysis of images. She planned the observation of the moons Phobos and Deimos while also searching for a ring or other moons. From this work, NASA published a Phobos atlas, which was used by the Russians in planning the mission to that moon. In 1977, Ocampo received her associate degree in science from Pasadena City College, and in 1980, she became a U.S. citizen.

LIFE'S WORK

Ocampo began work on the *Voyager* mission in 1980 with the navigation and mission planning team. An ephemeris (a calendar showing the position of space bodies over a period of time) for Saturn had to be developed so the instruments would be directed at the right place. Ocampo also developed skills in image processing, image visualization, and analysis using computers. She was named science coordinator for the *Mars Observer* mission, which malfunctioned and crashed before Ocampo could complete her analysis.

In 1983, Ocampo received her bachelor's degree in geology from California State University at Los Angeles and began to work full time for JPL. In 1984, she was named science coordinator for the *Galileo* mission to Jupiter. The *Challenger* space shuttle's explosion delayed the *Galileo* mission until 1989.

Ocampo also developed skills at imaging planets from satellites. Using these skills, Ocampo used satellites and *Galileo*'s instruments to detect atmospheric methane, which indicates life on a planet. Not only humans but also bacteria and other forms of life produce methane. Ocampo was responsible for the Near Infrared Mapping Spectrometer (NIMS), which uses reflected sunlight and heat to determine the composition, temperature, and cloud structure of planets. She used this and other instruments to study Venus, Earth, and the asteroid belt including the asteroids Gaspra and Ida, before *Galileo* reached Jupiter. Besides studying Jupiter, Ocampo focused on Europa, one of Jupiter's moons. In 2002, she went to the Netherlands to join two projects by the European Space Agency, the *Mars Express* and the *Venus Express*. After the *Mars Express* lifted off, Ocampo returned to JPL in 2004 to join the *Mars Odyssey* mission.

Ocampo stays constantly busy with various projects. In 1988, while looking at aerial photographs, she was the first to connect the ring of *cenotes* (sinkholes) around Mexico's Yucatan Peninsula to a meteor impact. With Kevin Pope, she led several expeditions to explore the possibility. With the data that they and other scientists gathered, it is now believed that the Chicxulub crater in Yucatan, Mexico, was caused by a meteor. The impact of the meteor is believed to have caused a layer of iridium to cover the Earth, which led to the extinction of the dinosaurs. Ocampo used the meteor research to earn her master's degree in geology from California State University at Northridge in 1997. She married Pope on November 3, 1989. They were divorced in 1998.

SIGNIFICANCE

Ocampo has been not only a leader in developing the meteor impact analysis and a scientist on several of NASA's space missions, but also a leader in developing methods to spread the knowledge of science to others, especially developing nations. She organized the first planetary sciences workshop in 1987, and the United Nations has used it as a pattern for continued education projects. She has been an inspiration and a role model for Hispanics and for women of all nations.

C. Alton Hassell

FURTHER READING

Guidici, Cynthia. *Adriana Ocampo.* Chicago: Raintree, 2006. This book is intended for a juvenile audience.

It tells of her early interest in space, her work with NASA's Jet Propulsion Laboratory, and her work with the impact crater in Mexico.

Hopping, Lorraine Jean. *Space Rocks: The Story of Planetary Geologist Adriana Ocampo.* New York: Franklin Watts, 2005. This book is intended for a juvenile audience. It is a very personal story of how Ocampo dreamed of space and became a planetary geologist.

Oleksy, Walter G. *Hispanic-American Scientists.* New York: Facts On File, 1998. This book profiles ten Hispanic-American scientists who have advanced science by their efforts. Ocampo's profile is short but detailed.

See also: Luis W. Alvarez; Walter Alvarez; France Anne Córdova; Ramon E. Lopez.

ELLEN OCHOA

American astronaut and inventor

Ochoa was the first Latina to become an astronaut. She had flown on four space flights by 2011 and holds three patents as an inventor or coinventor of optical systems used for space imaging. Ochoa was named deputy director of Lyndon B. Johnson Space Center in Houston, Texas, in 2007.

Latino heritage: Mexican
Born: May 10, 1958; Los Angeles, California
Also known as: Ellen Lauri Ochoa
Area of achievement: Science and technology

EARLY LIFE

Ellen Lauri Ochoa (oh-CHOH-ah) was born May 10, 1958, in Los Angeles, California, to Rosanne Deardorff Ochoa, a homemaker, and Joseph Ochoa, the manager of a retail store. Ochoa grew up in La Mesa, California. The third of five children, Ochoa was an outstanding student who excelled in the sciences and mathematics. In her family, education was considered very important, and the children were encouraged in their intellectual activities. Ochoa had many interests. At age thirteen, she won the San Diego County spelling bee. She also played classical flute and was a member of the Civic Youth Orchestra in San Diego.

Ochoa's parents divorced when she was twelve years old. Even with the changes in her family life, she continued to excel academically and graduated with honors as the class valedictorian from Grossmont High School in La Mesa in 1975. Ochoa was offered a four-year scholarship to Stanford University but turned it down to stay near home and help her mother raise her younger siblings.

Ochoa instead went to San Diego State University as a music major. She changed her major five times before graduating in 1980 as class valedictorian with a bachelor of science degree in physics. She then went to Stanford University on an engineering fellowship and received her master's degree in electrical engineering in 1981. Ochoa received an IBM Pre-Doctoral Fellowship from 1982 to 1984 and focused her work on designing optical systems for information processing. Her doctoral dissertation on the use of photorefractive crystals to filter images from space resulted in a patent in 1987. While at Stanford, Ochoa also played the flute and was an award-winning soloist in the Stanford Symphony Orchestra. In 1985, she received her doctorate in electrical engineering.

LIFE'S WORK

From 1985 to 1988, Ochoa was a researcher in imaging technology at the Sandia National Laboratories. She continued her work on optical systems used for filtering space images and developed an optical system to guide robots. After three years, Ochoa joined the National Aeronautics and Space Administration (NASA) at Ames Research Center and worked with a research team developing optical recognition systems as applied to space images. She also helped develop computer systems for aeronautical expeditions. Ochoa's work resulted in two additional patents as coinventor of an optical object recognition system and a method for noise removal in images.

Although Ochoa became interested in the astronaut program while she was at Stanford, NASA was not accepting female candidates. After two other attempts, Ochoa was chosen in January, 1990, as one of five women and eighteen men to begin training at Lyndon B. Johnson Space Center in Houston, Texas. That year, she married Coe Fulmer Miles, a computer research engineer she met at Ames Research Center. They later had two sons, Wilson and Jordan.

In July, 1991, Ochoa finished training and qualified as a mission specialist. Her first mission was on the April 4-17, 1993, flight of the space shuttle *Discovery*, followed shortly thereafter by the *Atlantis* shuttle flight November 3-14, 1994. Both the May 27-June 6, 1999, *Discovery* flight and the April 8-19, 2002, *Atlantis* flight visited the International Space Station. In total, Ochoa logged more than 978 hours in space. She was awarded a 1995 NASA Outstanding Leadership Medal, four NASA Space Flight Medals, a 1991 NASA Group

Ellen Ochoa. (AP Photo/NASA, Bill Ingalls)

Achievement Award for photonics technology, a NASA Distinguished Service Medal, and NASA's Exceptional Service Medal in 1997.

While in the Astronaut Office, Ochoa served in various roles and became the deputy director of flight crew operations in December, 2002. In September, 2006, Ochoa was named the director of flight crew operations, in which capacity she managed and directed the Astronaut Office and aircraft operations at Johnson Space Center. On September 17, 2007, Ochoa was named deputy director of Johnson Space Center, where her responsibilities include planning and organizing the day-to-day management of the space shuttle program.

SIGNIFICANCE

In interviews, Ochoa has indicated that she never felt that her Latina heritage helped or hindered her. She has, however, served as a role model for minorities and women in the fields of science and engineering. She has talked with thousands of students, sharing her life experiences and encouraging young people to set goals and stay in school. Ochoa is passionate about encouraging students to follow their dreams and not be discouraged, thus inspiring young women to choose fields that challenge them and benefit society.

Ochoa has received numerous awards and honors, including having two schools named after her: Ellen Ochoa Middle School in Pasco, Washington, and Ellen Ochoa Learning Center in Cudahy, California. She also was the first woman to be named engineer of the year by the Hispanic Engineer National Achievement Awards Conference. The award, which she won in 2008, recognizes overall leadership and technical achievement in science, technology, engineering, and mathematics.

Virginia L. Salmon

FURTHER READING

Hasday, Judy L. *Ellen Ochoa.* New York: Chelsea House, 2007. Offers basic biographical information and details Ochoa's space flights. Includes a time line, index, and bibliography.

Paige, Joy. *Ellen Ochoa: The First Hispanic Woman in Space.* New York: Rosen, 2004. Overview of Ochoa's life that explains many aspects related to space travel. Includes photographs, index, further reading, and glossary.

Schraff, Anne. *Ellen Ochoa: Astronaut and Inventor.* Berkeley Heights, N.J.: Enslow, 2010. Focuses on her astronaut career and includes a general discussion of the missions. Includes chronology, notes, index, and further reading.

Woodmansee, Laura S. *Women Astronauts*. Toronto: Apogee Books, 2002. A collection of interviews

and histories of several female astronauts, including Ellen Ochoa.

See also: Franklin Ramón Chang-Díaz; Sidney M. Gutierrez; Carlos Noriega.

ESTEBAN OCHOA

Mexican-born entrepreneur and politician

When the Arizona Territory was still largely unsettled, Ochoa helped bring the vast territory economic stability by establishing a network of transportation routes that provided vital supplies to the most remote areas of the territory. In the process, he became one of the wealthiest entrepreneurs west of the Mississippi, wealth he used to fund a significant legacy of public-spirited endeavors, most notably in education, for his adopted community of Tucson.

Latino heritage: Mexican
Born: March 17, 1831; Chihuahua, Mexico
Died: October 27, 1888; Las Cruces, New Mexico
Also known as: Estevan Ochoa
Areas of achievement: Business; education; government and politics

EARLY LIFE

Esteban Ochoa (EHS-teh-bahn oh-CHOH-ah) was born in the northern Mexican state of Chihuahua on March 17, 1831. He was well-educated and enjoyed a life of privilege—his father ran a mercantile concern that transported local goods as far north as Missouri via long mule trains. The work was grueling but lucrative, and young Ochoa often accompanied his father on the arduous routes. Hence, he grew up in a bicultural environment.

As a youth, Ochoa demonstrated business savvy and a hunger for success, and at the conclusion of the Mexican-American War, Ochoa, like other Mexican business visionaries of his generation, headed north for the promise of prosperity. Initially, he went to Mesilla (later Las Cruces), New Mexico. There he began his first freighting service. By 1860, Ochoa was restless. Recognizing the potential for such transportation services in the vast Arizona Territory, he moved to Tucson, which was little more than a dusty crossroads. In Tucson, he met Pinckney Randolph Tully, an enterprising former post trader who had worked in the Southwest for years. In 1864, they started Tully and Ochoa, a small

freight-hauling company (fewer than ten wagons) modeled after Ochoa's father's enterprise. They began by establishing trading routes connecting Mesilla to Tucson but quickly expanded their operations.

LIFE'S WORK

Tully and Ochoa wagons followed the Santa Fe Trail into some of the most forbidding territory west of the Mississippi. The mule trains, maintained at Ochoa's direction by Mexican immigrant laborers, faced daunting conditions: extreme heat and monsoon rains, a scarcity of water and food, and the possibility of wild animal attacks and Apache raids. Nevertheless, Ochoa was determined to establish a working network of reliable trails. The wagon trains brought much-needed food and supplies, as well as eagerly anticipated news, to remote army posts, small settlements and farms, and hundreds of scattered silver-mining camps. In the process, Ochoa's success helped make Tucson a transportation hub for the territory (indeed, it served as the territory's capital from 1867 to 1877, when its population boomed to more than seven thousand).

In a frontier business long known for unsavory characters and unscrupulous practices, Ochoa earned a reputation for honesty and diligence. By 1870, he was wealthy—he had a taste for ostentation, and his home in Tucson was widely known for its luxurious appointments and lavish landscaping. However, Ochoa was interested in establishing Tucson as not only an economic hub but also a community with cultural integrity and long-term viability. Over the final decades of the nineteenth century, as white settlers came in waves to the Southwest, the traditions of the first Mexican settlers were lost. Not so in Tucson, a town that during Ochoa's life was nearly 80 percent Hispanic. Ochoa dedicated much of his time (and his considerable fortune) to maintaining Tucson as a model bicultural town, welcoming Anglo settlers while preserving Mexican traditions (for instance, funding the construction of the city's first cathedral).

Ochoa became a leading figure in the city—in 1875, he was elected the city's mayor and served two additional terms. He served as justice of the peace and as the town representative to the territorial legislature. During that time, Ochoa undertook the task of providing the town, still just a generation away from being a remote desert outpost, with a public education system, which he saw as the soundest strategy for securing the territory's economic future. The success was remarkable: By 1875, the territory staffed more than one hundred public schools. Ochoa himself served as president of Tucson's school board and not only provided funding for the construction of schools but also helped direct the development of the school's curriculum, which became a model of biculturalism.

It is a measure of Ochoa's civic spirit and his dedication to the Tucson community that when the railroad first appeared in the early 1880's, he did everything he could to encourage the growth of the transportation system that would guarantee the end of his own highly profitable business. Indeed, within a decade of the railroad's arrival in the Arizona Territory, freight-transport concerns such as Ochoa's were largely out of business. Ochoa's final years were spent in Las Cruces, where he died on October 27, 1888.

SIGNIFICANCE

Although his entrepreneurial success would be eclipsed by the economic renaissance introduced first by the railroad and later by the discovery of copper and the rise of cotton farming and cattle ranching, Ochoa made an indelible impression on the political and cultural evolution of Tucson. He emerged as one of the earliest and most respected Hispanic civic leaders in the American Southwest; his passionate dedication to creating a stable and prosperous city rich with cultural and religious traditions and anchored to a well-funded public education system became a template for urban development in the Southwest well into the twentieth century.

Joseph Dewey

FURTHER READING

Officer, James E. *Frontier Tucson: Hispanic Contributions*. Tucson: Arizona Historic Society, 1987. Historic survey of Ochoa's era with special interest in Ochoa's freighting empire and how it brought a sense of community to the Arizona Territory. Offers assessment of Tucson as a singularly Hispanic community.

Sheridan, Thomas E. *Los Tucsonenses: The Mexican Community in Tucson, 1854-1941*. Tucson: University of Arizona Press, 1992. Seminal work on Hispanic contributions to Tucson's early development. Focuses attention on Ochoa's civic and entrepreneurial work and provides a look at his lavish estate.

Woosley, Anne I. *Early Tucson: Images of America*. Mt. Pleasant, S.C.: Arcadia, 2008. Adds helpful context on Ochoa's era through rare archival photos with detailed historical explanations.

See also: Gertrudis Barceló; Pío Pico; Vicente Martinez Ybor.

SEVERO OCHOA

Spanish-born biochemist

Although Ochoa made significant discoveries about the metabolism of glucose, he is best known for his discovery of polynucleotide phosphorylase (PNP), which led to the deciphering of the genetic code. He won a Nobel Prize in 1959 for his work on the synthesis of ribonucleic acid (RNA).

Latino heritage: Spanish
Born: September 24, 1905; Luarca, Spain
Died: November 1, 1993; Madrid, Spain
Also known as: Severo Ochoa de Albornoz
Area of achievement: Science and technology

EARLY LIFE

Severo Ochoa de Albornoz (seh-VEH-roh oh-CHOH-ah) was born on September 24, 1905, in Luarca, Spain, to Severo Manuel Ochoa and Carmen de Albornoz. He attended grade school in Málaga and then went to Málaga College, a state school equivalent to an American high school, from which he received a bachelor's degree in 1921.

Ochoa's interest in the biomedical sciences was stimulated by Santiago Ramón y Cajal, a Spanish biologist and 1906 Nobel laureate. To further his knowledge of the biomedical sciences, Ochoa attended medical

Severo Ochoa. (The Nobel Foundation)

school at the University of Madrid, from which he received an M.D. degree in 1929. As a medical student, Ochoa worked with Juan Negrín y López, a physician and head of the department of physiology. Working with Negrín, Ochoa and another student, José Valdecasas, developed a method to assay small amounts of creatinine and subsequently isolated creatinine from urine. In the summer of 1927, after his fourth year of medical school, Ochoa worked with Diarmid Noël Paton at the University of Glasgow. There, he discovered that the compound guanidine stimulated the contraction of melanophores (pigment cells) in frog skin.

After medical school, Ochoa held several positions that gained him considerable expertise in experimental biochemistry. From 1929 to 1930, he worked with Nobel laureate Otto Fritz Meyerhof in Germany, where he studied muscle metabolism and biochemistry. Upon returning to Madrid in late 1930, Ochoa collaborated with Francisco Grande Covián to study the effect of the adrenal gland on muscle contraction. These studies formed the basis of his thesis, which was a requirement for the M.D. degree. After completing his thesis in 1931, Ochoa was appointed lecturer in physiology at the University of Madrid. Also in 1931, he married Carmen García Co-

bián. From 1932 to 1933, Ochoa studied with Harold Ward Dudley and Henry Hallett Dale at the National Institute for Medical Research in London. When Ochoa returned to Madrid in 1933, he again joined the Negrín laboratory as an assistant professor in biochemistry and investigated glycolysis in the heart muscle.

LIFE'S WORK

In 1934, Ochoa was appointed lecturer in physiology and biochemistry; he later was appointed head of the physiology division of the Institute for Medical Research at the University of Madrid. When the Spanish Civil War erupted in 1936, Ochoa left Spain and returned to the laboratory of Meyerhof to pursue research focusing on carbohydrate metabolism.

Before Meyerhof fled Nazi Germany for France, he arranged a six-month fellowship for Ochoa with Archibald Vivian Hill at the Plymouth (England) Marine Biological Laboratory. From 1938 to 1941, Ochoa worked on vitamin B1 with biochemist Rudolph Albert Peters at Oxford University, where he became interested in oxidative phosphorylation—a metabolic pathway that uses energy released from nutrients to produce adenosine triphosphate (ATP), a coenzyme used in cells. During his tenure in the Peters laboratory, Ochoa discovered the coupling of phosphorylation to the oxidation of pyruvic acid and demonstrated that three phosphates were fixed for each oxygen atom consumed.

Ochoa left for the United States in August, 1940, and was appointed instructor and research associate in pharmacology at Washington University School of Medicine in St. Louis. There, he worked with Carl Cori and Gerty Cori. Under the tutelage of the Coris, Ochoa pursued studies involving the isolation, purification, and characterization of enzymes. In 1942, Ochoa was appointed research associate in medicine at New York University (NYU) School of Medicine. He spent time in the Department of Biochemistry and in the Department of Pharmacology, but by 1954 he was professor of biochemistry and chairman of this department. Ochoa became a U.S. citizen in 1956. He remained at NYU until he retired in 1974.

Through the early 1950's, Ochoa's research focused on various aspects of intermediary metabolism and oxidative phosphorylation and culminated with the isolation of nicotinamide adenine dinucleotide (NAD), a coenzyme found in living cells. By the mid-1950's, his attention had turned to the synthesis of nucleic acids. In 1955, while studying the mechanism by which the energy of glucose is stored as ATP, he and Marianne Grunberg-Manago discovered an enzyme known as

Significance of Ochoa's Work on RNA Synthesis

Severo Ochoa and Marianne Grunberg-Manago's discovery of polynucleotide phosphorylase (PNP) directly led to the determination of many of the ribonucleic acid (RNA) codons for amino acids. A codon is a sequence of three adjacent molecules, called nucleotides, that constitute the genetic code and determine the insertion of amino acids during protein synthesis in living cells.

The laboratories of Ochoa, Marshall Nirenberg, and Har Gobind Khorana used PNP to synthesize RNA molecules of known nucleotide composition that could be used as templates in cell-free polypeptide synthesis experiments. In 1961, Nirenberg and Heinrich Matthaei used a synthetic mRNA composed only of uracil (U), poly U, to assign the first codon (UUU) to phenylalanine. Later, other codon assignments were made by Ochoa, Nirenberg, and Khorana using synthetic mRNAs composed of either single nucleotides or two or more nucleotides. The final codon assignments were made by Nirenberg and Khorana using other techniques. By 1966, all sixty-four codons had been assigned.

polynucleotide phosphorylase (PNP), which could polymerize (unite molecules in a chemical reaction to form three-dimensional networks or polymer chains) ribonucleoside diphosphates into a polynucleotide chain without a deoxyribonucleic acid (DNA) template. This was the first enzyme discovered that could polymerize ribonucleotides into ribonucleic acid (RNA), and although it was subsequently shown that within living organisms the enzyme degraded RNA, under laboratory conditions PNP ran in the reverse direction and synthesized RNA.

The discovery of PNP was instrumental in the synthesis of synthetic messenger RNAs (mRNAs) used in the unraveling of the genetic code. In separate laboratories, Ochoa, Marshall Nirenberg, and Har Gobind Khorana used PNP to synthesize a variety of synthetic mRNAs, including copolymers consisting of two or more different nucleotides. In 1961, Ochoa, Peter Lengyel, and Joseph Speyer discovered that copolymers such as those made with uracil and cytosine promoted the synthesis of polypeptides consisting of phenylalanine, serine, and leucine. It only took five years for the laboratories of Ochoa, Khorana, and Nirenberg to completely decipher the genetic code.

Ochoa's later research contributed to the understanding of the mechanisms of replication of RNA viruses and the translation of mRNA into polypeptides. Upon his retirement from NYU School of Medicine in 1974, Ochoa became a distinguished member of the Roche Institute of Molecular Biology. There, he studied protein biosynthesis and the replication of RNA viruses. In 1985, he returned to Madrid as a professor of biology at the Autonomous University of Madrid.

Ochoa published more than two hundred scientific articles during his distinguished career and received numerous honorary degrees and awards. In 1959, Ochoa shared the Nobel Prize in Physiology or Medicine with Arthur Kornberg. In 1961, he was elected president of the International Union of Biochemistry, a position he held until 1967. Ochoa died on November 1, 1993, in Madrid.

SIGNIFICANCE

Although Ochoa's work on carbohydrate metabolism and oxidative phosphorylation contributed significantly to the understanding of energy transfer between glucose and ATP, it was Ochoa's discovery of PNP and his work on the genetic code for which he is best known. The use of PNP by Ochoa, Nirenberg, and Khorana to synthesize synthetic mRNAs of known composition significantly contributed to the elucidation of the genetic code, one of the most important accomplishments in the history of science.

Charles L. Vigue

FURTHER READING

Garretson, Gregory. *Severo Ochoa.* Chicago: Heinemann/Raintree, 2005. Aimed at young adult readers, this book summarizes the life and work of Ochoa.

Grunberg-Manago, Marianne. "Severo Ochoa." *Biographical Memoirs of Fellows of the Royal Society* 43 (November, 1997): 351-365. This obituary of Ochoa was written by one of his postdoctoral students, with whom he discovered polynucleotide phosphorylase.

Kornberg, Arthur. "Severo Ochoa." *Proceedings of the American Philosophical Society* 141, no. 4 (December, 1997): 478-491. Obituary of Ochoa written by Kornberg, who shared the 1959 Nobel Prize in Physiology or Medicine with Ochoa.

Ochoa, Severo. "Pursuit of a Hobby." *Annual Review of Biochemistry* 49 (1980): 1-30. Autobiographical sketch describing Ochoa's early life and scientific career.

See also: Anne Maino Alvarez; Luis W. Alvarez; Albert V. Baez; Elma González.

TONY OLIVA

Cuban-born athlete

A hard-hitting outfielder, Oliva spent his entire Major League Baseball career with the Minnesota Twins, compiling a lifetime batting average over .300.

Latino heritage: Cuban
Born: July 20, 1938; Pinar del Rio, Cuba
Also known as: Antonio Oliva Lopez Hernandes Javique; Pedro Tony Oliva, Jr.; Tony-O
Area of achievement: Sports; baseball

EARLY LIFE

Tony Oliva (oh-LEEV-uh) was born Antonio Oliva Lopez Hernandes Javique in Pinar del Rio, a western province in Cuba. There were ten children in the Oliva family, five boys and five girls. Although Oliva's given name was Pedro, when he signed his first professional baseball contract he needed a passport in order to travel to the United States. He didn't have one and didn't have time to get a birth certificate that was necessary to get the passport, so he used his older brother Antonio's birth certificate and passport. That is why everyone started calling him Tony.

Oliva started playing baseball because his father, Pedro, Sr., loved baseball and encouraged all his children to play. Oliva started playing baseball at age seven and began playing organized baseball on a country team at age fifteen. He signed a contract to join the Minnesota Twins when he was nineteen. A former outfielder in the Washington Senators' farm system, Roberto Fernandez, recommended Oliva to Joe Cambria, a top scout in Cuba for the Twins.

Oliva was in the last group of baseball players allowed to leave Cuba before Fidel Castro began prohibiting such emigration. Oliva was among twenty-two Cuban baseball players who left Havana for Jacksonville, Florida, in early 1961. He got to play in four games as part of his tryout but was released. He was picked up by the Wytheville, Virginia, team, a Twins affiliate in the Appalachian League. In his first season as a professional baseball player, he won the Silver Louisville Slugger for leading all of organized baseball with a .410 batting average. He then played the 1962 season with Charlotte of the Sally League and was named the player of the year after hitting .349.

LIFE'S WORK

Oliva was a September call-up for the Twins in 1962 and 1963, but his first full season in major league baseball came in 1964, and it was outstanding. He started the season with an eight-game hitting streak and was elected as a starter in right field for the All-Star Game. He went on to lead the league in hits (217), times at bat, batting average (.323), total bases (374), doubles (43), and runs scored. He walked away with rookie of the year honors in the American League, getting nineteen out of twenty votes. He was the first black to win an American League batting title and the first black to be named rookie of the year in the American League.

He had even greater success in his second season as he won another batting title in 1965 with a .323 average. He is the only player ever to win batting titles in his first two seasons. He was named Player of the Year by *The Sporting News* and helped lead the Twins to an American League pennant and a spot in the World Series against the Los Angeles Dodgers.

While he didn't win the batting title in his third season, he did lead the league in hits with 197 and won his only Gold Glove award for his play in right field. He continued to excel year after year, eventually retiring in

Tony Oliva. (Getty Images)

1976 after playing all fifteen of his major league seasons with the Twins. He finished his major league career with a .304 batting average, 1,917 hits, and 220 home runs. Among his many career highlights: he holds the major-league record for being named to the American League All-Star Team his first eight seasons in the league; he led the American League in hits five times; he won the American League batting title three times; and he was the first rookie to win the batting title in 1964.

SIGNIFICANCE

Hundreds of Latin American-born players have played in Major League Baseball. However, when Oliva left Cuba in 1961 with little money and scant knowledge of the English language, he became part of a group that would break down many racial barriers within baseball as well as the nation. During his last year in baseball he began to make the transition to coaching, becoming a player-coach in 1976. As a coach, Oliva served the Twins as a first-base coach and batting instructor and also served as a hitting instructor in the Twins' minor-league system. He helped pave the way for other Latin Americans to serve as coaches and managers. However, Oliva was best known for his ability to hit the baseball, and the only team he ever played for, the Minnesota Twins, acknowledged his unique ability when the team retired his number 6 in 1991.

Paul Finnicum

FURTHER READING

Brackin, Dennis, and Patrick Reusse. *Minnesota Twins: The Complete Illustrated History*. Minneapolis, Minn.: MVP Books, 2010. A comprehensive review of the teams, the players, and the highlights through the years.

Oliva, Tony, and Bob Fowler. *TONY O! The Trials and Triumphs of Tony Oliva*. New York: Hawthorn Books, 1973. A look at Oliva's life from his beginnings in Cuba to his career with the Twins.

Regalado, Samuel O. *Viva Baseball! Latin Major Leaguers and Their Special Hunger*. Champaign: University of Illinois Press, 2008. A combination of existing literature and interviews that describes the efforts of Latin American professional baseball players in the United States from the late 1800's to the present.

Thielman, Jim. *Cool of the Evening: The 1965 Minnesota Twins*. Minneapolis, Minn.: Kirk House, 2005. A series of interviews with players from the 1965 team that won the American League Championship.

See also: Felipe Alou; Juan Marichal; Minnie Minoso; Luis Tiant.

FRANCISCO OLLER

Puerto Rican-born artist

Oller was a pivotal Latin American figure of the Impressionist art movement, which was dominated by French artists such as Claude Monet, Camille Pissarro, and Pierre-Auguste Renoir in the late nineteenth century. His paintings combined European elements with folk scenes from his native Puerto Rico. Many of his renowned works depict the island's culture and landscapes.

Latino heritage: Puerto Rican
Born: June 17, 1833; Bayamón, Puerto Rico
Died: May 17, 1917; San Juan, Puerto Rico
Also known as: Francisco Manuel Oller y Cestero
Areas of achievement: Art

EARLY LIFE

Francisco Manuel Oller y Cestero (OH-yehr) was born in Bayamón, Puerto Rico, in 1833 to an affluent family. He was one of four children born to Cayetano Juan Oller y Fromesta and María del Carmen Cestero Dávila. His paternal grandfather was a doctor who famously introduced the smallpox vaccine to the island and was hailed as a national hero.

Oller began studying art with Juan Cleto Noa when he was twelve years old, but after less than a year of lessons, the teacher declared that he had nothing else to teach his pupil, who had expertly reproduced a painting of his grandfather by renowned Puerto Rican artist José Campeche. Thus, from an early age, Oller displayed an amazing artistic aptitude, a talent that also resulted in his dismissal as a clerk at the Royal Treasury in 1848. After losing his post for drawing unflattering caricatures of his supervisors, he was offered an opportunity to study in Rome. Citing his young age, his mother promptly denied the offer.

At the age of eighteen, Oller traveled to Madrid, Spain, to study art at the Royal Academy of Fine Arts of San Fernando with Federico de Madrazo y Kuntz, who later became the director of the Prado Museum. After two years, Oller returned to Puerto Rico, where he stayed for five years before going back to Europe to study art. In 1858, he began studying with Charles Gleyre in Paris, where he became acquainted with Édouard Manet, Claude Monet, Pierre-Auguste Renoir, and Camille Pissarro.

LIFE'S WORK

Oller was influenced by his time in Europe with Impressionist painters, although he said that he was most affected by the work and technique of Gustave Courbet, with whom he studied art at the Louvre. He had several lengthy stays in Spain and France and traveled back and forth between Europe and Puerto Rico until he settled in his homeland in the 1890's.

Several of Oller's works were exhibited alongside paintings by Impressionists Jean-Frédéric Bazille, Monet, Renoir, and Alfred Sisley in 1859. His first significant solo show took place in San Juan in 1868, the year he also married and received permission to open his first art academy. Oller painted many cultural and military leaders in Puerto Rico before producing his most recognizable masterwork, *El velorio*, which was first displayed at the Paris Salon in 1895. He captured rural life on the island in a scene depicting a child's wake, and as in many of his paintings, Oller offered commentary on the prevailing social system of his day. While depicting the culture and landscape of Puerto Rico, he also used his art to denounce colonialism and slavery. A talented baritone who sang with the Philharmonic Society of Puerto Rico, Oller also gave concerts when his economic situation necessitated such performances. In addition, he was friends with both Pissarro and Paul Cézanne, the latter of whom was his pupil for a short time but cut ties after a disagreement.

Oller established the Free Academy of Art of Puerto Rico in 1868, and in 1884, he opened the Universidad Nacional, an art school for women. In addition, he was an official court painter for Amadeo I, who ruled Spain from 1870 to 1873. During this time, he also was named a Cabellero de la Orden de Carlos III (Knight of the Order of Carlos III) and exhibited some of his works in Vienna, Austria.

After settling permanently in Puerto Rico, Oller was a drawing professor at the Escuela Normal, which later became the University of Puerto Rico. After two years, he was dismissed in 1904. Little is known about Oller's later life, which ended in 1917 when he died in San Juan at age eighty-three.

SIGNIFICANCE

Oller is considered the only Hispanic Impressionist, although he often is overlooked as an important participant in that art movement. His uniqueness was further defined by his choice to portray realistic native scenes of the culture and landscape of Puerto Rico, including sugar plantations and slaves, among other views of rural life. Offering a commentary on the island's repressive social system, Oller challenged traditional notions of art as well as prevailing practices of colonialism and slavery. His paintings have been exhibited around the world and are housed in numerous museums, the most famous of which is the Louvre.

Alyson F. Lerma

FURTHER READING

Manthorne, Katherine. "Plantation Pictures in the Americas circa 1880: Land, Power, and Resistance." *Nepantla: Views from South* 2, no. 2 (May, 2001): 317-353. Discusses Oller's representations of rural life and its political implications.

Raynor, Vivien. "Art: Francisco Oller, Puerto Rico Glimpsed." *The New York Times*, Feb. 10, 1984. Brief review of Oller's work and a biographical sketch.

Soto-Crespo, Ramón E. "The Pains of Memory: Mourning the Nation in Puerto Rican Art and Literature." *MLN* 117, no. 2 (March, 2002): 449-480. Article discusses the importance and centrality of Oller's most famous work, *El velorio*. Soto-Crespo argues that this painting metaphorically portrays Puerto Rico as it mourned its failed nationhood.

See also: José Aceves; Lorenzo Homar.

EDWARD JAMES OLMOS

American actor and director

Olmos is one of the premier Latino actors working in Hollywood. Through his performances, he has created more positive portrayals of Latino characters in American entertainment. He also has used his fame to advance social causes and famously took part in the efforts to clean up Los Angeles and heal ethnic rifts in the aftermath of the 1992 riots.

Latino heritage: Mexican
Born: February 24, 1947; Los Angeles, California
Areas of achievement: Acting; radio and television; activism

EARLY LIFE

Edward James Olmos (OL-mohs) was born in East Los Angeles on February 24, 1947, to a Mexican immigrant father and a Mexican American mother. He was initially interested in music but ultimately decided his future lay in acting.

Olmos's rise to fame began with his role in the play *Zoot Suit* (1978), which debuted in Los Angeles before moving to Broadway. The production dealt with racism against Latinos during World War II; in 1981, it was adapted into a critically acclaimed film of the same name, and Olmos reprised his role. He also starred in the television film *The Ballad of Gregorio Cortez* (1982), another critically acclaimed film about ethnic tensions. Both films remain important parts of Latino studies curricula in the United States.

LIFE'S WORK

After his roles in *Zoot Suit* and *The Ballad of Gregorio Cortez*, Olmos began to be cast in higher-profile roles, such as Gaff in *Blade Runner* (1982) and Lieutenant Martin Castillo in the television series *Miami Vice* (1984-1989). The police show gave him a stable job for five seasons, allowed him to portray a character that was widely respected, and made him a well-known actor in Hollywood.

Olmos's most famous role is arguably that of award-winning mathematics teacher Jaime Escalante in the biographical film *Stand and Deliver* (1988), which rewarded his interest in presenting a positive portrayal of a Latino character in a mainstream film. Olmos received an Academy Award nomination for best actor in 1989. In *Stand and Deliver*, he plays a Bolivian American teacher who believes in his inner-city students' capacity to learn advanced mathematics. Although his

students do so well on a standardized test that they are accused of cheating, Escalante continues training and encouraging them until their innocence is proved when they retake the test. This role was iconic in part because it reinforced a belief in urban education. Among other high-profile Latino projects, he had a supporting role in Gregory Nava's *My Family* (1995), about the trials and triumphs of three generations of an immigrant clan, and played Abraham Quintanilla, father of slain singer Selena, in *Selena* (1997). Made only two years after Selena's death, the film starred Jennifer Lopez in the title role. Olmos's interest in Latino issues also is evident in some of his later projects. In 2006, he directed *Walkout*, an HBO film about the uprising of Latino students in 1968 East Los Angeles.

Olmos's most prominent role in the 2000's came in the television remake of the 1970's show *Battlestar Galactica*. In the science-fiction series, his character, Adama, is ethnic but is not supposed to be Latino. Instead, he hails from the planet Taurus, whose citizens often suffer injustice based on racial prejudice. Adama

Edward James Olmos. (AP Photo)

Activism During the 1992 Los Angeles Riots

During the 1992 Los Angeles riots, the city was engulfed in an ethnic revolt that led to widespread destruction and violence among people of different races and law-enforcement officials. Edward James Olmos was one of the local celebrities who sought to bring peace to the city by organizing members of local communities and speaking to the news media in a bid to discourage looters, appease combatants, and save lives. He famously appeared with a broom and organized cleanup brigades for three days to help clean the streets of debris from the riots. Nationwide, the revolt was perceived to be the work of local hooligans, but Olmos saw it as a consequence of the ethnic segregation in the city, the harsh economic climate for the working class, and the government's ineffective attempts to deal with gang warfare and its social roots. His work in the reconstruction of Los Angeles after the riots is one of his most important achievements.

ultimately becomes the leader of the military and the character that everyone in the series looks up to. Olmos was the first Hispanic actor to have such a high-profile role in a science-fiction series. The series became a cult hit and attracted the attention of critics and academics because it dealt metaphorically with the social and political climate in America after the September 11, 2001, terrorist attacks. After the series ended in 2009, Olmos directed a tie-in television film, *The Plan* (2009), set in the same universe.

Offscreen, Olmos has continued to promote the Latino community. He cofounded the Los Angeles Latino International Film Festival, which offers some of the most significant displays of Latin American cinema in the United States. He also is active in encouraging underprivileged youths to strive to overcome hardships and take lives in their own hands. In 1998, he cofounded and chaired Latino Public Broadcasting, a nonprofit organization that funds the creation of programs specifically for the Latino community in the United States. In 2001, he took part in protests against the U.S. Navy practice bombings in Vieques, Puerto Rico.

By 2010, Olmos had been married three times, including an eight-year marriage to actor Lorraine Bracco, whom he divorced in 2002.

Significance

Olmos is one of the most important Latino actors of the late twentieth century. He was able to achieve mainstream success in Hollywood by portraying complex Latino characters as well as characters of other ethnicities in projects such as *Blade Runner* and *Battlestar Galactica*. Olmos also has directed for television and participated in important Latino-centric initiatives. Meanwhile, he has expressed and demonstrated his dedication to activism on behalf of the Latino community and underprivileged youths.

Enrique Garcia

Further Reading

Beltrán, Mary. "The Face of the 'Decade': Edward James Olmos and Latino Films from the 1980's." In *Latino/a Stars in U.S. Eyes: The Making and Meanings of Film and TV Stardom*. Urbana: University of Illinois Press, 2009. A book chapter focusing on Olmos's early career in the context of the growth of Latino cinema and the rising number of Latino directors.

Dockser, Amy. "Making Sure There Are Alternatives: The Ballad of Edward James Olmos, Tom Bower, and Gregorio Cortez." *Imagine: International Chicano Poetry Journa*l 1, no. 1 (Summer, 1984): 1-9. An article that examines *The Ballad of Gregorio Cortez*, including the role of Olmos in the film.

Goulart, Woody, and Wesley Y. Joe. "Inverted Perspectives on Politics and Morality in *Battlestar Galactica*." In *New Boundaries in Political Science Fiction*, edited by Donald M. Hassler and Clyde Wilcox. Columbia: University of South Carolina Press, 2008. Discusses the fictional universe of *Battlestar Galactica* and its controversial depictions of political issues.

Latino Public Broadcasting. http://www.lpbp.org. The official Web site of the organization cofounded and chaired by Olmos.

Wilkinson, Tracy. "Street Drama: Actor Edward James Olmos Plays Leading Role in Cleanup Effort." *The Los Angeles Times*, May 5, 1992. Details Olmos's involvement in cleanup work after the Los Angeles riots, including recruiting and organizing volunteers.

See also: Hector Elizondo; Andy Garcia; Raúl Juliá; Cheech Marín; Martin Sheen.

LUPE ONTIVEROS

American actor and activist

Although relegated throughout her career to small, supporting roles, mostly stereotypical in nature, Ontiveros provided a constant presence as a Latina in entertainment and a role model for Latino actors who follow in her footsteps.

Latino heritage: Mexico
Born: September 17, 1942; El Paso, Texas
Also known as: Guadalupe Ontiveros; Guadalupe Moreno
Areas of achievement: Acting; theater; social issues

EARLY LIFE

Guadalupe Ontiveros (gwah-duh-LEW-pay ahn-tih-VEH-rohs) was born Guadalupe Moreno in El Paso, Texas, on September 17, 1942, to poor Mexican immigrants. Ontiveros's father, Juan Moreno, and mother, Lucita Castanon, sold sombreros and shoes out of the bed of a Ford pickup truck until they saved enough money to start their own tortilla stand. Eventually Ontiveros's parents opened a Mexican restaurant, which later grew to become two El Paso restaurants and a tortilla factory.

Ontiveros was the fifth child born to Juan and Lucita; the first four children died in infancy before Ontiveros was born, largely because of extreme poverty and insufficient medical care. Ontiveros was named for the Virgen de Guadalupe, as her parents' thanks for her being born healthy and surviving childbirth. A lover of her family-like Latino community in El Paso, Ontiveros thrived in her family's restaurants, and she worked with her parents in their tortilla factory before leaving for college. After graduating from El Paso High School in 1960, Ontiveros attended Texas Woman's University in Denton, Texas. Never having been away from home before, Ontiveros was isolated and homesick, and she begged to come home, but her mother insisted that she stay and complete her education. Ontiveros graduated with a bachelor's degree in social work and returned to El Paso, where she was employed as a social worker until marrying Elias Ontiveros and moving to California in 1968.

For sixteen years, Lupe Ontiveros continued her employment as a social worker until, disillusioned and unhappy in her work, she saw an advertisement in the newspaper calling for film extras. Curious, Ontiveros tried out for a part, became an extra, and discovered a passion for acting. Still employed as a social worker by

day, Ontiveros began appearing at Nosotros, a Los Angeles community theater, by night, where she perfected her skills and gained increasing recognition as an actor. In 1976, Ontiveros appeared as a maid on ABC's television phenomenon *Charlie's Angels*.

LIFE'S WORK

Ontiveros worked as one of the founding members of the Los Angeles Latino Theater Company and appeared in small, supporting roles throughout the late 1970's: as a prostitute in *The World's Greatest Lover* (1977) and as a maid in Neil Simon's *California Suite* (1978). The critically acclaimed play *Zoot Suit* (1978), by Luis Miguel Valdez, marked a major turning point for Ontiveros, who for two years performed on stage in Los Angeles and in New York as Dolores, the first Chicano mother character to appear on Broadway. In 1981, the highly successful film *Zoot Suit* was released, gaining Ontiveros national attention for her performance.

In 1983, Ontiveros received critical recognition for her portrayal of Nacha in the independent film *El norte*

Lupe Ontiveros. (AP Photo)

(1983), directed by Gregory Nava. Ontiveros plays a maid who becomes surrogate mother to a young immigrant girl who has just arrived in the United States from Guatemala. Ontiveros has acknowledged repeatedly that Nacha is the favorite role of her career and that *El norte* is her greatest film because it best captures the life of the poor Latino immigrant.

Her performance in the blockbuster *Goonies* (1985) remains for many filmgoers Ontiveros's most memorable role, as the high-strung maid Rosalita. In 1987, Ontiveros was unforgettable as Rudy's mother in Cheech Marín's hugely successful *Born in East L.A.* Appearing as Camilla in the horror film *Dolly Dearest* (1992) and as Irene Sanchez in *My Family* (1995) with Jennifer Lopez, Ontiveros enjoyed continuing success. Ontiveros's most challenging role came in 1997, however, when she played Yolanda Saldivar, the woman who went from fan club to killer of Tejano singer Selena in the enormously popular film *Selena*. In addition, Ontiveros worked alongside Jack Nicholson as Nora Manning in the Academy Award-winning film *As Good as It Gets* (1997).

After twenty-five years of acting in films and plays and on television, Ontiveros received her first role as a white woman, a theater director named Beverly, in the film *Chuck and Buck* (2000), for which she was nominated Best Supporting Actress at the Independent Spirit Awards. Ontiveros's portrayal of Carmen Garcia, a controlling reactionary Latina mother, in the independent film *Real Women Have Curves* (2002), earned her a Special Jury Prize at the prestigious Sundance Film Festival.

Ontiveros has appeared in dozens of television series, notably *Veronica's Closet* in 1997 as Louisa, for which she was awarded an American Latino Media Arts Award in 1998. Ontiveros starred as grandmother Magdalena in the series *Greetings from Tucson* (2002-2003), and she was nominated for an Emmy Award for playing mother-in-law Juanita in the series *Desperate Housewives* (2004-2005). In 2007, Ontiveros appeared as Adelfa with George Lopez in *Tortilla Heaven*, and in 2010, Ortiz starred as Momma Cecelia in *Our Family Wedding*.

Ontiveros lives in Pico Rivera, California, with her husband and three sons.

SIGNIFICANCE

Ontiveros is significant because her long career in the public eye provides a visible mirror image of the inequality and racism Latinos have encountered in their struggle to succeed. There is a direct correlation between

Ontiveros's inability to access popular roles in film and Latinos' denial by mainstream American society. When Ontiveros first began acting professionally in the mid-1970's, very few opportunities were available to her as a Latina actor, unlike her Caucasian counterparts, who, though often less talented, educated, beautiful, and skillful, nonetheless obtained superior roles in films, plays, and television. Likewise, in American society at large, Latinos often found themselves locked into inferior positions professionally, victims of detrimental stereotyping, relentless marginalization, and pervasive bigotry.

For decades, Ontiveros was allowed to play only working-class characters on screen, inasmuch as Latinos were presumed by white audiences to occupy blue-collar positions, regardless of qualifications. In later years, however, Ontiveros gradually assumed alternative roles in films, while modern Latina actors such as Lopez, Salma Hayek, and America Ferrera have

Ontiveros and Typecasting of Latina Actors

Lupe Ontiveros has played the role of a maid or nanny on television or in films more than 150 times. Although she has auditioned for a wide variety of acting roles for decades, she has been continually typecast in housekeeper positions, with an occasional role as a prostitute.

Additionally, all of the maids portrayed by Ontiveros in her acting career have been deliberately designated with Mexican names, further perpetuating the stereotype so often portrayed by Latina women in the mainstream media.

Ontiveros, who speaks perfect English, devoid of any trace of a Spanish accent, has found that if she speaks proper English during an audition, she will either be denied the part in question or the director will demand that she speak broken English with a Spanish accent, the thicker the better. Finally, after decades spent performing stereotyped housekeeper roles, in 2000 director Miguel Arteta offered Ontiveros a role playing a white woman named Barbara in the film *Chuck and Buck*. Ontiveros was so overjoyed to be offered a nonstereotyped ethnic role for the first time in her life that she accepted the part, sight unseen, without even reading the script. In 2004, because she had portrayed repeatedly the role of a maid in plays, films, and television, Ontiveros was chosen to narrate *Maid in America*, a documentary examining the social, political, and racial aspects of Latina women working as maids in the United States.

assumed dramatic leading roles, benefitting greatly from Ontiveros's indefatigable efforts to achieve equality in the media for Latino actors.

Mary E. Markland

FURTHER READING

Benavides, Oswald. *Drugs, Thugs, and Divas: Telenovelas and Narco Dramas in Latin America.* Austin, Tex.: University of Texas Press, 2008. The significance of Ontiveros repeatedly playing the role of a maid is analyzed, with Ontiveros saying that she is proud to have played the role of a maid so many times, emphasizing that she has never employed a maid herself.

O'Brien, Soledad, and Rose Marie Arce. *Latino in America.* New York: New American Library, 2009. Ontiveros talks about her roots in El Paso, Texas, her Mexican immigrant parents, and her family's transition from Texas to California once her acting career took off.

Valdivia, Angharad. *Latina/os and the Media*, Malden, Mass.: Polity Press, 2010. Ontiveros's increasing number of roles in recent years playing traditional Latina women, particularly those who are controlling or anachronistic, in film is discussed.

See also: America Ferrera; Luis Miguel Valdez; Elena Verdugo; Carmen Zapata.

ANTONIO ORENDAIN

Mexican-born migrant farmworker and labor leader

Orendain was the first secretary-treasurer of the United Farm Workers labor union that was established in California in 1962, following the Delano grape boycott. He was later appointed to lead the grape and lettuce boycott office in Chicago. Years later, Orendain organized the Farm Workers Union in Texas, after years of fighting for civil rights alongside César Chávez, Delores Huerta, and Gilbert Padilla for migrant workers in California.

Latino heritage: Mexican
Born: May 28, 1930; Etzatlán, Jalisco, Mexico
Areas of achievement: Activism; social issues

EARLY LIFE

Antonio Orendain (an-TOH-nee-oh ohr-EHN-dayn) was born in Etzatlán, Jalisco, Mexico, on May 28, 1930, at a time when poverty was pervasive in Mexico. He managed to complete only elementary school before leaving home to work as a migrant farmworker across the border in the United States. Orendain came as an illegal immigrant in 1950 at the age of twenty. He secretly crossed the border into San Ysidro, California, shortly after the end of World War II in hopes of earning $1.60 an hour.

Orendain shared his immigration story with interviewer Charles Carr Winn on July 20, 1974, and again with interviewer Allen McCreight on November 14, 1978. Orendain stated that although Mexico was close to the United States it seemed to be far away from God because of the impoverished lives that Mexicans lived from day to day. He had heard that life in the United States was easier, so he planned his migration to build a better life.

LIFE'S WORK

In 1962, migrant workers started an insurgency of boycotts that would last for nearly two decades. The Delano, California, grape boycott anchored the beginnings of a soon-to-be-powerful labor union, the National Farm Workers Association (NFWA). The NFWA was established under the tireless leadership of César Chávez, and it was supported by Orendain and others.

In 1966, the NFWA became known as the United Farm Workers (UFW). Chávez was elected president, Dolores Huerta and Gilbert Padilla became vice presidents, and Orendain took the position of secretary-treasurer. The union adopted a flag with a black eagle that represented the farm workers' dark situation, a white circle that signified hope, and a red background that represented the sacrifices the UFW would have to make in order to gain justice. Its official slogan was "Viva La Causa" ("Long Live Our Cause"). Farmers across the United States began to take note, and most responded favorably to needed changes that improved migrant workers' lives. Orendain and Chávez were responsible for numerous labor boycotts against grape and lettuce farm owners during this period. The list is extensive and the years were long. Most work actions (boycotts) were significantly effective under their leadership. Congressional hearings were held and laws were passed to protect the migrant workers.

SIGNIFICANCE

Orendain worked alongside Chávez, leader of the United Farm Workers of America. In 1966, the UFW merged with the American Federation of Labor and Congress of Industrial Organizations (AFL-CIO). As a result of this merger, Chávez's labor union was renamed United Farm Workers Organizing Committee (UFWOC). Chávez and Orendain's supporters included priests, nuns, and many other nonviolent community groups. During Chávez's later years, the United Farm Workers and La Causa experienced dissent among the ranks, causing a decrease in union membership from 100,000 to approximately 20,000. In August, 1975, Orendain organized the Texas Farm Workers Union (TFWU) to put an end to the exploitation of workers by Texas farmers, just as Chávez had done in California.

Orendain is characterized as the hot-tempered labor leader, in contrast to Chavez, whose calm demeanor and strategic-planning skills kept the union moving in a positive direction. "Si, se puede" ("Yes, It Can Be Done") was chanted by the union organizers and their followers at staged events throughout the farming communities. This motivational language encouraged migrant workers to press on for better days. Orendain significantly impacted working conditions for poor farmers and helped forge the creation of labor laws that were established to protect migrant workers from abuse. A notable law was the Federal Immigration Act of 1986, which granted amnesty to seasonal immigrant farmworkers.

Sandra W. Leconte

FURTHER READING

Ferriss, Susan, and Ricardo Sandoval. *The Fight in the Fields: Cesar Chavez and the Farmworkers Movement.* New York: Harcourt Brace, 1997. Chavez relates Orendain's role in the grape boycott.

Meier, Matt S., and Margo Gutierrez. *Encyclopedia of the Mexican American Civil Rights Movement.* Westport, Conn.: Greenwood Press, 2000. Several references to Orendain's role in securing rights for seasonal workers.

Orendain, Antonio. "Farm Workers and the 1980's." *Appeal to Reason* 5, no. 4 (Winter, 1979/1980). Orendain gives his philosophy on how farm workers can get the rights they deserve.

See also: César Chávez; Gus C. Garcia; Dolores Huerta; Reies López Tijerina.

FELIPE DE ORTEGO Y GASCA

American writer, scholar, and educator

In Chicano literature, Ortego y Gasca is the critic who dubbed the movement between 1966 and 1975 the "Chicano Renaissance." As a pioneer in the field of Mexican American literary history, he taught the first-ever U.S. college course in Chicano belles lettres in 1969 . He also wrote nonfiction, fiction, poetry, and drama.

Latino heritage: Mexican

Born: August 23, 1926; Blue Island, Illinois

Also known as: Felipe Ortego; Philip D. Ortego; Philip Darragh Ortego; Philip D. Ortego y Gasca

Areas of achievement: Literature; scholarship; education

EARLY LIFE

Felipe de Ortego y Gasca (ohr-TEH-goh ee GAHS-kah) was born in 1926 to itinerant Mexican parents Luis Mendes Ortego and Anita Campos Gasca. Spanish was his first language and he struggled to learn English in school, repeating the first and fourth grades. Although he was born in Illinois, he lived in San Antonio, Texas, until 1936; and in Chicago and Pittsburgh, Pennsylvania, from 1936 to 1943. Ortego y Gasca quit high school at age seventeen to join the Marines. During his military years as a Marine (1943-1946) and Air Force officer (1953-1962), he began to write.

LIFE'S WORK

Ortego y Gasca is a true renaissance man. Over the course of his career, he has worked as an actor, director, playwright, magazine editor, newspaper publisher, and consultant to national agencies and corporations. He earned a Ph.D. in English in 1971 from the University of New Mexico at Albuquerque. In 1970, he was founding director of the first Chicano studies program at the University of Texas at El Paso; that year, his article "Montezuma's Children" was recommended for a Pulitzer Prize. He also has received several awards, including the 2007 Letras de Aztlán Award from the National Association for Chicana and Chicano Studies and the 2005 Patricia and Rudolfo Anaya Critica Nueva Award from the University of New Mexico for his contributions to Chicano literature and critical theory.

Ortego y Gasca has taught at a number of educational institutions, is a world traveler, and has lived in a number of foreign countries. Starting in 2007, he served as a scholar in residence and chair of the Department of Chicana/Chicano and Hemispheric Studies (CCHS) at Western New Mexico University in Silver City.

Ortego y Gasca's major publications have included the essay "The Chicano Renaissance" (1971), *Backgrounds of Mexican American Literature* (1971), and "Chicanos and American Literature" with Jose Carrasco(1972); some of his most memorable plays were *Voices of Women/Voces de Mujer* (1993) and *Madre del Sol/Mother of the Sun* (1981). Overall, Ortego y Gasca has written more than 450 articles, essays, poems, plays, and edited the anthology *We Are Chicanos: An Anthology of Mexican American Literature* (1973).

SIGNIFICANCE

Ortego y Gasca's 1971 dissertation on Mexican American literature was considered the first ever taxonomic study in the field of Chicano literary history. As a scholar of Chicano literature, he argued that the seventeenth century colonial roots of American literature in New England were actually superseded by the colonial influence of late sixteenth century New Spain. Especially in the American Southwest, Mexican Americans were in fact producing literature in America's pre-Revolutionary period, contributing a plethora of literary influences to American culture—as much, Ortego y Gasca claimed, as the British literary output of the Atlantic frontier.

Furthermore, Ortego y Gasca asserted that Chicano literature began with the end of the Mexican-American War in 1848 but was rendered invisible and actually forced underground until the flowering or "rebirth" of Chicano literary expression as a major offshoot of the Chicano movement in the late 1960's and early 1970's. Ortego y Gasca also was one of the first writers with the prestigious Quinto Sol publishing house, and was a strong proponent of Latino civil rights. He was an erudite literary critic and prolific writer who brought to mainstream attention a flourishing of Mexican American works, stamping the imprint of "Chicano literature" on the American literary landscape.

Itzcóatl Tlaloc Meztli

FURTHER READING

Ortego, Philip D. "The Chicano Renaissance." In *Introduction to Chicano Studies,* edited by Livie Isauro Duran and H. Russell Bernard. New York: Macmillan, 1973. Ortego's seminal essay announcing the "awakening" of Chicano literature in the American mainstream, claiming that Mexican American literature has been in existence in the United States since 1848.

Ortego, Philip D., and Jose A. Carrasco. "Chicanos and American Literature." In *Searching for America,* edited by Ernece B. Kelly. Urbana, Ill.: CCCC & NCTE, 1972. Critique of the absence of Chicano literature in the American literary canon, blaming an Anglo ethnocentric point of view.

Ortego y Gasca, Felipe de. "Millennial Reflections on the Chicano Renaissance." *Voices: San Antonio College Multicultural Journal* 4 (2009). The author describes the academic circumstances that led to the writing of his most famous essay, "The Chicano Renaissance," and explores at length the historical roots of Chicano literature.

See also: Edna Acosta-Belén; Rodolfo F. Acuña; Fernando Alegría; Juan Bruce-Novoa; Lourdes Casal.

DAVID ORTIZ

Dominican-born baseball player

Ortiz is best known as one of Major League Baseball's great power and clutch hitters. His laid back and pleasant personality has made him a fan and clubhouse favorite. David will most likely be best remembered for helping the 2004 Red Sox win their first World Series title in 86 years.

Latino heritage: Dominican

Born: November 18, 1975; Santo Domingo, Dominican Republic

Also known as: David Américo Ortiz Arias; Big Papi;
   Señor October; Cookie Monster

Area of achievement: Baseball

EARLY LIFE

David Américo Ortiz Arias (or-TEEZ) was born November 18, 1975, in Santo Domingo, Dominican Republic. His father, Enrique, played semiprofessional and
professional baseball throughout the Dominican leagues
for many years. Growing up, Ortiz emulated his father
and other local players; however, unlike his father, who
was best known for his fielding, Ortiz developed into a
power hitter. While his natural talent and athletic build
allowed Ortiz to excel in both basketball and baseball
while at Estudia Espallat High School, it was his ability
to hit the ball that garnered interest from Major League
Baseball (MLB) scouts.

In 1992, shortly after his seventeenth birthday, Ortiz was signed by the Seattle Mariners organization. He
spent the following summer playing for the Mariners'
Dominican Summer League team and earned a spot on
the Mariners' rookie-level club in Peoria, Arizona, for
the 1994 and 1995 seasons. After the 1995 season, he
was named the team's most valuable player and voted
to the Arizona League All-Star team.

The following summer, Ortiz was promoted to
th Mariners' Class-A affiliate in the Midwest League,
where he batted an impressive .322, hit 19 home runs,
and tallied 93 runs batted in (RBI). During the offseason
that followed, he was traded to the Minnesota Twins.
That September, the Twins called up Ortiz to the major
leagues, where in fifteen games he batted .327, drove in
6 runs, and hit his first big-league home run.

Awarded a roster spot for the 1998 season, Ortiz
broke his wrist and was forced to miss much of the season's first half. The following season, the Twins sent
him back to the minor leagues, and he spent the entire
1999 season with the team's Salt Lake City affiliate.
However, in 2000, Ortiz was back in the majors with
the Twins.

LIFE'S WORK

During the 2001 and 2002 seasons with the Twins, Ortiz was somewhat hampered by injuries. However, during the second half of the 2002 season, Minnesota fans
watched as Ortiz went on a tear. He finished the season
with 20 home runs and 75 RBI, helping the Twins win
the division title for the first time since 1991.

The following season, Ortiz signed a one-year
contract with the Boston Red Sox. He helped lead the
Red Sox into the postseason only to see the team lose
to the New York Yankees in the 2003 American League
Championship Series.

After the 2003 season, Ortiz signed a two-year
contract with the Red Sox. In 2004, he belted a career-
best 41 home runs, 47 doubles, and 139 RBI. This season produced Ortiz's first All-Star Game selection, and
he was instrumental in helping the long-suffering Red
Sox win their first World Series since 1918. During
the American League Division Series, he secured a
sweep of the Anaheim Angels by crushing a walk-off
two-run home run over Fenway Park's Green Monster.

In the best-of-seven American League Championship Series, the Red Sox fell behind the Yankees three
games to none. No team ever had overcome such a deficit. Making matters worse was the humiliating 19-8 loss
the Red Sox suffered in game three. In the bottom of the
ninth inning of game four, the Red Sox rallied to tie the
game and force extra innings. Then, in the bottom of the
twelfth inning, Ortiz crushed a two-run game-winning
home run. The following night, he solidified his place in

David Ortiz. (AP Photo)

Red Sox lore by driving in the game-winning run in the bottom of the fourteenth inning. The Red Sox and Ortiz never looked back, becoming the first team in history to win a seven-game series after trailing by three games. Ortiz then helped lead his team to a World Series sweep of the St. Louis Cardinals.

The following two seasons, Ortiz continued to improve. He ended the 2005 campaign with 47 home runs and 148 RBI, and followed that performance in 2006 by leading the league with 54 home runs and 137 RBI.

In 2007, Ortiz led his team to a second World Series victory, as the Red Sox swept the Colorado Rockies in four games. In 2009, his image was clouded by a report that his name appeared on a 2003 list of players who had tested positive for performance-enhancing drugs. Ortiz denied ever using steroids or other such drugs and said that he believed legal supplements and vitamins had caused his positive test. Through 2010 he remained one of the top power hitters in baseball and an integral part of the Red Sox lineup.

SIGNIFICANCE

In the Dominican Republic, *papi* is slang for "daddy." With Ortiz's impressive size, powerful bat, and relaxed demeanor, the Red Sox leader earned the nickname "Big Papi." He has firmly established himself as a fan favorite and one of the top clutch and power hitters of his era. In 2006, he created the David Ortiz Children's Fund to raise funds for children in need of critical pediatric care in the Dominican Republic and the northeastern United States. He also volunteers his time at various baseball clinics for children in the Boston area and the Dominican Republic. In 2008 Ortiz was awarded the Children's Champion Award by the United Nations Children's Fund.

Michael D. Cummings, Jr.

FURTHER READING

Ortiz, David, and Tony Massarotti. *Big Papi: My Story of Big Dreams and Big Hits*. New York: St. Martin's Press, 2007. Ortiz's autobiography covers his journey from the Dominican Republic to baseball stardom in Boston.

Simmons, Bill. *Now I Can Die in Peace: How the Sports Guy Found Salvation and More, Thanks to the World Champion (Twice!) Red Sox*. Rev. ed. New York: ESPN Books, 2009. Collection of columns documenting the Red Sox's 2004 and 2007 championship runs. Offers a compelling look at Ortiz's postseason heroics from a fan's point of view.

Verducci, Tom. "Who's Your Papi?" *Sports Illustrated* 104, no. 25 (June 19, 2006): 42. A feature story that provides insight into Ortiz's career and the impact his mother had on him.

See also: Miguel Cabrera; José Canseco; Pedro Martinez; Manny Ramirez; Alex Rodriguez; Freddy Sanchez; Sammy Sosa; Miguel Tejada.

JUDITH ORTIZ COFER

Puerto Rican-born writer and educator

Best known for her depiction of Puerto Rico and her upbringing in New Jersey, Ortiz Cofer has had a successful career as a writer and educator. Her writings, which are often interspersed with Spanish, portray the multicultural struggles of an adolescent Latina.

Latino heritage: Puerto Rican
Born: February 24, 1952; Hormigueros, Puerto Rico
Also known as: Judith Ortiz
Areas of achievement: Literature; poetry; education

EARLY LIFE

Judith Ortiz Cofer (or-TEEZ COH-fur) was born in Hormigueros, Puerto Rico, on February 24, 1952, to Fanny Morot and Jesus Logo Ortiz. Jesus was a career military man, and soon after his enlistment in the U.S. Navy (1955), he relocated the family to Paterson, New Jersey. His duty assignment was on a ship in Brooklyn Navy Yard, New York City. Even though Fanny did not want to leave Puerto Rico, she did not resist the move. Jesus was convinced that a move to the U.S. mainland would provide his children a successful life through education. In Paterson, Ortiz Cofer's family settled into a tenement filled with newly arrived New York City Puerto Ricans. In her work, she often refers to this tenement as "El Building."

Ortiz Cofer's family was first introduced to racism while living in Paterson. The landlords and shopkeepers feared the influx of Latinos into the community. Thus, her father's goal became to move his family out of

Autobiographical Elements in Ortiz Cofer's Work

Judith Ortiz Cofer's *The Latin Deli: Prose and Poetry* (1993) is a collection of fiction, poetry, and essays inspired by her bicultural upbringing. The first poem in the collection, "The Latin Deli: An Ars Poetica," depicts the sense of longing to find "home." While walking through a grocery store that caters to Latinos, the narrator's senses transport her back to Puerto Rico. She smells the dried codfish and green plantains, and she hears the voices of Cubans, Mexicans, and Puerto Ricans. A prolific writer, Ortiz Cofer explores the conflict inherent in the straddling of two cultures, and the role of women within this context. In her writing, she attempts to resolve her conflicts but acknowledges that she might never find closure. Nonetheless, she attempts to do so in her novel *The Line of the Sun* (1989) and in her collection of prose and poetry *Silent Dancing: A Partial Remembrance of a Puerto Rican Childhood* (1990). Both works take their titles from incidents in Ortiz Cofer's life.

the "barrio" as soon as possible. As a result of the isolation the father imposed on the family, Ortiz Cofer developed a love of reading. She spent a great deal of time at the local library but was frequently harassed by white and African American children because she was of Puerto Rican descent.

Jesus was away often because of his military career. When he feared the neighborhood had become too dangerous, he ordered his wife and children to travel to Puerto Rico and live with Ortiz Cofer's grandmother while he was away on tours of duty. It is during these extended visits to Puerto Rico that Ortiz Cofer learned from her grandmother the art of storytelling

When Ortiz Cofer was fifteen years old, Jesus relocated the family to Augusta, Georgia. Upon graduating high school, Ortiz Cofer attended Augusta College (now Augusta State University) and received an undergraduate degree in English in 1974. She also received an M.A. from Florida Atlantic University in 1977. During her college studies, she married Charles John Cofer on November, 13, 1971. From 1974 to 1984, Ortiz Cofer taught extensively at public schools, community colleges, and universities.

In 1984, Ortiz Cofer joined the English faculty at the University of Georgia at Athens. In 2006, she was named a Regents and Franklin Professor of English and creative writing at the university.

LIFE'S WORK

Only after receiving a graduate degree did Ortiz Cofer attempt to write poems. Her first published poem, "Latin Women Pray," was published in the national journal *New Mexico Humanities Review*. To Ortiz Cofer's astonishment, she had success publishing individual work, but when she attempted to send out manuscripts, they were rejected. This period was the late 1970's, and publishing houses felt that her work was not commercial enough. Nevertheless, Ortiz's early chapbook *Latin Women Pray* was published in 1980. She went on to release numerous other books of poetry, including *The Native Dancer* (1981), *Among the Ancestors* (1981), *Peregrina* (1986), *Terms of Survival* (1987), and *A Love Story Beginning in Spanish* (2005).

Peregrina won the Riverstone International Chapbook Competition. Ortiz Cofer's first major work of prose fiction, *The Line of the Sun* (1989), was nominated for the Pulitzer Prize. In 1990, she wrote an autobiographical collection of prose and poems, *Silent Dancing: A Partial Remembrance of a Puerto Rican Childhood*. This collection received the 1991 PEN/Martha Albrand Special Citation in nonfiction and was awarded a Pushcart Prize. In 1993, Ortiz Cofer published *The Latin Deli: Prose and Poetry*. A winner of the Anisfield Wolf Book Award, *The Latin Deli* is a combination of poetry, short fiction, and personal narrative.

Ortiz Cofer also has written *An Island Like You: Stories of the Barrio* (1995), *The Year of Our Revolution: New and Selected Stories and Poems* (1998), and *Woman in Front of the Sun: On Becoming a Writer* (2000). *Woman in Front of the Sun* won an award from the Georgia Writers Association.

In 2003, she published the young-adult novel *The Meaning of Consuelo*. This novel, like *An Island Like You*, is aimed at young adults. *An Island Like You* received the 1995 Pura Belpré Medal and the Fanfare Best Book of the Year award and was listed among the best books for young adults by the American Library Association. In 2010, Ortiz Cofer was inducted into the Georgia Writers Hall of Fame. She was the first honoree of Latino descent.

SIGNIFICANCE

In her literary work, Ortiz Cofer explores topics such as religion, sexuality, and gender. As an adolescent, Ortiz Cofer's frequent commutes between the U.S. mainland and Puerto Rico gave her a distinctively bicultural perspective. In her work, she attempts to resolve the conflicts between those two points of view.

She uses storytelling as a form of empowerment and depicts the power of stories.

Gabriela Ybarra Lemmons

FURTHER READING

Marshall, Joanna Barszewska. "Translating 'Home' in the Work of Judith Ortiz Cofer." In *Writing Off the Hyphen: New Critical Perspectives on the Literature of the Puerto Rican Diaspora*, edited by José L. Torres-Padilla and Carmen Haydée Rivera. Seattle: University of Washington Press, 2008. Analyzes depictions of Puerto Rico and the United States in Ortiz Cofer's work.

Ortiz Cofer, Judith. "An Interview with Judith Ortiz Cofer." Interview by Margaret Crumpton. *Meridians* 3, no. 2 (2003): 93-109. Examines the significance of an adolescent muse in Ortiz Cofer's writing.

_____. "A MELUS Interview: Judith Ortiz Cofer." Interview by EdnaAcosta-Belen. *MELUS* 18, no. 3 (1993): 83-97. Ortiz Cofer discusses gender, race, culture, class issues, and being a Latina author in mainstream America.

_____. "Speaking in Puerto Rican: An Interview with Judith Ortiz Cofer." Interview by Rafael Ocasio and Rita Ganey. *Bilingual Review* 17, no. 2 (1992): 143-146. Discusses the importance of poetry in Ortiz Cofer's life and women who have influenced her writing.

_____. *Woman in Front of the Sun: On Becoming a Writer*. Athens: University of Georgia Press, 2000. A useful source for understanding why Ortiz Cofer became a writer. This collection of essays, poems, and folklore explores her love of words and language.

See also: Julia Alvarez; Gloria Anzaldúa; Norma Elia Cantú; Sandra Cisneros; Carmen Tafolla; Helena María Viramontes.

MIGUEL ANTONIO OTERO

American politican and writer

Otero was the first Hispanic territorial governor of New Mexico in fifty years and later served as marshal of the Panama Canal Zone. Otero also wrote a three-volume autobiography and a biography of Billy the Kid that questions Anglo American myths surrounding the traditional Western narrative.

Latino heritage: Mexican

Born: October 17, 1859; St. Louis, Missouri

Died: August 7, 1944; Santa Fe, New Mexico

Also known as: Miguel Antonio Otero II; Miguel Antonio Otero, Jr.; Miguel A. Otero; Gillie

Areas of achievement: Government and politics; literature

EARLY LIFE

Miguel Antonio Otero II (oh-TEH-roh) was born to Miguel Antonio Otero and Mary Josephine Blackwood on October 17, 1859, in St. Louis, Missouri. Otero had an older brother, Page Blackwood, and two younger sisters, Gertrude Vicentia and Mamie Josephine. When Otero was born, his father had just been appointed for his third term as delegate to the United States Congress from the New Mexico Territory. When his father completed that term, he chose to dedicate himself to his business interests, so the family began its journey throughout the Southwestern frontier. Otero's early education was in various private and boarding schools. The family eventually settled in Las Vegas, New Mexico.

Otero studied at St. Louis University in Missouri and the University of Notre Dame in Indiana. He also received an appointment to the U.S. Naval Academy in Annapolis, Maryland, but stayed only a short time. His education often was interrupted by poor health, but he seemed to thrive in the Western deserts. On May 30, 1882, when Otero was just twenty-two years old, his father died of pneumonia.

On December 11, 1888, Otero married Caroline Virginia Emmett. In 1891, they had a son, Miguel Antonio Otero III, who lived only eight days. On August 30, 1892, the Oteros had a second son, named Miguel Antonio Otero IV. In his autobiography Otero often referred to his son as "Junior," adding to the confusion over the names of the various generations of Otero men.

LIFE'S WORK

Otero's political career began when he met William McKinley at the 1892 Republican National Convention. It was because of the relationship formed at that convention that President McKinley decided in 1897 to appoint Otero as the first Hispanic territorial governor of New Mexico since Donaciano Vigil in 1847. At the age of thirty-seven, Otero also was very young for a governor. In 1898, when the Spanish-American War became inevitable, Otero was instrumental in organizing the military regiment known as the Rough Riders.

During Otero's second term as territorial governor, he rigorously opposed President Theodore Roosevelt's plan to set aside timber lands as national forests. Otero's opposition cost him a third term as governor. He stepped down as territorial governor on January 1, 1907, and changed his political allegiance to the Democratic Party. Otero led the New Mexico delegation to the Democratic National Conventions in 1912 and 1916. Subsequently, he accepted an appointment by President Woodrow Wilson as marshal of the Panama Canal Zone. He served in Panama from 1917 to 1921.

Otero began his career as a writer during the 1920's. In 1925, he published *Conquistadores of Spain and Buccaneers of England, France and Holland*, followed by *Colonel José Francisco Cháves, 1833-1924* (1926). He then wrote his memoirs in three volumes: *My Life on the Frontier, Volume One: 1864-1882* (1935), *My Life on the Frontier, Volume Two: 1882-1897* (1939), and *My Nine Years As Governor of the Territory of New Mexico, 1897-1906* (1940). The three volumes later were reissued under the title *Otero: An Autobiographical Trilogy* (1974). Otero also wrote the biography *The Real Billy the Kid: With New Light on the Lincoln County War* (1936). He died in Santa Fe, New Mexico, in 1944.

SIGNIFICANCE

While Donaciano Vigil was the first Hispanic territorial governor of New Mexico, he took office only after the assassination of the man appointed to the office, Charles Bent. Otero was the first Hispanic to be appointed as territorial governor by the president of the United States. As territorial governor, Otero worked tirelessly for statehood, which was not achieved until 1912, six years after he left office. His personal and political life both focused on defining the position of the New Mexicans within the Anglo imagination. His writing also works to clarify the historical perception of New Mexicans to recast them in a more favorable light.

Norma A. Mouton

FURTHER READING

Leal, Luis, and Ilan Stavans. *A Luis Leal Reader*. Evanston, Ill.: Northwestern University Press, 2007. Devotes one chapter to Otero, discussing his historical significance as well as his literary production.

Otero, Miguel Antonio. *Otero: An Autobiographical Trilogy*. New York: Arno Press, 1974. Otero's complete three-volume autobiography is reprinted in this edition.

Padilla, Genaro M. *My History, Not Yours: The Formation of Mexican American Autobiography*. Madison: University of Wisconsin Press, 1993. Presents historical background on Otero and places his autobiography in the context of other such works by Mexican Americans.

Rivera, John-Michael. *The Emergence of Mexican America: Recovering Stories of Mexican Peoplehood in U.S. Culture*. New York: New York University Press, 2006. Discusses the importance of Otero's political position focusing one chapter on the intended social impact of Otero's writing.

See also: Dennis Chavez; Joseph Marion Hernández; Joseph M. Montoya; Pío Pico.